'This is required reading for both scholars of insurgency and counterinsurgency strategists. After decades of stasis, the analytical literature on insurgency is experiencing a renaissance, driven by major shifts in the security environment and innovation by insurgent actors. Erudite, persuasive, and an important contribution.'
—Steve Metz, Professor of National Security and Strategy,
US Army War College

'This book puts insurgency into a much wider strategic context, offering an analysis that ought to make readers think carefully about what leads to success in twenty-first-century irregular warfare.'
—Matthew Ford, Senior Lecturer in International Relations,
University of Sussex, and co-author of *Radical War*

'An important new entry into the ongoing debate in military and strategic studies over the last twenty or more years. This is a useful exercise in rethinking the nature of insurgencies and counter-insurgency, especially with its discussion of state theory.'
—Paul B. Rich, consultant for TRENDS Research & Advisory,
and editor, *Small Wars and Insurgencies*

THE INSURGENT'S DILEMMA

DAVID H. UCKO

The Insurgent's Dilemma

A Struggle to Prevail

OXFORD
UNIVERSITY PRESS

OXFORD

UNIVERSITY PRESS

Oxford University Press is a department of the
University of Oxford. It furthers the University's objective
of excellence in research, scholarship, and education
by publishing worldwide.

Oxford New York

Auckland   Cape Town   Dar es Salaam   Hong Kong   Karachi
Kuala Lumpur   Madrid   Melbourne   Mexico City   Nairobi
New Delhi   Shanghai   Taipei   Toronto

With offices in

Argentina   Austria   Brazil   Chile   Czech Republic   France   Greece
Guatemala   Hungary   Italy   Japan   Poland   Portugal   Singapore
South Korea   Switzerland   Thailand   Turkey   Ukraine   Vietnam

Oxford is a registered trade mark of Oxford University Press
in the UK and certain other countries.

Published in the United States of America by
Oxford University Press
198 Madison Avenue, New York, NY 10016

Library of Congress Cataloging-in-Publication Data is available

ISBN: 9780197651681

Printed in Great Britain by Bell and Bain Ltd, Glasgow

CONTENTS

ABOUT THE AUTHOR

David H. Ucko is Professor and Department Chair at the College of International Security Affairs (CISA), National Defense University, Washington DC. He is also an adjunct professor at Johns Hopkins University and a senior visiting research fellow in the Department of War Studies, King's College London.

ACKNOWLEDGEMENTS

The thoughts and ideas within this book speak to an intellectual journey undertaken over several years. As my itinerary developed, I benefited from the guidance of others—those who pointed me in new directions and helped me when I got stuck. Much as I hope this book may inform the paths of future travelers, it is important for me to acknowledge those who showed me the way and inspired me to keep going.

The core of my thinking about insurgency and political violence has been powerfully molded by my many years at the College of International Security Affairs of the National Defense University. In particular, it has been a joy and privilege to work so closely with Thomas A. Marks, a veritable giant in the field and someone who has greatly expanded my academic horizons. I should also thank the many colleagues at NDU, both past and present, who have inspired my writing, including Kirklin Bateman, David Oakley, Frank Hoffman, Hassan Abbas, Sean McFate, Carlos Ospina-Ovalle, Michael Sullivan, David Spencer, Kevin Whitaker, John Creamer, Geoffrey Gresh, Peter Eltsov, and T. X. Hammes. Much of what is in this book reflects my conversations and collaboration with these fine thinkers and doers.

Still at CISA, this book would have been impossible were it not for the daily interactions with our international student body: senior practitioners from around the world, with first-hand experience in addressing both insurgency and instability. I wish to thank all our alumni for their willingness to engage on difficult topics, for sharing their stories, and for teaching me all the while I sought to teach them.

The topic of this book stems from a June 2018 session of the RAND Insurgency Board on the future of insurgency. I would therefore be remiss if I did not thank Ambassador James Dobbins and Patrick Johnston for commissioning me to write, and David Kilcullen, Steve Metz, Kimberley Kagan, Austin Long, and Bryan Frederi for their comments on the paper that ensued.

My thinking then evolved via several opportunities to brief preliminary findings and engage with different audiences. For these opportunities, I would like to thank the organizers of the 2018 Colombo Defence Seminar, in particular Brigadier Shewanth Kulatunge of the Sri Lankan Army; the S. Rajaratnam School of International Studies in Singapore, in particular Rohan Gunaratna, Sabariah Hussin, and Wei Chong Ong; and Tim Huxley of the International Institute for Strategic Studies–Asia, also in Singapore. I want to thank Major General Kurt Sonntag for taking an interest in my work and inviting me to share my paper with the special operations community under the auspices of a US Army Special Operations Command workshop on resistance. I was also fortunate to be able to share my thinking at the National Defense University 2018 Global Alumni Summit in Rabat, Morocco, for which I thank my institution and colleagues. Finally, I extend my gratitude to the Bangladeshi National Defence College for inviting me to present and discuss my findings with its faculty and students.

The writing of this book benefited tremendously from the input of a select few research assistants. I have nothing but admiration for the drive and dedication of Toshiro Baum, Susan Stalter, and James Suber, all of whom provided invaluable support as I tried to complete the manuscript. It is humbling and encouraging to see such excellence in the next generation. I have also been privileged to receive the advice and guidance of friends and colleagues who patiently reviewed early drafts and provided feedback. I would like to thank, in particular, Hannes Ebert, Raffaello Pantucci, Christopher Coker, Mark Stout, and Peter Neumann.

ACKNOWLEDGEMENTS

The superb team at Hurst Publishers greatly facilitated the eventual publication of this book. I want to thank Michael Dwyer for his belief in the manuscript and his faith in me as an author. I also want to thank Christopher Coker and Hassan Abbas for their guidance throughout the publishing process. Mats Berdal, my erstwhile doctoral supervisor, has continued to be an invaluable source of reassurance and advice, and I remain forever in his debt.

To conclude, a personal note: writing a book during a global pandemic brings its own challenges and my wife and children bore additional burdens as a result. I wish to thank you, Kate, and my daughters, Magdalena and Charlotte, for your love, patience, and sense of humor throughout it all. Finally, while writing this book I often thought back to my own parents, Hans and Agneta, and the intellectual and nourishing environment that they created and continue to provide. Anything I've ever accomplished is thanks to you.

1

INTRODUCTION

Insurgency, it is said, is the 'graduate level of war.' This honorific was earned through the countless traumas experienced by states at the hands of seemingly inferior foes: in Iraq, Afghanistan, Vietnam, Algeria, and going all the way back to Napoleon's Peninsular War and beyond. Indeed, insurgency can induce an acute case of helplessness among states; when well led and organized, these movements seem to hold a power that all but nullifies the state's many advantages. Shortly after the Vietnam War, Henry Kissinger gave voice to the frustration: 'The guerrilla wins if he does not lose. The conventional army loses if it does not win.'[1] This war in Southeast Asia, so dark and haunting for the United States, spawned another telling aphorism: responding to a US colonel's claim that the Americans had never lost a single firefight, his Vietnamese counterpart quipped: 'That may be so, but it is also irrelevant.'[2] On the political plane, the Americans had lost—technology and firepower notwithstanding.

Some decades later, the US military once again confronted the limits of its power in the face of insurgency. Stuck in Iraq, the US Army and Marine Corps published new doctrine to explain the unfamiliar 'paradoxes' of counterinsurgency to an increasingly exasperated force; these included insights such as 'Some of the Best

1

Weapons for Counterinsurgents Do Not Shoot' and 'Tactical Success Guarantees Nothing.'[3] In Afghanistan, yet another maxim appeared, apparently uttered by Taliban commanders, that further underlined the counterinsurgent's dilemma: 'You have the watches. We have the time.'[4] The cutting prescience of this aphorism became painfully clear in the summer of 2021, when after 20 years of occupation NATO forces finally withdrew and, in doing so, abandoned the government in Kabul, and the nation of Afghanistan, to the Taliban's rapid advance.

The maxims that have emerged from such failures are pithy and revealing, but they can also be overly fatalistic, or outright inaccurate, in describing the true power of states—even those confronting a concerted insurgency. Not only do several governments threatened in this manner do quite well; according to some, governments have since the Cold War experienced decisive victories more than thrice as often as their non-state challengers.[5] More fundamentally, and very much contrary to Kissinger, in most contemporary cases (seven out of ten for the same time period), the struggles simmer, maybe occasionally rise to a boil, but do not boil over or threaten state collapse.[6] In many nations affected by insurgency—places like Nigeria, Colombia, the Philippines, Pakistan, Peru, even Myanmar—the conflict becomes a nuisance, or something to manage, but does not amount to a primary or particularly urgent concern. The government may not be 'winning,' or win decisively, but it remains in power and thereby denies the insurgents their own victory.

This trend will strike many as counterintuitive given the high-profile loss in Afghanistan and the other setbacks of the so-called War on Terror. Adopting a broader lens, however, the Taliban's swift victory in the summer of 2021 emerges as a notable exception to a more general trend of state survival. It is also an exception shrouded by its exceptional circumstances. Though most states threatened by insurgency are weak, few are as artificial and hollow as was the Kabul government that the international community sought to build and legitimize for almost 20 years. Through a half-baked 'nation-building' experiment cooked up in the West, with scant regard for Afghan cultural and political norms, a highly centralized national government was created that ran counter to the fragmented nature of the Afghan state. As that government, while also corrupt and criminalized, was then charged with instilling democracy, a liberal economy, and social justice, it could rightly be said that, in this instance, it was the counterinsurgents that were the revolutionaries, seeking as they were to graft a radical political project onto an unwilling body.[7] Meanwhile, this was also a case where the insurgents received strong state support, primarily via Pakistan's military intelligence service. Few other challengers benefit from such a ripe and forgiving context and imitators hoping to export the Taliban's approach can expect an altogether different result.

Indeed, in broader terms, insurgents are no longer defeating states militarily; most do not even try, and those that do suffer the consequences. The combined track record of recent insurgencies brings the point home: there are exceedingly few cases where they have subdued and successfully replaced their government adversary. For the most part, they have not even secured sufficient military gains to achieve meaningful concessions at the negotiating table. Sure enough, coups and revolutions still occur with some frequency (witness for example the convulsions of the Arab Spring), and those insurgents blessed with the military support of capable states—in Libya, Ukraine, or Afghanistan as mentioned—can often do rather well (though they also struggle—even fail—to consolidate their gains). For most, however, the fight goes on, or simmers, leading to eventual state victory or, at least, its survival.

On this basis, an update on Kissinger may be in order: it is the *state* that wins by not losing, and the *guerrilla* that loses by never getting to win. After all, it is the insurgent that must reverse the balance of power—a far more onerous task than hanging on to the status quo. During the Cold War, Mao Tse-tung famously advocated a three-phased approach to insurgency, each involving ever-growing popular and military mobilization. The theory was immensely influential and instrumental in several rebel victories that followed. Today, however, the state's adversaries become stuck in the phase of harassment and fail to progress. Without a very generous and brazen state sponsor, insurgent organizations rarely acquire the combat capability and lethality of states, and few therefore can—or even seek to—go toe to toe against their armed forces. So long as they remain in the shadows, they may survive to fight another day, and even impose some costs along the way, yet there is no real possibility of victory, at least not by force of arms.

Two recent cases of insurgent defeat bring the point home. The mighty Liberation Tigers of Tamil Eelam (LTTE) prosecuted a lethal insurgency over several decades, owned its own counter-state in the north and east of Sri Lanka, and developed state-like military capabilities, including a navy and even a modest air force. Yet once the Sri Lankan government decided it had had enough and, in 2006, launched a massive military onslaught, the Tigers were roundly defeated within less than three years. Then, in 2014, the Islamic State emerged in Iraq and Syria as one of the most resourced and threatening insurgent groups the world had ever seen. It attacked both countries conventionally, using tanks and self-propelled artillery, and amassed manpower from across the globe. Yet despite (or because of) its initial successes—in standing up in this manner, in gaining territory and proclaiming a state—ISIS also exposed itself to military counterattack that, again in less than three years, demolished its ambitions and overall plan. It is true that the counteroffensive in this case called upon a vast military coalition of states, all galvanized by the rapid advances of the group, but this in itself signals the hostile global environment for insurgent groups—even those that prove effective during the mobilization stage.

When insurgency reaches a certain level—where it claims territory, usurps governmental prerogatives, and actually threatens the state—it opens itself to a military backlash too powerful for most embryonic proto-states. In counterinsurgency theory, the government would use the space thus created to address the political roots of the conflict, so that the problem of insurgency does not reappear. This rarely happens. Instead, states end up reapplying military force as necessary to suppress rather than ever quite resolve the matter. 'Mowing the grass,' as this approach has been termed, is deemed a suboptimal response to political violence, and yet for the insurgent the grass is nonetheless mowed, and the armed struggle must start over—often with great effort.[8] Thus, despite pronounced concern about the Tigers rising again from the blood-soaked ashes of

4

Sri Lanka's final offensive, signs of a rebirth are modest at best. And while ISIS persists with launching terrorist attacks worldwide and strikes targets opportunistically in Syria and Iraq, their efforts must necessarily remain below the threshold of consolidating territory— or at least showing off about it.[9]

This is a costly approach to business. Some insurgents may conclude that they require the military backing of powerful states, but most cannot expect or easily secure such support. Others may learn not to fight a state power conventionally, but for this reason they will also struggle to impose costs or seize power. Others yet may restrict their use of violence to softer targets than the state, or use mostly terrorism, yet these will confront issues of legitimacy and political isolation, making it difficult to build a new political order. Some may go in another direction altogether, seeking to avoid launching attacks lest they invite 'unwanted government attention' and become counterproductive.[10] As Jacob Shapiro concludes in his study of violent covert organizations, 'conducting too many attacks can be as damaging as conducting too few.'[11]

The need for such awkward compromises represents *the insurgent's dilemma*: the difficulty of asserting oneself as a start-up, of challenging authority violently, and establishing oneself sustainably as the new source of power, without suffering devastating retaliation along the way. Because of this dilemma, insurgency—defined broadly as a politico-military campaign against the writ of the state—at once remains the most common form of conflict and yet is also experiencing dwindling returns. But how long can this track record of failure persist? How long can states expect to maintain the upper hand? Clausewitz characterized warfare as the competition of wills, and so adaptation is to be expected.

As it turns out, the balance of power is already being challenged. States have managed well enough by doing just enough, but in the face of continued failure some insurgents are learning to overcome the dilemma laid out above. As a result, while states lament their poor performance in recent counterinsurgency campaigns, greater trouble may lie ahead. Insurgency is being reinvented—it is being tailored to the vulnerabilities of our times and with new strategic salience for tomorrow. As successful approaches are copied, refined, and repurposed, what we think of as counterinsurgency will also need to change.

On this basis, this book seeks to capture emerging trends in insurgent strategy. It asks how pioneering insurgent organizations are moving beyond the traditional model of politico-military overthrow and what avenues they are exploring instead to capture and retain power. By contextualizing insurgency within the social and political norms of today and tomorrow, it maps and explains such adaptation, focusing on the strategic approaches that look most likely to produce viable and sustainable political outcomes.

In short, this book is concerned with the future of insurgency— or with the theories of victory that will guide insurgents' paths to power. It is a topic that matters for at least three reasons:

- First, insurgent adaptation will seek to undo the military trump card that many states rely upon as a crude but effective way of staying in power. Without this trump card, states will be far more vulnerable to extra-legal and subversive attack. Some of these states may anyway deserve replacement, but a better outcome, even in these instances, is productive engagement with the internal challenge rather than chaotic devolution into violence and war.

- Second, within an increasingly multipolar balance of power globally, state rivals will be looking to foster and fuel insurgencies as one way of undermining their strategic competitors. Much as during the Cold War, insurgency will therefore assume greater meaning as a component of great-power competition. In tandem, state backing will compound the destabilizing effects of internal strife, while insurgency, reinvented for our times, will offer these states more potent ways to undermine their adversaries.

- Third, with democracy in retreat on a global scale, the opportunities for peaceful transfers of power will also shrink. This narrowing of political opportunity leaves the window open for the increased use of subversion, force, and crime to claim and hold on to power, not just in the non-democratic world but also in those countries where democracy is being challenged or even discredited. As contestation blends with conflict, as formal politics mesh with illicit methods, states will be faced with fundamental ethical and strategic problems both of diagnosis and of response. Studying what to expect is one critical way of navigating these murky waters.

If the future of insurgency is an important topic, it is also one rife with methodological challenges. The broad range of the subject matter makes it difficult to generalize and, for this reason, the approaches detailed here are presented neither as entirely distinct nor as exhaustive of other ways that may also be attempted. Similarly, it should be stated up front that none of the adaptive insurgent strategies explored in this book are altogether new. Instead, the treatment of the topic purposely allows the present, even the past, to shape analysis and prognosis. As war theorist Christopher Coker frames his own approach to forecasting, we must in these exercises 'have an ear attuned to the secret harmonies of everyday life, for the present may persist longer than we think and the future may be more familiar than we expect.'[12] The key lies not in pronouncing historical watersheds, but in examining how and why strategic approaches already with us today may be adjusted and used on a far wider scale tomorrow, to mount a strategic threat to democratic norms and stability.

Whether insurgency's strategic rebirth is a good or a bad thing is of course a matter of political prerogative, or of how we perceive the state's legitimacy and right to govern. It is an axiom within studies of insurgency that states confronting this challenge already suffered from some major legitimacy deficit to begin with, hence the will and ability of small groups to threaten their writ. Bolstering the state to withstand such efforts can therefore seem perverse, as it reinforces the authority of a government that is misusing its power and position. In response, it should be noted that counterinsurgency theory seeks not a return to a status quo ante—the conditions that obtained before it came to blows—but *change* to that system, precisely to address the government's legitimacy deficit and the 'roots of the conflict.' Still, this is a topic where strategic and ethical perspectives mesh, making dispassionate academic treatment difficult. Even the terms of the discussion (*insurgency*, *counterinsurgency*, never mind *terrorism*) come with significant baggage.

We will return to this question, but at the most basic level this book is concerned with what to expect from the insurgents of tomorrow; it does not provide a priori judgement of the causes pursued by these groups, the grievances that fuel their struggles, or the moral right of the governments to survive. To the degree that this approach has a normative mission beyond the pursuit of knowledge, it is to obviate violent and subversive challenges by encouraging more enlightened and productive management of political change. Counterinsurgency, after all, is best thought of as 'armed reform': beyond its undeniable security component, the heart of the matter is political, or the reasons why so many revolt and accept, even embrace, violent solutions.

Structure and Argument in Brief

With these caveats in mind, the book argues that, for insurgents across the world, military confrontation against the nation-state has become a far less salient road to power, and change is therefore in the air. Chapter 2 lays out the backdrop for this evolution, but it is a discussion that presupposes a decent understanding of what insurgency is and has been. Though definitions are typically an inauspicious point of departure for any engaging discussion, exploration of the terms involved is in this case made necessary by the common tendency to confuse the matter at hand. Analysis is prone to militarize the treatment of insurgency, focusing almost exclusively on its use of terrorism and violence, and forgetting thereby its political and social essence. To reframe the discussion and promote the intensely political nature of insurgency, the chapter relates this phenomenon to social movement organizations, but with violence added to the mix.

On this basis, the chapter then surveys the collective experience of insurgents, during the Cold War and more recently, to reveal the strategic contradictions that they face today. Framing insurgency as a reflection of the political and social context in which it unfolds, the chapter demonstrates how the factors that made insurgency work during the Cold War have since changed. Though these changes may not be realized by all or even most of today's insurgency movements, any dispassionate overview of trends, quantitative as well as qualitative, lays bare the impasse that they are at. Simply put, the traditional avenue to state capture appears to be closing, producing an insurgent's dilemma that is compelling, in different ways, strategic adaptation.

While old paths to power have shrunk, new opportunities have emerged. The next few chapters—chapters 3 to 5—explore in depth various approaches that look to become more common precisely because of their adaptiveness within the present strategic context. These chapters use as evidence those cases wherein insurgents have prevailed against ostensibly strong states, or at least secured most of their aims. It teases out why the selected approaches worked and how they have been, or may yet be, replicated or recycled also by others. Discussion focuses on three areas of convergence:

- In *localized* insurgency, the group aims not for regime change, but for informally delineated spheres of influence, so that its subversive agenda can be pursued locally and without provoking an overwhelming armed response. By never triggering the state's defense mechanism, the struggle can go on, yet, over time, this coexistence costs the government both its coherence and legitimacy.
- In *infiltrative* insurgency, the group removes from view all that may justify and enable military targeting—still the state's forte—and instead penetrates the state quasi-legally, with violence used covertly to clear the way. Camouflaged as a legitimate political party, the insurgents attain power through the democratic system, which they then go on to dismantle from within.
- In *ideational* insurgency, the power of spin and narrative is used, typically online, to build political momentum and legitimacy, mimicking the sway of mass movements yet in a de-territorialized and, often, highly deceptive way. Violence occurs sporadically and unpredictably as a force multiplier, to polarize society, alter its norms, and create an environment in which the insurgency and its ideology can grow.[13]

What unites these approaches is a shift from traditional insurgency, whereby state capture would be achieved militarily, to struggles wherein non-violent lines of effort dominate and violence is added tactically in support. Ironically, this subservience of the military line of effort is taken straight out of Mao Tse-tung's playbook, but, whereas Mao saw military domination of the state as the unavoidable requirement for victory, insurgent struggles now proceed according to a different, and altogether more subtle, logic. In seeking victory by other means, these approaches are exceptionally adaptive, as they render unusable the state's military superiority and strike it instead where it is weak—in its management of society, politics, and overall legitimacy. Given this commonality, these three approaches could also be combined, plausibly to even greater effect.

What is fascinating, and of concern, is that this emerging theory of victory is reflected in the strategies adopted also by revisionist states, not least the People's Republic of China and the Russian Federation. In their own ways, states seeking to challenge international order are eschewing direct confrontation in favor of weaponized ambiguity, compelling narratives, and blended lines of effort, with military realities hovering in the wings but only occasionally making themselves known.[14] The so-called Gerasimov Doctrine is neither doctrine nor the intellectual creation only of General Valery Vasilyevich Gerasimov, the Russian chief of general staff, but it does provide a coherent theorization of the overall approach. It deserves to be quoted at length:

> The very 'rules of war' have changed. The role of nonmilitary means of achieving political and strategic goals has grown, and, in many cases, they have exceeded the power of force of weapons in their effectiveness. The focus of applied methods of conflict has altered in the direction of the broad use of political, economic, informational, humanitarian, and other nonmilitary measures—applied in coordination with the protest potential of the population. All this is supplemented by military means of a concealed character, including carrying out actions of informational conflict and the actions of special-operations forces. The open use of forces—often under the guise of peacekeeping

and crisis regulation—is resorted to only at a certain stage, primarily for the achievement of final success in the conflict.[15]

Where this philosophy is applied, ambiguity delays response and, when one is urgently needed, the lack of clear military targets means the favored instrument of states—armed superiority—can anyway not be used. Instead, whether blended or used separately, these approaches force the state to rethink its application of politics, its building of narrative, and its aggregation of legitimacy among alienated and contested populations.

Animated by this challenge, chapters 6 to 8 explore the paths available to the state as it seeks to counter each of the three emerging approaches under review. The assessment of response builds on past cases and relevant precedent, producing in this manner a menu of practical options that a state might consider as part of an overall strategy. The purpose is not to argue for any one solution in particular—this would anyway be inappropriate given the general nature of the treatment. Instead, the main recommendation to emerge from these chapters is to move the discussion of counterinsurgency beyond the military institutions that have to date owned this space. This exhortation has always been central to counterinsurgency theory and scholarship, but it has also been overwhelmingly ignored. If insurgency evolves in the manner anticipated here, such neglect will no longer be an option. Instead, it will be necessary for those charged with response to master not just matters of security, but the art of governance, how society functions, and the struggle for legitimacy, as these are the areas where the state will be most systematically under attack. On this basis:

- Chapter 6 reviews the challenge of *localized insurgency* and questions the potential of traditional counterinsurgency and state-building practices in fusing societal schisms and political divides. As the chapter argues, this question strikes at the very heart of our international system of ostensibly sovereign states and may require a reinterrogation of the Weberian norms on which this blueprint is based.

- Chapter 7 evaluates the possible responses to *infiltrative insurgency*, wherein anti-democratic parties engage democratically to seize and destroy the system. Whether the response is to ostracize, integrate or proscribe the subversive actor, democracy emerges as uniquely vulnerable to this type of attack. The response must be capable of turning this weakness into a strength.

- Chapter 8 considers various countermeasures against *ideational insurgency*, homing in on the possible regulation of social media so as to stymie its reach and strength. To this end, the discussion also touches upon efforts to boost individual and social resilience. Mass production of disinformation, filtered through today's technological architecture, mounts a truly epistemological threat to modern democracies, and the response will need to engage delicately but deftly with questions of truth, trust, and credibility.

Conclusion

The historian Jeremy Black has noted that, where issues of winning over a population or of fomenting legitimacy are concerned, it is critical that 'military history becomes an aspect of total history; not to "demilitarize" it, but because the operational aspect of war is best studied in terms of the multiple political, social and cultural contexts that gave, and give, it meaning.'[16] This direction is perhaps particularly pertinent to the study of insurgency, which as a political and social phenomenon feeds off and reflects the structural conditions in which it unfolds. Seeking to understand insurgency in the absence of this context is futile, even counterproductive.

It is a central contention of this book that the context for insurgency is changing—and that states must change with it. For long, states have been able to use their superior military capability to fend off insurgent challengers, even if outright victory has proven a bridge too far. Counterinsurgency theory pushes states to engage with the root causes of insurgent conflicts, yet states generally fail to address the contradictions that enable these movements to grow. By merely suppressing the insurgents militarily, however, the state blocks their path to power and lives to rule another day. In this manner, insurgent challenges drag on, but, contrary to the prophecy of Henry Kissinger with which this chapter began, it is the state that survives, copes, and perhaps even thrives, dismissing the periodic ups and downs of an ongoing insurgency as a subsidiary concern. The track record speaks for itself: in contrast to the Cold War, it is now very rare that insurgent groups defeat the state and claim political control over the long term, particularly when they lack a state sponsor.

This picture will be highly unsatisfying to insurgent challengers hungry for change or, simply, power. Already today, there are signs of adaptation—these are likely the pioneers of new forms of insurgency that will become more common tomorrow. On the basis of a broad review of recent practice, particularly cases where non-state challengers have sought to overcome the insurgent's dilemma detailed above, this book considers three particularly potent ways forward. Before going into detail, however, and before considering how the state should react, we must first understand the roots and nature of the insurgent's dilemma prompting such change.

2

UNRAVELING THE DILEMMA

Insurgency means to rise, take up arms, and mobilize against the state. The effort is motivated by grievances with the status quo and the search for a new political order. As such, insurgency pits the challenger against the powers that be, forcing a gradual shift in position until the state must accept the demands being made or be vanquished and replaced. According to the leading theories, this transition requires the conversion of political capital into increasingly potent military capability. The group begins by harnessing a mass base, using grievance and ideology to recruit and indoctrinate. It then directs the resulting momentum at the state, chipping away at its power and finding opportunities to grow. Over time, a losing state will find its security forces overrun, its resources depleted, and its territory and popular legitimacy taken over by its insurgent adversary. In the face of increasingly violent confrontation and a people in revolt, the government must either accept defeat or be defeated, resulting in a new political accommodation.

This logic informed the theories of victory of both Mao Tse-tung and Che Guevara and was reflected in the relatively frequent instances of regime change throughout the twentieth century. Because of its prevalence and success rate, it also informed the key theories of how to counter insurgency—or how states should organize to resist attempts at armed overthrow. Since May 2009, however, when the Sri Lankan military defeated the Liberation Tigers of Tamil Eelam (LTTE), only a select few insurgent groups have attempted this traditional approach—and hardly any of them succeeded. Specifically, it is now very uncommon for insurgents to progress to the final phase of the prescribed strategy: the attempted defeat of the state by force of arms. During the Cold War, subduing the state, either to defeat it or to achieve significant concessions via a peace agreement, stood out as a realistic theory of victory; today it is beyond the ambition of most insurgent groups—and the outliers are overwhelmingly movements sponsored by other states. For the rest—the majority—the military path to power appears largely closed, though not necessarily for want of trying.

Islamic State produces a telling arc. Though it distinguished itself by acquiring conventional capability and squaring off with notable success against both Syria and Iraq, it quickly confronted the limits of its own power and, within a year, began losing the territory it had gained. The lesson from ISIS, and from the defeat of LTTE, is that when a group claims territory and directly threatens governmental prerogatives, it will typically face a military backlash too powerful for the 'counter-state' that the insurgent has sought to fashion. In the unique case of ISIS, its explosive emergence and initial strength required a robust international response; in lesser cases, the outcome has been much the same, yet on a smaller scale. Across the board, the insurgent's advantage lies in dispersion, camouflage, and fluidity, yet these are difficult to maintain when it is committed to territorial defense of a controlled area or engaged in head-on clashes against the military forces of the state. Insurgents trying to set up shop therefore find themselves defeated or, like ISIS, forced below a particular threshold, where they can inspire and launch attacks but never quite realize the political aspirations that such violence is meant to serve.

If the use of military confrontation to defeat the state no longer appears possible, at least not without a state sponsor, it is not necessarily because counterinsurgents have gotten better. The state response to insurgent challenges tends to diverge starkly from the established counterinsurgency principles and best practices found in the doctrine and relevant literature. Most often, states privilege palliative strikes and raids and neglect the reasons for mobilization, for violence, and for the continued recruitment into the group. And yet the application of force, repeated if need be, does seem to block the insurgent's strategic progress. Each raid may create new martyrs and ignite fresh passions among affected populations, but it also forces the insurgent to start over, thwarting its claim to power. For this reason, insurgents are forced to cede a path to power that, historically, had served them well.

Combat and warfare are said to be the ultimate Darwinian laboratory, in that the fittest adversaries learn to overcome the challenges faced while the unfit perish.[1] Given this selective pressure for change, we should expect insurgents to learn from one another and adapt—exactly how will be the topic of ensuing chapters. Yet to understand the logic and purpose of such evolutions, we must first grasp the dilemma that confronts insurgents today and that they seek to escape. This chapter begins with a discussion of insurgency as a phenomenon, which is necessary given the many ethical and strategic ambiguities related to this term. The chapter then reviews data on conflict termination since the turn of the century to demonstrate a recent trend of insurgent defeat or, at best, stalemate. It explains the normative changes that are contributing to this trend and thereby frames the discussion in subsequent chapters of the strategic adaptations that it has fueled.

The argument, in short, is that the traditional approach to insurgency worked during the Cold War because it was keyed directly to the vulnerabilities of states at that time. In part because of ensuing successes, this period had a disproportionate influence on how modern insurgency, and also counterinsurgency, are viewed and practiced. The problem for insurgents is that the vulnerabilities of states have changed since the Cold War, forcing evolution also in how insurgency should be designed. Until such changes are made, the traditional path to power will yield diminishing returns.

Terrorism, Insurgency, and Counterinsurgency

It is true, also for armed groups, that 'nothing comes out of nothing.' In the case of insurgencies, it is helpful to view these groups as outgrowths of social movement organizations—the difference being that, at some point, the insurgent added violence to its repertoire. Still, for all the violence, insurgents and social movements share key traits. Both are collective actors, motivated by perceived grievances, and seeking social or political change. Both use predominantly social, political, and informational methods, mobilize resources (whether manpower or materiel), and organize these assets to serve political objectives. In insurgencies, violence acts as an enabler for the broader political project, yet it is but one method among many and does not necessarily define either the strategy or the challenge at hand.

The political nature of insurgency must be restated to counteract a common tendency to militarize this topic.[2] Because the use of terrorism or guerrilla warfare is the most visible and immediately unsettling aspect of insurgency, it is also this facet that tends to dominate analysis of the overall phenomenon. Perhaps as a result, scholarly treatment of insurgency and counterinsurgency occurs primarily within the fields of defense, security, and strategic studies, with retired officers or academics interested in military affairs opining about the role of government forces in combating armed rebels. In the policy world, the seductive simplicity of eliminating armed threats by force encourages the further militarization of counterinsurgency in practice, which then shapes how the term is understood within the public imagination. As a result of all these factors, the violent competition assumes center stage, obscuring the political purpose of the conflict and the need for states to respond through engagement and reform. It is, for example, very telling that, in many states, not least the United States and most of Europe, insurgency and counterinsurgency are hardly discussed, let alone practiced, outside military contexts.[3]

The problem with this militarized lens is that it lets the tail wag the dog. If war is truly a continuation of politics by other means, it is necessary to broaden the discussion of insurgency from the military domain and to consider also, even principally, its political essence: the drivers of mobilization into violence and the deals, bargains, and processes that may produce paths out of conflict. For this reason, insurgency may be more successfully framed as a form of violent politics and, hence, as a subset of contentious politics—the term used in social movement theory to analyze the strategies of social groupings pushing for change.[4] As sociologist William A. Gamson has argued, 'rebellion is simply politics by other means ... as instrumental in its nature as a lobbyist trying to get special favors for his group or a major political party conducting a presidential campaign.'[5] Indeed, much like an electoral campaign, insurgency is about the whys and wherefores of mobilization.

This positioning of insurgency is not meant to eclipse its violent expression. Violence is inherent in insurgency, yet it is the lubricant for political action, not an end in itself. For this reason, there is also an important difference between insurgency and terrorism, one that is poorly understood and that generates confusion both in diagnosis and in response. Terrorism is the non-state group's violent targeting of innocents for the purpose of political communication—this much is clear.[6] However, the term has become over-used and therefore deeply unhelpful, as it is now (for largely political reasons) made to describe all sorts of violent efforts. The point is not that insurgencies do not use terrorism—they almost always do—but rather that they do far more, and signify something bigger, and therefore should not be confused with the narrower problem set presented by the tactic of terrorism.

To be clear, this is not an ethical statement. It is a tired cliché but also a fallacy that 'one man's terrorist is another man's freedom fighter'; the phrase conflates the reasons for violence with its manner of execution.[7] Ethical treatments may concern themselves with the circumstances and causes that may morally justify internal revolt, even violence, yet this book is not a work of ethics. Instead, the concern here is with the strategic context of violence: its placement within a broader organizational repertoire, the relationship of its perpetrators to their purported mass base, and the function of violence in achieving political goals. In interrogating these questions, terrorist actors turn out to be of far lesser interest than their insurgent brethren. But what is the difference?

The French sociologist Michel Wieviorka put it very well when he noted that some groups use terror as one of many 'methods,' yet for others that method becomes all-consuming, that is, it becomes the 'logic' of the entire political project.[8] Herein lies the key distinction between insurgents and terrorists: both use terrorism, but terrorists have failed to achieve a constituency, be it willed or coerced, and cannot engage society except through repeated attacks. Isolated, radicalized, and with no other channels through which to communicate, terrorists adopt a punishment strategy as a relatively low-cost way of being heard, and yet, as society is not mobilized in support, these attacks only further divorce the group from its purported base.[9] Achieving political change therefore becomes very difficult. The state's response may be bedeviled by the group's clandestinity and small size but, ironically, these same factors also make it politically self-contained. The few key actors involved are, in effect, the sum total of 'the movement'—in reality there is no such thing—and the group becomes highly reliant on the minimal manpower that it has been able to attract.[10]

It is this limitation that allows the state to pursue a terrorist group by focusing on its members rather than its cause. With insurgency, however, a focus on rooting out 'the terrorists,' to the exclusion of finding political solutions to sources of conflict, often leads to new cycles of violence that an astute challenger will exploit to improve its position. Quite often, insurgent groups combine violence with a political strategy of mobilization, resulting in pockets of support and, even, the perception of legitimacy among a significant portion of the population. Elsewhere, it may be that the insurgent group is not supported, but that the government is absent or in a sorry state, leaving no option but to join the rebellion. Either way, it is far more complex and demanding to counter such a group than one with minimal ties to society and its politics.

Ironically, then, despite the great hype surrounding terrorism, it is really the insurgent that poses the more formidable threat. States get into the habit of labeling their insurgent foes as terrorists because the term is pejorative and brings in legal authorities—there simply is no comparable body of legislation for insurgencies.[11] Nonetheless, this practice is self-defeating when it obscures analysis of the problem at hand. When in 2005 US Secretary of Defense Donald Rumsfeld banned the word 'insurgency' from the Pentagon, for instance, it only delayed an appropriate response to the situation in Iraq at that time. Rumsfeld stated that he did believe the Sunni armed resistance 'merited' the word 'insurgency,' yet he failed to appreciate that it was not really his call to make.[12] The confused nature of the debate was also evident in President Barack Obama's bold assertion, in September 2014, that Islamic State 'is a terrorist organization, pure and simple.'[13] Perhaps not intended for academic evaluation, the statement nonetheless indicated a dangerously incorrect analysis (after all, this 'terrorist organization' was then mobilizing thousands of recruits and governing a significant counter-state).

The confusion can be traced to the very origins of the 'War on Terror' and the growing role of the military in subsequent 'counterterrorism' campaigns—tasks previously assigned to law enforcement agencies. The Obama administration shelved the 'War on Terror' moniker in 2009, yet the answer to the 9/11 attacks has remained largely consistent: engaged as it is in counterterrorism, there is little in the overall response to address the isolated yet significant pockets of support for al-Qaeda or the factors that might spread it further. This shortcoming is significant, given the findings in a Pew poll of 2013 that more than 15 percent of respondents in several Muslim-majority states had a 'favorable' view of al-Qaeda.[14] As Charles Lindholm and José Pedro Zúquete convincingly argue, this is not just a terrorist group; its self-proclaimed 'jihad' reflects a transnational social movement using violence to propel its concerns onto the global stage, so as to awaken and extend a pre-existing network.[15] Not only was the War on Terror negligent of this focoist insurgent strategy, it was also conducted in a bullish manner that all but ensured the empowerment of al-Qaeda's counter-hegemonic ideology.[16]

As al-Qaeda's ambiguous nature as an organization suggests, telling apart a terrorist group from an insurgent movement is not always so simple. After all, the carnage of terrorism looks more or less the same regardless of the type of group involved. Analysis and response must therefore carefully consider broader questions relating to the strategic function and context of the violence. Are those responsible a self-contained unit or, more worryingly, the vanguard of a mass movement? Is the group isolated and alone, or does it represent segments of the population who view it as somewhat legitimate? This last question must encourage dispassionate analysis of political realities, not opinion or preference about how matters 'should be.' We must be ready to acknowledge that our adversary may be more than a bandit, that its acts generate support at the expense of the state, and that even an ideology deemed toxic may be fueled by broad-based grievances and therefore find acceptance among those yearning for change.

The issue of legitimacy lies at the heart of counterinsurgency, at least in its theory. Because the state is pitted against an actor signifying far more than just its use of terror, the response must go beyond this security concern and consider also the social, economic, and political drivers that fuel support for violent solutions. Derided by its detractors as a euphemism for death squads and massacres, counterinsurgency theory succumbs instead to a liberal script: that through stability and reform to the social contract, the state becomes more inclusive and removes both the opportunity and the motive for violence.[17] Where the insurgent ideology cannot be accepted, it is the state's charge to reduce its appeal among the population, thereby isolating and rendering irrelevant a die-hard fringe that can be dealt with through proper law enforcement and traditional counterterrorism. This focus on addressing the drivers of alienation is reflected in the official definition of counterinsurgency as a set of 'comprehensive civilian and military efforts designed to simultaneously defeat and contain insurgency *and address its root causes*.'[18] For this reason, in successful counterinsurgencies, a government going in never looks quite the same as it does coming out.

It would be an understatement to say that this focus on reform and legitimacy does not always carry over from theory into practice.[19] As has happened throughout the history of counterinsurgency, threatened governments cast a wide net and punish entire segments of society, hoping in this manner to kill off incipient challenges and deter further violence. The use of force is indiscriminate or excessive or both. Even where governments mean well and seek to do better, the approach taken typically privileges the immediate need for security, seen as a precondition for any progress at all, and then neglects or fails at the political efforts that security is meant to make possible. It is worth asking why practice so often differs from theory in this manner—and it is a question to which we must now turn.

Deuce; Advantage State

Counterinsurgency analysts rightly decry the sorry track record of governments engaged in these efforts, specifically their inability to translate military gains into politically meaningful and sustainable goals. In theory, counterinsurgency should operate like an 'oil slick,' a metaphor coined by French colonial officers to denote the progressive expansion of state control and legitimacy, 'from the center to the periphery,' so as to undo the insurgent project.[20] In the Anglo-Saxon tradition, the imagery of choice was that of the ink spot, spreading across blotting paper, but the gist was much the same. Translated into the more prosaic vernacular of military organizations, the approach is that of 'clear-hold-build': the state gains control of contested territory, expands such control throughout the country, and while doing so establishes a new contract with the population, built on legitimacy and consent. Zones of government control are created, which grow over time until the insurgency is defeated.[21]

In practice, instead of government control spreading like oil slicks or ink spots, counterinsurgent armies commonly find themselves 'mowing the grass'—a more recent metaphor denoting the repeated clearing of the same territory only for it to be retaken by the enemy.[22] Despite the great efforts of many, this fitful, indecisive, and cyclical approach characterized much of the counterinsurgency seen both in Afghanistan and in Iraq. In Afghanistan, NATO forces launched several large-scale operations against the Taliban, harrying them elsewhere, yet failed to set up the security, development, and governance reforms for which the clearing of terrain was intended.[23] In theory, these lines of effort should have been led by the Afghan government, whose legitimacy was at stake and who would need to bind the state following the eventual departure of foreign troops. In reality, as NATO troops departed one 'cleared' area, the Taliban returned and swiftly punished whoever might have cooperated with the government in Kabul. As a result, by 2016 the Taliban—once facing near defeat—had overrun at least a third of the country.[24] By the summer of 2021, with NATO forces leaving, the Taliban took over the rest of Afghanistan and claimed national power, illustrating just how superficial past claims of government control had been.

In Iraq, for several years following the overthrow of Saddam Hussein, most US troops were confined to large forward operating bases and left their compounds only for discrete raids, typically to find, capture, and kill suspected insurgents.[25] Any security gains made in this manner were ephemeral, or even counterproductive, in that they inflamed relations between the occupying forces and the local population and neglected the insurgency's political drivers. The rediscovery of counterinsurgency doctrine in 2006 enabled more enduring stabilization during the so-called surge years of 2007–10. Still, even at this time, the consequences of having empowered sectarian Shia elements within the government were never addressed, leading to schisms and further violence once US troops left—and they left quickly.[26] The jury is still out as to whether the latest mowing of the grass—the military dismantling of the ISIS counter-state—will be politically sustained or have a more transient effect.[27]

The lawn-mowing dilemma also characterizes local efforts at counterinsurgency that do not involve US or NATO troops. In Nigeria, various cycles of military operations against the Islamic State West Africa Province (ISWAP) have expelled the group from the cities and limited its area of operations but have failed to address the factors that allow it to survive, even grow, within the country's northeast.[28] In the Philippines, thinly deployed local security forces and a lack of civil–military coordination have complicated the consolidation of military gains, leading the armed forces to conduct repeated security operations with inadequate follow-up.[29] In Colombia, save for a period in the early 2000s, the armed forces have operated essentially as firemen: 'the initiative may be wrested from the enemy, but victories cannot be solidified in the absence of government popular mobilization to hold ground.'[30] In Brazil, the Unidades de Polícia Pacificadora (UPP) approach, steeped in the clear-hold-build philosophy, succeeded in temporarily undermining the gangs that had claimed ownership of entire *favelas*, yet the lack of consolidation and rushed expansion of the program to other areas resulted in the gradual loss of initial gains and the re-emergence of criminal elements.[31]

The United Nations, in its efforts at 'robust peacekeeping,' faces the same inability to translate military gains into political progress.[32] In Haiti, where UN forces mounted impressive operations against entrenched gangs, 'tactical success through the use of force led to only limited strategic payoffs … with MINUSTAH [the UN peace operation] struggling to integrate the use of force into a larger project for Haitian political and economic transformation.'[33] As Mats Berdal notes, a similar verdict applies to the many applications of 'robust force' in the Democratic Republic of Congo, whose stabilizing effects have been 'highly localised and displaced violence, including widespread atrocities, elsewhere.'[34] In the same vein, various French interventions in Africa, for example operations Serval and Barkhane in the Sahel, have kept insurgents on the run yet failed to make possible political progress, or even a sense of sustainable security.[35]

Overall, the collective experience with counterinsurgency reveals a pattern of states not doing enough or doing the wrong thing. Repeated missteps, failures, and quagmires have informed cautionary remarks that counterinsurgency is 'messy and slow, like eating soup with a knife.'[36] To a large degree, such warnings are entirely apt: these missions demand deft diplomatic action, persuasive information campaigns, accurate intelligence on murky clandestine structures, swift institutional specialization for the task, and, perhaps most elusively, the ability by fundamentally weak states to (re)gain legitimacy and mobilize an alienated population for support. The political challenge is—in one sense—compounded for the United States and other actors whose engagement with counterinsurgency occurs primarily in other countries. While these expeditionary actors may appreciate their remove from the problem, the vicarious approach to counterinsurgency must contend not only with the rebellion but also with a host nation government over which external parties have only so much influence or control.

And yet, despite all of this—despite states lacking the necessary capabilities and ignoring most of the best practices in the field—in recent times the incidence of insurgent victory has been extremely low. During the Cold War, it was relatively common to see insurgents overthrow the government and become the new state. This was how China went communist, Vietnam ejected the French and then the Americans, Israel was created, Che Guevara won Cuba, the Sandinistas gained power, and Laos became a people's republic. More generally, during these years, successful insurgency also brought about regime change in Angola, Bangladesh, Cambodia, Costa Rica, Guinea-Bissau, Iran, Mozambique, and Zimbabwe. In the 1990s, Eritrea, the Republic of Congo, Rwanda, the Democratic Republic of Congo, Kosovo, and Timor Leste followed suit, with new regimes installed as a result.

In contrast, insurgent victories have become far less frequent since the turn of the century. There are good reasons to treat with caution the large quantitative datasets that claim to track conflict outcomes, but it is still notable that, according to Uppsala University's prestigious Conflict Termination dataset, there were only *two* decisive insurgent victories in all the armed conflicts occurring between 2000 and 2015.[37] The first of these two refers, strangely, to the highly transient control of northern Mali by the National Movement for the Liberation of Azawad—its grip on the territory lasted about a year. The second case was not an insurgent victory but rather the coup led by François Bozizé in the Central African Republic. Coups, of course, are not the same as insurgencies: one is a swift seizure of power through the support of some of the state's own military, the other a protracted armed struggle that targets these very same forces and involves, to a far greater degree, the population (even then, it is notable that successful coups have also declined steadily from 61 in the 1960s to fewer than 10 in the 2010s).[38]

The Uppsala dataset is clearly incomplete. For one, it has yet to account for the conquest of Kabul by the Taliban in August 2021—a clear and resounding insurgent victory. It also misses five other relevant cases. In Liberia in 2003, the Liberians United for Reconciliation and Democracy (LURD) and the Movement for Democracy in Liberia (MODEL) ousted the Charles Taylor regime; in Côte d'Ivoire, the military activities of the Forces Nouvelles led to the arrest of President Laurent Gbagbo, who had refused to cede power following his electoral defeat; in Libya in 2011, the National Transitional Council (NTC) overthrew the government of Muammar Gaddafi; and in Sudan, the Sudan People's Liberation Movement (SPLM) was able to fight its way to a peace agreement and referendum, leading the way to South Sudan's secession and independence in 2004.[39] Coming back to Afghanistan, one could also count the earlier instance of regime change there, in 2001, when the Northern Alliance successfully toppled the Taliban regime, such as it was.

These six cases, while notable, also remain exceptions to a striking trend. As striking, in all six cases, albeit to varying degrees, foreign state sponsorship was critical to the insurgents' success.[40] The Northern Alliance had been losing ground throughout the 1990s yet it all but defeated the Taliban in three weeks following the US intervention prompted by 9/11. Later, as the Taliban fought back and eventually swept Kabul, it was aided by the support and sanctuary received in Pakistan.[41] In Liberia, LURD benefited from the support of Guinea, and therefore indirectly also from Europe and the United States, whereas MODEL acted, in effect, as an extension of the Ivorian government, even operating from its territory. In Côte d'Ivoire itself, French-led UN forces helped separate the two combatants and then struck directly at sites held by forces loyal to Gbagbo.[42] In Libya, it was NATO's military intervention, ostensibly to prevent atrocity, that sealed Gaddafi's fate. Finally, the military stalemate that led to the peace agreement between Sudan and South Sudan related closely to Ugandan, Ethiopian, and also US support for the forces of John Garang.[43] Notably, other than in Liberia and Côte d'Ivoire, the aftermath of these conflicts was marked by intense warfare, rendering these would-be insurgent 'victories' far from conclusive. It is still too early to say which way the Taliban victory will go—whether it will realize its political project of an Islamic Emirate or succumb to infighting within a seemingly never-ending civil war.

State support has always been important to insurgents, yet these days they appear not to manage without it. As we have seen, this shift is not because of some qualitative improvement in the execution of counterinsurgency. If we return to the Conflict Termination dataset, 38 percent of all conflict 'episodes' that ended between 1950 and 1989 resulted in a decisive victory for the state; from 2000 to

2014, this figure dropped to 14.7 percent, amounting to only 13 government victories out of a total 88 relevant outcomes.[44] Writing in 2017, Seth G. Jones found just two clear government victories against insurgents since 9/11: the Guinean War of 2000–2001 against the Allied Democratic Forces of Guinea (RDFG), a relatively minor rebel group, and Sri Lanka's military defeat of the Tamil Tigers, a far more formidable adversary. Depending on one's standards, one might include the defeat of Islamic State, at least in Iraq but also in the Philippines, as a third and fourth contender. Nevertheless, the overall picture suggests that most conflicts since 9/11 have failed to be resolved decisively one way or the other—and, indeed, the struggles against ISIS have hardly ended, either in the Middle East or in Asia.

Statistics back up this trend. Joakim Kreutz demonstrates, for example, that the proportion of intra-state conflicts 'ending' without a decisive outcome (victory for either side or peace agreement) has increased from 33.3 percent during the Cold War to 68 percent since 1990.[45] Between 1950 and 1989, a fifth of 'intense' conflicts (those causing an annual death toll of above 1,000) would end decisively, yet from 2000 to 2014 the rate declined to 6 percent (Sri Lanka and Libya).[46] Looking at the average experience, insurgency and counterinsurgency are today best characterized by the vast majority of cases where the outcome is unresolved; this is our new normal.

The problem for today's insurgents, then, is not that the state is necessarily better at counterinsurgency, but rather that the insurgents are no longer succeeding in claiming power in the way they did during the Cold War. In datasets, these types of conflict may be coded 'indecisive,' but over time they do allow the state to live on and plausibly even grow stronger. Without necessarily winning, states thus survive challenges to their writ and thwart insurgent projects of violent change, which—to many of them—will be as good as victory, particularly when it requires less effort and little or no reform. To understand why this minimalist approach to counterinsurgency may work better today than it did in the past, it is necessary to review the conditions for insurgent success back then and to query whether they are still in place.

The Etiology of Insurgency

Today's theory and practice of insurgency were forged in the decades following the Second World War. At this time, the crumbling of empires and the ideological backdrop of the Cold War provided an auspicious laboratory for any challenger seeking to upset the status quo. Serendipity also produced a roadmap for insurgency early in this period, with the victory of the Chinese Communist Party (CCP) in 1949 and the codification of, and intent to export, the best practices of this effort to other revolutionaries around the world. As James C. Corum highlights, the CCP 'developed a comprehensive theory of insurgency … a quantum leap forward … drawn from classical military and Marxist theory, military history, and an analysis of China's conditions.'[47] For decades, even to this day, the approach taken by the communists in China would act as a blueprint for insurgents elsewhere.

As is implied, what Mao prescribed was not entirely new—far from it—though he was responsible for turning the approach into a form of war. Thomas Marks explains: Mao 'combine[d] the parts into a systematic whole, complete with doctrine, in a manner that put any state at risk. Indeed, the combination, built as it was upon ideological mobilization of inferiority, proved so baffling that for a time it appeared well-nigh unstoppable.'[48] A key innovation was to marry a military approach to rebellion with the political exploitation of 'contradictions,' or the vulnerabilities in society that could be used to mobilize a movement. With a tireless focus on the political, Mao constructed a revolutionary apparatus capable of penetrating entire societies, translating mobilization into military capability, and deploying such assets in potent confrontations against the state. Victory progressed along three phases, never quite contiguous or linear, whereby the insurgents (1) mobilized and built support, (2) established base areas and upped their attacks, and finally (3) formed regular units for the ultimate overthrow of the state.

Mao was not alone in either building or exporting 'people's war.' In Vietnam, almost in parallel and benefiting from some historical linkages to the situation in China, Ho Chi Minh inspired a closely related form of insurgency, further articulated by Vo Nguyen Giap and Truong Chinh. It was this Vietnamese variant that made its way, via Havana, to El Salvador and Nicaragua. Because the Cold War was now a more pressing reality, and local dynamics meshed with great-power politics, a growing focus would be devoted to stemming international support for the local government, thereby facilitating an eventual military victory. Notwithstanding differences in emphasis and nuance, however, it was still a fundamentally Maoist theory that 'influenced, and continues to influence, insurgent groups throughout the world.'[49] In all these cases, 'the key was mobilizing the counter-state so as ultimately to be able to project superior combat power against the state.'[50]

Mao's insistence on politics and patient mobilization of the masses was evidently difficult to replicate, and his 'people's war' did not always travel well. Mao had acknowledged the protracted duration of the struggle, yet 'he was convinced that as long as the insurgents remained active and followed his theory, they would eventually win.'[51] In contrast, for many revolutionaries, those seeking quicker results, violence—not politics—became the defining feature of the struggle. It is indeed rather telling that Mao's approach to insurgency became popularized through his *On Guerrilla Warfare*, which was in fact merely a training manual for military operations, released in 1937 as 'a stepping stone to a much larger and more complex body of "people's war" work.'[52] It would appear that insurgents, as well as states, seek the quick and bloody way out.

Violence mattered also to Mao, yet—again—only within its political context: its use was to neutralize 'the armed capacity of the enemy; but, more fundamentally, to carve out the space necessary for the political activities of (alternative) state-building achieved through mobilization and construction of capacity.'[53] Thus, even as a young insurgent, Mao chastised those who 'think the task of the Red Army ... is merely to fight. They do not understand that the Chinese Red Army is an armed body for carrying out the political tasks of the revolution ... Without these objectives, fighting loses its meaning.'[54] In contrast, many followers of Mao were too impatient, or misread local conditions, leading to rushed efforts marked by the hasty and foolhardy adoption of violence. In many of these cases, the state was still too strong, and so the insurgent rushed toward a predictable defeat.

At its most extreme, Che Guevara, while he lauded Mao's legacy, proposed what was in fact its very antithesis: a form of top-down mobilization where violence against the state would ignite the political movement, rather than the other way around. Walter Laqueur explains the deviation: Che 'regarded armed insurrection not as the final, crowning phase of the political struggle, but expected on the contrary that the armed conflict would trigger off, or at least give decisive impetus to, the political campaign.'[55] What was lost in translation was Mao's emphasis on tactical alliances with societal powerbrokers (the united front), the mobilization of the masses (the mass line), the shaping of the international environment, and the construction of clandestine infrastructure (the counter-state). Partly for this reason, and despite Che's international image as a leading revolutionary of the twentieth century, his overall track record is rather damning, as is most serious analysis of his efforts.[56] Christopher Hitchens was not too far off in suggesting that Che may retain 'a hint of charisma' but 'made no contribution whatsoever to the battle of theories and ideas.'[57]

If Mao and Che occupy opposite sides of the spectrum of insurgent strategy, most movements fell somewhere in-between. In Thailand, the Philippines, El Salvador, Colombia, Peru, Nepal, India, Zimbabwe and beyond, various insurgent outfits claimed to be adopting the Maoist people's war approach to local struggles.[58] In almost all cases, these efforts replicated Mao's primary focus on rural mobilization. This focus, which had worked well in China, represented a philosophical break with the traditional Marxist focus on the urban proletariat; it also seemed better suited to the developing world, as it was easier both to recruit and to survive the onslaughts of the state when far removed from its urban centers.[59] Though urban guerrilla attacks occasionally featured as a way to sap or distract the state, it was the patient build-up of military capability in the countryside that promised eventual success.[60] As Paul Rich notes in an extensive deconstruction of Che's legacy, even the insurgency in Cuba—the presumed standard-bearer of his city-based *focismo*—was in reality 'as much an urban as a rural revolt.'[61]

Having spread throughout the world, the Maoist approach shaped understandings of insurgency well beyond the Cold War and well beyond just communist struggles.[62] In 1993, when the jihadi theorist Abu Musab al-Suri provided guidance for how to launch successful insurrection, he went so far as to steal Mao's metaphor of insurgents swimming like fish in the sea of the masses.[63] When al-Qaeda strategist Abu Bakr Naji in 2004 published *Management of Savagery* as strategic guidance for the Islamist project, he proposed a path to power very heavily influenced by Mao's teachings.[64] Echoing Mao's three phases of mobilization (harassment, establishment of base areas, and overthrow of the state), Abu Bakr Naji proposed phases of vexation and exhaustion, administration of loosely governed areas, and the final establishment of the caliphate (the jihadi counter-state).[65] As Craig Whiteside has demonstrated, the later rise of Islamic State also used an 'adaptation of Mao's revolutionary warfare concept—as executed by the Vietnamese communists and modified to fit its Islamist ideology.'[66]

Given his continued influence well into the twenty-first century, Mao also became the foundation for how states framed insurgency. As the topic once again became strategically relevant, as a subset of the War on Terror and against the backdrop of an escalating war in Iraq, the US military released an updated counterinsurgency manual that resonated loudly with Cold War-era texts on the topic.[67] By and large, the new field manual assumed a Maoist insurgent adversary, devoting most of its energies to 'protracted people's war.' Digging into this approach, it explained how the insurgent's 'transition from guerrilla warfare to conventional warfare,' in combination with 'political action,' would cause 'the government's collapse or the occupying power's withdrawal.'[68]

In this manner, the Maoist blueprint for insurgency powerfully shaped the West's rediscovery of counterinsurgency early in the twenty-first century. As set out in the field manuals, the role of the US military was, at a minimum, to prevent the escalation from 'strategic stalemate' to 'strategic counteroffensive,' in which an insurgency takes on 'the characteristics of a full-scale civil war.'[69] While it acknowledged that the insurgent was unlikely to engage in open battle until conditions were correct, the point was to reclaim the insurgent's 'expanding areas of control,' where its 'subversive activities' were contributing to the emergence of a 'counterstate.'[70] Following a similar logic, NATO in 2009 explicitly identified 'clear-hold-build' as its 'preferred operational approach' to counterinsurgency.[71] If Mao and Abu Bakr Naji had their three phases, so did the state, and if their guerrillas were going to swim like fish in the sea of people, the state would reclaim both fish and sea through oil slicks and ink spots expanding across blotting paper.

It is ironic that just as Mao's followers often failed to replicate his insistence on the political process, so counterinsurgents have often struggled to translate clearing and holding into something more politically sustainable. In many places, a militarily driven adaptation of Maoist insurgency has squared off against a militarily driven approach to counterinsurgency, producing a dialectic, or a competition of wills, that begins to explain the increasing prevalence of undecided or indecisive outcomes in these struggles. Yet, whereas during the Cold War this stalemate would often favor the insurgents, it is now far more difficult for them to push home the advantage. Today, the dialectic instead benefits the state, as it appears increasingly capable of managing insurgency without addressing its root causes and by relying on military fixes rather than political solutions. To explain this shift, it is necessary to interrogate the ways in which the context for insurgency has evolved.

Insurgency amid a Shifting Context

Four major changes explain why the dialectic mentioned above, which used to provide a promising path for insurgents, now favors the state. These factors did not develop simultaneously, but their admixture over time has proved particularly fatal for the militarized insurgent approach practiced during the Cold War. Any one or two of these factors can be effectively overcome by sound strategy and an entrepreneurial spirit, but confronting all four at once appears near impossible to all but the most innovative of insurgent organizations.

First, urbanization is depleting the rural countryside of people and resources. Between 1950 and 2015, the extent of urbanization in the world's 'less developed regions'—where insurgency has always been more likely—almost tripled from 17.7 to 50.6 per cent.[72] This creates a problem for the traditional approach to insurgency, which relied on the rural population to build a movement and to find shelter from the state. Already during the Cold War, insurgent movements struggled, mostly unsuccessfully, to operate in urban settings and to integrate these efforts within an overall strategy. Certainly, the Vietnamese grasped 'the symbiotic relationship between rural and urban space,' but, as Marks notes, the approach formulated there 'was not well understood, even by those who sought explicitly to adopt it.'[73] For example, in Latin America, the most urbanized continent and one where insurgency moved early on to the city, most groups found it difficult, despite great theorization on the topic, to mobilize the urban population and to survive so close to the state without a rural rearguard.[74]

As Jennifer Taw and Bruce Hoffman predicted back in 1994, 'as rural populations, uprooted by poverty, hunger, and conflict, continue to migrate to the cities, the guerrilla forces dependent on them for food, information, concealment, and support will have no choice but to follow.'[75] Yet operating in the cities invites risk; at the very least, the crowded terrain and the oversight of the state make it difficult to build up the conventional combat capabilities necessary to confront the government militarily.[76] Recent advances in technology, not least in artificial intelligence and surveillance, make the urban terrain even more inhospitable to clandestine movements seeking to gain power gradually before finally taking on the state. Thus, much as during the Cold War, it is likely that urban campaigns will produce attacks and harassment, violence and bloodshed, but little with which to build strategic momentum.

Second, the normative environment facing insurgents is less auspicious today than during the twentieth century. Amid decolonization, the world faced, and the international community tolerated, a number of violent regime changes brought about by armed movements of 'national liberation.' The end of colonialism was underpinned by a 'moral revolution,' allowing nationalists to claim the mantle of legitimacy and an acceptable narrative, not only domestically but also internationally.[77] This stance—that empire had had its day—was one point on which both the United States and the Soviet Union could agree. Also, as William Reno points out, because these anti-colonial rebels ultimately sought state sovereignty, 'the results of their struggles were easy to incorporate into the international system, and this was formalized in these rebels' acceptance of the established international order.'[78] The concomitant emergence of an ideological competition, between capitalism and communism, further normalized the use of violence as a way of restructuring these societies, whose character and trajectory were anyway still in play.

In contrast, since the end of the Cold War and the 9/11 attacks in particular, the struggles of rebel groups have become less politically palatable, much as the very art of insurgency, executed by unaccountable groups that employ terrorism, has become a source of vulnerability. In the past groups could argue a distinction between their violent activity and their political work and ideals, and thereby retain some measure of international support. These days, they find themselves proscribed outright by an increasing number of states. This shift applies, naturally, to the groups behind the 9/11 attacks, but it has extended far beyond al-Qaeda or even Islamic State. In 2002 and 2003 respectively, Canada and the European Union banned Hamas, dismissing its purported distinctions between aid work, politics, and violence as empirically untenable. They added LTTE to the list in 2006. A number of states long tolerated Hezbollah as a primarily political movement, albeit with a military wing, yet since 9/11 it has been blacklisted in its entirety in the Netherlands (2006), the United Kingdom (2019), Germany (2020) and elsewhere. More generally, states are quick to foist the 'terrorist' label on any non-state adversary as soon as, or even before, it launches its first attack, so as to benefit from a zeitgeist in which armies of liberation have lost their glory.[79]

Third, and conversely, states are now benefiting from more support, more power, and greater legal authority when combating insurgent adversaries. The 9/11 attacks produced international legislation that tightened loopholes used by non-state armed groups, complicated money transfers to proscribed organizations, and empowered states to do more against the scourge of terrorism.[80] Simultaneously, third-party assistance to counterinsurgency efforts has increased, while military technology has advanced, specifically with regard to stand-off weaponry, mobility, and surveillance.[81]

Because of these capabilities and support, it is now more difficult for insurgents to mass forces and structures beyond the state's reach and to compete with it militarily—those that do prove only 'their willingness and readiness for martyrdom.'[82]

Fourth, whereas insurgency used to feature as a fairly common instrument of foreign policy for the superpowers of the Cold War— as the mechanism by which to flip hostile governments and score points in a global battle for ideology—such sponsorship is now less overt and less generous. The practice of sponsoring insurgency still goes on, but those most active in this arena tend to be neighbors to the conflict rather than superpowers competing for global dominance, and the sums involved are far more modest than before.[83] Also, reflecting the changed zeitgeist alluded to above, the states involved in sponsoring insurgency tirelessly insist that they play no role in the conflict at all. Be it Pakistan's funding of the Taliban in Afghanistan, Iran's sponsorship of the Houthis in Yemen, or even Russia's role in eastern Ukraine, such claims are clearly contestable, but they do limit the extent to which aid can be visibly tendered.[84]

These four factors aggregate into an insurgent's dilemma, imposed upon challengers to the state as they square up against its military might. Insurgents have always faced the challenge of superior state adversaries and the 'dilemma of conflicting goals': growth and exposure versus stasis and security.[85] Charles, Louise and Richard Tilly captured this dilemma in 1975, describing it as the difficult choice 'between taking actions which have a high probability of bringing on a violent response (but which have some chance of reaching the group's goals) and taking no action at all (thereby assuring the defeat of the group's goals).'[86] The balancing act is age-old, and yet in contrast to the Cold War, the dilemma has now become razor-sharp.

In the past, the relative weakness of states, the ample spaces and populations in and among which to organize, and generous state support to boot meant insurgents could amass impressive military capability, often rivalling those of the state.[87] As Stathis Kalyvas and Laia Balcells conclude, 'the Cold War benefited rebels more than governments because it turned their "deep weakness," which had prevented many budding rebellions from reaching the stage of civil war, into "relative weakness," which allowed them to mount an effective military challenge against a stronger state.' Kalyvas and Balcells refer to the outcome as a 'robust insurgency,' which in practice takes on the form of civil war.[88] As an example, even though it, too, faced the 'dilemma of conflicting goals'—and was in fact crushed by the state—a group like the Democratic Army of Greece was first able to muster 25,000 fighters, organized into brigades and divisions and equipped conventionally.[89] Similarly, FMLN in El Salvador, FARC in Colombia, UNITA in Angola, SPLA in Sudan, the LTTE in Sri Lanka and many others also acquired state-like armies and military capability with which to confront, and occasionally defeat, government forces.

This trend meant that an insurgent theory of victory based on the armed overthrow of a seated government, while ambitious, was not entirely unrealistic. Certainly, it would be possible, under such circumstances, to impose sufficient military costs on the regime so as to achieve key concessions. Indeed, to most theorists and practitioners of the time, insurgents were *required* to become a regular army, and insurgency a conventional war, because (in the words of one noted revolutionary) 'only such an army can stage an offensive of the nature that will subdue the enemy.'[90] Today, in contrast, owing to the factors proposed above, it is difficult to conceive of an insurgent army organizing itself into divisions or outgunning the state, let alone defeating it and becoming the new authority. Instead, groups that have sought regularization in this manner have given up their key asymmetric advantages (the fluidity, camouflage, and dispersion) and thereby become relatively fixed targets for the state's military. At the same time, limiting armed actions to softer targets, typically through terrorism, further isolates the group societally and internationally, which is bad for business and can result in pariah status.[91]

In parallel, the absence of state sponsors and the disappearance of a taxable rural population have forced insurgent groups to look elsewhere for support. Owing in part to the effects of globalization and easier access to international markets, some groups have generated significant resources through criminal activity, be it the trafficking of drugs, precious stones, lumber, or—indeed—people. The growth of such activity stems from the deregulation of key industries, the increased mobility of capital, and the vastly improved communications technology and can result in untold wealth.[92] Still, in an international environment that is already hostile to insurgency, criminal ventures have further sullied armed movements and their causes, greatly complicating the leap from rebel to statesman. In Colombia, where Marxist guerrillas were once framed as 'politically-driven, heroic, revolutionary victims, fighting to redress authoritarianism,' after 9/11 'rebel groups in general, from the left to the right, appeared less heroic, particularly as the academic and policy emphasis on the economics of war had uncovered its "dirty" financial aspects and greed.'[93] In other contexts, the emergence of illicit political economies has tended to distract ideologically driven movements, leading to their fracture and loss of direction. As Mats Berdal notes, 'where economic agendas have played a prominent part,' armed groups typically fragment, as local commanders and strongmen seek to reap the benefits of war rather than engage in 'costly and drawn-out battles.'[94] In many ways, therefore, the search for new sources of funding has further diminished the likelihood of traditional insurgent success, at least as conventionally defined.

These contextual factors, and their impact, help us understand the prevailing trends of contemporary insurgency and counterinsurgency, as described above: a tendency toward stalemate; military confrontations that harass but never defeat the state; and outcomes that benefit neither the state nor its challengers but also perpetuate the status quo. The US military's 2006 counterinsurgency manual unintentionally hit on this reality when it stated that 'insurgents succeed by sowing chaos and disorder anywhere'; this may very well be what we expect insurgencies to do, but is it how they *succeed*— and, if so, how? How do they transform the instability they sow into a durable political order, or move from troublemaker to state-taker? As it turns out, they often cannot, because, owing to certain contextual factors, the progression expected by Mao and other Cold War revolutionaries is blocked.

Many groups have failed to realize this change, or failed to adapt to it, and go on without truly challenging the state. Still, these realities are shaping the global experience of insurgency today. To William Reno, despite a long list of grievances to draw on, 'the age of the committed guerrilla fighters in the countryside, battling state forces to control and administer populations, appears to have largely disappeared from the African scene.'[95] In Asia, 'the last two decades have seen both a dramatic decrease in insurgency-related violence and a noticeable growth in state coercive power.'[96] ISIS still plans its resurgence and talks confidently about frustrating the enemy and draining his energy, but it is far from clear how any of this will allow the envisaged 'semi-conventional' military units to be fielded without running into the same fate as their predecessors in Mosul, Raqqa, or Marawi.[97] The Taliban's victory in Afghanistan may offer some inspiration to insurgents elsewhere, yet they will quickly discover just how contingent this case was on a specific and irreproducible set of circumstances. In more general terms, the traditional insurgent theory of victory is blocked—and yet, if this is today's insurgent's dilemma, some groups will adapt.

Conclusion

During the Cold War and the era of imperial decline, leading revolutionaries such as Mao Tse-tung and Che Guevara posited insurgency as an armed political competition to seize state power. Though theorists differed on what to emphasize and on questions of sequence, the proposed method of wresting power relied largely on mobilization, the construction of clandestine infrastructure, and violence of an increasing intensity. By coupling dispersed small-unit attacks with organized big-unit violence, the approach forced government troops to be everywhere, making them vulnerable to attack anywhere. Over time, escalating military harassment would allow for a conventional attack on the armed forces of the government, leading to state capture.

Back then, regime change through force of arms was relatively common, producing what Kalyvas and Balcells call 'a remarkable reversal in the outcomes of irregular wars.'[98] Indeed, it was precisely the severity of this challenge that fueled concern about counterinsurgency and broader theorization about how states ought to react. More recently, however, only a select few insurgent groups have attempted to go toe to toe against the organized units of a state, let alone succeeded in doing so. In reality, since the attacks of 9/11, insurgents on the whole are no longer winning.

This presents a puzzle, as there is also no compelling evidence to suggest states are doing much better, or that they have mastered the art of counterinsurgency. Despite great exhortations in the attendant theory and the valuable efforts of many, states typically fail to address the political aspects of insurgency or to undergo those reforms that might bring sustainable results. Across the globe, whether it be third-party interventions by the United States and its allies, robust peace operations by the United Nations blue helmets, or host nation efforts against homegrown adversaries, the common experience of counterinsurgency today is cyclical and at best palliative. And yet, while scholars of counterinsurgents decry the low number of success stories and apparent lack of progress, this suboptimal approach does appear sufficient in tamping down rebellion and keeping it at a level of intensity deemed acceptable. The net outcome of these simmering confrontations is that the state survives and, in some cases, grows stronger.

It is this record that creates the insurgent's dilemma: the difficulty of asserting oneself as a start-up, of violently challenging authority, and establishing oneself sustainably as the new source of power. While this dilemma is certainly not new, it is becoming more acute, owing to mutually reinforcing contextual changes. Urbanization has emptied the rural countryside of both manpower and materiel, forcing mobilization within cities, where the state is more present and the build-up of military capability more hazardous. Whereas newly independent states were once weaker and vulnerable to armed challengers, they are today more established and militarily capable, with surveillance and stand-off weaponry allowing them to see and reach further than before. The international community has also become increasingly intolerant of non-state armed groups, given their use of terrorism, and therefore resists their efforts to claim authority through violent means. Meanwhile, overt state sponsorship of rebellion has subsided, forcing insurgents to self-finance, often in ways that contribute to the stigmatization and fragmentation of their cause.

In short, the current operating environment has made it more difficult for insurgents to reach the military strength of states. These groups can sustain campaigns of low-level destruction, with AK-47s, IEDs, and ideology squaring up against the armed forces deployed in response. And yet, despite the great harm that can be caused in such confrontations, it is not a promising path to significant political gains. Indeed, while sub-state conflict and intra-state conflict by far remain the most common forms of conflict, they increasingly lead to indecisive outcomes.[99] This trend will not be entirely satisfying to either side, but it nonetheless favors the state, which, in the absence of being overthrown, remains the constituted authority.

In the face of this abysmal track record, amid this butting of heads between insurgents and states, some groups will adapt. Warfare is a competition of wills, as Clausewitz reminds us, using the metaphor of a wrestling match.[100] More recent war theorists describe strategy as a process of co-evolution, whereby opposing sides reciprocally drive each other's development in a battle for fitness—that is to say, for survival.[101] Regardless of metaphor, it should be expected that insurgents, stuck in a dilemma, will seek a way out. If Cold War insurgency was keyed to the vulnerabilities of the states of that era, savvy insurgents will be looking for, and some have already found, the vulnerabilities of our own era—those that allow for fresh paths to power.

3

LOCALIZED INSURGENCY
PARA-STATES AND PERIPHERIES

If insurgents can no longer expect to defeat the state militarily, or achieve sufficient gains to force concessions, how can they nonetheless satisfy their political objectives? One possible approach relies on localizing the struggle, or limiting it to the subnational level, so as to stay below the threshold where the state is compelled to respond. By eschewing the lofty goals of regime change and focusing instead on peripheral territories or populations that the state has already lost, or over which it is less likely to fight, the group can find space to operate, even thrive. Over time, this approach may even lead to an awkward accommodation, whereby the state and challenger learn to coexist in both productive and deeply destructive ways.

The localized approach to insurgency is hardly new, but it benefits from structural conditions accentuated in recent years. Specifically, opportunities to share sovereignty with the state are made more abundant by the global process of urbanization and its fragmentary effects on governance, both within its cities and in their relation to the periphery. The parallel globalization of economics and trade makes it easier for elites to capitalize on what interests them without having to carry the populations and parts of the country deemed less profitable. In the places left behind, insurgents find that by moderating their approach they can obtain ample space in which to create and maintain an illicit political project. Indeed, in this more globalized environment, actual control of the capital is no longer as necessary as before to project a narrative, mobilize resources, and stake a claim for power.

The localized approach relies upon and also contributes to the incidence of 'failed' or 'fragile' states. In its logic and effect, it challenges the notion of a monolithic or cohesive nation-state, often assumed to be the building block of international society. More than an inability to exert government authority from border to border, in line with the Weberian norms of sovereignty, a number of states evince a lack of interest in such grand ideals. Instead, they make shrewd assessments of what to prioritize, leading to political oligopolies, or archipelagos of political power, all within one nation-state. As accommodative arrangements congeal, localized insurgency also challenges the traditional conception of rebels and governments pitted against one another in a zero-sum game. Instead, both co-exist within a conception of the state largely unrecognized by political theory yet increasingly prevalent across the globe.

This chapter sets out the nature of localized insurgency, distinguishing it both from the traditional form of insurgency and from its close brethren: secessionist struggles. It weaves theory with a series of cases to illustrate how this approach works in practice, both in urban and in rural environments. The chapter concludes by commenting on the dangers of localized insurgency. Indeed, though states may dismiss the very localization of insurgency as a sign of success, in that it does not threaten the capital or governing elite, over time this approach still has a way of hollowing out the state and existentially undercutting its institutions to the point of collapse. Given their foundation in informal and precarious balances of power, between the state and the challenger, localized struggles also risk inviting outsiders—both states and others—who seek to exploit the ongoing fragmentation to serve broader and more destabilizing ends.

Struggles in a Segmented City

In the *favelas* of Rio de Janeiro, Brazil, the presence of the state might best be described as 'patchy': there are signs of its systems and structures, but its provision of services, including that of security, cannot be relied upon. With no functioning or persistent form of governance provided by the state, gangs and criminal syndicates have arisen and become the most influential powerbrokers. For the *favelados*—the residents of the slums and shantytowns—this transfer of authority away from the state has required evolving new ways of dealing with the powers that be. Comando Vermelho, or CV, is one of the most prominent of these organizations. Born as a prison gang, it controls the drug trafficking and use of violence in several *favelas*, targeting rival gangs, law enforcement, and the local community. The group has a cell structure, with gangs operating semi-autonomously within separate *favelas*, yet it is also centrally managed and has cultivated international links, in Latin America and beyond, to help it push drugs and grow its market.

Gangs such as CV are typically viewed as criminal organizations guided primarily by profit. This characterization is not incorrect but misses important characteristics that CV shares with insurgent groups.[1] Unlike your typical criminal outfit, CV relies on the cooperation and consent of the community within which it operates. Unlike ordinary criminals, it avoids legal sanction not through clandestinity—by finding refuge in the underground—but by creating a new world wherein to exist.[2] In effect, it forms the same 'liberated zones,' and uses the same patterns of mobilization, as any insurgent organization would. These are what Mançur Olson might have called 'stationary bandits': criminal enterprises that remain in one area for profit and therefore also come to depend upon its population and resources for security and manpower.[3] The enduring bond between criminal group and population encourages a symbiosis to emerge whereby the informal rulers ensure the well-being of their informal subjects so as to sustain the base and labor that they provide. In his work on organized crime, James Cockayne refers to the ensuing configuration of power as one of 'criminal autonomy,' a set-up defined by territorial segmentation, alternative

45

governmental capabilities, and ineffective state enforcement capabilities, particularly among specific communities.[4]

As with Mao's construction of a counter-state, CV's carving out of territory requires both repelling the state and co-opting the local population. On these fronts, CV is helped by the fact that the authorities in Rio have historically displayed limited interest in the *favelas*, contributing over time to a sense of bifurcation between the city's haves and have-nots. In the 1920s and 1930s, the *favelas* absorbed the spillover of Rio's rapid urbanization, producing slums that were infrastructurally ill-equipped for the swelling population. Neglected by the state and with few options, the communities that gravitated toward these areas were vulnerable to criminal influences, even if only as a coping mechanism.[5] As gangs established themselves, the state intervened in the *favelas* through aggressive raids, further alienating its residents.[6] Given such a foothold, CV entrenched the division between *favela* and the state by launching guerrilla attacks whenever the government was seen as intruding on 'its turf.' In this manner and with time, these *favelas* grew into no-go areas for the state, in the sense that the state could not provide security and services to their residents even if it wanted to.[7]

This approach would not be as effective unless CV also worked to co-opt the local population and make itself an attractive source of protection and resources. Thus, while denying the state access, the gang ensured local cooperation by providing employment and rudimentary state functions, including governance, taxation, arbitration, and the supply of basic services.[8] It also organizes social functions and events—most infamously the baile funk parties—which serve to glorify the gang's role and contributions. As the absentee state loses legitimacy, these communities come to see the local powerbrokers as their protectors and representatives.[9] In this manner, they can also be recruited as workers within the criminal enterprise, providing functions of drug packaging and distribution, sales, surveillance, muscle, and logistics.

It is in this blending of criminal motive and insurgent method that one finds CV's evolution into a 'criminal insurgency.'[10] Although the term is in some ways an oxymoron, it is appropriate for at least two reasons. First, regardless of its pecuniary intent, CV politically controlled, at its height, 40–50 percent of Rio's slums, which along with the local populations were cut off from the state and owned by the gang.[11] Where it rules, CV determines who lives and dies, or 'who gets what, when'—the very essence of politics.[12] Second, it has become clear that, to counter this threat, governments must themselves engage in the 'armed politics' typical of counterinsurgency; a crime-fighting approach will not win over contested (or lost) populations or restore the social contract necessary for success.[13]

Much like traditional counterinsurgency, the struggle against CV is fundamentally a contest for legitimacy. CV has understood the core premise of people's war, that 'active support from the population' is a pre-eminent condition for success.[14] Needless to say, just as with Mao's own approach to insurgency, those who do not volunteer their support risk elimination by force. Either way, by blending coercion and co-option the gang has, in effect, claimed and held on to territory, which it proceeds to govern, however rudimentarily. Through this approach, CV is satisfying its objectives of acquiring untold profits in a generally secure environment. Using a conservative estimate, a 2009 study pegged the value of the annual drugs sales in Rio at R$316m (US$182m) and annual profits for Rio's dealers at R$27m (US$15m).[15] Because of the government's inability to win back its lost citizens and neighborhoods, CV is, unlike many other insurgents, winning.[16]

CV epitomizes a broader trend of urban localized insurgency. Gangs such as MS-13 and MS-18 have, in a similar fashion, established footholds in the slums of Guatemala, El Salvador, and Honduras, as has the First Capital Command (PCC) in São Paulo, Brazil.[17] In Mexico, writes John P. Sullivan, 'it has been estimated that up to 71.5% of *municipios* (cities and towns) have been captured or are under control of *narcos*.'[18] Criminalized urban insurgency of this type is particularly common in Latin America, probably because of the continent's early and rapid urbanization and its location along a key vein of the drugs trade. As that trade and its profits have shifted to the Caribbean, similar gang formations and behaviors can now be seen in Jamaica, Haiti, and Trinidad and Tobago.[19] The approach uniting these gangs is comparable to that of the mafia, in that they exert control over local communities and even protect 'their' territories against ordinary criminality, thereby generating a stable business environment.[20]

Localized urban insurgency need not be criminal in nature or aim for illicit profit. Another prototypical variant can be found in Moqtada al-Sadr's control of Sadr City, Baghdad, through his Jaish al-Mahdi militia. Jostling for political power in the aftermath of the US invasion of Iraq, Sadr was able to turn parts of northeastern Baghdad into a no-go area for both Iraqi and US troops. Sadr City became the informal name for this vast and densely populated slum, perversely to honor Shi'ite leader Mohammad Mohammad-Sadeq al-Sadr, Moqtada's father, who was slain by the Saddam Hussein regime. Given this legacy, even as a young radical, Sadr had a certain religious authority among the two million or so inhabitants of Sadr City. Crammed into its squat cement buildings, narrow streets, and alleys, they provided a popular base that Sadr learned to mobilize to shape government policy and behavior. Yet, much as in Rio, this power required Sadr to displace the central government from 'his' turf and for him to become the sole hope for the abandoned slum dwellers.

In the turbulent 'post-war' environment of Iraq, Moqtada al-Sadr founded a new Shia militia, the Jaish al-Mahdi, or JAM. The militia was to safeguard Sadr's political project and allow him to compete against the other Shia militias left in place following the US invasion.[21] Amid an unstable political environment, in which Sunni insurgent adversaries were the government's first priority, Sadr was able to grow this militia and movement using his charisma and credibility among the masses of dispossessed Shia youth. By 2006, he had accrued significant combat power, a base for operations, and an armed political following, demonstrated through regular uprisings in Najaf, Karbala, and Basra. To consolidate and extend its *de facto* control of Sadr City, JAM launched attacks on the limited US military presence there. Over time, this undermanned force transferred its responsibilities to the Iraqi Army, whose unwillingness to confront Sadr meant that 'JAM now owned the district in almost every way.'[22]

JAM divided Sadr City into 80 sectors, each of which had a mosque, a school, and its own militia group to administer justice and provide basic yet essential services.[23] As the RAND Corporation points out in its strategic assessment of JAM, 'to the extent that the legitimate government of Iraq had established any presence in Sadr City at all, al-Sadr's people had thoroughly infiltrated that presence to the point that any government efforts were actually seen as JAM's doing.'[24] Because of his legitimacy and control over Shia communities, Sadr could combine the threat of violence against the government with that of political consequences, such as lost votes, and was therefore able to extract from the Iraqi prime minister, Nouri al-Maliki, a guarantee that US forces would no longer enter Sadr City.[25] Though this guarantee did not last—Sadr City was the site of a largely successful joint Iraqi–US operation in March 2008— Sadr did sustain the political power accrued through this strategy: remnants of his streamlined militia participated in operations against ISIS and, to this day, he remains a powerful force in Iraqi politics. Arguably, he also achieved his main objective of securing the withdrawal of US forces from the country.

Urban Localization: A Distinct and Growing Approach

Though still uncommon, the concentration of insurgent struggles within shantytowns and slums is not an altogether new phenomenon. In 1991, Sabri Sayari and Bruce Hoffman produced a study of a similar approach applied within the rapidly expanding *gecekondus*, or squatter settlements, of Turkey's main cities. Between 1976 and 1980, some far-left, and also far-right, insurgent groups exploited the limited state and police presence within these slums to position themselves as an alternative government. Blending force with co-option, these groupings claimed the local population as theirs and began to meet some of their basic needs, thereby creating 'liberated zones' close to the seat of government and yet also beyond its reach. As Sayari and Hoffman explain, the exploitation of the *gecekondus* resolved the insurgents' earlier inability to establish territorial control, with the countryside having proved too treacherous and the city too impenetrable.[26]

In a similar vein, Jennifer Taw and Bruce Hoffman in 1994 noted the potential for insurgency within Latin America's growing slums, known variously as 'the *callampas* ("mushrooms" because of the way they suddenly appear) …, as *favelas* (squatter towns) in Brazil, as *villas miserias* ("miserable villages") in Argentina, as *pueblos jóvenes* ("young towns") or *invasions* ("invasions") in Peru,' and so on.[27] As they predicted, these slums provided would-be insurgents with the 'same benefits and advantages that they have traditionally enjoyed in rural areas: control over territory, the allegiance (whether voluntary or coerced) of a considerable part of a country's population, inaccessibility to security forces, and a reasonably secure base for operations around the heart of the government.'[28]

The nexus of slums and insurgency is therefore not new, but the logic of localized insurgency differs in one important respect from these early prototypes. Whereas Taw and Hoffman argued that urban insurgents sought 'to eventually take power, first in the cities, and then in the rest of the country,' this progression goes against the logic of localized struggles.[29] Similarly, while the insurgents in the *gecekondus* sought, much as in Rio and Sadr City, 'to sever the government's authority over its urban centers,' they also 'hoped to take all power from the government'—something that we do not see in localized insurgencies.[30]

Rather than build a 'counter-state' that over time grows and seeks the violent replacement of the state, both criminal insurgencies and outfits such as JAM seek a para-state that can coexist, in parallel, with the state to build power and profit. These groups realize that their theory of victory relies squarely on not overplaying their hand; if, like Pablo Escobar in Colombia, the criminality and violence threaten to turn the entire country into a full-blown narco-state, a more concerted state response can be expected, which would disrupt the entire project.[31] Rather than seek to overthrow or overpower the state in this manner, insurgencies localized within its sprawling cities will typically work with the powers that be, all the while using violence to signal red lines and to configure favorable forms of coexistence. Sovereignty is contested but is also in some ways split: the insurgent will insist—violently if necessary—on exclusive control of its areas of operation, but otherwise will benefit parasitically from some of the state's services and power.[32]

In that sense, it is misleading to speak of state and non-state governance as a dichotomy, as this method of insurgency purposely seeks to blend the two.[33] In these settings, the urban fragmentation produces segmented 'spheres of influence,' underpinned by 'tacit coexistence,' as the state is not entirely absent in the slums but, rather, overlaps with the informal governance provided by the insurgency.[34] It is a set-up that challenges the foundational Weberian understanding of the state as enjoying a monopoly on the legitimate use of force, and the assumption that any infringement on this right would be actively resisted. The accommodation that develops between challenger and state also forcefully undercuts the presumed dyadic relation between these two, or the notion that parties to an intra-state war are pitted against each other in a zero-sum game.[35] Instead, the arrangement can come to resemble 'passive cooperation,' defined by 'live-and-let-live bargains structured around norms of acceptable violence.'[36]

This form of coexistence works to the insurgent's advantage, as it obviates a conventional showdown that the challenger would typically lose. Instead, in this approach, the violence used—to coerce locals or to force the state out—need never exceed the low-level and opportunistic strikes that favor non-state armed groups. Meanwhile, the defense against the state's military overmatch is at once rudimentary—just the shantytown and its people—and also formidable, as offensives in such cramped conditions risk great 'collateral damage.' For some states, next to the political costs of urban annihilation 'low-level militancy is acceptable in comparison.'[37] Even where states do intervene, often very heavily, they quickly realize that strikes and raids depend for their effectiveness on a longer-term program of socio-political integration for which there is insufficient interest or competence. Thus, in terms of the insurgent dilemma noted in the previous chapter, the abandoned community provides a path by which to coerce the state, all the while avoiding the head-on confrontations that have blocked more traditional paths to power.

If the purpose of urban insurgency has changed since the 1990s, in that it now emphasizes para-states rather than counter-states, the circumstances that foster this approach have also become more pronounced and pressing. Specifically, three developments have emerged in recent decades that make the strategies adopted by Comando Vermelho and Moqtada al-Sadr more relevant than ever: cities have become bigger, more socio-economically fractured, but also more transnationally connected to the world. The effects of these developments are manifold, and include the rise of empowered, localized insurgencies.

In 2016, 54 percent of the world's population lived in urban settings.[38] In that same year, it was predicted that the urban population of developing countries, where most conflicts occur, would double by 2030, and the area covered by cities triple.[39] By 2050, three-quarters of the world's population will be living in urban environments, as cities contend with millions of migrants from rural areas and with the effects of population growth, which are particularly explosive in the developing world.[40] To Ronak Patel and David Palotty, global warming will further compound this trend, as the hundreds of millions of environmental migrants projected for the coming decades follow current refugee flows into the cities.[41] David Kilcullen draws out the meaning of all this in an accessible yet staggering manner: the world's cities, he warns, will 'absorb— in just one generation—the same population growth that occurred across the entire planet in all of recorded history up to 1960.'[42]

Underpinning this urbanization, and turning it into a veritable security concern, are the growing levels of inequality in the cities, primarily in the developing world but also beyond. Urbanization is driven by an individual search for opportunity, yet in today's cities the gap between rich and poor is 'at its highest level since 30 years.'[43] The situation is unlikely to improve; in 2016, the United Nations estimated that by 2030 urbanization would see demand for energy and water in developing countries increase by 40 and 50 percent respectively.[44] As cities grow in this manner, so will the slums; already today, in an average developing city, they account for 43 percent of the population.[45] Within these sprawling, unequal metropoles, hermetically sealed gated communities sit atop expanding seas of slum dwellers, each living according to a different social contract. Nils Gilman frames the implications of such a set-up: 'rather than a single national space in which power is exercised and all residents enjoy rights in a consistent and homogeneous way, the cartography … consists of diverse enclaves of heterogeneous political authority and of non-standardized social-service provisioning arrangements.'[46]

Christopher Coker provocatively describes the slum dwellers of the world's mega-cities as the 'cast-offs of late modernity,' or as 'the "collateral damage" of capitalism.' [47] Indeed, at some point it is necessary to acknowledge that the conditions for localized urban insurgency are the direct outgrowth of our neo-liberal world order, which also looks unlikely to change. [48] The Washington Consensus— the global agreement to pursue trade liberalization, deregulation, and limitations on public expenditure—has generated untold wealth and lifted millions out of poverty. However, since 1980, the same economic model has also seen the global top 1 percent of earners capture twice as much of the growth in global income as the 50 percent of poorest individuals. [49] Thus, the United Nations now estimates that the one billion people who lived in slums in 2016 will 'double or even triple by 2050.' [50]

There is clearly no direct causation between even widespread poverty and violence, but rampant urbanization does seem to bring the correlation between the two into sharper focus. As one example, Latin America, the most urbanized continent, represents just 8 percent of the world's population yet 38 percent of its criminal killings. [51] The scholarly literature also suggests that whereas inequality is not conflict-generating per se, the *perception* of inequality often is. [52] Notably, it is also the feeling of poverty, not poverty itself, that predicts poor health. [53] This psychological component is what makes economics a political issue and, in some circumstances, a violent one; hence the focus on 'relative deprivation' rather than outright 'poverty' in explaining the onset of armed conflict. Given the forced proximity of urban environments, not to mention the claustrophobic closeness brought on by social media, the awareness of relative deprivation is higher than ever; it is in your face and on your screen. The flagrant inequity is what brings on a legitimacy crisis and a search for new solutions. Meanwhile, where institutions are weak and insecurity high—as in the growing slums of the metropoles—motivation for rebellion meshes with opportunity, either to exploit the absence of the state or to replace it with something deemed better. [54]

A final factor that brings untold power and reach for localized urban insurgents is the globalization both of information and of commerce.[55] For 'criminal insurgencies' such as CV, a globalized economy makes possible the accumulation of vast wealth through engagement in transnational criminal activity. As Gilman argues, these are 'the unsung globalizers of the 1990s and 2000s,' who 'rapidly scaled up their local mom-and-pop graft organizations to become globe-spanning deviant commercial empires.'[56] From the *favelas* in Rio, the reach of its drug trafficking stretches across the Atlantic into Africa, Europe, and even Asia, with minimal need for the local state. For more politically engaged local insurgencies, those focused on cause rather than commerce, the ability to reach broader audiences and build transnational networks will act as a force multiplier, to spread awareness, internationalize the struggle, and mobilize additional resources. From the relative safety of the urban para-state, they make full use of the transnational networks of social media to wage a battle of ideas, all the while avoiding an unwanted final showdown with the state.

Recognizing these trends, Robert Muggah and other academics now write of 'fragile cities,' not 'fragile states,' and identify the urban terrain as 'the new frontier of warfare.'[57] Indeed, it looks more than likely that urban dysfunction will provide increasing breeding space for violent non-state enterprises of various types, with urban militia leaders, city warlords, and drug-cartel barons operating 'their own micro-sovereign structures, weakening the state and challenging its monopoly of violence, and fatally eroding its authority to govern.'[58] These actors rely upon the effects of mass urbanization, inadequate government presence within the resultant shantytowns, and the ability to co-opt and in this way control masses of dispossessed peoples with few options other than to obey the local strongman. Underlying and enabling this trend is not the physical distance that benefited insurgents of years past, but a political distance that is fueled by elite apathy and that entrenches the very fragmentation on which it is built.

Localized Insurgency: The Rural Variant

Growing urbanization does not mean that rural insurgency will end. On the contrary, the fragmentation allowing for localized insurgency manifests itself not only within cities but also between these growing urban spaces and the emptying hinterland. As cities become globalized, and the periphery is left behind, states cede what they cannot hold and focus instead on where they think the future lies. Much as this prioritization creates opportunities for insurgency in the sprawling cities, it also opens space for localized, limited struggles in the countryside, so long as what happens on the periphery remains precisely that—peripheral to the concatenations of power and privilege in the big cities. It may be true, as we discussed in the previous chapter, that states can today see and reach further than during the Cold War, but, given the changing structure of socio-economic opportunity, many of them are also far less concerned with the hinterland so long as it does not interfere with elite interests.

This absence of the state on the periphery produces both the motivation and the opportunity for localized struggles to emerge, as militias, insurgents, and strongmen claim power for themselves and seek to make the best out of a bad situation. In contrast to traditional insurgency, these insurgent projects are rarely driven by a desire to claim ownership of the state. Even at the local level, there is no search for independence or formal political recognition. Instead, the populations that reside in the insurgent para-states are typically twice victimized, first by the state's neglect and then by the insurgent's predation. It is a tragic outcome, yet one that is not only tolerated but even sustained by the government's ceding of space and the insurgent's decision not to poke the bear.

The recent history of Jama'at Ahl al-Sunnah li-l-Da'wah wa al-Jihad (JAS), commonly known as Boko Haram, provides a telling illustration. When, in 2014, JAS established swift territorial control in Nigeria's northeastern states of Borno, Adamawa and Yobe, it was not because it was powerful enough to overthrow the institutions of state, but because in this rural part of the country there were hardly any institutions of state to begin with.[59] Far removed from the economic hub of Lagos, the political capital of Abuja, and the oil-based patronage system of the elite, these states have suffered from decades of isolation and under-governance. In 2014, an estimated 72 percent of northerners lived in poverty, with the region displaying 'some of the worst human development indicators in the world.'[60] Within the northeast alone, millions of school-aged children have been left to beg on the streets, to survive but also to support the underfunded Islamic boarding schools where they are ostensibly enrolled.[61] As they reach adulthood, a combination of desertification, under-investment, and insecurity provides scant opportunity for employment.

Within such a context, it was relatively easy for JAS—hitherto a fringe movement—to establish itself, just as it was difficult for outsiders to get a clear sense of what was going on. Seeking to contain rather than respond to the problem, the state initially attempted to deny its loss of control; it then downplayed the ongoing terrorist attacks and has on a number of occasions since declared victory.[62] Spurious claims such as these are made more plausible by the conflict's unfolding on the periphery. As a measure of its remoteness, observers are uncertain even what to call the group, opting first for the 'Nigerian Taliban' and then a nickname—Boko Haram—that the group itself never used and that has since been so repeatedly mistranslated in commentary as to distort what the struggle was all about.[63] The neglect of the budding insurgency is striking, in that JAS, in 2015, was the world's most lethal insurgency, even more so than ISIS.

Once the crisis reached a certain threshold, the Nigerian government responded with force. In 2015, a military coalition involving regional players and South African mercenaries helped expel the insurgents from the main cities. Even then, a basic lack of ownership and of political engagement has allowed both JAS and its now more powerful splinter group, Islamic State West Africa Province (ISWAP), plenty of space to roam. Disgruntled observers even from within Nigeria's military refer to the stalemate as a 'political economy of crisis,' whereby local governors, the federal government, and also the Islamist outfits benefit more from sustaining the status quo than by seeking an all-out victory.[64]

Like other localized insurgencies, this rural struggle is unlikely to result in a march on the capital—or the attempted conquest of the state. Nonetheless, even within its present margins, it allows insurgent outfits sufficient opportunity to showcase their power, not least because of the reach afforded by social media (for which control of the capital is unnecessary). As Leena Koni Hoffmann argues, 'the connectedness of today's globalized world has allowed local extremists like Boko Haram to graft themselves onto universalized debates on Muslim resistance to domination through Jihad in order to puff up their otherwise local profile.'[65] This type of connectedness, and the growing role of narratives and branding, have fundamentally changed the nature of insurgency from its Cold War heyday.

Nigeria's south hosts a similar, yet different, type of localized rural insurgency. Animated by perceived inequity in the distribution of oil wealth and the concomitant environmental destruction of the south, from where most of this oil is sourced, a number of social movements and insurgent outfits have long rallied against the state in search of reform. Much as in the north, the state response has oscillated between neglect and repression, but it has never actually addressed the roots of the conflict. The conditions would seem ideal for separatist rebellion: there are chronic problems of corruption at every level, the region hosts fantastic resources, and yet it is woefully neglected by the same federal government that it effectively bankrolls. In spite of this set-up, the local insurgent groupings exhibit little ability or desire to combat the state or seek its overthrow.[66] Instead, they opt for tacit agreements with the federal government and local oil companies, allowing all sides to profit while they ignore their mutual antagonism as well as the deeper societal problems that are fueling the conflict.

Through these agreements, the state sustains its control over the oil resources, the oil companies can continue to operate as before, and the insurgents enrich themselves through the deals they strike. Initially, these deals reached only as far as local politicians; William Reno alludes to pacts whereby local armed groups 'received offers of political protection, including license to carry out profitable bunkering operations [oil theft], if they would help drive out opposition party campaigners and candidates.'[67] In 2009, the federal government stepped in, providing the Delta militants with generous payouts for giving up their weapons and abandoning violence.[68] Millions of dollars flowed into the region each year. Attacks on oil infrastructure did decline, but the payments also fueled corruption and a proliferation of new armed groups, often with access to better arms and with fresh demands.[69] Moreover, by funneling the payments through the leaders of militant groups, the amnesty has strengthened their patrimonial networks and allowed some of them to establish themselves as benefactors of the community, further eroding the legitimacy of the absentee state.[70]

Nigeria is far from alone in facing this type of fragmentation. The Middle East and Africa host a disturbing number of rural localized insurgencies. The most extreme examples may be drawn from Syria, Libya, or Yemen, where multiple groups combine into a patchwork of control.[71] The eastern regions of the Democratic Republic of Congo (DRC) are the site of a localized insurgent struggle likely to persist indefinitely without ever encroaching physically upon the capital, Kinshasa. It is also unclear whether Kinshasa seriously intends ever to reclaim control and govern the conflict-affected eastern regions of Ituri, Kasai, and Kivu. Born out of a proxy war between the DRC and Rwanda, the conflict has dragged on since 1994, with 'a series of tenacious local insurgencies' surviving precisely 'by avoiding direct confrontation with UN and government soldiers while continuing to terrorize villagers and exploit local resources.'[72]

Governance in eastern and also northern Iraq, both pre- and (even more so) post-Islamic State, has been split between state, non-state, and hybrid actors, often characterized by ethnicity and benefiting from a militia. As Damian Doyle and Tristan Dunning explain, 'These alternative sources of authority exercise their own sovereignty, particularly in the sense that they control the use of coercion in the territories they control.'[73] Into this loose distribution of control comes post-caliphate ISIS, which exploits the central government's patchy governance to assert itself and sustain its insurgency at the local level. Having failed to accrue power in the traditional manner of Cold War insurgencies—by proclaiming and holding on to territory—ISIS now emphasizes in its directives the need to remain below the threshold of armed confrontations. It exhorts its fighters to seize and hold territory but to retreat 'before large enemy forces are present' and to avoid 'a battle of mutual confrontation that is not in the interest of the mujahideen.'[74]

What underlies these localized struggles is the fragmentation of nation-states and the turn toward 'heterarchical' governance, a term denoting a multiplicity of political power structures coexisting within one national space, each with its own coercive capabilities.[75] In this sense, localized rural struggles are reminiscent of the early processes of state formation in Europe, wherein local strongmen acquired titles and legitimacy by filling the political and institutional voids of the medieval era.[76] Parallels could also be drawn with the informal orders (and disorders) of imperial borderlands, especially as they expanded and shrank.[77] The difference today, or since decolonization, is the normative expectation for the nation-state to control its own territory and to live up to the Weberian ideal whereby states enjoy 'full internal and external sovereignty, a legitimate monopoly on the use of force, and checks and balances that constrain political rule and authority.'[78]

This Weberian ideal is largely a fiction. It may serve a normative purpose, and help states pretend to exercise the control they are nominally expected to wield, but as a descriptor of actual capacity and power it is a chimera—a myth.[79] Recognition of this fact matters; as Thomas Risse puts it, 'if one of the key concepts of modern social sciences is not applicable to two-thirds of the international community, we face not only theoretical challenges but also eminently political and practical ones.'[80] For one, it appears that in many cases the state either cannot or will not extend governance to particular sections of its population. Unsurprisingly, such limitations are most common in the 20 percent of states now deemed 'fragile' and in places where one may find large 'areas of limited statehood' or 'hybrid political orders.'[81] Because of the factors highlighted above—specifically, urbanization and fragmentation—this ceding of space is often tolerated, or even allowed to happen, because the costs of preventing or reversing it are deemed incommensurate with the gains involved. This leads to real opportunities for those capable of mobilizing materiel and manpower, resulting in what some scholars call an 'oligopoly of violence.'[82]

The phenomenon is similar to but different from its close relative, secessionism—or the attempt by set regions or enclaves to split off politically from the nation-state. Localized insurgents also seek to split from the center, yet, as Charles Thomas and Toyin Falola specify, secession is defined by 'the creation of a *new and recognized sovereign body'*—something that we do not see in localized struggles.[83] Indeed, in their study of separatism, Thomas and Falola note a 'tacit rejection of formal secession' among insurgents across the developing world, particularly in Africa, and a turn instead toward 'limited separatist or reform conflicts among the currently dispossessed or discontented political groups.'[84] This development encourages the localization of insurgency as a mutually acceptable compromise: the state is allowed to feign sovereign control, sustaining mythical Weberian ideals, and the group achieves some autonomy while retaining the benefits of belonging to a recognized state.

Mali is, in this vein, another key case, given the bifurcation of its south, along with the national capital, Bamako, and the vast arid north that cuts deep into the Sahara. The disconnect in Mali stems from the preferential treatment of the south during the colonial era and the difficulties for the national government, once independent, to assert itself across a sparsely populated and under-developed north. Yet the difficulty reflects also a lack of interest; as Edoardo Baldaro explains, 'central authorities in Bamako have tended to distinguish between a Mali *utile* [useful] and a Mali *inutile* [useless], considering northern regions as the most peripheral and less attractive area of the country.'[85] The resulting lack of investment and patchy provision of services have contributed to historical forces of irredentism, not least among the Tuareg community, and fueled a number of rebellions: in 1962–64, in 1990–95, in 2007–9, and since 2012.

These flare-ups have been tolerated, because—even today—the state has preferred instability, crime, and periodic bursts of violence to the requirements of nation-wide government control. Even with the escalation of the conflict since 2012, and the deployment of international forces to assist, it has proved extremely challenging to sway the 'indifferent political elite in Mali,' which is perceived as doing 'the bare minimum … to invest in the violence-wracked north and central regions of the country.'[86] This elite has most of its voters down south, does not believe the trouble in the north will affect the capital, and therefore views it as 'politically impractical to divert current development and education programs to more vulnerable regions.'[87] The implicit contract contends that the state is here, the insurgency is there, and never the twain shall meet.

In Mozambique's north, or Cabo Delgado, we see a similar pattern. Nicknamed Cabo Esquecido or 'Forgotten Cape,' the province has suffered long-standing neglect, resulting in living conditions worse than elsewhere in the country. 'There has been little investment in education, health services, water and sanitation systems, public transport and telecommunication infrastructure. As a result, of the country's 10 provinces, Cabo Delgado ranks at the bottom in human development indicators.'[88] The government is at least indirectly present, in that it profits from the extraction of natural resources and the drug trade in the north, but there is no sense of formal or of functioning governance. Where the state has sought to clamp down on the illicit trade, it has done so to shore up relations with foreign corporations, which are invested in the country's ruby mining and timber sector. Indeed, without local consultation, the government licensed crucial parts of the province to foreign contractors, crushing the informal ruby mining business that had provided some form of opportunity to the local population.[89]

As in Nigeria's northeast, the combination of neglect, poverty, corruption, and desperation generated anger at the elite and invited a homegrown type of radicalization benefiting from global ties. In Mozambique, the result was the Islamic State-associated Ahlu Sunnah wal-Jama'a (ASWJ), a group also known as al-Shabaab. 'Under the unconcerned eye of local and central government authorities,' ASWJ spent years in the north engaging in 'social and psychological work to recruit, indoctrinate, brainwash and transform the youth.'[90] Despite being warned of the phenomenon, the government 'chose inaction and turned a blind eye.'[91] Then, in October 2017, ASWJ launched a two-day attack on police stations and government buildings in Mocímboa da Praia. Thereafter, the government could no longer so blatantly ignore the problem. Mercenaries were called upon to contain the rebellion by military means, without addressing its root causes. The philosophy is not unlike that seen in Nigeria or—for that matter—within Rio's *favelas*. In keeping with these cases, ASWJ is unlikely to seek control of Maputo, the capital of Mozambique, but will use the safe haven within the neglected territory to showcase, over social media, its localized successes and its placement within a global Islamic State movement.

A final example may be drawn from Asia, or more specifically the long-standing insurgency in Baluchistan, Pakistan's largest yet least densely populated province. This conflict has been ongoing since the establishment of Pakistan in 1948. To the insurgents, the state has since then discriminated against the Baluch people and marginalized the province, all the while profiting from its mineral, gas, and oil resources.[92] During its most intense flare-ups in the 1970s, the conflict pitted tens of thousands of fighters on each side in direct combat. The intensity has since diminished, but the conflict persists, as factions within the government elite reject the Baluch demands for greater autonomy, over both its resources and politics. We are now in the fifth round of the insurgency, the longest in Baluchistan's history and one complicated by the apparent merger of the province's two dominant armed groups.[93]

The question in Pakistan, as in the other cases given above, is whether the state truly cares. The government tends to frame the struggle as driven by greed and the province as almost immutably 'restive.'[94] The violence is still significant—some analysts describe it as a 'cauldron of ethnic, sectarian, secessionist and militant violence, threatening to boil over at any time'—yet others concede that it 'does not currently pose a severe threat to state power.'[95] It is perhaps for this reason that the Baluch insurgency has been termed Pakistan's 'other war,' or that the government—unable to impose its writ— has instead privileged a low-level military response, using hired guns and other unaccountable, and often brutal, proxies.[96] Money poured into the province to win hearts and minds 'does not seem to have reached its targets'; instead, 'industry has collapsed … teachers and professionals have left the province, while infrastructure, health, and sanitation lie neglected.'[97] With all of this occurring 'away from the media glare, the violence has continued unabated' and is 'likely to endure.'[98]

The Dangers of Localized Insurgency

Localized insurgency suggests that the heuristic of 'the state' has been extended too far, with many (particularly Western) observers confusing lines on a map for actual delineations of government writ.

On the ground, there is little space for such confusion. Instead, in the face of fragmented control, governments must learn to accept that areas of its territory are denied to them by ethnic militias, criminal organizations, or tribes and clans. In many cases, *de jure* authorities strike an understanding with their *de facto* equivalents at the local level, putting the latter in charge of the 'shadow state.'[99] As elite accommodations congeal, these arrangements can result in a patterned form of complicity, or what Ken Menkhaus refers to as 'mediated states' and Paul Staniland calls 'shared sovereignty.'[100] The lines of control between these entities may not be found on a map, but they are arguably more real than the borders of any world atlas.

Despite the occasional violence, cooperative systems such as these can appear relatively stable, in that they threaten neither the elite nor the government, as traditional insurgency would. For instance, Menkhaus has illustrated how in Somalia, supposedly one of the world's most anarchic states, informal power-sharing produced fairly predictable patterns of governance, albeit 'governance without government.'[101] As Menkhaus goes on to explain, 'through an amalgam of customary law, sharia law, and the influence of business people and various professional associations, a messy, loose and fluid mosaic of authorities emerged that collectively added up to something far removed from anarchy.'[102] While Somalia remained dangerous, the results were astonishing: along with fostering pockets of stability, Somalia became one of the leading African countries in telecommunications, remittance companies, and transit trade. Politically, some of the sub-state polities emerging from this trend 'assumed a fragile but nonetheless impressive capacity to provide core functions of government.'[103]

If such stability is possible in Somalia—given its history—it follows that the same can and, indeed, does often occur elsewhere. Violence is certainly a fundamental component of these fragmented political economies, yet it is typically less intense than that seen in civil wars. As Clionadh Raleigh notes, 'civil wars involve a primary cleavage of rebels against an established government, where the objective is to replace the regime or establish a separate state,' yet in the more ambiguous arrangements of power—in less dyadic contests—'conflicts are frequently limited in spatial scope and fatalities are significantly fewer.'[104] This stabilizing potential, or at least the basic predictability of state fragmentation, is a major reason why systems like these persist. Weberian ideals notwithstanding, if there is no incentive for states to extend their governance to the periphery, they most likely won't, particularly when the elite and the state can make do by focusing on the center.[105]

Yet there can be significant costs to this fragmentation, even when it appears stable. First, there is no guarantee that the red lines governing localized insurgency will remain in place and, when circumstances shift, it is through violence that old arrangements are revisited. It may be possible to ignore the *favelas* and to let the gangs there rule supreme, but a state has to take notice when the same gang reaches a strength of 30,000 fighters, as a recent intelligence report suggested, and recruits advisors from Africa and Eastern Europe to provide military training.[106] Similarly, it is one thing to accept the brutal violence of 'Boko Haram' in Nigeria so long as it mostly affected the local population, but when ISWAP in 2018 started targeting the security forces more than the people, and began endearing itself to the local community, the threat to Nigerian statehood underwent a step change.[107] Since it had previously failed to engage meaningfully in this part of the country, it is unclear whether the state has enough cachet with the local population, or military capability even, to claw its way back.

A similar slippage can be seen in Nigeria's south. The agreement and payouts to militants contained the crisis yet also turned militancy into a form of self-enrichment. When the government sought to end the payouts in 2015, it encountered fierce resistance. New groups emerged, demanding sovereignty for the Niger Delta, or at least continued disbursement of funds.[108] This pattern continues to the present day, illustrating that the deal proffered by the state has generated perverse incentives and, indeed, encouraged the very behavior it sought to stem.[109] The tacit understanding with the militants also did not foresee the dip in oil prices from 2015 onward, which has led local armed factions to adopt new forms of attack, trading sabotage of oil infrastructure for piracy and maritime kidnapping for ransom. The result is that Nigerian waters and the wider Gulf of Guinea have since become 'the world's worst piracy hotspot.'[110]

The fluidity of localized insurgency can be seen also in Iraq. Given the fissiparous nature of the JAM militia, it was always doubtful how accurately and for how long Sadr could rely upon it to shape the Iraqi government's behavior. During 2006, elements of the militia strayed increasingly toward crime and self-enrichment, with renegade units turning on each other and on civilians—even in Shia areas.[111] With violence escalating, the movement was jeopardizing Sadr's hopes for greater influence. Though Sadr denounced the rogue units, and tacitly worked with the US military to hunt some of them down, the splinter groups proliferated, with some sponsored by Iran and pursuing sectarian agendas, and others driven by criminal interest and engaging in murder-for-hire and extortion.[112] In this manner, the relatively fixed margins of Sadr's localized insurgency gave way to chaos and violence, which were difficult to understand, never mind control.[113]

Second, even without escalating their use of force or increasing their level of ambition, localized insurgency groups have a way of hollowing out the state. By controlling access to populations or communities, these groups can sell their services or access to votes to more 'cooperative' politicians, thereby undermining democracy and corrupting the state. In Rio, the CV gang sells willing politicians licenses to campaign in the *favelas*; according to Antonio Sampaio, this fee can reach up to R$100,000, or US$40,544.[114] Similar stories have emerged from Mexico and from El Salvador, where politicians are alleged to have struck deals with the country's most powerful gangs in return for electoral support.[115] Kickbacks can involve illicit campaign financing or blocking certain candidates from gang-owned territory; during the 2014 electoral campaign in Rio, for example, CV banned placards or campaign staff related to a particular candidate, as he represented a security policy not to the gang's liking.[116] More habitually, these gangs pay off the police so as to limit intrusion or interference, or other government bodies for them to turn a blind eye.[117] In many ways, therefore, while the localized insurgents design their projects so as to eschew direct attacks on the government, their net impact can be just as harmful, albeit in more gradual and subtle ways.

Third, informal orders built upon basic failures in governance readily invite new champions of insurrection, who seek (quite

65

justifiably) to purge the old and create something new. In Colombia in the 1980s and 1990s, the government's prolonged inability to check various left-wing insurgencies within its own territory spawned the rise of 'self-defence' forces—the Autodefensas Unidas de Colombia, or AUC—which then evolved into a separate problem for the state to manage.[118] Though the AUC was initially a local reaction to a well-founded need for protection and security, it grew to control 50 percent of drug trafficking in the country, became as violent as the insurgents, and engaged in extortion, kidnapping, and massacres.[119] Similarly, though on a lower scale, the unchecked activity of JAS in Nigeria's northeast created the rise of the 'Civilian Joint Task Force'—a vigilante movement to protect against insurgent predation. The vigilantes are credited with mitigating the effects of conflict, but they have also been accused of indiscriminate violence, sexual exploitation, and abuse.[120] In Colombia, Nigeria, and elsewhere, the allegation of government complicity with vigilantes tears at the state's legitimacy.

Localized insurgency has fostered vigilante paramilitaries also in 'abandoned' urban settings. In Rio, self-defense forces have emerged, structured around ex-police, to protect against gang violence. As seen elsewhere, the cure has become the disease. By 2019, these militias—really a mafia organization—were said to control 'roughly a quarter of the Rio de Janeiro metropolitan region,' or 45 percent of the city's roughly one thousand *favelas*.[121] Much like the gangs, they provide services in exchange for cash, extort, and engage in organized crime; they also violently eliminate those who stand in their way. The main difference is that they benefit from a more openly cozy relation with the state, which presents them as a bulwark against crime and also uses them to buy votes.[122]

A final vulnerability stemming from localized insurgency is, ironically, its internationalization. It may have been acceptable for Mali to stomach the occasional paroxysm of Tuareg irredentism, or the routine involvement of the northern communities in illicit trading and other crimes. Yet, aided by the influx of arms and fighters following the collapse of Libya in 2011, these very factors allowed a more lucrative lawlessness to take hold (cocaine smuggling, people trafficking, and kidnapping for ransom) and a far more radical and well-armed opposition to emerge.[123] Indeed, the entry of al-Qaeda in the Islamic Maghreb (AQIM) into northern Mali in the early 2000s showcased the exact utility of these lost spaces, at least for insurgent groups seeking space to operate and thrive. As the alliance of Islamists and ethnic militias seized two-thirds of the country, the red lines had to be renegotiated, very much to the detriment of the state.[124]

A similar internationalization is now emerging in the conflict in northern Mozambique, with ASWJ benefiting militarily from an influx of foreign fighters, drawn to the conflict because of the group's high-profile attacks.[125] So far, these fighters have come mainly from countries neighboring Mozambique, but the trend illustrates the transnational ideological reach of localized insurgency and thus the great difficulty of sustaining the red lines by which these struggles are so often 'managed.'[126] Indeed, evidence from other conflict zones suggests that with foreign fighters comes not only enhanced military capability but also the potential destabilization of the group structure, ideology, and cohesion.

Indeed, in Baluchistan, sustained conflict and neglect have invited more extremist outsiders, who are bringing with them a more virulent and sectarian Islamist ideology. In this instance, this development is the by-product of the province's proximity to the war in Afghanistan and its significant refugee flows. Though still not a leading force in the insurgency, 'radicalization is on the rise and sectarian groups have stepped up their activities in the region.'[127] Another contributing factor has been the state's military response to the insurgency, which has dislocated the traditional social structures of the province and thereby made it more vulnerable to co-option by hardliners.[128] The compounding of the conflict is particularly ill-timed for Pakistan, as Baluchistan has become more interesting to the state since the development of the China–Pakistan Economic Corridor, which cuts through Baluchistan and promises great revenue but is now the target of increasing insurgent attack.

Non-state networks are not the only outsiders to see opportunity in the neglected, localized insurgencies of the world. Already, as Russia seeks to re-establish itself as a global power, it has sought to weaken its enemies, real and perceived, by exploiting and exacerbating their internal fault lines.[129] Russia's handiwork is clear enough in Ukraine and Georgia, where it has stoked ethnic tensions to create 'break-away' regions and frozen conflicts that now harm these countries' sense of national unity. Along with media control and disinformation, Russia's actions include also so-called 'passportification,' whereby it issues Russian citizenship to the residents of the ethnic enclaves in targeted societies, thereby 'creating new demographic facts on the ground,' derailing efforts at reconciliation, and mounting a future 'legal right to intervene at will' in these countries' internal affairs.[130] The strategy is rooted in a deep tradition, going back to the Soviet Union, of supporting separatist-irredentist groupings.

Russia has also interfered, albeit in less forceful ways, in the Catalan region of Spain, in Scotland, in the Balkans, and even in the United States, where its online operations sought to inspire southern secessionism.[131] In 2015 and 2016, it helped fund conferences in Moscow convening separatists from Texas, Hawaii, Northern Ireland, Ukraine, Italy, Catalonia, and beyond to stir up irredentist agendas and sow dissension in the countries represented.[132] In its search for points of leverage, the Kremlin focuses on these internal schisms, which may be conflict-generating or at least undermine national resolve.

It does not take a major leap of logic to see how this approach can also exploit the divisions that underpin localized insurgency, or the informal rules by which it works. To take one example, Stephen Blank rightly interrogates Russia's motives in calling for Kurdish 'cultural autonomy' in any post-war Syrian state, in building a military facility in the Kurdish People's Protection Unit (YPG)-controlled territory, or in allowing YPG to expand its territory within Syria and its political arm to open an office in Moscow. As Blank concludes, Russia appears intent on using 'the Kurds, as it has for over a century, to weaken Turkey as well as keep Syria in a state of dependence upon Moscow, and thereby gain leverage over both states—and over the Kurds, as their main foreign protector.'[133]

In all these cases, we can see how localized insurgency, even if it is designed not to attack the government head-on, and indeed to avoid the capital as the seat of power, readily undermines the state's writ and legitimacy and generates vulnerabilities that others may exploit.

As they feed upon government neglect, or at least its acceptance of fragmented rule, localized insurgencies are rooted in a seedbed of dysfunctional governance and are, therefore, typically poor indicators of longer-term stability. In effect, these wartime political 'orders' serve to randomize the state's supposed monopoly on the use of force, ceding power to the highest bidder or to those with the greatest coercive skill. In so doing, it creates flux, perpetuates insecurity, and challenges the coherence of an international system based on nominally capable states.

Conclusion

In the last two decades, only a few insurgent groups have achieved the military capability necessary for head-on confrontations with the state—and in almost all these cases, the assistance and sponsorship of another state accounted for any gains made. For most other challengers, it has been necessary to find new ways to sustain power and influence, without provoking a military backlash that forces the insurgency project to start over again.

As this chapter has detailed, one potential avenue lies in localizing the struggle within areas of the state, either rural or urban, that have anyway been neglected or forgotten and where insurgents can set up shop. As cities grow beyond control and the state loses oversight, perhaps even interest, in the vast abandoned hinterland, there is ample space in either environment to pursue alternative political orders. So long as their activities remain below a particular threshold, these insurgent groups can sustain local influence and power, all the while internationalizing their activities through social media, illicit networks, and other transnational ties—whatever it takes to make ends meet. In these struggles, the violence used is of the kind that most benefits insurgency—low-level, unpredictable, and opportunistic—and it is used to keep the state out of areas that it anyway would rather not own.

This is a form of insurgency that bypasses the traditional norms of the government as the most relevant actor and seat of power. The common understanding of insurgency tends to stipulate a zero-sum competition between state and challenger in which both actively seek the same prize. Instead, localized insurgency exists awkwardly in parallel with the government and results in shared power and sovereignty within one 'state' (in reality, what emerges is very different from what we associate with this term). In this manner, localized insurgency also challenges the notion of an international system based on essentially coherent states, capable to some degree at least of controlling their territory and people. This Westphalian system of states has never been a particularly realistic lens through which to understand international relations; to Michael Phillips, it mostly represents 'a utopian allegory exemplifying the American [or Western] experience.'[134] Even so, this allegory has grown to the point of paradigm and underwrites both expectations and policy; hence the need for it to be further challenged.

Localized insurgency is also distinct from secessionist struggles—violent uprisings that seek to create a new sovereign state and therefore reinforce the normative standing of this political unit. Localized insurgency persists without such lofty goals. Rhetoric may suggest a clear telos, yet in practice the struggles go on without major progression or movement toward climax. The state is instead able to live on, while its adversaries benefit from the goods it provides and the weaknesses it reveals. So long as it does not overly threaten or embarrass elite concerns, the insurgency will not invite a concerted response. When the troubles of the 'other world' become too much, or an international embarrassment, states will swat at the problem and claim credit for the temporary calm rather than repair the fractures of a damaged society. In that sense, these struggles count on the state's inability or unwillingness to assert its authority over its own territory—or its acquiescence in a degree of instability in less relevant areas.

This reality promises to become more prevalent as the factors underpinning localized insurgency grow: the urbanization, the growing inequality, and the transnational connections that cut across fragmented states. Whereas some states may interpret the limited objectives of localized insurgency as a sign of having successfully managed the threat, the track record in several cases suggests a need for far greater caution. Indeed, without launching or even aiming for outright attacks on the state, localized insurgencies tend to compound the very conditions that led to their emergence. If, in some instances, the implicit modus vivendi with the state slips, resulting in a new (and usually more destructive) pattern of violence, in others it engenders corruption, exploitation, and abuse, and thereby hollows out the state from within. Finally, wartime political orders between the state and the challenger cannot always control third-party actors, whether from within or beyond, whether state or non-state, that seek to upend old orders and create something new. For all these reasons, localized insurgency must be studied in greater detail, along with possible options for how its problems may be addressed.

4

INFILTRATIVE INSURGENCY
THE TROJAN HORSE

Of late, insurgent groups are failing to defeat or subdue their state adversaries militarily, something that happened with notable regularity during the Cold War and that informed the theories of insurgency expounded at that time. These theories are still with us, furnishing the norms of the struggle, yet they no longer appear to describe the reality and options for insurgent outfits. In the previous chapter, we discussed one form of adaptation to this change, which saw insurgents localize their struggle in areas where the state is less strong, less vigilant, and less likely to insist on control. Another approach, discussed here, relies not on avoiding the state but on co-opting it, using seemingly legal mechanisms yet also covert illegal and violent means to clear the path. The theory of victory in this approach, here termed infiltrative insurgency, is to combine the benefits of legality with those of illegality, to exploit the state's openness, all the while persisting with violence, so as to ensure electoral success and, from there on, dictate political change.

Much like localization, infiltration avoids the insurgent's dilemma by eschewing the attempted overthrow of the state. Compared with the traditional strategies of insurgency, it is a subtler method of seizing power—one that minimizes international censure and also removes opportunities for an armed repressive response. Rather than confronting the state on this military plane, where it is strong, the approach hits the state where it is weak: in its handling of social and political rupture. Though the exploitation of contradictions has been a fundamental component of insurgent strategy ever since the days of Mao, the contest for legitimacy in this infiltrative approach is accentuated by the group's supposed rejection of violence, its purported interest in 'peace,' and its alliance-building with mainstream civil society actors. Through this deft weaponization of narrative, the group can make its project seem socially and politically irresistible, allowing for sustained control.

What distinguishes these efforts from standard party politics and social movement mobilization is the continued use of violence, which is disguised, unattributed, and therefore capable of achieving effect without significant political costs. Furthermore, because this violence is covert, so as not to sully the image of the above-ground effort, the approach imposes significant analytical and ethical duties on the state so as to foster an appropriate response. It becomes of paramount importance, for example, to assess political adversaries dispassionately and fairly, to be ready to compete against legitimate political rivals within the democratic parameters of the state yet suppress those who are participating in this system only to subvert it in pursuit of illegal ends. The challenge is that infiltrative insurgency trades in ambiguity. A similar analytical and ethical minefield complicates also the study of this phenomenon and underlines the need for great care in uncovering what is meant never to be seen.

To untangle the infiltrative strategy, this chapter sets out its nature and functioning, blending theory with a series of cases to illustrate how it works in practice. As with the other approaches detailed in this book, this method of insurgency is not altogether new, and so insight can readily be drawn from historical precedents, going back to the Russian Revolution of 1917 and to the overthrow of the Weimar Republic by the Nazi Party in 1933. Still, much as with the localized approach to insurgency detailed in the previous chapter, the strategy discussed here also benefits from specific enablers that are more common today and whose salience is likely to grow. The approach has also become particularly responsive to today's strategic conditions, in which direct and stark exercises in power work less well or, at least, less often. Given this context, the chapter discusses the dangers of infiltrative insurgency to political openness and state legitimacy—and therefore to democratic societies most of all—so as to help inform a possible response.

A 'Brilliantly Executed' Insurgency in the Andes

In October 2003, 100,000 protesters marched on Bolivia's political capital, La Paz. Following years of heightened instability, the crowd demanded fundamental political changes to address the ongoing economic recession, the social exclusion of marginalized communities, and the planned export of gas to Chile. The protest convened a range of the country's most powerful social movements: trade unionists, miners, peasants, representatives of the indigenous population, and members of the Movement for Socialism (MAS), a party controlled by the Cocaleros (the coca-leaf growers) and led by Evo Morales. To at least some of these protesters, the change needed was nothing less than the resignation of President Sánchez de Lozada. His position already weakened by months of protest, episodes of violence, the resignation of cabinet members, and the public withdrawal of support from his vice-president, Lozada was cornered and yielded to the pressure.[1] His vice-president, Carlos Mesa, took over and would proceed to govern for two years while under the growing influence of the Cocalero organization. In 2005, another massive protest in La Paz led to Mesa's own resignation. Following a brief interregnum by a caretaker president, fresh elections were held in which MAS won and Evo Morales became president.

In their detailed study of these events, based on extensive fieldwork and several senior-level interviews, David Spencer and Hugo Acha Melgar call Evo Morales's rise to power a 'brilliantly executed insurgency'—so brilliant, in fact, 'that the victory was not really perceived by the international public as an insurgency.'[2] From this perspective, what happened in Bolivia is a prime example of an infiltrative insurgency, by which the cocaine cartels, with Evo Morales in the lead, oversaw a gradual transfer of power that was largely constitutional but also fueled by subversion and violence.

75

By appealing to legitimate grievances in society and using drug money to put pressure on the government, this infiltrative approach succeeded in replacing a democratically elected administration with a narco-funded party, and then used this official power to enable and expand the Cocaleros' trafficking business.

The backdrop to this case lies in Bolivia's long-standing relation to coca, the relation of that plant to cocaine, and the country's legacy of social exclusion, social movement mobilization, and protest. These forces converged violently in the 1980s, when traditional coca cultivation gave way to increasing cocaine production and collided, therefore, with the US-driven War on Drugs. An important marker was the 1980 'coca coup,' which was financed by a drug lord and which led to the two-year reign of General Luis García Meza. As a 'narco-state' during these years, the government worked to expand coca cultivation in the Chapare province, a dense area of rainforest in Bolivia's Cochabamba Department. When democracy was restored, Bolivia's subsequent presidents sought to undo the economic damage of the Meza years, which caused conflict with the entrenched and now increasingly prosperous Cocaleros.

During the first phase of this conflict, the insurgency took on the character of a localized struggle, similar in nature to the contexts seen in the previous chapter. The Cocaleros were uninterested in central power but used protest and violence to keep the state out of the cocaine-growing regions of the country, particularly the Chapare.[3] As the United States upped its pressure on Bolivia and the government took aggressive actions against the Cocaleros, the movement reacted by using its significant wealth to buy off politicians and thereby shape policy. This approach worked to some degree, yet by the 1990s—with coca growth in decline—frustration led some within the movement to push for more concerted action, so as to overthrow the state and put a stop to its counter-narcotics operations. Sensing the 'insurgent's dilemma,' senior ideologues intervened, warning that 'an all-out guerrilla war would only attract the wrath of the United States, and the movement would eventually be crushed.'[4]

Herein lies the logic of the infiltrative approach. Facing insufficient returns on the corruption of willing politicians, yet unable to progress militarily without causing a backlash, the

Cocalero movement sought to create its own party—one that it could control and use to set, rather than subvert, state policy. As Filemón Escobar, one the MAS founders, puts it, 'it was necessary to take a great turn and adopt the line of participation in the elections of representative Western democracy, which for the traditional left was the dictatorship of the bourgeoisie.'[5] The hardliners were indeed reluctant, with Evo Morales exclaiming, '*Yo soy "fierrero" y no creo en las elecciones*' (I am 'iron man' and I don't believe in elections).[6]

Still, it soon became clear that party-political competition would not mean abandoning the struggle but merely its continuation by other means. All while setting up a political infrastructure, for example, 'the Cocalero military wing harassed military units from the moment they entered the Chapare, attacking their patrol camps day and night with sharpshooters, only desisting when they left.'[7] This 'complementarity of opposites' would go on to define the strategy.[8] While retaining the option of violence and subversion, the narco-traffickers used their funding to build bridges within civil society and to control the MAS party, thereby producing both social and political pressure on the government.

On the social front, the financial crisis of the late 1990s, the illegitimacy and several missteps of the government, and the legacy of protest movements provided ample opportunity for the Cocaleros to ally themselves with a whole network of disgruntled groupings. In these dealings, the Cocaleros presented themselves as champions of indigenous rights, which made sense as many within the Cocalero leadership were of Aymara origin and as the coca leaf has such significance within Bolivia's indigenous culture. Still, it bears noting that the coca grown in Chapare—the Cocalero homestead—has historically been for cocaine production; that intended for traditional uses grows best at higher altitudes, which is also why the government had specifically allowed its cultivation in the mountainous Yungas region.[9] Nevertheless, by 'divide and conquer' and through their superior resources and organization, the Cocaleros were able to displace the leadership of the indigenous rights movement and take the helm.[10]

In parallel, the Cocaleros in 1997 took over the MAS party, with Evo Morales—hitherto refusing a political role—becoming an increasingly prominent leader. In that same year, he won a seat in the lower house of Congress. In the general elections of 2002, MAS came in second place. Its success stemmed from effective bridge-building with other social movement organizations and their united protestations against the very real social, economic and political plight within Bolivian society at this time: the rural poverty, stagnant economic growth, government corruption, abusive security operations, and mounting social conflict.[11] A particular, and promising, target was the government's unpopular austerity measures, such as the introduction of an income tax bill to address the country's economic woes.[12] Amid the outrage sparked by poorly executed policies to privatize water, or the plans to export gas to Chile, it was easy for the Cocaleros to add the government's aggressive drug eradication to the list of grievances. It was through effective 'frame alignment' of this type that MAS could, in the midst of heightened instability, amass 100,000 protesters to descend on La Paz in October 2003.

During all this time, the Cocaleros never stopped—indeed, it actively relied upon—the use of violence: to produce incidents, to fire up the masses, and to protect areas needed for cocaine production.[13] It was in response to such transgressions that the lower house of the Bolivian Congress expelled Morales in January 2002, charging him with inciting violence and subversion. The move did not, however, change his chosen strategy. Instead, throughout these years, the Cocaleros blocked highways and engaged in offensive maneuvers, ambushing security forces and setting booby traps. In some of these clashes, MAS relied upon a formation of 'paramilitary shock troops,' the Ponchos Rojos, to fight it out with the state.[14] As a result, casualties in Chapare doubled in 2001 and 2002, reaching over 200—almost one-third of which, in 2002, represented military and police victims.[15] In the midst of one ambush in 2003, guerrillas and armed fighters sought to assassinate the minister of defense, Carlos Sánchez Berzaín; he survived by boarding a helicopter rather than traveling by land.[16] In that same year, leading up to the mass protests in La Paz, 60 operatives from the Colombian insurgent group FARC were reportedly brought to Bolivia to provide arms and training.[17]

This type of violence acted as a lubricant, but it was important for the instigators that it should not taint the image of the broader struggle. Whenever possible, confrontations were presented as government repression rather than organized clashes; such framing was made easier by the state's frequent heavy-handedness. More broadly, social protests, front organizations, and information operations remained by far the most visible components of the strategy—and the preferred method for extracting concessions from the state. Even at the campaign's acme, in October 2003, the Cocalero leadership rejected calls for a military showdown, as this would alienate the international community: 'it would be obvious that the constitutional order had been broken and that power had been seized through insurrection.'[18] Instead, following the resignation of President Sánchez de Lozada, the cartels oversaw a gradual transfer of power to a politician who could be controlled but who was then later also forced out, leaving the space open to the populist and narco-funded MAS. To Spencer and Melgar, Morales's election as president in 2006 was a brilliant insurgent victory, so much so that it is rarely recognized as such.[19]

Unsurprisingly, once in power, Morales employed the same tactics as before, projecting a narrative of authentic righteousness to cloak a systematic attack on state institutions.[20] By 2009, so many judges had been driven away that there was no longer a quorum for the Constitutional Court and only one member on the Supreme Court.[21] Underlying this institutional onslaught was a disturbing record of intimidation, bullying, and even violence (rarely condemned by the government), targeting the press and political opponents; Douglas Farah details the continued use of the Ponchos Rojos to do the government's dirty work.[22] Following a drive to 'decolonise the judiciary' (the choice of language is itself a weapon), the newly constituted Supreme Tribunal of Justice in 2017 cleared the way for Morales to run for a fourth consecutive term.[23] It was only when Morales was accused of rigging the eventual election, in 2019, that society turned on him and (ironically, through vast social movement mobilization) forced his resignation.

Nepal: 'A Model of Revolution in the Twenty-First Century'

The strategy in Bolivia purposely combined covert or non-attributed violence with mass protests and political infiltration by a Cocalero-controlled party. In Nepal, the Communist Party of Nepal (Maoist) attempted a similar approach. Having since 1996 privileged violence as a method of state capture, the group came to realize that its objectives would be more readily achieved and, more importantly, sustained by infiltrating the state rather than overthrowing it. This required a change in strategy and yet, contrary to much of the commentary, the insurgency lived on, even if its violence took on more discreet forms so as not to tarnish the project at hand. Nepal serves as a potent example of the overall infiltrative approach, given that the Communist Party of Nepal (Maoist) has achieved what no other Maoist group in Asia has been able to accomplish since the Vietnam War: gain a slice of power.

From 1996 to 2006, the Maoists engaged in violence as part of a people's war strategy that shared much with its Cold War antecedents. The violence associated with this insurgency began, as it usually does, with the use of terror to ensure compliance in the base areas, remove key individuals, and destroy symbols of the state. The emerging insurgent infrastructure soon came to be supported by guerrilla units charged with attacking state targets or reinforcing the political cadres. In extending the counter-state, the main target of guerrilla action was the police force: patrols sent to the scenes of incidents were ambushed and police stations overrun. Over time, the small guerrilla units were linked to main force units of battalion strength and equipped with weaponry similar to that of the government. The mobile warfare phase began with an offensive in November 2001 and would see several instances in which Royal Nepalese Army main units were overwhelmed and badly beaten.[24] Yet despite this formidable evolution in the use of force, the group concluded in 2005 that the violent line of effort had climaxed and that gaining political power—the objective—would require a different and altogether more creative strategy.

What led to the change? For one, the Maoists discerned the difficulty of advancing the revolution through a purely rural approach. Its military effort in the countryside had yielded impressive returns, but the group struggled to build upon the territory it ostensibly controlled.[25] Meanwhile, attempts to infiltrate the cities brought no decisive results, in part owing to the increasing international support provided to the state's military.[26] Indeed, the global environment proved unexpectedly hostile, with India actively opposing the Maoists and the recent 9/11 attacks stigmatizing the use of violence by non-state armed groups.[27] Between 2001 and 2003, the governments of Nepal, India, and the United States branded the group 'terrorists.' Therefore, despite the notable gains made through overt war, the Maoists' strategy was failing: 'they needed either vast popular support or clear military superiority but they discovered they had neither.'[28]

Standing face to face with the insurgent's dilemma, the Maoists adopted a new approach. As Baburam Bhattarai, their chief ideologue and 'number two,' explains: 'if you don't take note of the existing balance of forces, both politically and militarily in the country and outside, firstly it will be difficult to capture state power and secondly even after capturing state power it will be difficult to sustain it. That's why we introduced certain new features.'[29] These 'new features' relied on infiltration and, much as in Bolivia, exploited legitimate grievances to build alliances and the perception of legitimacy. In this case, the assumption of autocratic power by the king in 2005, though itself a response to Maoist violence, allowed these very forces to make common cause with major parties in government in seeking a return to democracy. Second, the Maoists also gauged correctly the domestic and international appetite for 'peace'—the Nepalese conflict having been exceptionally bloody—and used their ability to deliver on this desire to gain concessions. Yet all this would require a change in rhetoric, in ideology, and in overall approach.

A strategy session in September 2005 decided upon the shift: a political line of effort consolidated support in the base areas, an alliance line of effort built a united front against the increasingly isolated monarchy, a non-violent line of effort (also known as 'political warfare') exploited the widespread war fatigue, and an international line of effort ensured other states put pressure on the government to recognize the Maoists as a legitimate 'partner for peace' (while cutting off lethal aid to Kathmandu). The shift led to the Comprehensive Peace Agreement of 2006, which granted the Maoists an opportunity, fully exploited, to combine party politics with continued covert terrorism—frequently less lethal, but still brutal. Within the turbulent post-war context, the Maoists were in this manner able to control elections and then thrice hold the prime ministership, allowing them to solidify their position, fundraise, and neutralize resistance within the increasingly demoralized security forces.[30]

The key ingredient in Nepal, as in Bolivia, was the appearance of legitimacy, which led mainstream reporting and international coverage, even policy, to miss the strategic innovations at play. International observers tend to laud the shift to peace as definitive, if at times regrettably messy. The Nepali press made mention of the Nobel Peace Prize as a fitting tribute to Pushpa Kamal Dahal, aka Prachanda—the head of the Maoist war effort.[31] In 2008, he joined Jimmy Carter, Nelson Mandela, and Mahatma Gandhi in receiving Nepal's most prestigious peace award; the press release spoke of his 'unwavering contribution to establishing a democratic federal republic in Nepal, implementing the constituent assembly agenda and restoring lasting peace.'[32] If one scratches the surface, however, it becomes clear that deception was very much the name of the game, complicating not only government responses but also academic research into what was truly going on.

In the case of Nepal, looking behind the curtain is made easier by the candid utterances, and several leaked testimonies, of leading Maoist ideologues. Witness, for example, the staggering admission by Bhattarai, speaking in 2009: 'we have not abandoned the path of PPW [Protracted People's War]. What we have done is suspended that part of the activity … After some time we will be able to combine both aspects of PPW and general insurrection to mount a final insurrection to capture state power.'[33] Bhattarai, it is worth noting, was not only the 'number two' of the Maoist organization during the overt war years, but he then went on to serve as Nepal's prime minister from August 2011 to March 2013. His reflections on the Maoists' transition are therefore worth careful consideration:

For the time being we cooperated with the interim government also, because by participating in that coalition government we thought we could work within the bureaucracy, within the army, within the police and within the judiciary, in order to build our support base through those state structures, which would help us for future revolutionary activities ... What we have been doing since 2005 is the path of preparation for general insurrection through our work in the urban areas and our participation in the coalition government.[34]

Lest there be any confusion about a case that is often celebrated as a largely successful transition from war to peace, the sentiment and tone exhibited here are echoed by Prachanda, who twice served as prime minister, from 2008 to 2009 and 2016 to 2017. Caught on tape in 2008, he explains how the Maoists used intimidation and force to subvert parliamentary democracy, how their intent was to infiltrate the army through the mechanisms of the peace agreement, so that it could be 'politicized' and fall under Maoist influence, and how the group was deceiving the United Nations in presenting vastly inflated figures for the People's Liberation Army so as to produce, in peacetime, a larger force than before. As Prachanda clarifies, 'This is the truth. We cannot tell others, but you all and I know the truth.'[35] In other words, the shift to democracy, as expressed by Bhattarai, was an indirect means of 'cutting up the state part by part,' ultimately 'to smash it and then replace it with a new state.'[36]

Violence was deployed in support of this project, yet it was made covert and sporadic, allowing the Maoists to 'continue their campaign of terrorism within the very structure and protections of democracy, often with the support of misguided international actors (both state and non-state).'[37] Research and extensive fieldwork by Thomas A. Marks reveal a pattern of systematic low-level violence, only a fraction of which was reported in the press—in part because much of it occurred on the rural periphery where access is anyway limited and also because major outlets seldom devote space to intimidation and other lesser forms of violence. Among the Nepalese population, however, the method was not unlike that of the mob, with violence and the threat thereof becoming known to those who need to know, yet without tarnishing the 'legitimate' face of the business.[38] To this end, a particular victim has been those journalists who threaten to expose the method at hand, or intellectuals who speak out against Maoist intimidation.[39] Violence need not be fatal for the point to be made; attacks may include threats, assault, slashing, torture, and—in the case of women—rape.[40] Thus, even during Nepal's supposed years of peace, from 2007 to 2014, more than 3,000 emigrants were granted political asylum in the United States alone—despite a highly adversarial legal system—on the basis of known and credible threats to their lives.[41]

A main force behind this pattern of covert and low-level violence was the Maoist Young Communist League (YCL), which emerged in 2006 as a paramilitary force and replaced the People's Liberation Army. Denoting a shift from the large-scale violence associated with the overt phase of the conflict, the YCL has instead engaged in politically motivated 'extortion, abductions, intimidation, threats and murder.'[42] This is the same force that Prachanda boasted of in the leaked recording of 2009, when he explained the Maoists' continued fighting power: 'We have not shrunk; we have grown. And on the outside, we have created the YCL infrastructure, and we have thousands in the YCL.'[43] A similar grouping, the All Nepal National Independent Students' Union (Revolutionary), or ANNISU-R, was used to coerce, intimidate, punish, and put pressure on political opponents; stories detail the instigation of riots, vandalism, arson, and attack, all to complete the 'unfinished revolution.'[44]

Marks calls this approach 'the unrecognized second coming of people's war,' with violence used as a preparatory shaping mechanism for other, more dominant political and social tools. 'Ironically,' he adds, 'no context is better suited for such an approach than "peace."'[45] Under the cover of peace, the decision-making autonomy of elected governments and, by extension, of the electorate is gradually eroded or attacked outright from a series of directions, some involving covert violence, others threatening the chaos and disruption associated with violence, but all achieved without significant bloodshed. Over time, the conditions become ripe for a political takeover, from which point power can be exercised without backlash or major interruption.

It is a clever approach and, in Nepal, has helped the Maoists sidestep the insurgent's dilemma. Through the infiltrative strategy, the Maoists not only won the prime ministership on three occasions, but—as a seemingly legitimate actor—they could also partner with more moderate allies, primarily the United Marxist-Leninists (UML), as one restored Nepal Communist Party (NCP). Through this 'united front' method, the Maoists were able to achieve a significant share in the two-thirds majority that exercised political power, while simultaneously being given the home ministry (which controls the police) and a dominant role within NCP party affairs, which, as Marks points out, is all the 'more important in a party-state wherein all major government decisions are first decided upon in party deliberations.'[46] Given the current trajectory, Bhattarai's original intent is not so implausible: 'We will complete the revolution in a new way and we have to show that revolution is possible even in the twenty-first century. And Nepal can be a model of revolution in the twenty-first century.'[47]

Filling a Lacuna in Theory

There are fascinating and concerning parallels between the infiltrative approach to insurgency and the subversive methods used by Russia to control events in its 'near abroad' and beyond. As we have seen, the unfortunately named Gerasimov Doctrine speaks of 'political, economic, informational, humanitarian, and other nonmilitary measures—applied in coordination with the protest potential of the population' and 'supplemented by military means of a concealed character.'[48] Thus, the method captures the three main components of infiltrative insurgency. First, it operates by societal penetration, exploiting the population's ability to bestow legitimacy through mass mobilization. Some analysts of the approach have even come to term it 'society-centric warfare,' encompassing strategies that 'influence, engage and penetrate, at an early stage, *all* of the societies relevant to a conflict.'[49] Second, the approach operates through above-ground political action, using proxies or organizational structures that remain sufficiently respectable to compete within formal institutions. Third, it uses violence, but of a cloaked variety, to clear

85

obstacles in the way of political change without undermining the social and political standing of the above-ground element. Like many irregular strategies, violence becomes the shaping, or supporting, mechanism for the non-violent center, which is political action both among the people and across society.[50]

There is nothing new in states employing this type of approach, and insightful analysts have long sounded the alarm as to its implications. In 1946, American diplomat George Kennan issued a stern note of caution about what he termed 'political warfare'— 'the logical application of Clausewitz's doctrine in time of peace.'[51] Similar warnings have become more common of late, in response to Russian and Chinese assertiveness that, while systematic, deliberately remains below the threshold of outright war.[52] Indeed, though Kennan accurately discerned a lag in understanding in the West—due in part to a 'popular attachment to the concept of a basic difference between peace and war'—we are now fairly familiar with state use of subversion, of ambiguity, and of all 'means at a nation's command, short of war, to achieve its national objectives.'[53] In contrast, it is difficult to find scholarship on or acknowledgement of the same approach being used *within* states. The infiltrative approach remains, for a variety of reasons, a lacuna in our study of political violence.

Traditionally, within peace and conflict studies, it is assumed that party-political competition represents the laying down of arms and that democracy and warfare are two separate and mutually exclusive paths to power. Commentary discusses armed groups disarming so as to attempt peaceful politics, and then potentially returning to the armed struggle should this process fail, but seldom is the focus on bullets and ballots combined. The vast majority of work that does treat this topic is concerned with electoral violence, and for good reason: according to some estimates, in 2020, one in two national elections featured violence of some type.[54] In general, however, the assumption is that protracted and systematic violence cannot coexist with above-ground politics because it would mean combining illegality with legality and alienate voters all while relying on their support.[55] What is missed here is the political utility of violence, even in the midst of democracy, so long as it is employed in a carefully tailored way.

A select few works have sought to conceptualize the shrouded space occupied by infiltrative insurgency. Aila Matanock and Paul Staniland offer a helpful mapping of the many ways in which armed groups use elections as part of their strategy. They propose a two-by-two matrix of possibilities, ranging across the axes of overtness (the degree to which the armed group is open about its participation in party politics) and directness (the vicariousness of this involvement). The taxonomy is provided because, as the authors note, there is 'little overarching conceptual and theoretical development' around the question of how armed groups navigate elections, beyond—at best—their use simply as 'the pawns of politicians.'[56] One reason for the gap is precisely the 'subtleties and ambiguities that accompany several of the strategies,' which make empirical research into this topic 'a major, and daunting, task.'[57]

Within the taxonomy provided, infiltrative insurgency approximates best to the overt and direct participation of armed groups in elections. The difference, however, is that in infiltrative insurgency the party denies or deliberately camouflages the armed group or, at least, any link to its violence. In that sense, while helpful, Matanock and Staniland's taxonomy does not quite capture the strategy at hand, as their study presupposes the existence of an armed group and only then queries whether it has an acknowledged political wing, not the other way around. This route makes the violent component the focus rather than the adjunct of the political effort and therefore obscures the duplicitous nature of infiltration as a strategy.

The literature on how and why political parties adopt terrorism helps to close the loop, but, again, minimal consideration is given to groups that deliberately constrain and deny their use of violence, or to militant undergrounds kept hidden, yet operational, by the above-ground element of the same organization.[58] Typically, analysis of the use of force by political groupings looks upon the violence in binary terms, either as an overt component of strategy or as not there at all. This approach provides little by way of nuance and is less than helpful in navigating the murkier aspects of politico-military strategies. Relatedly, the scale of violence tends to be measured in fatalities, belying the use of non-fatal force as a superior form of terror within many contexts.

There are legitimate reasons for this dearth of scholarship. First, there are only so many cases in which this infiltrative strategy has been attempted; and, second, where it has been tried, it has been specifically to dupe observers, and so academic analysis becomes even more difficult. As Cynthia Irvin points out in her study of armed movements-turned-parties, research in this area is 'impeded by the obvious difficulties faced by researchers who want to "get inside" these revolutionary organizations, which often inhabit a very gray and narrow political space between legality and proscription.'[59] And yet, despite these methodological hurdles—hurdles that also subvert strategies of response—there are sufficient historical precedents, both theoretical and in practice, to suggest an approach with growing potential also for the future.[60]

Historical Precedents: Hitler and His Party

As an insurgent method, the infiltrative approach was responsible for some of the most consequential insurrections of the twentieth century. In his writing on revolution, Vladimir Lenin foreshadows the approach, noting the importance of 'combining illegal forms of struggle with *every* form of legal struggle.'[61] To Lenin, while the Marxist project would countenance no compromise as to its ultimate objectives, it could benefit from tactical pacts along the way, 'between the old, which is no longer strong enough to completely negate the new, and the new, which is not yet strong enough to completely overthrow the old.'[62] Thus, he advocated combining an ideologically pure clandestine organization of revolutionaries, who were never to lose sight of the bigger prize, with above-ground efforts in less radical social and political forums. Much as in Bolivia or Nepal, the key lay in simultaneously 'infiltrating, "capturing", and manipulating smaller groups, but also finding temporary "allies" with whom to work in larger arenas of power.'[63]

Despite Lenin's great theorization, and his major influence on revolutionaries throughout the Cold War and beyond, the clearest practical precedent for the infiltrative approach is found in Adolf Hitler's rise to power in the late 1920s and early 1930s. As in the cases cited above, Hitler followed a carefully designed strategy that blended party-political competition, societal infiltration, and the deliberately restrained use of violence so as to clear the path to state power without suffering a backlash along the way. The precedent warrants in-depth review not only because of its instructional and prototypical nature but also because of its transformative implications—for the German democratic experiment of the 1920s, for German society itself, and, along with it, for the course of world history.

Hitler's strategy combined three elements—the very same seen, with some variation, in Bolivia and Nepal. First, he charted the rise of the National Socialist movement through a formal political party—the National Socialist German Workers' Party (NSDAP). After joining the party in July 1919, Hitler rose swiftly through its ranks owing to his oratorical skills and mobilizing powers. He became chairman of the party in July 1921 and quickly boosted its support base by playing on the anxieties of the time: Germany's post-war traumas, the weakness of the Weimar Republic, and the fear of a socialist takeover. Though the party was briefly banned in 1923, it resumed operations as the NSDAP in 1925 and would thenceforth be the mechanism through which Hitler legally seized power. Like a Trojan horse, he and the NSDAP used the very openness of German parliamentary democracy—and its unpreparedness for exactly this type of threat—to dominate the state. As H. W. Koch explains, the Weimar Constitution simply 'contained no article making it illegal to attack the republican form of state, or even to abolish it, as long as the aim was pursued legally, within the framework of the Constitution.'[64]

Second, to guarantee the electoral base necessary for this strategy, the NSDAP designed itself as more of a movement than a party. By infiltrating clubs and communities, and by building structures and leagues across different strands of society, the Nazis could extend their reach—and their perception of legitimacy—far beyond what would have been possible through political mobilization alone. Helmut Anheier notes that Nazism suffused these 'pre-political' fields, spread across various cultural and social contexts, and 'transcending narrow ideological, religious, and economic boundaries.'[65] Thomas Childers and Eugene Weiss refer to the approach as a 'revolutionary catchall strategy.'[66] The demographically diverse networks thus created would be critical to the party-political strategy and, also, to the totalitarian reach of the movement once in power.

Third, the NSDAP employed violence as a force multiplier to make possible its political rise. Hitler's use of violence evolved over time, as he too confronted the insurgent's dilemma. The NSDAP created the *Turn- und Sportabteilung* (Gymnastics and Sports Unit) in November 1920, which (despite its name) took the form of a 'self-protection' militia similar to that used by other parties at this time. Soon, however, the Nazis established the *Stoßtrupp*, or shock troops, and went on the offensive, attacking or intimidating political opponents and disrupting their meetings and events.[67] The violence escalated following the establishment of the Nazi *Sturmabteilung* (or SA) in August 1921. Facilitated by former army man Ernst Röhm, the SA received weapons from the military as a paramilitary *Wehrverband* committed to protecting the nation against communism.[68] The SA then engaged in various street fights and provoked other violent incidents, leading to major pitched battles such as during 'German Day' in Coburg on October 14–15, 1922.

The insurgent's dilemma came into sharp relief when the Nazis doubled down on violence and attempted an armed insurrection. Hitler sparked the revolt in Munich in November 1923—this was the so-called Beer Hall Putsch. The sudden escalation provoked clashes with government forces in which the Nazis lost 14 men and Hitler was wounded and later imprisoned. Following the violence, the Nazi Party and militia were banned. The lesson drawn by Hitler was that 'armed insurrection against a government which commands the loyalty of the police and the army is foredoomed.'[69] Upon his release from prison, Hitler changed strategy, setting the Nazi Party—and the SA—on 'the path of legality'; thenceforth, the SA would be 'used first and foremost for propaganda, but would not seek out military confrontation with the legal forces.'[70]

Neither Hitler's embrace of parliamentarianism, nor the new role for the SA, changed the fundamental objective of seizing power and creating a fascist state. Indeed, once it was again allowed to operate, the SA emerged from the underground with new allies and influence, reaching 30,000 men by August 1927 and 60,000 by

1929. The pitched battles were now rare, but the force was used to clear the streets of political enemies, disrupt the meetings of rivals, terrorize opponents, and create an image of power (such as with the 'token mobilization' in Brunswick of some 104,000 uniformed forces in October 1931).[71] As David Littlejohn explains, 'without actually challenging the government to a head-on confrontation, Hitler was able to blackmail and intimidate it with the size and discipline of his brown-shirted army.'[72]

As a central yet also potentially inflammatory ingredient, the violence used by the SA had to be carefully calibrated. Where circumstances and political forces allowed, it would engage in bloody confrontations, either with the communists or with the Social Democrats, but it would present these as self-defense and as supporting 'law and order.'[73] In more delicate situations, the SA would 'create incidents' that could be exploited for political purpose, by provoking a reaction and then sending reinforcements, or by marching onto enemy turf in the hope of sparking a fight.[74] More than the tally of casualties, it was the 'emotional dynamics' of these incidents that mattered: their mobilizing potential externally and their internal spurring of *esprit de corps*.[75] In fact, the Nazis often lost more men than they claimed, but such outcomes were all the more effective in selling the threat of communism, the heroism of lost martyrs, and the need both for the SA and for a radically new political leadership.[76]

Because strategic objectives were privileged over tactical outcome, much was achieved through indirect violence, such as threats, intimidation, or just gatherings of forces—referred to, at the time, as *Versammlungsterror* (loosely translatable as 'gathering terrorism').[77] In a proto-Maoist way, the SA were deployed not just as agents of violence but as 'political soldiers,' engaged in 'the varied political activities deemed necessary by the political leadership to mobilize support for the NSDAP at the polls.'[78] By keeping violence below the threshold at which it could no longer be ignored, Hitler derived the benefits of terror and intimidation without enduring the feared response. Even the media were circumspect in reporting on the matter, owing partly to the low profile of the violence and partly to the climate of fear that it nonetheless—and very effectively—

spawned. In the words of journalist Gabriele Tergit (later attacked by the SA), 'People know it—when Sturm 33 [a Berlin-based SA chapter] is involved, ... there is terror. But no newspaper says as much any longer, no police pass it on as news—it is civil war as habit.'[79]

Hitler's approach did not proceed without a hitch. His SA proved difficult to control; its fighters often did not understand the legal path or the 'repeated postponements' of armed insurrection, and as violent incidents increased in the early 1930s, they began to threaten Hitler's success at the polls.[80] In the end, however, through an admixture of strategy and contingency, Hitler legally gained the chancellorship in 1933 and went on to destroy what he had conquered, having in this time also prepared the ground—socially, politically and through terror—for his totalitarian project. Ultimately, his strategy worked as planned, and the case warrants our attention. As Daniel Siemens concludes, 'the history of the SA is in many respects paradigmatic of the way politics, media coverage, violence, and grassroots activism were interwoven in the twentieth century.'[81]

Infiltrative Insurgency on the Rise

Indeed, the twentieth century proved well suited to the infiltrative approach. A key requirement for this path to power is the existence of a political competition whose openness can be subverted to claim power indefinitely. It was in the last three decades of the nineteenth century that the world witnessed the formation of mass political parties—a development that coincided with the spread of democracy and the mass circulation of newspapers.[82] From then on, democratic means became far more common. Freedom House finds that whereas there was not one democracy at the onset of the twentieth century, at least not by today's standards, by 1950 'one third of the population of the world lived under democratic rule.'[83] Democratic governments then grew from representing 29 percent of the total in 1945 to 57 percent in 2017, a figure that does not account for the 28 percent of 'mixed' cases that blend, each in a unique way, characteristics of both democracy and authoritarianism.[84] Indeed, even dictators now hold elections, producing a growing number of 'anocracies' and 'democratic authoritarian' regimes.[85] Few of these systems would qualify as credible experiments in party-political democracy, but the very fact of elections, and the need to cheat somewhat inconspicuously, do create 'arenas through which opposition forces may—and frequently do—pose significant challenges.'[86]

A second, parallel, development of the twentieth century, also enabling an infiltrative approach, was the expansion of civil society in many countries around the world. In their work on global social movements, Charles Lindholm and José Pedro Zúquete present a century of socio-political mobilization, from the utopian impulses of communism and fascism in its early decades, to the anti-colonial movements in the Third World mid-century, and, from the 1960s on, the 'liberation theologies, hippie and drug subcultures, civil rights crusaders, antiwar activism, feminist protests, and a New Left committed to overturning "the system."'[87] This vitalization of civil society dovetailed with the process of democratization noted above, extending the role of social movements to new contexts and fueling a growing challenge, following the Cold War, to the supposed 'end of history' proclaimed by the status quo.

With this opening up of the political space—this democratization of both state and society—new opportunities for gaining power also presented themselves. At its Second World Congress in July 1920, the Communist International officially endorsed Lenin's method of making tactical alliances for strategic ends. At the Third World Congress, held the following year, the approach was refined and codified as the 'united front.'[88] Throughout the 1930s, Trotskyists in Europe and the United States promoted the 'French turn,' whereby communists would partner with, and seek to dominate, more moderate leftist outfits. At no point was this strategic feint a matter of capitulation or a dilution of ideological standing; the aim throughout was to gain power in numbers and pursue common aims, all the while proselytizing 'our temporary semi-allies' as well as their constituents.[89] This ruse informed subsequent strategies of entryism, used by communists throughout the Cold War to penetrate and seize larger, more mainstream organizations. To Rudi Dutschke, the German communist student activist, victory required a 'long march through the institutions,' or the infiltration of societal groupings in preparation for eventual revolution, by 'working against the established institutions while working in them.' As he explained, the approach implied not just 'boring from within,' but the development of skills and funding necessary to 'build up counterinstitutions.'[90]

The imagery of a 'long march,' never mind the mention of counterinstitutions, evokes—quite deliberately—Mao Tse-tung's theory of protracted warfare, his emphasis on clandestine infrastructure, and the legendary Long March from Jiangxi to Shaanxi provinces in October 1935. In retrospect, Mao was perhaps the twentieth century's most proficient 'united front' strategist, starting with the pact struck with the Kuomintang (KMT) to end warlordism in China and continuing with the one formed some years later to combat the Japanese invasion. Though in a vastly different context—that of wartime—Mao drew on, and developed further, the very stratagem first proposed by Lenin and Trotsky, namely 'to get inside the foe and use his strengths to build your own.'[91] By uniting with KMT, Mao removed the pressure it had exerted on the communists, gained an ally in opposing the greater adversary, and could meanwhile work to turn those who were receptive to the communist ideology—all in return for a few tactical concessions.[92] In Mao's own words, it involved 'developing the progressive forces, winning over the middle forces, and combating the die-hard forces.'[93]

In this way, rather than a departure from Maoist insurgent techniques, the infiltrative approach is really a reaffirmation of its political core. At the same time, it is also a reaction to the militarized misapplication of the Maoist model by several would-be emulators—those who failed to follow through on Mao's exhortations to let politics lead and all else follow. As we have seen with the insurgent's dilemma, there is today limited scope for such a militarized approach. Innovation can also be seen in the application of this method in times of relative peace, allowing the strategy to unfold without triggering the panic and responses that result from armed conflict. Indeed, Mao never dreamt of denying or seeking to disguise his use of violence; operating in the midst of the most lethal civil war of the twentieth century, there was no need to be bashful. In contrast, the infiltrative approach is designed for more brackish environments, in which violence must take on ambiguous and shapeless forms. It exploits democratic inroads, uses civil society connections for momentum, and carefully adds covert or below-the-radar violence to clear obstacles along the way.

It is this final innovation that makes the approach so complex and difficult to counter. Infiltrative insurgency cloaks its defining characteristic—the violence, coercion, and terror—and presents itself therefore as a social movement organization, a political party, a non-violent force for change. The ostensible rejection of violence not only legitimizes the movement; it also removes from view the types of military targets whose elimination states tend to rely upon as a form of counterinsurgency. As Spencer and Acha Melgar note with regard to the infiltrative approach, 'We have built very sophisticated military capabilities to defeat irregular military forces, but the same sophistication does not exist in the non-military arena ... Without completely discarding the military struggle, it is into this gap that new forms of insurgency are stepping.'[94]

If the method is designed to confuse analysis and response, its effects can be as stark as those of any other type of insurgency. Even if operating through the institutions and gaining ground by means of the ballot box, groups that use subversion and violence to succeed at democratic mobilization do not generally gain newfound respect for democratic principles once in power. Hitler was quite candid: 'we have openly declared that we would deploy democratic means only to attain power, and after our assumption of power we would deny our enemies all those means which are allowed to us while in opposition.'[95] Lenin, too, was clear: nothing in the tactical compromises would 'in the least prevent Marxism, as a living and operating historical force, from fighting energetically against compromises.'[96] Morales and Prachanda may have been less forthcoming, but in both cases their infiltration of the state resulted in its politicization and corruption. Though neither fully succeeded—Morales was ousted, and Nepal has yet to be 'totally destroyed and replaced,' as Bhattarai had hoped—the two cases, and the historical precedents of the approach, are troubling in their implications.[97]

Recent and Contemporary Cases

Given increasingly enabling conditions, there is a range of cases that, already today, illustrate the potential of the infiltrative approach. We can turn, for example, to Golden Dawn in Greece, a European fascist party that experienced unparalleled success at the polls by emulating the approach mastered by Hitler in the 1920s. Buoyed by an economic crisis, a wave of migration, and a pattern of corruption and cronyism in government, Golden Dawn partook in electoral politics as an anti-systemic challenger, seeking to win democratic support for the creation of a fascist anti-democratic state. Still, by selectively downplaying its fascist nature and posing as just another political party, the group arrogated to itself a veneer of legitimacy while it also engaged in violence and paramilitarism targeting immigrants and political opponents. This strategy enabled the party to poll in double-digit figures, to win 7 percent of votes in Greece's national elections of 2012, and send 18 members to Greece's 300-strong parliament. When the legal system sought to ban the party as a criminal organization, it appealed to its freedom of speech and democratic credentials to seek legal protection.[98]

Golden Dawn used the same admixture of violence and politics as seen in the Weimar Republic, but it borrowed also from Lenin. In a way similar to his emphasis on a small yet ideologically pure cadre of professional revolutionaries, Golden Dawn cultivated a core of carefully selected and dedicated followers so as 'to avoid incoherence and opportunism.'[99] Only when followers had proved their loyalty, or had undergone an ideological 'boot camp,' were they granted power within the party. This distinction between true believers and hangers-on guaranteed the movement's strategic direction and also cloaked the true intentions of the party so as to make possible its social acceptance and penetration.

Indeed, like Hitler's NSDAP, Golden Dawn positioned itself as a movement rather than just a party. By playing on the traditional concerns of mainstream Greek nationalism (pride in Orthodox Christianity, resentment of the EU, of Turkey, and of North Macedonia), the group established roots in local communities and a basis for their gradual radicalization. It further consolidated support by offering social services: security patrols against the supposed immigrant menace, loans to hard-up followers, employment opportunities in shipyards or construction, and 'Greek-only' food banks and blood donation drives.[100] As Antonis Ellinas explains, although these efforts were typically 'limited in scale, the media attention amplified the party's local community work, allowing it to claim social legitimacy while retaining its ethnocentric message.'[101] As a stark reminder of Nazi techniques of the 1930s, Golden Dawn also engaged in patriotic education to brainwash children in line with its ultra-nationalist and xenophobic agenda.[102]

To this strategy, Golden Dawn added violence—to strengthen the movement, to create a climate of fear, and to win support among those frustrated by government inaction and desperate for quick 'solutions.' The violence ranged from seemingly spontaneous low-level attacks on immigrants to targeted assaults on opposing, or 'traitor,' politicians—those championing inclusion, tolerance, and pluralism. To give a sense of scale, between 2010 and 2011, 200 such incidents were recorded (presumably many others were not).[103] The group also engaged in 'cleansing operations' targeting areas heavily frequented by immigrant populations and turning these into its own meeting grounds. Sporadically, and when expedient, the party denied any direct involvement in the racist attacks; at other times, it publicized its role, so as to brandish its anti-systemic and nationalistic credentials.[104] The violence also made possible criminal activity—intelligence reports mention blackmail, protection rackets, human trafficking, and prostitution—which funded the group but, ironically, also caused its ultimate disestablishment through trial in 2020.

Despite this failing, 'Golden Dawn pulled off something that should be impossible in an advanced democracy—the simultaneous operation of a legal, parliamentary party and a violent racist militia.'[105] That this combination could occur in peacetime within a European democracy is alarming, yet the basic approach is not so unusual. Apart from the racism, we see a similar effort on the left side of the political spectrum with the Colombian Communist Party (PCC), both before and after its legalization in 1957. Indeed, in the decades preceding FARC's creation in 1964, and against the backdrop of Colombia's violent politics, the PCC simultaneously engaged in above-ground mobilization in the cities and strategic direction of 'self-defense' forces in the countryside (the euphemistic labeling of these armed revolutionary units was to some degree justified by the pattern of violent persecution in Colombia at this time).[106] The PCC perceived these rural guerrillas as part of its overall struggle and, when FARC was created, the party used it as a clandestine armed wing, offering ideological guidance and political support to its rural operations.[107] Actual linkages and support structures remained clandestine, to the point where even the CIA concluded that the PCC firmly adhered to the '*via pacífica* or mass struggle'; any talk of 'armed struggle,' the CIA assumed, was just 'a matter of shrewd semantics' and intra-movement positioning.[108] This was a misreading of the strategy at hand, which the communists termed *la combinación de todas las formas de lucha* (or 'the combination of all forms of the struggle') and which drew directly on the writing and theories of Lenin.[109]

To the *combinación* approach, FARC (and by extension the PCC) in 1982 added the Unión Patriótica, a political party created during a truce between FARC and the Colombian government. According to FARC leader Jacobo Arenas, UP was to operate overtly as FARC's political arm (in contrast to the clandestine relation it enjoyed with PCC), and thereby extend the guerrillas' appeal and mobilizing potential to a broader audience.[110] Internal FARC documents from the period reveal that, for the leadership, 'this was not a party to substitute for armed revolution, but rather a party to create the revolution.'[111] Thus, while the UP experienced notable electoral success—particularly at the local level—FARC almost doubled its number of 'fronts' from 27 to 48.[112] The potential of this experiment remains unknown, as the UP became the target of a brutal campaign of annihilation at the hands of paramilitaries, some with connections to Colombia's armed forces. The dirty war that followed decimated UP and ended the *combinación* strategy.

This violent denouement should not shroud the intent and logic of the method. Though it was little understood outside Colombia, it was fear of precisely this type of approach that led many to doubt FARC's later effort to disarm, within the context of peace talks in the mid-2010s. FARC was then facing diminishing military returns and a global environment hostile to narco-insurgents. In response, the group reframed its fight: it recruited allies in promising societal sectors—coca growers, marginalized members of organized labor, and alienated left-wing elements—and presented itself as a viable negotiating partner. Dangling the prospect of peace, FARC then talked its way to guaranteed parliamentary power and the possibility of shaping the nature of the state.[113] It insisted upon overseeing its own disarmament within FARC-controlled territories ('peace zones') and an end to aerial and even manual eradication of coca crops, which was to be undertaken by local communities in return (and only in return) for adequate service delivery by an increasingly cash-strapped state. The Colombian people rejected this initial draft of the agreement, and a second, more stringent version was approved by parliament. Though evidence does not suggest a return to the *combinación* strategy, violence by FARC dissidents has continued and coca production has surged.[114]

In Colombia, the military arm—FARC—gradually grew to dominate and ultimately sideline the political party, the PCC. In another major case of infiltrative insurgency, Northern Ireland, the relation between the political and military wing evolved in the opposite direction. Here, we see a struggle to end British rule involving both the Sinn Féin party and the Provisional Irish Republican Army (PIRA), two 'umbilically linked' organizations denying the fact of working together.[115] Whereas it was the armed element that dominated this partnership for much of the twentieth century, by the late 1970s the prospect of a military victory was fading, and a new strategy was needed. Sinn Féin was then elevated as a political tool to develop and extend grassroots support and to translate this backing into formal power. To enable the strategy, by the early 1980s PIRA ended its previously steadfast position of abstentionism—neither recognizing nor engaging in Irish state institutions—and adopted instead the 'Armalite and ballot box strategy,' where party-political and military efforts would work together to force Britain out.[116]

The new strategy allowed Sinn Féin to build formal political power and earn international recognition. In government, it expanded its base and 'established a sort of Republican veto' on any conciliatory move by more moderate parties.[117] In the streets, it used electoral participation to legitimize the armed struggle and demonstrate public support. On the international stage, it established ties with sympathetic audiences and lobbied foreign governments, not least the United States.[118] All the while, PIRA acquired arms from Libya and launched terrorist attacks in Northern Ireland, England, and beyond; as Sinn Féin president Gerry Adams had explained, the armed struggle 'provides a vital cutting edge' without which 'the issue of Ireland would not even be an issue.'[119] Internal PIRA documents confirm the overall approach: engagement in politics 'may ameliorate conditions from time to time, but will not and cannot, because of the nature of those institutions, bring about the fundamental changes needed ... A big and successful heave to topple and replace is what is needed rather than tinkering with the existing system.'[120]

To exert influence and control, PIRA maintained parallel security structures and meted out low-level vigilante violence. The attacks were systematic and planned, yet, much as in Nepal, they were often non-lethal, making them difficult to account for and easy for Sinn Féin to dismiss as unrelated to its own political campaign. Andrew Silke notes that between 'accidental' deaths and suicides, PIRA vigilante actions produced just one fatality for every 250 attacks, a ratio that reveals both the calibration and the prevalence of violent incidents.[121] Despite such 'restraint,' it should be noted that PIRA still killed an average of 50 people per year from 1980 to 1993.[122] When challenged on this topic, Sinn Féin 'tended to downplay the involvement of the republican movement, and instead stress that many so-called punishment attacks are carried out by ordinary people who are simply fed up with the crime problem.' As Silke shows in some detail, whereas this was the official party line, 'the reality of course is quite different.'[123]

Over time, as Sinn Féin mobilized and sought mainstream legitimacy, it became increasingly critical for it to 'assert its separate identity from the IRA'—despite nagging evidence to the contrary.[124] In Northern Ireland, the subterfuge consisted of Sinn Féin presenting itself as a partner for peace and as a possible bulwark against PIRA violence—so long as its demands were met. Playing up the rhetoric of peace was to grant Sinn Féin access to legitimate political forums where it could negotiate its way to victory, and yet its main bargaining chip in these talks was its implicit influence over PIRA's violent campaign. The central conceit was that the violence was not Sinn Féin's doing, but that it knew what would make it stop.[125] Whenever critics pointed out the far more cozy relationship between the two and demanded greater accountability, Sinn Féin would accuse them of threatening the 'peace process,' which, in this sense, had become 'an instrument of coercion.'[126] In other words, the party expropriated the language of peace and made warmongers of those rejecting its subterfuge—a very effective use of 'guilt transfer.'[127]

Did it work? Ultimately, PIRA's strategy was constrained by its own contradictions. Sinn Féin's effort to deny any link with PIRA was never entirely convincing, with its international partners condemning it for continued violence during negotiations. Abandoning the violence became the price of admission to a real seat at the table, yet, as Kevin Bean points out, 'decommissioning, disbandment of the IRA, and explicit recognition of the state's law and order structures were cards that could be only played once.'[128] Once violence had been forsworn, even 'skilful negotiation would yield only limited advantage because it was impossible to win at the conference table what republicans had failed to gain either on the battlefield or through the ballot box.'[129] As a result, while Sinn Féin has succeeded electorally in recent years, Northern Ireland remains part of the United Kingdom and PIRA officially laid down its arms in 2005.

For hardcore republicans, to whom the outcome of the strategy may very well appear pyrrhic at best, the mistake lay in the faulty timing of the strategic shift, in giving up on the coercive component too soon, and being left with just a political party when all the strategic objectives had still to be met. And yet it should be recognized that an alternative path was highly unlikely given the specific conditions in Northern Ireland at this time. Most fundamentally, PIRA was so thoroughly penetrated by British intelligence services as to cripple its capacity for armed action. By the late 1980s an estimated 85 percent of its operations had to be aborted, either because the plans had been compromised or because of the paralyzing paranoia that now pervaded its ranks.[130] This domination forced PIRA to decentralize even more than before, greatly complicating the execution of a seamless 'Armalite and ballot box' strategy. Rather than reinforcing one another, each facet of the struggle tripped up the other, making a change in strategy again seem necessary.[131]

Despite all this, PIRA's strategy still holds great lessons for future insurgents regarding the synergy of legal politics and illegal violence. By claiming separation from PIRA, Sinn Féin legitimized itself as a champion of peace and whitewashed its own responsibility for terrorism over several decades. With significant success, it played a double game of political integration and armed coercion, all the while pretending that one component of this struggle was separate from the other. In this manner, PIRA sought to benefit from the best of both worlds: the expedience and power of illegal methods and the acceptability and access of the legal path. Conditions greatly stunted what it was able to achieve politically through infiltrative insurgency, and yet it is not difficult to imagine how a different set of factors, perhaps in a different context, might have generated a different result.

A Note on Militias

Whereas PIRA provides a clear illustration of an armed group adopting party politics as a complement to its strategy, there are several other cases of political parties using military wings to extend their possible repertoire and boost their democratic fortunes. Indeed, in our discussion of infiltrative insurgency, some note must be made of the extensive use of militias as components of multiparty democracy. This phenomenon has much in common with the infiltrative approach to insurgency, though it also represents an evolution from the cases laid out above. Militias generally are not said to be engaging in insurgency, as they represent factions within the government and operate, over the long term, on its behalf. Also, in contrast to the infiltrative efforts highlighted above, the relationship between party and militia is typically not covert, but rather a feature of democracy 'as is.' And yet, when we look at insurgency through the lens of infiltration, the relevance of militias to the topic becomes clear.

First, in democracies where militias are a feature, they provide a coercive component to electoral parties, allowing them to operate both within and outside state institutions. Thus, both infiltrative insurgents and militia-wielding parties emphasize the simultaneity of licit and illicit action and reveal the gains made possible by gaming the system in this manner. Second, whereas the existence of a militia is often openly acknowledged, its exact activities and uses by the party tend to be a source of intrigue and allegation, revealing another similarity with the cases of infiltrative insurgency addressed above. Third, both militias and infiltrative insurgency represent a conceptual challenge of analytical and practical importance, in that they render razor-thin the line dividing insurgent challengers subverting the system from outside and incumbents doing the same from within. Militias, then, can be seen as the consequence of prolonged infiltrative insurgency, or as what happens when illicit and licit forms of competition are blurred and allowed to coexist as a permanent feature of democracy. In such a context, violence, intimidation, and party politics go hand-in-hand.

The case of post-Saddam Iraq is helpful in making the point, as it featured an armed political competition unfolding from within state institutions. Shortly after its invasion, the United States helped elevate to positions of democratic power various political parties, each of which entered government with its own armed militia. Prime among these parties were the Supreme Council for the Islamic Revolution in Iraq (SCIRI, later renamed ISCI), the Islamic Da'wa Party, and the two major Kurdish parties (the Patriotic Union of Kurdistan and Kurdistan Democratic Party). These paramilitary organizations had long opposed the rule of Saddam Hussein and had operated from various sanctuaries—typically Iran in the case of the Shia militias or in Iraq's protected north in the case of the Kurdish forces. With Saddam's overthrow, they were brought back in, with their militias in tow. The initial US intention had been to 'DDR sub-state militias'—to disarm, demobilize, and reintegrate their members into society—yet amid the mounting insecurity of 'post-war' Iraq, and the professed desire of the militias' sponsoring parties to lend a helping hand, it became too tempting to partner with them instead.[132]

In this manner, the parties returning from exile were given a seat on the Iraqi Governing Council. The Kurdish Peshmerga continued to dominate in the north, where it had long operated, and in the south, SCIRI's Badr Corps—swiftly renamed the Badr Organization for Reconstruction—was allowed to remain essentially intact, while it infiltrated local security units. Yet with the possible exception of the Peshmerga, none of the parties enjoyed much public support, even among their supposed constituents.[133] Instead, their promotion was based on their unmistakable opposition to Saddam Hussein, their clearly pronounced ethnic identity (allowing for the semblance of a 'representative government'), and the power they held through their control of armed forces. By October 2004, even the recalcitrant Moqtada al-Sadr had joined the feast, following a deal whereby members of his Jaish al-Mahdi militia were paid to disarm and Sadr was invited to join the government. As with the other militias, there was no expectation or demand that all arms be handed over or that JAM disband or shift allegiance. The reintegration, here too, was largely unconditional.[134]

The missteps of American nation-building in Iraq gave what was in fact an armed competition for state power the veneer of democratic legitimacy—and blurred the line between the two. This competition not only pitted the Shia against the Sunnis, as is commonly assumed, but also saw different Shia parties feud for power, through sermons in the mosques as well as violence in the streets.[135] Armed with militias, these parties fought for and assumed the space left behind by the crumbling regime and then competed for control of ministries and government assets. With the exception of JAM, the militias tried to avoid armed confrontations with the occupying forces, but they all insisted— at times violently—on total freedom of action.[136] Not only did this threaten the state-building enterprise in Iraq; it also raised the question of who, exactly, was in charge. Larry Diamond frames the contradiction well: 'the menace of radical, Iranian-backed armed militias ... [was] mounting rapidly ... even as the leaders of their sponsoring political parties were sitting in Baghdad on the Iraqi Governing Council, signing democratic declarations and professing sweet moderation and restraint to the Americans.'[137]

Elevated by the occupying authorities, the position of militia-wielding parties would be consolidated further through the elections of January and December 2005. Henceforth, the arrangements of the Iraqi government were spun to serve the interests of particular leaders and groups rather than, necessarily, those of Iraq. The constitution written by this government was rightly recognized by Sunnis as a 'sectarian text'—one that would leave that community both landlocked and without oil.[138] Unsurprisingly the constitution also condoned the continued existence of militias, though these were anyway increasingly infiltrating the official security services of the state, which accordingly took on a highly sectarian character. Similarly, once firmly in government, the militia leaders also claimed specific ministries, which they quickly 'turned into party fiefdoms directly breaking governmental coherence': Sadr loyalists gained control of the ministries of health and of transportation, which were purged of their Sunni employees, while SCIRI appointed a former commander of its Badr Organization to the post of interior minister.[139]

Democratic participation allowed these sectarian actors to whitewash their violent agendas. When Sadr gained the health ministry, two of his officials—the deputy health minister and the commander of the ministry's security force—turned Baghdad's hospitals into 'death zones for Sunnis seeking treatment there': the two 'were accused of organizing and supporting the murder of Sunni doctors; the use of ambulances to transfer weapons for Shi'ite militia members; and the torture and kidnapping of Sunni patients.'[140] Under the leadership of Badr commander Bayan Jabr Solagh, the interior ministry was purged of Sunnis and then used by SCIRI to execute and torture to death hundreds of Iraqis each month.[141] When Bayan Jabr was dislodged from the interior ministry and moved sideways to become minister of finance, he allegedly used this position to obstruct reconstruction projects in Baghdad's Sunni areas. Meanwhile, Sadr exploited the newly created power vacuum in the interior ministry to penetrate its security forces, to provide thereby legal cover for sectarian attacks, protect Sadrist-controlled areas from police interference, and allow his militants to pass through checkpoints unimpeded.[142]

Rather than fighting the state from outside, these political parties were competing for power from within. The result has been a seemingly irredeemable corruption of Iraqi governmental affairs, not only in its devastating effects but also because any corrective measure must itself rely on the very structures that are to be reformed. Consequently, it is unsurprising that the militia problem has persisted, allowing parties to pursue sectarian (in place of national) and patrimonial (in place of societal) goals. Some may celebrate the use of these same militias and their offshoots in combating ISIS (the Iraqi national forces having proved too weak), yet the increased ownership of Iraqi politics by Iran, the frustration of Iraqis with sectarian and corrupt governance, and the unchecked crime and violence of some of these same militias augur very badly for the future of the country.[143] While themselves destabilizing and volatile, the mounting public protests and outcry against this set-up offer a source of hope, but, should reforms fail to impress a population hungry for change, the seeds sown in 2003 may well generate another bloody harvest in years to come.[144]

Pakistan provides a different, though in some regards comparable, setting. While the major parties in Pakistan do not use militias, there are local cases where militias and parties have worked together in ways that perforate the democratic fabric of society. Reflecting Pakistan's disrupted democratic path and its frequent periods of military rule, these parties at once contest elections and wield distinct militant wings that engage in violence, 'often under the command of the main party leadership.'[145] At times, the political leadership will prosecute its above-ground activities using a different name, thereby seeking to cloak its parallel involvement in violence. In other cases, maintaining plausible deniability is less of a concern. In either case, these entities provide another instance where the exact difference between party-political participation and infiltrative insurgency is difficult to parse.

The Muttahida Qaumi Movement (MQM) is a case in point. Since its founding in Karachi in 1984, MQM has actively participated in provincial and general elections and has formed multiple coalition governments with more powerful parties. It has laid out specific policy goals in its manifesto and promotional materials relating to the removal of what it sees as Pakistan's 'feudal system' and its replacement by a form of 'grassroots democracy.'[146] In practice, its exact political ambitions fluctuate according to need and appear largely patrimonial. Indeed, MQM emerged in reaction to ethnic discrimination against the Urdu-speaking Muhajirs and continues to rely extensively on that community's support; efforts to expand the party and seek broader appeal among the working and lower classes have been only marginally successful. Even so, a strategy of combining coercion with co-option has allowed MQM to gain and maintain significant influence as a political party, leading to various alliances and coalitional arrangements in Sindh Province and beyond.[147]

In establishing itself as a major political force in Karachi, MQM made extensive use of violence. In the words of Niloufer Siddiqui, 'it continues to function as much outside the system as a pressure group as within it.'[148] Throughout the 1990s, there were frequent allegations of targeted killings, extortion, torture, and kidnapping. This type of violence was used predominantly to fight off contenders, to facilitate electoral success, and to gain resources. In July 1995, 'the rate of political killings in the port city reached an average of ten per day, and by the end of that year more than 1,800 had been killed.'[149] Violence then ebbed, but rose in a crescendo in 2007, culminating in a yearly toll of more than 2,100 killings in 2012.[150] Clearly, not all of this bloodshed can be attributed to MQM, yet violence has served the group well, in 'attacking rivals, protecting its members, moving into new territory, building lucrative extortion rackets, and gaining leverage over the government.'[151]

MQM's path to power included, but was never defined by, the political party and its dealings within government. In ways that echo Lenin, MQM founder Altaf Hussain differentiates between a movement and a political party thus: 'sometimes a Movement is compelled to participate in politics, however, its aim remains the completion of its mission, whereas the purpose of a political party is to get into power.'[152] This perspective explains the instrumentalization of democracy as but one of many ways to achieve stated aims. It also clarifies the apparent compatibility of this party-political competition with other efforts, even those that weaken the formal political institutions in which MQM is a major force. The result for Karachi, however, has been ruinous, particularly as other political hopefuls have replicated MQM's approach and sought to compete with it by using both ballots and bullets. The result, writes Laurent Gayer, was a state of 'ordered disorder'—a 'complex ecology of violence co-produced by the city's belligerents in the course of their interactions.'[153]

For many decades, the Pakistani government proved unable to respond to this situation. Periodically, its security forces would be called on a major offensive, which would target MQM—a recognized political party—as a terrorist organization. These operations at times forced MQM to tone down its violence and rhetoric, yet its modus operandi would soon return, along with the bloodshed. In contrast, the latest major offensive, in September 2013, was wider in scope and sought to 'cleanse' Karachi of its long-running violence and crime. The International Crisis Group calls the offensive 'an indiscriminate, opaque crackdown' that is 'increasing ethno-political tensions.'[154] Still, during the first six months of 2015, murders were down by 60 percent on the previous year; also, 'bank robberies, extortion attempts, and kidnappings—all key ways to fund militarized political parties and terrorist organizations—have dropped between 70 and 83 percent.'[155] Amid unprecedented improvements in public security, many analysts speak of a city breathing again.[156]

Though such reports are not unprecedented and have not held up well in the past, for MQM something does appear to have changed. The 2013 offensive combined with other latent and longer-running factors to defang the organization, in part by disrupting its ability to shut down the city through strikes, but also by accelerating its splintering and political moderation.[157] The question is whether enough has been done, through the offensive, to prevent another violent political grouping like MQM from taking its place. Indeed, even if MQM remains dormant and abandons violence, its history has reinforced a dangerous precedent. As Omar Shahid Hamid explains, 'every party over the past 30 years has felt that it needs to follow the MQM pattern if it wants to make inroads into Karachi. That has created the need for a close alliance between militancy and local politics … While MQM can change, reform or go away, the fear that ordinary people suffer from comes from that'—the proximity between militancy and politics.

This pattern extends beyond Karachi. The Deobandi party Jamiat Ulema-e-Islam (JUI) enjoys 'informal connections with insurgent groups focused on the Kashmir struggle as well as the Afghan–Pakistan border'; it has opened its *madaris* (Islamic seminaries) to recruitment by violent sectarian groups (this is how the original Taliban emerged); and it spawned the Sipah-e-Sahaba splinter, which in turn formed an armed wing—Lashkar-e-Jhangvi—that is 'responsible for much of the sectarian violence occurring in Pakistan today.'[158] The Jamaat-e-Islami party holds alliances with Kashmiri insurgent groups and comprises a violent student wing, the Islami Jamiat-e-Talaba, while the Tehreek-e-Labbaik Pakistan (TLP) party has commissioned targeted assassinations and encouraged violence against minorities.[159] Notably, TLP, which came in third place in its first-ever election in Punjab, has since demonstrated its crippling leverage over the government by organizing vast, violent street protests.[160]

As Siddiqui has argued, for these political parties, violence plays four key roles. It allows them to lobby the government 'from outside of the legislative system' so as to achieve political and ideological objectives. Second, it signals to both the government and society 'that the party is willing to go to great lengths to have its voice heard,' thereby boosting its leverage. Third, it 'serves an ideological function by, for example, targeting specific sects and minority groups' and, in so doing, woos militant actors who may prove useful allies. Finally, the use of violence can serve electoral purposes, by playing to sectarian agendas or aggravating social schisms.[161] Seeking to get in on this action, even the internationally renowned terrorist group Lashkar-e-Taiba has created a political party—the Milli Muslim League—though it has thankfully not been recognized by Pakistan's Election Commission. Even so, the broader point is clear: that so many parties 'engage in both vigilante activities and formal politics has contributed significantly to one of the more worrisome dynamics of post-9/11 Pakistan: the blurring of the line that should demarcate the realm of formal politics from anti-state violence.'[162]

Conclusion

Infiltrative insurgency emerges as an insidious way of resolving the dilemmas of rebellion that inform this book. Rather than trying to outgun the government, the insurgent produces a party to compete with it openly, using in this manner the inclusivity of the political system to steer policy. The search for votes and political support generally requires intense bridge-building—what sociologists call frame alignment—to extend the struggle and link it to disparate interest groups. But the secret ingredient, or the ace up the sleeve, is the continued use of low-level or covert violence to facilitate the rise to power through the system. Because the agenda remains subversive, because it uses the system to destroy it, the infiltrative insurgent can be likened to a Trojan horse.

The infiltrative approach allows the insurgent to game the current system and combine the best of both worlds—that of party politics and that of armed politics. The path may therefore seem alluring, yet, as seen in the cases mentioned above, not least in Bolivia, Nepal, and Northern Ireland, it also carries significant risks for the insurgent movement. First, the downplaying of violence (even if partial) can run counter to the constituents' preferences for radical action, threatening a loss of support (recall the disaffection within the SA for the Nazi Party's policy of 'legality') or outright splintering (witness the factionalism within the Maoist camp in Nepal and also for PIRA). United front activities are meant to be duplicitous, but duping your own side risks confusion and dissent.

Second, it takes a disciplined organization and effective leadership to coordinate the above-ground and underground activities in a way that is synergistic.[163] If Golden Dawn's political strategy suffered because of its criminal and violent excesses, PIRA's ambitions to join the mainstream ultimately forced it to shelve its Armalites before it had achieved its political objectives—which to this day remain unfulfilled. As the architect of the 'Armalite and ballot box' strategy later conceded, 'I wanted to reassure people that it was possible to support the waging of an armed struggle and simultaneously take part in electoral politics—even though deep down I knew there were contradictions. I knew there was a ceiling to how far you could go.'[164]

These constraints will no doubt limit the prevalence and effectiveness of the infiltrative approach to insurgency, but two points bear noting. First, the approach clearly still has remarkable potency. It has allowed armed political movements to legitimize their struggle, to cloak their violence, and to tap support from more sources all at once. Second, even where it derails or fails, the infiltrative approach still carries potentially devastating consequences for democracy and society. Regardless of outcome, the danger of infiltration is that it cynically twists that which defines and is best about democracy— open political competition—into a mere component of a coercive, violent project. The most cherished assets of democracy—its thriving civil society, its representative government, and the political opportunities for groups and citizens—are also those used by the infiltrative insurgent to gain strength and seize power.

Responding to this phenomenon represents further challenges. Diagnosis of the problem at hand suffers because of the deliberate ambiguity of the approach, which is designed to confound analysis. Specifically, the link to violence is denied and obscured so as to obfuscate and potentially paralyze the response needed. State and society must therefore work hard to identify infiltrative efforts for what they are: an attempt to use the rhetoric of 'peace' and 'democracy' to tear the guts out of both. It is a task that requires the utmost care: much as insurgents have historically hidden among civilians to avoid state sanction, these groups are hiding behind legitimate labels to cloak a project driven by subversion. Thus, states must distinguish between actual social movements and the insurgent variations of the same, and both are likely to coexist and interact within one political space. Indeed, it is by piggybacking on the existing and prevalent grievances of a community that more violent elements catapult themselves into positions of power.

Errors of omission are matched only by errors of commission. Missing the central insurgent intent and seeing democracy subverted is a heavy price to pay, and yet over-correcting can be as harmful if it results in the pre-emptive closing down of civil society and tarnishing of political opposition groups. As with the term 'terrorism' immediately following the 9/11 attacks, there is ample space within the ambiguity of the infiltrative approach for states to make bad calls, either unwittingly or deliberately, and attack the very system that they seek to defend. In other words, any proliferation of infiltrative insurgency will have potentially devastating impacts on the meaning and practice of democracy, further undermining and weakening a form of government that is already challenged, messy, and yet also an apex achievement of human civilization.

5

IDEATIONAL INSURGENCY
THE DIGITAL COUNTER-STATE AND BEYOND

Narratives played a major role in the form of insurgency detailed in the previous chapter. Indeed, the importance of information and framing is today such that it requires more detailed scrutiny as a major component of future struggles. In this discussion the internet looms large; though it is now well into its thirties, the continued democratization of the 'world wide web' is allowing virtual connections to unfold faster, further, and by more sources simultaneously than before. The peer-to-peer networks thus enabled are central to our lives, and it is not unusual for people to devote more time, and derive more meaning, from these parallel universes. The implication for insurgency is that there are now new spaces to organize and recruit, even plan and conduct attacks, without creating physical targets that the state can strike. In this manner, information technology, and social media in particular, are leading to the third insurgent approach detailed here, the *ideational* approach.

Faced with the insurgent's dilemma—to wit, the difficulty of massing above-ground without facing the coercive response of states—ideational insurgency moves its organization to the virtual plane, using social media and internet communications. This emphasis on online as opposed to 'on-the-ground' assembly provides camouflage, but it also generates alternative realities that extend in-group loyalty even in the absence of in-person contact. The result is a de-territorialized movement whose members exist at once within a digital counter-state and also within the state itself, each world operating by very different norms. Within the epistemically bound network of believers, both radicalized and radicalizing, the individual experiences a sense of belonging and meaning; away from the screen there lurks a reality that cannot compete and must be attacked, even destroyed.

Violence is quick to emerge from the tensions separating these two worlds—but it can also be carefully planned and calibrated for effect. Either way, the system and society under attack face the challenge of unraveling and mapping a movement that has no physical location, no set geographic spread, and whose involvement in violence—both punitive and polarizing—is therefore very difficult to predict. Underlying and informing this violent assault is a political competition for influence and control, spearheaded by an online counter-state spinning out of cyberspace and making itself known 'in real life' (or IRL, to use the telling abbreviation). In this manner, through mobilization, intimidation, and alteration of the narrative, political and social change becomes possible. Insurgent success need not take the form of a direct attack or the overthrow of the system but proceeds more incrementally—by changing values and norms, mainstreaming fringe or extremist ideas, and moving society to accommodate the undeniable sway of the movement.

To explore this method of insurgency, this chapter sets out the evolution of the ideational approach and the reasons for its growth. There is a distant past to consider here, relating to clandestine networks and their use of rudimentary communications to conspire and subvert. After all, political violence has always been about discourse. Still, in the context of the insurgent's dilemma, it was only with the birth of the internet that ideational insurgency began to reach its full potential. It was only when it became possible to exist online that this approach became effective, not just as a component of strategy but as its core and driving force. Our story therefore begins with the dawn of a global internet in the mid-1990s and the early pioneers of ideational insurgency that emerged, not coincidentally, around the same time. Tracing the approach from these humble origins, the chapter reviews its evolving application by both ISIS and far-right violent extremists—two movements whose ideological differences belie a shared strategic logic. These case studies, and the underlying theory from which they spring, illustrate the serious challenges of ideational insurgency—to societal stability, coherence, and norms. There is reason to expect that the potency of the approach will continue to grow.

Insurgency, the Internet, and the Power of Ideas

In Jean Lartéguy's *Centurions*, Amar, a leader of Algeria's Front de Libération Nationale, illustrates the value of ideas in insurgency. Conversing with a French colonial officer, he explains:

> There's only one word for me: *Istiqlal*, independence. It's a deep, fine-sounding word and rings in the ears of the poor fellahin more loudly than poverty, social security or free medical assistance. We Algerians, steeped as we are in Islam, are in greater need of dreams and dignity than practical care. And you? What word have you got to offer? If it's better than mine, then you've won.[1]

The exchange demonstrates the decisive meaning of 'meaning,' or the importance of framing political action in a way that resonates with relevant audiences. Indeed, narratives play a major role in insurgency—contests, it should be recalled, in which perceptions of legitimacy aggregate into political power. Much like any movement, insurgency needs a good story to survive; as sociologist and political scientist David E. Apter has put it, 'people do not commit political violence without discourse.'[2]

The centrality of narrative is reflected in the emphasis placed on information by the world's leading practitioners of insurgency, both past and present. In preparing for the 1917 revolution, Vladimir Lenin saw 'systematic, all-round propaganda and agitation' as 'the pressing task of the moment.'[3] Hitler famously weaponized the radio and used state propaganda to radicalize an entire nation. On the Vietminh revolutionary war, General Vo Nguyen Giap noted that 'the most essential and important task was to make propaganda among the masses and organise them.'[4] Osama bin Laden picked up on the theme, arguing that 'the media war' is 'one of the strongest methods ... [reaching] 90 percent of the total preparation for the battles'; Ayman al-Zawahiri, somewhat more modestly, saw 'more than half of this battle' as 'taking place in the battlefield of the media.'[5] Al-Shabaab has compared the power of narratives favorably with 'the war of navies, napalm, and knives,' and ISIS—always seeking to outdo—claimed it can 'be more potent than atomic bombs.'[6]

Though the war for hearts and minds is as old as insurgency itself, the role of information became more complex when it could be captured and disseminated in virtually any medium both instantaneously and globally. More than that, as the internet evolved into an increasingly user-participatory platform—also known as Web 2.0—new social linkages and networks could be established online that, for many, are more authentic than connections made 'IRL.' Meanwhile, the internet has democratized the production of news, setting established media with clear journalistic standards in direct competition with amateur broadcasters—a competition for immediacy, trust, and, also, truth. As these factors combine, parallel communities have emerged online feeding on parallel sources of information, fragmenting society, and undermining any sense of shared epistemology. Within this context, it has become far easier to use information to build and erode legitimacy, constrain government options, and alter the strategic balance of power.

Perhaps the first internet-enabled insurgency to tap into this power was the Zapatistas of Chiapas, Mexico, whose struggle gained worldwide attention just as the world wide web was becoming mainstream. Often discussed in the context of 'netwars,' the Zapatistas used this new platform to generate protection and resilience against a state far stronger and more capable than itself.[7] The case is instructive not only because of its prototypical nature, but because it illustrates forcefully how ties and networks developed online can have real consequences on the ground, by targeting political will and offsetting military capability.

Southern Mexico has long been disadvantaged socially, economically and politically. Within Chiapas, Mexico's southernmost state, chronic inequality and ineffective governance provided the kindling for sporadic revolts not only against the central government, but also against its neo-liberal policies and, by extension, against Mexico's neighbor to the north. These grievances against the state have fueled a sentiment of difference and resistance, shaped also by the relatively high indigenous population in Chiapas relative to the rest of Mexico. Following in this tradition of confrontation, the Zapatista Army of National Liberation (EZLN) emerged in the 1970s as a fairly conventional guerrilla force, inspired by Maoist revolutionary doctrine and seeking to achieve political redress through the use of force. Once it came to blows, however, armed confrontations imposed devastating losses on EZLN, forcing it into dormancy. For many years, throughout the 1980s, it concentrated mainly on building up support networks within Chiapas and refrained from further attack.

In 1994, EZLN re-emerged. Following various divisive reforms to land distribution in the preceding years, and the perceived failure to mediate these grievances by peaceful means, it was the signing of the North American Free Trade Agreement (NAFTA) that triggered a renewed attack.[8] The very day NAFTA was signed, on January 1, EZLN launched a bold military offensive, with 2,500 lightly armed guerrillas making surprising territorial gains at the expense of the state. Using the media spotlight provided by the attack, the masked leader of the group, Subcomandante Marcos, broadcast the Zapatista grievances and manifesto worldwide. The Mexican state was wholly unprepared but put together a forceful military response that looked to nip the rebellion in the bud. David Ronfeldt and John Arquilla detail how, owing to various miscalculations and mismatches in capability, 'the insurgents were quickly pinned down and exposed to heavy fire from artillery and helicopters.'[9] Bloody losses forced a swift retreat from territory that had been briefly captured.

It is at this critical juncture that we see the logic of the ideational approach take hold. To Clifford Bob, the EZLN 'realized that forcing radical economic and political reform in Mexico, let alone overthrowing the president, was well beyond their capabilities acting alone.'[10] What it needed was partners, or a support network, capable of ensuring the group's survival and advancing its goals by other means. As we have seen, EZLN had already built strong

117

networks among peasant organizations and civil society in Chiapas. The shock value of its January 1994 offensive allowed it to extend this networking effort to the global stage. Having in fact instigated the attack, the Zapatistas were nonetheless able to draw in an international support base by presenting themselves as the dignified yet beleaguered voice of the indigenous, as the authentic alternative to a soulless and abusive state.[11] The EZLN thus positioned itself within a web of solidarity that would 'bear witness' to the stand-off. Using the heroic posture of victimhood, the EZLN turned Mexican military might, and the undeniable excesses of its response, into just another weakness to exploit.[12]

The strategy of internationalization relied on networks made robust by globalization, which bridged the local plight of indigenous actors in Chiapas and various anti-establishment, pro-indigenous movements abroad. Specifically, the connections enabled by the internet—though still primitive in the mid-1990s—acted both as shield and as megaphone. Via listservs, emails, fax, newspaper websites, blogs, news aggregators, and conferencing systems such as PeaceNet and Mexico's La Neta (which came online in 1993), the international support network was kept alive, aware of the goings-on in remote Chiapas, and strong enough to put pressure on the Mexican government.[13] Few of these capabilities were actually owned or maintained by the EZLN itself, and yet they made possible visits to Chiapas by supportive NGOs and individuals, energized by the conflict and eager to play a part.

Most observers agree that 'this multiform assistance, seemingly so unlikely at the start of the rebellion, has been crucial to the Zapatistas, repeatedly saving them from army attacks and helping them achieve significant gains.'[14] Twice, in 1994 and 1995, the Mexican government called off offensives intended to reclaim the territory still held by the rebels. As Arquilla and Ronfeldt conclude, 'the transnational activist netwar—particularly the information operations stemming from it—was a key contributing factor,' in that it aroused media attention, alarmed foreign partners of the Mexican state, and kept the conflict on the radar across communities distributed around the world.[15] As a result, thirty years on, 300,000 Zapatistas still inhabit the *Municipios Autónomos Rebeldes Zapatistas* (or

MAREZ for short)—autonomous areas controlled by the EZLN and governed separately from and in opposition to the state.[16]

Refinements to the Approach: Anonymous

The case of EZLN is relevant because the group deliberately transitioned from a failing military approach to an information-enabled strategy that not only prevented further losses but allowed for some measure of success. Even in this early case, by internet standards, it is possible to discern how the nexus of globalization, information technology, and political violence would transform the role of framing and narrative, allowing for new sources of resilience and strength. As Thomas Marks notes, 'On the one hand, threat groups, using the astonishing capabilities inherent to cybercommunications, can theoretically reach a universe of potential sympathizers, supporters, and recruits. On the other hand, they can leverage intangible images and tales of injustice and suffering as any kinetic effort would deploy tangible weapons systems.'[17]

If the Zapatistas showed the way and earned their status as the 'first informational guerrilla movement,' the case lacks dimensions that have since matured and helped the ideational method achieve greater potence.[18] Specifically, in this case, the internet- and information-enabled components of the strategy were 'an adjunct to physical based insurgency,' or what was unfolding territorially in Chiapas.[19] As such, it also relied upon the Mexican government tolerating the Zapatista occupation of territory and its creation of a counter-state, currently the size of New Hampshire or Vermont. To the degree that the Zapatistas could mount a protective 'informational shield' around these autonomous municipalities, much relied upon the group's renunciation of violence following 1994, as this made possible the international bridge-building with civil society and has tempered the state's urge to react.

Where these conditions do not apply—in the many instances where insurgent violence continues, or governments refuse to relent—more emphasis yet will need to be placed on the virtual domain to compensate for the impossibility of maintaining a fixed presence in the physical world. As it happens, since the 1990s technology has evolved to a point where such a shift is possible, so that the virtual realm is not just an adjunct but its own reality and an independent, or at least dominant, stage for insurgency.[20] This distinction matters greatly if the intent is to avoid a forceful state response.

The history of Anonymous is an early but telling illustration of how the approach evolved. Anonymous emerged in 2003 out of a communications forum within the site 4chan, an online discussion board where users, rather than identifying themselves by name, simply appear as 'anonymous.' Within the /b/ section of the site, the combined outcome of this communication engendered a very loose sense of collective identity, marked by in-jokes, the self-referential posting of memes, and a deeply ironic sense of humor in which anything went. The board was characterized by its transgressive style and topics of conversation, encouraging a counter-systemic culture where the norms of 'real life' were systematically broken, not to serve a particular ideology or purpose comprehensible to the uninitiated (the 'normies') but mostly just 'for the lulz' (or the laughs).[21] Yet, from the unfiltered streams of consciousness and the growing ties among returning posters, a political purpose soon emerged; fleeting, contested, yet persistent, it would inform interactions by Anonymous with the outside world.

The initial premise concerned freedom of speech, which was to be promoted unconditionally. In the face of perceived censorship or attempts to control the internet, Anonymous would take what it had practiced on random victims—through pranks as well as cyberbullying—and apply it to new and more meaningful targets. Perpetrators worked apart but together, much like a flock of birds, to coordinate online hacking operations against Sony, the Church of Scientology, VISA and Mastercard, white supremacists, and others accused of some objectionable behavior, which might include mere criticism of the group.[22] The attacks were virtual and never crossed the threshold of inflicting violence, yet they demonstrated two important points: the possibility of engendering a sense of community even without meeting or sharing names and faces, and the possibility of such a collective inflicting damage in the real world, be it psychological, financial, or reputational.

Much like the Zapatistas, Anonymous benefited from online connections, yet, in contrast to the Chiapas-based group, it had no physical presence: everything was done online. Recruitment took the form of voluntary traffic and engagement with the 4chan message board, which grew as Anonymous began to advertise its agenda online and attract media attention. Planning was conducted through more-or-less secure online channels. Attacks would be carried out by self-organized volunteers—those who might be available and interested, and have the technical skill (and, where skill was lacking, tools and knowhow could easily be provided).[23] Going deeper, the online environment also created for Anonymous a new social reality, allowing virtual identities to form and settle. Meanwhile, the anonymity encouraged a sense of disinhibition, much as it had done with the jokes and memes, and so individuals would more readily transgress and push the limits without fear of repercussion.[24]

Because Anonymous was so fluid, and hence its ideology too, it proved difficult to predict or prevent its attacks. Yet the movement committed several unforced errors, resulting in fragmentation and its separate splinters turning on each other. The in-fighting and lack of discipline provided a trail of evidence used by law enforcement agencies to remove the veil of anonymity surrounding the movement's main users.[25] Once the authorities had identified and arrested key individuals, who then faced significant jailtime, the same assets were used to roll up the broader network. Whereas Anonymous claimed to be a 'hydra' ('cut off one head and we grow two back'), the lack of a consistent worldview, mobilizing message, or stated purpose appears to have stemmed the supply of willing recruits—particularly as the increasingly likely costs of participation became clear.[26] The collective remains active, but far less so than before, and it hardly ever conducts, or at least it does not own up to, major offensive campaigns.[27]

What made for the strength and weakness of Anonymous, then, was that it was never an insurgency group—first, because it never amounted to a group, and, second, because it never followed a unified political agenda or goal.[28] This odd set-up brought flexibility and unpredictability, but it also deprived it of a purpose that might withstand opposition. Still, the method represented by the case remains very much with us—and it has been appropriated and further developed by a slew of online groupings that do have a pronounced political vision and are less readily deterred. Marching in the footsteps of the Zapatistas, and of Anonymous, these groups have learned to use the internet, the networks, and the virtual world as a potent launch pad for ideational insurgent struggles—campaigns that, while developed in the Petri dish of the internet, then bloom to drive narratives and actions far beyond.

The Theory and Practice of Ideational Insurgency

The word 'netwar' was used previously and now warrants elaboration, given that its attendant theory explains presciently the potential and challenges of ideational insurgency. In their work on netwar, published initially in the 1990s, Arquilla and Ronfeldt defined it as 'an emerging mode of conflict (and crime) at societal levels, involving measures short of war, in which the protagonists use—indeed, depend upon using—network forms of organization, doctrine, strategy, communication.'[29] The term is apposite as it was precisely in the network that the Zapatistas found their resilience and Anonymous its power. Arguably, the analysis has only become more relevant since then, given the advances in internet communications and, particularly, in social media.

Arquilla and Ronfeldt propose and map out a variety of networks—the 'chain,' the 'star or hub,' and the 'all-channel' configuration. Of these, it is the last that has the greatest relevance to today's ideational insurgents, as it describes a multitude of nodes connected to one another with limited hierarchy and few gatekeepers.[30] Arquilla and Ronfeldt base their work in this area on previous theory by Luther Gerlach, who in 1987 described these all-channel structures as 'segmented, polycentric, ideationally integrated networks.' Gerlach shortens this mouthful to SPIN, an acronym that 'helps us picture this organization as a fluid, dynamic, expanding one, spinning out into the mainstream society.'[31] The image presciently describes today's amorphous social media networks; they are structurally dispersed, strategically decentralized, yet bound together by a common ideology.

In still earlier work, in 1970, Luther Gerlach and Virginia Hine elaborated on the organizational strengths of these networks in ways that speak directly to the insurgent's dilemma. The network 'limits the ability of the establishment to penetrate, gather intelligence about, and counteract the movement. It protects the identity of leaders; more importantly, it assures a constant supply of leaders and replacement, should any be lost.'[32] In other words, these movements are able to maintain security simply by providing no targetable hierarchy or fixed leadership for the government to strike. Also, because there is no central command, 'the failure of one does not jeopardize the entire system.'[33] Thus, as Arquilla and Ronfeldt also conclude, 'such network designs can be quite difficult to crack and defeat as a whole.'[34] The network is deliberately duplicative and therefore resilient.

Thirty years on, with the birth and evolution of the internet, it has become far easier both to picture and to create such an organization. Yet in assessing in full how this model of insurgency works, it is instructive to apply the theory to two contemporary cases. The first case is Islamic State, given its pioneering work online not only to plan and launch attacks, or even to recruit, but to foment a virtual movement. Needless to say, ISIS has had to rely on this approach more extensively since the loss of its physical so-called caliphate—or when it, too, fell victim to the insurgent's dilemma. As we shall see, the shift in strategy has allowed ISIS to exist online even as it was dismantled on the ground, and to find thereby a new sanctuary, a measure of security, and, most fundamentally, a virtual counter-state.

In understanding ISIS's use of information operations, an instructive starting point is their origins and development within the violent radical Islamist movement, or how they came to differ from what al-Qaeda and other similar groupings had previously attempted. Indeed, by the time ISIS advanced across Iraq and Syria in 2014, much had already been written on the nexus of internet and insurgency, in large part because of al-Qaeda's reliance on virtual networks to recruit and radicalize. As a global movement lacking one central geographical front, al-Qaeda faced the problem of coordinating and communicating across vast distances and letting gains in one theater inspire and motivate followers in another.

The 9/11 attacks on Washington, DC, and New York had been tremendously successful in reaching and awakening a worldwide audience, but how to sustain coherence across this movement and retain momentum in the absence of regular large-scale attacks?

In addressing this challenge, al-Qaeda was assisted by the internet's quick progression in the first decade following the attacks, with YouTube emerging in 2005, Twitter and Facebook becoming available in 2006, and the first iPhone launching in 2007. These advances rapidly aged the group's original methods of engagement: the black-market DVDs, amateur footage, and various murky internet websites. Through social media and the advances of Web 2.0, it was possible to reach across the world and inculcate a countercultural rhetoric of revolt among those susceptible to the ideological message. In Western societies struggling with questions of integration, for instance, some Muslims found within al-Qaeda's image a redemption of the Islamic identity and a renewed sense of respect, albeit through fear.[35] More hopeful adherents saw within al-Qaeda's ontology a bridge from the purported 'golden era' of Islam to a future representing salvation and justice and, between these two points, a struggle against all that is inauthentic and wrong.[36] Finally, there were those who perceived a Western war on Islam internationally and wrestled with how to respond. Through the rapidly developing architecture of Web 2.0, al-Qaeda could more easily speak to these various audiences, ensuring greater reach and resonance.

Despite this evolution in capability, al-Qaeda's information operations remained top-down and didactic rather than participatory. Even its most infamous innovation on this front, the *Inspire* magazine—a much-vaunted and professionally produced publication circulated digitally from out of Yemen between 2010 and 2016—ultimately represented another one-way flow of information, where the masters spoke and the students listened.[37] The role of the audience was to follow guidance, to learn, and to engage in 'do-it-yourself jihad,' be that through local terrorist attacks or merely the adoption of traditional dress codes, more pious mores, and other trappings of 'jihadi cool.' In this way, being part of the scene was very much being part of the gang.[38]

Yet a gang is no mass movement. In contrast, when ISIS emerged in 2013, it did so by means of an 'all-channel' information strategy that reflected a fundamentally more participatory approach. By counting not just on its senior leadership but also on followers to pass on, amplify, and contribute content, the group's proselytism reached further and faster. As communications were disseminated and repeated, they blurred the line between authorship and readership, reinforced in-group identities, and, over time, extended receptivity to the message far beyond what al-Qaeda had achieved. Though commentary on Islamic State's communications strategy tends to focus on its high-quality magazines and videos, it was its participatory nature that helped create a true movement, by providing supporters with 'a competitive system of meaning.' As Haroro Ingram perceptively notes, it is here that we find 'the true potency' of ISIS's information operations.[39]

Such a strategy required organization. To launch the online offensive, ISIS created specialized units—the *mujtahidun* (or industrious)—to act as 'electronic brigades,' aggressively pushing and promoting social-media content.[40] Twitter, barely used by al-Qaeda, emerged as a particularly promising platform. Not only did it offer the possibility of anonymity, but it also encouraged and rewarded virality—or the saturation of the internet with specific messages and hashtags. By 2009 it had introduced its 'retweet' button, allowing for seamless mass production and adaptation of online content. ISIS developed its own app, Dawn of Glad Tidings, to exploit this platform: it translated Twitter messages into Arabic, allowed adherents to communicate, and channeled information to users; most crucially it also accessed its users' own Twitter accounts and automatically retweeted messages produced centrally.[41] When a particular line or hashtag succeeded, Twitter itself would promote it as a trending topic and thereby push it further and to more people than before. ISIS also achieved virality by hijacking trending hashtags, for instance those relating to the World Cup, and turning the conversation toward itself, thereby benefiting from the extensive reach established by others.[42]

For some crucial years, and in a variety of ways, ISIS made Twitter the 'useful idiot' of its struggle—an unwitting agitator for its cause. Once Twitter and Google suspended 'Dawn,' the group moved to bots, programmed to retweet ISIS messages on a massive yet distributed scale so as to avoid spam filters. As Twitter began to suspend the group's main accounts (see chapter 8 for more on this), these users reappeared with more discreet profiles, deployed familiar hashtags to reconnect with the flock, and became another voice in a decentralized process of amplification and saturation.[43] By this stage, the mass dissemination of threats and graphic videos of violence had been credited with successfully intimidating ordinary Iraqis, including its military, into submission.[44] Further from the battlefield, it emphatically conveyed that ISIS was a force to be taken seriously, that its messaging was resonating and its ideology spreading.

Measuring the extent of ISIS's Twitterstorm is not easy, yet an authoritative study estimated that, in 2014, there were between 46,000 and 90,000 active ISIS-affiliated accounts, not including bots. As the study also found, a typical account would generate an average of 15.6 tweets per day during surge periods, resulting in hundreds of thousands of tweets per day from all members combined.[45] Quantitative dominance meshed with mastery of content, as ISIS demonstrated the ability to speak in a way that was both accessible and mobilizing to would-be supporters. The group engaged in what has been termed 'cultural' or 'political jamming,' to wit, the delivery of pro-jihadist messages using the rhetoric and imagery typical of memes and Western pop culture, thereby making its propaganda seem both authentic and satirical.[46] As with Russian information operations during the 2016 American presidential elections, ISIS proved capable—plausibly because of its broad-based recruitment—of tapping into audiences that traditional media struggled to reach, precisely by using the very language, symbols, and (often very ironic) register that these audiences themselves employ online.[47]

The lynchpin of all this online activity was the participatory nature of ISIS's online operations. Much like al-Qaeda, it united actual fighters, those wanting to fight, and the many 'jihobbyists,' or self-starters curious about the movement. In contrast, however, it actively encouraged onlookers to become participants.[48] ISIS communications venerated the individual poster or social media user, showering praise on their important role in the overall struggle. As

Charlie Winter notes, 'this promise of active, lower-risk participation in jihad has proven to be an intoxicating idea for many thousands of individuals around the world.'[49] Given its massive scale and alluring style, ISIS's online communications created the semblance of a global resistance movement, producing a gravitational effect for those seeking an easy yet seemingly meaningful platform for revolt.[50]

The participatory nature of this operation carried an important psychological dimension. Over time, mass participation in ISIS's online campaign helped generate an actual 'culture of extremism.'[51] Immersive, social, and empowering, this culture proved as comforting to insiders as it was alluring to those seeking to belong. Members of ISIS's Twitter campaign described their community as the Baqiya family—as Amarnath Amarasingam explains, 'Baqiya means enduring, and is often used as a war cry by members of the Islamic State.'[52] As with any family, the online community provided meaning and a sense of togetherness: members 'cared for each other, celebrated the birth of children, respected online boundaries of marriage and gender ("I'm married, no DMs from brothers please"), developed relationships and got married, expressed condolences at the loss of a fighter, shared news, and served as a support group.'[53] Demonstrating the sophistication of this online universe, subgroups were created to cater to the interest or background of specific types of members: for female participants, for those from a particular country, or for communication in different languages.[54] Of course, discussions and disagreement might occur, but an underlying bond was sustained by a similar worldview and a sentiment of 'mutual love and support.'[55]

Indeed, underlying all this was an echo chamber for the ISIS ideology. Thus, because its ideology, message, and community still reverberate and provide meaning, the idea of ISIS has been able to survive the destruction of its physical caliphate. As Winter notes, 'the organisation has used propaganda to cultivate digital strategic depth and, due to this effort, the caliphate idea will exist long beyond its proto-state.'[56] Rather than on the ground, ISIS is now operating through a digital counter-state, one similarly marked by a separate language and culture, and inhabited by a chorus of followers eagerly braying the same slogans and songs. Yannick Veilleux-Lepage terms this a 'paradigmatic shift' in online operations, allowing ISIS, through empowered unaffiliated sympathizers, to 'normalize and legitimize IS' existence through the domination of the so-called "Twittersphere."'[57] It is also what makes this approach relevant to the insurgent's dilemma at the core of this book.

Violence has remained a central component of ISIS's struggle, yet its use and meaning have also shifted as the group has transitioned to a digital counter-state. Indeed, what ISIS has achieved online— and what other groups can mimic and have mimicked—threatens to turn the distinction between terrorism and insurgency on its head. As we have seen in chapter 2, whereas insurgent movements use terrorism as but one of many methods, for purely terroristic groups it becomes the sum total of their entire strategy, that is to say its 'logic.'[58] With such terrorism, the assault on the system is divorced from the purported mass base in whose name action is undertaken, so the state response can focus on the few perpetrators and members that the group has been able to attract. With insurgency, however, a focus on rooting out 'the terrorists,' to the exclusion of finding political solutions to sources of conflict, often leads to new cycles of violence that the operationally astute challenger will exploit to mobilize additional support.[59]

Within the globally distributed ISIS network, each terrorist attack appears, at first glance, as self-contained and isolated; indeed, they are commonly referred to as 'lone wolf' attacks precisely because it is thought each perpetrator was individually radicalized and acted on his or her own. This frame obscures the fundamental movement that binds these seemingly random attacks and gives each political meaning within a broader project.[60] Because of the investment of ISIS in an online community, the attackers are not alone, but grow out of close connections within a virtual, transnational network. Indeed, these attacks follow exactly the anticipated logic of netwar, whereby, even in the apparent absence of leadership or of coordination, members 'know what they have to do': there is 'an ideational, strategic, and operational centrality that allows for tactical decentralization.'[61] What may therefore appear as a terrorist attack is often just another flashpoint in a broader insurgent struggle, carried out by a movement benefiting from a de-territorialized presence and digital counter-state.

The phenomenon is occasionally referred to as 'stochastic terrorism': the attacks are 'statistically predictable but individually unpredictable.'[62] ISIS calls upon its followers to launch attacks in its name and—because of its online reach and immersive persuasiveness—some followers heed its call.[63] The circumstances triggering each attack are unique and therefore difficult to anticipate, yet they all contribute to the same ideology and movement. This distributed responsibility to keep the cause alive harks back to the theory of 'individual terrorism' proposed by Islamist ideologue Abu Musab al-Suri, and yet, writing in 2005, al-Suri could not have imagined the future potency and potential of the approach.[64] Making full use of information technology and the pervasiveness of social media in particular, ISIS has showcased how online mobilization can combine with violence so as to produce a mode of insurgency that is both effective and very difficult to stop; attacks are polarizing, intimidating, and self-perpetuating, but the only consistent target for state response is their shared ideology.

Ideational Insurgency in the United States

Despite its loss of a physical counter-state, ISIS continues to inspire terrorist attacks, thereby upholding its status as a counter-hegemonic movement. Internet communications have been a central ingredient in most ISIS attacks, at least those conducted outside active war zones: the 2015 San Bernardino attack in California, the July 2016 massacre in Dhaka, the Nice truck attack in France later that month, the 2017 London Bridge attack, the ramming attack in New York City in 2017, the Easter Sunday attacks in Sri Lanka in 2019, the November 2020 shootings in Vienna ... the list goes on. These and other attacks are a product of, and contribute to, ISIS's online strategy: they energize a de-territorialized network, ensconce its brand in our consciousness, and sustain the underlying ideology as an accessible and meaningful vehicle of dissent.

In this sense, ISIS highlights effectively the potential of ideational insurgency. On the other hand, the group has, to date, struggled to translate the influence and presence achieved online into concrete political objectives. Beyond the countermeasures imposed by social media platforms and governments (more on this later), the weakness stems fundamentally from ISIS's uncompromising objectives, which necessitate the military overthrow of the state. As a physical counter-state, the envisaged 'caliphate' cannot be reached solely by shifting social norms, which is what ideational insurgency does best. Instead, for ISIS, this phase is necessarily a precursor to a more climactic confrontation; one in which the group is likely to suffer the same fate as in Iraq, Syria, and wherever else it has sought to seize and retain land. It is, at present, sticking with a theory of victory that forces repeated collision with the insurgent's dilemma and that, therefore, will not work.

In contrast, the 'alt-right' in the United States, along with its right-wing extremist and white-supremacist bedfellows, has proved more adept at channeling the gains of ideational insurgency into something resembling political and social power. This collection of far-right and anti-establishment extremists have done so, ironically, by emulating precisely the approach employed by ISIS, showing quite neatly how *les extrêmes se touchent*. In contrast, however, the movement has eschewed the Islamists' insistence on a physical counter-state (something the alt-right and their cohorts never enjoyed anyway) and therefore also the need for a military struggle to reach this goal.[65] Instead, the theory of victory speaks to a relocation of norms and values so as to polarize, build receptivity to the message, and over time align society with the ideology.

'Politics is downstream from culture'—the remark is Andrew Breitbart's, founder of *Breitbart News*, which years after his death went on to become 'a platform for the alt-right.'[66] Following this very logic, the alt-right's ideational insurgency seeks to transform culture—first within the in-group, then among sympathizers, and then within society—so as to produce, gradually, a new polity. As Daniel Trilling notes, the approach draws indirectly on the Italian Marxist philosopher Antonio Gramsci, who ascribed the failure of various left-wing movements to the cultural and normative hegemony of the dominant political order.[67] From the late 1960s onward, this same theory—that cultural acceptance was a necessary precondition for political power—was adopted by far-right French intellectuals within the so-called Nouvelle Droite, and it has since become central to the alt-right.[68]

The focus on cultural conquest is particularly germane to the alt-right, given the toxicity of its belief system within liberal democratic societies. Indeed, with an ideology of racial purity, anti-Semitism, and misogyny, the far right faces an uphill battle in most contexts. The alt-right emerged with a social media strategy designed to overcome this obstacle, allowing it to spread the word, attract new recruits, and seep into society.[69] The name itself derives from the Alternative Right website, which was launched in 2010 by the white supremacist Richard Spencer precisely to reinvent and revive American white nationalism following 'decades of gradual fragmentation and growing social stigma.'[70] Not only did this website give the movement its name, but it also kickstarted its online mode of operations. Indeed, since then—and in contrast to previous far-right efforts at change— it has revealed a clear 'prioritization of cultural awareness over organizational activity.'[71]

Though the exact contours of the alt-right are difficult to trace, it is clear that it does not operate alone. Instead, this amorphous network sits within a broader ecosystem of neo-Nazi outfits (such as the Atomwaffen Division or The Base), neo-fascists (such as the Proud Boys), and militias (such as the Oath Keepers and Three Percenters). The ideologies of these various groups overlap but are not entirely congruent, as they cover a spectrum of nativism, populism, white nationalism, and white supremacism. On the whole, however, the idea is to restructure society on the basis of race, ethnicity, and gender, so that the 'in-group' (typically white males) rules supreme, those deemed undesirable are excluded or marginalized, and everyone knows their place. Added to the mix are followers of various conspiracies, including, most infamously, QAnon, and oddball outfits like the Boogaloo movement, both of which are less readily placed ideologically but share the far right's anti-establishmentarianism and yearning for violent change.[72]

There are clearly important distinctions between all these groups, and yet the alt-right is used here as a pragmatic shorthand for the right-wing extremist movement as a whole. The conflation is in part heuristic, or a matter of analytical convenience, but it also reflects the overlap between separate outfits and the deliberate ambiguity of their respective structures.[73] All these groups have also benefited from the alt-right's social media strategy, designed to mainstream fringe ideas and the major concern of the study at hand. Through online action, this strategy has achieved mass radicalization, created virtual communities of belonging, mobilized 'real-world' activity, and intimidated and terrorized opponents. As a measure of the overlap of the actors involved—in cause, membership, and prominence—on January 6, 2021, they together stormed the Capitol building in Washington, DC, elevated by a sea of disgruntled Republicans whose entire political party had, by then, shifted significantly to the right. This is, for now, the acme of the ideational insurgency, driven by a segmented, polycentric, ideationally integrated network 'spinning out into the mainstream' very much as Gerlach had anticipated.

Authorities in Washington, DC, are now protecting the Capitol against another attack, yet the more meaningful assault is likely to be indirect, ideological, and intangible. It is on this front—via the shifting of norms—that the movement seeks victory, with violence acting as an accelerant. What happens with this movement from here on is uncertain, but it has already showcased the effectiveness of its approach. For this reason, the alt-right provides a helpful prototypical case study of ideational insurgency and how it drives political change without inviting military backlash. To assess this approach, the analysis that follows proceeds along three necessary categories: the enabling social and political conditions for ideational insurgency, the strategy and methods used in this case, and the effect and effectiveness of the overall approach. As is apparent, nothing within this strategy is confined to the cause of 'white power' or 'white nationalism' in the United States; instead, this is a form of violent contestation that is likely to mark other insurgencies in years to come.

Origins and Enabling Circumstances

Much like Anonymous, the alt-right originated on the 4chan platform, where in the /pol/ board a group of like-minded posters produced an online environment of racism, sexism, and the systematic violation of social and political norms. Amid the black-humored memes and graphic jokes that dominated the forum, the broader intent was to resist and reject the perceived 'culture war' of the progressive left.[74] The sentiment was that a white- and male-owned America was under attack by immigration, feminization, and racial equality—an assault cloaked by the self-censorship of political correctness. Through words, memes, and deeds, the group fought back, seeking to transgress the 'pacifying moral order' and, in a quasi-Nietzschean sense, end the 'slave morality' that it was thought to impose.[75] As a marker of this collective identity and purpose, when five Black Lives Matter protesters were shot in Minneapolis in November 2015, two of the perpetrators filmed a shout-out to the board: 'We just wanted to give everyone a heads up on /pol/ ... Stay white.'[76]

4chan and its spin-off, 8chan, illustrate the power of the internet in bringing together outsiders and helping them form groups. This development is, in and of itself, a key feature of contemporary mobilization, as it lowers the entry barriers to group creation and allows fringe causes to gain greater prominence. As military historian Robert Bateman put it: 'Once, every village had an idiot. It took the internet to bring them all together.'[77] Yet this development is not the whole story, nor necessarily its most interesting part. White supremacists have been convening online since the early 1980s, using internet prototypes and virtual bulletin boards, yet somehow the phenomenon looks larger and more menacing today.[78] What we witness with the alt-right is the ability of these murky networks to rev up and spin out, drawing in more members until the movement shapes the mainstream. For this reason, 'idiocy' may be the wrong frame, as whatever is driving this phenomenon appears to be both widespread and contagious.[79]

Indeed, the alt-right is fueled by a sense of societal malaise, or what Émile Durkheim might have called a state of anomie. Writing in the late nineteenth century, Durkheim proposed that when society changes rapidly, the norms and expectations that govern communal living are ruptured, producing a period of flux and uncertainty. As the bonds that tie individuals to groups, and groups to society, begin to fray, some individuals find themselves unmoored, isolated, and without clear placement or purpose. This deregulation of social life can, other sociologists suggest, lead to 'deviance.'[80] In this case, the alt-right emerged as one of those deviant coping mechanisms, because it provided a soothing narrative to those who in the midst of disconcerting change sought solace, answers, and a path to redemption. Once its narratives gained momentum, through social media, they assumed a gravitational pull. Accordingly, alt-right quickly outgrew 4chan, took on a more mainstream character, and was able to reach deep into society and eventually all the way into the White House.

Today's anomie, which is driving this phenomenon, is rooted in the history of the United States, where white skin has long denoted social, economic, and political advantage. As this country has become more diverse, leading to an expected 'majority-minority' flip by 2044, sections of the white population have come to fear their replacement as the central pillar of American society.[81] This fear is triggered by the United States' halting march toward greater inclusivity, as accommodation of non-white races, or non-Christian religions, is seen as a threat to once-dominant identity markers. Similarly, with respect to gender, some males see danger also in society's move toward greater gender equality, as this shift challenges the traditional framing of men as both stronger and superior. In these ways and others, society threatens to exclude those who had previously thrived on exclusion. To some, it all amounts to a multifaceted attack on 'white man's country.'[82]

The fear of these societal shifts is compounded by a sense of acute vulnerability among pockets of the white population. Economic anxiety is often trotted out as the go-to explanation for alienation and radicalization—and it is true that the United States has, much like other countries, experienced a growing gap between rich and poor over the last four decades. Still, as a macro-trend affecting millions (one in eight American families now lives in poverty), economic anxiety is simply far too broad to explain fairly specific behaviors. Although these economic patterns are still relevant, rather than indigence or absolute dearth, it is the perceived loss of status that matters, as it leads to resentment and fear. As James C. Davies's so-called J-curve theory of social crisis predicts, deprivation, poverty, and a fair degree of misery will be tolerated so long as there is faith in a better tomorrow, in a natural order of things, yet it is when these expectations fail that crisis ensues and extreme measures are taken to regain status.[83] In this instance, declining economic fortunes most offend those who feel that they deserve social primacy and who believe that poverty in America was supposed to be for 'the others.'

Whatever the admixture of grievances, the resulting disappointment with the system has largely predictable consequences: a sense of anger, even of humiliation, fuels a search for redemption and revenge. A critical part of this process is the creation of in- and out-groups: fellow victims on the one hand and those held responsible for the hardship on the other. Studies within the field of biology already confirm the troubling immediacy with which we, as a species, identify superficial differences and discriminate accordingly.[84] Such framing is made all the easier within the racially charged context of the United States—a country that has never thoroughly dealt with its own legacy of racism.[85] Thus, beyond hatred of the government and an abstract 'elite,' many of those aggrieved by their lot in life point to those of a different race, national origin, gender, or sexual orientation. In this manner, an adversary is constructed that is readily identifiable and upon whom blame can be shifted, turning self-regarding disappointment into outward-facing rage.

There is nothing terribly new or surprising about this process, yet social media transforms such scapegoating in two related ways. First, more than half of Americans get their news from social media, which pegs their intake of information about the world to a pre-existing peer group.[86] Social media also facilitates the spread of 'fake news' (a combination of misinformation and disinformation), because its deliberate shock value encourages sharing, because the fabricated stories come to users via a trusted network of friends, and because the online algorithms of social media platforms reward engagement of any type with heightened visibility. When these patterns are meshed with the historically low faith of American society in mainstream news outlets, the results are fairly self-explanatory.[87] Indeed, the overall effect is to produce echo chambers of like-minded people, all but eliminating the prospect of new and challenging perspectives.

Second, social media allows like-minded individuals to find one another through the click of a mouse. As fringe views develop, it is therefore far easier today to find corroboration by others, resulting in the building of networks that, intramurally, normalize and further develop the shared ethos. The sense of belonging is of course comforting and encouraging to the individual, but the process also produces what Donatella Della Porta calls 'spirals of encapsulation,' or the gradual loss of contact with the moderating influences of the outside world.[88] In such conditions, in-group reinforcement leads to collective radicalization, until prejudice is reified into hatred. As an illustration of the problem, in 2020 Facebook's own assessment found that 70 of its 100 most active 'Groups' dedicated to civics— that is, politics and society—were 'considered non-recommendable for issues such as hate, misinfo, bullying and harassment.'[89]

Both these effects of social media—how we acquire information and organize socially—stem from our naturally coded preference for bias confirmation: we seek out and are more willing to receive stories that validate our worldview.[90] The alt-right is aware of this very dynamic and positions itself accordingly. As analysts from the Southern Poverty Law Center explain, 'for a recruit, the alt-right helps explain why they don't have the jobs or the sexual partners or the overall societal and cultural respect that they believe (and are told) to be rightfully theirs.'[91] A writer on the alt-right website explains the narrative in further detail: 'all of modern society seems to offer literally nothing to young White men. It's as if society doesn't *want* them to tune in, show up and have a stake in the future of that institution. As a result, new institutions step up to pick up the slack.'[92]

Scholars of conspiracy theories suggest that these are the exact conditions in which such tales are spun and succeed. Joseph Uscinski and Joseph Parent make the point that 'sharing conspiracy theories provides a way for groups falling in the pecking order to revamp and recoup from losses … The tendency of conspiracy theorists to scapegoat, however reprehensible, channels anger, avoids internecine recriminations, and aims at redemption.'[93] Political scientists have also found that adherents of conspiracy theories tend to be those who are politically informed yet evince minimal trust in traditional institutions and authorities.[94] Such a personality type is more likely to dismiss mainstream politicians, mainstream media, and mainstream society if they do not provide the sought-after explanations and answers. The internet then emerges as an ideal platform for 'do-it-yourself' research into the 'hidden' truth behind the headlines; pursuing such research as a group lends credence to claims made and fosters a sense of solidarity among supposed 'victims.'

The focus on conspiracy theories applies, in spades, to QAnon, the cultish online community that believes an all-powerful Donald Trump was waging a secret war against a 'Deep State' cabal engaged in satanism and pedophilia. QAnon is clearly on its own plane in terms of the complexity and ludicrousness of its ideas, but the alt-right as a whole also trades in discredited myths. Be it the globalist 'Zionist plot'—the bête noire of the far right—the rigging of the 2020 US election, the imminent socialist takeover of America, the imposition of Sharia by Islamist radicals, or the Jewish-immigrant pact to replace the white race, conspiracy theories lie at the heart of the movement, providing both meaning and useful scapegoats.[95] In effect, these narratives all suggest that a nefarious elite is secretly in control, that it can be blamed for all that is wrong, and that the mission of exposing and defeating these forces is both urgent and just.[96] In this case, as in many others, conspiracy theory and extremism go hand in hand.[97]

These are the social and political dynamics that have made possible the alt-right's emergence and growth. These forces also go far beyond the United States. In March 2019, a young white man attacked a mosque in Christchurch, New Zealand, killing 49, because he feared the 'great replacement' of the white race. That attack was inspired by a mass killing in Oslo, Norway, in 2011, which claimed 77 lives and was intended to popularize the notion of a 'Muslim world-conspiracy.'[98] In Germany, a heady brew of xenophobic conspiracy theories, spread online, led to a Christchurch copycat attack on a synagogue and the murder of German politician Walter Lübcke.[99] In August 2020 in Berlin, protests against coronavirus-related restrictions saw far-right elements and conspiracy theorists storm the steps of the Reichstag, a harbinger of what was witnessed in Washington, DC, some months later. Germany also hosts a strong QAnon presence, which has meshed with the country's far-right extremist movement, replicating a pattern seen in the United Kingdom, France, and elsewhere in Europe.[100] In Holland, for example, the government's 2020 terrorist threat assessment spoke of 'far-right groups and individuals' latching on to 'conspiracy theories circulating online,' which have spread 'quickly from the margins of the internet to mainstream channels.'[101]

This is a response to the anomie of our times. The globality of the phenomenon speaks to the reality of a post-truth environment, filtered through social media, in which individuals feel at once powerless and empowered, atomized yet connected. This is both the age of individualism and the age of populism; it is the age of information overload and of striking, almost willed ignorance. It is an age of global integration but therefore also of extreme tribalism. It is the age of materialism and of economic insecurity. More than anything, it is the age of outrage—and there is much to be outraged about. In such circumstances, conspiracy theories abound, weaponizing weakness and vulnerability into self-righteous anger, even violence. Any ideology that can tap into this fury guarantees for itself both prominence and power.

The Method

A concerted strategy is required to turn societal malaise into ideational insurgency. The alt-right's approach is three-pronged: (1) organization of a robust digital counter-state, serving the function of a base area, (2) infiltration of the mainstream, so as to achieve social and political influence, and (3) the use of violence to polarize, show power, and accelerate change. Each step warrants close attention. Because the alt-right is anything but cohesive, mapping the strategy in this manner may overstate its coherence. At the same time, it is precisely the polycephalous nature of 'netwar' that makes this phenomenon so powerful. The loose borders, lack of structure, and amorphous membership are a feature, not a bug.

The digital counter-state serves the same purpose as the Maoist original: it is the 'building of a new world to challenge the existing world.'[102] Traditionally, a counter-state would have geographical boundaries and be governed by the insurgent group ideology; it is where the insurgents first test out their chops as a governing authority. In an ideational context, the boundaries are clearly not so territorial, but through persistent online interaction, members, and the group, achieve a comparable sense of unity and collective validation. In both settings, therefore, the counter-state is both the epicenter of the insurgent's political project and the home for its 'mass base.' US military doctrine describes how, in traditional insurgencies, 'mass base members provide intelligence and supplies. Mass base members may continue in their normal positions in society, but many will either lead second, clandestine lives for the insurgent movement, or even pursue new, full-time positions within the insurgency.'[103] That same function applies in ideational insurgency, except it is undertaken online. Members lend their resources and time to disseminate information, induct new recruits, and strengthen the ideological fabric of the new world.

We have seen how, for the alt-right, the counter-state began modestly on 4chan. Yet /pol/ was not the only refuge where the group's identity could congeal. During the Obama years, online meeting spaces for the alt-right proliferated, spreading to My Posting Career and Salo Forum, to gaming platforms like Discord, and—following Trump's announcement of a presidential run—to the r/The_Donald subreddit. As George Hawley notes, each space 'has its own style and rules, and many of the most memorable Alt-Right memes seem to have originated at these sites.'[104] In parallel, the more traditional white-power movement had already established an elaborate online presence, with neo-Nazi blogs, discussion boards, music-sharing sites, and stores peddling extremist merchandise just a few clicks away.[105] A stalwart in this field was Iron March, which emerged in 2011 as an online, anonymous meeting place where neo-Nazis and white nationalists could share material and message one another privately; from 2013 to 2017, members produced more than 200,000 (at times more than 300,000) posts per year.[106] For neo-Nazis, it is a method that dates back to the mid-1980s when 'proto-internet message boards' pioneered a form of social network organization. Needless to say, advances in information technology have allowed this activity to become both louder and more effective.[107]

Indeed, these online meeting places have evolved into parallel worlds, each assisting in normalizing the deviance of its members. In the corporate domain, 'normalization of deviance' is the process by which transgressions of acceptable behavior go unpunished and therefore become habitual.[108] In this instance, individuals curious about the white-power movement but too afraid to be associated with it can engage anonymously through the internet and receive a warm welcome rather than condemnation.[109] Exposed to a veritable vortex of memes and propaganda, adherents are then immersed in the worldview of the collective and come to accept its ideology not as aberrant but as an increasingly compelling truth. The use of counter-states to inculcate propaganda has long been a favored insurgent technique: Maoist organizations are infamous for their brutal 'self-criticism' sessions wherein cadres collectively affirm the ideology and reject the outside world. Yet in a world in which actual insurgent counter-states are few and far between, it is notable just how easy it is to enter their virtual equivalent, each with its own twist on proselytization.

The psychological effect achieved in the digital counter-state is akin to that of the 'mass meetings' instigated by the National Socialists of the 1930s. In *Mein Kampf,* Hitler underlined the 'strengthening and encouraging effect' of precisely such gatherings: as the individual steps into the mass meeting, he 'is now surrounded by thousands and thousands of people with the same conviction' and 'succumbs to the magic influence of what we call mass suggestion.'[110] In a similar vein, Nazi propagandist Eugen Hadamovsky saw in the mass meeting 'the strongest form of propaganda ... [because] each individual feels more self-confident and more power in the unity of a mass.'[111] This is precisely the purpose of the online communities, both for ISIS and for the alt-right: they create the semblance of consensus and momentum, draw in those with questions, and create a safe space for prejudice and hate. As the longtime editor of the white-nationalist journal *American Renaissance* puts it: 'It's just wonderfully refreshing to be with people who view the world as you do.'[112]

If bias confirmation helps to produce the initial spark, the alt-right and ISIS both use their websites and online spaces to guide the curious to increasingly extreme views and material.[113] The inculcation operates by means of a psychological quirk termed 'illusory truth,' namely the human tendency to believe information and claims that are repeated.[114] Gradually, new theories are introduced to compete with the dominant narratives of society, resulting in a schism with the outside world. At this point, the online building of camaraderie is critical in resolving the inevitable cognitive dissonance that results from inhabiting two moral universes all at once. Through in-jokes, a common argot, and other shibboleths, a feeling of belonging is generated that can replace the vestigial bonds of the outside world. For many, the digital counter-state takes over, becoming not just an ideology, but 'elements of a support group, a political party, a lifestyle brand, a collective delusion, a religion, a cult, a huge multiplayer game and an extremist network.'[115]

Though mobilization begins online, it is typically cemented through 'real-life' engagement as a final demonstration of group power and pull. Pete Simi and Robert Futrell detail the 'hate parties' set up by various neo-Nazi outfits, allowing members who might have met online to establish stronger bonds at ideologically themed 'bonfire parties, house parties, backyard barbeques, Bible study meetings, bars, and campouts.'[116] The alt-right holds speaking events in hotel conference rooms and stages rallies, such as the Unite the Right march in Charlottesville, VA, so as to demonstrate group solidarity and strength. Always quirky, QAnon had plans for a themed 'For God and Country Victory' boat cruise, intended to convene 'digital soldiers' in a joint celebration of the 'patriot family.'[117] They also hold conferences and rallies, with security provided (in at least one instance) by the Proud Boys.[118] Even in a world where so much can be done online, these types of meetings retain value. As one member of Anonymous put it following that group's first major in-person get-together: 'the idea of an anon is that you are fucking alone until you get to 4chan ... Then all of a sudden you are not alone, you are with 500 others, they all know the same jokes as you and they all clearly have similar interests to you. Here is your culture. You meet your own people finally.'[119]

With the digital counter-state established, the second prong of the ideational strategy is to move on to the mainstream. It is, in fact, at this point that ideational insurgency distinguishes itself from the traditional use of the internet by other white-supremacist movements.[120] Given its emphasis on changing the norms of society, it is not sufficient to create and cater to the mass base. Instead, the counter-state must take on the state. Accordingly, a primary objective for the far-right movement is 'red-pilling the normies'—that is to say, converting the uninitiated to the group's worldview.[121] Over time, the objective of such activity is to shift the 'Overton window'—a political science concept which denotes the range of ideas that society deems acceptable and which the alt-right glommed on to as a theory of change.[122] Karl Marx would have called this a struggle against 'false consciousness'; as with Marx, the aims are to awaken the people and to create a movement that simply cannot be ignored. In this manner, the alt-right seeks to become a social and political phenomenon, a consideration in electoral politics, and a primary determinant in defining values and norms.

This 'Overton window' requires some elaboration given how central this somewhat wonky concept has become to the alt-right's theory of change. The concept was developed in the mid-1990s by Joseph Overton, a free-market libertarian, yet it only became formalized posthumously when Overton's colleagues at the Mackinac Center developed the initial idea.[123] The Overton window, then, speaks to the process of changing norms in society: whatever is within the window is deemed acceptable and whatever lies beyond is rejected. There really is not much to the theory, but a key insight holds that it is not the politicians and lawmakers who 'shift' the window, but rather social movements, thinktanks, and opinion leaders. Thus, it is the job of the politician to detect such shifts in the Overton window—or what society regards as normal or even desirable—and to move policy accordingly.[124] Transposed onto the world of ideational insurgency, we return to the Gramscian notion that it is through cultural struggle that one enables political change; that revolution requires a 'war of position' to transform and mobilize civil society, so that a 'war of maneuver' can attack and overpower the state.[125]

In the alt-right's war of position, the first offensive targeted Twitter. Much as ISIS had done, the alt-right exploited the platform's own protocols to dominate the forum, thereby generating attention, credibility, and—along the way—recruits. Using its digital counter-state as a staging ground, it created and retweeted communications on an industrial scale, oftentimes with the help of bots, purchased followers, and sock puppets (multiple accounts owned by one individual). It hijacked hashtags and created its own (such as #BLMKidnapping, which popularized the false notion that Black Lives Matter had been behind the torture of a mentally disabled man in Chicago).[126] One of its most successful hashtags, '#cuckservative,' to denote conservative 'pandering' to non-white interests and communities, went viral and was used more than 5,000 times per day; it effectively created a new frame through which to view Republican politics.[127] Where the polemic did not arise naturally, the alt-right used Twitter's own ad function to force its tweets into the feeds of selected audiences, where it would appear as Twitter-'promoted' content and thereby suggest that the platform supported the message.[128]

This offensive succeeded in expanding the counter-state and stirring up the middle ground. From 2012 to 2016, American white-nationalist movements witnessed a 600 percent growth in followers.[129] Though estimates are necessarily vague, by 2018 there were more than 100,000 and possibly more than 200,000 alt-right accounts on Twitter (including bots and sock puppets).[130] Yet Twitter was not the only battleground. Online message boards, blogs, or comment sections even of major news sites became the stomping grounds of the alt-right. Its approved or manufactured reports were spread on Facebook's 'news feed,' videos of conspiracy theories and other radicalizing content were posted on YouTube, and, on both platforms, the comment sections were overrun by alt-right trolls. Because of these sites' algorithms, any users who engage with the alt-right's posts are guided toward related content, creating a trail of breadcrumbs until entire feeds are overtaken.[131] For those curious about the buzz generated in this manner, Google's own algorithms would respond to search queries by linking users directly to the alt-right's discussion boards; this was how Dylann Roof became interested in white supremacy, ending with his killing of nine black churchgoers.[132]

Social media sites presented clear vulnerabilities to be exploited. In parallel, the alt-right studied how best to convert the new members washing up on its shores. Whereas on 4chan and its spin-off, 8chan, the aim was to shock and excel in transgression, on more mainstream platforms the approach was designed to win hearts and minds, or at least trigger a war of narratives. Evidence suggests some schooled themselves on classic media studies, marketing, and sociology texts, including the work of Marshall McLuhan and Gustave Le Bon— though the effect of this effort is difficult to discern.[133] Either way, the strategies used were sophisticated.

One favored method was to start slowly and emphasize fairly mainstream concerns as a stepping stone to the ideology. As Don Black, founder of the white-nationalist site Stormfront, explains, 'It's important to be able to talk to people without coming across as a raving Nazi or white supremacist … So if we focus on the border, the economy, whatever's upsetting people right now, we're in a stronger position.'[134] From then on, it is a matter of hinting at 'the small thing that they're thinking but don't have the courage to say' or letting the recruits feel liberated in expressing prejudiced opinions not accepted by society.[135] Another approach is to emphasize the higher 'intellectual' tenets of the movement—'conscious idealism, futurism and a deep reverence for objective, scientific data.'[136] Through this twisted lens, racist theory becomes a set of necessary if unpleasant truths whose suppression through political correctness is to blame for all of society's ills. Salvation would then be achieved by uncompromisingly and courageously accepting what science anyway proves correct and by arguing forcefully for the white ethno-state, no matter the social and personal consequences.

A far more prosaic method to gain recruits, or to spark interest, involves discrediting the opposition, often by 'gaslighting,' or dressing up the ideology as so eminently reasonable that it makes the outrage it provokes seem out of line. An effective alt-right slogan reads 'It's Okay to Be White'; in its allusion, the racist intent is clear and objectionable, yet in the phrasing it disguises itself as benign. Polemics created in this manner are designed to put anti-racists on the back foot, by forcing them to engage with readily deniable subtexts. Another ploy was the hijacking of the ubiquitous 'OK' hand gesture, which the alt-right presented as a symbol of 'white power' (the fingers and hand spelling, vaguely, the letters 'W' and

'P'). Unfolding online, the move prompted heated debate until it became a mainstream talking point, triggering controversies as to intent each time the sign was used. This was precisely the aim: to spark liberal outrage over something seemingly trivial, to discredit their political correctness, and to co-opt the middle-ground.[137] A similar approach was employed when the alt-right appropriated the image of a badly drawn but otherwise innocuous frog, which the Anti-Defamation League subsequently felt compelled to include in its database of hate symbols.[138]

The subtlety of some of these information operations does not mean that the alt-right had eschewed its cruder methods of gaining attention. Nonetheless, there was a balance to be struck. As one alt-right author explains, 'opinions inside the Overton window are useless, while Ben Garrison [an alt-right political cartoonist] levels of hatred will simply get us ignored and shunned ... we should strive for this level of edginess: probably racially aware, but with plausible deniability.'[139] Memes played a vital role in striking the balance; quite simply image-and-text combinations meant to convey a point ironically, they aid communication because they are designed to be humorous, accessible, and easy to share and replicate. A successful meme is defined by its immediate penetrative potential and reach, making it perfect for propaganda. Indeed, psychology tells us that the very fact of adding pictures to text increases the likelihood that a claim will be believed.[140] Given all of this, memes have clear strategic potential, or as the Christchurch mosque shooter argued, they 'have done more for the ethno-nationalist movement than any manifesto.'[141]

The far right has appropriated 'memetic warfare' both as a term and as a method, so as to 'bring our narratives to the people.'[142] Alice Marwick and Rebecca Lewis report on the 'memetic Monday' hosted by the neo-Nazi blog *Daily Stormer*, during which community members create images that are then shared on Facebook and Twitter. As the report explains, 'these images, which espouse ideas from the openly racist to the mainstream conservative, function as "gateway drugs" to more radical ideas.'[143] In a similar vein, some alt-right supporters have formulated specific instructions for prosecuting 'Advanced Meme Warfare,' because 'meme magic is real and our collective effort has the power to produce some pretty incredible results.'[144] In general, however, the process is largely uncoordinated and self-perpetuating. Some memes fail, others go viral, but because the resource requirements are so low, and the participants so numerous, proceeding by trial and error is more than manageable.

Whatever the form of online propaganda, the secret ingredient is typically its comedic payload. To Keegan Hankes, senior research analyst with the Southern Poverty Law Center, 'if you make racism or anti-Semitism funny, you can subvert the cultural taboo. Make people laugh at the Holocaust—you've opened a space in which history and fact become worthless.'[145] An alt-right poster confirms this method: the humor, he explains, is necessary for the meme to 'make it past any memetic defenses of the brainwashed ... it sticks in their brain and circumvents their shut-it-down circuits.'[146] Satire works particularly well, given its interlacing of political and comic effect. This duality also serves a separate purpose, granting plausible deniability to transgressions that go too far: 'Labelling the meme retrospectively as "satire" gives them the opportunity to claim, "it wasn't meant like that."'[147] Of course, by this point, the cat is out of the bag, normalizing and radicalizing regardless of purported intent. Richard Spencer invoked precisely this technique when he defended his Nazi salute in a crowded conference room, suggesting feebly that it was done in a spirit of 'irreverence and fun.'[148] The alt-right thrives on this ambiguity, allowing its subversive ideology to be heard before it is rejected, or to speak in two tongues all at once. As we shall see, it uses the same double-dealing in its promotion of violence.

This edgy satire, generation of talking points, and pretense to respectability allowed the alt-right to 'trade up the chain'—or to elevate content from lowly blogs to major news outlets, thereby increasing its cultural credibility and influence.[149] A particularly effective meme might, for example, compel explanation by others, either to educate or to warn of the subliminal intent; 'such exposure,' writes Maxime Dafaure, 'subtly contributes to the spread of the worldview behind those memes.'[150] Similarly, hashtag dominance on Twitter allows an alt-right talking point to become a potential news item, to be repackaged and repeated to a far broader audience. The 'It's OK to Be White' slogan (naturally shortened on Twitter to

#IOTBW) sparked an online wildfire and was then picked up by right-leaning news outlets, which mainstreamed (and sugar-coated) the alt-right's ideology every step along the way.[151] In a similar vein, the lies behind #BLMKidnapping did not prevent this hashtag from trending across the United States—it was used 480,000 times within 24 hours—and the theory was then included in most mainstream reporting on the kidnapping.[152]

Arch-conservative news sites (such as *Gateway Pundit*, the *Daily Caller,* and *InfoWars*) proved way stations in the alt-right's effort to 'trade up the chain.' Commentary tends to refer to these forums as the 'alt-light,' as they share the basic ideological premises of the alt-right but espouse them with less fervor and to a broader audience. Even mainstream yet still right-leaning outlets—specifically Fox News's opinion shows—repeatedly proved their willingness to shine a positive light on alt-right ideology, yet without ever quite endorsing it. In particular, pundits like Tucker Carlson, Laura Ingraham, Glenn Beck, and Ann Coulter have often stoked fears about immigrants replacing Americans, a takeover by the 'radical left,' and the dangers of diversity and of political correctness—all alt-right talking points.[153] It bears noting that, during all of this, Fox News was consistently the most watched cable network in the United States and therefore a potent ally for the alt-right.[154] The network's success encouraged the creation of copycat outlets, such as One America News Network and Newsmax, which doubled down on Fox's partisanship and were able to steal its viewers when this veteran network seemed insufficiently radical, such as with its acknowledgement of Joe Biden's victory in the 2020 presidential elections. The alt-right helped encourage the growth of the alt-light and used its mainstream platforms to reach the masses. Suddenly, talk of Overton windows shifting was not so far-fetched.

A notable alt-light ally was *Breitbart News*, the online outlet for reactionary and highly conservative stories. Beyond spreading its talking points to a broader market—in 2017 *Breitbart* was the 29th most popular site in America ('bigger, even, than Pornhub')—this partnership also linked the alt-right to Cambridge Analytica, described by one of its former employees as a 'psychological warfare firm.'[155] The connection was Steve Bannon, who, before he became a key advisor to Donald Trump, served both as executive chairman at *Breitbart* and on the board of Cambridge Analytica; his mission in all these roles was to redefine and radicalize the American right. To this end, Cambridge Analytica systematically harvested data from social media interactions and used this data to micro-target content and sway public opinion. Content would typically play on xenophobic conspiracies and sensationalist stories of mendacity within the Democratic Party. The precise shaping of messaging to fit the audience helped generate a new and more extreme right-wing political base. In the words of a whistleblower and former data consultant at the firm, these were the foundations for 'Cambridge Analytica's work catalyzing an alt-right insurgency in America.'[156]

As the alt-right traded up the chain, the final link was Donald Trump himself. From the moment Trump announced his presidential ambitions, the alt-right championed him relentlessly.[157] His unapologetic promotion of illiberal and xenophobic causes made him a talisman for the movement. Trump's rise not only helped attack the tamer conservatism that had long dominated the Republican Party, but he also represented a troll capable of haunting the liberal mind. Beyond this ideological congruence, Trump promoted the movement directly when he retweeted white-supremacist accounts, refused to condemn far-right extremists, and recruited arch-conservatives as members of his team. In short, Trump was alt-right's 'ice-breaker'—both in style and in substance—clearing the way for its own mainstreaming.[158] Prior to the election, Richard Spencer predicted that if Trump won, 'people will have to recognize us.'[159] When the results came in, he boasted, 'The Alt-Right has been declared the winner … We're the establishment now.'[160]

The successful mainstreaming of the alt-right did not go unopposed, yet, perversely, resistance was often counterproductive. Seeking to expose and stem the rise of the group, Hillary Clinton in 2016 brought the alt-right's playbook out in the open. In a major speech late in her campaign for the US presidency, Clinton spoke of Trump taking 'hate groups mainstream and helping a radical fringe take over one of America's two major political parties.' She called out the alt-right specifically, describing it as 'a loosely organized movement, mostly online, that "rejects mainstream conservatism, promotes nationalism and views immigration and multiculturalism as threats to white identity.'"[161] This was a blunt and prominent deconstruction. And yet its effect was to cement the perceived bonds between Trump and the alt-right, pushing the most ardent supporters of the former to accept also the latter. Among the alt-right, one blogger delighted in 'receiving so much press, negative or inaccurate as it may be, because it is driving curious people to our cause in droves'; another rejoiced that, following the speech, 'Google searches for "alt-right" have completely exploded, being at least 20x greater than last week.'[162]

The search for negative reactions also informed the speaking tours of leading white supremacists, who would deliberately visit liberal university campuses to spread their message. Beyond the platform they provided, such events would almost invariably elicit protests by anti-racists and generate the very real potential for scuffles, perhaps even violence.[163] Placed in the limelight in this manner, well-meaning universities faced an impossible position, either to remain impartial and host the alt-right, but thereby further its proselytism, or to bar them and be accused of elite censorship. Because these events touched upon sensitive issues relating to civil rights, freedom of speech, and race relations, they were also sure to reach broad audiences and, even, place the alt-right in a sympathetic light.

Indeed, mainstream media emerged as a major ally in the alt-right's information operations. Even on the left, efforts to explain the alt-right inadvertently normalized its ideas and leaders. For starters, the alt-right has a more polished pitch for outlets like the *New York Times* and the *Washington Post*, focusing on relatable concerns such as 'uncontrolled immigration,' 'basic' border security, and the importance of 'traditional family values.' This type of whitewashing was deliberate; indeed, it had been the whole point for the 'alt-right' label to begin with, as it repackaged old-fashioned white supremacism as something new, ambiguous, and worthy of a second look.[164] Furthermore, to unpack the story, and out of a fear of not seeming impartial, mainstream coverage also turned staggeringly neutral.[165] In bizarre long-form profiles, therefore, with titles like 'The Neo-Nazi Next Door,' prominent white supremacists received a far-reaching rostrum from which to present a tailored version of their ideology.

The third prong of the alt-right's strategy involves the use of violence, through which it has concretized its struggle and accelerated political change. Violence is deemed necessary to give real-world substance to online (i.e. virtual) activity; it complements the propaganda with 'propaganda of the deed.' In this regard, the movement again draws on its 1930s' forebears: to Hadamovsky, the Nazi politician and radio director, 'power formations which have their origin in mere propaganda are fluctuating and can disappear quickly unless the violence of an organization supports the propaganda.'[166] Following precisely this logic, the alt-right used violence to attract more attention, to polarize society, and to communicate 'real-world' power both to friends and to foes. The line of effort can be split into three major campaigns: (1) terrorist attacks on perceived adversaries; (2) shows of force; and (3) online harassment and intimidation to shape behavior.

With the use of terrorism, the alt-right adheres to the 'leaderless resistance' model of famed neo-Nazi Louis Beam (though the approach is also very similar to al-Suri's theory of 'individual terrorism,' as used by al-Qaeda and ISIS).[167] As with the ISIS case examined above, the terrorism is stochastic, that is to say united in ideological intent but distributed in all other respects. This feature makes the attacks statistically predictable but otherwise random, frustrating attempts at prevention. Indeed, the strategy is an explicit attempt to overcome the insurgent's dilemma, in that the only consistent target for state response is the ideational foundation of the movement. As with ISIS, however, the attacks are connected, making the metaphor of a 'lone wolf' highly problematic. To give scale to the resulting activity, the Anti-Defamation League has found right-wing extremism to have motivated 274 of the 389 extremist-related murders in the United States between 2008 and 2017, amounting to 70 percent of the total.[168]

A 2018 report by the University of Warwick demonstrates a clear correlation between social media hate speech and violent crime.[169] The online discourse is how these attacks are motivated and encouraged, even if they are never quite commissioned. The style guide of the neo-Nazi blog *The Daily Stormer* explains the logic: 'The unindoctrinated should not be able to tell if we are joking or not.' The author continues by clarifying that, for legal reasons, the blog would not openly incite violence, yet 'whenever someone does something violent, it should be made light of.' The aim is to 'dehumanize the enemy, to the point where people are ready to laugh at their deaths.'[170] In a similar vein, when QAnon notables like Congresswoman Marjorie Taylor Greene speak of 'going after swamp creatures' in Washington, DC, 'to take this global cabal of Satan-worshipping pedophiles out,' it is not difficult to see why some die-hard adherents might hear therein a call to violence.[171] Even if just a small proportion see within the fear-mongering and endless dehumanization a mandate to act, violence will follow. As Dylann Roof explained following his murder of nine black churchgoers, 'no one is doing anything but talking on the Internet. Well, someone has to have the bravery to take it to the real world, and I guess that has to be me.'[172]

It is noteworthy that this violence has yielded relatively few fatalities—one database suggests 117 deaths throughout the 2010s—yet, as Kathleen Belew explains, 'the casualties wrought by this movement are not, in themselves, the movement's goal.'[173] Terrorism—even if stochastic—is still about political communication: to awaken the masses to the threat, spread ideology, and influence fellow adherents. The footage or manifestos associated with attacks are therefore of key importance, with the bloodshed acting merely as amplification. A second function behind the violence is to accelerate conflict by goading the state into a concerted response that will enrage the unaffiliated and push them toward the far-right's anti-establishment agenda. One theory suggests that, with enough attacks, the US government will soon enough want to regulate access to guns, a rational response to the mass violence yet a move that would immediately alienate many Americans and allow the alt-right to swoop in. Another method is to use 'violent opportunists' to infiltrate peaceful protests, presumably with the intent of attacking the police and triggering an overwhelming armed response that would delegitimize the state.[174] This is the tried-and-tested 'provocation strategy' of insurgents past and present.

Beyond terrorism, another type of violence used by the alt-right takes the form of aggressive rallies. This method is akin to the *Versammlungsterror* of the Nazi Party of the 1920s, or the use of gatherings to spread fear and threaten violence. The act may be seen as a form of 'swaggering,' the term developed by Robert Art and Kenneth Waltz to explain the actions of states, but which applies equally well to non-state armed groups. For states, swaggering entails 'displaying one's military might at military exercises and national demonstrations and buying or building the era's most prestigious weapons.'[175] These acts are primarily psychological in nature. Similarly, for white supremacists, swaggering entails public displays of military gear at protests, so as to show power, intimidate adversaries, and 'enhance the national pride of a people.'[176] Needless to say, the power of the internet greatly amplifies the psychological payload.

The violence inherent in these acts can be implicit, such as when hundreds of militarily trained and armed white supremacists convene in front of mosques or other targets.[177] Yet to many observers, the gatherings of the alt-right and neo-Nazis are designed to escalate, hence the increasing incidence of violence at such events.[178] In Charlottesville, the 'Unite the Right' rally famously led to clashes and to one follower ramming counter-protesters with a car, killing one and injuring 19. In Washington, DC, in January 2021, the protest supporting Donald Trump culminated in the storming of the Capitol building, resulting in five deaths and the creation of a truly international incident. In both cases, there is ample evidence to suggest prior planning, specifically for violence, so as to bring home the message of terror and recruit new members.[179]

The third function of violence is the online harassment and intimidation of the alt-right's opponents. Through the creation of large cybermobs, the alt-right is able to subject perceived enemies to a swarm of threats and abuse, including the revelation of home addresses and other personal details for others possibly to act upon.[180] Even if no action is taken as a result of being 'doxed' in this manner, the psychological toll is severe and is compounded by the relentless hounding occurring online. Indeed, the approach is similar to the 'night letters' hand-delivered by the Taliban to targeted individuals, in which the group makes demands and threatens violence and death in case of non-compliance. For an ideational insurgency, the message is sent electronically, but with the same intent and effect. The difference in ideational insurgency is that the internet affords the ability to target and punish without bloodshed, thereby avoiding police attention. Arquilla and Ronfeldt presciently anticipated this advantage of netwar—its ability 'to inflict costly, disruptive damage but without inflicting the physical and human destruction that so often arouses the ire of victims, or that may even alienate the affections of the terrorists' sponsors or constituencies.'[181] Illustrating the value of this approach, posters to *The Daily Stormer* have organized themselves into a 'Stormer Troll Army' (also known just as 'Stormers') so as to carry out harassment campaigns at the behest of the site's founder.[182]

The Strategic Effectiveness of Ideational Insurgency

In biology, neoplasia is the process of cells proliferating abnormally, or growing rapidly in numbers, leading to the swelling of tissue and the possibility of it turning cancerous. The analogy is not entirely inappropriate in explaining the alt-right's insurgency, given the abnormal rise of its membership and its attack on the society that hosts it. From its humble origins on 4chan, the alt-right quickly multiplied, invading Twitter and other social media platforms from where its ideas could spread further. Over time, this growing movement began to affect actions and expectations away from the computer screen, reaching out onto the street and all the way into the White House. Fueling it all was a narrative, fed by the alt-right to those seeking solace or power, to explain grievances and provide a path toward redemption. Once these narratives took root and a movement started to form, they metastasized and drew in others desperate for answers.

This strategy appears to be successful, but how does one gauge its effectiveness, particularly given the amorphous and shifting nature of the alt-right itself? Analysis often centers on the use of violence, as this is what most immediately harms societies and threatens state authority. In this instance, according to the Global Terrorism Index, from 2014 to 2019 the number of far-right-inspired attacks increased by 250 percent and the number of deaths by 709 percent.[183] At the same time, the total numbers are relatively low. Even the 89 deaths in 2019 that were caused by right-wing violence pale in comparison with the more than 16,000 homicides in the United States that year. Any observer of the alt-right and white supremacy would be forced to conclude that its influence far outweighs the number of casualties wrought.

Indeed, though tallying violent acts can help measure the fervor and growth of a movement, much depends on the political meaning of the violence, its calibration, and its relation to the broader base. In this case, at least until January 6, 2021, violence remained under the threshold where it would trigger a concerted societal response, yet it was sufficiently elevated to make the ideology a recognizable brand and a commonplace concern. It remains an open question whether this will change now that the Biden administration has promised a more purposeful response to the problem of 'domestic terrorism.'[184]

A more troubling indicator than violence is the shifts in membership seen in recent years. Once the online community was formed, it has proved challenging to stop its momentum. Though social media platforms have taken to banning alt-right accounts, many have migrated to Parler or Gab (Twitter replicas championing 'free speech'), Voat (a Reddit clone with a similar philosophy), Discord (initially an online gaming platform), and other more obscure meeting places.[185] Telegram proved particularly useful, given its encryption and anonymity; one channel promoting accelerationist neo-Nazi violence had more than 5,900 members when it was taken down and then quickly reconvened hundreds of its fans within just days of its reconstitution.[186] Fueling this online growth, record highs have also been reported by the Southern Poverty Law Center in the number of active hate groups in the United States, up from 599 in 2000 to 1,020 in 2018. Though this number decreased in subsequent years, this decline is ascribed to greater use of encrypted online platforms and the possibility, therefore, for 'individuals to engage with potentially violent movements like QAnon and Boogaloo without being card-carrying members of a particular group.'[187]

The impossibility of knowing the size of the movement can benefit the group. Indeed, in their original work on this topic, authored in 1970, Gerlach and Hine noted presciently that a main advantage of 'segmented, polycentric, ideationally integrated networks' is their ambiguous size and composition: 'To some it seems as if they are facing, on the one hand, a spontaneous explosion at the grass roots level; and, on the other, a many-headed hydra.'[188] It is by appearing consequential and being heard that the alt-right can affect norms, influence society, and therefore shift Overton windows—that concept so central to the alt-right's machinations. Indeed, in today's social media-suffused society, P. W. Singer and Emerson Brooking note, power is 'measured not by physical strength or high-tech hardware, but by the command of attention.'[189] On this front, the alt-right does very well.

Yet in measuring the alt-right's social penetration, we face the immediate dilemma of separating its impact from that of other related, yet distinct, societal forces. The alt-right liked to claim credit for 'meme-ing Trump into the White House,' yet did it truly cause this outcome or did the influence flow the opposite way?[190] Even with Trump installed, the alt-right proved unable to implement its agenda: America is not currently on the verge of turning into a fascist state and, according to some polls, 'American attitudes toward racial integration and immigration have become more open among liberals and conservatives alike.'[191] In so far as politics in the United States have become more polarized, and the Republican Party has moved distinctly to the right, it could be legitimately argued that this was the result of Trump's outlandish imprimatur rather than the online actions of Nazi trolls.[192]

And yet, there is reason to take note of the alt-right and of the strategy that it has used. Certainly, the movement has been helped by parallel forces and actors within the American body politic, yet the same can be said for any successful insurgency. As collective movements exploiting social and political contradictions, insurgencies can hardly take off without an enabling context or thrive without promising allies. Relying on structures that share one's agenda, either partly or fully, need not represent an abdication of control or loss of initiative; it is in fact what an insurgency must do to have effect. The troubling quandary in measuring outcomes is that, in contrast to traditional insurgency, there is no explicit seizure of power but rather a shifting of norms, which takes time, is difficult to measure, and has a multitude of causes. Even so, in this case, there is sufficient data to suggest strongly that the alt-right has been more than just an opportunistic bystander claiming credit for something it did not also help shape.

According to a 2017 ABC News/*Washington Post* poll, a full 9 percent of the US population—equivalent to about 22 million Americans—find it 'acceptable to hold neo-Nazi or white supremacist views.' In the same poll, 10 percent declared support for the alt-right, with only 50 percent of respondents opposing the movement.[193] For both questions, self-censorship by respondents is likely and the poll also surveyed people of all races. In three polls taken in the November 2020—January 2021 time frame, both before and after the Capitol attack, 23–41 percent of self-identified Republicans espoused a favorable view of QAnon or said they believed in the conspiracy theory of a deep-state cabal made up of pedophiles and satanists.[194] Following the Capitol attack, Twitter's initial purge of QAnon on its platform netted 70,000 accounts.[195] Even three months after the riot in Washington, DC, 'about half of Republicans believe[d] the siege was largely a non-violent protest or was the handiwork of left-wing activists.'[196] These figures speak to a phenomenon—one bigger than Donald Trump. 'In fact,' writes conservative political commentator David French, a focus solely on specific politicians 'understates the extent to which "alt-right" ideas and themes have infiltrated American discourse in ways that have energized a fringe movement and given it life and reach beyond the Oval Office.'[197]

Going further, there are clear signs of the alt-right's epistemological influence on US society. It is, for example, disturbing that when President Joe Biden used his inauguration speech to call out the threat of 'political extremism, white supremacy, [and] domestic terrorism,' the response from mainstream voices on the right was to feel targeted and to protest against the 'thinly veiled innuendo.'[198] As Tucker Carlson noted on his highly popular Fox News talk show, 'Now that we're waging war on white supremacists, can somebody tell us in very clear language what a white supremacist is?'[199] Regarding Fox News, it is further telling that this standard-bearer of the right wing is now competing for viewers with yet more extreme networks, where conspiracy theories and intolerance spread like viruses.[200] And it is telling, and frankly disturbing, that more than a fifth of polled Republicans believe the storming of the Capitol was justified and at least somewhat support the attackers.[201]

The true potence of ideational insurgency lies in this impact on broader society. In the place of armed overthrows and climactic battles, information and narratives mount an epistemological challenge that subverts society incrementally, until a new normal has emerged and must be reckoned with. Arquilla and Ronfeldt anticipated this component of netwar: 'It means trying to disrupt, damage, or modify what a target population "knows" or thinks it knows about itself and the world around it.'[202] Indeed, if we return to Andrew Breitbart's motto that 'politics is downstream from culture,' ideational insurgency changes the culture of society by working first in online spaces, where its citizens spend so much time and have most of their engagements, and then letting its norms spill over into 'real life.' In this manner, 'virality can overwhelm truth.'[203] Many of those who end up taking on the movement's talking points as their own may not consider themselves as alt-right, or even recognize their role within the 'alt-light,' but they tacitly fuel its struggle and enable its agenda. Achieving this measure of acceptability allows for unprecedented opportunities for recruitment and above-ground organization, turning shadowy networks and taboo causes into a fully fledged social movement.

Conclusion

The alt-right ideational struggle is the culmination of an approach that has evolved over decades and finds its antecedents in pre-internet information operations. From the EZLN's initial experimentation with online community-building, to the *netkrieg* of rightist militias, to Anonymous's entirely online mode of existence and attack, and to ISIS's 'virtual caliphate,' we see in the alt-right the model example— to date—of how to mobilize violently against the state, all the while undoing or at least avoiding its coercive powers. The alt-right may not have vanquished the insurgent's dilemma—at least not yet—and it may not have turned the United States into a white ethno-state, but it shows avenues that will have potential and use for movements to come.

Indeed, going forward, the threat of ideational insurgency— and of its epistemological charge in particular—is likely to grow, given the increased fervor of disinformation, intense polarization, and the anomie of our times, all combined with more sophisticated technology. Micro-targeting of social media messaging has already proved effective in manipulating the attitudes and behavior of individuals and groups; it is a capability that is likely to evolve and become more prevalent.[204] As the technology of 'deep fakes' becomes more advanced and accessible, allowing for AI-generated simulations, both in photo and video form, it will become easier to manufacture outrage, to mobilize popular movements, and also to inject uncertainty as to what is really going on. Writing in 1999, Stephen Sloan predicted the possibility of 'virtual insurgency': 'a war of abstraction, of images, ... used by skillful adversaries who will have the ability to modify reality to achieve their goal.'[205] Two decades on, this scenario no longer seems so distant.

Information is power and, if it is misused, the threat to democracy is clear. The confrontation has been a long time coming. In 1849, Alexis de Tocqueville reported upon the 'axiom of political science in the United States,' that 'the only way to neutralize the influence of newspapers is to multiply their number.' Tocqueville saw within the newspaper 'an association which is composed of its habitual readers' and expressed concern that 'excessive dissemination' would splinter society into ever-smaller epistemic groupings.[206] Following in these footsteps, Walter Lippmann wrote in 1921, one century ago now, about the hazardous interplay of media and democracy, noting in particular the danger of special interest groups that have a monopoly on information and can therefore 'manufacture consent.' His warning back then was that 'there can be no liberty for a community which lacks the information by which to detect lies.'[207] Needless to say, these are both warnings with even greater poignancy today, given the erosion of truth, of society, and of trusted expertise.

6

MIND THE GAP
COUNTERING LOCALIZED INSURGENCY

The key to victory in ideational and infiltrative insurgencies is to subvert the state without giving it physical targets that it can legitimately strike. In localized insurgency, by contrast, the group does not necessarily cloak its insurgent project, but instead locates it in areas where the state is weak or uninterested in claiming control. This approach reduces the signature of the insurgent project and therefore also the likelihood of a concerted military response. At the same time, this strategy rests on an implied assumption: that the state will tolerate localized instability or at least 'shared sovereignty' rather than assert itself fully as the legal authority.

This calculation is a precarious yet not at all unrealistic gamble on the part of the insurgents. As we have seen, states threatened in this manner tend toward entrenchment, doubling down on developed areas and leaving the rest to their own devices. Underlying the antagonism between these two worlds, a tacit agreement may even take form between the state and the challenger whereby they learn to coexist in ways that may seem mutually beneficial. If and when matters get out of hand, the state will respond with an aggressive raid, which, while strictly palliative in terms of actually countering the insurgency, is also not terribly demanding, requires little to no political reform, and may even invite military aid and assistance from other countries pushing fruitlessly for a more enlightened approach. The military then becomes a reaction force, swatting at insurgents wherever they may be found yet never stopping to boost defenses against their reappearance or giving the local population a reason to side with the state.

As we have seen in chapter 3, this is an inauspicious response to localized insurgency, because it does not stem—and indeed accelerates—the fragmentary and destabilizing effects of this approach. Not only does this stance deepen political and social fault lines, but the unchecked dysfunction also invites new challenges to government writ, be they vigilante actors reacting to the chronic instability, the corrupting influence of accommodating illicit groups, or third-party actors from further afield seeking to exploit the situation. Though states may never have been monolithic, the erosion of sovereignty caused by localized insurgency puts the whole notion of statehood into doubt, raising questions as to who, ultimately, is in charge.

A better response is of course possible, and this chapter considers a few alternatives—first in rural and then in urban settings. The broad argument to emerge from this review, however, is that the first and necessary condition for countering localized insurgency is for the state to muster the necessary political will to control its own land and govern its own people. Regrettably, there are only a handful of cases where such a shift has taken place—where the state has reclaimed its lost territory, reversed the process of fragmentation, and consolidated control over an alienated population. The first two steps are already extremely demanding, but the third, and most political, is all but impossible without a new social contract and revived sense of political solidarity. As they say, miracles do happen— but it seems more realistic, in many settings, to acknowledge the limits of the Weberian ideal and to consider instead alternative ways of structuring states so that they function. As this chapter suggests, one option—promising but perilous—is to focus on the quality of governance rather than on who is doing the governing.

Fusing the Divide: Clear, Hold, Build

Localized insurgency implies a division of the nation-state into areas controlled by the government and those held informally by the challenger. In contrast to traditional insurgency, this division is here enduring, or at least there appears to be no real intent by either side to prevail over the other and establish cohesive and coherent control over the state as a whole. Countering localized insurgency would necessarily imply a change to this arrangement. Specifically, to fuse the divide that localization thrives upon, the government would need to (re)assert control and reach into parts of the country that it had long ago abandoned. On the back of a legacy of neglect, winning back the perception of legitimacy will be an uphill battle, not least if it must begin with the military clearing and holding of territory so as to resume control. Even if intended to build legitimacy, this process will typically be inflammatory and destabilizing, thereby undermining the ultimate objective of restoring good faith and repairing state failure.

In querying whether and how this can be done, we must interrogate those instances where a state has reconquered lost territory and held on to it, thereby fusing the divides of its political geography. There are curiously few examples to go on, at least within recent history. Within this limited sample space, however, Sri Lanka's final confrontation with the LTTE in 2006–9 emerges as a key case. After decades of insurgency, the government was growing increasingly frustrated with the LTTE's cynical use of peace talks and its continued violence, not least the assassination attempts on senior military leaders in early 2006. When the Tigers closed the sluice gates of the Mavil Aru dam in July of that year, threatening the water supply of tens of thousands of people, the government embarked upon a major offensive intended to crush the group once and for all. This effort was successful and saw the restoration of government writ in the northern and eastern areas previously claimed and governed by the Tigers. Twelve years on, the LTTE remains defeated and its 'once impregnable' insurgency is no more.[1]

The case of the LTTE is particularly relevant because, over time, the conflict had become very similar to the localized insurgencies discussed in chapter 3. Notwithstanding periodic escalations in the conflict, the LTTE maintained informal control over the north and the east, while the government held the rest of the island. The LTTE did maintain a desire to secede and dreamt of an independent Tamil state, yet in practice the conflict had evolved into something far more stable, with the two entities coexisting awkwardly within one national space. For example, despite the great antagonism between the two sides, the government of Sri Lanka continued to fund public services within the Tamil counter-state, seeking in this manner to retain some sort of linkage with its lost citizens.[2] The puzzling arrangement speaks to an institutionalized fragmentation that both sides could abide by. Indeed, an indirect cause behind the final offensive was the LTTE's attempt to untether itself from the government's services and set up truly parallel structures, using the significant humanitarian aid that flowed into the northeast following the December 2004 tsunami.[3] Consequently, this conflict is a relevant example of localized insurgency, and there is therefore good reason to ask how the state reversed course and reclaimed what it had lost.

It may seem perverse to draw lessons from the Sri Lankan offensive, which has elicited strong condemnation internationally for excesses in the use of force and many human rights abuses. Estimates of the number of people killed in the war range from 7,000 (as per the government) to 40,000 (according to the United Nations).[4] Allegations have been made about war crimes and the mass disappearance of Tamils during the conflict. Because of the lack of independent investigations, the situation remains difficult to assess, yet it is clear that even by the standard of other civil wars the offensive was certainly brutal. Still, the humanitarian aspect—albeit difficult to ignore—is not the relevant aspect here. Instead, what makes the case apposite to this discussion is that the state not only conquered territory long controlled by the Tigers but also claimed it as its own. More than a decade on, this achievement has not been contested, though efforts at reconciliation have yielded mixed results. Even so, this case still distinguishes itself from most contemporary counterinsurgency efforts and should be studied for the lessons it may impart.

The reassertion of state control required, in the first place, reconquering the ceded territory where this resistance took place. The offensive started in 2006, following years of military build-up, and proceeded quickly. Traversing difficult terrain, government forces had by July 2007 seized control of several well-defended bases in the east. The government then pivoted to the north, scoring victories against the Tigers and confining the group to an ever-shrinking area. In January 2009, Sri Lankan troops captured the LTTE's *de facto* capital in Kilinochchi, then the Jaffna Peninsula, and finally the last LTTE stronghold of Mullaitivu. On 17 May, the LTTE admitted defeat and, two days later, their iconic leader, Velupillai Prabhakaran, was killed by government forces. Only years earlier, the group had controlled nearly a third of the island and governed this territory with its own courts, schools, and civil service.

Though these military successes were impressive (and signaled a step change in Sri Lankan military performance), clearing the Tigers was only one part of the eventual response. In preparing and executing this offensive, the Sri Lankan government had taken measures to ensure that its military conquests would be enduring. From the moment the government came to power in 2005, it added 5,000 recruits per month to the army, thereby tripling its size—from 100,000 to 300,000 personnel—within just three years.[5] The expansion enabled the armed forces to overwhelm the LTTE, but it also generated sufficient follow-on units to hold conquered territory and thereby reassert state control. As Ahmed Hashim notes in a major study of the offensive, 'the operational methods of the past, whereby the army would clear an area of the LTTE and then vacate it—allowing the insurgents to reinfiltrate—would now be avoided.'[6]

The Sri Lankan case demonstrates the need for sustained control—to clear territory, but also to hold it—in order to set the conditions for political consolidation. In this endeavor, the government was helped by the fact of Sri Lanka being an island, and a relatively small one at that. Hemmed in on all sides, and with a naval blockade to boot, the LTTE found it impossible to evade or escape the government's onslaught, resulting in their decimation and eventual defeat. Still, this geographic reality should not obscure the heavy and deliberate investment in the endeavor: at the war's end, the former Tamil heartland in the north and east was the most militarized region in South Asia in terms of force density, with 200 soldiers deployed per 1,000 civilians.[7] Under such conditions, any re-emergence of Tamil militancy was impossible.

Ironically, this militarization has led to new grievances, as it created a political economy in the east and north controlled by the armed forces at the expense of the local Tamil population. Critics of the government denounce the continued occupation for causing displacement within semi-permanent shelters and limiting livelihood options.[8] Indeed, it is fair to say that while Sri Lanka successfully cleared and held territory, it has largely squandered the opportunity to build government legitimacy among the population 'reclaimed' in this manner. The matter goes beyond the excesses of the offensive itself, as the government has also not seriously addressed the grievances of the Tamil community or accepted accountability for wartime abuses.[9] Enveloping all of this is the sense of Sinhala Buddhist chauvinism prevalent among some sections of the ruling elite, which encourages the exclusion and subordination of minorities as second-class citizens.[10] Thus, whereas the case is a rare contemporary illustration of effective clearing and holding, and even the *de jure* unification of the country, it also constitutes a highly illiberal case of state-building.[11]

The case of Colombia provides a different lens on how to extend the state to previously lost peoples and lands. According to some estimates, in the 1990s 'as much as 40% of Colombian territory was controlled by the FARC forces and the state had no presence in 158 (16%) of Colombia's 1,099 municipalities.'[12] For this reason, the Colombian government in 2002 adopted a new strategy to unite the country under the democratic governance of the state. As in Sri Lanka, the turning point was a mounting crisis: FARC forces were deployed around Bogotá, the capital, blockading the most important national highways and stifling trade and travel, and a steep rise in crime, such as kidnapping and drug trafficking, led to fear, even panic. Elected on a platform of defeating FARC, President Álvaro Uribe set out on a new approach—the Democratic Security and Defense Policy—'to strengthen and guarantee the rule of law throughout Colombia, through the reinforcement of democratic authority.'[13]

This new ambition would require a different military approach. Hitherto, while the armed forces had made gains at FARC's expense, they had struggled to retain territorial control. In effect, the Colombian Army, 15,000–30,000 strong—was rotating in and out of guerrilla-affected areas as if in a 'perpetual shell game,' never gaining the initiative or setting the conditions.[14] The approach was neither logistically sustainable nor terribly effective. For one, it did not seriously threaten FARC's control of the hinterland, because it did not reoccupy territory or mobilize the people in these areas in support of the state. The continued instability also prompted the emergence of paramilitaries which, over time, grew to be yet another problem for the state to solve.

To make possible a different approach, Colombia reinforced its already significant military. The new-found ability, after 9/11, to direct US assistance toward counterinsurgency rather than just counter-narcotics (the distinction had anyway been largely artificial) allowed for the construction of specialized assets, designed to roll back FARC's country-wide presence. Particularly useful, in this regard, was the increase in mobile brigades (or BRIM) to help spread government forces across the country. Each of these brigades comprised four counter-guerrilla battalions, organized and equipped to be self-sustaining. As Thomas Marks explains, 'this resulted in the sustained pursuit of FARC units in even the most remote regions and their permanent harassment, while regular units exercised area control in the heavily populated areas.'[15] Block leave was instituted to ensure longer-term operations rather than just 'search and destroy'; 'FARC thus found all possible space progressively closing, even in the jungle sectors it had once "owned."'[16]

With FARC on the run, the fundamental challenge lay in holding the liberated villages and towns. Crucial to this effort was the establishment of local security forces drawn from these very places and, appropriately, named the Soldados de Mi Pueblo (soldiers of my village). No fewer than 600 of these 40-man units were created, charged with maintaining local security and guarding against FARC reinfiltration. This sort of effort has often been found necessary in counterinsurgency settings, so as to extend security over large areas and act as back-up to local police assets, and yet relying on and empowering local security actors in this manner typically raises questions about their ability and accountability. As it turns out, handing out arms to the general population in hope of achieving greater security can be stunningly counterproductive.[17] In this instance, the risk of blowback was addressed by incorporating the platoons directly into the national government's chain of command; each was trained and armed but also officered by regulars, thereby ensuring oversight and unity of purpose, and increasing professionalization.[18]

The alignment of command and control was important, but it belies the most critical factor in making the Soldados de Mi Pueblo program work. Beyond the significant requirements of recruiting, screening and partnering with local forces, the enabler for all that followed was the political mobilization of the population to work with the government in the service of a mutually desirable goal. Despite the long-term absence of the state, it enjoyed sufficient vestigial legitimacy among FARC-controlled populations, primarily because FARC had done an even worse job of co-opting this middle ground. For sure, the failure of governance in the hinterland had to be addressed, yet in embarking upon this challenge the government did not face the additional burden of operating in 'enemy territory,' or amid a population that perceived it as an occupier. Instead, most Colombians resisted FARC and were willing to give the state another shot, so long as it offered some nominal promise for a better tomorrow.[19]

To build on this goodwill, and in furtherance of the new strategy's focus on reclaiming as true Colombians populations long abandoned by the state, the government created local security councils (*consejos de seguridad*) and local governance councils (*consejos comunales de gobierno*) in cleared villages.[20] This process was intended to take the strategic approach from the holding phase into one of building—building institutions, democracy, and legitimacy. To this end, Colombian president Álvaro Uribe personally and repeatedly toured the country, particularly war-torn towns and villages, to engage with communities previously neglected by the state. On each visit, Uribe sought to demonstrate the state's commitment: he explained the emerging strategy, registered local need, and arranged for a state response. In the first eight years, according to government figures, about 5,400 projects were drawn up in this manner, 4,700 (88 percent) of which were completed.[21] The investment was meant to give a voice to the local communities and a sense of self-determination in a new Colombia, thereby generating national unity.

Colombia presents an instructive case of how to clear, hold, and build over large territories, thereby reconsolidating legitimate state control. However, it is also a cautionary tale. The Democratic Security and Defense Policy began with great urgency, with FARC mounting an existential threat to the nation. As FARC was put on the back foot, however, and the threat subsided, it proved too tempting to dismantle—or too expensive to maintain—the comprehensive outreach and engagement envisaged by the new strategy. From 2006 onward, security efforts shifted increasingly to search-and-destroy operations targeting FARC remnants, while the broader intent of extending control and stability fell by the wayside.[22] The political core of the strategy also suffered, as did the expansion of Colombian governance into the countryside. Over time, this neglect recreated spaces and opportunity for FARC splinter groups to exploit, particularly as the military pressure waned following the peace agreement of 2016. Indeed, in the years following that agreement, coca production again surged by 50 percent per year, and the countryside is now witnessing increasing numbers of massacres, homicides, and incidents of displacement.[23]

The reasons for Colombia snatching defeat from the jaws of victory are all too familiar. A full 95 percent of the Colombian population live in the *sierra* region in the west of the country, where the country's major cities are located. Only 5 percent inhabit the savanna (the *llanos*) and the Amazon region, which are under-developed and difficult to traverse and where, not coincidentally, FARC operated and lived.[24] Given the incentives of electoral democracy and the strict limitations on national resources, there are compelling arguments for any government to focus on the developed majority rather than the more vulnerable minority. Meanwhile, given the lack of alternative livelihoods, the profits of the drug trade, and the power of local gangs, there are compelling arguments for the rural population to return to coca cultivation. The urgency that motivated the Democratic Security and Defense Policy proved too fleeting to change these hardwired patterns of governance, both national and informal. To a large degree, the periphery has remained peripheral.

This outcome reflects the particular complexity of the build phase. Whereas clearing and holding call for fairly traditional military tasks—combat operations and area security—building implies establishing a 'new normal,' requiring intimate engagement with local structures, capabilities, aspirations and fears. As can be seen in Colombia, it also requires the political will to construct and sustain a reformed political contract between a government that has long been absent and a population traumatized by war and that has every right to distrust central authority. In that sense, building brings to the fore intensely political questions of control and legitimacy. It involves that most delicate task of repairing past fractures and finding a new political compact as a unified state.

Building Mediated States

The case of Colombia raises the crucial question of whether it is possible to redeem the Weberian ideal of the state in countries affected by localized insurgency. In Colombia, the effort benefited from professional and capable security forces, generous US military aid, and a tradition of democracy reaching all the way back to the late nineteenth century. Even in this context, however, the 'successful integration of Colombian society' envisaged in the Democratic Security and Defense Policy proved too demanding—both politically and materially.[25] For all the successes experienced as part of this strategy, the case raises legitimate concerns about the likely outcomes of countering localized insurgency in less stable countries, operating with fewer resources, on a less solid footing politically, and in a worse neighborhood.

If, in these contexts, the Weberian ideal will likely remain a myth, how can insurgency-threatened governments nonetheless exercise control over their territory and govern their people? Countering localized insurgency in such a setting will likely require an alternative basis for order—one that acknowledges the fissiparous nature of statehood yet retains sufficient central oversight to avert conflict. A possible recourse lies in what Ken Menkhaus terms the 'mediated state'—one in which 'the government relies on partnership (or at least coexistence) with a diverse range of local intermediaries and rival sources of authority to provide core functions of public security, justice, and conflict management in much of the country.'[26] Others have called such arrangements 'hybrid political orders' and lauded this lens as a pragmatic recognition of how many states function in reality rather than in theory.[27] Instead of viewing any aberration from the Weberian ideal as an undifferentiated sign of 'state failure,' the goal is to acknowledge the great heterogeneity of such entities and to govern accordingly. Specifically, this approach would involve engaging with the 'informal structures and war economies that have crystallised during periods of protracted violence'—structures that are 'resilient, adaptable and difficult to transform by outsiders.'[28]

The mediated state may not only be a more realistic response to the artificiality of the state in many of those countries most threatened by localized insurgency, but it also recognizes that, in these very contexts, the attempted imposition of the state can have dramatically counterproductive consequences. In Somalia, the source of much of Menkhaus's work, the 'state' that Western interventions typically seek to recreate has, historically, been a catalyst for criminality, violence, and communal tensions. As a result, the international focus on recreating this leviathan as a cure for 'state failure' has repeatedly reawakened the 'worst instincts of Somalia's elites,' which may help explain the checkered record of 'state-building' in that country.[29] Similarly, in Afghanistan, local communities rejected the authority imposed upon them by the center, in part owing to vivid memories of abuse, injustice, and cruelty perpetrated by people within or allied with the state.[30] In post-war Iraq, the continued empowerment of an increasingly sectarian Shia government to deal with a Sunni insurgency led to predictable outcomes, with death squads in government uniforms cleansing entire neighborhoods and pushing their Sunni compatriots into the arms of al-Qaeda.[31]

In these cases, as well as others, 'more state' is not a recipe for more stability, and so creative ways are needed to tie the periphery to the center by other means. This insight runs counter to most counterinsurgency theory, which tends to equate progress with the gradual expansion of governance to previously 'ungoverned areas.'

A key assumption herein is that the absence of the state has led to the collapse of institutions and capacity and that integration of these lands will require the state to reassert itself and provide these functions. This type of thinking is not always wrong, but it can be dangerous. For one, while the theory emphasizes that government control spreads like ink spots across paper, it does not evince much concern for what was on that paper before the ink reached it. In fact, the analogy is critically flawed, as there is really no societal equivalent to a blank piece of paper.

Rather than viewing 'ungoverned,' 'stateless,' or 'post-conflict' territory through the metaphor of oil spots and paper—black on white—one must understand and approach each locality as heaving with activity, intrigue, and politics. This point matters, because how these areas are understood determines how they are handled. If these stateless peripheries are seen as places where politics have broken down and institutions are absent, the go-to solution will be to quickly impose the state so as to fill the vacuum. US general Stanley McChrystal, normally an astute observer of politics and strategy, demonstrated this problem in spades when in Afghanistan he optimistically explained that once NATO forces had cleared a particular town, 'we've got a government in a box, ready to roll in.'[32] As it happened, 'no one who planned the operation realized how hard it would be to convince residents that they could trust representatives of an Afghan government that had sent them corrupt police and inept leaders before they turned to the Taliban.'[33] Thus, for a combination of factors, as Brown puts it, 'the district governor "rolled in" to take charge ... was rolled right out ... in the same proverbial box in which he came.'[34]

Rather than viewing the periphery as 'ungoverned' and therefore attempt to reimpose control, a more promising lens is to recognize patterns of informal governance. This perspective seeks to identify the local structures that regulate life away from the state, so that they may be co-opted to benefit both center and periphery within the context of a new national compact. Be they systems of governance, security, justice, or dispute resolution, the local institutions developed bottom-up are often seen as more effective and also as more meaningful by the local population. In

Afghanistan, for example, the thin spread, many deficiencies, and impoverished state of the national courts meant that most Afghans preferred informal bodies—such as *jirgas* and *shuras* of local elders—for conflict resolution and adjudication.[35] In Mali, surveys have found that popular trust in traditional structures by far exceeds that placed in the police and national courts.[36] In post-conflict Timor Leste, rural areas far away from the administrative reach of the state are instead governed through 'customary forms of community organisation, decision-making and conflict mediation.'[37] As Bjoern Hofmann notes, state-based institutions 'acknowledge these forms of self-governance and work alongside them, while at the same time aiming to strengthen the new administrative structures staffed by elected representatives.'[38]

The point, here as elsewhere, is to identify those informal structures that enjoy local legitimacy, which Seymour Martin Lipset helpfully defines as 'the belief that existing political institutions are the most appropriate or proper ones for the society.'[39] So long as this condition is met, local divergences from the norm, or adaptations of the rule of law, may be tolerated, or even encouraged, to compensate for the many shortcomings of the state. Indeed, attempts to enforce convergence in the face of such difference, and to insist on homogeneity as a marker of sovereignty, are likely to backfire, particularly where the state lacks any centripetal logic or the government's reach is anyway hampered. The best hope for these states may be to combine a top-down and a bottom-up process of state-building, the former focused on professionalizing the central institutions of state and the latter on integrating within this structure local initiatives, diversity, and customs.

Afghanistan looms large, given the high-profile failure— despite several attempts—to manage this balancing act between the local and the central. Contrary to the self-serving myth that Afghanistan was always unruly, and that working to create a stable state was therefore a fool's errand, Olivier Roy makes the critical point that 'From 1880 to 1978, (from the accession to power of Amir Abdurrahman to the communist coup) Afghanistan enjoyed greater stability than many European countries [and since] the end of the 1940s until the communist coup of April 1978, the

Afghan central state was able to curb armed local opposition and establish an extensive network of military and administrative posts as well as schools all over the country.'[40] The issue is that the state envisaged through the Bonn process was created in a Western image rather than according to what had worked in Afghanistan. As Roy goes on to explain, the Afghan state has derived legitimacy to the extent that it embodies a concept of Afghanistan as 'a Muslim and always independent territory,' acts as 'a (relatively) honest and distant broker between local factions,' and 'channels funds and international help and provides some minimum services.'[41] In contrast, the state-building process post-9/11 centralized political power and made provincial preferences an afterthought. A system developed where virtually all senior provincial and district officials were appointed by the president; similarly, the bulk of NATO's efforts for many years flowed through the capital, with scant regard for the periphery over which it was to govern.[42] A different path may have been possible, but it would have required far more creativity in defining the state.

Accepting divergent patterns of governance and social organization allows states that never had a sense of unity to survive their own contradictions. Yet, there are limits to the flexibility. First, what is traditional or homegrown is not necessarily correct, or even wanted locally.[43] As Mats Berdal notes, there is a tendency in these conversations to view whatever happens away from the center as an 'authentic response of "civil society" to the predation, manipulation and violence of outsiders.'[44] This analytical tendency is particularly common where the state displays abusive behavior or is simply incompetent. It results in characterizations of villagers as simple folk, apolitical, and as wanting most of all to be left to their customs and mores. Samuel Popkin called this the 'myth of the village': the notion that politics at the local level represent some sort of refuge from politicking, graft, and day-to-day venality.[45] The problem with this myth is that it cloaks local-level dynamics that may require urgent redress. Indeed, local politics can be as corrupt, unaccountable, and brutal as those of the center; local mechanisms—be they councils, justice systems, or industry—can be equitable or exploitative, legitimate or coercive.

172

There must therefore be a distinction between devolution of decision-making on the one hand and laissez-faire on the other. In countering localized insurgency, the state cannot achieve buy-in purely through its absence—this would be pointless. If the state tolerates predatory local leaders, for example, their 'constituents' will be pushed to revolt, with attendant costs to national stability and government legitimacy. Instead, the state must ensure that the leaders and structures that it empowers can win community support and wield legitimacy, for themselves and—by proxy—for the state. The burning question is what to do when local coping mechanisms and definitions of legitimacy differ starkly from, and also undermine, those of the state. Drug eradication provides a key example. Few states will want to turn a blind eye to entrenched criminality of this sort, particularly given its destabilizing effects on society, yet, whether in Colombia, Afghanistan, or Peru, ill-sequenced or poorly executed efforts to eradicate drug cultivation have unwittingly raised the profitability of narcotics cultivation and deprived poor and desperate farmers of income—and both those outcomes benefited the insurgents.[46]

What is the lesson for countering localized insurgency in states incapable of reasserting themselves? Even if authority is ceded to the periphery, the state must nonetheless understand exactly what divergence to tolerate and be capable of effective interventions to reinforce the social contract (such as it is). The key lies in the state underwriting and even supporting informal variations on the periphery, thereby satisfying local needs, empowering local political allies, and contributing to a desire to be part of, rather than resist, the state at the center of it all. Needless to say, while the mediated state provides a way out of chronic localized insurgency, it does not significantly simplify the task of keeping the state together and functional.

... and the Cities?

The study of localized insurgency in chapter 3 began with the urban variant, or the use of slums and their residents as a base by gangs, warlords, and militias. As with rural localized insurgency, the location—in this case the less prosperous, less regulated, and less safe sections of town—is chosen because the state is absent and unlikely to visit, or at least to stay. Once established, therefore, these alternative power structures become the new governing authority, all while they exploit what the state can provide by way of public goods. In this sense, the relationship between the localized urban insurgent and the state is not entirely unlike the one that developed between the LTTE and the Sri Lankan government: in both settings, the state sustains some level of support for a population controlled by its ostensible adversary, thereby inadvertently legitimating the former as a somewhat competent service provider and enabling its continued criminality.

The gangs also use their local population as a source of labor and resources, and as a human shield to deter an offensive by the state. When states do launch into these areas, to repress crippling gang problems in the inner cities, the results tend to be hugely dislocating to the local community and ineffectual in slowing the longer-term growth of gangs. In most cases, the state's repression either empowers the gang by cementing its bonds with a beleaguered population or it creates a power vacuum over which rival gangs feud for control. Even so, these strategies are remarkably common, as can be seen with the so-called *mano dura* (firm hand) or *cero tolerancia* (zero tolerance) strategies adopted by Guatemala, Honduras and El Salvador.

The case of El Salvador warrants further attention, given its unenviable world record both for the number of active gang members and also for national murder rates.[47] Its *mano dura* strategy was first launched in October 2003, resulting in surged security operations targeting the gangs, ramped-up arrests and incarcerations, and greatly loosened legal criteria for such enforcement. The results were overwhelmingly negative: they caused destruction and death, the gangs survived—even thrived—and the operations put additional burden on an already overstressed justice system.[48] Nonetheless, this same approach was recycled and reapplied, resulting in a *súper mano dura* plan in 2006 and variations on the same theme in later years. In one two-year period, El Salvador managed to achieve 30,934 arrests of gang members (42 per day), and yet 84 percent of cases were dismissed owing to flimsy evidence or legal inadmissibility, often due to age.[49] Those who were nonetheless funneled to prison contributed to the dramatic overcrowding of these facilities (reaching 338 percent in 2014) and encountered conditions ideal for fostering gang identity and continued recruitment.[50] Though the approach gradually placed greater emphasis on prevention of recruitment and rehabilitation of gang members, poor resourcing and synchronization made the effect of such programs all but negligible.

As mentioned, the suppressive approach has proved surprisingly prevalent despite its extremely limited returns. At best, repression has produced periodic dips in violence, suitable for when a city is hosting a major international event, or it has allowed politicians to appear 'tough on crime' and win an election.[51] At worst, however, it has increased bloodshed and even legitimized and strengthened the gang as protectors of the targeted community. This phenomenon was seen also in Rio. Through schemes such as the 'Wild West bonus'—a financial award based on the number of criminals killed—the relationship between the police and the *favelas* grew to be purely adversarial.[52] From 1995 to 2003, police-caused deaths in Rio rose from 355 to 1,195 per year.[53] It was a strategy that not only failed to generate sustainable results in the territory that the state had *de facto* lost, but also provided a propaganda coup for the gangs, reinforcing its claims of solidarity with the *favelados*.[54]

A final example deserves mention. In Haiti, shortly after the *coup d'état* in 2004, a newly deployed UN stabilization force (MINUSTAH) turned its sights on the gangs threatening public security in the country. Initial forays into the slums of Port-au-Prince established temporary territorial control, but, as troops withdrew, the gangs either re-established themselves or fought one another to fill the void left behind. As James Cockayne explains, 'while this "gang-clearing" approach quickly and substantially increased freedom of maneuver in the area, it was not matched by a reinsertion of Haitian state authority, such as the PNH [the national police], to "hold" the territory.'[55] As the situation continued to deteriorate, the UN forces launched their own 'Iron First' operations, resulting in extensive firefights, including the use of grenades and mortars, all within densely populated slums offering the local population little by way of protection. Cockayne's verdict is damning but fair: it was a failure, he concludes, 'at both a tactical and strategic level,' as MINUSTAH secured neither the area nor the population, but rather pushed the locals toward the gangs, which now posed as resistance to 'foreign occupation.'[56]

The brutality and futility of the *mano dura* measures have encouraged some governments to seek negotiations with the gangs instead, as if these criminal insurgencies were indeed expressively political entities. In El Salvador in 2012, government figures struck a truce with the country's two major gangs, Mara Salvatrucha 13 and Barrio 18, aimed at reducing violence in return for the government transferring some gang members out of maximum security prisons. Following the truce, the homicide rate in El Salvador dipped by 50 percent, indicating the success of the approach, and yet long-term progress remained elusive. Because the local population vehemently rejected the notion of striking deals with the gang, the government never grew comfortable owning the process and the pact soon unraveled. Either way, it was a sham. As one study notes, 'the truce hinged on the *visibility* of gang violence,' not its incidence.[57] With an entire power structure predicated on coercion, the gangs proved incapable of stopping the violence, though they did find ingenious ways of cloaking its occurrence so as to milk continued favors from the state. Indeed, the decline in homicides coincided with an increase in disappearances, and when the truce broke, violence resumed— yet at higher levels than before.

The outcome underlines the difficulty of holding successful talks with criminal insurgents, at least as a stand-alone solution. As the International Crisis Group points out, even where gangs are willing to reduce homicides, at least temporarily, 'an effective agreement would require that they abandon extortion and other criminal practices, and eventually disarm and demobilize.'[58] Such an outcome is not impossible, though it 'depends intimately on the depth of the group's cohesion *and* its desire to continue existing in another form.'[59] In most cases, these pacts are embarked upon because the state is in a position of weakness, and so it is also poorly placed to compel a meaningful surrender by the gang.[60] Negotiating with violent community-based gangs also risks further enhancing their standing, all the while casting the government as incompetent and illegitimate. As Moritz Schuberth therefore concludes, 'if mediation with criminal gangs seems unavoidable to immediately lower escalating levels of violence, they must be complemented with and followed up by efforts to tackle the underlying conditions that contributed to the emergence and consolidation of gangs in the first place'—yet this would involve tasks of far greater magnitude and ambition.[61]

If confrontation and conciliation are both fraught with risk, a third approach seeks to address recruitment into the gang rather than the gang itself. In the 1990s, in the aftermath of its civil war, Nicaragua faced the steady growth of gangs to a point where they controlled territory, engaged in violence and drug trafficking, and attracted local youth. In contrast with other Central American contexts, however, Nicaragua's response was marked by 'relative restraint in police operations,' and—in its stead—an emphasis on 'proactive civil policies' in gang-affected neighborhoods. With the aim of co-opting the services and functions that gangs provide to the local population, NGOs and civil society organizations sought to ensure 'regular employment, paid labor, and involvement at the micro level in local politics.'[62] These measures have been credited with reducing the gang problem in Nicaragua and with preventing more established gangs, such as those dominating El Salvador and Honduras, from spreading south. As a result, Nicaragua's approach came to be known as a model for counter-gang action, based on prevention of recruitment and the rehabilitation of those already involved.

Cases like Nicaragua are intriguing, yet the search for lessons is a perilous undertaking. First, as José Luis Rocha argues, Nicaragua differs in important historical and political respects from its northern neighbors. El Salvador's gang problems stem in part from the deportation of Salvadoran gang members from Los Angeles and other cities on America's west coast, to which they had fled as migrants during El Salvador's war. Nicaragua never experienced this phenomenon, as wartime emigrants clustered in other locations, notably Miami, and were more successfully integrated within these communities.[63] Other factors, such as the legacy of the country's revolution, the relations between security forces and the local population, and even the far lighter population density in Nicaragua, are all relevant and make it difficult to generalize from this one case. To a large degree, Nicaragua's approach was possible because the gang problem was less pronounced to begin with. To attribute the absence of more sophisticated gangs to the approach is, to some degree, to reverse cause and effect.[64]

These contextual variables must be taken into account but do not invalidate the underlying principle. Haiti, too, has experimented with various 'Community Violence Reduction' (CVR) programs intended to 'stabilize communities in the short term by providing alternative means of income to at-risk youth while simultaneously improving community cohesion in the long term.'[65] As in Nicaragua, such efforts have been lauded for providing employment opportunities for community members as well as training in professional and practical skills.[66] Still, as Schuberth convincingly explains, in areas where the gangs rule supreme there are distinct dangers to a bottom-up approach. Participating organizations seeking to reach at-risk youth are in effect forced to choose between working with the gangs in these areas, even paying them off—with all the attendant strategic and ethical hazards—and bypassing them altogether and thereby missing the most urgent demographic.[67]

Middle paths through this dilemma are theoretically possible but difficult to navigate in practice. Furthermore, if conditions remain largely unchanged, and the gang therefore benefits from a fresh batch of recruits on a daily basis, measures to sway at-risk youth will necessarily tweak only the margins of the problem.[68] The sustainability of such programming is also in doubt as long as systematic incentive structures remain the same. As an example, just the matter of leaving the gang, in such contexts, raises serious risks, not least the real possibility of retaliation or life-long supervision and possible punishment for perceived transgressions.[69] It is in part for this reason that crime experts question the possible impact of violence-prevention initiatives within contexts of chronic insecurity.[70]

Though the repressive approach of *mano dura* clearly does not work, non-violent methods appear equally ineffectual in displacing entrenched gangs and their influence. As efforts to work with, or in parallel with, the gang in almost all contexts serve its interests, we return unavoidably to the need for some form of confrontation. To argue for the use of force has become a contentious undertaking, perhaps because so many states have woefully mismanaged their security operations against gangs. Amid the militarization of police in several of these cases, and the cynical use of repression despite full awareness of its strategic and ethical shortcomings, the suggestion that states use force in their counter-gang operations has become anathema—particularly in academic treatment of the topic and among advocacy organizations. Yet this is an unhelpful, if understandable, overreaction. As Timothy Donais and Geoff Burt note, though regrettable, it is 'also difficult to avoid the conclusion that robust enforcement operations may—at certain junctures—be necessary components ..., both as a means of combating impunity and as a way of creating conditions in which other kinds of violence-reduction programming can unfold.'[71]

It follows that, rather than debating whether the use of force should be part of efforts to counter urban insurgencies, the more relevant and difficult question is what type of force is needed and alongside what other efforts it must occur to be strategically meaningful. In answering these questions, much depends clearly on the permissiveness of the environment, or—to put it more plainly—whether the state is allowed to operate without armed resistance. The more impeded its access, the greater need there is—regrettably yet unavoidably—to establish a foothold by force, not primarily with a view to targeting the gang but rather to allowing new connections with the population it controls. Indian police director general K. P. S. Gill, though himself a contentious figure, is nonetheless right when he defends the use of such measures. He writes:

> The 'liberal' mind has always remained ambivalent when confronted by the fact that the State, among other things, is a coercive instrument, and that it must, from time to time, exercise its option of the use of force—albeit of judicious, narrowly defined and very specifically targeted use of force—if it is not to be overwhelmed by the greater violence of the enemies of freedom, democracy and lawful governance. To fail to exercise this legitimate coercive authority is, thus, not an act of non-

179

violence or of abnegation; it is not a measure of our humanity or civilisation. It is, rather, an intellectual failure and an abdication of responsibility that randomises violence, alienating it from the institutional constraints of the State, and allowing it to pass into the hands of those who exercise it without the discrimination and the limitations of law that govern its employment by the State. In doing this, it makes innocents the victims of criminal violence, instead of making criminals the targets of its own legitimate and circumspect punitive force.[72]

It is from this ambivalence regarding the use of force that we derive the traditional counterinsurgency principle of the 'minimum use of force'—or the imperative to apply only as much coercion as necessary to achieve strategic objectives. One manner of making this balancing act less prohibitive is to rely on proper intelligence, as illustrated by the case of MINUSTAH's counter-gang operations in Haiti. Its strategic performance was dramatically elevated with the creation of a Joint Mission Analysis Cell (JMAC) in late 2006. As an intelligence fusion center, the JMAC systematically collected both human intelligence (through tip-offs, clandestine outreach, and informants) and image intelligence (by aerial photography and satellite surveillance), which were then used to analyze gang patterns and vulnerabilities. As Cockayne explains, such intelligence allowed the mission to determine which gang members could be bought off and which had to be fought, how to distance the latter from their support base, and how best to structure the eventual armed offensive.[73] For one, it revealed the gang structure in Port-au-Prince to be 'heavily dependent on the personality and power of each gang leader,' prompting a concerted effort to target these figures (though in ways congruent with broader objectives).[74]

Largely owing to this intelligence-driven approach to operations, the eventual anti-gang efforts, in late 2006 and 2007, succeeded in pushing back the gangs, liberating territory for the local population, and allowing for the possibility of community-based initiatives. Walter Dorn notes how MINUSTAH 'transformed the Haitian slum of Cité Soleil from a foreboding place inaccessible to police for years to one in which the UN workers could safely walk [the] streets.'[75]

Polls taken in November 2007 suggested that '98 percent of Cité Soleil residents felt safer than they had six months earlier, and 85 percent reported that they could conduct their daily activities without fear of intimidation or extortion.'[76] The achievement is impressive and was sustained at least until the devastating earthquake in Haiti in 2010, which quite literally collapsed the state, cracking open its prisons, and quashing its capacity for justice, policing, and security. The fact that gangs have since returned may also stem, as Cockayne argues, from a lack of focus on the forces that generate the problem of criminality in Haiti, or the 'hidden powers that stand behind these groups'; for all the operational gains, the lack of such a focus means that 'the use of force may, ultimately, prove futile.'[77]

Rio's Unidades de Polícia Pacificadora (UPP) offers similar lessons on the use of force in counter-gang strategies (though here, too, enforcement suffered from a lack of follow-through). Launched in 2008, the UPP was meant to improve on the aggressive raids that had hitherto characterized the state's approach to gangs, not by jettisoning security operations altogether, but by incorporating them within a broader strategy. Indeed, in spite of its name (UPP translates as 'Pacifying Police Units'), the program was to be a whole-of-government effort unfolding across four phases: tactical intervention, stabilization, unit establishment, and evaluation and monitoring. Much as with clear-hold-build, the initial expression of the strategy would be familiar to any *favelado*: more security operations. In theory, however, clearing was meant to produce sustained public security, first through the specially trained UPP police and then through community policing involving the local community. In the final phase, social and public services were to be developed and the *favela* was to be integrated into the formal city.[78]

Where implemented, UPP showed initial signs of success. Homicides in 'pacified' areas were 10 percent those of other *favelas*.[79] Fatal police killings were reduced by more than 40 percent and, in around 60 percent of the territories where interventions occurred, murders, extortion, and burglaries all declined.[80] The gangs, specifically Comando Vermelho, could no longer operate freely or publicly carry weapons. An analysis of UPP after five years noted that residents generally felt safer, and had improved access to

181

education, health care, and public services, and that the gap between the pacified *favelas* and the city was being bridged.[81]

Much like the Haiti case, the UPP experience points to the potential of area and population security as precursors of governance, so long as the state is invested, can connect with the local community, and can generate social and political legitimacy. Much as in Haiti, however, it was also in this latter phase that UPP stumbled. First, when results looked promising, UPP expanded too quickly to other communities, thereby stretching resources and hampering implementation.[82] Cutting corners, or seeking to do more with less, invited violent counterattack and seriously undermined the intended psychological message.[83] Second, in many *favelas*, the UPP failed to engage with and empower the local community and therefore came to be resented as an illegitimate occupier.[84] Third, the UPP strategy did not gain the backing of the agencies and departments responsible for its implementation. Security forces struggled to transition from the mentality of short-term raids, and civilian agencies evinced reluctance or an inability to get involved in the strategy's later phases.[85] As the program cracked under pressure, violence increased, rupturing the emerging bonds between state and citizen and leading to a remilitarization of the response. For the gang, it was then easy to discredit the entire approach as 'more of the same.'[86]

Despite this flaw, the UPP experience provides helpful precedents in how to blend coercion with co-option. Similar lessons emerge from the far more concerted operations launched in spring 2008 against Moqtada al-Sadr's localized insurgency, both in Basra and in Sadr City. In Basra, Britain's mismanaged occupation had turned the city into a militia stronghold, resulting in violence, terror, and crime. The Iraqi Police Service was infiltrated, the local Iraqi Army was too weak to guarantee security, and the provincial council was corrupted by extremist elements. Unemployment soared while militias ruled with impunity. It was to redeem this situation that Iraq's prime minister launched Operation Charge of the Knights on March 25, 2008. US and UK assistance proved crucial in the early phase, with attack helicopters, unmanned aerial vehicles, air controllers, and intelligence assets helping to support Iraqi units against aggressive counterattacks. As security gains were made, the

Iraqi forces established joint security stations throughout the city to maintain control. Pockets of stability allowed the Iraqi Army to involve local residents in reconstruction and neighborhood patrols, thereby helping to address a drastic problem of unemployment and giving locals a stake in security. On March 31, Sadr agreed to a ceasefire. With the operation completed, a full 20,000 troops remained in Basra to patrol and return Iraq's only port to government control. Meanwhile, US and UK assistance allowed for the provision of essential services and infrastructure development to kickstart Basra's economy and boost investment. By 2009, estimates of unemployment had fallen from 70 to 17 percent.[87]

A similar trend can be seen in Sadr City. Earlier incursions into this Baghdad slum had been largely counterproductive, resulting in extensive collateral damage and a public outcry that Sadr and his Jaish al-Mahdi militia could exploit.[88] In contrast, the operation launched in spring 2008 had the more ambitious aim of reclaiming Sadr City and creating productive new links between its citizens and the state. Beginning on April 4, US and Iraqi forces fought their way into the slums and held their newly gained positions in spite of incessant attacks by the JAM militia. With the help of US military assets, Iraqi forces struck JAM leaders and weapons, while a hastily constructed wall denied the militia tactical movement and access to the population. On May 12, Sadr again declared a ceasefire. The Iraqi Army and national police forces were now providing security, while US units worked to ensure reconstruction and economic activity, thereby involving the local population in building a new normal.[89]

The Iraqi cases, and those in Rio and Haiti, underline the value of what some scholars have termed 'substitutive security governance.' This concept involves eliminating the functions provided by the urban insurgent—'the security they provide for their community, the income-generating role they play for their members, and the political function they fulfil for their sponsors'—and replacing these with a legitimate and competent state.[90] In all cases, however, it is this last effort where progress is the most elusive. In Iraq, the operations 'reduced JAM's military strength, removed a safe haven from the militia, and severely undermined both JAM's social control and its dominance in criminal markets.'[91] Yet progress has been less apparent in addressing the plight of the local population, reintegrating them and where they live, and building a more inclusive polity in order to reduce the risk of future conflict. Basra City fared well for some years but suffered because of the reallocation of resources once ISIS emerged as the bigger threat. Since then, corruption, government dysfunction, and criminality have again forced the city into a familiar trap, one between Iranian-sponsored militia and government neglect.[92] Meanwhile, in Sadr City conditions never truly improved.[93] Ironically, the continued neglect led Sadr City's inhabitants to vote for a somewhat reformed Sadr in the 2018 elections, giving him a surprise victory over his erstwhile rivals. It has also generated forceful protests against the government, leading to violent confrontation. These pressures, and the government's response, do not augur well for the future of the country.

In three ways, therefore, the armed approach to countering localized insurgency in Iraq, and also in Rio and Haiti, resembles Colombia's experience with the Democratic Security and Defense Policy. First, the *sine qua non* for action is achieving security for the civilian population and for those seeking to provide it with alternatives to the gangs, thereby allowing the restoration of a legitimate social and political contract between citizen and state. Second, this type of strategy is clearly demanding, requiring integration both horizontally (among different instruments of state) and vertically (between different levels of state and down to the local community). Such coordination and unified action are not feats that states typically handle very well, and yet the requirement for precisely such organization is common to virtually all 'success stories' throughout time and space.

Third, the final stretch of these operations consistently fails. To some degree, doing better on this front may be beyond the scope of counterinsurgency operations. One can argue that successful counterinsurgency will create a political process that precludes violence but will not necessarily see that process through to its distant conclusion.[94] And yet, to avoid precisely the type of fragmentation that localized insurgency exploits and entrenches, it becomes necessary for states to do more and go further: to unite their polities and address long-standing patterns of inequality and neglect. The task goes beyond simply declaring solidarity with the downtrodden; it calls upon states, and elites in particular, to consider their own role in fostering corruption, in benefiting from breakdown, and in perpetuating instability. Where these tasks are resisted, no amount of local stabilization or development is likely to make a difference—at least not in the long term.

This point, of course, forces us back to the original logic of localized insurgency, which prevails by operating precisely below the threshold where the state is galvanized to act. It is perhaps naive to hope for a concerted, resource- and time-intensive response in the face of what appears to be a 'manageable' or limited concern. Greater awareness of the adverse consequences of localized insurgency, whether in the city or in the countryside, along with closer study of promising past campaigns to replace illicit structures with legitimate governance, may provide both the impetus and the inspiration for how to do things differently. Either way, without the 'armed reform' that is intrinsic to counterinsurgency in its theory, the incentives for localized urban struggles—whether criminally or politically motivated—are likely to remain.

Conclusion

Localized insurgency thrives in places abandoned by the state. Countering localized insurgency therefore requires the state to go back on entrenched calculations of interest and extend itself in areas that have long been neglected. 'Political will' is an unsatisfying unit of analysis, as it is largely impossible to measure and difficult to define (at least in advance). Still, the notions of will and of interest go to the heart of countering localized insurgency, because these efforts survive by positioning themselves precisely below the threshold where the government is driven to act. The task of altering such conceptions of interest is daunting, yet the challenge is mitigated by fostering greater awareness of what inaction will yield and of what has shown promise in other settings.

This review of precedent leads to a second problem, namely the very few instances in which a government has, with success, reclaimed lost lands and peoples and unified the state. In urban as well as rural environments, even operations launched with the best intentions struggle with the most politically demanding aspect, namely the creation of a new social and political contract that is more inclusive and functioning than what came before. Clearing and holding are difficult enough; building brings sensitive political issues to the fore and requires the rewiring of entire societies. For this reason, in many of the countries confronting localized insurgency, the Weberian ideal of a sovereign state—one that controls both people and territory—remains abstract and largely unrealistic. How then to fuse the state and bring peoples together as part of a common and functioning political compact?

As this chapter demonstrates, there are creative ways to address this problem, by institutionalizing the informal political structures that can rule locally yet under the auspices of a central government. It is a response that accepts the inevitability of an absentee state, that empowers instead local mechanisms of control, but seeks to ensure that the latter respond to the non-negotiable values of the former. It will in all cases require a delicate discussion about what it is that defines a society, the norms that can and cannot be altered, and the importance of some form of common national identity despite variations in governance. Such variation also cannot be accepted as a good in itself, but must actively serve the people concerned, and enhance the legitimacy of their leaders and, in turn, the state compact of which they form part.

This requirement raises the central contradiction at the heart of this response: the state relinquishes control (a control it maybe never had) but will still need to insist on the conditions of local governance. As we have seen in the many contexts of criminal insurgency, simply ceding space to the most coercive and powerful actor—in this case, the gang—is not a sign of strategic ingenuity but merely the abdication of responsibility. The key, therefore, lies in balancing just how distant the state can be before it loses control and how it can productively exercise its authority to set the parameters for devolution. The mediated state may be a more realistic blueprint than the Weberian one, but state-building remains as complex and politically delicate as ever.

IN DEFENSE OF DEMOCRACY
COUNTERING INFILTRATIVE INSURGENCY

Insurgents using the infiltrative approach present themselves as a legitimate political party, even as a social movement, yet retain the use of violence and terrorism to clear the path and implement their agenda. Using seemingly legal means affords the group the protections given to other political parties, allowing it to hijack the state from within. While this veneer of respectability avoids the backlash that confronts starker expressions of power, it also renders any gains made more sustainable. Victory in infiltrative insurgency need not necessarily mean being elected to the head of government; mere participation in the state machinery can provide ample influence, key benefits, and the shield needed against repression. In short, this approach harnesses the advantages of extra-legal methods more typical of insurgency while also insisting on the benefits inherent in political participation. It is, in fact, within the mingling of these ways that the approach gains its potency.

This approach denotes evident risks. For an insurgent pursuing an unrestrained revolutionary project, operating in the open implies clear vulnerability to sanction, arrest, or worse. The only protection offered by the infiltrative approach is that the state will be incapable of moving against the group, either because it is unaware of its continued violence or because of the political costs of doing so. To cloak the project and build up defenses, it is of utmost importance that the group establish sufficient links above-ground. What is sought is a network of solidarity or a range of allies that will support and 'bear witness' to the legitimate aspects of the struggle, thereby enabling the sustained use of illicit means without fear of repression. Legitimation of this type requires abundant ambiguity and duplicity, so as to deny or downplay any link to violence. The onus is then on the state to establish not only the necessary legal evidence, but also the legitimacy, to assert itself and protect its institutions and constitution from subversion.

To be clear, infiltrative insurgency presents the state with severe ethical and strategic hazards. To respond to the Trojan horse of anti-democratic forces—those who seek to use the system only to destroy it—the government must engage in the delicate task of unraveling a conspiracy located within the central institutions of state. This is a territory where governments must tread carefully: much as insurgents have traditionally used a sympathetic civilian population as camouflage, the infiltrative variant uses democratic ideals and the openness of the party system to obscure its real method and intent. The challenge for the state is to distinguish, within a highly charged political terrain, between rival and adversary, between democratic competition and existential threat. It is also likely that any movement will encompass both sides of this spectrum all at once, compounding both assessment and response. Against this complexity, a historical review of past precedents reveals a range of options, but all require great care.

Taming the Beast with Kindness

When faced with an insurgent organization that elects to participate in the democratic competition, the initial and perhaps most intuitive response might well be to celebrate the shift and to anticipate further regularization of its struggle. Indeed, in political science as in the practice of peacebuilding, there is a broad consensus that a group's inclusion in the political system either represents or will at least cause its moderation. Moderation, in this respect, implies growing respect for other viewpoints and agendas (a moderation in ideology) and the renunciation of violence in attaining political ends (a moderation in behavior). Regardless of whether the group's involvement in democracy is entirely sincere from the outset, it should—according to this theory—be welcomed as a step in the right direction and as the likely precursor of more to come.

The 'inclusion-moderation' thesis, as it is termed, rests on three main pillars.[1] In the first place, it is assumed that groups resort to violence when peaceful channels for change have been exhausted or blocked.[2] Sociologists tend to argue that it is when the 'political opportunity structure' for peaceful change proves inadequate—when reform through the political system is perceived as unlikely—that social movement organizations take up arms and fight the state instead.[3] Some scholars take this argument a step further by arguing that democracies therefore face fewer risks of conflict, as their inclusivity and representativeness provide functioning alternatives to violence.[4] In contrast to authoritarian regimes, the openness of democratic systems may provide the opportunity for rebellion, but not the motivation, meaning a greatly reduced threat of rupture overall (in fully authoritarian regimes, the motivation may be there but the opportunity is lacking).[5]

This logic informs both the theory and practice of peacebuilding. A major emphasis is placed on liberalizing and improving the political system of war-torn states so as to create stronger and more representative democracies. In turn, such institutions will encourage and allow erstwhile enemies to hash it out in parliament rather than on the battlefield. In post-conflict environments, the sequence implied by 'DDR'—disarmament, demobilization, and reintegration—suggests precisely that a precondition and precursor for rejoining society is the laying down of arms, at which point there is a possibility of political reintegration and an attendant transition from war to peace. There is no shortage of examples to illustrate this point: insurgent movements demobilized, abandoned violence, and turned into political parties in Mozambique, Sierra Leone, South Africa, and Angola, in El Salvador, Uruguay, and Colombia—both with the M-19 and, more recently, with FARC. The underlying conditionality in these and other cases is that in return for moderating their ways and means, formerly armed groups evade state sanction and instead gain access to political openings and democratic opportunities for change.[6]

The second pillar points to the dynamics of institutionalization. The argument here is that the act of participating in electoral politics ensconces violent actors within new structures and methods that, over time, come to appropriate their entire project. Be it the acquisition of new skills for political campaigning, the adherence to at least some mainstream norms, greater awareness of how the system can generate change, the search for alliances and coalitions, the concomitant acceptance of compromise, or simply the growing familiarity with a 'political other,' the very medium of electoral participation is said to carry home the message of moderation.[7] To paraphrase Nietzsche, once you gaze long into the system, the system gazes also into you. Organizationally, power therefore shifts toward the more politically astute members of the movement—those who can compete within the democratic system—and radicals unable to adapt become an outdated liability to be marginalized.[8]

The institutional lens is often used to explain the evolution of the Provisional Irish Republican Army (PIRA). As we have seen in chapter 4, in the 1980s PIRA changed its position and opted to engage, via Sinn Féin, in party politics. The influence of this political front within the movement grew so that, by the Good Friday Agreement of 1998, it was the pragmatists rather than the hardliners that represented the organization. This shift led not only to a settlement that fell some distance short of PIRA's absolutist goals but also to sustained peace. The recommendation drawn from the case, as well as from Spain's engagement with Basque militancy, and from South Africa and Colombia, is that 'allowing insurgents to contest elections and offering them the opportunity to participate in the negotiation and decision-making process may result in a permanent cessation of violence.'[9] Adding some nuance, Lise Storm suggests that so long as the political environment is seen as functioning—that is, democracy works—it will come to moderate the behavior and agendas of participating 'post-rebel parties.'[10]

The third pillar of the 'inclusion-moderation' thesis concerns the moderating effects of societal dialogue. Once an armed group participates in democracy, it must engage with the electorate, which in a variety of ways will cause it to soften its methods and beliefs. For one, groups forced to hide underground in order to survive also cut themselves off from the moderating influences of broader society. Once fully encapsulated, the group is stuck within an ideological silo, or echo chamber, resulting in what Michel Wieviorka calls 'inversion,' or the process by which a 'political actor slides into terrorism as he drifts away from the social movement whose views he claims to be voicing.'[11] In contrast, proximity to one's constituents is said to have the reverse effect, introducing fresh perspectives, different avenues, and more productive ways of building political momentum.

As concerns the use of violence, for example, it seems largely intuitive that people generally abhor brutality and that groups seeking popular support will therefore be discouraged from engaging in such behavior.[12] This premise is supported by Lindsay Heger's assessment of 'bullets and ballots,' which indicates that groups looking for votes will downplay violence and terrorism, as bloodshed alienates mainstream audiences.[13] Similarly, Sara Polo has found that groups reliant on local support are far more restrained, whereas those with transnational sponsors evince less concern in their use of violence and targeting.[14] The underlying principle is that armed groups that want to succeed in elections, because these provide undeniable proof of political support of the type unavailable to clandestine actors, will, through their engagement with the electorate, be encouraged to moderate.

Clearly, there are sound reasons for promoting the political participation of armed actors, as it may reflect or at least encourage moderation, bringing forth a shift from violent to non-violent competition. And yet, there are significant dangers within this approach. Though there is no shortage of cases that support the inclusion-moderation thesis, it fails to explain why, in other cases, groups opt for inclusion and yet sustain their extremist or revolutionary agenda. In such circumstances, the gamble that the group can be tamed with kindness, or that the mere fact of inclusion will be moderating, can set the state up for veritable ambush, causing grave damage to the credibility and functioning of the democratic system. As we have discussed in chapter 4, there is good reason to expect these 'outliers' to become more common.

Indeed, infiltrative insurgency mounts a forceful challenge to the inclusion-moderation thesis, forcing a fresh look at each of its core pillars. First, there simply is no guarantee that providing democratic space to a militant armed group will persuade it that the use of arms, coercion, and terrorism is therefore no longer needed or desirable. Whereas participation in elections certainly provides a path to institutional power, it does not necessarily secure the achievement of strategic objectives. It is not just that democratic competition is challenging and can yield disappointing results, but rather that a group's agenda may require more drastic measures than those available through party politics. As Peter Neumann has argued, 'by definition, terrorism is about effecting radical political change, and it seems implausible that "access to the electoral arena" alone would persuade a terrorist group to abandon its military campaign.'[15]

What is plausible, however, is that an armed group may seek the advantages of participatory democracy without necessarily accepting its costs. Astute challengers understand that the institutions of state are themselves 'weapons' that can be added to their arsenal.[16] By establishing a legal front, a violent group can broadcast its ideology, undertake above-ground fundraising, negotiate as a legitimate actor, recruit others into the movement, and present itself as respectable and worthy of support. The broader objective is to institutionalize the movement to a point where its repression becomes impossible. None of these functions need imply moderation or even a basic acceptance of democratic principle. Much depends instead on the acumen of the group in proceeding along two seemingly contradictory yet also highly complementary paths all at once.

Second, whereas the process of institutionalization may itself be moderating, by imparting new skills and shifting the internal power balance of the group, much depends on the reasons why it decided to engage in party politics in the first place. If adherence to democratic principle is insincere, it seems wishful to think that the experience and perspective of the political wing will trump the ideological fervor of the real leadership. One should recall, from chapter 4, the repeated stress by insurgent leaders not to compromise on strategic matters and not to confuse means with ends. In such settings, rather than the system imparting norms of civility to the group, it may be the group that taints the system—and in very destabilizing and harmful ways. Short of actually subverting the entire state, as both Hitler and Lenin did, the mingling of violence with party politics may, more typically, set off an arms race among other political actors until party militias become the norm. As we have seen, it can also so politicize state institutions, not least its security forces and judiciary, that the very meaning of democracy is discredited, and more authoritarian or repressive alternatives swoop in to clean out.[17]

Similarly, as regards the organizational effects of prioritizing party politics, these are clearly unknowable without considering the broader hierarchy of the movement: the politicians sitting in parliament may still be distinctly subordinate to militant hardliners, serving as a legitimizing front while others run the show. Even in the case of Sinn Féin—typically the example invoked to make the case—its institutionalization and growth never altered the fact that it was PIRA's Army Council that decided on the strategic direction of the movement. Furthermore, as Neumann also points out, 'the leadership's ultimate priority was to avoid the fracturing of the movement, which meant that—whatever the precise numerical balance between "hawks" and "doves"—the concerns of the militarists needed to be addressed before any further move into the direction of constitutional politics could be implemented.'[18] While the group did of course soften its agenda and behavior throughout the late 1980s and 1990s, this related to shifts in leadership and strategy brought on by changing circumstances rather than a mere influx of new members.[19] To expect a similar shift in other contexts may therefore be wishful thinking.

Finally, as to the purported civilizing effects of public opinion, here too questions of context obtain. A public can grow to accept extremism and even violence depending on how, when, and why it is used.[20] Though many purely terroristic groups struggle to achieve a mass base, there are any number of insurgent movements that have attained thousands of adherents all while they maintained an armed wing and engaged in attacks—even against civilians. There are also several examples of violent actors doing well in democratic elections: witness the rise of Hitler's party in Nazi Germany, the success of Benito Mussolini's National Fascist Party in Italy, or the more recent cases of Sinn Féin during the 'Troubles' and of various militia-wielding parties in 'post-war' Iraq. Notwithstanding the exceptional circumstances at hand, the success of Hamas and Hezbollah as elected entities are but two prominent examples of precisely how well terrorism can mesh with party-political success. There simply is nothing inherent in democracy that would tame or pacify extremism within the body politic; it can instead arouse passions and divide society—particularly when elections near (as John Finn notes, 'on a fundamental level an election *is* conflict, albeit of a highly stylized sort').[21] Especially in a fractured states, elections tend to generate a centrifugal effect whereby competitors for key constituents engage in a bidding war for support; the ensuing polarization, it is suggested, can encourage and extend to the adoption of violence.[22]

It should also be recalled that infiltrative insurgency trades in ambiguity: it cloaks what it does underground, so as not only to prevent a backlash by the state but, plausibly, also to minimize potential censure from a resistant public. The deception is central to the approach and allows the group to project a simulacrum of innocence. This element is, however, lacking in the rational-actor-type thinking that the inclusion-moderation thesis uses to predict behavior. Though its implied causality appears intuitively correct, the model underestimates the advantages of gaming the system and expects—often as an article of faith—that any foul play will be temporary and quickly subside. Such assumptions may in several cases prove correct—but they require evidence and validation, not unquestioned acceptance.

Indeed, given the emphasis on duplicity, the first task in mustering a response to infiltrative insurgency is to demand more systematic assessment of the challenge at hand. It is, for example, crucial not to overstate the regulating effects of democracy or to accept inclusion as an end in itself. In some ways, democracy is far more vulnerable to infiltration than other forms of government: there is ample space for political organizations to form, freedom of speech allows for extensive propaganda, and there are stricter limits on state interference and oversight. As a defining criterion, democracy also encourages and accepts political challenge of the system—so long as political rivals play by the rules. This aspect of democracy can easily be corrupted; as Joseph Goebbels tauntingly put it, the best joke of democracy is 'that it gave its deadly enemies the means by which it was destroyed.'[23] In the light of this vulnerability, granting access to the innermost structures of the state cannot be done on the basis of inclusivity alone, or the promise of peace, or other lofty ideals, but must accord with legal standards and the demands of strategy.

First, integration should be conditions-based rather than unquestioningly embraced. Key questions may, for example, be asked regarding the nature of the group's aims, their attainability within the constitutional framework, the positioning of the party within the movement, and the relative importance of its hardline elements. The transition from armed actor to integrated party is also more likely where the group (1) demonstrates a high internal commitment to change, (2) is under institutional pressure to expand its sources of support, *and* (3) sees an 'opening' of the political opportunity structure that might allow for meaningful change to occur peacefully.[24] Ideally all three of these conditions should be in place; picking and choosing among them will increase the likelihood of false diagnosis and of a failed integration process.

Critics will charge that these conditions present the ideal scenario, and that integration should not be written off as a policy option for what may be more ambiguous, but will certainly be more likely, circumstances. Indeed, as some peacebuilding practitioners have argued, even when there is doubt as to a group's sincerity and agenda, there can be reasons for welcoming its creation of a political wing and democratic participation. In mediating an end to the Troubles in Northern Ireland, for example, former US senator George Mitchell and others were unsure of the exact links between PIRA and Sinn Féin yet found it pragmatic to leave the matter unknown rather than insist on clarity. At worst, even if Sinn Féin was just a PIRA puppet, 'if peace was to be achieved, the negotiations had to include the groups involved in making war.'[25] In such a case, negotiations allowed for continued engagement with an unreformed violent terrorist organization, thereby sustaining channels of communication that might yield opportunities over time.[26] In the interim, the Mitchell Principles, or the conditions underpinning the talks, would insist on a commitment to non-violence, which could be used to shape PIRA's decision-making and punish it for transgressions.

A similar level of pragmatism is often seen in the implementation of DDR programs, resulting in the reintegration and normalization of armed groups even without their full disarmament. Astute observers of this process note, for instance, that there is 'no automatic or inherent relationship between the process of disarmament and the creation of a secure environment'; on the contrary, insisting on full disarmament when the group still feels unsafe is likely to be destabilizing and squander opportunities for peace. Thus, rather than being approached sequentially, DDR must form 'part of a broader political process that seeks to reconcile conflicting parties and enhance security by an admixture of confidence-building means.'[27] That process, in turn, presupposes engagement, even when initial signs of moderation are mixed, as it opens channels of communication through which to reach an eventual outcome. Though such a gamble necessarily raises thorny ethical and strategic challenges, it is also the actors most capable of coercion and predation that are most likely to upset a peace that does not take account of their interests.

If this pragmatic path is to be taken, the key lies in balancing accommodation with the deeper ideals of the state, neither neglecting the need for expedience nor allowing it to undermine the 'peace' being built. This is a tough balancing act. To take the example of Tajikistan, Stina Torjesen and Neil MacFarlane note that the political reintegration process following the war in that country might well have 'worked precisely because it did *not* follow a liberal democratic script.'[28] Indeed, this was a process that set aside any attempt at disarmament, overlooked transitional justice issues, and offered instead comprehensive amnesties, positions in government, and even economic assets to ex-fighters and ex-commanders. Though this approach did create 'a number of important goods for Tajikistan in the immediate years after the war'—principally an absence of post-war conflict and the survival of a Tajik state— the expedience may well have come at a heavy long-term price: repressive authoritarianism, corruption, and what Steve Swerdlow describes as 'a full-blown human rights crisis.'[29]

The case of Tajikistan therefore points us back to the dilemmas of how to engage politically with murky violent actors whose intent is difficult to ascertain. The ideal conditions may never materialize and there may be reasons to compromise on standards to allow for longer-term progress. Yet, as Torjesen and MacFarlane ask, 'is there a breaking point when an "over-facilitation" of former combatants' interests will jeopardise the overall economic wellbeing of a country and perpetuate cycles of underdevelopment, grievance and insecurity?'[30] When can the inclusion and integration of an illicit actor help encourage reconciliation and longer-term stability, and when does it set up the state for a subversive or even violent takeover? The only definitive conclusion that can be made, simple yet seemingly necessary, is to approach with caution, to trust but verify, and to understand the risks involved even in the embrace of 'peace.'

Tolerance and Intolerance

If inclusivity can bring a violent challenger to bay, it may also expose the central nervous system of a democratic society to irreversible harm. It is for this reason that many practitioners and analysts of these tumultuous processes opt for restricting access to the political system and shutting down the democratic avenues of illicit or revolutionary actors, even when they evince peaceful intent or may plausibly moderate in return for participation. This approach may seem simpler and safer than the perilous path of political reintegration, and yet it raises its own sets of challenges and dilemmas, relating predominantly to the democratic bona fides of the state.

Specifically, in the state's efforts to repress those who may harm the system, key questions must be asked about what constitutes illegitimate political discourse and behavior. A code of conduct seems necessary to ensure the political playing field remains open to those willing to compete according to the parameters at hand but closed to those seeking to exploit inclusivity for subversive ends. Problematically, when this code is promulgated by political forces, it can too easily become a tool to restrict the democratic options of legitimate, yet disliked, political competitors. Even in the best of circumstances, which should not be assumed to apply, gaining consensus on who meets what criteria is also likely to be divisive. Indeed, the question opens a strategic and an ethical minefield: the balance between, on the one hand, the purpose of democracy as an inclusive system and, on the other, the limits that must be placed on this very system in order for it to survive.

The dilemma is age-old and was given prominence through the writing of the political philosopher Karl Popper. As a left-leaning Jew growing up in 1920s' Vienna, Popper was concerned with the fascist exploitation of democracy to subvert the system, incite persecution, and set up a dictatorship. In *The Open Society and Its Enemies*, published in 1945, Popper lays out the 'paradox of tolerance' that confronts democratic states when threatened by anti-democratic parties such as these. The treatment of the paradox is limited to a footnote (probably the most quoted footnote of all time), but it articulates compellingly the prerogative of a state to decide what its people may democratically support. He writes:

> unlimited tolerance must lead to the disappearance of tolerance. If we extend unlimited tolerance even to those who are intolerant, if we are not prepared to defend a tolerant society against the onslaught of the intolerant, then the tolerant will be destroyed, and tolerance with them.—In this formulation, I do not imply, for instance, that we should always suppress the utterance of intolerant philosophies; as long as we can counter them by rational argument and keep them in check by public opinion, suppression would certainly be most unwise. But we should claim the *right* to suppress them if necessary even by force; for it may easily turn out that they are not prepared to meet us on the level of rational argument, but begin by denouncing all argument; they may forbid their followers to listen to rational argument, because it is deceptive, and teach them to answer arguments by the use of their fists or pistols. We should therefore claim, in the name of tolerance, the right not to tolerate the intolerant. We should claim that any movement preaching intolerance places itself outside the law, and we should consider incitement to intolerance and persecution as criminal, in the same way as we should consider incitement to murder, or to kidnapping, or to the revival of the slave trade, as criminal.[31]

Samuel Issacharoff summarizes Popper's point well: 'the ability of extremism to find its way into the protective crevices of a liberal democratic order requires anticipatory defenses to resist capture—in one form or another—by antidemocratic forces.'[32] It is a contentious argument, one made more contentious yet by the range of anticipatory measures that states can take and have taken ostensibly for the sake of self-protection. Once it is handed these powers and authorities, it is not difficult to imagine circumstances where the cure for extremism appears worse than the disease.

Still, the abuse of democratic intolerance does not necessarily invalidate its occasional use; witness the naivety and helplessness of the Weimar Republic when faced with Hitler's 'legal revolution,' leading to authoritarian domination.[33] Instead, the rise of infiltrative insurgency requires further study as to how best, and with what safeguards, an inherently open democratic system can nonetheless close off certain actors and still serve the ideals for which such action is taken. In resolving this conundrum, context rules supreme and generalizations are difficult. Still, there is sufficient insight in the historical record to start a discussion. Specifically, it is worth considering three key ways by which states have attempted to resolve the Popperian dilemma: through coercion, ostracism, and proscription.

Coercion

When Popper sets out the rights that a democratic state should reserve for itself to protect against hostile takeover, he refers explicitly to the possibility of suppression 'by force.' Indeed, this is probably the most common—or at least the most visible—manner whereby states seek to expunge political forces that are said to threaten its constitution and stability. It is, however, the most contentious approach, as it hands tremendous power—over life and death, even—to the ruling party and violently short-circuits the open competition of ideas that is meant to define democracy.

Witness the fate of the Unión Patriótica (UP) in Colombia, the political party created in 1985 by FARC and the Colombian Communist Party. As we have seen in chapter 4, the UP was a major

199

initiative within FARC's strategy of *combinación de todas las formas de lucha*, whereby it sought to combine violence and subversion with above-ground political mobilization. Created during a ceasefire with the Colombian government, UP allowed FARC to communicate directly with the people, both as part of the continued peace talks and as a political party seeking to engage the electorate. On this latter front, its gains were modest but significant. In the 1986 general elections, it received only 1.4 percent of the vote, though this was enough to claim seats at both the national and local levels. In March 1988, UP was the fourth most prominent party, gaining 14 out of 1,008 mayoralties; these were anyway FARC strongholds, but areas where it could now exert formal control.[34]

There are doubts as to FARC's influence and power over UP or how closely all UP leaders followed FARC's line. Nevertheless, the gradual rise of the party in the late 1980s made it a concern to FARC's many enemies. Because they perceived UP as an outgrowth of FARC, and because UP was also an easier target than the guerrilla group, it became the victim of a protracted dirty war. Within a six-year period, paramilitaries and drug cartels, at times working closely with sections of the military and police, eliminated thousands of UP's members.[35] Though newcomers initially kept joining the movement, as the repression continued and more senior leaders of the party were killed, so its ability to sustain itself declined. Amid an exodus of members and FARC's eventual abandonment of the party, it limped on for a bit but then died. As its party president put it, 'No one wants to join a party whose leaders are still getting assassinated.'[36]

UP was successfully repressed, but at what cost? The popular charge of a 'political genocide' may not pass legal muster, but it does speak to the scale of death, terror, and bloodshed. Nor were the many violent actions and disappearances targeting the UP investigated, thereby contributing to a climate of impunity that would haunt Colombia for years to come—as would the accusations of collusion between the military and the paramilitaries. As concerns FARC, the repression of the UP may have undermined its *combinación* strategy, yet the insurgent group clearly did not suffer unduly from the systematic elimination of its political front. On the contrary, Steven Dudley suggests that FARC saw benefit in the repression, in that it delegitimized the state (at the very least among the political left), showcased the impossibility of change through the system, and therefore entrenched and, to some degree, ennobled FARC's violent resistance. In his memoir, even Carlos Castaño—later Colombia's most notorious paramilitary leader—seems to acknowledge that had the UP been handled differently, perhaps it might have splintered the extreme left and weakened its ideological hard core.[37]

Although there are few positive lessons to be drawn from the elimination of UP, there are more strategically sound and ethically responsible ways in which repression could be undertaken to resolve Popper's dilemma of democratic intolerance. Specifically, by narrowly pursuing the component of the organization that is violating the rules, rather than the licit component that may be closer to hand, it is possible to channel group behavior as a whole toward greater institutionalization. Ironically, the key example here is PIRA—commonly the poster child for the inclusion-moderation theory. Indeed, as Neumann and others have argued, a forceful driver of its moderation was not so much the fact of inclusion as the complete penetration of its militant cadres by British intelligence, making it extremely difficult to sustain the armed struggle even if PIRA's Army Council had wanted to.[38]

Throughout the 1980s, the British government launched a sophisticated and multipronged assault on all PIRA operations. One important aspect was the availability and better exploitation of intelligence, through the introduction of high-powered aerial and miniature cameras, sensors, advanced computers for data management and sharing, jamming devices to prevent explosions, and infrared surveillance and thermal imaging to detect command-wire bombs and arms caches.[39] In parallel, the use of informants increased both in scale and in value, given the maturation of intelligence assets into positions of real responsibility within PIRA ranks.[40] As evidence was amassed, changes in legal rules brought on by the 1972 Diplock Commission—specifically as they related to the admissibility of evidence collected during interrogations and the shift away from jury trials—also made it far easier to prosecute PIRA militants. In combination, these efforts forced PIRA to adopt a more dispersed, cellular structure, and—concomitantly—the size of the organization fell from 1,000 members in the mid-1970s to about 250 one decade later. The group found itself incapable of imposing costs on British security forces in Northern Ireland, and the later shift to softer targets on the UK mainland did not help, given the outrage provoked by the high number of civilian casualties thus caused.[41]

These trends had two complementary effects: they revealed the diminishing returns of PIRA's military operations, and they encouraged the shift toward a political path, so as to perhaps achieve change or at least restore the group's links with the local population. In terms of solving the Popperian dilemma, therefore, repression succeeded, in that it extirpated behavior that could not be tolerated and channeled the group toward peaceful participation in the democratic system. The key to the success lay in accurate targeting so as to squeeze the militant hard core while encouraging the further growth of Sinn Féin. Another equally important factor was that repression proceeded discreetly and discriminately, making deft use of intelligence in order to rupture the group's military activities without imposing on the surrounding population (notwithstanding legitimate concerns about civil liberties in the midst of mass surveillance). In this manner, the case does illustrate that in exercising democratic intolerance, coercion can still play a helpful role.

Ostracism

A precondition for the approach used in Northern Ireland was increased British knowledge of PIRA's militant activities and whereabouts, producing targets that could be exploited so as to channel the behavior of the movement as a whole. This precondition—a clear set of targets—is not a common feature in infiltrative insurgency. Instead, as we have seen, the group usually tries hard to disguise its use of violence. Another precondition in Northern Ireland was a state of sufficient capacity to penetrate the entire militant organization; this, too, is not a common feature in counterinsurgency settings. Third, the PIRA case features a national actor involved in constituent but dissimilar subnational spaces, providing distance between the insurgent's infiltration and the government responsible for countering it. In most cases, the state responding to infiltration is also the one being infiltrated— 'the "enemy" is not only *ante portas* (at the gates) ... they are also *intra moenia*, that is, inside the citadel of democratic political institutions.'[42] This set-up significantly restricts a government's practical options.

As a result, there may only be limited cases in which one might hope to replicate Britain's success. Still, this does not mean that the channeling of behavior seen in Northern Ireland cannot be achieved by other means, namely through the political and social isolation of the offending party. In contrast to the ingratiating logic of the 'inclusion-moderation' thesis, this approach seeks to moderate through exclusion. In plain terms, instead of the group being welcomed into the system in exchange for it adapting to its constraints, the intent is to punish the extremist element through ostracism with a view to encouraging moderation. Much like the repressive route, the 'exclusion-moderation' thesis is grounded in clearly declared intolerance, but it is of a non-violent sort and, as such, less technically demanding and less likely to rupture the very democracy it seeks to defend.[43] Collective ostracism also relies on establishing a common front based on shared underlying norms, which are if anything reinforced by this banding together of political parties against the transgressor in their midst. The offending party is, in a sense, placed in 'moral quarantine,' which at once protects and enhances democracy.[44]

Ostracism does not break the rules of democracy to save it but instead relies upon the system to self-regulate in the face of extremist challenges. In his first inaugural address as president, Thomas Jefferson put it this way: 'If there be any among us who wish to dissolve this union, or to change its republican form, let them stand undisturbed, as monuments of the safety with which error of opinion may be tolerated where reason is left free to combat it.'[45] In other words, Jefferson asked that those seeking to undo the political union he himself had helped to create be allowed to compete fairly, so that their ideas might also be fairly discredited within democracy's marketplace of ideas. Rather than the state's iron fist, it would be the invisible hand of reason that protects threatened democracies, and—in so doing—reinforces and further defines their common values.

This approach finds extensive precedent. Indeed, going back in history, Giovanni Capoccia suggests that many of the democracies of the interwar period that survived the assault by anti-democratic political forces were precisely those whose main parties agreed to isolate the extremist adversary before it could seize power. Capoccia notes that in the cases of Finland, Austria, and Czechoslovakia—and in contrast to Germany and Italy—infiltration was thwarted through the admixture of three factors: (1) proper recognition of the democratic challenger as fundamentally anti-democratic, (2) the maintenance of a common front against this threat, and—from then on—(3) a combination of accommodative and coercive techniques to splinter it and complicate its activities.[46]

If one puts to one side the *sine qua non* of proper assessment, the crucial component appears to be the creation of stable political coalitions in the face of an anti-democratic threat. In Germany, Italy, and other cases, the infiltrative strategy worked best where it could tempt groupings in society and within government to strike deals or attempt conciliation through power-sharing. A steadfast consensus closes the entry points for such a strategy. Regrettably, however, splintering of the consensus appears to be a common and logical product of electoral competition, in which ideologically proximate parties seek to "ride the tiger" in search of narrow political gains. Indeed, as Capoccia cautions, 'for the sake of the survival of the system, the whole front will have to support strategies that will, in the end, favor one constituent party more than the others—which, again, goes against a purely partisan logic.'[47] The outcome is typical; its avoidance requires mobilization toward higher ideals and purpose, even at the risk of short-term costs.

Civil society can play an indispensable role in compensating for the parochialism and occasional pettiness of party politics. If we look again at Golden Dawn, the fascist party in Greece, it took concerted mobilization by civil society organizations—and of society as a whole—to compel the Greek government finally to act against this deeply anti-democratic and violent party. Daniel Trilling demonstrates how, because of some latent tolerance of racism within

Greek society, possible sympathy among the security forces, and the role that it played as a foil to other democratic parties, Golden Dawn was able to grow roots and thrive—all in spite of its violence and fascist ideology.[48] It took the paroxysm of anger following the killing of Pavlos Fyssas, the Greek musician, by a Golden Dawn member to spur action. Major protests erupted throughout Greece, and also across Europe, and all Greek government parties (even Golden Dawn) felt compelled to condemn the murder. The momentum led to a five-year trial and the conviction of Golden Dawn's leadership for heading a criminal organization, a verdict that destroyed the party. Still, the outcome did not come easily. As Trilling concludes, 'without the human rights activists and investigative journalists who painstakingly documented racist violence, the anti-fascist activists who organised mass protests, the volunteer legal teams who brought private prosecutions, and the victims and witnesses who gave evidence in court, this verdict would not have been reached.'[49]

The central role of civil society is underlined in other relevant cases. Francesco Cavatorta and Fabio Merone argue that, in Tunisia, the Islamist Ennahda party moderated its ideology and action in part because of the 'strong rejection' it faced across 'large sectors of Tunisian society,' turning an anti-democratic, illiberal, and occasionally violent actor into a peaceful contender within Tunisia's post-Arab Spring democracy.[50] In the Netherlands, as Joost van Spanje and Wouter van der Brug argue, it was the strong response by anti-fascist groupings that compelled the country's political parties to boycott and denounce the Centre Party, an extreme right-wing body, following its win of a single parliamentary seat in 1982. The CP declared bankruptcy only four years thereafter.

Although civil society mobilization clearly has potential in isolating an anti-democratic party, resulting in it either changing its ideology or being isolated, when these anti-democratic parties are armed—as is the case with infiltrative insurgency—it is precisely the ability to mobilize openly and to resist that they will target. As we have seen in Nepal, as well as in the other cases of infiltration considered in chapter 4, violence and intimidation are used to shut down dissent, to target independent journalism, and to attack social criticism. In such contexts, relying on civil society to do what is right, to protect the state against itself, is to invite substantial risk. As we saw with the moderation-inclusion thesis, there is also no guarantee that 'civil society' will evince much interest in democratic principle or in opposing the populist forces seeking to take over.[51] Even in Greece, Golden Dawn for long managed to evade societal censure and, in a different context, might have operated with more discipline or entrenched itself more fully to survive the backlash whenever it might arrive.

In other words, ostracism may work best when the state and society are strong and the threat relatively weak, which is also when the strategy is least needed. In cases where the entity to be isolated is nonetheless able to establish a foothold in government, it greatly increases the political costs of excluding it and risks breaking the coherence of any government-wide response down the line.[52] Given these risks, a more aggressive tack is often considered, allowing the state to move more decisively and more pre-emptively against anti-democratic forces, yet without incurring the risks and abuse related to violent repression. This compromise—between constitutionalism and armed confrontation—is found in the process of party proscription.

Proscription

Short of violently repressing an anti-democratic threat, proscription of a party is the most forceful and definitive way of making it go away. The practice is far from uncommon and also has long historical roots. Following the American Civil War, the US constitution was amended for a fourteenth time to bar from political office those who had previously engaged in insurrection or rebellion against the US government. Following the Second World War, Germany introduced and then twice used the legal right to proscribe Nazi and communist parties, seeking in this manner to avoid the fate suffered by the Weimar Republic. Italy, too, banned a post-war fascist party from participating in its democracy. Given their past, Ukraine and other former Soviet-controlled countries in Eastern Europe have similarly banned communist parties from competing electorally. In 1988, and again in 1992, Israel banned the Kach movement on the basis of its anti-Arab agitation and racism. In 2003, the Spanish government proscribed the Herri Batasuna party as the political front of the ETA terrorist organization. Turkey barred the Kurdistan Workers' Party, or PKK, and the Czech Republic the far-right Workers' Party. According to one compilation, there were a full 46 cases of party proscription in Europe alone between 1945 and 2015.[53]

In implementing what is sometimes called 'militant democracy,' or 'intolerant democracy,' each state draws its own line.[54] Some present the limits of tolerance within their constitution, others approach the matter through statutory means. Some bar parties of a particular ideological persuasion, others focus on their potentially violent or secessionist agendas, and others yet distinguish between banning electoral participation and existence *tout court*. Regardless of formulation, party proscription remains highly contentious. By denying some parties the right to engage in what is intended to be a participatory system, and by denying voters the right to vote for their own political preferences, proscription appears to limit both the scope and quality of democracy. As one critic notes, if the state removes options from the electorate in the name of higher ideals that the electorate itself was not involved in crafting, 'there had better be a more compelling argument for democracy than that it enables the people to choose.'[55]

Political philosophy acknowledges the contentiousness of the practice yet tends to provide it with a qualified defense. Popper— as we have seen—came down squarely on the need for democratic intolerance, though only in the limited context of groups that refuse 'to meet us on the level of rational argument ... forbid their followers to listen to rational argument ... and teach them to answer arguments by the use of their fists or pistols.'[56] In similar terms, though he recognizes the scope for abuse, Michael Walzer nonetheless finds that excluding programmatically anti-democratic actors is not about being intolerant to difference; rather, 'it is merely prudent.'[57] John Rawls wrestles long and hard with the ambivalence of democratic intolerance and concludes almost reluctantly that 'the limitation of liberty is justified' though 'only when it is necessary for liberty itself, to prevent an invasion of freedom that would be still worse.'[58]

The hesitation of these philosophers is understandable because, while eminently arguable in theory, the practical implications of party proscription are often less clear. Quite simply, 'claims of insurrectionary ambitions easily turn into a pretext for enabling a "lockup" of the political process—a scenario in which incumbents entrench and immunize themselves against electoral challenges.'[59] In Egypt following the Arab Spring, for example, the swift oscillation between incumbent parties led to a flurry of attempted and actual bans that shot massive holes through the fabric of that country's burgeoning democracy.[60] Even where a major threat is truly imminent, proscription can still be damaging in its implications, as when during the interwar period several European states reacted to the creeping infiltration of communists or fascists by short-circuiting the democratic system and imposing outright autocracy.[61] Here, too, the cure can easily become worse than the disease, as when the banning of other parties leads to a one-party state, for example in Tanzania, Kenya, and Cameroon during the Cold War and in China, Vietnam, and Cuba to this day.

As Walzer argues, separating the proper use of democratic intolerance from its abuse presupposes a responsible distinction, namely 'that of politics itself from the state.'[62] In theory, political parties compete for power and decision-making authority, yet the state exists on a more fundamental plane and exerts a force of continuity on both polity and society, regardless of the governing party. Democracy, therefore, does not yield absolute power even to the winner of popular elections and means more than simply 'one man, one vote.' At a most basic level, this 'thin definition of democracy' belies a 'background set of rules, institutions and definitions of eligible citizenship' that circumscribe the notion of a truly popular choice.[63] More fundamentally, even developed democracies have permanent and even unalterable clauses within their constitutions to safeguard the basic structure of the democratic system.[64] This structure necessarily limits what the majority party can do at any given point, not least because it has to protect the mechanisms by which it might itself become the minority. Democracy implies freedom to choose, but always within certain limits.

Granting the state the power to ban parties outright extends the remit of this underlying entity. Still, Issacharoff presents an intriguing analogy that helps explain and defend the state's power in these circumstances. Comparing it to a market, he proposes that 'it does not seem too fanciful a notion to imagine that even the night watchman state has an obligation to maintain the openness of the instrumentalities of political competition in much the same way as the state must protect the integrity of economic markets from theft, fraud, and anticompetitive behavior.'[65] The state, therefore, becomes the 'guardian of the vitality of the democratic process as a whole.'[66] It should be noted, however, that it is the state that assumes this role, though—unavoidably—it typically acts through the political party that inhabits its government at any given time. This awkward compromise is, it would seem, the source of potential abuse.[67]

Attempts have been made to diminish the scope for such abuse. A fundamental dilemma concerns whether to use the hostile intent or hostile acts of the offending party as the criterion for exclusion. Unsurprisingly, as in any courtroom, it is far less controversial, and far more definitive, to judge an actor on the basis of its behavior rather than its intent. The same principle appears to hold true in the case of party proscription, not least when the behavior involves the use of force or the threat thereof. After all, where society operates by a credible system of peaceful political change, there should be no need or excuse for the use of coercion to tip the scales. This logic informs the US Supreme Court's distinction between protected anti-democratic speech and unprotected incitement or involvement in anti-democratic action, with the latter leading to potential proscription.[68]

Infiltrative insurgency is defined by its prosecution of violence—this is what separates it from the also problematic but distinct problem of radical parties and extremist social movements. Given this definitional point, the focus on violent deeds seems like a promising method for the state to protect itself, as it limits proscription specifically to insurgent actors and thereby militates against abuse. And yet, difficulties immediately surface. First, we return, inescapably, to the tendency for subterfuge within the infiltrative strategy—there precisely because of the obvious vulnerability that comes with being associated with violence. It is the commission of violence that facilitates government sanction and so it is this exact feature that must be camouflaged or denied. This duplicity, at the very core of the program, will complicate the state's efforts to bar the party on these legal grounds—at the very least, such an effort will require a more concerted effort, more time, and more political will on the part of the state.

Second, the use of actions as the grounds for proscription raises the question of imminence—or how close the anti-democratic threat is to seizing power. It is worth recalling the perceptive way General Valery Vasilyevich Gerasimov frames the use of violence in political warfare: 'The open use of forces,' he notes, 'is resorted to only at a certain stage, primarily for the achievement of final success in the conflict.'[69] The implication for infiltrative insurgency—also a form of political warfare—is clear. As the use of force grows starker, it becomes easier to justify proscription but also more difficult for the state to carry through on it. The more readily such violence can be connected incontrovertibly to the group, the more vulnerable the state will be to irreversible incapacitation. Conversely, the further away from this apogee, the more likely it will be 'that civil disorder and insurrection themselves can never be distinguished from lesser breaches of the peace by any precise line.'[70]

Third, where the violent acts are committed by actors that have already to some degree infiltrated the government, the process of accountability will be subverted by their power and influence over the very authority required to act. The case of 'post-war' Iraq is relevant, in that the sectarian parties involved in violence were already well represented within government and therefore proved very difficult to remove. Even as prime minister, Nouri al-Maliki found himself constitutionally incapable of moving against the sectarian and militia-wielding parties, as doing so would require the buy-in of ministers—and these ministers were loyal to the parties that they represented and that had appointed them. Politically, meanwhile, Maliki's own fortunes were dependent on the United Iraqi Alliance (UIA) coalition, which comprised SCIRI as well as Sadr. 'Efforts to go after these groups risked defection, a threat the Sadrists carried out twice over the course of 2006–7 with devastating impact on the capacity to govern.'[71] Even when violence escalated sharply, the state had precious few options left.

As Carl Friedrich argues, a party's engagement in violence— although 'relatively objective'—may indeed be an 'insufficient criterion for determining the propriety of emergency action in cases of this sort.'[72] To Gregory Fox and Georg Nolte, the result of using violence as the threshold—as the Rubicon that cannot be crossed— is that 'democratic parties, in essence, become the unfair victims of a process dedicated to fairness—a process they themselves seek to preserve until the end.'[73] Instead, what is needed is some anticipatory rather than retroactive protection against anti-democratic threats. Such anticipatory defense makes proscription all the more contentious and open to abuse, yet it may also be necessary for protection to be effective. Alexander Kirshner expresses the dilemma well: he acknowledges that although 'preventive party bans or preventive interventions of any sort are democratically illegitimate ... it may be democratic for individuals to take illegitimate action, just as it may be democratic to act without a democratic imprimatur when rebelling against authoritarian regimes.'[74]

On this precarious basis, anticipatory self-defense lowers the evidentiary threshold from matters concerned narrowly with acts (which must necessarily be addressed retroactively) to matters relating to intent (which can be judged pre-emptively). Despite the increased scope for abuse, this is not an uncommon standard. The European Court of Human Rights (EHCR), hardly an authoritarian institution, centers its criteria for banning parties on their promotion of violence, which 'may involve both explicit calls for violence or ambiguity about the appropriateness of violence for achieving political ends.'[75] Neither of these amounts to the commission of violent acts. Following a similar logic, and bearing the scars from Weimar's collapse, German constitutional law declares as 'unconstitutional' parties that 'by reason of their aims or the behaviour of their adherents, seek to undermine or abolish the free democratic basic order or to endanger the existence of the Federal Republic.'[76] Also, Czech law demands that parties not only commit themselves to democratic principles but actively 'renounce force as a means of promoting their interests.'[77]

Again, this criterion is some way removed from actual involvement in violence.

The principle at play here, as phrased by the ECHR, is that a 'state cannot be required to wait, before intervening, until a political party has seized power and begun to take concrete steps to implement a policy incompatible with the standards of the Convention and democracy.'[78] Still, in having broadened the criteria for proscription, the next few questions must necessarily concern how far this can and should be stretched. The danger of going too far is that the state effectively criminalizes speech and ideology in the name of pre-emptive government self-protection, causing fatal harm to the democratic system. It is for this reason that Kirshner suggests 'defensive practices should be used as often as necessary, but as infrequently as possible,' so that the state avoids 'the Scylla of Weimar' without steering into 'the Charybdis of McCarthyism.'[79]

The onus, then, is on establishing guidelines. The European Court of Human Rights sets out three conditions for anticipatory proscription: (1) it must accord with the state's existing law, (2) it must serve a legitimate aim, and (3) it must be actually 'necessary in a democratic society.'[80] Focusing more narrowly on the offending party, Fox and Nolte suggest that pre-emptive proscription of a group can be justified on the basis of '(1) its members holding anti-democratic beliefs, *and* (2) a manifest intent to act on those beliefs through the vehicle of the party.'[81] In similar terms, Friedrich asks three questions: 'How great is the insurrectionary intent of the people who have yet to engage in insurrectionary action? (2) What is the probability that this intent will be translated into action? (3) Will the action constitute a serious threat to the maintenance of public order?' As he adds, however, 'To answer such questions correctly is no easy matter.'[82]

Indeed, when distilling these conditions into three pillars and considering them in turn—the intent of the party, the imminence of the danger, and the legitimacy of the state's response—difficulties immediately appear. On the question of intent, many states effectively ringfence certain core ideals of the state (such as constitutional design, territorial integrity, or the commitment to democracy) so that they cannot be challenged, regardless of the method used. Still, this approach relies on the group's intent being fairly unambiguous. As Fox and Nolte argue, 'Few parties will call for an outright end to future elections. Others may adopt the rhetoric of committed democrats as a tactical device.'[83] Indeed, much as with their use of violence, infiltrative insurgents will also calibrate their rhetoric so as to allow for continued participation in the very mechanisms of state they seek to subvert. Thus, as Issacharoff explains, 'the effort to define with precision the exact ideas or advocacy that should be proscribed is unlikely to be fruitful. If advocating overthrow is prohibited, then it is easy to advocate for resistance—and if that too is banned, then the language of choice might be freedom.'[84] The issue is further compounded by the possibility of these disparate causes coexisting within one movement aimed collectively at some form of fundamental reform yet on vastly different scales.

On the imminence of the threat, this criterion forces us back to the availability of irrefutable evidence. We have already discussed how engagement in violence provides too little warning for self-protection; so what then is the appropriate indication of a threat being imminent? One common metric concerns the electoral fortunes of the offending party, with more votes and more seats denoting a greater threat and a greater justification for action. For example, even though the German state determined in 2017 that the National Democratic Party was unconstitutional given its intent 'to replace the existing constitutional system with an authoritarian national state,' it also elected not to proscribe the party because there were 'no specific and weighty indications' that any of its 'endeavours might be successful.'[85]

This focus on capacity and capability makes sense yet raises two difficulties. First, the approach assumes that the electoral fortunes of a threatening party will not change over time. Should a certain number of seats be gained (perhaps because violence and intimidation are used to facilitate this outcome), proscribing the party's elected officials will become a more politically contentious act, not only because of its growing capacity to interfere in government affairs but also because it would effectively disenfranchise a larger segment of society.[86] Second, and more fundamentally, it is difficult to assess in advance how much governmental power will be needed for the infiltrative trap to be sprung.

The Weimar experience demonstrates both points. When the Nazi Party successfully took over the German state, it did not control a majority of parliamentary seats. Even when Hitler was appointed chancellor, in 1933, the party held slightly less than one-third of the Reichstag. However, as Fox and Nolte caution, despite the Nazis' lack of a governing majority, beginning with the elections in the summer of 1932, they 'held, together with the Communist Party, a "negative" majority' that 'allowed them to block the formation of any government with parliamentary support.'[87] From this foothold, the Nazis fought their way to secure enough political capital, not to control government, but to pressure parliamentary deputies to vote for the Enabling Act, which nullified the separation of powers and effectively legalized dictatorship.[88] At what point, exactly, would an emergency measure to proscribe the party have been appropriate? The Weimar government never could answer the question. It should also be borne in mind that Hitler himself was publicly committed to constitutional means, thereby complicating any precipitate removal of his party.[89]

From this experience and others, it is clear that attempts to ban political parties are inherently contentious. The final criterion of legitimacy therefore seeks to ensure that, when the call is made, it passes muster even with those who do not stand to benefit politically from the act. The common method is to use an independent judicial review mechanism to certify the government's reasoning and, also, to allow the victim a chance of appeal. For instance, the Spanish legislature requested that the country's Supreme Court ban the Basque militant party Batasuna, given its failure to condemn the violent activities of ETA. In the subsequent deliberations, this charge was found lacking, and so the case against Batasuna shifted to its being 'inseparable from ETA, providing the military operation both funding and logistic support'—and it was on this basis that the ban went through.[90] The case then passed to Spain's Constitutional Court, which upheld the ban, and then to the ECHR for external review, where the judgment was again sustained. The outcome allowed Spain to crack down on the party with some legitimacy, resulting in ETA's overall failure to prosecute an infiltrative approach similar to that attempted by PIRA.

Judicial review clearly will not always side with the state or else it would lose its legitimizing function. It should be noted, therefore, that in contrast to the Spanish case, the ECHR has reversed several attempts by Turkey's Constitutional Court to ban various Kurdish parties owing to their terrorist links or secessionist agendas. The ECHR has in these instances either cited a lack of evidence for the supposed ties to violence or argued that the main effect of a proscription would be to threaten the party's freedom of association under European law rather than protect Turkey's territorial integrity. Respectively, the verdicts appealed to the principles of necessity and of serving a legitimate aim. In contrast, however, the ECHR did accede to Turkey's electoral banning of the Islamist party Refah on the grounds that it threatened Turkish democracy. The verdict explicitly endorsed the anticipatory right of states to defend themselves against anti-democratic challengers, and yet it has also encountered vociferous opposition among legal scholars.[91]

Certainly, judicial review will never be infallible, and ECHR's treatment of Turkey—and of Refah in particular—suggests some inconsistency and even a possible bias against Islam.[92] Ultimately, courts are not bodies of science but of argumentation. Still, an authoritative and independent external review does appear to boost the legitimacy of proscriptions while limiting the scope of abuse. Of course, this recourse does depend on the state acceding to the higher authority in the first place and on it allowing those charged to appeal their case in a functioning and legitimate court of law. For this reason, several democratic states have the right to judicial review inscribed within the very clauses that also authorize proscription, providing by design both the possibility of sanction and that of appeal.[93] Again, however, such countermeasures are largely voluntary and seem to be most effective where the scope for abuse is also the least pronounced. In the obverse case, there is no guarantee that the judiciary itself is not politicized, at which point it no longer provides any real safeguard against government abuse.[94]

Another method of enhancing the legitimacy of state action against anti-democratic forces is to lessen the sanction by focusing on the party's activities rather than its right to exist. In the case of Refah, for example, the consequence of the court's actions was not to proscribe the movement as a whole but rather to deny it a right to participate in elections. Similarly, in sanctioning the Kach party, Israel only limited its electoral participation, but did not outlaw the party. Confining anti-democratic parties to civil societal rather than parliamentary positions sustains the possibility of democratic expression but makes it theoretically impossible for these forces ever to claim state power. It also assumes that the infiltration can be stymied by denying the party formal political standing.

Another related option, again short of outright proscription, is to subject the offending party to legal or bureaucratic harassment. In other contexts, such weaponization of legal checks and procedural requirements has been termed 'lawfare,' or the 'use of law as a weapon of war.'[95] Issacharoff explains, for example, that 'Belgium does not permit the banning of political parties, but reserves the right to deny state support to parties that "show clearly and repeatedly their hostility toward the rights and freedoms protected in the European Convention on Human Rights and its additional protocols."'[96] In the interwar period, before the Convention had been drafted, Belgium was faced with the seemingly inexorable rise of a far-right nationalist movement—the Rex party—and responded by prohibiting its marches, refusing it broadcast time, arresting party-affiliated journalists (who later had to be released), and pursuing the members of the party through the courts.[97] Such constant interference can be debilitating, yet—as Issacharoff adds—'while this is a type of sanction less onerous than the outright prohibition of a party, it paradoxically may raise more concerns about state censorship.'[98]

A third legal way of countering infiltrative insurgency short of actual proscription involves legal sanctions against specific behaviors or actors rather than the party as a whole. This targeting leaves the party intact and thereby minimizes the overall harm to democracy. It may be possible, for example, to audit a political party so as to ensure that it is not funneling resources and finances into a military wing. Kirshner suggests that the state might also oversee internal elections for party leadership or use the type of oversight and accountability mechanisms that helped the United States rid American labor unions of mob influence.[99] Where legitimate social movement meshes with infiltrative insurgent, as is often the case, this type of precision-guided sanction may be promising, as it 'would balance the communities' dual interests in curbing criminal activity and in allowing the broadest possible political participation.'[100]

To some degree, these 'lighter sentences' block the infiltrative approach, protect the state, and cause only so much damage to its democratic credentials—for these reasons, they may therefore be seen as more legitimate. Yet, as with any precision instrument, the measure of effectiveness is not the ability to target discriminately but the strategic outcome of doing so. The Weimar state imprisoned Hitler, then released him, it banned his paramilitary outfits, then allowed them to resume operations, and in general it sought to do in small doses what it dared not do completely, which is also why these half-measures remained just that.[101] And if the state proved too weak, the party proved too wily. Indeed, Capoccia describes how Hitler ordered the SA and the SS to submit to their ban without resistance, yet they were never disbanded and therefore continued to ready themselves for the moment when the ban was rescinded, which it soon was. Similarly, various attempts to bar militias from Iraq's government resulted in a 'false process of political reintegration' by which the targeted leaders hid their own fighters within the emerging security structures.[102] As we have seen with the case studies considered in chapter 4, one should expect subterfuge and duplicity also from other infiltrative insurgents. In that sense, seeking greater legitimacy by lessening the attack may only induce hesitance when resolve is needed.

Regardless of the scale and scope of the ban, a final consideration—or, ideally, a condition—should be borne in mind. As Kirshner argues, 'the dilemmas raised by those who oppose democracy will be more tractable if we treat defensive policies as efforts to augment the democratic character of flawed regimes, instead of as attempts to preserve a perfect moral community or any other idealized status quo.'[103] In other words, we return to the traditional emphasis within counterinsurgency theory on political reform as the critical condition for strategic and long-term success. On this basis, the proscription of parties as a counterinsurgency practice can only be expected to hamper the threat group and must therefore be complemented by political measures to address the reasons for its existence in the first place. Without a broader approach of this kind, proscription may very well 'miss the point,' providing 'the illusion of an easy answer to social problems of complex origin.'[104]

Indeed, even when legally authorized and legitimate, proscription only addresses symptoms. The fuller response, therefore, lies in querying why these parties are created and appear to resonate in society. This, in turn, should lead to more effective engagement with those constituents and causes that, left unheard, lend themselves to exploitation and radicalization. Sociologists speak frequently of the 'political opportunity structure,' or the ability in society to seek change through legitimate political contention.[105] While seeking to police which parties are acceptable within a polity, and who can say what, the state must also underline and demonstrate the real possibility of political and social change afforded by a functioning democracy. While seeking to deter and punish abuse, it must also leave the door wide open to legitimate, even sharp-elbowed competition.

Conclusion

Infiltrative insurgency is challenging because it blurs the line between legitimate political competition and illicit, coercive subversion. As such, it places the state in an awkward position, having to limit its democracy in order to save it. The dilemma is to some degree resolved when the challenger employs violence, a definitional characteristic of insurgency, yet infiltrative methods complicate this aspect by shrouding the use of force or denying any connection to it. This duplicity affords the insurgent the advantages of above-ground status as well as those of underground subversion. When traditional insurgents deliberately swim like fish among the sea that is the people, they use the population as camouflage but also as a human shield, gambling that the state will not dare attack or—at least—will suffer severe consequences when it does. In similar vein, infiltrative insurgents use party politics and parliamentary participation as camouflage, forcing the state to attack these systems in order to address the threat. It is easy to see how such action can become deeply counterproductive.

This chapter has laid out a few options that are available for those seeking a way out of the dilemma. Scholars and practice are clearly divided on whether to tame the beast with kindness—to encourage democratic participation so as to compel moderation—or whether to punish the transgressor, through repression, ostracism, or legal proscription, so as to limit its influence and channel its behavior. The particulars of context must drive the elaboration of strategy, and so no template or silver bullet can be proposed. A combination of approaches may also be possible—or even advisable. What is clear, however, is that regardless of the path taken, this type of challenge presents the state with an ethical and strategic minefield—one where missteps can cause grave and enduring harm to what is being protected: the democratic functioning of society. When a society embarks on this journey, it engages with the most intimate aspects of its being: its rules, values, and integrity. Whatever approach it takes must be unambiguously legal, transparently executed, and clearly explained; anything less will play into the enemy's hands and legitimize more radical solutions to political differences.

8

DUELING NARRATIVES
COUNTERING IDEATIONAL INSURGENCY

The challenge of ideational insurgency is that it does not provide the state with a physical target at which to aim its response. Instead of involving a group with a set hierarchy and specific location, the insurgency is spread out like a mist, yet it remains capable of harnessing collective effect. In countering these effects, the state often finds itself without a theory of victory, or a central idea of how to prevail. It proves extremely difficult to predict and prevent the group's use of stochastic terrorism, given the unpredictability of its timing, targeting, and authorship. Meanwhile, the ideology and cause that nonetheless unite these ruptures fester in online spaces that the democratic state can neither suppress nor control. Thus, the ideational approach surges, making 'useful idiots' out of social media's algorithms and exploiting the growing dominance of virtual connections and parallel existence. The result is not a cataclysmic defeat or overthrow of the state, but more like a death by a thousand cuts, as societal norms and values shift to accommodate an increasingly unassailable force.

For all this, the foundational problem with ideational insurgency may just be that it is seldom recognized as such. Instead, talk of 'lone wolves' masks the connective tissue and the deeper strategy at hand.

221

In this manner, rather than being understood in their political and social context, individual attacks are treated in isolation or as the product of mental-health issues. For instance, when Anders Breivik killed 77 people, including many children, in Norway on July 22, 2011, some commentators spoke of a 'meaningless and random' act, perpetrated by a 'madman.'[1] With hindsight, we now know the attack gained iconic status within the far right and energized a transnational network of fellow believers—including a few copycats. Accordingly, the classification and treatment of this type of incident have rightly changed. Still, the incident points to the analytical ambiguity surrounding this approach, given its subtlety, the incremental nature of its gains, and the lack of an overall architect.

Assuming that the thorny issue of assessment can be addressed, there are options available to governments and societies targeted by ideational insurgency. Three major categories of response obtain—disruption through law enforcement, suppression through online censorship, and the fostering of individual and societal resilience, be it through counter-messaging, preventive interventions, or education. This chapter lays out these three approaches in some detail, pointing in particular to the US context (given its targeting by both ISIS and the alt-right ideational insurgencies studied in chapter 5). What quickly becomes clear is that the best strategy will in all likelihood combine elements of each of these three components. What they all share, however, is a requirement for sophisticated counterinsurgency capabilities that go way beyond the military connotations of the term and call instead upon the smooth integration of disparate instruments of power.

Disruption through Law Enforcement

In contrast to the archetypal insurgent challenge, ideational insurgency will rarely feature ongoing armed confrontations between the government and the group. Instead, the violence is distributed and of a lower intensity, as it is intended to promote and reinforce a polarizing narrative rather than necessarily weaken the coercive capabilities of the state. A caveat is needed here, because another central feature of ideational insurgency is that its violent acts are not directed and, as such, could theoretically take a variety of forms. Still, by the very fact of decentralization, the usual attack will involve just one or a small group of perpetrators and therefore be fairly primitive while also focused on softer targets rather than the state. This lowered ambition does not matter much, in that the violence is anyway meant to be expressive rather than instrumental.

A typical state response to such a strategy is found within the realm of policing. Following the January 2021 Capitol attack—a wake-up call for the United States as to the right-wing ideational insurgency under way—President Joe Biden pledged that the 'diffuse and dispersed threat to Americans' would be met with 'robust law enforcement and intelligence capabilities, as well as strong cooperation and appropriate information sharing.'[2] This approach follows a similar logic to the militarized search-and-destroy missions seen in several counterinsurgency campaigns. Though it unfolds at a far lower intensity and within a different legal framework—that of human rights law rather than the law of armed conflict—the theory of victory in both settings is that by neutralizing enough of the organization's members, it is possible to make the movement fall.

This type of criminal pursuit is what counterterrorism is all about—at least prior to 9/11. However, back then the threat took the form of stable groups with a sufficiently constant cast of characters, allowing a case to be built over time. This approach is challenged when, precisely to evade law enforcement, groups such as the alt-right eschew a fixed hierarchy and membership and instead operate as a self-organizing network. Indeed, in revisiting the strategy of the alt-right (see chapter 5), there are only really two sets of behavior that are susceptible to disruption through law enforcement: the actual violence or threat thereof, and the extensive communications and activity online. Neither component is ideal: the former emanates from anonymous virtual networks and involves unknown assailants; the latter is for the most part protected by fundamental freedoms of speech and association.

If we look first at the violence, this is clearly the juiciest target for law enforcement. When an attack is executed, there is a clear legal basis for response, and it also becomes far easier to meet the evidentiary threshold necessary for pursuit. Thus, in the United

States, virtually all arrests connected to right-wing extremism have been connected in one way or another to the use of violence. In this case, legal efforts of this type are helped by the attackers' habit of filming their actions and promoting such footage online. Virality is very much a force multiplier in ideational insurgency, but the associated tendency to self-incriminate is also a vulnerability that the state can exploit.[3]

Pursuing the perpetrators of violent acts is a necessary response, but as a counterinsurgency strategy it falls short. Police action can easily become predominantly retroactive, in that it responds to violent acts rather than deters them. The only preventive aspect here is the hope that legal consequences for an individual attacker will discourage others who might be inspired to follow a similar path. Such an effect seems at odds with the ideological fervor of those taking up arms against the state and their fellow citizens. These attackers view themselves as warriors and are unlikely to be put off by the obvious dangers involved in their act. If anything, the hype generated by past attacks is likely to inspire others to fight on, regardless of the fate that befell their perpetrators. The very fact of suicide missions illustrates this point, though it can also be seen in the number of incidents in which 'active shooters' turn their weapons on themselves. Meanwhile, with each attack not deterred, community relations and society suffer in ways that are difficult to undo.

For all of these reasons, there is a need for more anticipatory knowledge of the threat and an ability to prevent attacks rather than just deal with their aftermath. It is for this reason that various governments faced with the threat of terrorism have sought to enact special or emergency regulations that allow them to do more, at an earlier stage, before the attack takes place. Still, the further removed from the attack itself, the more uncertain the target for law enforcement and the greater the risk of trampling on the rights and freedoms of innocent populations. This conversation plays itself out in every country confronted with terrorism and—given its anonymity and overall murkiness—it is particularly acute in cases of ideational insurgency.

To provide an example: France has faced the most severe threat of online-based Islamist terrorism within Europe and it also has some of the sternest counterterrorism laws to help the state combat this trend. Its counterterrorism legislation criminalizes otherwise legal actions if they form part of a longer-term conspiracy to commit terrorism; this extends the state's prosecutorial reach far beyond the attack itself.[4] In the face of growing Islamist terrorism in Europe, Switzerland is considering a similar legal standard, though it is facing significant opposition from civil society groups.[5] In France, meanwhile, even the 'failure to account for resources on the part of any person habitually in contact with one or more persons engaging in terrorist acts' is a punishable offense.[6] Under the two-year state of emergency that followed the bloody terrorist attacks of 2015, 11 religious centers were shuttered 'for incitement to commit terrorist acts' and '41 individuals were placed under house arrest for harboring extremist sympathies.'[7]

To take this tack one step further, other states have sought to disrupt violent groups by proscribing them in their entirety, thereby criminalizing their very existence. Such a sanction makes possible the seizure of assets and property relating to the group and the penalization of individuals attending its events or purchasing its merchandise. In other words, the government would then no longer require evidence of a violent act to pursue and dismantle; the group is prima facie guilty. Following the January 2021 assault on the US Capitol, the Canadian government banned the Proud Boys, alleged to have masterminded the attack, along with three other far-right organizations. The move allowed the state to check any movement, recruitment, funding, or training relating to these groups. The rights of their members (at least when operating as such) are thereby severely curtailed. Europe has also been active in this regard, allowing for the freezing of funds of both groups and members along with strict limits on the type of support that they can legally receive.[8]

In the United States, several groups are included on its list of designated terrorist organizations but, notably, this mechanism is only available for international groups, not domestic ones. As a result, whereas the US government can isolate, criminalize, and punish most actions relating to organizations such as ISIS or al-Qaeda, or even international neo-Nazi movements, those groups that conduct their actions 'primarily within the territorial jurisdiction of the

United States' face a lesser degree of disruption. As one FBI agent explains, 'There has to be a credible allegation or a threat of violence before someone opens a case.'[9] The distinction between domestic and international is often quite flimsy, not least given the globalized nature of most violent extremist ideologies, and yet it is a dichotomy that goes to the very heart of US counterterrorism.

Following the January 6, 2021 attack on the US Capitol, there were renewed calls to bring American domestic counterterrorism legislation in line with its international counterpart. The issue at hand, it is argued, is that whereas US law acknowledges domestic terrorism as a crime, it does not set out clear associated charges.[10] This reasoning is open to challenge,[11] yet it has prompted repeated calls for a domestic terrorism statute so that the United States can prosecute such terrorism consistently and coherently.[12] The introduction of fresh legislation would, it is argued, add prosecutorial powers to the government's domestic counterterrorism work and allow it to criminalize acts that currently do not fit well within existing statutes, such as the stockpiling of firearms with the intent of undertaking a domestic terrorist attack, or engagement in domestic terrorism using knives, firearms, and vehicular ramming.[13]

Still, there are reasons for caution here. Michael German persuasively lays out the extensive statutes and regulations already available to the state, even for domestic counterterrorism, and argues that the limited response to right-wing extremism to date stems not from a lack of statutes and laws but from issues of policy and, even, bias.[14] Adding powers, therefore, might encourage prosecutorial overreach—against activists, political opponents, or other civil society organizations—without fixing the problem it is meant to address. Indeed, the very reason for limiting the FBI's remit in respect of domestic terrorism in the first place was that it abused its authority in the 1970s. More recently, German adds, the FBI has used its domestic counterterrorism powers to pursue relatively peripheral threats, such as environmental activists or what it curiously has called 'Black Identity Extremists'; without a change in policy, added authorities would likely compound rather than resolve this tendency.[15]

There is also a very pragmatic and yet disconcerting reason why the United States does not pursue domestic right-wing extremism as it does groups like ISIS, namely the far greater integration of the former within the fabric of American society. This issue goes beyond the very real signs of support for right-wing extremism among US law enforcement officials—though this is in itself highly problematic.[16] More broadly, targeting far-right violent organizations as terrorists would likely infringe upon and criminalize the many who support the ideology, or who provide services to the groupings and their members, wittingly or otherwise. By way of illustration, for internationally designated groups, even innocuous training programs, for example in how to 'use humanitarian and international law in peaceful dispute resolution,' are deemed illegal, because they constitute 'material support' to a proscribed terrorist organization.[17] Holding funds for such an organization, providing services to it, enabling it to access arms or materiel, or circulating its literature would all be serious criminal offenses. Applying such a standard to far-right extremism would clearly be unimaginably disruptive, given its embeddedness in American society and the great sensitivity within this broader community about government overreach.[18]

On this basis, Dan Byman tentatively concludes that 'treating domestic extremism just like foreign terrorism would be a mistake, but moving a bit in that direction would be desirable.'[19] A key innovation, one that would not require a change in laws, would be to properly assess right-wing terrorism by tracking and labeling its incidents as just that—as terrorism, used as one method within a broader insurgency. German has long argued that by sometimes treating these crimes as 'hate crimes,' and sometimes as 'civil rights violations,' or simply as 'violent crimes,' the government obscures not only the scale of the problem but also the common ideological foundation from which these attacks stem. Properly accounting for the threat in this manner would bring more resources to bear, a more concerted response, even a national strategy, and greater awareness and use of the laws already available.[20]

Indeed, such a response could fall short of proscription and still be effective, as there are other ways to target violent organizations collectively. German cites the impressive track record of the Southern Poverty Law Center in launching civil suits against various KKK chapters, using any criminal conduct to seek damages.[21] Such actions hem in the movement and have in many cases caused financial ruin. It is a type of response that could equally well be undertaken by the Justice Department, which has a track record of bringing civil suits in the context of white-collar and environmental crime.[22] The defamation suit brought by Dominion Voting Systems against the peddlers of conspiracy theories relating to the 2020 US presidential elections provides a possible example of how to target the extremist rhetoric of the alt-right, thereby serving to correct the record in the court of public opinion while also punishing and deterring the disinformation on which this movement thrives.[23]

German's own professional experience points to a further possibility, namely the penetration of domestic terrorist groups and the accumulation of evidence to make possible successful prosecutions. Indeed, German spent the better part of the 1990s as an FBI undercover agent infiltrating white-supremacist groups and far-right militia movements. These investigations occurred following the Rodney King beating and the riots that ensued, when the FBI began to pay serious attention to far-right agitation and the incitement of a potential race war. Thus, German was deployed to gain the trust of the main movements and, in so doing, collected evidence of their extensive weapons trafficking, manufacture and use of explosives, and conspiracies to engage in violent activities. This evidence was then used in federal domestic counterterrorism cases that powerfully undermined the targeted organizations.[24]

These types of efforts can be tremendously successful, and some of them are already being implemented.[25] Still, the key limitation in countering an ideational insurgency lies in the virtual nature of the struggle. The entire purpose of Louis Beam's 'leaderless resistance' was to protect right-wing extremists and neo-Nazis from government infiltration and surveillance. As can be seen in the US response to Islamist 'homegrown' terrorism, it is an approach that can confound law enforcement activity. Fearful of another attack, yet lacking known targets, the FBI has had to resort to various sting operations wherein agents bring and, sometimes, even goad a willing target to the brink of an attack and then arrest them.[26] The method typically begins with scouring the social media sites where ideational insurgencies unfold; this leads to the identification of individuals who appear supportive of Islamic State or violent extremism. At that point, however, it has not been uncommon for the FBI to provide both the means and the opportunity for attack, requiring therefore only an acknowledgement of intent from the would-be terrorist—individuals who, in at least some cases, likely would not have participated on their own initiative.[27]

Though sting operations have clear potential in countering a diffuse and unpredictable network, the approach has been condemned as little more than entrapment. Supporters of the practice point to the fact that, to date, no terrorism case based on this method has been thrown out of court.[28] On the other hand, there are minimal costs attached to charging seemingly willing jihadists, however hapless or mentally unstable they may be. Indeed, a number of judges have cited concern with this practice, but then ruled as expected.[29] The strategic cost, however, is that entire communities are made to feel preyed upon and under siege, resulting in their alienation from the justice system along with the state it serves.[30] In this manner, sting operations can fuel exactly the insurgency that they are meant to prevent. Indeed, questions must be asked about the method by which the FBI finds its perpetrators and whether the nets it uses really catch the right fish.

A more promising approach may be to treat ideational insurgency's reliance on social media as a vulnerability and to roll up entire networks through infiltration and the turning of likely assets. The legal effort that went into countering Anonymous is instructive. Anonymous is also based on a 'lack of hierarchy'; according to Hector 'Sabu' Monsegur, a key leader of the group, this attribute was meant to protect it against the type of misinformation and subversion used by the FBI in the 1960s and 1970s.[31] And yet, advanced surveillance of its online communications and proper exploitation of factionalism within its ranks gave the FBI enough to work with. As it turned out, despite the movement's amorphous nature, its sustained interactions—although anonymous and online—generated patterns and persistent identities that the FBI could use to build a case.[32] In this manner, the FBI in 2012 managed to out Sabu himself, along with several other senior leaders, all of whom faced significant charges.

Based on his extensive hacking, online theft, and other crimes, Sabu faced a possible 125 years of jail-time. Rather than going down this route, however, the FBI offered this influential member of the Anonymous collective the possibility of working undercover as an agent and bringing in other Anonymous leaders. Most emerging plots made their way to Sabu, as his position and status made others seek his participation or praise. Such information could then be relayed to the authorities, resulting in countermeasures to address vulnerable sites and the arrest of those involved.[33] According to his sentencing memorandum, Monsegur's substantial cooperation 'contributed directly to the identification, prosecution, and conviction of eight of his major co-conspirators'; the FBI further suggests that he helped disrupt or prevent 'at least 300 separate computer hacks.'[34] It is true that Anonymous as a phenomenon survived the attack, but, with its participants spooked, the movement was definitely weakened.

Organizations such as the Proud Boys, the Three Percenters, or the Atomwaffen Division also have some form of hierarchy that could be exploited. Similarly, it does not require extensive research to identify the key characters involved in the alt-right and its associated networks. Still, a *sine qua non* of the approach used against Anonymous was the target's commission of a crime—in this case, hacking and fraud—as it was the ability to present charges that generated the leverage needed for cooperation. In the case of the alt-right or other ideational insurgents, this precondition may be more difficult to meet, as their strategy relies predominantly on rhetoric and radicalization. In seeking criminal charges, much will therefore come down to where individual states draw the line between protected speech, even if odious, and unprotected incitement of violence.

We move, then, to the question of legally sanctioning the second component of ideational strategy, namely its extensive online speech and activity. It is a sensitive topic, given the charged polemic in most democratic societies between counterterrorism concerns on the one hand and civil liberties on the other. Since 9/11, this tug of war has definitely favored the security community, as laws have been drafted that dramatically increase the scope of government powers. As al-Qaeda and ISIS have shifted to emphasizing online mobilization, and as the attacks keep on coming, the laws have tightened further. Though there is clear utility in having the tools necessary to pre-empt and counter these dispersed and atomized networks, the scope for abuse and potentially adverse consequences for democracy is also extremely high.

To give an idea of current practice, in 2005 the Council of Europe agreed to a counterterrorism convention that made it illegal to distribute 'a message to the public' with the intent and effect of inciting a terrorist offense.[35] Through its 2006 Terrorism Act, the British government criminalized statements that are 'likely to be understood … as a direct or indirect encouragement' of acts of terrorism, including their glorification.[36] In 2019, through the Counter-terrorism and Border Security Act, the list of offenses was extended to include specifically 'clear expressions of support for terrorist organisations' and 'recklessness' about such statements encouraging the support of others.[37] Spain also bans the glorification of terrorism, and France criminalizes 'speech which "provoke[s] discrimination, hatred, or violence" … on the basis of several categories, including race, religion, and ethnicity.'[38] Similarly, in Singapore, Sedition Act 28 'makes it an offence to promote feelings of ill-will and hostility between different races or classes.'[39] With broad and vague laws like these, there are clearly many ways in which the online activity of ideational insurgents can be targeted—indeed, many question whether these powers are in fact too broad.

The United States takes pride in the high level of protection it affords to freedom of speech; the general impression among Americans is that the harm of offensive language, including the possibility of violence, is 'simply a cost of doing business for the First Amendment.'[40] And yet, the powers arrogated by the United States in the aftermath of 9/11, and in the context of mass casualty terrorism, have significantly narrowed the gulf separating it from its European allies.[41] US law makes several exceptions to protected speech and these could, in specific circumstances, be used to penalize the online communications by ideational insurgents. As we have seen, the designation of terrorist groups criminalizes 'material support,' which effectively prohibits speech in the form of advice, services, or even praise (at least when it is seen as increasing the likelihood of a terrorist act).[42] When a group is proscribed as a foreign terrorist organization, most of its online activities are effectively banned, because its virtual existence implies the provision of some type of service to the group.[43]

The situation concerning 'domestic' terrorism is somewhat different but still leaves options open for criminalizing online speech. Since 1969, the American criteria for prosecuting incitement of terrorist actions have been based on the so-called Brandenburg standards: 'free speech and free press do not permit a State to forbid or proscribe advocacy of the use of force or of law violation except where such advocacy is [1] directed to inciting or producing [2] imminent lawless action and [3] is likely to incite or produce such action.'[44] Thus, there is a basis in the United States to pursue speech that incites, yet the difference with other countries is that the Brandenburg standards were arrived at to protect speech rather than to regulate it and, in this spirit, the Supreme Court has only very rarely dismissed First Amendment protection on this basis. When it is applied to regulate online speech, questions of imminence and of direction are likely to become thornier yet, given the tangled and indirect links between speaker and audience.[45]

Because of the high bar set by Brandenburg, a more likely option for criminalizing online speech is 'true threat' situations, where an individual communicates his serious intent to cause unlawful violence or harm to his envisaged victim(s). In these cases, expression is interpreted not as an exchange of ideas to be covered by the First Amendment, but as 'intimidation, coercion, and terror'; in effect, Martin Redish and Matthew Fisher explain, 'a true threat is a coercive act, not speech.'[46] This principle has been used in a number of cases where defendants made significant threats of violence and were accordingly charged. What is particularly relevant to ideational insurgency is that cases have succeeded even where the violence was to be carried out by third-party intermediaries rather than by the person making the threat.[47]

There are clear implications here for the incitement and threats seen within ideational insurgency. Still, it is less clear how courts might distinguish between 'true threat' situations and protected expression, or how targeted the threat must be for the speech to become prosecutable. It is also worth noting that the alt-right has made a habit of speaking in code, using metaphors, and deploying thick irony to obfuscate any definitive meaning. Violence is certainly encouraged, yet a legal case would need to engage with its plausible deniability. For example, when an alt-right podcast popularized the placement of triple parentheses around the names of Jewish individuals or supposedly Jewish-owned industries, like (((this))), the intent was quite clearly for those targeted to be harassed and attacked by the online hordes of anti-Semitic trolls. Jewish individuals subjected to this method reported relentless abuse in the form of messages, phone calls, photographs and even death threats.[48] Given the ambiguity of the method (its progenitors claim the parentheses symbolize an echo, to denote the reverberance of Jewish influence) and of the perpetrators, it is difficult to see how even repeated death threats of this type might go to trial or be used by law enforcement.

A third approach, and the one most commonly used, concerns the distinction between 'protected expression' and restrictions on 'nonexpressive conduct.'[49] The meaning here is that courts can regulate terrorist use of the internet to organize, recruit, train, and fundraise because these actions, although they necessarily also involve communication, do not legally constitute speech. The same argument is made with regard to 'attempts, conspiracies, solicitations, and instructional speech.'[50] Though the conditions for regulating such activity are manifold, the legal consensus is that in cases of strong government interest (such as in combating terrorism), actions can be controlled 'even if the regulation incidentally burdens speech.'[51]

The question is how far this standard can be stretched before it becomes a mere contrivance to avoid cherished First Amendment principles. When is speech instrumental to the act of terrorism? What does recruitment mean in an insurgent movement that is largely non-hierarchical and in which membership is informal? What is the difference between advocacy and conspiracy? Legal scholars are torn. Jon Sherman argues that any invocation of speech acts to criminalize internet-based terrorist communications would require extreme specificity, such as exact instructions for the conduct of an attack.[52] Taking this one step further, others argue that to be prohibited, such speech would need to go beyond online communications and actually result in or significantly risk real-world harm.[53] At that point, however, the pre-emptive effect of controlling internet communications will have been lost.

It is difficult to know whether to celebrate or bemoan these obstacles to state regulation of online terrorist communications. Several legal scholars have sought to address the state's limited reach or improve the accuracy of its targeting so that it can more discriminately and nimbly stop what must be stopped.[54] Any such new law would need to demonstrate not only precision in targeting, but also 'compelling government interest.'[55] Some rightly counter that, at least in the United States, terrorism represents a far less lethal threat than commonly thought; as the line goes, you are more likely to be accidentally shot by an armed toddler.[56] As a basis for diluting constitutional rights, therefore, counterterrorism simply does not measure up. And yet, the threat of terrorism should be measured not only by its violence, but by its overall societal effect. On this basis, there are sound reasons for governments to check the radicalizing efforts of ideational insurgency, lest it damage the fabric of society and shift norms toward violent extremism. In this endeavor, however, it would be tragically ironic if the state itself harmed the very values that it was attempting to protect.

De-platforming, or Suppression by Online Censorship

Ideational insurgency derives much of its power from online interactions, yet policing this sphere runs up against fundamental concerns relating to freedom of speech. An alternative way to target this strategy is to focus on the online account and content rather than the individual user. The idea here is to eschew criminal proceedings but to prevent the individual from sharing and expressing radicalizing content online, thereby sapping its societal reach and effect. The method relies upon 'de-platforming'—the cancellation of social media accounts, the disappearance of content deemed radicalizing, or the elimination of virtual groups and other online meeting places where members convene. A key advantage is that rather than brushing up against constitutional constraints, this approach stems from the ability of private companies to impose sanctions based on their own terms of service. Still, as quickly becomes clear, the broadness of 'de-platforming' as an activity belies a range of options and parameters that need to be carefully studied and tailored for optimal effect.

De-platforming already plays a major role in controlling online communication by violent extremist organizations. In the first nine months of 2018, Facebook removed 14.3 million pieces of content related to Islamic State, al-Qaeda and their affiliates, preventing untold exposure to radicalizing material.[57] Between August 2015 and December 2016, Twitter launched a spate of suspensions, terminating 636,248 accounts 'primarily related to ISIS.'[58] In mid-2018, it announced it was 'locking' almost '10 million suspicious accounts per week'—mainly bots—so as to combat the malign use of the platform to manufacture virality, spread misinformation, and create influence.[59] Similarly, Facebook has reworked its timeline so as to minimize the incidence of fake news and is encouraging users to flag suspicious news sources.[60] WhatsApp limited the number of times that any one message can be forwarded, so that its platform can less readily be used to spread incendiary disinformation and create violent mobs.[61] Reddit in June 2015 announced a new anti-harassment policy that led to the deletion of white-extremist subreddits.[62] In a similar vein, internet company Cloudflare, whose CEO once loudly protested that '[a] website is speech. It is not a bomb,' decided in 2017 to terminate its hosting of the white-supremacist Stormfront site and in 2019 kicked 8chan off its network.[63] Even PayPal and other financial services are regularly barring identifiable members of violent extremist organizations, complicating their fundraising operations.

If we put aside the ethical aspects of denying service on the basis of content (more on this later), critics of de-platforming often raise two practical concerns. First, it is argued that de-platforming treats only the symptom of the disease, as those banished can easily return with a new account and handle. Accordingly, the method is likened to the fairground game of Whack-a-Mole, wherein the player strikes animatronic talpids only to face more of them reappearing at an ever-faster rate. The criticism is correct in so far as deleted users have been found to return and seek to re-establish their erstwhile networks. Indeed, some simply add a number to their handle, at times as a boastful counter of just how many times they have been suspended. Ensuring that a ban is definitive, or that material is not reposted in altered form, requires either well-programmed algorithms or very diligent human trackers, neither of which is likely to strike the average social media company as a smart investment.

Despite this flaw, the deletion of content and suspension of users do disrupt online networks, even if they are not eliminated. J. M. Berger and Heather Perez found that Twitter's assault on pro-ISIS accounts 'held the size and reach of the overall network flat, while devastating the reach of specific users.'[64] Separate analysis concludes ISIS was 'significantly disrupted' by this attack, particularly in its 'ability to develop and maintain robust and influential communities.'[65] ISIS itself has described the suspensions as 'devastating,' and despite concerted efforts, it has failed both to replace deleted accounts and to restore lost networks.[66] When the group now uses Twitter, it creates a swarm of new accounts for each 24-hour news cycle, spewing out information in rapid bursts until they are taken offline and the process must start all over again. This may seem like a pyrrhic victory for the hall monitors of cyberspace, yet it imposes significant costs in time and effort and makes it near impossible to sustain an actual community, at least as compared to the 'golden era' when the group's communications were largely unimpeded.[67]

A second concern is that those banished from a particular platform will simply find a home elsewhere. Both Stormfront and 8chan reacted to their cancellation by Cloudflare by moving to other hosting services; they remain operational to this day. ISIS videos banned on YouTube have been found on Tune.pk, a similar site hosted in Pakistan.[68] Likewise, efforts to de-platform the alt-right prompted a flow of adherents toward 'alt-tech' platforms: Voat replaced Reddit, Hatreon replaced Patreon, YouTube became BitChute, Twitter Gab, and—showcasing their renowned wit—GoFundMe became GoyFundMe.[69] These platforms are not as closely monitored or they officially abjure 'censorship' of any type, and therefore allow extremists greater freedom of movement. They also provide a refined echo chamber where the likelihood of moderating voices is all but nil. Thus, it is further argued that the main effect of de-platforming is to encourage continued radicalization all the while complicating surveillance of online activity by law enforcement and intelligence agencies.[70] ISIS, for example, caused some headaches for counterterrorism practitioners when it shifted to Telegram and began using its encrypted messaging service to reconstitute broken links, converse, and plot attacks.

Needless to say, the internet is fungible; the closure of one area will open another one elsewhere. Still, de-platforming pushes extremists further and further down the chain, from Facebook to Telegram and from Telegram to obscure platforms such as Rocket.Chat, Riot, TamTam and Hoop Messenger.[71] This may be frustrating, yet as ideational insurgents must influence society to be effective, these ersatz sites are by themselves insufficient, in that they are less frequented by the regular 'normies' whom the extremist seeks to sway. To use the terminology of chapter 5, it might be possible to recreate the digital counter-state, but the insurgency cannot take on the mainstream—a limitation that invalidates their theory of victory. It is telling that the ISIS émigrés to the dark web and other obscure corners of the internet have been implored by their ideological masters to return to Twitter.[72] More prosaically, the 'alt-tech' is often buggy, less user-friendly, less popular even with the movement's own members, and generally less satisfying than the mainstream platforms, all of which undercuts the online campaign.[73]

As to the argument that de-platforming pushes insurgents toward platforms that are more difficult to monitor, the implications of this critique are puzzling. First, it seems perverse to allow dangerous activity to proceed only to make possible its surveillance. The precarious gamble of such an approach is that law enforcement can both amass evidence and intervene to prevent attacks before they occur. Given the total sum of racist, incendiary, and bigoted communications online, this wager presents extensive risk. For every incident prevented, how many more will be generated, and missed, by giving insurgents unfettered access to a base of potential attackers? Finally, it is also possible to monitor some of the more secure sites to which extremists flock; Amarnath Amarasingam, Shiraz Maher, and Charlie Winter detail how Europol's cooperation with Telegram—known for its encryption and, hence, a common refuge for extremists—resulted in the location (and suspension) of several accounts breaking that platform's terms of service.[74] The effect, here too, was to profoundly reduce the number of extremist posts over the long term.

There is another component to this discussion: the further away from the mainstream, the less likely it is that the terrorist attacks associated with ideational insurgency will succeed. It is not just that there will be fewer would-be attackers exposed to the noxious ideology and, therefore, fewer attacks, but when one does occur, it will also lack the communicative payload afforded through more mainstream channels. With the restriction of the movement and its propaganda to the far reaches of the internet, the meaning of an attack will be defined not by the insurgent group but by the society with which it now struggles to connect. This does not mean that the terrorism will necessarily stop, but, much as in other counterinsurgency settings, turning an expansive insurgent movement into an isolated problem of terrorism is in itself a marker of success. The residual problem remains serious, but it will struggle to effect social and political change, can more easily be dealt with through traditional law enforcement, and, therefore, will contain the seeds of its own destruction.

De-platforming clearly has several beneficial effects and should be included as part of a broader strategy to counter ideational insurgency. Still, key strategic and moral questions are raised whenever this type of approach is considered. These questions can be grouped into three broad and necessarily overlapping categories: *what* are the criteria for de-platforming, *how* is it to be done, and *who* is responsible for initiating and deciding upon this type of action? These questions do not pose insurmountable obstacles to the overall effort, but they must be considered for the measure to be effective. It is also crucial that de-platforming, as a contribution to an overall strategy, is not confused with the strategy itself.

On the question of what to regulate, it is difficult to target precisely speech advocating violence and terrorism without again confronting questions of intent, imminence, and interpretation. Thus, de-platforming initiatives must strike a delicate balance between removing enough of the offending material for the effort to be worthwhile yet without overstepping the mark and violating the openness of the internet as a forum for communication. One method of drawing this line is to focus the effort on specific groups; indeed, within the Islamist online ecology, pro-ISIS accounts have been regulated far more strictly and systematically than those from ideologically linked yet separate movements. This approach derives in part from ISIS's international proscription, making its online presence a priori unlawful. It was also facilitated by ISIS's extensive use of officially sanctioned media, which had a tremendous impact on the base but also acted as a homing device for de-platforming efforts. The narrow, intense focus on this group has made it prohibitively difficult for it to sustain this model of communications. For Charlie Winter, 'this is not just a media decline—it is a full-fledged collapse.'[75]

Focusing on ISIS in this manner worked, yet the approach had the unintended side effect of leaving significantly more leeway for other organizations, even those sharing a similar intent and international ambition.[76] The conundrum of this type of targeting is compounded as groups dissolve into a more nebulous movement and their online activity becomes miasmic. Indeed, even as ISIS faced higher entry barriers to online communication, its 'virtual caliphate' evolved, giving greater prominence to more ambiguous posts, also known as 'gray content,' which trackers struggle to catch. In parallel, the group has also shifted from centrally produced media and encouraged its followers, 'once considered to be the peanut gallery of the Islamic State jihad,' to take on greater responsibility for content generation.[77] Its less organized, less stylized contributions may appear innocuous by comparison, but in intent and effect they provide the comforting lining for online echo chambers, enabling the enculturation and radicalization of others.[78] They also make it far more difficult for social media companies to target clearly illegitimate use of their platforms.

These challenges are yet more pronounced with the alt-right, given the very loose boundaries of this movement. As we have seen, the talking points of the alt-right are shared with a larger non-violent constituency in society. The use of linguistic subterfuge, irony, and memes further mainstreams the group's content and erases any hard line between it and the broader public. To pick an example from the United Kingdom, before it was banned from Facebook, the far-right and fascist organization Britain First had a following of 1.8 million users and more than 2 million likes, 'making it the second most-liked Facebook page within the politics and society category in the UK, after the royal family.'[79] The group amassed this audience precisely by cloaking its intent, intermixing light racism with unrelated memes, and using dog whistles to radicalize. What, in this context, amounts to terrorist content, what is potentially radicalizing, and what is just 'trolling' and 'shitposting'?

The fundamental reality of ideational insurgency is that radicalization does not necessarily come from the starkest imagery or word choice, but through prolonged exposure to a community trading in satire and subtext. Dialogue is not one-way but participatory, its effect is cumulative rather than direct, and it is over time that the epistemological fix sets in. Locating the offensive content within such communities is akin to finding needles in haystacks—but more challenging yet, as auditors of these sites will likely fail to see and experience the content like an insider. Meanwhile, blanket bans will be perceived as digital disenfranchisement, even political censorship, and run up against the desire of social media companies to maximize rather than suppress their user base.[80]

If the alt-right demonstrates the significant hurdles in the way of effective countermeasures against right-wing extremism, at least online, it does not follow that social media companies are entirely powerless. Twitter, to name but one prominent example, has focused on the big fish, deleting and suspending the accounts of the major voices in the community. Shortly after Donald Trump's presidential victory of 2016, Twitter banned Richard Spencer along with many of his alt-right outlets on the basis of abuse and harassment.[81] Following the Charlottesville 'Unite the Right' rally, these efforts accelerated. The January 2021 attack on the Capitol saw the crackdown spread to other major platforms and led to the de-platforming of many of the alt-tech apps developed as safe havens for the fleeing hordes. At this point, Twitter targeted Trump himself for having glorified violence and encouraged the insurrection at the Capitol. It also updated its terms of service relating to 'civic integrity' and purged more than 70,000 accounts 'engaged in sharing harmful QAnon-associated content at scale.'[82] The conspiracy continues to thrive but mainly on less regulated sites and, thus, with reduced contact with the 'non pilled.'

These moves may have been correct and appropriate, but they also raise unsettling precedents—and speak to the targeting difficulties in countering a truly ideational insurgency. Trump's glorification of violence was indirect and highly arguable; his suspension appears to have related more to his position and amplifying potential, raising questions as to whether it is audience or content that counts.[83] As concerns QAnon, Sophia Moskalenko and Clark McCauley rightfully remind us that, in spite of its off-kilter belief system, QAnon is not a terrorist group and the vast majority of its adherents will never engage in violence.[84] Indiscriminately targeting followers of this bizarre cult might be the right thing to do—not least given its disturbing growth and millenarian ideology—but the legal basis and normative precedents of doing so will require further thought and a better argument.

The question of what to regulate is related to the second question of how to do it. Clearly, the less ambiguity in online content, the easier it is to program automatic moderation efforts that track and remove offending materially autonomously. Indeed, automation of this type is becoming the norm, at least for major platforms. Facebook, for instance, reported in 2017 that through 'automated systems like photo and video matching and text-based machine learning,' it was able to remove 99 percent of ISIS- and al-Qaeda-related material before it had a chance to be flagged by users.[85] Some of this content did not even have a chance to make it onto the site before being deleted. Similarly, Twitter claims that its algorithms can identify and suspend 95 percent of all terrorist-related accounts, three-quarters of which are removed even before the first tweet is sent.[86]

Still, these accomplishments may raise more questions than they answer. As Brian Fishman, who heads Facebook's counterterrorism efforts, notes, 'it may seem easy for a company to simply "prohibit terrorism" on their platform, but putting in place a robust policy is far more complex.'[87] Variables to consider include what content is legitimate versus what is not; whether to prohibit the material, the account, or the user; whether to ban for life or suspend temporarily; whether to grant rights of appeal; and whether to derive intent through context (connections, repeat offenders) or to focus more narrowly on the material itself. All questions dealing with sanctions presuppose an ability to locate the material in the first place, raising wholly separate parameters regarding computer or human tracking systems along with protocols for user-generated flagging. Human review is more flexible and creative but is subject to error and bias; automated solutions are fast and efficient but can be more easily fooled.[88] Both require extensive resources.

These considerations all matter, because to be effective de-platforming must be seen as legitimate, and to be legitimate it must abide by a consistent and somewhat accessible set of rules. The downside of having standards and communicating them publicly, however, is that it allows targeted organizations to game the system. ISIS users on Telegram routinely circulate 'tricks and tips' to avoid contravening Twitter's terms of service, for example by avoiding certain words and phrases.[89] Fishman also relates how, by slightly altering their graphics, extremists can throw off carefully honed automatic tracking techniques and force a far more laborious human review.[90] In a similar vein, Moustafa Ayad demonstrates how ISIS networks manage to avoid Facebook's automated and manual moderation efforts, through the hijacking of accounts and hashtags, content masking, link sharing, and posting in languages other than Arabic. In one case, a network of nearly 300 accounts was thereby able to remain online while posting 'clearly terrorist content' viewed by tens of thousands of users within just a month.[91]

The method of de-platforming must also confront the problem of 'gray content' alluded to earlier. Most companies are responding to this challenge by erring on the side of the user, avoiding the false positives and charges of over-censorship yet assuming, therefore, that the content will not result in radicalization or terrorist attack.[92] It is a risky but understandable stance, given the ambiguity involved. An intriguing middle way may be possible, namely to eschew the outright banning of this type of material in favor of its marginalization. The argument here is to 'de-prioritize' violent extremism, plausibly by identifying it as misinformation, providing links to fact-checking sites, or programming bots 'to identify extremist rhetoric and enter the conversation with automated or targeted responses' (both Google and Facebook have already implemented this type of action).[93] A still more insidious type of marginalization would be to surreptitiously reduce the visibility of those problematic accounts that do not quite warrant expulsion, thereby enabling the unwitting user to proceed uninterrupted yet with reduced connectivity and to diminished effect.

Whatever measures are taken, and however well the issue is handled, it is easy to see how the effort to de-platform can ensnare social media companies in a cat-and-mouse game requiring ever more vigilance and resources. Whereas larger and better-endowed social media companies like Facebook and Twitter can sink assets into pursuing terrorist content online without overly threatening their bottom line, smaller or less developed players will struggle to follow their lead. Efforts are under way for different companies to help one another, via initiatives such as the Global Internet Forum to Counter Terrorism's content database, whereby offending material is shared across platforms to speed up identification and removal.[94] Still, this is definitely an area where the search for perfection is likely to disappoint, resulting in companies being accused of not doing enough, or of doing too much. It is worth recognizing, in this context, just how difficult it is to identify and to regulate speech across vast networks, the number of tough decisions that companies must make in formulating a policy and approach, and their constant battle against movements that adapt to whatever they come up with and seek to do.

This leads to the third major question, namely who should be in control of de-platforming initiatives. Clearly, the companies that own the spaces that are to be policed will be centrally involved in the process, yet they are also frequently accused of not caring or not doing enough to face up to the growing misuse of their platforms. To Jonathan Greenblatt, CEO of the Anti-Defamation League, 'the few meaningful steps taken by the large social media companies to self-regulate came about only when the companies also faced a combination of legislative and regulatory pressure, as well as public outrage and significant reputational damage.'[95] Fishman, of Facebook, acknowledges that social media companies 'were late to address the threat,' but adds that accusations of neglect are by now 'outdated.'[96] Certainly, since the rise of ISIS and its successful use of the internet, the dark side of social media has become more difficult to ignore.

Still, the underlying issue of who should own this process remains. The argument for private sector control centers on its greater access to the material, its greater capacity to control it, and the fact that it is according to the platform's terms of service that content may be deleted, obviating a feisty constitutional battle regarding free speech. As Fishman therefore concludes, while the government will play its role, 'the voluntary efforts made by these companies are likely to have a far greater impact on addressing the problem of terrorist exploitation of the Internet.'[97] At worst, as the government gets involved, it will seek to politicize what content must go, which introduces a harmful degree of bias, threatens democracy, and places social media companies in a difficult position.[98]

Arguments for greater government control stress that governments are beholden to society and the population in a way that private enterprises are not. It was in response to the apparent apathy of social media companies that governments around the world pushed these entities to do more. The expectation was that the big-tech companies should not just rely on users flagging content to be addressed but that they search proactively for such material using automation, artificial intelligence, and human review teams. The pressure worked in the sense of compelling a response from the private sector. Still, as Yochai Benkler argues, there are good reasons not to put 'more editorial responsibility on the shoulders of a tiny number of monopolistic or at least oligopolistic companies that have their bottom line as their primary consideration.'[99]

The better solution may be to generate a better share of responsibility, and better coordination on this question, between government and private actors. Seeking to build such collaboration, world leaders and technology providers on May 15, 2019, signed on to the Christchurch Call, named after the recent far-right terrorist attack in New Zealand. The call is a commitment by its supporters 'to prevent the upload of terrorist and violent extremist content and to prevent its dissemination on social media and similar content-sharing services, including its immediate and permanent removal, without prejudice to law enforcement and user appeals requirements, in a manner consistent with human rights and fundamental freedoms.'[100] Nineteen countries and the European Union were founding supporters of the call, along with ten online service providers, including Facebook, Google, Twitter, and Microsoft. By 2020, 51 nations and multilateral bodies were signatories and, in 2021, another 7 joined, including—most notably—the United States.

It is gratifying to see companies cooperate with the international community of states in this manner. Yet bold proclamations do not resolve the underlying issues of primary responsibility. In April 2021, two years after it had joined the Christchurch Call, the European Union passed legislation that forces online platforms to remove terrorist content within one hour of it being flagged by a specialized government agency.[101] The bill also sets out sanctions for non-compliance. Though this instrument is plainly well-intentioned, questions abound regarding its implementation and the risk of adverse effects—on smaller companies, on free speech, and on the internet writ large. Because governments clearly felt that social media giants were not doing enough, complex notions of what constitutes terrorist content will now have to be expediently resolved; when combined with the inadequate resources of smaller companies to engage with this broad question, the outcome is likely to be rampant over-deletion.[102] Tellingly, similar legislation was attempted by the French government, but for a day's notice rather than an hour, and it still had to be significantly watered down owing to its unrealistic timeline and lack of judicial review.[103] Germany has also passed this type of bill, stipulating one day's notice for 'obviously illegal' content but a week, and possibly longer, for more ambiguous cases.[104] Regardless of configuration, the signal from European governments is that the private sector cannot be relied upon to do the work itself.

Indeed, these laws spring from a groundswell of anger at social media companies and pressure for truly fundamental reform.[105]

The United States has taken a different tack. Through the Communications Decency Act (CDA) of 1996, specifically section 230, social media companies are not held responsible for the content that users of these platforms upload and share.[106] The principle underpinning this approach is 'to prioritize economic development and free expression on the internet at the cost of imperfect enforcement.'[107] Yet this interpretation of CDA is not beyond reproach. Danielle Citron and Benjamin Wittes make the cogent point that §230 was never intended to immunize 'platforms for destructive third-party content they encourage or intentionally tolerate.'[108] The Act was initially an attempt to ensure that those companies that act as 'good Samaritans'—that look after their platform—were protected both for the prohibited content that they miss and for erroneous decisions to purge. It does not follow, argue Citron and Wittes, that the Act should, across the board, shield 'businesses that are not merely failing to take "Good Samaritan" steps to protect users from online indecency but are actually being "Bad Samaritans."'[109]

This argument has garnered significant support and the fate of §230 is now in doubt.[110] The point would not be to scrap the legislation, as it has had key benefits for the development and openness of social media. Instead, it would be a matter of giving the government greater flexibility to intervene as needed, to prevent the serious social hazards caused by irresponsible companies, yet without harming the original spirit of the Act. For instance, it would be possible for the government to keep working as before with the many social media companies that do act as 'good Samaritans,' while also intervening against those companies that fail to respond to repeated notifications of terrorist content or activity on their platforms.[111] In this manner, and as suggested in a variety of legislative attempts to amend the CDA, the United States would move ever so slightly closer to European praxis.[112]

This compromise position between the US and the EU legal systems may just be the sweet spot for partnerships between companies and governments. Still, regardless of how this relation is modulated, three fundamental principles obtain. First, most social media companies, in particular the major ones, work hard to clean their platforms of pro-terrorism material, not only as a counterterrorism policy but because the majority of internet users want a relatively sanitized online environment. Despite these efforts, it is simply impossible to remove violent extremism from the internet altogether; there is simply too much gray-area content and adversaries learn how to game the system. Consequently, even with the significant efforts of the private sector, internet-born terrorist attacks will persist. This does not signify the failure of Silicon Valley's efforts—it would be an impossible and also dangerous standard to meet. Instead, it simply reinforces the need to try harder and do better (which is not necessarily the same as simply doing more).

Second, if social media companies should not be charged with the impossible, it must also be recognized to what degree they themselves generate the problem at hand. Social media monetizes outrage and emotion, as both are crucial to sustained engagement. For the sake of ad revenue, then, these companies fashion online worlds that exploit our data, feed us information that cements our bias, and create the very echo chambers in which ideational insurgencies take root. More pointedly, Sasha Havlicek notes how this technological architecture 'inorganically amplifies extreme messaging and content, and ultimately drives people into spaces that they otherwise may not have been driven into.'[113] So, while the discussion on deleting or retaining individual posts is important, it also risks obscuring this deeper structural reality. No doubt, unraveling that reality will force an unpleasant conversation with and among social media companies, but greater transparency is needed on how their algorithms work, the incentives that they cause, and their effects on society. It is a conversation in which government and civil society should both have a major say.

Indeed, as a third and final principle, the conversation of terrorism, free speech, and social media is one that should involve not just government and companies but also society at large. Havlicek, again, gets at this point, arguing for big-picture thinking 'around our digital policy strategy [and] our vision for the internet.'[114] Authoritarian regimes have already laid out a clear and fairly consistent blueprint for what they want the internet to be, yet in liberal democracies—despite signs of heightened public concern—this conversation has lacked structure and direction.[115] As the users most affected by both freedom of speech concerns and terrorism, democratic citizens cannot sit idly by and expect others to make choices on their behalf. Instead, education, debate, and advocacy are needed, regarding the use of our data, what we want social media to be, and the safeguards taken both by public and by private actors to regulate our 'digital public square.'[116]

Fostering Individual and Societal Resilience

Talk of societal inclusion introduces a third major response to ideational insurgency. Given the significant difficulties in eliminating exposure to the hateful rhetoric of violent extremism, a safer bet might just be to reduce its effect. Thus, rather than focusing on the supply side of radicalizing content—what is posted online—this approach homes in on the demand, or the interest and receptivity of users to such messaging. After all, a tweet is only a tweet; it is really its effect on specific individuals that matters.

There are two broad paths to challenging the appeal of extremist ideologies: discrediting the extremist rhetoric itself (the pull factors for radicalization) and addressing susceptibility to this message (the push factors). Both paths can yield positive results, and there is a significant overlap between the two. Regardless of approach, however, this type of work produces a wide margin for missteps and own goals. Indeed, it is instructive to revisit both the positive and the negative lessons that have emerged from 20 years of seeking to marginalize the ideological appeal of al-Qaeda, ISIS, and their affiliated movements.

Counter-messaging

The intent of counter-messaging is to confront and discredit violent extremist rhetoric, thereby reducing its appeal to consumers of such material. Efforts center on raising awareness, correcting misinformation and misinterpretation, providing positive alternatives to the extremists' often hateful ideology, and challenging preconceived notions and biases through logic, fact or humor.[117] Though these types of actions may not sway the hardliners, they are intended to provide the curious and onlookers with a different narrative, thereby stemming their process of radicalization. One might surmise that liberal democracies would perform rather well in these contests of credibility, particularly when pitted against hateful groups preaching violence and intolerance, and yet practice reveals counter-messaging to be a peculiarly fine art. Questions abound regarding how to engage, who can best do it, whom should be targeted, and how to measure success.

The US Center for Strategic Counterterrorism Communications (CSCC) is a frequently cited illustration of how counter-messaging can go wrong. Seeking to respond to the ideational onslaught of al-Qaeda and other affiliated movements, the US government created CSCC in 2011 as a component within the State Department. Its role grew as ISIS took to the internet and was able to draw thousands of youths from around the world into its fight for a caliphate in the Middle East. Seeking ways to counter ISIS's radicalizing message, CSCC created various Twitter accounts, an Arabic YouTube profile, and a Facebook page. The highest-profile effort was the 'Think Again Turn Away' Twitter account, which posted content meant to fact-check ISIS propaganda and, even, engage with its sympathizers. One of its most notable moments involved a minute-long video, 'Welcome to ISIS Land,' which sought through irony and grisly images of ISIS brutality to expose the group's hypocrisy. By 2016, this Twitter account had amassed close to 22,000 followers.[118]

CSCC was a bold and creative initiative. It was an attempt to replicate the agility and modern methods of malign networks yet use this approach for good.[119] Yet as many observers of this program have concluded, the overall effort was undermined by an admixture of errors. As a US government entity, CSCC lacked the reach, reaction time, and credibility necessary to influence the audiences that mattered. Also, the war of narratives against ISIS too often degenerated into exchanges of 'snarky jabs' between the State Department and anonymous pro-ISIS Twitter users, who were greatly elevated and amplified as a result.[120] Many saw it as both unseemly and ineffective to have an official US government account involve itself in petty disputes, attempt sarcasm, and engage with attention-seeking trolls. Furthermore, even if CSCC did turn someone away from extremism, to demonstrate this return on investment was all but impossible.

CSCC represents an unfortunate but instructive episode, and many of its lessons have been absorbed. For starters, CSCC was in 2016 replaced with the Global Engagement Center (GEC) and its Twitter handle was terminated. In contrast to its predecessor, GEC does not seek to engage in its own messaging, but instead focuses on supporting the communication efforts of others—those with the credibility and vernacular necessary to reach the most critical audiences. To this end, GEC has built links with think tanks, academia, civil society, and the private sector to ensure that communication campaigns are more carefully designed and executed. This approach reflects best practices in the field. Facebook, for instance, has worked with civil society groups to help them design anti-extremist campaigns, which the social media platform can then amplify. Various grassroots tech companies are providing training to youth in how to create high-quality media that can challenge extremist views and ideologies.[121] The focus of these efforts is on finding the most authentic interlocutors and enabling them to reach vast audiences, all the while speaking in their own voice.

This approach has promise, yet it is difficult to know whether the related efforts are influencing the right individuals, and at the right time, or whether they merely preach to the converted. Even when optimally targeted (a challenge in and of itself), how can episodic engagement replicate the sustained influence that a participant in ideational insurgency draws from the online spaces created by the movement? A further obstacle concerns 'disconfirmation' bias, or the common tendency to reject messages that run counter to hardwired ideological convictions. Indeed, psychological studies confirm that directly challenging people's 'core worldviews' often evokes 'a defensive emotional reaction' and can therefore 'counterproductively lead people to fortify their belief systems.'[122] This limitation points to the key conundrum within counter-messaging, namely how to reach, from outside, those who explicitly reject the outside world, or how to disrupt the relentless reinforcement of an insular echo chamber. The dilemma is age-old: Hannah Arendt captured well the firm grip of totalitarian propaganda, describing it as 'foolproof against arguments based on a reality which the movements promised to change, against a counterpropaganda disqualified by the mere fact that it belongs to or defends a world which the shiftless masses cannot and will not accept.'[123]

A precondition for success in this field is using an interlocutor that members of the targeted movement can accept as credible. Some governments have reacted to this finding by seeking out extremist yet non-violent partners, in the hope of thereby increasing their reach. Clearly, this presents a quandary between working with questionable actors, and thereby enhancing their standing, and sticking with politically safer interlocutors who may have no sway over the ideological hard core.[124] Another way forward is to work with 'formers'—ex-members of the group—who can relate to current group members in a way that is both authentic and sensitive to their experience. Indeed, this approach was central to the comparative successes of ExitUSA, an American initiative of the Life After Hate organization that targets white supremacism.[125] Yet another option is to use survivors of terrorism, so as to humanize the 'other' and bring awareness of the human costs of violent extremism.

Regardless of interlocutor, counter-messaging faces a more fundamental challenge. It is facile to point out that group members are radicalized for different reasons and that counter-messaging must adjust accordingly. The deeper and thornier point is that adherence to a group—and acceptance of its ideology—are typically not the result of rational discourse, which can be challenged empirically, but stem from a protracted and ongoing socio-psychological process. Narrative, in this context, is less a message, and more a matter of 'socialisation, meaning-seeking and identity formation,' buttressed by online bonds and friendships.[126] These links, and the meaning they provide, will not be undone merely by appealing to reason. Indeed, counter-messaging must then go beyond 'direct rebuttals' and engage with 'the social processes and broader factors driving radicalization.'[127] This might imply exploring 'the interests, anxieties and frustrations of "vulnerable individuals" ... so as to help dissolve

251

the binary comparisons that often underpin extremist narratives.'[128] It might also require affirming the self-worth of targeted members, to build them up to a point where they no longer react defensively but feel empowered to address uncomfortable thoughts and realities.[129] All of this, however, presumes a deep level of engagement, over the long term, and the development of trust—even intimacy, so that the targeted individual derives the same psychological benefits from the interlocutor that he or she normally would enjoy with the group.[130]

Given these sensitivities and requirements, the odds against successfully inducing disengagement from a violent extremist organization seem vanishingly small. Reassuringly, there is anecdotal evidence of such efforts working, yet because of major methodological issues in measuring and tracking effectiveness, it is unclear whether these positive cases were due to the intervention or to other causes. Intuitively, creating off-ramps for members of an ideational insurgency would seem more productive where these individuals are already contemplating disengagement but need a way out. Another possible target is those group members facing minor charges, who might be better rehabilitated through counter-messaging rather than through serving time (particularly given the common effect of prisons in spreading and strengthening violent ideologies). These specific sorts of contingencies may in themselves justify continued investment in counter-messaging, yet it should be borne in mind that, much as with CSCC, these efforts can be counterproductive rather than just ineffectual.

Preventing Violent Extremism

A different, and plausibly more promising, road to individual resilience would involve earlier engagement, before the process of radicalization has truly taken hold. This is the field of 'Preventing Violent Extremism,' or PVE, which has gained global prominence in recent years as a non-coercive counterterrorism tool aimed at averting radicalization rather than dealing with its aftermath. PVE aims to identify and reach individuals drawn in by extremist ideologies and to change their trajectory by addressing the factors fueling their alienation. Thus, PVE opens up space for a range of non-security-related actors, from the community or civil society, to engage in counseling, interventions, religious rehabilitation, prison reform, skills training, and other similar efforts. In theory, then, this approach generates new opportunities for state and society to work together to help those who are being led astray.

In the last two decades, PVE has gained popularity as governments sought a more flexible approach to the problem of terrorism. A typical PVE program will resemble the British government's Channel initiative, which aims to provide early assistance to those identified as 'vulnerable' to terrorism. Vulnerability, in this context, is determined on the basis of several factors, including access to extremist materials, the promotion of scripted extremist narratives, experience of trauma in conflict zones, and expressed acute intolerance of people of different backgrounds and faiths.[131] Frontline staff—teachers, counselors, law enforcement, members of the community—make referrals to the Channel program, leading to a comprehensive assessment by a multidisciplinary panel. When intervention is considered appropriate, a plan is put together based on the exact nature of the case. Consent is obtained either from the individual or from his or her legal guardian, and the program is launched. Depending on need, support may take the form of mentoring, guidance, anger management, theological or ideological dialogue, therapy, or skills training. Progress is regularly and thoroughly reviewed until the desired dissociation from the ideology or group is complete.[132]

Though it is difficult to measure its effectiveness, there is ample anecdotal evidence to suggest that PVE activities can work.[133] Intuitively, it is easy to see how this method could be a helpful complement in addressing ideational insurgents. By providing an alternative, challenging extremist narratives, and creating spaces and institutions where those drawn in can safely reassess their views and possibly disengage, it may be possible to reverse the gravitational pull of online radicalization before it is too late. And yet, much as with counter-messaging, PVE is not just a field of opportunity, but also one of great ethical and strategic peril. Indeed, the seductive simplicity of this type of work belies the very sensitive dilemmas surrounding its implementation.

Specifically, because PVE is a preventive approach, it must necessarily deal with the precursors of terrorism, or with the incipient signs of radicalization. Consequently, it relies upon the ability to locate, in an accurate and pre-emptive manner, those individuals who urgently need help. The traditional method of doing so is to work with the community and to respond to its appeals for help. Achieving this type of partnership, however, has been the thorniest part of it all. In both the United Kingdom and the United States, PVE initiatives to counter Islamist violent extremism were introduced in such a way as to make the Muslim community feel less like a partner addressing a common concern and more like a security risk or a problem to be managed.[134] Given the already fraught state–community relations, not least in view of the recent 9/11 attacks and the ongoing War on Terror, this outcome should have been anticipated.[135] Instead, mismanaged communications strongly undermined PVE's implementation, with civil society, civil rights organizations, and religious organizations rejecting the effort as a fig leaf for espionage, profiling, and marginalization.

The role of the community in PVE is crucial but also ambiguous, which explains to some degree the difficulties of engagement. On the one hand, the invocations of religion and community are far too sweeping, as the individuals of concern are a tiny minority, and at times not even members, of either. Of approximately three million British Muslims, about 0.0003 percent (or 850) left to become foreign fighters in the Middle East. A similarly negligible percentage of American Muslims have been charged with ISIS-related crimes.[136] In that sense, identifying a tie between the community and the problem of radicalization can rightly be seen as misguided and even insulting. And yet the Muslim community cannot be made irrelevant to PVE efforts targeting ISIS and its related ideology. Because the majority of those who join this group, or launch attacks in its name, do self-identify as Muslim, it is crucial that, when signs of radicalization are seen, members of that community are aware of the preventive measures that the state provides and can trust the system to engage appropriately.

Without community support, the state operates in the dark.[137] When it comes to finding partners, however, most states have struggled. In the United States, it certainly did not help that PVE efforts for long focused near exclusively on the problem of Islamist terrorism, even as right-wing extremism became a growing, even dominant, concern. The Trump administration doubled down on this narrow focus and, given the incendiary Islamophobic policies and rhetoric emerging from the White House at this time, relations with the Muslim community soured further.[138] Because the FBI has been a lead participant in several PVE efforts, the entire endeavor is also easily mistaken for another coercive instrument in the state's arsenal, camouflaged by a gentler vocabulary and, for that reason, perhaps all the more sinister. For all of these reasons, it is now difficult to see how PVE efforts can go on, at least using this nomenclature (indeed, though the Biden administration will be sustaining this type of work, it has shut down PVE centers and established a Center for Prevention Programs and Partnerships).

Rebranding may help achieve buy-in but, without reform, the fundamental contradictions of practice will return to haunt the associated programs. The difficulties of successful PVE will also be compounded now that the tool is, belatedly—after the Capitol riot—applied to the problem of far-right violent extremism. Clearly, even though all the rioters that day were Trump supporters, casting all Trump voters as in some way relevant to this brand of terrorism would be to tar about 74 million Americans with the same brush. And yet, much as with the Muslim community, the state requires the assistance of these families, networks, and people to identify and help address the proportionally few instances of right-wing violent radicalization in their midst. As any observer of American politics will testify, the chances of fostering such a partnership are slim.[139]

PVE targeting right-wing extremism will be further complicated by the fact that, as discussed earlier, large parts of the American right wing share the talking points that motivate the very violence that is to be prevented. Between 65 and 71 percent of registered Republicans supported Trump's proposal 'to temporarily halt Muslims from entering the United States.'[140] Only 49 percent of Republicans polled in 2015 believed that 'the religion of Islam should even be legal in the United States with 30% saying it shouldn't be'; among Trump voters, the split was virtually even.[141] We saw in

255

chapter 5 how, depending on the poll, between 23 and 41 percent of self-identified Republicans hold a favorable view of, or believe in, the QAnon conspiracy theory.[142] Similarly, nearly half of polled Trump voters lend credence to the bizarre Pizzagate saga connecting Hillary Clinton, a child sex-trafficking ring, and a Washington, DC, pizzeria.[143] In polls taken shortly after January 6, 2021, 'roughly 15 percent of Republicans openly endorsed the rebellion,' even when it was explicitly described as an 'attack,' as 'storming,' and as 'taking over' the Capitol. On other questions in the same poll, 23 percent of Republicans agreed that 'in America today ... it can be acceptable for people to use force or violence to try to achieve political goals.' So far, these sentiments do not seem to have waned.[144]

The point should be clear but it goes to the heart of a political reality in America that must be internalized before any effort of 'preventing violent extremism' can take root. It will be a highly fraught endeavor to establish a partnership to prevent radicalization with a community of which large parts are themselves radicalized. There is a key distinction to be made between radicalization of belief and radicalization of deed, as clearly not all those espousing radical opinions will be involved in or favorably predisposed toward violence. And yet, even with this narrower and more appropriate scope, partnering with a community that not only is hostile to government but operates in a separate epistemic realm will bring immense challenges. Eric Rosand notes in a separate context that 'in many respects, the broader aims of strengthening the relationship between the state and its citizens and building trust between all levels of government and local communities lie at the heart of the P/CVE agenda.'[145] In this instance, this agenda will call for nothing less than healing the rifts of a deeply divided America, something that probably goes beyond the PVE ambit.

Though this issue of community relations is by far the largest obstacle in the way of effective PVE, accumulated practice with such programming also reveals significant down-river challenges. It is, for example, ironic that, for all the negative attention, PVE activities are typically resourced on an ad hoc basis or out of existing budgets. As a result, for all the opprobrium, the agenda has had a fairly minimal effect on counterterrorism practice.[146] More than undercutting the impact of this programming, such deficiencies in resourcing and interest also increase the danger of it badly misfiring. For one, the necessary engagement across the federal government, including the agencies devoted to education, social outreach, and human services, has not matured. As a result, the FBI has taken the lead, which undercuts the intent for PVE to be a non-prosecutorial and non-security-oriented approach. Second, the federal government has not established the necessary partnerships with city officials, civil society organizations, and other local-level structures—those that should always steer the associated programming. Addressing this shortfall will be crucial in any PVE work within the United States, given the apparent toxicity of federal engagement at the local level.[147]

Underpinning these questions of resourcing and structure, PVE also requires a far more disciplined empirical foundation, with more energy devoted to clarifying the theory, method, and metrics relating to such work. To date, insufficient focus and interest have resulted in a lack of rigor, allowing any number of projects to claim PVE relevance even when their link to drivers of alienation is indirect at best. Because measuring the success of PVE is anyway challenging—in effect it requires proving a negative, or the non-event of an averted attack—there is plenty of scope for less effective programs to go on uncontested. J. M. Berger's observation is therefore caustic but fair: 'Programmes built on false or ambiguous correlations diminish confidence in policy leaders, and in the very concept of [PVE] itself, as millions of dollars are wasted on efforts that can be charitably described as irrelevant, and less charitably described as the funding of pet projects under the auspices of fighting terrorism.'[148]

The rather haphazard, lackadaisical, and often tone-deaf approach with which the US government has engaged with PVE will seal the fate of this approach unless quickly addressed. In future, projects must not only engage with communities productively—a tall order—but also arrive at truly targeted interventions that identify and address drivers specific to the individual case. This requirement will be both analytically and strategically challenging, yet it is through interventions such as these that violent extremism is observably prevented and PVE as an approach gains credibility.

Media Literacy

If PVE seeks preventive intervention, it is possible to get further 'left of bang,' to use the military term, by focusing not on specifically vulnerable individuals but rather on the societal weaknesses that render us susceptible to the forces unleashed through ideational insurgency. Given the distorting epistemological effects of social media, there is growing need for concerted instruction and measures to assist adaptation to this new reality. This conversation goes beyond the topic of violent extremism, touching upon the 'filter bubbles' created by online algorithms and their harmful effects on discourse, expertise, and democracy.[149] Still, it is also a conversation that is relevant to the more specific discussion of this chapter, in that the ideational onslaught depends so fundamentally on shifting facts to effect political change.

It is said that we now live in a 'post-truth' environment—one where a 'content-overladen and hyper-pluralistic public sphere has generated a culture of relativism' in which 'every fact and opinion can be found online and so can their counterparts.'[150] As social media has democratized the internet and led to a proliferation of voices, it has also led to an erosion of trust in traditional knowledge-producing institutions (including the media). The upshot is that 'we have lost our capacity to agree on shared modes of validation as to what is going on and what is just plain whacky.'[151] Though some utopians envisaged that an open marketplace of ideas would lead to a more diverse and productive competition of ideas, they did not anticipate that the playing field would be so tilted: by an outrage-driven information economy, manipulative players demanding attention, and populist leaders peddling simple answers to complex questions.[152] Within the resulting cacophony, truth has lost all meaning.

Problematically, once society loses its tethering to a particular method for validating truth, it is difficult to reverse this process. One prominent response seeks to educate the population on basic media literacy, so as to build the skills needed to navigate the information landscape of our times. The notion here is that 'separating fact from opinion, evaluating text and image for bias, and constructing and deconstructing a text based on principles of logic are teachable skills.'[153] By learning to identify misinformation and propaganda in this manner, it might be possible to disarm the actors responsible for such content. This theory is not new; in fact, it reappears at regular intervals whenever a new informational medium emerges that challenges how societies communicate and learn.[154] Within its latest iteration, the desired end state has been called 'cognitive resilience,' that is, 'the ability to withstand pressure from various ideas spread, for instance, through disinformation.'[155] Others go further, seeing a need for a more systemic state of 'digital resilience' that protects 'the public sphere itself against the threat of dissolution.'[156]

Media literacy would help counter ideational insurgency by empowering societies to resist and challenge the conspiracy theories, cant, and sophistry used to radicalize individual users. In contrast to PVE and counter-messaging, the method is pre-emptive and systemic, targeting entire societies before the fact and preparing them for the dangers that lurk online. In that sense, this approach acknowledges the difficulty of pinpointing exactly who will succumb to radicalization and the challenge of addressing this process once it is under way. Instead, media literacy casts a wide net and catches its targets while they are young, or before the corrupting influences of the internet have had a chance to unalterably close their minds.[157]

A number of media literacy programs are already under way in a variety of contexts—some more well developed than others. Schools across Europe and the United States teach media literacy in one form or another as part of their curriculum. In many cases, these efforts are undertaken with the support of social media, traditional media, and civil society organizations, which have developed tools and content tailored for specific purposes and age groups. Interactive programs, apps, and material have been formulated to simulate online encounters with disinformation and 'fake news' so as to inculcate best practices and foundational principles for twenty-first-century living. Signatories to the EU Code of Practice on Disinformation, which include the major social media companies, have all 'made progress in creating and supporting media literacy programs,' such as Facebook's Digital Literacy Library and support for related regional programs, Twitter's provision of grants to grassroots programs, and Google's funding of similar initiatives in Finland, France, and Portugal.[158] In 2018, the

OECD introduced a 'global competence assessment' as part of its Programme for International Student Assessment (PISA), including a notable emphasis on digital media literacy.[159]

There is typically a common structure to these endeavors. The first step involves raising students' awareness of their own biases and how they affect news consumption and comprehension. The training then points to best practices to stymie the effects of filters and prejudice, for example by questioning content that emotively feels right and by seeking out information and perspectives from a variety of sources.[160] As Alan Miller adds, 'another teaching tool is to urge students to try to withhold judgment when they first learn of an event, especially on fast-breaking, chaotic and polarizing stories such as the recent shootings by or of police.'[161] A deeper topic of discussion might be why we even share information online: whether it is to inform and discuss or mostly to build our own brand.

Another way of fostering the digital resilience sought through these programs is to 'inoculate' media users against disinformation and propaganda. Developed by W. J. McGuire and D. Papageorgis, this approach seeks to build up resistance against disinformation by priming the brain before the fact. Inoculation is the term used because, much like a vaccine, the user is exposed to a weakened dose of the lie (or an allusion to its content), along with a 'weakened' (not fully developed) counter-argument, so they will be able to reject the attempted manipulation when it comes.[162] Working with Jigsaw (of Google), Kurt Braddock has found that, in a controlled environment, 'participants who read a text-based inoculation message prior to seeing an extremist propaganda post were less willing to support the extremist group and had lower perceptions of the extremist group's credibility relative to a control group that hadn't been inoculated.'[163]

More work is expected from Jigsaw on this front. Already, social media platforms are attempting to automate the delivery of counter-arguments and forewarnings whenever disinformation is found on their platforms. The exact mechanisms of how to simulate the controlled-study environment of psychological experimentation are still being determined. An initial attempt by Facebook to 'flag' suspect material was found to boost engagement precisely with these posts and was therefore dismissed as counterproductive.[164] More helpful is appending links to false posts that provide further context and counter-arguments. Links to fact-checking conducted by independent third parties can also work, though these types of efforts will clearly rely on the user believing that Facebook has his or her best interests at heart and that its preferred sources are trustworthy.

There is ample and convincing evidence that training in media literacy can boost resilience against propaganda, disinformation and fake news, yet the effects of such programming in addressing the online world of violent extremism are less clear. Three major caveats should be borne in mind. First, the process of radicalization is not always a product of disinformation and conspiracy theories, making it difficult to see where better media literacy would make a difference. To take the example of Islamist groups like ISIS, adherents are generally motivated by genuine and, to some degree, legitimate objections to US foreign policy, or to the perception (again at times legitimate) of societal racism and poor integration. In these cases, the receptivity to the Islamist ideology is based on feelings rather than poor information or research skills.

Conspiracy theories and disinformation play a more prominent role in the far-right ideational insurgency. One may, for instance, cite the anecdote of Dylann Roof, whose curiosity about 'black on white crime' led him to disinformation about racial violence in the United States and, in turn, to his violent assault on black parishioners in South Carolina. Similarly, it was exposure to the so-called Pizzagate conspiracy theory that led so many to harass the restaurant's owner and staff and to one individual barging in armed and looking for evidence of child abuse. The myth of a Jewish conspiracy, or of election fraud, or of eugenics might also be countered by greater media literacy and critical thinking. By building skills necessary to debunk such disinformation, at least some of the armed attacks of the far right may be prevented.

This conclusion, however, invites a second caveat, namely that what media literacy seeks to correct is in fact societal cracks and divisions that require more fundamental redress. Advocates of media literacy frequently point to Finland or Estonia as countries where advanced programming in this area has allowed for a robust defense against Russia's repeated onslaughts of disinformation. In Finland, for example, a 'strong public education system emphasises digital and media literacy, teaching citizens to identify bias or skewed narratives in their information sphere and to critically engage with new technological platforms like social media.'[165] Similarly, in the Estonian school curriculum, students are expected to master 'communication competence' and 'digital competence.'[166] Yet in both cases, such proficiency reflects a deeper societal foundation which, in comparison with the programs themselves, will be more difficult to copy. 'The answer, in the Finnish case,' write Corneliu Bjola and Krysianna Papadakis, 'rests with the issue of social trust': Finnish people enjoy a long track record of journalistic integrity, a 'positive relationship with traditional news sources,' and a 'neutral media space' free from 'heavily partisan political reporting.'[167] In Estonia, the defense against Russia's active measures relies on the high levels of societal integration and trust in government and in one another; other than seeking to exploit the Russian-speaking minority in the country, the Kremlin has therefore struggled to find entry points for its disinformation campaigns.[168]

These societal attributes appear to be prerequisites for the sought-after resilience. Lance Bennett and Steven Livingston argue, for example, that it is precisely 'the breakdown of trust in democratic institutions of press and politics, along with educational and civil society institutions in more advanced cases,' that lies behind the emergence of the current 'disinformation order.'[169] As others also point out, the issue is not really social media or online manipulation, but rather how these mesh with local context: 'it is only where the underlying institutional and political-cultural fabric is frayed that technology can exacerbate existing problems and dynamics to the point of crisis.'[170] Like so many other solutions to ideational insurgency, or insurgency *tout court*, the toolkit of media literacy appears least likely to work where it is most urgently needed.

Third, and relatedly, in truly epistemologically fractured societies—and the United States belongs in this category—there is good reason to ask what media literacy even means. If it means consulting more sources and being a critical thinker, it is easy to see how media literacy can inadvertently encourage the very conspiracism that it seeks to counter: it all depends on what types of sources are deemed legitimate. Media literacy programming operates by an implied 'universal agreement that major news outlets like the *New York Times*, scientific journal publications, and experts with advanced degrees are all highly trustworthy.'[171] This assumption will not raise concern among left-leaning and progressive crowds, but it leaves unaddressed the question of why faith in these institutions is more defensible than that placed by others in their own sources of knowledge. Cory Doctorow summarizes the dilemma cogently:

> The 'establishment' version of epistemology is, 'We use evidence to arrive at the truth, vetted by independent verification (but trust us when we tell you that it's all been independently verified by people who were properly skeptical and not the bosom buddies of the people they were supposed to be fact-checking).'

> The 'alternative facts' epistemological method goes like this: 'The "independent" experts who were supposed to be verifying the "evidence-based" truth were actually in bed with the people they were supposed to be fact-checking. In the end, it's all a matter of faith, then: you either have faith that "their" experts are being truthful, or you have faith that we are. Ask your gut, what version *feels* more truthful?'[172]

Without some common ground, how can media literacy help prove that the alt-right's replacement theory is incorrect, that a Jewish cabal does not control the world, or—even—that Hillary Clinton is not involved in a child sex-trafficking ring? The lack of evidence is the very best argument, and yet it quickly loses its potency when it is meant to shut down speculation on topics that by their nature were always supposed to be clandestine. Instead, we are left with the open-ended notion that 'where there is smoke there is fire,' which makes the truly media literate those who reject the wool pulled over their eyes by the establishment and who consider sources far beyond those that the establishment has decided are trustworthy. Danah Boyd's question is therefore unsettlingly apropos: 'You Think You Want Media Literacy ... Do You?'[173]

Conclusion

One year before her death, Hannah Arendt was interviewed by the French writer Roger Errera. On the topic of totalitarianism and the free press, she noted that 'What makes it possible for a totalitarian or any other dictatorship to rule is that people are not informed; how can you have an opinion if you are not informed?'[174] In a twist of irony, the democratization of information seen since the advent of social media threatens modern society with a similar ignorance to that observed by Arendt in totalitarian settings. In this sense, *les extrêmes se touchent*, as both the dearth and the overabundance of information generate the same helplessness.

Ideational insurgency targets the very fabric of society: our norms, our values, and the implicit contract that regulates our coexistence. The challenge is compounded by the epistemological nature of the attack. Arendt again provides a frightening parallel: 'a people that no longer can believe anything cannot make up its mind. It is deprived not only of its capacity to act but also of its capacity to think and to judge. And with such a people you can then do what you please.'[175] Therein lies the most fundamental charge of ideational insurgency: the ability to inject so much doubt, so much disinformation, that alternative—even extreme—ideas can be accepted. Social media, with its expansive virtual worlds and algorithms, acts as the perfect stage for the assault, but it is an attack with deeper roots within the schisms and contradictions of society. Any response must be similarly profound and touch upon issues of legitimacy (and the lack thereof), civil rights (and their limitation), freedom of speech (and its abuse), and our core values (if they exist).

This chapter has offered some ways whereby this undertaking can be approached, yet clearly there are no silver bullets. Law enforcement always has a place in counterterrorism and can disrupt subversive networks. However, its effects are too often retroactive, and when it seeks to engage with the precursors of the attack, it often succeeds only at great cost to civil liberties. Censoring the rhetoric that allows ideational insurgents to thrive can stymie both the reach and the potency of the movement. Still, policing the internet is a vast, delicate, and ever-shifting undertaking, even for the companies that give us our social media, and gains made can quickly become pyrrhic. Seeking to reduce the appeal of extremist ideology through counter-messaging, or by addressing the drivers of alienation, can limit the occurrence and scope of radicalization. Yet establishing the credibility necessary to change minds, and locating those most in need of help, are tall obstacles to overcome. Finally, training society as a whole against disinformation seems promising as a way to defend democracy, yet it may be overly broad for the specific threat of violent extremism and is also unlikely to rise above the epistemological crisis that it seeks to address.

A strategy to counter ideational insurgency would need to select aspects of these approaches, and others, and then approach with caution. Regardless of the strategy crafted, it must counter a societal attack by harnessing a societal response, requiring deft engagement with civil society, the private sector, media, and academia—and also with the 'ordinary' citizen. It is necessary to confront the frames and narratives that fuel ideational attacks and to respond to a movement defined neither by structure nor by location. Responses must neither overreact to mindless trolling nor allow social and political subversion to go unchecked. And while challenging their narrative, the state must also work on its own storyline; strategies of suppression, of censure, even of engagement, will fail if the state has no credible and unifying vision of its own.

This leaves one final and unsettling question. Counterinsurgency is sometimes referred to as 'armed reform' because the military or security component is only there to make possible the critical political changes that address the roots of the problem. To what degree does a counterinsurgency campaign against an ideational challenge require a similar type of reform—to what degree can it politically address, or even accommodate, the factors that mobilize a group toward violence against the state? Returning to Durkheim, can the response be expected to address the anomie that is fueling alienation, or somehow change society to lower its incidence?

Given the two major case studies used to examine the phenomenon of ideational insurgency—that of ISIS on the one hand and the far right on the other—the likelihood of finding common ground or of negotiating core grievances seems very low. Still, ways forward

265

can be found by distinguishing the leadership of these movements (those stressing 'ideological solutions to grievances') from their followers (those 'galvanized by local particulars, whatever their economic-social-political nature').[176] Much as in counterinsurgency campaigns of the past, the key may lie in persuading the latter to buy into and engage through the political opportunity structure, thereby severing their bond with, and isolating, the anti-systemic figures and ideologies that are left behind. Needless to say, this is easier said than done.

CONCLUSION

From Darius's frustration at his enemy's evasion in the Scythian campaign of 513 BC, to Napoleon's anger at guerrilla resistance during the Peninsular War (his 'Spanish ulcer'), it has become an axiom of strategic studies that states struggle when faced with insurgency. And yet, in reviewing the overall insurgent experience in recent years, there are exceedingly few instances where they have toppled an established government and seized sustained power. Indeed, rather than being overthrown one after the other, most states survive the onslaught of insurgency, often by relying on their superior resources and military capabilities. Though the counterinsurgency manuals preach mobilization and hearts and minds, it is typically through suppression that states contain their adversary, causing their movement either to fizzle out or to become a peripheral concern. Outright victory may elude both sides, but the stalemate nonetheless favors the state, which in the absence of a decisive outcome remains the constituted authority.

This trend represents a dilemma for the world's insurgents. During the Cold War and into the 1990s, insurgents found ways to mobilize rural populations and build coercive capability, making a conventional showdown against the state an ambitious yet feasible path to power. Today, this approach is less likely to succeed and is therefore also rare. For sure, those few groups that act as proxies for states can expect more, yet for most the path to military victory is blocked. Even insurgent heavyweights such as ISIS and LTTE were denied their counter-state and experienced military defeat within three years. For other insurgents, most of whom will not amass similar capability, the overall track record raises legitimate questions of how to prevail in today's strategic environment. 'Do we get to win this time?'—the question was of course Rambo's, that quintessential American warrior, when first told that he was to return to Vietnam.[1] Today, the question belongs to the insurgents. How can they do better against stronger states? How can they overcome the insurgent's dilemma?

In examining this question, it is important not to draw too many conclusions from the singular, and exceptional, Taliban victory in Afghanistan. Indeed, rather than represent the future of insurgency, the movement's conquest of Kabul in the late summer of 2021 has more in common with insurgency's distant past, during the era of empire and the Cold War. In Afghanistan, we saw an insurgent group capable of mobilizing a primarily rural population against a distant state, much as movements of national liberation did during the Cold War. We also saw a central government in Kabul so dependent on foreign forces that it harks back to the puppet regimes of colonial times. Similar to those regimes, which were overthrown or defeated with some regularity, the Afghan state proved itself not just artificial but therefore also incapable of exerting itself beyond the capital. And, finally, we saw a non-state armed group receiving military assistance and sanctuary from a neighboring state, namely Pakistan. In these three ways, the context in Afghanistan resembles that faced during the heyday of insurgency rather than the decidedly less forgiving conditions that today's and tomorrow's movements confront.

Indeed, the decline in insurgent fortunes since the 1990s relates to contextual shifts that have altered the vulnerabilities of states in relation to their adversaries. Though the comparative strength and reach of states have always mounted difficulties for insurgent start-ups, the change in strategic environment has made the gap in capability more pronounced. The vast hinterlands where insurgents used to find their manpower and materiel have been emptying out for decades, forcing would-be challengers to contend in urban settings and under the gaze of the state. Also, despite the recent re-emergence of great-power competition, the superpowers of today are not sponsoring insurgencies on nearly the same scale as they did during the Cold War. Instead, since 9/11, the notion of seizing control through force of arms has become politically stigmatized, and groups must therefore tread carefully when using violence as part of their political strategy. Even the Taliban will likely struggle to convert their military victory into a sustainable and accepted political order.

Some discern within these shifts a possible, if gradual, end to war as we know it. To Steven Pinker, the picture is clear: he sees a decline in violence on a global scale, a trend he frames as maybe 'the most significant and least appreciated development in the history of our species.'[2] Pinker suggests the tighter regulation of states, the benefits of trade, and changing cultural mores have so lowered the benefits of aggression that actors now prefer peace and expect peace from others. Such norms, he argues, affect the cost-benefit analysis of aggression—or what Pinker terms the 'pacifist's dilemma.'[3] Following this logic, Bruno Tertrais concludes that 'we are nearing a point of history where it will be possible to say that war as we know it, long thought to be an inevitable part of the human condition, has disappeared.'[4]

This may be going too far—and the notion of collective violence being out of fashion took a serious knock with the Syrian civil war and the emergence of Islamic State. Still, despite plenty of countervailing evidence—none of which Pinker necessarily refutes—violence has come to mean something different from what it did in decades, even centuries, past. Even revisionist world powers, such as China and Russia, make concerted if patently transparent attempts to cloak their coercion with narratives, posing as innocents while extending their reach. As regards insurgency, rather than striving for a decisive military endgame, the art of rebellion has also become less stark, more ambiguous, and the violence must therefore be calibrated more carefully. This does not necessarily mean that the 'better angels of our nature' have prevailed—as Pinker suggests—but rather that different calculations have to be made. Writing on realism, Hedley Bull astutely observed that 'the only rules or principles' that govern behavior are those 'of prudence or expediency'—it would seem as if global norms now compel many insurgents to focus more squarely on the former.[5]

It is within this crisis of insurgency that one finds the emergence of adaptive strategies, designed to undo the state's coercive advantage and allow for sustained power in a new security environment. In this context, what appears to show promise is the adoption of subtler methods, the avoidance of open battle, and instead the use of spin and subversion to score incremental gains. Violence still plays an important role, but it tends to be limited in scope and dominated by non-violent efforts, be they deception, propaganda, above-ground mobilization, or alliance-building. This moderation of violence allows the insurgent to do more without suffering military consequences or reputational cost, either domestically or abroad. Thus, whereas traditional insurgency threatened the state with increasingly forceful strikes and assaults, the approaches explored here result in its power being gradually sapped, sometimes without governments showing much awareness or an ability to react.

This theory of victory informs the three insurgent approaches considered in this book. In *localized* insurgencies, the group seeks survival by limiting its objectives to the local level. Rather than aim for regime change, and thereby produce a climactic confrontation that it is unlikely to win, these groups establish informally delineated spheres of influence, incrementally forcing the state to share sovereignty with them. Much like squatters, yet with more violence thrown in, with time these groups establish *de facto* rights over key territory, mostly because that territory has anyway been abandoned by the state. And yet, whether urban or rural, these informal divisions of control tend to slip, as the realities of either world creep across established lines and cause confrontation. Elsewhere, the tacit 'arrangements' between the government and challenger corrupt and delegitimize the state, thereby inviting new sources of instability. The task for the state lies in somehow fusing the divide upon which localization rests, either by reconnecting with lost populations, or through more indirect forms of governance that acknowledge the practical limitations of sovereignty.

In *infiltrative* insurgencies, the group competes quasi-legally within the political opportunity structure all the while using violence behind the scenes to facilitate its assumption of power. By ostensibly engaging in legal politics, these movements protect themselves with the cloak of legitimacy yet retain a low-level use of terror and intimidation as a force multiplier—one that is more effective precisely when it does not tarnish the above-ground efforts under way. Once the group has gained access to the formal instruments of state, these are used as but another avenue of attack and source of power. The dilemma for the state lies in establishing, dispassionately and fairly, which democratic rivals are legitimate yet sharp-elbowed political opponents and which are Trojan horses, exploiting political openness to tear the whole system down.

In *ideational* insurgencies, movements are united by an idea rather than territory and, therefore, become difficult to locate and to suppress militarily. The advent of social media provides the means necessary to de-territorialize insurgency, to radicalize and recruit, and to trigger violence and intimidation 'IRL' (in real life). Violence, in these cases, has been termed 'stochastic,' in that it occurs randomly, albeit according to a common ideology and in the service of the same movement. In this way, ideational insurgencies combine the advantages of dispersion with the traditional benefits of mass, presenting analytical and strategic challenges for those charged with response. Indeed, the state must in such contexts not only predict and prevent largely randomized terrorist attacks but also contain the polarizing influence of the underlying movement, both societally and online. The challenge is compounded by the globalized spread of these struggles and their acquisition of mainstream partners that launder their ideology and legitimize their cause.

These three approaches are exceptionally adaptive. They have, to various degrees, demonstrated their value against stronger states and look likely, therefore, to be adopted, adapted, and refined by others. There is also ample opportunity for these methods to be combined. In Iraq, Moqtada al-Sadr both localized his struggle within Sadr City and other urban centers, and later transitioned to an infiltrative strategy based on the political cachet and following thus achieved. Hezbollah has arguably pursued a similar strategy in Lebanon, operating from a state-within-a-state, using violence (though predominantly against external adversaries) and also competing in electoral democracy. The alt-right in the United States at one point looked likely to pursue and extend its ideational insurgency by penetrating the US government itself through infiltrative tactics. Other cases obtain.

Notably, major revisionist states have picked up on the potency of these methods and sought to use them to boost their influence abroad, or simply to destabilize state rivals. In contrast to the sponsorship of armed movements during the Cold War, the emerging forms of insurgency provide the state sponsor with a greater measure of deniability and also an approach that, in today's environment, may generate more promising results. Thus, Russia has effectively spawned or sponsored *localized* insurgencies in Ukraine, Georgia and elsewhere, creating political schisms in these countries which are now begrudgingly tolerated by the international community.[6] Iran has long sponsored *infiltrative* insurgency in Palestine, Lebanon and Iraq, whereby political groupings with armed wings or militias have claimed government institutions or representation and used these, alongside threatened and actual violence, to pursue their particularist agendas.[7] Russia, again, has been key in sponsoring *ideational* insurgency in the United States, most prominently in relation to the 2016 election but also to sap state power and societal cohesion. Its sponsorship of extreme-right actors in several European countries and its involvement in various 'active measures' operate by a similar logic.[8]

Given these trends, it is becoming increasingly important to rethink insurgency and also the strategies of response. For too long, efforts to defeat insurgency have been overly militarized. In Iraq and Afghanistan, and also in Nigeria, the Philippines, and most other countries affected by insurgency, it is the military that owns the topic and practice of counterinsurgency. Rhetorical invocations of civilian participation or of 'whole-of-government' approaches to countering this challenge have too often failed to translate into the necessary resource allocation or the organization of relevant structures. It is therefore a long-running trend, and a long-running complaint, that counterinsurgency efforts miss the heart of the matter. Whereas all agree that counterinsurgency is in its essence political, far less attention is devoted to understanding and studying what politics is, what it means, and how it works.

Change is clearly necessary. Suppressive firepower may have helped states survive past struggles, but it looks likely to yield ever-diminishing returns as insurgents solve the dilemma that was thus imposed upon them. At that point, states will require an analytical approach that maps more carefully the full totality of insurgent strategy and produces on this basis a tailored and integrated response. Indeed, the three types of insurgency highlighted here will call on new repertoires, approaches, and capabilities, stretching far beyond the military. In broad terms, the social, political, economic, and informational components of state power must work, in concert with the security sector, to enable both proper assessment and the possibility of appropriate response to insurgent threats that, themselves, are similarly diversifying their approach.

Ironically, change of this type would mean grasping, much belatedly, enduring realities about insurgency. Throughout the ages, insurgency has been a violent political competition for legitimacy and influence. The point for insurgents, working from the ground up, was always to apply their strengths against the government's weaknesses and to avoid the application of government strength against their own vulnerabilities. The problem for counterinsurgents is that we no longer interrogate the correlation of forces that inform insurgent strategy, but proceed with an unshakable response inherited from the Cold War.[9] States are stuck fighting the last war, which works well enough when the enemy is doing the same. As the adversary adapts, however, counterinsurgents will need to adopt a similarly flexible understanding of the insurgent phenomenon and of how counterinsurgency will need to change in response.

In his writing on irregular warfare and insurgency, Thomas Marks suggests a way to analyze insurgent strategy that places military tasks in their proper supporting relation vis-à-vis the political and that identifies and explores their interaction with other, non-military lines of effort.[10] Analytical frameworks are no panacea for poor strategy, but they are an indispensable starting point for all that must follow. Thus, Marks proposes five key questions that must be asked of any challenge of political violence, and that may help us discern, without prejudice or preconceived notions, the full logic of the strategy at hand:

1) What is the insurgent doing politically?
2) How is the group exploiting domestic alliances to better reach its objective?

3) How is violence used in support of its political project?
4) How is non-violence used?
5) What is the role of internationalization in the group's struggle?

In considering these questions, one arrives at a potential blueprint for the *how* of strategy, or of the lines of effort used to bridge means and ends. This blueprint, crucially, acknowledges the coexistence of violence and non-violence, and even the subordination of the former to the latter, without losing focus on the overall strategic intent. The framework also indicates the importance for states to diversify their response, thereby to meet the many lines of effort by which the threat strategy operates. In turn, this would entail a veritable broadening of counterinsurgency thinking and practice, beyond the use of the military, to include—as well, and depending on the threat faced—a range of political, social, informational, economic, and even psychological considerations.[11]

In *localized* insurgency, for example, it will not suffice to use violent raids to tamp down the insurgent effort whenever it is deemed out of hand. Response will also require addressing the national economic, social, and political fault lines that allow these struggles to fester. Such work requires renegotiation of both sovereignty and its meaning so as to draw up a social contract that unites people across entrenched dividing lines. The implied need for effective mobilization and communication is clear, but both must also be buttressed by a creative approach to state-building. The point is not necessarily to (re)constitute the Weberian ideal of a nation-state, particularly in places where it has never really applied, but rather to find new modalities of co-option, and more fitting national compacts, that allow for decentralization and divergence all within one political system.

In *infiltrative* insurgency, response cannot rely on the use of force, or at least states must approach the use of repression with utmost care so as not to damage the democracy that they seek to protect. Instead, the key requirement will be to address the alliance-making of the insurgent, to mobilize legitimate political forces against anti-democratic infiltrators, and to ensure the rule of law is applied fairly but effectively and in a non-politicized manner. Theories of militant democracy may be helpful in guarding the unique vulnerabilities of participatory democratic systems, yet this countermeasure can easily be abused to target legitimate political rivals. Some thought must also go into how non-democratic and extremist parties gain electoral support, or to the grievances that they exploit to mobilize. Legitimacy is central to this type of struggle, and so the response must also address the insurgent group's non-violent activities, be they service delivery or social movement agitation, and respond, not with force, but in a manner that responsibly stems a violent, yet camouflaged, project of state capture.

In *ideational* insurgency, state response must account for the group's extensive use of information operations, alliance-making in society, and political mobilization online. There are many options for the state, but targets for security operations are few and far between. Instead, the state must grapple with difficult decisions as to what speech to allow online, how to reach at-risk individuals, how to foster better ties with relevant communities and civil society, and how to build resilience within the population to resist radicalization. This battle of norms and values forcefully underlines the central role of legitimacy in counterinsurgency. Even then, however, states face the challenge of how to communicate this legitimacy in a way that is strategically effective, not least to those who are already alienated and unwilling to engage.

In all three approaches, and in the discussion of response, legitimacy emerges again and again as the center of gravity.[12] It is by delegitimizing government action, by making it go against the grain of public opinion, that oppositional actors gain allies and strength. In creating a hostile political environment for the state, insurgents constrain its perceived options even as it leaves its military power largely intact. As crisis sets in, the insurgent project takes over and grows until, to contested populations, it becomes simply irresistible. States can avert this fate, but they must recall and work harder to articulate exactly what it is they are fighting *for*, not just the threats they seek to defeat. In recent counterinsurgency campaigns, this process of building legitimacy has been an under-developed and under-prioritized area of investment, yet it only promises to become more salient in years ahead.

NOTES

1. INTRODUCTION

1. Henry A. Kissinger, 'The Viet Nam Negotiations,' *Foreign Affairs* 11, no. 2 (1969): 38–50.

2. Harry G. Summers, *American Strategy in Vietnam: A Critical Analysis* (Mineola, NY: Dover Publications, 2012), 1, http://public.eblib.com/choice/publicfullrecord.aspx?p=1890088.

3. US Department of the Army and United States Marine Corps, *FM 3-24/MCWP 3- 33.5. Counterinsurgency* (Washington, DC: US Army, 2006), 1-26, 1-27.

4. Evan Solomon, 'Fighting in Afghanistan: "You Have the Watches. We Have the Time,"' *Maclean's*, September 2, 2017, https://www.macleans.ca/news/fighting-in-afghanistan-you-have-the-watches-we-have-the-time/.

5. See the Uppsala Conflict Termination dataset. Specifically, among decisive outcomes favoring the government or the rebels between 1990 and 2014, the government tallies 30 and the rebels 9 wins. As will be discussed in chapter 2, these figures should be taken with a pinch of salt, yet they are still indicative of a trend.

6. See Joakim Kreutz, 'How and When Armed Conflicts End: Introducing the UCDP Conflict Termination Dataset,' *Journal of Peace Research* 47, no. 2 (March 2010): 246, https://doi.org/10.1177/0022343309353108.

7. Robert Egnell, 'A Western Insurgency in Afghanistan,' *Joint Force Quarterly* 70, no. 3 (2013): 8–14; Ucko and Egnell, *Counterinsurgency in Crisis*, 35.

8. The phrase was used to signal the return of insurgents to supposedly 'cleared' areas as soon as NATO forces moved on.

9. Sam Heller, 'When Measuring ISIS's 'Resurgence', Use the Right Standard' (Commentary, International Crisis Group, May 13, 2020), https://www.crisisgroup.org/middle-east-north-africa/gulf-and-arabian-peninsula/iraq/when-measuring-isiss-resurgence-use-right-standard.

10. Jacob N. Shapiro, *The Terrorist's Dilemma: Managing Violent Covert Organizations* (Princeton, NJ: Princeton University Press, 2017), 6, https://doi.org/10.23943/princeton/9780691157214.001.0001.

11. Ibid., 6.

12. Christopher Coker, *Future War* (Malden, MA: Polity Press, 2015), 10.

13. These three approaches have featured, among many others, in past works on insurgency's future. See for example Robert J. Bunker, *Old and New Insurgency Forms* (Carlisle, PA: Strategic Studies Institute and US Army War College Press, 2016); Ian Beckett, 'The Future of Insurgency,' *Small Wars and Insurgencies* 16, no. 1 (March 2005): 22–36, https://doi.org/10.1080/0959231042000322549; Steven Metz, 'The Future of Insurgency' (Carlisle Barracks, PA: Strategic Studies Institute, US Army War College, 1993).

14. On this point, see David H. Ucko and Thomas A. Marks, 'Violence in Context: Mapping the Strategies and Operational Art of Irregular Warfare,' *Contemporary Security Policy* 39, no. 2 (April 3, 2018): 206–33, https://doi.org/10.1080/13523260.2018.1432922.

15. General Valery Gerasimov, 'The Value of Science in Prediction,' *Military-Industrial Kurier*, no. 8 (476) (March 27, 2013), http://vpk-news.ru/sites/default/files/pdf/VPK_08_476.pdf.

16. Jeremy Black, *Rethinking Military History* (London: Routledge, 2004), 19.

2. UNRAVELING THE DILEMMA

1. The Darwinian nature of warfare is explored in further detail in David Kilcullen, *The Dragons and the Snakes: How the Rest Learned to Fight the West* (London: Hurst Publishers, 2020), chap. 2.

2. One leading work on insurgency defines this phenomenon as 'a technology of *military conflict*'; another presents its three 'strategies' as 'guerrilla warfare, conventional warfare, and punishment'—all distinctly *military* options. See respectively James D. Fearon and David D. Laitin, 'Ethnicity, Insurgency, and Civil War,' *American Political Science Review* 97, no. 1 (February 2003): 75, https://doi.org/10.1017/S0003055403000534 (my emphasis) and Seth G. Jones, *Waging Insurgent Warfare: Lessons from the Vietcong to the Islamic*

State (New York: Oxford University Press, 2017), 11. Another major work equating insurgency with its *military* approach is Gil Merom, *How Democracies Lose Small Wars: State, Society, and the Failures of France in Algeria, Israel in Lebanon, and the United States in Vietnam* (Cambridge: Cambridge University Press, 2003).

3.　Irvin points to 'This overarching concern with the military operations of revolutionary organizations,' which she blames for 'a significant theoretical gap in our understanding of the political wings of these movements and their impact on democratic politics.' See Cynthia L. Irvin, *Militant Nationalism: Between Movement and Party in Ireland and the Basque Country*, Social Movements, Protest, and Contention 9 (Minneapolis, MN: University of Minnesota Press, 1999), 7.

4.　See Charles Tilly and Sidney G. Tarrow, *Contentious Politics*, 2nd rev. ed. (New York: Oxford University Press, 2015).

5.　William A. Gamson, *The Strategy of Social Protest* (Homewood, IL: Dorsey Press, 1990), 139.

6.　Struggles to define the term 'terrorism' revolve around two main, yet deeply flawed, arguments: (i) that the term seeks to delegitimize the national liberation struggles of the weak and (ii) that states are anyway responsible for the greater 'terror' and should therefore be included in discussions of terrorism. Yet, as argued by the High-Level Panel on Threats, Challenges and Change, set up by Secretary General Kofi Annan in September 2003, (i) 'there is nothing in the fact of occupation that justifies the targeting and killing of civilians' and (ii) 'the legal and normative framework against State violations is far stronger than in the case of non-State actors.' See High-Level Panel on Threats, Challenges, and Change, *A More Secure World: Our Shared Responsibility* (New York: United Nations Publications, 2004), para 160. These points are still being debated, but in practice organizations such as the United Nations, while it still lacks a formal definition of terrorism, operates by a common understanding of the term as laid out in 16 international counterterrorism conventions, international customary law, the Geneva Conventions and Rome Statutes.

7.　Fred Halliday, 'Terrorism in Historical Perspective,' *Arab Studies Quarterly* 9, no. 2 (1987): 140.

8.　Michel Wieviorka, 'Terrorism in the Context of Academic Research,' in *Terrorism in Context*, ed. Martha Crenshaw (University Park, PA: Pennsylvania State University Press, 1995). I am grateful to Thomas A. Marks for alerting me to this work.

9.　Donatella Della Porta, *Clandestine Political Violence* (New York: Cambridge University Press, 2013), 282–94, https://doi.

org/10.1017/CBO9781139043144; Michel Wieviorka, *The Making of Terrorism* (Chicago: University of Chicago Press, 2004), 61–77; Donatella Della Porta, *Social Movements, Political Violence, and the State: A Comparative Analysis of Italy and Germany* (Cambridge: Cambridge University Press, 2006), 113–32.

10. This distinction draws heavily on the work of Thomas A. Marks. See, for example, Thomas A. Marks, 'Counterinsurgency in the Age of Globalism,' *Journal of Conflict Studies* 27, no. 1 (2007); Thomas A. Marks, *Maoist People's War in Post-Vietnam Asia* (Bangkok: White Lotus, 2007).

11. This limitation creates its own confusion. Witness, for example, the US State Department's list of 'designated terrorist organizations,' which forces together a whole array of outfits on the basis of their one shared tactic, which has been stripped of any context. At the time of writing, the list involves not just governments (Hamas) but Maoist insurgents (Communist Party of the Philippines and Sendero Luminoso) and defunct cults (Aum Shinrikyo). 'Foreign Terrorist Organizations,' US Department of State, accessed June 14, 2017, http://www.state.gov/j/ct/rls/other/des/123085.htm.

12. Referring to the armed opposition to US nation-building, Rumsfeld insisted that 'this is a group of people who don't merit the word "insurgency" ... You know, that gives them a greater legitimacy than they seem to merit.' Dana Milbank, 'Rumsfeld's War on "Insurgents,"' *Washington Post*, November 30, 2005, sec. Opinions, http://www.washingtonpost.com/wp-dyn/content/article/2005/11/29/AR2005112901405.html.

13. 'Transcript: President Obama's Speech on Combating ISIS,' CNN, September 10, 2014, http://www.cnn.com/2014/09/10/politics/transcript-obama-syria-isis-speech/index.html.

14. The states in question are Egypt, Tunisia, Indonesia, the Palestinian territories, and Malaysia. The median approval rating for al-Qaeda across the 11 Muslim-majority countries included in the poll was 13 percent, with 23 percent undecided or refusing to answer. See Andrew Kohut and James Bell, 'Muslim Publics Share Concerns about Extremist Groups' (Pew Research Center, Washington, DC, September 10, 2013), https://www.pewresearch.org/global/2013/09/10/muslim-publics-share-concerns-about-extremist-groups/.

15. Charles Lindholm and José Pedro Zúquete, *The Struggle for the World: Liberation Movements for the 21st Century* (Stanford, CA: Stanford University Press, 2010). The notion of a global insurgency was popularized by David Kilcullen. See David J. Kilcullen, 'Countering

Global Insurgency,' *Journal of Strategic Studies* 28, no. 4 (August 2005): 597–617.

16. On the notion of the 9/11 attacks as a focoist insurgent attack, see Kenneth Payne, 'Building the Base: Al Qaeda's Focoist Strategy,' *Studies in Conflict and Terrorism* 34, no. 2 (January 24, 2011): 124–43.

17. Joint Chiefs of Staff, 'Counterinsurgency' (Department of Defense, Washington, DC, April 25, 2018), 1–6.

18. Ibid., xiii. Emphasis added.

19. The limitations of counterinsurgency in practice are discussed in M. L. R. Smith and David Martin Jones, *The Political Impossibility of Modern Counterinsurgency: Strategic Problems, Puzzles, and Paradoxes* (New York: Columbia University Press, 2015) and in Celeste Ward Gventer, David Martin Jones, and M.L.R. Smith, eds., *The New Counter-Insurgency Era in Critical Perspective* (New York: Palgrave Macmillan, 2014).

20. Général Galliéni, *Neuf ans à Madagascar* (Paris: Librairie Hachette, 1908), 48. Author's translation.

21. For a longer assessment of this approach, see David H. Ucko, 'Beyond Clear-Hold-Build: Rethinking Local-Level Counterinsurgency after Afghanistan,' *Contemporary Security Policy* 34, no. 3 (December 2013): 526–51.

22. Dexter Filkins, 'Afghan Offensive Is New War Model,' *New York Times*, February 12, 2010, sec. World, https://www.nytimes.com/2010/02/13/world/asia/13kabul.html.

23. Stephen Grey, *Operation Snakebite: The Explosive True Story of an Afghan Desert Siege* (London: Viking, 2009), 61–65. See also David H. Ucko and Robert Egnell, *Counterinsurgency in Crisis: Britain and the Challenges of Modern Warfare* (New York: Columbia University Press, 2013).

24. Theo Farrell, 'Unbeatable: Social Resources, Military Adaptation, and the Afghan Taliban,' *Texas National Security Review* 1, no. 3 (May 2018): 58.

25. Thomas E. Ricks, *Fiasco: The American Military Adventure in Iraq* (New York: Penguin Books, 2007); Thomas E. Ricks, *The Gamble: General Petraeus and the American Military Adventure in Iraq* (New York: Penguin Books, 2010).

26. Ned Parker, 'The Iraq We Left Behind: Welcome to the World's Next Failed State,' *Foreign Affairs* 91, no. 2 (2012): 94–110; Steven Simon, 'The Price of the Surge,' *Foreign Affairs* 87, no. 3 (May/June 2008). For background, see also David H. Ucko, 'Militias, Tribes and Insurgents: The Challenge of Political Reintegration in Iraq,' *Conflict, Security and Development* 8, no. 3 (October 2008): 341–73.

27. Sam Heller, 'When Measuring ISIS's "Resurgence," Use the Right

Standard,' Commentary, International Crisis Group, May 13, 2020, https://www.crisisgroup.org/middle-east-north-africa/gulf-and-arabian-peninsula/iraq/when-measuring-isiss-resurgence-use-right-standard.

28. International Crisis Group, 'Facing the Challenge of the Islamic State in West Africa Province' (Africa Report, Brussels, May 16, 2019), 1.

29. Observations gleaned through continuous engagement with members of the Philippines armed forces, Washington, DC, 2011–20.

30. Thomas A. Marks, 'Colombian Army Adaptation to FARC' (Strategic Studies Institute, Carlisle, PA, 2002), 23.

31. See Claudio Ramos da Cruz and David H. Ucko, 'Beyond the Unidades de Polícia Pacificadora: Countering Comando Vermelho's Criminal Insurgency,' Small Wars and Insurgencies 29, no. 1 (January 2, 2018): 38–67.

32. Mats Berdal and David H. Ucko, 'The Use of Force in UN Peacekeeping Operations: Problems and Prospects,' RUSI Journal 160, no. 1 (March 13, 2015): 6–12.

33. James Cockayne, 'The Futility of Force? Strategic Lessons for Dealing with Unconventional Armed Groups from the UN's War on Haiti's Gangs,' Journal of Strategic Studies 37, no. 5 (July 29, 2014): 738, https://doi.org/10.1080/01402390.2014.901911.

34. Mats Berdal, 'The State of UN Peacekeeping: Lessons from Congo,' Journal of Strategic Studies 41, no. 5 (July 29, 2018): 745, https://doi.org/10.1080/01402390.2016.1215307. To this list may also be added the much-vaunted Force Intervention Brigade, which defeated the rebel group M-23, yet whose gains failed in 'addressing the underlying political issues at the heart of conflict and the complex political economy that drives much of the violence' (pp. 736–37).

35. Ruth Maclean and Finbarr O'Reilly, 'Crisis in the Sahel Becoming France's Forever War,' New York Times, March 29, 2020, sec. World, https://www.nytimes.com/2020/03/29/world/africa/france-sahel-west-africa-.html. See also Sergei Boeke and Bart Schuurman, 'Operation "Serval": A Strategic Analysis of the French Intervention in Mali, 2013–2014,' Journal of Strategic Studies 38, no. 6 (September 19, 2015): 801–25, https://doi.org/10.1080/01402390.2015.1045494.

36. T. E. Lawrence, Seven Pillars of Wisdom (Ware: Wordsworth, 1977), 182. For an appropriately dizzying list of attributes desired in the 'post-modern warrior,' see John Kiszely, 'Post-Modern Challenges for Modern Warriors' (The Shrivenham Paper, Defence Academy of the United Kingdom, December 2007), 8.

37. The reason for caution stems from the questionable or at least inconsistent coding within many of these datasets, resulting in them contradicting one another and generating highly contestable findings. For the most recent datasets, see the website of the UCDP Conflict Termination Dataset at https://ucdp.uu.se/downloads/index. html#termination.

38. Drew Desilver, 'Coups Have Become Less Common Worldwide,' *Pew Research Center* (blog), November 17, 2017, https://www. pewresearch.org/fact-tank/2017/11/17/egypts-coup-is-first-in-2013-as-takeovers-become-less-common-worldwide/.

39. UCDP codes Afghanistan 2001 as not terminating, and thus no outcome is given; Liberia as a Peace Agreement; Libya 2011 as a government victory; and Sudan as not terminating in 2004 but rather in 2012 and with a Peace Agreement. Côte d'Ivoire is not included in the dataset.

40. This was also the case for many of the insurgent victories in the 1990s, such as that of the Kosovo Liberation Army, the success of the Cobra militia in the Republic of Congo, and the toppling of Mobutu Sese Seko by the Alliance of Democratic Forces for the Liberation of Congo-Zaire (AFDL).

41. See Matt Waldman, 'The Sun in the Sky: The Relationship Between Pakistan's ISI and Afghan Insurgents,' Discussion Paper 18, Crisis States Research Centre: London School of Economics (June 2010); Mark Mazzetti et al., 'Pakistan Aids Insurgency in Afghanistan, Reports Assert,' *New York Times*, July 25, 2010; 'Leaked NATO Report Shows Pakistan Support For Taliban,' *Radio Free Europe*, February 1, 2012, https://www.rferl.org/a/leaked_nato_report_shows_pakistan_support_for_taliban_awire/24469649.html.

42. See the helpful analysis in Alexandra Novosseloff, 'The Many Lives of a Peacekeeping Mission: The UN Operation in Côte D'Ivoire,' *International Peace Institute*, June 2018, https://doi.org/10.2139/ssrn.3261285.

43. Matthew LeRiche and Matthew Arnold, *South Sudan: From Revolution to Independence* (Oxford: Oxford University Press, 2013), 102.

44. A separate outcome, peace agreement, could—depending on its content—favor either the state or the challenger and therefore does not lend itself to quantitative comparisons of this type.

45. See Joakim Kreutz, 'How and When Armed Conflicts End: Introducing the UCDP Conflict Termination Dataset,' *Journal of Peace Research* 47, no. 2 (March 2010): 246, https://doi. org/10.1177/0022343309353108.

46. Bizarrely, the Uppsala Conflict Termination dataset codes Libya as a 'government win.'

47. James S. Corum, 'Development of Modern Counterinsurgency Theory and Doctrine,' in *The Ashgate Research Companion to Modern Warfare*, ed. John Buckley and George Kassimeris (London: Routledge, 2010), 35–36.

48. Marks, *Maoist People's War in Post-Vietnam Asia*, 8. See also Thomas A. Marks and Paul B. Rich, 'Back to the Future: People's War in the 21st Century,' *Small Wars and Insurgencies* 28, no. 3 (May 4, 2017): 414, https://doi.org/10.1080/09592318.2017.1307620.

49. Corum, 'Development of Modern Counterinsurgency Theory and Doctrine,' 35–36.

50. Marks, *Maoist People's War in Post-Vietnam Asia*, 11.

51. Thomas X. Hammes, *The Sling and the Stone: On War in the 21st Century* (St. Paul, MN: Zenith Press, 2006), 63.

52. Thomas A. Marks, 'Mao Tse-tung and the Search for 21st Century Counterinsurgency,' *CTC Sentinel* 2, no. 10 (October 2009): 17.

53. Marks and Rich, 'Back to the Future,' 411.

54. As cited in John Costello and Peter Mattis, 'Electronic Warfare and the Renaissance of Chinese Informational Operations,' in *China's Evolving Military Strategy*, ed. Joe McReynolds (Washington, DC: Jamestown Foundation, 2017), 191.

55. Walter Laqueur, *Guerrilla Warfare: A Historical and Critical Study* (London: Transaction Publishers, 1998), 330–31.

56. Paul B. Rich, 'People's War Antithesis: Che Guevara and the Mythology of Focismo,' *Small Wars and Insurgencies* 28, no. 3 (May 4, 2017): 451–87, https://doi.org/10.1080/09592318.2017.1307616.

57. Christopher Hitchens, 'The Old Man,' *The Atlantic*, July 1, 2004, https://www.theatlantic.com/magazine/archive/2004/07/the-old-man/302984/.

58. For an extensive review of these cases, see Marks, *Maoist People's War in Post-Vietnam Asia*.

59. Hammes, *The Sling and the Stone*, 46.

60. Jennifer M. Taw and Bruce Hoffman, *The Urbanization of Insurgency: The Potential Challenge to U.S. Army Operations* (Santa Monica, CA: RAND Corporation, 1994), 7–15.

61. Rich, 'People's War Antithesis,' 460.

62. Indeed, there is nothing inherently communist about People's War. When it is removed from its Marxist-Leninist framework and specific vocabulary, there are few divergences tactically, operationally, or strategically from the approach of the Patriots in the American

independence war against Britain. Unlike key communist figures, however, central players in the American Revolution produced no handbooks on revolutionary war. Secondary sources help fill in the blanks: John W. Shy, *A People Numerous and Armed: Reflections on the Military Struggle for American Independence*, rev. ed., Ann Arbor Paperbacks 2A (Ann Arbor, MI: University of Michigan Press, 1990); Paul Hubert Smith, *Loyalists and Redcoats: A Study in British Revolutionary Policy* (Durham, NC: University of North Carolina Press, 1964). I am grateful to Thomas A. Marks for alerting me to the parallels.

63. Abu Musab al-Suri, 'Lessons Learned from the Armed Jihad in Syria' (Harmony Program, West Point Combating Terrorism Center, n.d.), 17, https://ctc.usma.edu/wp-content/uploads/2013/10/AFGP-2002-600080-Translation.pdf. As Whiteside points out, the metaphor was used without any mention of Mao, 'a clever dodge to avoid tainting the message with the messenger for virulent Salafi–jihadis who hated communism as a source of disbelief and atheism.' See Craig Whiteside, 'The Islamic State and the Return of Revolutionary Warfare,' *Small Wars and Insurgencies* 27, no. 5 (September 2, 2016): 747, https://doi.org/10.1080/09592318.2016.1208287.

64. Tomáš Kaválek, 'From al-Qaeda in Iraq to Islamic State: The Story of Insurgency in Iraq and Syria in 2003–2015,' *Alternatives: Turkish Journal of International Relations* 14, no. 1 (December 26, 2015): 20.

65. Ibid.

66. Whiteside, 'The Islamic State and the Return of Revolutionary Warfare,' 744.

67. This argument is the foundation for John Mackinlay, *The Insurgent Archipelago: From Mao to Bin Laden* (London: Hurst Publishers, 2009). It is possible to quibble with the stark bifurcation he draws between 'Maoist' and 'post-Maoist' insurgency, but Mackinlay convincingly captures the many sources of change separating the Cold War from the 'War on Terror' environment.

68. US Department of the Army and United States Marine Corps, *FM 3-24/MCWP 3- 33.5. Counterinsurgency* (Washington, DC: US Army, 2006), 1-7.

69. Ibid., 1-6–1-7.

70. Ibid., 1-7.

71. NATO, 'Allied Joint Doctrine for Counterinsurgency (COIN)' (NATO, Brussels, 2009), 5–13.

72. UN, Department of Economic and Social Affairs, 'World Urbanization Prospects: The 2018 Revision' (United Nations, New York, 2019), 11,

https://population.un.org/wup/Publications/Files/WUP2018-Report.pdf.

73. Thomas A. Marks, 'Urban Insurgency,' *Small Wars and Insurgencies* 14, no. 3 (September 2003): 103, https://doi.org/10.1080/0959231041 0001676925.

74. As Taw and Hoffman explain: 'In each case, urban populations seemed impervious to the claims of the insurgents and would not be mobilized … Logistical and security complications in the cities also made insurgent operations difficult to maintain over a prolonged period.' See Taw and Hoffman, *The Urbanization of Insurgency*, 9.

75. Ibid., 8.

76. See Hammes, *The Sling and the Stone*.

77. See David Tucker, *Revolution and Resistance: Moral Revolution, Military Might, and the End of Empire* (Baltimore: Johns Hopkins University Press, 2016).

78. William Reno, *Warfare in Independent Africa* (Cambridge: Cambridge University Press, 2011), 243.

79. Elena Pokalova, 'Framing Separatism as Terrorism: Lessons from Kosovo,' *Studies in Conflict and Terrorism* 33, no. 5 (April 9, 2010): 429–47, https://doi.org/10.1080/10576101003691564.

80. Kent Roach, *The 9/11 Effect: Comparative Counter-terrorism* (Cambridge: Cambridge University Press, 2011).

81. According to the UCDP Armed Conflict Database, the percentage of total conflicts in which external states supported governments was 10 percent between 1990 and 1999, then increased to 22 percent between 2000 and 2009, and increased again to 27 percent between 2010 and 2017. See also Anthony James Joes, *Urban Guerrilla Warfare* (Lexington: University Press of Kentucky, 2007), 5; Steven Metz and Raymond Millen, 'Insurgency and Counterinsurgency in the 21st Century: Reconceptualizing Threat and Response' (Strategic Studies Institute, US Army War College, Carlisle, PA, November 2004), 12.

82. The phrase is that of al-Qaeda strategist al-Suri, used to describe the Muslim Brotherhood's botched attempt to 'liberate' the city of Hama in 1982. See al-Suri, 'Lessons Learned from the Armed Jihad in Syria,' 5.

83. As a RAND study on the topic notes, 'hundreds of millions of dollars no longer regularly flow from Washington's and Moscow's coffers. Iran and Pakistan are two of the most significant post–Cold War backers of insurgencies, but the resources they devote for this purpose pale in comparison to the support once offered by the United States and the Soviet Union.' See Daniel Byman, Peter Chalk, Bruce Hoffman,

William Rosenau, and David Brannan, *Trends in Outside Support for Insurgent Movements* (Santa Monica, CA: RAND Corporation, 2001), 2.

84. Carlotta Gall, *The Wrong Enemy: America in Afghanistan, 2001–2014* (Boston: Houghton Mifflin Harcourt, 2014); Steve Coll, *Directorate S: The C.I.A. and America's Secret Wars in Afghanistan and Pakistan, 2001– 2016* (New York: Penguin Press, 2018). See also 'Iran Denies Providing Missiles to Yemen's Houthi Rebels,' *Middle East Eye*, December 20, 2017, http://www.middleeasteye.net/news/iran-denies-providing-missiles-yemens-houthi-rebels. For Russia, see Karoun Demirjian, 'Putin Denies Russian Troops Are in Ukraine, Decrees Certain Deaths Secret,' *Washington Post*, May 28, 2015, sec. World, https://www.washingtonpost.com/world/putin-denies-russian-troops-are-in-ukraine-decrees-certain-deaths-secret/2015/05/28/9bb15092-0543-11e5-93f4-f24d4af7f97d_story.html.

85. 'To achieve their objectives, they must be expansive and aggressive. In order to survive, they must take precautions and prize security.' Andrew R. Molnar, William A. Lybrand, Lorna Hahn, James L. Kirkman, and Peter B. Riddleberger, *Undergrounds in Insurgent, Revolutionary, and Resistance Wars* (Washington, DC: Special Operations Research Office, 1963), 51.

86. See Charles Tilly, Louise Tilly, and Richard H. Tilly, *The Rebellious Century, 1830–1930* (Cambridge, MA: Harvard University Press, 1975), 283. More recently, Jardine has used the term 'insurgent's dilemma' to describe the choice between large-scale organization and presence, inviting counterattack, or clandestine approaches, inviting irrelevance. See Eric Jardine, 'The Insurgent's Dilemma: A Theory of Mobilization and Conflict Outcome' (doctoral thesis, Carleton University, Ottawa, 2014), https://curve.carleton.ca/4043e1a5-90ab-4835-bafe-96274c75ce2a.

87. Kalyvas and Balcells call these 'robust insurgencies' and link the phenomenon to the Cold War via three channels: material support, revolutionary beliefs, and military doctrine. See Stathis N. Kalyvas and Laia Balcells, 'International System and Technologies of Rebellion: How the End of the Cold War Shaped Internal Conflict,' *American Political Science Review* 104, no. 3 (August 2010): 419, https://doi.org/10.1017/S0003055410000286.

88. Ibid., 421.

89. Jones, *Waging Insurgent Warfare*, 45.

90. See Abdul Haris Nasution, *Fundamentals of Guerrilla Warfare* (New York: Praeger, 1965), 17. As Molnar et al. explain, the theory was that 'guerrilla forces led by the Communist Party and backed by the masses

would eventually oust the incumbent government through military victory.' See Molnar et al., *Undergrounds in Insurgent, Revolutionary, and Resistance Wars*, 136.

91. Lindsay L. Heger, 'Votes and Violence: Pursuing Terrorism While Navigating Politics,' *Journal of Peace Research* 52, no. 1 (January 2015): 32, https://doi.org/10.1177/0022343314552984.

92. Jeroen de Zeeuw and Georg Frerks, Proceedings, Seminar on the Political Economy of Internal Conflict, 22 November 2000, Netherlands Institute of International Relations (Clingendael), December 2000, 5.

93. See Alexandra Guáqueta, 'The Way Back In: Reintegrating Illegal Armed Groups in Colombia Then and Now,' in *Reintegrating Armed Groups after Conflict: Politics, Violence and Transition*, ed. Mats Berdal and David H. Ucko (Abingdon: Routledge, 2009), 35.

94. See Mats Berdal, 'How "New" are "New War"? Global Economic Change and the Study of Civil War,' *Global Governance* 9 (2003): 486.

95. Reno, *Warfare in Independent Africa*, 245.

96. Paul Staniland, 'Political Violence in South Asia: The Triumph of the State?' (Carnegie Endowment for International Peace, September 3, 2020), https://carnegieendowment.org/2020/09/03/political-violence-in-south-asia-triumph-of-state-pub-82641.

97. Haroro J. Ingram, Craig Whiteside, and Charlie Winter, *The ISIS Reader: Milestone Texts of the Islamic State Movement* (New York: Oxford University Press, 2020), 291. See also Heller, 'When Measuring ISIS's "Resurgence," Use the Right Standard.'

98. See Kalyvas and Balcells, 'International System and Technologies of Rebellion,' 420.

99. Marie Allansson, Erik Melander, and Lotta Themnér, 'Organized Violence, 1989–2016,' *Journal of Peace Research* 54, no. 4 (July 2017): 576, https://doi.org/10.1177/0022343317718773.

100. Carl von Clausewitz, *On War*, ed. Michael Eliot Howard and Peter Paret (Princeton, NJ: Princeton University Press, 1989), 75.

101. Kilcullen, *The Dragons and the Snakes*.

3. LOCALIZED INSURGENCY: PARA-STATES AND PERIPHERIES

1.   For an excellent treatment of this crime–insurgent nexus, see Max Manwaring, *Street Gangs: The New Urban Insurgency* (Carlisle, PA: Strategic Studies Institute, US Army War College, 2005).

2.   Donatella Della Porta, *Social Movements, Political Violence, and the State: A Comparative Analysis of Italy and Germany* (Cambridge: Cambridge University Press, 2006).

3. Mançur Olson, *Power and Prosperity: Outgrowing Communist and Capitalist Dictatorships* (New York: Basic Books, 2000).

4. James Cockayne, *Hidden Power: The Strategic Logic of Organized Crime* (New York: Oxford University Press, 2016), 272–73. This strategy is also reminiscent of Sullivan and Bunker's description of warlords, or how Manwaring frames 'third-generation gangs,' in that these criminal entities also acquire political significance along with territorial control. See Max G. Manwaring, *Street Gangs: The New Urban Insurgency* (Carlisle, PA: Strategic Studies Institute, US Army War College, 2005), 9; John P. Sullivan and Robert J. Bunker, 'Drug Cartels, Street Gangs, and Warlords,' *Small Wars and Insurgencies* 13, no. 2 (August 2002): 50–51, https://doi.org/10.1080/09592310208559180.

5. Rolf Straubhaar, 'A Broader Definition of Fragile States: The Communities and Schools of Brazil's Favelas,' *Current Issues in Comparative Education* 15, no. 1 (2012): 44; Elizabeth Leeds, 'Rio de Janeiro,' in *Fractured Cities: Social Exclusion, Urban Violence & Contested Spaces in Latin America*, ed. Kees Koonings and Dirk Kruijt (London: Zed Books, 2007), 26–27; Luke Dowdney, *Children of the Drug Trade: A Case Study of Children in Organised Armed Violence in Rio de Janeiro* (Rio de Janeiro: 7Letras, 2003), 82.

6. Jefferson Puff, 'Como grupo de jovens virou referência internacional na denúncia de abusos policiais,' BBC Brazil, October 30, 2015, http://www.bbc.com/portuguese/noticias/2015/10/151028_coletivo_papo_reto_alemao_jp.

7. John P. Sullivan, 'How Illicit Networks Impact Sovereignty,' in *Convergence: Illicit Networks and National Security in the Age of Globalization*, ed. Michael Miklaucic and Jacqueline Brewer (Washington, DC: NDU Press, 2013), 173.

8. Ibid., 173.

9. Ibid., 176. See also Enrique Desmond Arias and Corinne Davis Rodrigues, 'The Myth of Personal Security: Criminal Gangs, Dispute Resolution, and Identity in Rio de Janeiro's Favelas,' *Latin American Politics and Society* 48, no. 4 (2006): 53–81.

10. Steven Metz introduced the concept in 1993 using the term 'commercial insurgency' and it was then developed further by others. See Steven Metz, 'The Future of Insurgency' (Carlisle Barracks, PA: Strategic Studies Institute, US Army War College, 1993); Sullivan and Bunker, 'Drug Cartels, Street Gangs, and Warlords'; John P. Sullivan and Robert J. Bunker, 'Rethinking Insurgency: Criminality, Spirituality, and Societal Warfare in the Americas,' *Small Wars and Insurgencies* 22, no. 5 (December 2011): 742–63, https://doi.org/10.1080/09592

318.2011.625720. See also Hal Brands, 'Criminal Fiefdoms in Latin America: Understanding the Problem of Alternatively Governed Spaces' (Western Hemisphere Security Analysis Center, Applied Research Center, Florida International University, Miami, 2010); John P. Sullivan and Adam Elkus, 'State of Siege: Mexico's Criminal Insurgency,' *Small Wars Journal*, 2008, 12.

11. Luiz Augusto Gollo, 'Vigilante Groups in Brazil Trump Drug Gangs and Become Rio's New Authority,' *Brazzil*, November 11, 2009, https://www.brazzil.com/23490-vigilante-groups-in-brazil-trump-drug-gangs-and-become-rio-s-new-authority/.

12. I am grateful to Tom Marks for alerting me to this phrase from Lasswell's classic 1936 work on power and manipulation among competing elites. As Lasswell notes, 'The study of politics is the study of influence and the influential ... The influential are those who get the most of what there is to get.' See Harold D. Lasswell, *Politics: Who Gets What, When, How* (New York: Meridian Books, 1958).

13. Vanda Felbab-Brown, 'Conceptualizing Crime as Competition in State-Making and Designing an Effective Response,' *Security and Defense Studies Review* 10 (Spring–Summer 2010): 156–57.

14. Mao Tse-tung, 'Problems of Strategy in China's Civil War,' in *Strategic Studies: A Reader*, 2nd ed. (Abingdon: Routledge, 2014), 283.

15. 'The Bottom Line,' *The Economist*, October 22, 2009, http://www.economist.com/the-americas/2009/10/22/the-bottom-line.

16. For more details, see Claudio Ramos da Cruz and David H. Ucko, 'Beyond the Unidades de Polícia Pacificadora: Countering Comando Vermelho's Criminal Insurgency,' *Small Wars and Insurgencies* 29, no. 1 (January 2, 2018): 38–67. See also Michael Jerome Wolff, 'Building Criminal Authority: A Comparative Analysis of Drug Gangs in Rio de Janeiro and Recife,' *Latin American Politics and Society* 57, no. 2 (2015): 21–40, https://doi.org/10.1111/j.1548-2456.2015.00266.x.

17. Douglas Farah and Kathryn Babineau, 'The Evolution of MS 13 in El Salvador and Honduras,' *PRISM* 7, no. 2 (September 14, 2017): 59–73; Brands, 'Criminal Fiefdoms in Latin America: Understanding the Problem of Alternatively Governed Spaces.'

18. John P. Sullivan, 'Narco-Cities: Mexico and Beyond,' *Small Wars Journal*, March 3, 2014, https://smallwarsjournal.com/jrnl/art/narco-cities-mexico-and-beyond#_edn17.

19. Max G. Manwaring, *A Contemporary Challenge to State Sovereignty: Gangs and Other Illicit Transnational Criminal Organizations in Central America, El Salvador, Mexico, Jamaica, and Brazil*, Security Issues in the Western Hemisphere (Carlisle Barracks, PA: Strategic Studies

Institute, US Army War College, 2007); David Kilcullen, *Out of the Mountains: The Coming Age of the Urban Guerrilla* (London: Hurst Publishers, 2013), 97–99; D.C. (David) Beer, 'Haiti: The Gangs of Cité Soleil,' in *Impunity: Countering Illicit Power in War and Transition*, ed. Michelle Hughes and Michael Miklaucic (Washington, DC: Center for Complex Operations (CCO) and the Peacekeeping and Stability Operations Institute (PKSOI), 2016), http://cco.ndu.edu/News/Article/780129/chapter-3-haiti-the-gangs-of-cit-soleil/;   James Cockayne, 'The Futility of Force? Strategic Lessons for Dealing with Unconventional Armed Groups from the UN's War on Haiti's Gangs,' *Journal of Strategic Studies* 37, no. 5 (July 29, 2014): 738, https://doi.org/10.1080/01402390.2014.901911; COHA, 'Gangs Are the New Law in Urban Trinidad & Tobago,' *Council on Hemispheric Affairs* (blog), October 11, 2013, https://www.coha.org/gangs-are-the-new-law-in-urban-trinidad-and-tobago/.

20. Alberto Aziani, Serena Favarin, and Gian Maria Campedelli, 'Security Governance: Mafia Control over Ordinary Crimes,' *Journal of Research in Crime and Delinquency* 57, no. 4 (July 2020): 444–92, https://doi.org/10.1177/0022427819893417; Olson, *Power and Prosperity*, 5–7.

21. Spencer Ackerman, 'Badr to Worse,' *New Republic*, July 11, 2005.

22. Christopher O. Bowers, 'Future Megacity Operations: Lessons from Sadr City,' *Military Review*, June 2015, 13.

23. International Crisis Group, 'Iraq's Civil War, the Sadrists and the Surge' (Middle East Report, Brussels, February 7, 2008), 7.

24. David E. Johnson, M. Wade Markel, and Brian Shannon, *The 2008 Battle of Sadr City: Reimagining Urban Combat* (Santa Monica, CA: RAND, 2013), 26.

25. Joel Rayburn and Frank K. Sobchak, eds., *The U.S. Army in the Iraq War* (Carlisle, PA: Strategic Studies Institute, US Army War College Press, 2019), 20–22; David H. Ucko, 'Militias, Tribes and Insurgents: The Challenge of Political Reintegration in Iraq,' *Conflict, Security and Development* 8, no. 3 (October 2008): 341–73.

26. Sabri Sayari and Bruce Hoffman, *Urbanization and Insurgency: The Turkish Case, 1975–1980* (Santa Monica, CA: RAND Corporation, 1991).

27. Jennifer M. Taw and Bruce Hoffman, *The Urbanization of Insurgency: The Potential Challenge to U.S. Army Operations* (Santa Monica, CA: RAND Corporation, 1994), 11.

28. Ibid., 12.

29. Ibid., 12–13.

30. Sayari and Hoffman, *Urbanization and Insurgency: The Turkish Case, 1975–1980*.

31. Escobar became the target of a US–Colombian manhunt, resulting in his going into hiding, the collapse of his Medellin cartel, and his eventual death at the hands of the Colombian National Police. For the full account, see Mark Bowden, *Killing Pablo: The Hunt for the World's Greatest Outlaw* (New York: Penguin, 2001).

32. Nils Gilman, 'The Twin Insurgency,' *American Interest* 9, no. 6 (2014): 3–11.

33. As Ralf Michaels notes, the very notion of 'non-state governance' is in fact conceptually, empirically and normatively unattractive, because it implies a false dichotomy between state and non-state, is exceedingly rare in its purported form, and provides no clue as to its desirability. See Ralf Michaels, 'The Mirage of Non-state Governance,' *Utah Law Review* 2010, no. 1 (2010): 31–46.

34. Paul Staniland, 'States, Insurgents, and Wartime Political Orders,' *Perspectives on Politics* 10, no. 2202 (June 2012): 243–64, https://doi.org/10.1017/S1537592712000655.

35. Tellingly, in coding civil war outcomes, many datasets unquestioningly assume that the challenger is bent on state capture and measure their success accordingly. In the UCDP Conflict Termination dataset, for example, localized insurgency would fit awkwardly within the broad (and notably overpopulated) 'other outcomes' category. See Joakim Kreutz, 'How and When Armed Conflicts End: Introducing the UCDP Conflict Termination Dataset,' *Journal of Peace Research* 47, no. 2 (March 2010): 246, https://doi.org/10.1177/0022343309353108. Getmansky's dataset, meanwhile, assumes that insurgent victory is limited to 'overthrowing the incumbent or gaining independence.' Anna Getmansky, 'You Can't Win If You Don't Fight: The Role of Regime Type in Counterinsurgency Outbreaks and Outcomes,' *Journal of Conflict Resolution* 57, no. 4 (August 2013): 716, https://doi.org/10.1177/0022002712449326.

36. Staniland, 'States, Insurgents, and Wartime Political Orders,' 248.

37. Paul Staniland, 'Cities on Fire: Social Mobilization, State Policy, and Urban Insurgency,' *Comparative Political Studies* 43, no. 12 (December 2010): 1630, https://doi.org/10.1177/0010414010374022.

38. UN Habitat, *Urbanization and Development: Emerging Futures*, World Cities Report 2016 (Nairobi: UN Habitat, 2016), 1.

39. Ibid., 7.

40. Kilcullen, *Out of the Mountains*, 28–29.

41. Ronak B. Patel and David P. Palotty, 'Climate Change and Urbanization: Challenges to Global Security and Stability,' *Joint Force Quarterly* 89, no. 2 (2018): 94.

42. Kilcullen, *Out of the Mountains*, 29.

43. UN Habitat, *Urbanization and Development*, 17.

44. Ibid., 87.

45. Giok Ling Ooi and Kai Hong Phua, 'Urbanization and Slum Formation,' *Journal of Urban Health* 84, no. S1 (May 2007): 27–34, https://doi.org/10.1007/s11524-007-9167-5.

46. Gilman, 'The Twin Insurgency.'

47. Christopher Coker, *Future War* (Malden, MA: Polity Press, 2015), 189.

48. A major UN study on slums describes how 'Increases in inequality can be traced almost directly to liberalization, which is also a proximate cause of globalization.' See United Nations Human Settlements Programme, ed., *The Challenge of Slums: Global Report on Human Settlements, 2003* (London: Earthscan Publications, 2003), 39, 46.

49. Facundo Alverado, Lucas Chancel, Thomas Piketty, Emmanuel Saez, and Gabriel Zucman, 'World Inequality Report 2018' (World Inequality Lab, 2017), 11, http://wir2018.wid.world/files/download/wir2018-full-report-english.pdf. For a fuller treatment of this point, see Gilman, 'The Twin Insurgency.' For a spirited defense of the Washington Consensus, see Kevin B. Grier and Robin M. Grier, 'The Washington Consensus Works: Causal Effects of Reform, 1970–2015,' *Journal of Comparative Economics*, September 2020, S0147596720300639, https://doi.org/10.1016/j.jce.2020.09.001.

50. John Friesen, Lea Rausch, Peter F. Pelz, and Johannes Fürnkranz, 'Determining Factors for Slum Growth with Predictive Data Mining Methods,' *Urban Science* 2, no. 3 (September 2018): 81, https://doi.org/10.3390/urbansci2030081. Whereas the world has actually made some progress in reducing the *proportion* of people living in slums in the developing world, from 46 percent in 1990 to 30 percent in 2014, the 'absolute number of slum dwellers increased from 690 million to 880 million over the same period.' See United Nations, *World Social Report: Inequality in a Rapidly Changing World* (New York: Department of Economic and Social Affairs, 2020), 120.

51. 'Shining Light on Latin America's Homicide Epidemic,' *The Economist*, April 5, 2018, https://www.economist.com/news/briefing/21739954-latin-americas-violent-crime-and-ways-dealing-it-have-lessons-rest.

52. See, for example, Frank J. Elgar and Nicole Aitken, 'Income Inequality, Trust and Homicide in 33 Countries,' *European Journal of Public Health* 21, no. 2 (April 2011): 241–46, https://doi.org/10.1093/eurpub/ckq068; Ted Robert Gurr, *Why Men Rebel* (Princeton, NJ: Princeton University Press for the Center of International Studies,

1970); Edward N. Muller and Mitchell A. Seligson, 'Inequality and Insurgency,' *American Political Science Review* 81, no. 2 (June 1987): 425, https://doi.org/10.2307/1961960; Frances Stewart and E. V. K. Fitzgerald, eds., *War and Underdevelopment*, vols. 1–2 (Oxford: Oxford University Press, 2001).

53. Robert M. Sapolsky, *Behave: The Biology of Humans at Our Best and Worst* (New York: Penguin Press, 2017), 294–95.
54. James D. Fearon and David D. Laitin, 'Ethnicity, Insurgency, and Civil War,' *American Political Science Review* 97, no. 1 (February 2003): 76, https://doi.org/10.1017/S0003055403000534.
55. This is one of the megatrends explored in Kilcullen, *Out of the Mountains*.
56. Gilman, 'The Twin Insurgency.'
57. Robert Muggah, 'Fragile Cities Rising.' *IPI Global Observatory* (blog), July 10, 2013, https://theglobalobservatory.org/2013/07/fragile-cities-rising/.
58. Coker, *Future War*, 189.
59. Observation based on interaction with senior military and civilian analysts in Abuja, Nigeria, May 2018.
60. Leena Koni Hoffmann, 'Who Speaks for the North? Politics and Influence in Northern Nigeria' (Research paper, Royal Institute of International Affairs, Chatham House, July 2014), 5. See also Patricio Asfura-Heim and Julia McQuaid, 'Diagnosing the Boko Haram Conflict: Grievances, Motivations, and Institutional Resilience in Northeast Nigeria' (Occasional paper, Center for Naval Analysis, January 2015), 16.
61. This 'system' of education is known as *almajiranci*. 'Mixing the Modern and the Traditional,' *The Economist*, July 26, 2014, https://www.economist.com/middle-east-and-africa/2014/07/26/mixing-the-modern-and-the-traditional.
62. 'Boko Haram Crisis: Nigeria Estimates Baga Deaths at 150,' BBC News, January 12, 2015, sec. Africa, https://www.bbc.com/news/world-africa-30788480; 'Commander Says Nigerian Army Completely Defeated Boko Haram,' *The Guardian*, February 4, 2018, https://guardian.ng/news/commander-says-nigerian-army-completely-defeated-boko-haram/.
63. Whereas *haram* indeed refers to that which is theologically forbidden, *boko* 'is a Hausa word that, originally, had nothing to do with a geographical designation (western) or even education. The word itself can be understood as conveying the meaning of something that is false, duplicitous, a lie, an illusion, inauthentic.'

'Boko Haram' therefore refers to the rejection of that which is not authentic, which in JAS's worldview encompasses all that goes against its strict Salafi ideology. See William Hansen, 'Boko Haram: Religious Radicalism and Insurrection in Northern Nigeria,' *Journal of Asian and African Studies* 52, no. 4 (June 2017): 4–6, https://doi.org/10.1177/0021909615615594.

64. Observation based on interaction with senior military and civilian analysts in Abuja, Nigeria, May 2018.

65. Hoffmann, 'Who Speaks for the North? Politics and Influence in Northern Nigeria,' 14.

66. William Reno, *Warfare in Independent Africa* (Cambridge: Cambridge University Press, 2011), 226–28.

67. Ibid., 233.

68. See Rebecca Golden-Timsar, 'Amnesty and New Violence in the Niger Delta,' *Forbes*, March 20, 2018, https://www.forbes.com/sites/uhenergy/2018/03/20/amnesty-and-new-violence-in-the-niger-delta/.

69. 'The relative stability gained through the amnesty program has been eroded by the emergence of new militant groups in 2016 and the rise of other forms of violent conflict in the region.' See Foundation for Partnership Initiatives in the Niger Delta, 'Niger Delta Annual Conflict Report: January to December 2020' (PIND, February 9, 2021), 2.

70. 'Ateke Tom Receives Winners of 2018 MBMN, Gets National Merit Impact Award,' *Vanguard News* (blog), January 4, 2019, https://www.vanguardngr.com/2019/01/ateke-tom-receives-winners-of-2018-mbmn-gets-national-merit-impact-award/; Ameh Comrade Godwin, 'Asari-Dokubo Establishes University in Benin Republic,' *Daily Post Nigeria*, October 11, 2013, https://dailypost.ng/2013/10/11/asari-dokubo-establishes-university-in-benin-republic/.

71. Maria-Louise Clausen, 'Competing for Control over the State: The Case of Yemen,' *Small Wars and Insurgencies* 29, no. 3 (May 4, 2018): 560–78, https://doi.org/10.1080/09592318.2018.145579; Raymond Hinnebusch, 'From Westphalian Failure to Heterarchic Governance in MENA: The Case of Syria,' *Small Wars and Insurgencies* 29, no. 3 (May 4, 2018): 391–413, https://doi.org/10.1080/09592318.2018.1455330; Andrea Carboni and James Moody, 'Between the Cracks: Actor Fragmentation and Local Conflict Systems in the Libyan Civil War,' *Small Wars and Insurgencies* 29, no. 3 (May 4, 2018): 456–90, https://doi.org/10.1080/09592318.2018.1455318; Philippe Droz-Vincent, 'Competitive Statehood in Libya: Governing

Differently a Specific Setting or Deconstructing Its Weak Sovereign State with a Fateful Drift toward Chaos?,' *Small Wars and Insurgencies* 29, no. 3 (May 4, 2018): 434–55, https://doi.org/10.1080/09592 318.2018.1455322. For an in-depth study of fragmented sovereignty in Liberia, see Christine Cheng, *Extralegal Groups in Post-conflict Liberia: How Trade Makes the State* (New York: Oxford University Press, 2018).

72. Council on Foreign Relations, 'The Eastern Congo,' CFR InfoGuide Presentation, n.d., https://on.cfr.org/21SfJBh.
73. Damian Doyle and Tristan Dunning, 'Recognizing Fragmented Authority: Towards a Post-Westphalian Security Order in Iraq,' *Small Wars and Insurgencies* 29, no. 3 (May 4, 2018): 537–38, https://doi.or g/10.1080/09592318.2018.1455324. See also International Crisis Group, 'Iraq's Paramilitary Groups: The Challenge of Rebuilding a Functioning State' (Middle East Report, Brussels, July 30, 2018).
74. Translation of contemporaneous article of the Islamic State's *al-Naba'* newsletter. See Aymenn Jawad al-Tamini, 'Islamic State Insurgent Tactics: Translation and Analysis,' *Aymenn Jawad al-Tamini's Blog* (blog), April 26, 2019, http://www.aymennjawad.org/2019/04/islamic-state-insurgent-tactics-translation.
75. Abel Polese and Ruth Hanau Santini, 'Limited Statehood and Its Security Implications on the Fragmentation Political Order in the Middle East and North Africa,' *Small Wars and Insurgencies* 29, no. 3 (May 4, 2018): 383, https://doi.org/10.1080/09592318.2018.145 6815.
76. See Robert J. Bunker, *Old and New Insurgency Forms* (Carlisle, PA: Strategic Studies Institute and US Army War College Press, 2016), 43–44; Charles Tilly, 'War Making and State Making as Organized Crime,' in *Bringing the State Back In*, ed. Peter B. Evans, Dietrich Rueschemeyer, and Theda Skocpol (Cambridge: Cambridge University Press, 1985), 169–91, https://doi.org/10.1017/CBO9780511628283.008.
77. See Mats Berdal, 'How "New" Are "New Wars"?': 493.
78. Thomas Risse, ed., *Governance without a State? Policies and Politics in Areas of Limited Statehood* (New York: Columbia University Press, 2011), 1.
79. Andreas Mehler, 'Hybrid Regimes and Oligopolies of Violence in Africa: Expectations on Security Provisions "from Below",' in *Building Peace in the Absence of States: Challenging the Discourse on State Failure*, ed. Martina Fischer and Beatrix Schmelzle, Berghof Handbook Dialogue Series 8 (Berlin: Berghof Forschungszentrum für Konstruktive Konfliktbearbeitung, 2009), 58.
80. Risse, *Governance without a State?*, 2.

81. Areas of limited statehood are defined as 'parts of a country in which central authorities (governments) lack the ability to implement and enforce rules and decisions or in which the legitimate monopoly over the means of violence is lacking, at least temporarily.' See ibid., 4. 'Hybrid political orders' is another attempt to elucidate the same phenomenon. See elaboration and critique in Martina Fischer and Beatrix Schmelzle, eds., *Building Peace in the Absence of States: Challenging the Discourse on State Failure*, Berghof Handbook Dialogue Series 8 (Berlin: Berghof Forschungszentrum für Konstruktive Konfliktbearbeitung, 2009).

82. Hinnebusch, 'From Westphalian Failure to Heterarchic Governance in MENA,' 396.

83. Charles G. Thomas and Toyin Falola, *Secession and Separatist Conflicts in Postcolonial Africa* (Calgary, Alberta: University of Calgary Press, 2020), 8, http://www.deslibris.ca/ID/459176.

84. Ibid., 15.

85. Edoardo Baldaro, 'A Dangerous Method: How Mali Lost Control of the North, and Learned to Stop Worrying,' *Small Wars and Insurgencies* 29, no. 3 (May 4, 2018): 585, https://doi.org/10.1080/09592318.2018.1455323. See also Morten Bøås, 'Crime, Coping, and Resistance in the Mali–Sahel Periphery,' *African Security* 8, no. 4 (October 2, 2015): 299–319, https://doi.org/10.1080/19392206.2015.1100506.

86. Judd Devermont, 'Politics at the Heart of the Crisis in the Sahel' (CSIS Briefs, Center for Strategic and International Studies, December 2019), 2, https://csis-website-prod.s3.amazonaws.com/s3fs-public/publication/191206_Devermont_SahelCrisis_layout_v5.pdf.

87. Ibid., 2.

88. David Matsinhe, 'Mozambique: The Forgotten People of Cabo Delgado,' *Daily Maverick*, May 28, 2020, sec. Opinion, https://www.dailymaverick.co.za/article/2020-05-29-mozambique-the-forgotten-people-of-cabo-delgado/.

89. Simone Haysom, 'Where Crime Compounds Conflict: Understanding Northern Mozambique's Vulnerabilities' (Global Institution Against Transnational Organized Crime, Geneva, October 2018), 13. See also Jacco van der Veen, 'A Very Private War: The Failure of Mozambique's Approach to Defeating an Islamist Insurgency,' *JASON Institute for Peace and Security Studies* (blog), July 19, 2020, https://jasoninstitute.com/2020/07/19/a-very-private-war-the-failure-of-mozambiques-approach-to-defeating-an-islamist-insurgency/.

90. David Matsinhe and Estacio Valoi, 'The Genesis of Insurgency in Northern Mozambique' (Southern Africa Report, Institute for Security Studies, October 2019), 8.

91. Ibid., 8.

92. Alok Bansal, 'Factors Leading to Insurgency in Balochistan,' *Small Wars and Insurgencies* 19, no. 2 (June 2008): 185, https://doi. org/10.1080/09592310802061356. See also Zeus Hans Mendez, 'Repression and Revolt in Balochistan: The Uncertainty and Survival of a People's National Aspirations,' *Journal of Indo-Pacific Affairs* 3, no. 3 (Fall 2020): 46–47, passim.

93. Umair Jamal, 'Amid a Pandemic, Pakistan Focuses on a Baloch Insurgency,' *The Diplomat*, June 16, 2020, https://thediplomat. com/2020/06/amid-a-pandemic-pakistan-focuses-on-a-baloch-insurgency/.

94. Frederic Grare, 'Balochistan: The State versus the Nation' (The Carnegie Papers, South Asia, Carnegie Endowment for International Peace, Washington, DC, April 2013), 3, https://carnegieendowment. org/2013/04/11/balochistan-state-versus-nation-pub-51488.

95. See, respectively, Naveed Hussain, 'Fiddling While Balochistan Burns,' *Express Tribune*, August 15, 2012; Paul Staniland, 'Political Violence in South Asia: The Triumph of the State?' (Carnegie Endowment for International Peace, September 3, 2020), https:// carnegieendowment.org/2020/09/03/political-violence-in-south-asia-triumph-of-state-pub-82641.

96. 'Balochistan: Pakistan's Other War,' Al Jazeera, January 9, 2012, https://www.aljazeera.com/program/episode/2012/1/9/ balochistan-pakistans-other-war/; Grare, 'Balochistan,' 14.

97. Grare, 'Balochistan,' 12–13.

98. See, respectively, Bansal, 'Factors Leading to Insurgency in Balochistan,' 182; Staniland, 'Political Violence in South Asia.'

99. William Reno, 'Clandestine Economies, Violence and States in Africa,' *Journal of International Affairs* 53, no. 2 (Spring 2000): 433–59.

100. Ken Menkhaus, 'Governance without Government in Somalia: Spoilers, State Building, and the Politics of Coping,' *International Security* 31, no. 3 (2006): 78; Staniland, 'States, Insurgents, and Wartime Political Orders,' 248.

101. Menkhaus, 'Governance without Government in Somalia.'

102. As cited in David H. Ucko, 'The Role of Economic Instruments in Ending Conflict: Priorities and Constraints' (International Institute for Strategic Studies roundtable, National Press Club, Washington, DC, 2009), 9.

103. Ken Menkhaus, *Somalia: State Collapse and the Threat of Terrorism*, Adelphi Paper 364 (Oxford: Oxford University Press for the International Institute for Strategic Studies, 2004), 11.

104. Clionadh Raleigh, 'Political Hierarchies and Landscapes of Conflict across Africa,' *Political Geography* 42 (2014): 93.

105. Jeffrey Herbst, *States and Power in Africa: Comparative Lessons in Authority and Control*, 2nd ed. (Princeton, NJ: Princeton University Press, 2014), 193, http://hdl.handle.net/2027/heb.34113.

106. Robson Bonin, 'Comando Vermelho vira preocupação do governo Bolsonaro—entenda,' *Veja*, sec. Radar, accessed September 29, 2020, https://veja.abril.com.br/blog/radar/faccao-criminosa-importa-mercenarios-para-o-rio-de-janeiro/.

107. Idayat Hassan, 'The Danger of a Better-Behaved Boko Haram,' *New Humanitarian*, August 21, 2018, sec. Opinion, http://www.thenewhumanitarian.org/opinion/2018/08/21/opinion-nigeria-militancy-peace-boko-haram. In one week in July 2018, ISWAP ambushed an army location, killing 23 Nigerian soldiers and destroying a dozen vehicles, and then overran a 700-man base, with hundreds of troops going missing.

108. 'Nigeria Arrests 'Avengers' Oil Militants,' BBC News, May 16, 2016, sec. Africa, https://www.bbc.com/news/world-africa-36301835.

109. Golden-Timsar, 'Amnesty and New Violence in the Niger Delta.' See also Emma Amaize, 'EndSARS: Tension as N'Delta Militants Roll Out 11-Point Demand,' *Vanguard News* (blog), October 25, 2020, https://www.vanguardngr.com/2020/10/endsars-tension-as-ndelta-militants-roll-out-11-point-demand/.

110. 'The Gulf of Guinea Is Now the World's Worst Piracy Hotspot,' *The Economist*, June 29, 2019, http://www.economist.com/international/2019/06/29/the-gulf-of-guinea-is-now-the-worlds-worst-piracy-hotspot.

111. International Crisis Group, 'Iraq's Civil War, the Sadrists and the Surge,' 6–10.

112. Suadad al-Salhy, 'Iraq Shi'ite Militia Splinters into Hit Squads, Gangs,' Reuters, July 21, 2011, https://www.reuters.com/article/us-iraq-violence-mehdi-idUSTRE76K22E20110721. See also Babak Dehghanpisheh, 'The Great Moqtada Makeover,' *Newsweek*, January 19, 2008, https://www.newsweek.com/great-moqtada-makeover-86687.

113. Philip Smyth, 'Beware of Muqtada al-Sadr' (Policy Analysis, Washington Institute, October 19, 2016), https://www.washingtoninstitute.org/policy-analysis/view/beware-of-muqtada-al-sadr.

114. Enrique Desmond Arias, 'The Impacts of Differential Armed Dominance of Politics in Rio de Janeiro, Brazil,' *Studies in Comparative International Development* 48, no. 3 (September 2013): 271; Antonio Sampaio, 'Out of Control: Criminal Gangs Fight Back in Rio's Favelas,' *Jane's Intelligence Review* 26, no. 12 (December 2014): 44–48. See also Wolff, 'Building Criminal Authority,' 25; Dowdney, *Children of the Drug Trade*, 53.

115. International Crisis Group, 'Miracle or Mirage? Gangs and Plunging Violence in El Salvador' (Latin America Report, Brussels, July 8, 2020), 9; International Crisis Group, 'Electoral Violence and Illicit Influence in Mexico's Hot Land' (Latin America Report, Brussels, June 2, 2021), 15.

116. Sampaio, 'Out of Control,' 47.

117. Imelda Cengic, 'Brazil Cracks Down on Gangs and Corrupt Government Agents' (OCCRP: Organized Crime and Corruption Reporting Project, August 16, 2019), https://www.occrp.org/en/daily/10493-brazil-cracks-down-on-gangs-and-corrupt-government-agents.

118. Thomas A. Marks, 'FARC, 1982–2002: Criminal Foundation for Insurgent Defeat,' *Small Wars and Insurgencies* 28, no. 3 (May 4, 2017): 510. See also Kent Eaton, 'The Downside of Decentralization: Armed Clientelism in Colombia,' *Security Studies* 15, no. 4 (October 2006): 556, https://doi.org/10.1080/09636410601188463.

119. W. Alejandro Sánchez, 'Sangre Joven? Understanding the New Wave of Armed Groups in Latin America,' *Security and Defense Studies Review* 12 (Fall–Winter 2011): 137. For a helpful problematization of the AUC, and the causes that led to its formation, see David J. Spencer, *Colombia's Paramilitaries: Criminal or Political Force?* (Carlisle, PA: Strategic Studies Institute, US Army War College, 2001).

120. As the Center for Civilians in Conflict explains, 'they intimidate civilians, employ punitive justice measures to settle personal scores, trade drugs, and have been implicated in the commission of extortion and theft, including the diversion of humanitarian aid.' Center for Civilians in Conflict, 'Civilian Perceptions of the Yan Gora (CJTF) in Borno State, Nigeria,' July 2018, 3, https://chitrasudhanagarajan.files.wordpress.com/2018/07/civilian-perceptions-of-the-yan-gora.pdf.

121. 'Mafias Run by Rogue Police Officers Are Terrorising Rio,' *The Economist*, May 30, 2019, http://www.economist.com/the-americas/2019/05/30/mafias-run-by-rogue-police-officers-are-terrorising-rio. See also Vanessa Barbara, 'The Men Who Terrorize

Rio,' *New York Times*, May 23, 2018, sec. Opinion, https://www.nytimes.com/2018/05/22/opinion/rio-janeiro-terrorize-militias.html.

122. Enrique Desmond Arias, 'How Criminals Govern in Latin America and the Caribbean,' *Current History* 119, no. 814 (February 2020): 43–45.

123. Benno Zogg, 'Organized Crime: Fueling Corruption and Mali's Desert War,' *IPI Global Observatory* (blog), February 27, 2018, https://theglobalobservatory.org/2018/02/organized-crime-corruption-mali/.

124. Thomas Shipley, 'Mali: Overview of Corruption and Anti-Corruption' (U4 Helpdesk Answers, Chr. Michelsen Institute, 2017), 1, https://www.u4.no/publications/mali-overview-of-corruption-and-anti-corruption.

125. Emilia Columbi and Austin C. Doctor, 'Foreign Fighters and the Trajectory of Violence in Northern Mozambique,' *War on the Rocks*, April 13, 2021, https://warontherocks.com/2021/04/foreign-fighters-and-the-trajectory-of-violence-in-northern-mozambique/.

126. Austin C. Doctor, 'The Looming Influx of Foreign Fighters in Sub-Saharan Africa,' *War on the Rocks*, August 18, 2020, https://warontherocks.com/2020/08/the-looming-influx-of-foreign-fighters-in-sub-saharan-africa/.

127. Grare, 'Balochistan,' 17. See also Muhammad Akbar Notezai, 'The Rise of Religious Extremism in Balochistan,' *The Diplomat*, January 9, 2017, https://thediplomat.com/2017/01/the-rise-of-religious-extremism-in-balochistan/.

128. Grare, 'Balochistan,' 24.

129. Geir Hågen Karlsen, 'Divide and Rule: Ten Lessons about Russian Political Influence Activities in Europe,' *Palgrave Communications* 5, no. 1 (February 8, 2019): 1–14, https://doi.org/10.1057/s41599-019-0227-8.

130. Peter Dickson, 'One Million Passports: Putin has Weaponized Citizenship in Occupied Eastern Ukraine,' *UkraineAlert*, Atlantic Council, June 17, 2020, https://www.atlanticcouncil.org/blogs/ukrainealert/one-million-passports-putin-has-weaponized-citizenship-in-occupied-eastern-ukraine/.

131. Stephen Daisley, 'Why Putin Wants Scottish Independence,' *The Spectator*, July 22, 2020, https://www.spectator.co.uk/article/why-putin-wants-scottish-independence; Óscar López-Fonseca and Fernando J. Pérez, 'Spain's High Court Opens Investigation into Russian Spying Unit in Catalonia,' *El País*, November 21, 2019, https://english.

elpais.com/elpais/2019/11/21/inenglish/1574324886_989244. html; Tim Lister and Clare Sebastian, 'Stoking Islamophobia and Secession in Texas—from an Office in Russia,' CNN, October 5, 2017, https://www.cnn.com/2017/10/05/politics/heart-of-texas-russia-event/index.html.

132. Alec Luhn, 'Russia Funds Moscow Conference for US, EU and Ukraine Separatists,' *The Guardian*, September 20, 2015, https://www.theguardian.com/world/2015/sep/20/russia-funds-moscow-conference-us-eu-ukraine-separatists; Mansur Mirovalev, 'Moscow Welcomes the (Would-Be) Sovereign Nations of California and Texas,' *Los Angeles Times*, September 27, 2016, https://www.latimes.com/world/europe/la-fg-russia-separatists-snap-story.html.

133. Stephen Blank, 'Imperial Strategies: Russia's Exploitation of Ethnic Issues and Policy in the Middle East,' in *Russia in the Middle East*, ed. Theodore Karasik and Stephen Blank (Washington, DC: Jamestown Foundation, 2018), 163–65.

134. P. Michael Phillips, 'Deconstructing Our Dark Age Future,' *Parameters* 39, no. 2 (Summer 2009): 95, https://doi.org/10.21236/ADA501234. A similar argument is proposed in Michaels, 'The Mirage of Non-State Governance.'

4. INFILTRATIVE INSURGENCY: THE TROJAN HORSE

1. Amnesty International, 'Bolivia: Crisis and Justice; Days of Violence in February and October 2003' (AMR 18/006/2004, November 2004), 2.

2. David E. Spencer and Hugo Acha Melgar, 'Bolivia, a New Model Insurgency for the 21st Century: From Mao Back to Lenin,' *Small Wars and Insurgencies* 28, no. 3 (May 4, 2017): 629–60. Spencer and Melgar's account is by far the most detailed and compelling, as it is based on extensive fieldwork and interviews with high-level protagonists within government, the security forces, media, civil society, and inhabitants of the Chapare, the Cocalero's base.

3. A General Accounting Office report suggests that during the 1980s, 'cocaine traffickers effectively ran the Chapare as a free-trade, free-fire zone for several years.' See US General Accounting Office, 'Efforts to Develop Alternatives to Cultivating Illicit Crops in Colombia Have Made Little Progress and Face Serious Obstacles' (Report to Congressional Requesters, Washington, DC, February 2002), 26. See also International Campaign to Ban Landmines and Human

Rights Watch, *Landmine Monitor Report 2004: Toward a Mine-Free World* (Washington: Human Rights Watch, 2004), 190.

4. Spencer and Acha Melgar, 'Bolivia, a New Model Insurgency for the 21st Century,' 637. See also the testimony of Filemón Escobar, one of the MAS founders: '*Sin embargo, habría sido una estrategia errónea, porque podía generar presencia militar norteamericana*' (However, it would have been a wrong strategy, because it could generate a US military presence). Alberto K. Rodriguez, 'Evitar la confrontación: Entrevista con Filemón Escobar,' *Encuentro* 44 (July 20, 2007): 101.

5. '*Por lo tanto, había que dar un gran viraje y adoptar la línea de participación en las elecciones de la democracia occidental representativa, que para la izquierda tradicional era la dictadura de la burguesía,*' See Rodriguez, 'Evitar la confrontación,' 101.

6. See ibid., 101.

7. Spencer and Acha Melgar, 'Bolivia, a New Model Insurgency for the 21st Century,' 639.

8. Filemón Escobar refers to it as '*complementariedad de opuestos,*' though he does not overtly acknowledge the role of outright violence in the strategy. See Rodriguez, 'Evitar la confrontación,' 102.

9. As Farah explains, 'the ideal climate for growing high quality, chewable coca leaf used in the traditional indigenous manner is found in elevations from 3,500 feet to 6,500 feet, far higher than the Chapare. As a result, almost all the coca used for chewing is found in the mountainous, semi-tropical Yungas region, the traditional home of coca leaf since Incan times. The vast bulk of the coca grown in the Chapare, since its inception, has been used for cocaine production rather than traditional uses because it is of greatly inferior quality.' See Douglas Farah, 'Into the Abyss: Bolivia under Evo Morales and the MAS' (International Assessment and Strategy Center, Alexandria, VA, June 18, 2009), 16, http://www.offnews.info/downloads/20090618_IASCIntoTheAbyss061709.pdf.

10. Spencer and Acha Melgar, 'Bolivia, a New Model Insurgency for the 21st Century,' 640. See also Donna Lee van Cott, 'From Exclusion to Inclusion: Bolivia's 2002 Elections,' *Journal of Latin American Studies* 35, no. 4 (2003): 762–64.

11. See Willem Assies and Ton Salman, *Crisis in Bolivia: The Elections of 2002 and Their Aftermath*, Research Paper 56 (London: University of London Institute of Latin American Studies, 2003).

12. The issue of income tax in the context of MAS mobilization is dealt with in detail in Tasha Fairfield, *Private Wealth and Public Revenue in*

Latin America: Business Power and Tax Politics (New York: Cambridge University Press, 2015), 224–37.

13. Spencer and Acha Melgar, 'Bolivia, a New Model Insurgency for the 21st Century,' 630. In January 2002, two days of confrontations between the Cocaleros and security forces resulted in seven deaths, including four members of the security forces, and 80 people being wounded. LADB, 'Bolivia Expels Cocaleros Leader' (Latin America Data Base, February 1, 2002), https://digitalrepository.unm.edu/cgi/viewcontent.cgi?article=13988&context=notisur. Around the same time, the two bodies of a policeman and a soldier were recovered, both bearing marks of torture.

14. 'Los Ponchos Rojos, la milicia aymara que se planta como la 'retaguardi' de Bolivia,' *Gestión*, December 16, 2019, sec. Internacional, https://gestion.pe/mundo/internacional/los-ponchos-rojos-la-milicia-aymara-que-se-planta-como-la-retaguardia-de-bolivia-noticia/. Farah, 'Into the Abyss,' 22.

15. William T. Barndt, 'Destroying the Opposition's Livelihood: Pathways to Violence in Bolivia since 2000,' *Journal of Politics in Latin America* 4, no. 3 (December 2012): 9, https://doi.org/10.1177/1866802X1200400301.

16. René Quenallata, 'El Mallku revela que falló una emboscada para matar a Sánchez Berzaín,' Eju!, August 4, 2013, Opinion edition, https://eju.tv/2013/08/el-mallku-revela-que-fall-una-emboscada-para-matar-a-snchez-berzan/.

17. 'Un abogado dice que las FARC actuaron el 2003,' Eju!, October 17, 2018, sec. Política, http://eju.tv/2008/10/un-abogado-dice-que-las-farc-actuaron-el-2003/. See also 'EEUU confirma presencia de las FARC y ELN de Colombia en Bolivia,' Agencia de Noticias Fides, May 8, 2003, https://www.noticiasfides.com/nacional/politica/eeuu-confirma-presencia-de-las-farc-y-eln-de-colombia-en-bolivia-46291; 'Las FARC estuvieron en Bolivia y expanden su dominio en la region,' Agencia de Noticias Fides, September 25, 2004, https://www.noticiasfides.com/nacional/sociedad/las-farc-estuvieron-en-bolivia-y-expanden-su-dominio-en-la-region-187050.

18. Spencer and Acha Melgar, 'Bolivia, a New Model Insurgency for the 21st Century,' 651.

19. Ibid., 651.

20. Farah, 'Into the Abyss,' 8.

21. Roger F. Noriega, 'Evo Morales's Reelection: Last Stand for Democracy?' (Latin American Outlook, American Enterprise

Institute, Washington, DC, December 2009), 2, http://www.aei.
org/wp-content/uploads/2011/10/No-%204-LAOg.pdf.

22. Farah, 'Into the Abyss,' 22. For Morales's attack on the press, see US
Embassy La Paz, 'Bolivia: Morales Manipulates Media Owners' (La
Paz, Bolivia, December 22, 2008), Wikileaks Public Library of US
Diplomacy, https://wikileaks.org/plusd/cables/08LAPAZ2623_a.
html.

23. Gabriel Elizondo, 'Bolivians Vote to "Decolonise Courts,"' Al Jazeera,
October 16, 2011, sec. Opinion, https://www.aljazeera.com/
indepth/opinion/2011/10/201110169924243497.html.

24. For a splendid treatment of this insurgency, see Thomas A. Marks,
Maoist People's War in Post-Vietnam Asia (Bangkok: White Lotus, 2007),
297–352.

25. International Crisis Group, 'Nepal's Maoists: Purists or Pragmatists?'
(Asia Report, Brussels, May 18, 2007), 2; Manish Thapa, 'Nepal's
Maoists: From Violent Revolution to Nonviolent Political Activism,'
in *Civil Resistance and Conflict Transformation: Transitions from Armed to
Nonviolent Struggle*, ed. Véronique Dudouet (London: Routledge,
2015), 196.

26. As Prachanda, leader of the Maoists, explains, 'We believed we could
conquer Kathmandu militarily. But later, when countries like the
U.S., the UK, and India started supporting the royal army militarily
... that posed some difficulties.' Cited in International Crisis Group,
'Nepal's Maoists: Purists or Pragmatists?,' 3.

27. Winne Gobyn, 'From War to Peace: The Nepalese Maoists' Strategic
and Ideological Thinking,' *Studies in Conflict and Terrorism* 32, no. 5
(May 2009): 427, https://doi.org/10.1080/10576100902831578.

28. See International Crisis Group, 'Nepal's Maoists: Purists or
Pragmatists?,' 2–3.

29. 'Interview with Baburam Bhattarai: Transition to New Democratic
Republic in Nepal,' *Monthly Review*, November 21, 2009, https://
monthlyreview.org/commentary/interview-with-baburam-
bhattarai/.

30. Thomas A. Marks, 'Terrorism as Method in Nepali Maoist Insurgency,
1996–2016,' *Small Wars and Insurgencies* 28, no. 1 (January 2, 2017):
81–118.

31. 'The Peace Prize,' *The Economist*, November 23, 2006, https://www.
economist.com/asia/2006/11/23/the-peace-prize. For examples
of the academic treatment, see Thapa, 'Nepal's Maoists'; Gobyn,
'From War to Peace.' To their credit, these sources are far from
alone in making definitive statements about the shift from violence

and acceptance of democracy. See also Aila M. Matanock and Paul Staniland, 'How and Why Armed Groups Participate in Elections,' *Perspectives on Politics* 16, no. 3 (September 2018): 710–27, https://doi.org/10.1017/S1537592718001019, which frames the Maoists as 'peaceful political parties' or as 'purely electoral actors embedded within mainstream politics.'

32. 'Maoist Chief Prachanda to Get Nepal's Top Peace Award,' Zee News, June 16, 2008, https://zeenews.india.com/news/south-asia/maoist-chief-prachanda-to-get-nepals-top-peace-award_449170.html.
33. 'Interview with Baburam Bhattarai.'
34. Ibid.
35. 'Maoists Tricked UNMIN,' *Nepali Times*, May 8, 2009, https://archive.nepalitimes.com/news.php?id=15924. Video and transcript available at https://www.youtube.com/watch?v=6EoQYZ2oa6M (accessed 8 October 2020).
36. 'Interview with Baburam Bhattarai.'
37. Thomas A. Marks, '"Post-conflict" Terrorism in Nepal,' *Journal of Counter Terrorism* 21, no. 1 (2015): 28.
38. Marks, 'Terrorism as Method in Nepali Maoist Insurgency, 1996–2016,' 105.
39. Guna Raj Luitel, 'Nepalese Journalist Defiant after Razor Slashing' (CPJ, January 12, 2010), https://cpj.org/blog/2010/01/tika-bista-heard-the-word.php.
40. Despite efforts to deter reporting on this violence, there are enough news clippings to suggest a pattern. See for example 'YCL Cadres Injure Nepali Congress Leader in Rukum,' *Himalayan Times*, April 14, 2016, https://thehimalayantimes.com/nepal/ycl-cadres-injure-nepali-congress-leader-rukum/; 'Fears over Nepal's Young Maoists,' BBC News, August 1, 2007, http://news.bbc.co.uk/2/hi/south_asia/6915564.stm. See also list of actions compiled by the South Asia Terrorism Portal: 'Nepal Terrorist Groups: Young Communist League (YCL),' South Asia Terrorism Portal, accessed August 6, 2018, http://www.satp.org/satporgtp/countries/nepal/terroristoutfits/YCL.html.
41. Marks, 'Terrorism as Method in Nepali Maoist Insurgency, 1996–2016,' n. 11. As Marks elaborates, 'These affirmative cases, of course, represent but an unknown segment of the pending cases in the adversarial system that is "immigration court."'
42. Refugee Review Tribunal, Australia, 'RRT Research Response: Nepal,' March 4, 2008, 1, https://www.justice.gov/sites/default/

files/eoir/legacy/2013/06/11/npl32984.pdf. See also Rameswor Bohara, 'An Armless Army,' *Nepali Times*, April 26, 2007.

43. 'Maoists Tricked UNMIN.'

44. See 'Riot Police Called In to Halt Nepali Student Violence,' *Daily Star*, August 16, 2007, https://www.thedailystar.net/news-detail-194; Refugee Review Tribunal, Australia, 'RRT Research Response,' 2; Thomas A. Marks, 'For Nepal's Maoists, the Cold War Continues,' *World Politics Review*, February 22, 2011, https://www.worldpoliticsreview.com/articles/7943/for-nepals-maoists-the-cold-war-continues.

45. Thomas A. Marks, 'Back to the Future: Nepali People's War as "New War,"' in *Countering Insurgencies and Violent Extremism in South and South East Asia*, ed. Shanthie D'Souza (London: Routledge, 2019).

46. Thomas A. Marks, 'Tenuous Security in the Himalayas: A Focus on Nepal,' in *Terrorism, Security and Development in South Asia: National, Regional and Global Implications*, ed. M. Raymond Izarali and Dalbir Ahlawat, New Regionalisms (Abingdon: Routledge, 2021), 64.

47. 'Interview with Baburam Bhattarai.'

48. Valery Gerasimov, 'The Value of Science in Prediction,' *Military-Industrial Kurier*, no. 8 (476) (March 27, 2013), http://vpk-news.ru/sites/default/files/pdf/VPK_08_476.pdf. On the unfortunate and misleading origins of the term, see Mark Galeotti, 'I'm Sorry for Creating the "Gerasimov Doctrine,"' *Foreign Policy*, March 5, 2018, https://foreignpolicy.com/2018/03/05/im-sorry-for-creating-the-gerasimov-doctrine/.

49. Ariel E. Levite and Jonathan (Yoni) Shimshoni, 'The Strategic Challenge of Society-Centric Warfare,' *Survival* 60, no. 6 (November 2, 2018): 96, https://doi.org/10.1080/00396338.2018.1542806.

50. On irregular warfare and strategies, see David H. Ucko and Thomas A. Marks, *Crafting Strategy for Irregular Warfare: A Framework for Analysis and Action* (Washington, DC: National Defense University Press, 2020).

51. George F. Kennan, 'The Inauguration of Organized Political Warfare [redacted version],' April 30, 1948, 1, Wilson Center Digital Archive, https://digitalarchive.wilsoncenter.org/document/114320.

52. For some notable examples, see Michael J. Mazarr, *Mastering the Gray Zone: Understanding a Changing Era of Conflict* (Carlisle Barracks, PA: Strategic Studies Institute and US Army War College Press, 2015), http://www.strategicstudiesinstitute.army.mil/pubs/display.cfm?pubID=1303; Mark Galeotti, *Hybrid War or Gibridnaya Voina? Getting Russia's Non-linear Military Challenge Right* (Prague: Mayak

Intelligence, 2016); James Q. Roberts, 'Need Authorities for the Gray Zone?,' *PRISM* 6, no. 3 (December 2016): 21–32; Frank G. Hoffman, 'Hybrid vs. Compound War,' *Armed Forces Journal*, October 1, 2009, http://armedforcesjournal.com/hybrid-vs-compound-war/.

53. Kennan, 'The Inauguration of Organized Political Warfare,' 1.

54. See Clayton Besaw, 'Election Violence Spiked Worldwide in 2020: Will This Year Be Better?,' *The Conversation*, February 18, 2021, http://theconversation.com/election-violence-spiked-worldwide-in-2020-will-this-year-be-better-153975. Numbers drawn from the ELection VIolence (ELVI) Events and Forecast dataset.

55. These hypotheses are proposed explicitly in Lindsay L. Heger, 'Votes and Violence: Pursuing Terrorism While Navigating Politics,' *Journal of Peace Research* 52, no. 1 (January 2015): 30, https://doi.org/10.1177/0022343314552984, which stipulates that 'groups actively participating in electoral politics are less likely to target civilians [because] (1) rebels care about generating local-level support and (2) civilian-targeted attacks counter these ambitions.'

56. Matanock and Staniland, 'How and Why Armed Groups Participate in Elections,' 712. See also Benedetta Berti, *Armed Political Organizations: From Conflict to Integration* (Baltimore: Johns Hopkins University Press, 2013); Thad Dunning, 'Fighting and Voting: Violent Conflict and Electoral Politics,' *Journal of Conflict Resolution* 55, no. 3 (June 2011): 327–39, https://doi.org/10.1177/0022002711400861.

57. Matanock and Staniland, 'How and Why Armed Groups Participate in Elections,' 721. Similarly, Berti notes that even though 'armed groups have shown an increased interest in creating political parties to take part in institutional politics ... this trend has been scarcely researched and analyzed.' Berti, *Armed Political Organizations*, 1.

58. Two thorough treatments of the topic are Berti, *Armed Political Organizations*; Leonard Weinberg, Ami Pedahzur, and Arie Perliger, *Political Parties and Terrorist Groups*, 2nd ed., Routledge Studies in Extremism and Democracy (London: Routledge, 2009). Both works distinguish themselves through their use of qualitative methods, which—given the ambiguity and subtleties of the topic—are more promising than the broad large-n quantitative overviews so typical of the field.

59. Cynthia L. Irvin, *Militant Nationalism: Between Movement and Party in Ireland and the Basque Country*, Social Movements, Protest, and Contention 9 (Minneapolis, MN: University of Minnesota Press, 1999), 8.

60. According to one dataset, of 430 terrorist groups, 203 had links with a political party but only 23 pursued 'a policy of jaw/jaw and war/

war simultaneously.' See Weinberg, Pedahzur, and Perliger, *Political Parties and Terrorist Groups*, 29, 79. Matanock and Staniland find that 'a *significant number* of armed groups use electoral and armed strategies simultaneously for long periods, and that many of them never moderate in the sense of ending their armed attacks.' See Matanock and Staniland, 'How and Why Armed Groups Participate in Elections,' 711 (emphasis added).

61. Vladimir Lenin, '"Left-Wing" Communism: An Infantile Disorder,' Marxist Internet Archive, June 1920, https://www.marxists.org/archive/lenin/works/1920/lwc/index.htm.

62. V. I. Lenin, 'Against Boycott: Notes from a Social-Democratic Publicist,' Marxist Internet Archive, 1907, https://www.marxists.org/archive/lenin/works/1907/boycott/i.htm#fwV13E005.

63. Andrew R. Molnar, William A. Lybrand, Lorna Hahn, James L. Kirkman, and Peter B. Riddleberger, *Undergrounds in Insurgent, Revolutionary, and Resistance Wars* (Washington, DC: Special Operations Research Office, 1963), 128. For the primary source, see Lenin, '"Left-Wing" Communism.' For useful commentary, Philip Selznick, *The Organizational Weapon: A Study of Bolshevik Strategy and Tactics* (Santa Monica, CA: RAND Corporation, 1952), 215–16, 255–66, https://www.rand.org/pubs/reports/R201.html.

64. H. W. Koch, '1933: The Legality of Hitler's Assumption of Power,' in *Aspects of the Third Reich*, ed. H. W. Koch (London: Macmillan, 1985), 46. Koch's work explores in detail the legal avenues that Hitler exploited. To this analysis, Finn adds that where the Weimar state did have emergency powers to proscribe anti-democratic parties, it 'could not respond to challenges to constitutionalism disguised in the language of democratic legality.' In other words, the failure was one of analysis, not institutional design. See John E. Finn, *Constitutions in Crisis: Political Violence and the Rule of Law* (New York: Oxford University Press, 1991), 137.

65. Helmut Anheier, 'Movement Development and Organizational Networks: The Role of "Single Members" in the German Nazi Party, 1925–30,' in *Social Movements and Networks*, ed. Mario Diani and Doug McAdam (Oxford: Oxford University Press, 2003), 51, https://doi.org/10.1093/0199251789.001.0001.

66. Thomas Childers and Eugene Weiss, 'Political Violence and the Limits of National Socialist Mass Mobilization,' *German Studies Review* 13, no. 3 (October 1990): 491.

67. Daniel Siemens, *Stormtroopers: A New History of Hitler's Brownshirts* (New Haven, CT: Yale University Press, 2017), 8.

68. David Littlejohn, *The SA 1921–45: Hitler's Stormtroopers*, Men-at-Arms 220 (Oxford: Osprey, 2001), 4.
69. Ibid., 4–5.
70. Koch, '1933'; Siemens, *Stormtroopers*, 35.
71. Littlejohn, *The SA 1921–45*, 5.
72. Ibid., 6.
73. Childers and Weiss, 'Political Violence and the Limits of National Socialist Mass Mobilization,' 493. One of the more notable confrontations was the 'Altona Bloody Sunday,' where 18 people died in clashes between Nazis and communists.
74. For more on the 'well-known National Socialist tactic' to 'provoke attacks from the political left' and exploit the resulting violence for their 'emotional dynamics,' see Siemens, *Stormtroopers*, 22–23, 183–84.
75. Peter H. Merkl, 'Approaches to Political Violence: The Stormtroopers, 1925–33,' in *Social Protest, Violence, and Terror in Nineteenth- and Twentieth-Century Europe*, ed. Wolfgang J. Mommsen and Gerhard Hirschfeld (London: Macmillan Press, 1982), 367–83. On the emotional dynamics of violent incidents, see Randall Collins, *Violence: A Micro-sociological Theory* (Princeton, NJ: Princeton University Press, 2008).
76. Merkl, 'Approaches to Political Violence,' 373. As an example, witness Hitler's own exaggerated spin on a particularly heavy defeat for the SA: 'More than 300 massacred—one could literally say, butchered—party comrades number among our dead martyrs. Tens of thousands and even more tens of thousands have been injured ... Only when the cup began to run over and the terror of the red bands of organized murderers and criminals became unbearable did von Papen's "National Government" rouse itself to take action ... Whoever of you harbours sentiments to fight for the honour and freedom of the nation will understand why I refuse to join this bourgeois Government ... Herr von Papen has thus engraved his name in German history with the blood of national fighters.' As cited in Siemens, *Stormtroopers*, xix–xx.
77. Childers and Weiss, 'Political Violence and the Limits of National Socialist Mass Mobilization,' n. 57. On the importance of threats, see Siemens, *Stormtroopers*, 73.
78. Childers and Weiss, 'Political Violence and the Limits of National Socialist Mass Mobilization,' 486. The authors cite a Nazi Party official who frames the purpose of the SA in terms very similar to those used by Mao in emphasizing the political nature of the Chinese Red Army: 'The SA man should not only be a soldier in a military sense, but

must also be a political soldier who views himself at all times as a representative of the National Socialist *Weltanschauung* and conducts himself in a manner consistent with that ideology' (p. 490).

79. As cited in Sven Reichardt, 'Violence and Community: A Micro-study on Nazi Storm Troopers,' *Central European History* 46, no. 2 (June 2013): 275, https://doi.org/10.1017/S0008938913000617.

80. See Childers and Weiss, 'Political Violence and the Limits of National Socialist Mass Mobilization,' 484.

81. Siemens, *Stormtroopers*, xxxiii.

82. Weinberg, Pedahzur and Perliger see the starting point as the emergence of modern political parties in 1849. See Weinberg, Pedahzur, and Perliger, *Political Parties and Terrorist Groups*, 5–14.

83. Freedom House as cited in Thomas Davies, 'Civil Society History VI: Early and Mid 20th Century,' in *International Encyclopedia of Civil Society*, ed. Helmut K. Anheier, Stefan Toepler, and Regina List, Springer Reference (New York: Springer, 2010), 362.

84. As cited in Drew Desilver, 'Despite Global Concerns about Democracy, More than Half of Countries Are Democratic' (FactTank, Pew Research Center, May 14, 2019), https://www.pewresearch.org/fact-tank/2019/05/14/more-than-half-of-countries-are-democratic/.

85. Brancati finds that between 2004 and 2014, 'about 70% of authoritarian states held legislative elections and 80% held elections for the chief executive.' Dawn Brancati, 'Democratic Authoritarianism: Origins and Effects,' *Annual Review of Political Science* 17, no. 1 (May 11, 2014): 314, https://doi.org/10.1146/annurev-polisci-052013-115248.

86. As Levitsky and Way note, these competitive authoritarians are unlikely to reduce elections 'to a mere façade'; 'rather than openly violating democratic rules (for example, by banning or repressing the opposition and the media), incumbents are more likely to use bribery, co-optation, and more subtle forms of persecution, such as the use of tax authorities, compliant judiciaries, and other state agencies to "legally" harass, persecute, or extort cooperative behavior from critics.' See Steven Levitsky and Lucan Way, 'The Rise of Competitive Authoritarianism,' *Journal of Democracy* 13, no. 2 (2002): 53–54, https://doi.org/10.1353/jod.2002.0026.

87. Charles Lindholm and José Pedro Zúquete, *The Struggle for the World: Liberation Movements for the 21st Century* (Stanford, CA: Stanford University Press, 2010), 4–8. See also Davies, 'Civil Society History VI'; Arnd Bauerkämper, 'Civil Society History VII: Late 20th and 21st Century,' in *International Encyclopedia of Civil Society*, ed. Helmut K.

Anheier, Stefan Toepler, and Regina List, Springer Reference (New York: Springer, 2010).

88. Thomas A. Marks, 'Maoist Conception of the United Front with Particular Application to the United Front in Thailand since October 1976,' *Issue and Studies* 16, no. 3 (March 1980): 47.

89. Leon Trotsky, *What Next? Vital Questions for the German Proletariat*, Marxist Internet Archive, 1932, https://www.marxists.org/archive/trotsky/germany/1932-ger/index.htm. See also Robert J. Alexander, *International Trotskyism, 1929–1985: A Documented Analysis of the Movement* (Durham, NC: Duke University Press, 1991), 348–50. For a detailed review of how the French turn worked in the United States, said to be its 'most decisive success,' see Bryan D. Palmer, 'The French Turn in the United States: James P. Cannon and the Trotskyist Entry into the Socialist Party, 1934–1937,' *Labor History* 59, no. 5 (September 3, 2018): 610–38, https://doi.org/10.1080/002365 6X.2018.1436946.

90. Herbert Marcuse, *Counterrevolution and Revolt* (Boston: Beacon Press, 1972), 55.

91. Interview with Thomas A. Marks (e-mail), 24 October 2020.

92. Marks, 'Maoist Conception of the United Front with Particular Application to the United Front in Thailand since October 1976,' 52–59.

93. Mao Tse-tung, 'Unite All Anti-Japanese Forces and Combat the Anti-Communist Die-Hards,' in *Selected Works of Mao Tse-tung*, vol. II (Peking: Foreign Languages Press, 1967), 389–94, http://marxism.halkcephesi.net/Mao/CACD40.html.

94. Spencer and Acha Melgar, 'Bolivia, a New Model Insurgency for the 21st Century,' 632.

95. As cited in Koch, '1933,' 45.

96. Lenin, 'Against Boycott.'

97. 'Interview with Baburam Bhattarai.'

98. Daniel Trilling, 'Golden Dawn: The Rise and Fall of Greece's Neo-Nazis,' *The Guardian*, March 3, 2020, sec. News, https://www.theguardian.com/news/2020/mar/03/golden-dawn-the-rise-and-fall-of-greece-neo-nazi-trial.

99. Antonis A. Ellinas, 'The Rise of Golden Dawn: The New Face of the Far Right in Greece,' *South European Society and Politics* 18, no. 4 (December 2013): 553, https://doi.org/10.1080/13608746.2013.782838; Trilling, 'Golden Dawn.'

100. Ellinas, 'The Rise of Golden Dawn,' 559; Tsoutsoumpis Spyridon, 'The Far Right in Greece: Paramilitarism, Organized Crime and the

Rise of "Golden Dawn,'" *Südosteuropa: Journal of Politics and Society* 66, no. 4 (2018): 526.

101. Ellinas, 'The Rise of Golden Dawn,' 559.

102. Mary Shiraef, 'From Fighting Nazis to Electing Nazis: The Rise of Golden Dawn in Greece,' *Cornell International Affairs Review* 7, no. 1 (2013), http://www.inquiriesjournal.com/articles/1486/from-fighting-nazis-to-electing-nazis-the-rise-of-golden-dawn-in-greece.

103. Spyridon, 'The Far Right in Greece,' 524.

104. Ellinas, 'The Rise of Golden Dawn,' 550.

105. Paul Mason, 'Golden Dawn Verdict: No Sunset for the Far Right,' *International Politics and Society*, October 14, 2020, https://www.ips-journal.eu/topics/human-rights/golden-dawn-verdict-no-sunset-for-the-far-right-4718/.

106. Gilberto Vieira and Marta Harnecker, *Combinación de todas las formas de lucha* (Bogotá: Ediciones Suramérica, 1988).

107. James J. Brittain, *Revolutionary Social Change in Colombia: The Origin and Direction of the FARC-EP* (London: Pluto Press; New York: Palgrave Macmillan, 2010), 14, 242.

108. Directorate of Intelligence, 'Foreign and Domestic Influences on the Colombian Communist Party, 1957 – August 1966' (Intelligence Report, Central Intelligence Agency, Langley, VA, March 1967), vii, passim.

109. Vieira and Harnecker, *Combinación de todas las formas de lucha*. On this strategy and its evolution, see also Steven S. Dudley, *Walking Ghosts: Murder and Guerrilla Politics in Colombia* (New York: Routledge, 2006).

110. Abbey Steele, *Democracy and Displacement in Colombia's Civil War* (Ithaca, NY: Cornell University Press, 2017), 123.

111. David Spencer, 'The Evolution and Implementation of FARC Strategy: Insights from Its Internal Documents,' *Security and Defense Studies Review* 12, nos. 1–2 (Fall–Winter 2011): 75. See also Dudley, *Walking Ghosts*, 50.

112. Spencer, 'The Evolution and Implementation of FARC Strategy,' 75.

113. Carlos A. Ospina, Thomas A. Marks, and David H. Ucko, 'Colombia and the War-to-Peace Transition: Cautionary Lessons from Other Cases,' *Military Review* 96, no. 4 (2016), http://usacac.army.mil/CAC2/MilitaryReview/Archives/English/MilitaryReview_20160831_art010.pdf. See also Adam Isacson, 'Why Colombia's Historic Peace Breakthrough Was the "Easy Part,'" *World Politics Review*, September 6, 2016, https://www.worldpoliticsreview.com/articles/19826/why-colombia-s-historic-peace-breakthrough-was-the-easy-part.

114. Angelika Albaladejo, 'Is Colombia Underestimating the Scale of FARC Dissidence?,' *InSight Crime* (blog), October 17, 2017, https://www. insightcrime.org/news/analysis/is-colombia-underestimating-scale-farc-dissidence/; Christopher Woody, 'Colombia Is Trying to Root Out the Cocaine Trade, but Farmers Are Relying on It as an "Insurance Policy,"' *Business Insider*, March 22, 2018, http://www. businessinsider.com/farmers-in-colombia-relying-on-economic-benefits-of-cocaine-production-2018-3; Tracy Wilkinson, 'U.S. Alarmed over Surge in Coca Production in Colombia,' *Los Angeles Times*, February 6, 2018, http://www.latimes.com/nation/la-fg-tillerson-colombia-20180206-story.html.

115. Anthony Richards, 'Terrorist Groups and Political Fronts: The IRA, Sinn Fein, the Peace Process and Democracy,' *Terrorism and Political Violence* 13, no. 4 (December 2001): 74, https://doi. org/10.1080/09546550109609700.

116. This evolution is laid out in detail in Berti, *Armed Political Organizations*, 148–56; Ian McAllister, '"The Armalite and the Ballot Box": Sinn Fein's Electoral Strategy in Northern Ireland,' *Electoral Studies* 23, no. 1 (March 2004): 123–42, https://doi.org/10.1016/j. electstud.2003.10.002; Richards, 'Terrorist Groups and Political Fronts'; Andrew Silke, 'Rebel's Dilemma: The Changing Relationship between the IRA, Sinn Féin and Paramilitary Vigilantism in Northern Ireland,' *Terrorism and Political Violence* 11, no. 1 (March 1999): 55–93, https://doi.org/10.1080/09546559908427495; Peter Taylor, *Provos: The IRA and Sinn Fein*, rev. ed. (London: Bloomsbury, 1998), chap. 20.

117. Gerry Adams, then vice-president of Sinn Féin, interviewed in Michael Farrell, 'We Have Now Established a Sort of Republican Veto,' *Magill*, June 30, 1983, https://magill.ie/archive/we-have-now-established-sort-republican-veto.

118. Gerry Adams, then the president of Sinn Féin, was for example able to reform a devoted yet insular US-based fundraising body, Noraid, into a political institution for lobbying and publicity. See Andrew J. Wilson, 'The Conflict between Noraid and the Friends of Irish Freedom,' *Irish Review*, no. 15 (1994): 40, https://doi.org/10.2307/29735731.

119. As quoted in Taylor, *Provos*.

120. As quoted in Irvin, *Militant Nationalism*, 161.

121. See Silke, 'Rebel's Dilemma,' 55, 71.

122. Peter R. Neumann, 'The Bullet and the Ballot Box: The Case of the IRA,' *Journal of Strategic Studies* 28, no. 6 (December 2005): 960, https://doi.org/10.1080/01402390500441081.

123. See Silke, 'Rebel's Dilemma,' 55, 71.

124. Berti, *Armed Political Organizations*, 141–42, 174.
125. Malachi O'Doherty, *The Trouble with Guns: Republican Strategy and the Provisional IRA* (Belfast: Blackstaff Press, 1998), 118–20. See also Berti, *Armed Political Organizations*, 138–39.
126. Rogelio Alonso, 'Terrorist Skin, Peace-Party Mask: The Political Communication Strategy of Sinn Féin and the PIRA,' *Terrorism and Political Violence* 28, no. 3 (May 26, 2016): 529, https://doi.org/10.1080/09546553.2016.1155934.
127. Ibid., 522.
128. Kevin Bean, 'Endings and Beginnings? Republicanism since 1994,' *Studies in Conflict and Terrorism* 37, no. 9 (September 2, 2014): 522, https://doi.org/10.1080/1057610X.2014.931211.
129. Ibid., 522.
130. Neumann, 'The Bullet and the Ballot Box,' 969.
131. See Warren Chin, 'Northern Ireland (1976–1994): Police Primacy,' in *Network Centric Operations (NCO) Case Study: The British Approach to Low-Intensity Operations: Part 2*, 1.0, Transformation Case Study Series (Washington, DC: Department of Defense, 2007), 101–48; M. L. R Smith, *Fighting for Ireland? The Military Strategy of the Irish Republican Movement* (Abingdon: Routledge, 2003), 146.
132. This section draws extensively on Ucko, 'Militias, Tribes and Insurgents.'
133. As Pollack notes, 'because Washington had not allowed enough time—let alone created the circumstances—for genuinely popular figures to emerge, the Coalition Provisional Authority (CPA) simply appointed twenty-five Iraqi leaders well-known *to them*.' See Kenneth M. Pollack, 'The Seven Deadly Sins of Failure in Iraq: A Retrospective Analysis of the Reconstruction,' *Middle East Review of International Affairs* 10, no. 4 (December 2006): 10.
134. Thomas S. Mowle, 'Iraq's Militia Problem,' *Survival* 48, no. 3 (October 2006): 49, https://doi.org/10.1080/00396330600905528; International Crisis Group, 'Iraq's Muqtada al-Sadr: Spoiler or Stabiliser?' (Middle East Report, Brussels, July 11, 2006), 1.
135. International Crisis Group, 'Iraq's Muqtada al-Sadr,' 9–10.
136. Andrew W. Terrill, *The United States and Iraq's Shi'ite Clergy: Partners or Adversaries?* (Carlisle, PA: US Strategic Studies Institute, 2004), 12. The one attempt to rein in these sub-state forces—a UK effort to disarm forcibly the town of Majar al-Kabir in June 2003—resulted in the deaths of six Royal Military Police and was the last such action in the southeast for some time. In the following months, the US coalition 'decided that dealing with the militias was not a high priority

[and], instead, Coalition military units made tactical arrangements with militias on an ad hoc basis.' See Andrew Rathmell, Olga Oliker, Terrence K. Kelly, David Brannan, and Keith Crane, *Developing Iraq's Security Sector: The Coalition Provisional Authority's Experience* (Santa Monica, CA: RAND Corporation, 2005), 66.

137. Larry Diamond, *Squandered Victory: The American Occupation and the Bungled Effort to Bring Democracy to Iraq* (New York: Henry Holt and Company, 2013), 8, http://rbdigital.oneclickdigital.com.
138. International Crisis Group, 'The Next Iraqi War? Sectarianism and Civil Conflict' (Middle East Report, Brussels, February 27, 2006), 12–13.
139. Toby Dodge, 'Securing America's Interest in Iraq: The Remaining Options' (Pub. L. no. S. HRG 110-153, Committee on Foreign Relations, United States Senate, 2007), 619.
140. Amit R. Paley and Zaid Sabah, 'Case Is Dropped against Shiites in Sunni Deaths,' *Washington Post*, March 4, 2008, http://www.washingtonpost.com/wp-dyn/content/article/2008/03/03/AR2008030300311.html.
141. Toby Dodge, 'The Iraq Transition: Civil War or Civil Society?' (Testimony before the Committee on Foreign Relations, Washington DC, April 20, 2004); Mowle, 'Iraq's Militia Problem.'
142. International Crisis Group, 'Iraq's Civil War, the Sadrists and the Surge' (Middle East Report, Brussels, February 7, 2008),' 4–5.
143. Michael Knights, 'Soleimani Is Dead: The Road Ahead for Iranian-Backed Militias in Iraq,' *CTC Sentinel*, January 2020.
144. Ibrahim al-Marashi, 'The Future of Militias in Post-ISIL Iraq,' Al Jazeera, March 27, 2017, sec. Opinion, https://www.aljazeera.com/opinions/2017/3/27/the-future-of-militias-in-post-isil-iraq; Douglas A. Ollivant, 'Why Washington Should Side with the Protesters in Iraq,' *Washington Post*, November 5, 2019, sec. Opinion, https://www.washingtonpost.com/opinions/2019/11/05/why-washington-should-side-with-protesters-iraq/.
145. Niloufer Siddiqui, 'Strategic Violence among Religious Parties in Pakistan,' in *Oxford Research Encyclopedia of Politics* (Oxford: Oxford University Press, 2019), 11, https://doi.org/10.1093/acrefore/9780190228637.013.842.
146. 'Empowering People: MQM Manifesto 2013,' January 4, 2013, http://www.mqm.org/Manifesto2013.
147. Amna Mahmood, 'Regional Political Parties: Challenge to Political Stability of Pakistan,' *Pakistan Vision* 15, no. 2 (2014): 39; Niloufer Siddiqui, 'The MQM and Identity Politics in Pakistan,' *Criterion*

Quarterly 3, no. 3 (November 20, 2020), https://criterion-quarterly. com/the-mqm-and-identity-politics-in-pakistan/.

148. Siddiqui, 'The MQM and Identity Politics in Pakistan.'

149. United States Bureau of Citizenship and Immigration Services, 'Pakistan: Information on Mohajir/Muttahida Qaumi Movement-Altaf (MQM-A),' February 9, 2004, https://www.refworld.org/ docid/414fe5aa4.html. A typical denial of violence: 'MQM Denies It Incites Violence,' BBC News, July 11, 2013, https://www.bbc.com/ news/av/uk-23270720.

150. Laurent Gayer, *Karachi: Ordered Disorder and the Struggle for the City* (New York: Oxford University Press, 2014), 10.

151. Matanock and Staniland, 'How and Why Armed Groups Participate in Elections,' 716. Though they were not solely the work of MQM, Karachi witnessed almost 18,500 homicides between 2000 and 2015 and a peak of almost 3,000 killings just in 2013. See Alison Brown and Saeed Ahmed, 'Local Government Dissolution in Karachi: Chasm or Catalyst?,' *Third World Thematics: A TWQ Journal* 1, no. 6 (November 2016): 882, https://doi.org/10.1080/23802014.2016.1315318.

152. As cited in MQM, 'Life and Death of Mohajirs Is Associated with Sindh Province,' January 6, 2006, http://www.mqm.org/English-News/Jan-2006/news060107.

153. Gayer, *Karachi*, 11–12, 51.

154. International Crisis Group, 'Pakistan: Stoking the Fire in Karachi,' (Asia Report, Brussels, February 15, 2017), 1.

155. Statistics drawn from Karachi's Citizens Police Liaison Committee, as cited in Arif Rafiq, 'Operation Karachi: Pakistan's Military Retakes the City,' *National Interest*, August 24, 2015), https://nationalinterest.org/ feature/operation-karachi-pakistans-military-retakes-the-city-13660.

156. Waseem Abbasi, 'Karachi Returning to Peace,' *The News International*, August 2, 2015, https://www.thenews.com.pk/print/54321-karachi-returning-to-peace; Syed Raza Hassan, 'Fearful for Decades, Pakistan's Main Parties Now Openly Campaign in Karachi,' Reuters, July 19, 2018, https://www.reuters.com/article/us-pakistan-election-karachi-idUSKBN1K9162.

157. See Abid Hussain, 'Dialogue: Laurent Gayer and Omar Shahid Hamid on Karachi,' *Herald Magazine*, October 26, 2016, http://herald. dawn.com/news/1153570.

158. Joshua T. White, 'Vigilante Islamism in Pakistan: Religious Party Responses to the Lal Masjid Crisis,' *Current Trends in Islamist Ideology* 7 (2008): 52–53; Siddiqui, 'Strategic Violence among Religious Parties in Pakistan,' 10.

159. Siddiqui, 'Strategic Violence among Religious Parties in Pakistan,' 12.

160. Ahmad Sabat, Muhammad Shoaib, and Abdul Qadar, 'Religious Populism in Pakistani Punjab: How Khadim Rizvi's Tehreek-e-Labbaik Pakistan Emerged,' *International Area Studies Review* 23, no. 4 (December 2020): 365–81, https://doi.org/10.1177/2233865920968657; Nirupama Subramanian, 'Explained: How Radical Outfit Forced Pakistan Hand in Move to Expel French Envoy,' *Indian Express*, April 27, 2021, https://indianexpress.com/article/explained/tehreek-e-labbaik-pakistan-saad-hussain-rizvi-protests-imran-khan-7281260/.

161. Siddiqui, 'Strategic Violence among Religious Parties in Pakistan,' 1, passim.

162. White, 'Vigilante Islamism in Pakistan: Religious Party Responses to the Lal Masjid Crisis,' 51.

163. This is the dilemma explored in Jacob N. Shapiro, *The Terrorist's Dilemma: Managing Violent Covert Organizations* (Princeton, NJ: Princeton University Press, 2017).

164. As cited in Richard English, *Armed Struggle: The History of the IRA* (London: Pan Macmillan, 2008), 223.

5. IDEATIONAL INSURGENCY: THE DIGITAL COUNTER-STATE AND BEYOND

1. Jean Lartéguy, *The Centurions*, trans. Alexander Wallace Fielding (New York: Penguin, 2015), 474.

2. David E. Apter, 'Political Violence in Analytical Perspective,' in *The Legitimization of Violence*, ed. David E. Apter (Houndsmills: Macmillan in association with UNRISD, 1997), 9.

3. V. I. Lenin, *Selected Works [of] V. I. Lenin* (New York: International Publishers, 1968), 40, https://books.google.com/books?id=y_sNAQAAMAAJ.

4. Nguyên Giáp Võ, *People's War, People's Army: The Viet Công Insurrection Manual for Underdeveloped Countries* (New York: Praeger, 1962), 78.

5. See Akil N. Awan, 'The Virtual Jihad: An Increasingly Legitimate Form of Warfare,' *Virtual Jihad* 3, no. 5 (May 2010), 10–13.

6. Jason Straziuso, 'US Team Using Twitter, Facebook to Fight Militants,' *Taiwan News*, April 13, 2012, https://www.taiwannews.com.tw/en/news/2195115; Charlie Winter, 'Media Jihad: The Islamic State's Doctrine for Information Warfare' (International Centre for the Study of Radicalisation and Political Violence, London, 2017), 18.

7. See for example John Arquilla and David F. Ronfeldt, *The Advent of Netwar* (Santa Monica, CA: RAND, 1996); David F. Ronfeldt, John

Arquilla, Graham Fuller, and Melissa Fuller, *The Zapatista 'Social Netwar' in Mexico* (Santa Monica, CA: RAND, 1998).

8. On the origins of the struggle, see Clifford Bob, *The Marketing of Rebellion: Insurgents, Media, and International Activism*, Cambridge Studies in Contentious Politics (Cambridge: Cambridge University Press, 2005), 120–24; Lawrence R. Alschuler, 'The Chiapas Rebellion: An Analysis according to the Structural Theory of Revolution,' *Estudios Interdisciplinarios de América Latina y el Caribe* 10, no. 2 (1999): 132–35; Juanita Darling, *Latin America, Media, and Revolution: Communication in Modern Mesoamerica*, Palgrave Macmillan Series in International Political Communication (New York: Palgrave Macmillan, 2008), 122–24.

9. John Arquilla and David F. Ronfeldt, 'Emergence and Influence of the Zapatista Social Netwar,' in *Networks and Netwars: The Future of Terror, Crime, and Militancy*, ed. John Arquilla and David F. Ronfeldt (Santa Monica, CA: RAND Corporation, 2001), 179.

10. Bob, *The Marketing of Rebellion*, 127.

11. On the framing techniques used, see Charles Lindholm and José Pedro Zúquete, *The Struggle for the World: Liberation Movements for the 21st Century* (Stanford, CA: Stanford University Press, 2010), 11–21; Darling, *Latin America, Media, and Revolution*, 127–30.

12. Though there is clear evidence of excesses in the initial response to the January 1994 offensive, there were also instances in which misinformation and possible disinformation by the EZLN and others greatly exaggerated the abuses of the military. See Darling, *Latin America, Media, and Revolution*, 126, 133.

13. The types of sites and capabilities used are detailed in Bob, *The Marketing of Rebellion*, 132–33; Arquilla and Ronfeldt, 'Emergence and Influence of the Zapatista Social Netwar,' 183.

14. Bob, *The Marketing of Rebellion*, 118. See also Alschuler, 'The Chiapas Rebellion,' 139; Darling, *Latin America, Media, and Revolution*, 133–34.

15. Arquilla and Ronfeldt, 'Emergence and Influence of the Zapatista Social Netwar,' 189.

16. Alschuler, 'The Chiapas Rebellion'; Bob, *The Marketing of Rebellion*.

17. Thomas A. Marks and Rodney S. Azama, 'Cyberterrorism,' in *The Fundamentals of Counterterrorism Law*, ed. Lynne K. Zusman (Chicago: American Bar Association, 2014), 259.

18. Manuel Castells, *The Power of Identity*, 2nd ed., The Information Age: Economy, Society, and Culture (Malden, MA: Wiley-Blackwell, 2010), 75.

19. Robert J. Bunker, *Old and New Insurgency Forms* (Carlisle, PA: Strategic Studies Institute and US Army War College Press, 2016), 49.

20. Stephen Sloan, 'The Challenge of Nonterritorial and Virtual Conflicts: Rethinking Counterinsurgency and Counterterrorism' (JSOU Report, Joint Special Operations University, MacDill AFB, Florida, March 2011).

21. See Angela Nagle, *Kill All Normies: The Online Culture Wars from Tumblr and 4chan to the Alt-Right and Trump* (Winchester: Zero Books, 2017).

22. For background, see the informative 2012 documentary directed by Brian Knappenberger, *We Are Legion: The Story of Hacktivists* (FilmBuff, 2012). See also Parmy Olson, *We Are Anonymous: Inside the Hacker World of LulzSec, Anonymous, and the Global Cyber Insurgency* (New York: Back Bay, 2013).

23. The app 'Low Ion Orbit' (or LOIC), for example, could be downloaded for free and used without any technical expertise to overwhelm and take down a targeted server or website.

24. Michael S. Bernstein, Andrés Monroy-Hernández, Drew Harry, Paul André, Katrina Panovich, and Greg Vargas, '4chan and /b/: An Analysis of Anonymity and Ephemerality in a Large Online Community,' in *Proceedings of the Fifth International Conference on Weblogs and Social Media* (Barcelona, 2011), 6; Olson, *We Are Anonymous*, 27–33.

25. Paul Roberts, 'Chats, Car Crushes and Cut 'n Paste Sowed Seeds of LulzSec's Demise,' *Threatpost*, March 7, 2012, https://threatpost.com/chats-car-crushes-and-cut-n-paste-sowed-seeds-lulzsecs-demise-030712/76298/; Knappenberger, *We Are Legion: The Story of Hacktivists*.

26. Anonymous (@YourAnonNews), March 6, 2012, https://twitter.com/YourAnonNews/status/177073022455398400.

27. See Dale Beran, 'The Return of Anonymous,' *The Atlantic*, August 11, 2020, https://www.theatlantic.com/technology/archive/2020/08/hacker-group-anonymous-returns/615058/.

28. In explaining the fizzling out of Anonymous's threatened 'war' on then-candidate Donald J. Trump, the movement's 'best-known' voice online notes: 'We believe that major Anonymous operations simply did not take place because of the divide of the collective on the political spectrums. The U.S. election pitted friend against friend, mother against son. It did the same within Anonymous.' See David Gilbert, 'Anonymous Declared War on Trump, and Then Disappeared,' *Vice*, November 28, 2016, https://www.vice.com/en/article/ywna4w/anonymous-declared-war-on-trump-and-then-disappeared.

29. Ronfeldt, Arquilla, Fuller, and Fuller, *The Zapatista 'Social Netwar' in Mexico*, 9.

30. Ibid., 11–12.

31. From Luther P. Gerlach, 'Protest Movements and the Construction of Risk,' in *The Social and Cultural Construction of Risk*, ed. B. B. Johnson and V. T. Covello (Boston: D. Reidel, 1987), 115.

32. See Luther P. Gerlach and Virginia H. Hine, *People, Power, Change Movements of Social Transformation* (Indianapolis, IN: Bobbs-Merrill, 1970), 65.

33. Gerlach, 'Protest Movements and the Construction of Risk,' 116–17.

34. Arquilla and Ronfeldt, *The Advent of Netwar*, 11.

35. These types of sentiments pervade the individual testimonies of individuals arrested on terrorism-related charges in France, as interviewed and presented in Farhad Khosrokhavar, *Quand Al-Qaïda parle: Témoignages derrière les barreaux* (Paris: Seuil, 2007). Second-generation Muslim immigrants and, seemingly at a higher proportion but fewer in absolute numbers, converts to Islam appear to have been particularly affected by the message.

36. Lindholm and Zúquete, *The Struggle for the World*, 122–51. On the historical myths of such atavism, see Mohammed Ayoob, 'The Myth of the Islamic State,' *Foreign Affairs*, April 4, 2016, https://www.foreignaffairs.com/articles/2016-04-03/myth-islamic-state.

37. Yannick Veilleux-Lepage, 'Paradigmatic Shifts in Jihadism in Cyberspace: The Emerging Role of Unaffiliated Sympathizers in Islamic State's Social Media Strategy,' *Journal of Terrorism Research* 7, no. 1 (February 5, 2016): 38, https://doi.org/10.15664/jtr.1183. For the background and context of *Inspire*, which is the most well-known al-Qaeda publication, see Julian Droogan and Shane Peattie, 'Reading Jihad: Mapping the Shifting Themes of *Inspire* Magazine,' *Terrorism and Political Violence* 30, no. 4 (July 4, 2018): 684–717, https://doi.org/10.1080/09546553.2016.1211527.

38. On this point, and on 'jihadi cool,' see Jason Burke, *The New Threat: The Past, Present, and Future of Islamic Militancy* (New York: New Press, 2015), 179–81. See also John M. 'Matt' Venhaus, 'Why Youth Join al-Qaeda' (Special Report, United States Institute of Peace, Washington, DC, May 2010), https://www.usip.org/sites/default/files/SR236Venhaus.pdf.

39. See Haroro J. Ingram, 'The Strategic Logic of Islamic State Information Operations,' *Australian Journal of International Affairs* 69, no. 6 (November 2, 2015): 730, https://doi.org/10.1080/1035771 8.2015.1059799.

40. See Jessica Stern and J. M. Berger, *ISIS: The State of Terror* (New York: Ecco Press/HarperCollins, 2016), 154–56.

41. Ibid., 149.

42. James P. Farwell, 'The Media Strategy of ISIS,' *Survival* 56, no. 6 (November 2, 2014): 51, https://doi.org/10.1080/00396338.201 4.985436.

43. J. M. Berger and Jonathon Morgan, 'The ISIS Twitter Census: Defining and Describing the Population of ISIS Supporters on Twitter' (Analysis Paper, Brookings Project on US Relations with the Islamic World, Center for Middle East Policy, Brookings, March 2015), 23. See also Maura Conway, Moign Khawaja, Suraj Lakhani, Jeremy Reffin, Andrew Robertson, and David Weir, 'Disrupting Daesh: Measuring Takedown of Online Terrorist Material and Its Impacts,' *Studies in Conflict and Terrorism* 42, nos. 1–2 (February 2019): 151, https://doi. org/10.1080/1057610X.2018.1513984.

44. Aymenn Jawad al-Tamini, 'Review of "ISIS: The State of Terror,"' *Syria Comment* (blog), March 27, 2015, https://www.joshualandis.com/ blog/review-of-isis-the-state-of-terror/; Craig Whiteside, 'Nine Bullets for the Traitors, One for the Enemy: The Slogans and Strategy behind the Islamic State's Campaign to Defeat the Sunni Awakening (2016–2017),' *Terrorism and Counter-terrorism Studies*, 2018, 1–36, https://doi.org/10.19165/2018.1.07.

45. Berger and Morgan, 'The ISIS Twitter Census,' 7, 29.

46. Laura Huey, 'This Is Not Your Mother's Terrorism: Social Media, Online Radicalization and the Practice of Political Jamming,' *Journal of Terrorism Research* 6, no. 2 (May 25, 2015): 2, https://doi. org/10.15664/jtr.1159.

47. An analysis by the International Centre for the Study of Radicalization notes how ISIS's communications were designed 'for swift memetic dissemination and capable of transcending both identity and culture,' thereby allowing the 'group to popularise its war in a manner unparalleled by any other insurgent actor, past or present.' See Winter, 'Media Jihad,' 6. On the Russian variant, see Philip N Howard, Bharath Ganesh, and Dimitra Liotsiou, 'The IRA, Social Media and Political Polarization in the United States, 2012–2018' (Computational Propaganda Research Project, University of Oxford, December 2018).

48. 'Jihobbyist' as a term was coined in Jarret Brachman, *Global Jihadism: Theory and Practice* (New York: Routledge, 2009), 19.

49. Winter, 'Media Jihad,' 19.

50. Ibid., 9.

51. Burke, *The New Threat*, 207.

52. Amarnath Amarasingam, 'Elton "Ibrahim" Simpson's Path to Jihad in Garland, Texas,' *War on the Rocks*, May 14, 2015, https://

warontherocks.com/2015/05/elton-ibrahim-simpsons-path-to-jihad-in-garland-texas/.

53. Amarnath Amarasingam, 'What Twitter Really Means for Islamic State Supporters,' *War on the Rocks*, December 30, 2015, https://warontherocks.com/2015/12/what-twitter-really-means-for-islamic-state-supporters/.

54. Conway et al., 'Disrupting Daesh,' 150–51.

55. Amarasingam, 'Elton "Ibrahim" Simpson's Path to Jihad in Garland, Texas.'

56. Winter, 'Media Jihad,' 17.

57. Veilleux-Lepage, 'Paradigmatic Shifts in Jihadism in Cyberspace,' 37.

58. Michel Wieviorka, 'Terrorism in the Context of Academic Research,' in *Terrorism in Context*, ed. Martha Crenshaw (University Park, PA: Pennsylvania State University Press, 1995).

59. Paragraph draws on David H. Ucko and Thomas A. Marks, 'Violence in Context: Mapping the Strategies and Operational Art of Irregular Warfare,' *Contemporary Security Policy* 39, no. 2 (April 3, 2018): 208, https://doi.org/10.1080/13523260.2018.1432922. See also the work of Tom Marks, for example Marks, 'Counterinsurgency in the Age of Globalism,' *Journal of Conflict Studies* 27, no. 1 (2007).

60. According to one study of 55 so-called 'lone wolf' attacks, 78 percent of the perpetrators 'were exposed to external sources of encouragement or justification for the use of violence' (in a further 9 percent of cases, the degree of such exposure was unknown). See Bart Schuurman, Edwin Bakker, Paul Gill, and Noémie Bouhana, 'Lone Actor Terrorist Attack Planning and Preparation: A Data-Driven Analysis,' *Journal of Forensic Sciences* 63, no. 4 (July 2018): 1195, https://doi.org/10.1111/1556-4029.13676.

61. Arquilla and Ronfeldt, *The Advent of Netwar*, 10.

62. Anonymous, 'Stochastic Terrorism: Part 1, Triggering the Shooters,' *Stochastic Terrorism* (blog), January 26, 2011, http://stochasticterrorism.blogspot.com/2011/01/stochastic-terrorism-part-1-triggering.html. The term 'stochastic' derives etymologically from the Greek words for aiming and guesswork, suggesting the admixture of purpose and randomness informing the phenomenon.

63. As a senior ISIS spokesperson puts it in one text, 'We will argue, before Allah, against any Muslim who has the ability to shed a single drop of crusader blood but does not do so, whether with an explosive device, a bullet, a knife, a car, a rock, or even a boot or a fist. Indeed, you saw what a single Muslim did with Canada and its parliament of shirk, and what our brothers in France, Australia, and Belgium did.'

See Abu Muhammad al-Adnani, 'Say "Die in Your Rage!"' (Al Hayat Media Centre, January 2015), 4. See also Thomas Wyke, 'Sharpen Your Knives. Prepare Your Explosive Devices' Urges Canadian Isis Fighter,' *International Business Times UK*, December 7, 2014, sec. Society, https://www.ibtimes.co.uk/sharpen-your-knives-prepare-your-explosive-devices-urges-canadian-isis-fighter-1478447.

64. See Paul Cruickshank and Mohannad Hage Ali, 'Abu Musab al Suri: Architect of the New al Qaeda,' *Studies in Conflict and Terrorism* 30, no. 1 (January 2007): 1–14, https://doi.org/10.1080/10576100601049928; George Michael, 'Leaderless Resistance: The New Face of Terrorism,' *Defence Studies* 12, no. 2 (June 2012): 257–82, https://doi.org/10.1080/14702436.2012.699724.

65. Some neo-Nazi outfits dream of seizing territory. The Base, for example, espouses 'a plan to forcibly seize the Pacific Northwest and bring it under the control of white supremacist militants.' Actual progress toward realizing this plan is modest at best, though the Base founder did purchase 'three 10-acre parcels of adjacent undeveloped land in Ferry County for a total of $33,000.' The entire gambit feels somewhat laughable. 'The Base,' Anti-Defamation League, accessed February 2, 2021, https://www.adl.org/resources/backgrounders/the-base.

66. Nagle, *Kill All Normies*, 40, 48.

67. Daniel Trilling, 'Tommy Robinson and the Far Right's New Playbook,' *The Guardian*, October 25, 2018, sec. World news, http://www.theguardian.com/world/2018/oct/25/tommy-robinson-and-the-far-rights-new-playbook.

68. Tamir Bar-On, 'The Alt-Right's Continuation of the "Cultural War" in Euro-American Societies,' *Thesis Eleven* 163, no. 1 (April 2021): 43–70, https://doi.org/10.1177/07255136211005988.

69. Nagle, *Kill All Normies*, 12.

70. J. M. Berger, 'The Alt-Right Twitter Census: Defining and Describing the Audience for Alt-Right Content on Twitter' (VOX-Pol, 2018), 5.

71. Ibid., 6.

72. For an authoritative take on this outfit, see Robert Evans and Jason Wilson, 'The Boogaloo Movement Is Not What You Think,' *Bellingcat*, May 27, 2020, https://www.bellingcat.com/news/2020/05/27/the-boogaloo-movement-is-not-what-you-think/. On the relation between QAnon and violence, see Amarnath Amarasingam and Marc-André Argentino, 'The QAnon Conspiracy Theory: A Security Threat in the Making?,' *CTC Sentinel* 13, no. 7 (July 2020): 37–43.

73. Even scholars who seek to emphasize the alt-right's distinctiveness

from the broader white-power movement acknowledge that 'people regularly circulate between groups and belief systems, that they often hold concurrent memberships, and that they use a wide variety of flexible and interchangeable symbols and ideologies.' See Kathleen Belew, 'The White Power Movement at War on Democracy' (Harry Frank Guggenheim Foundation, New York, January 2021), 5–6. Furthermore, as Marwick and Lewis also recognize, 'Attempting to form coherence out of this loose aggregate is very difficult. Ambiguity is, itself, a strategy; it allows participants to dissociate themselves with particularly unappetizing elements while still promoting the overall movement.' Alice Marwick and Rebecca Lewis, 'Media Manipulation and Disinformation Online' (Data and Society Research Institute, May 15, 2017), 11.

74. Nagle, *Kill All Normies*, 24. For background on 4chan channels and their evolution, see Brian Feldman, 'Inside /Pol/, the 4chan Politics Board Shouted Out in Minneapolis Gun Video,' *Intelligencer*, November 25, 2015, https://nymag.com/intelligencer/2015/11/inside-pol-4chans-racist-heart.html.

75. Nagle, *Kill All Normies*, 34.

76. Feldman, 'Inside /Pol/, the 4chan Politics Board Shouted Out in Minneapolis Gun Video.'

77. As cited in P. W. Singer and Emerson T. Brooking, *LikeWar: The Weaponization of Social Media* (Boston: Eamon Dolan/Houghton Mifflin Harcourt, 2018), 126.

78. Estes cites the moment in 1983 when 'a white supremacist named George Dietz connected his Apple IIe, one of the first personal computers, to the internet and took the Liberty Bell Network online. This dial-up bulletin board system (BBS), a precursor to the World Wide Web, allowed anyone with a modem and computer to read through endless screens of Holocaust denial literature and anti-Semitic diatribes.' See Adam Clark Estes, 'How Neo-Nazis Used the Internet to Instigate a Right-Wing Extremist Crisis,' *Vox*, February 2, 2021, https://www.vox.com/recode/22256387/facebook-telegram-qanon-proud-boys-alt-right-hate-groups.

79. As intelligence operative-turned-police detective Patrick Skinner put it in an interview shortly after the January 6, 2021 Capitol invasion, 'We're not even just talking about our mentally unstable people. We're talking about … what we used to call regular people … But now they are certainly unstable.' Cited in Andrew Feinberg, 'Intelligence Officials Warn of What Comes Next after Pro-Trump Capitol Riots,' *The Independent*, January 7, 2021, sec. Voices, https://

www.independent.co.uk/voices/capitol-riots-trump-dc-shooting-cia-b1783607.html.

80. See Emile Durkheim, *The Division of Labor in Society* (New York: Free Press, 2014); Emile Durkheim, *Suicide: A Study in Sociology* (New York: Free Press, 1951). On deviance, see Robert K. Merton, 'Social Structure and Anomie,' *American Sociological Review* 3, no. 5 (October 1938): 672–82, https://doi.org/10.2307/2084686.

81. In a 2012 analysis by the United States Census Bureau, it was calculated that by 2044, 49.7 percent of the US population will be white, compared to 50.3 percent of minority populations (25 percent Hispanics, 12.7 percent black, 7.9 percent Asian, 3.7 percent multiracial, and 1 percent 'others'). See Sandra L. Colby and Jennifer M. Ortman, 'Projections of the Size and Composition of the U.S. Population: 2014 to 2060' (Current Population Reports, United States Census Bureau, March 2015). A previous projection by the Census Bureau, in 2008, pegged the flip to 2042, which is also the date seen in a majority of white-nationalist writing and discussion of this issue. See Sabrina Tavernise, 'Why the Announcement of a Looming White Minority Makes Demographers Nervous,' *New York Times*, November 22, 2018, sec. U.S., https://www.nytimes.com/2018/11/22/us/white-americans-minority-population.html.

82. Nils Gilman, 'The Collapse of Racial Liberalism,' *American Interest* 13, no. 5 (March 2, 2018), https://www.the-american-interest.com/2018/03/02/collapse-racial-liberalism/; Thomas B. Edsall, 'White Riot,' *New York Times*, January 13, 2021, sec. Opinion, https://www.nytimes.com/2021/01/13/opinion/capitol-riot-white-grievance.html. See also Ashley Jardina, *White Identity Politics* (Cambridge: Cambridge University Press, 2019), 3–4, passim.

83. James C. Davies, 'Toward a Theory of Revolution,' *American Sociological Review* 27, no. 1 (February 1962): 5–19.

84. See Robert M. Sapolsky, *Behave: The Biology of Humans at Our Best and Worst* (New York: Penguin Press, 2017), 85–89.

85. Gilman, 'The Collapse of Racial Liberalism.'

86. Elisa Shearer and Amy Mitchell, 'News Use across Social Media Platforms in 2020,' *Pew Research Center's Journalism Project* (blog), January 12, 2021, https://www.journalism.org/2021/01/12/news-use-across-social-media-platforms-in-2020/.

87. On clearly fabricated stories outperforming regular news items, see Craig Silverman, 'This Analysis Shows How Viral Fake Election News Stories Outperformed Real News on Facebook,' *BuzzFeed News*, November 16, 2016, https://www.buzzfeednews.com/article/

craigsilverman/viral-fake-election-news-outperformed-real-news-on-facebook. On faith in mainstream media, see Megan Brenan, 'Americans Remain Distrustful of Mass Media,' Gallup, September 30, 2020, https://news.gallup.com/poll/321116/americans-remain-distrustful-mass-media.aspx. Polling in 2020 revealed that 'the percentage with no trust at all is a record high, up five points since 2019.'

88. Donatella Della Porta, *Social Movements, Political Violence, and the State: A Comparative Analysis of Italy and Germany* (Cambridge: Cambridge University Press, 2006), 12.

89. Jeff Horwitz, 'Facebook Knew Calls for Violence Plagued "Groups," Now Plans Overhaul,' *Wall Street Journal*, January 31, 2021, sec. Tech, https://www.wsj.com/articles/facebook-knew-calls-for-violence-plagued-groups-now-plans-overhaul-11612131374.

90. A helpful review of this concept is found in Raymond S. Nickerson, 'Confirmation Bias: A Ubiquitous Phenomenon in Many Guises,' *Review of General Psychology* 2, no. 2 (June 1998): 175–220, https://doi.org/10.1037/1089-2680.2.2.175.

91. Keegan Hankes and Alex Amend, 'The Alt-Right Is Killing People,' Southern Poverty Law Center, February 5, 2018, https://www.splcenter.org/20180205/alt-right-killing-people.

92. Vincent Law, 'What Exactly Does Modern Society Offer Young White Men Anymore?,' AltRight.com (blog), December 28, 2017, https://altright.com/2017/12/28/what-exactly-does-modern-society-offer-young-white-men-anymore/.

93. Joseph E. Uscinski and Joseph M. Parent, *American Conspiracy Theories* (Oxford: Oxford University Press, 2014), 132.

94. Joanne M. Miller, Kyle L. Saunders, and Christina E. Farhart, 'Conspiracy Endorsement as Motivated Reasoning: The Moderating Roles of Political Knowledge and Trust,' *American Journal of Political Science* 60, no. 4 (October 2016): 824–44, https://doi.org/10.1111/ajps.12234.

95. Maxime Dafaure, 'The "Great Meme War:" The Alt-Right and Its Multifarious Enemies,' *Angles*, no. 10 (April 1, 2020): 15–17, https://doi.org/10.4000/angles.369.

96. Russell Muirhead and Nancy L. Rosenblum, *A Lot of People Are Saying: The New Conspiracism and the Assault on Democracy* (Princeton, NJ: Princeton University Press, 2019), 2.

97. Studies suggest, rather uncontroversially, that extremists are more prone to conspiratorial thinking. See Sander Linden, Costas Panagopoulos, Flávio Azevedo, and John T. Jost, 'The Paranoid

Style in American Politics Revisited: An Ideological Asymmetry in Conspiratorial Thinking,' *Political Psychology* 42, no. 1 (June 24, 2020): 23–51, https://doi.org/10.1111/pops.12681. Some suggest the right wing of the political spectrum is particularly vulnerable to conspiracy theories; others disagree. See, respectively, Miller, Saunders, and Farhart, 'Conspiracy Endorsement as Motivated Reasoning'; Uscinski and Parent, *American Conspiracy Theories*, 88.

98. See, respectively, Adam Taylor, 'New Zealand Suspect Allegedly Claimed "Brief Contact" with Norwegian Mass Murderer Anders Breivik,' *Washington Post*, March 15, 2019, https://www. washingtonpost.com/world/2019/03/15/new-zealand-suspect-allegedly-claimed-brief-contact-with-norwegian-mass-murderer-anders-breivik/; Mattias Gardell, 'Crusader Dreams: Oslo 22/7, Islamophobia, and the Quest for a Monocultural Europe,' *Terrorism and Political Violence* 26 (2014): 135, passim.

99. See, respectively, Kai Biermann, Luisa Hommerich, Yassin Musharbash, and Karsten Polke-Majewski, 'Anschlag in Halle: Attentäter mordete aus Judenhass,' *Die Zeit*, October 9, 2019, sec. Gesellschaft, https://www.zeit.de/gesellschaft/zeitgeschehen/2019-10/anschlag-halle-helmkamera-stream-einzeltaeter; Marcel Fürstenau, 'Walter Lübcke: ein politischer Mord erschüttert Deutschland,' Deutsche Welle, June 2, 2020, https://www.dw.com/de/walter-l%C3%BCbcke-ein-politischer-mord-ersch%C3%BCttert-deutschland/a-53604759.

100. See QAnon Anonymous, 'International QAnon (The Netherlands) Feat. Marc-André Argentino,' December 30, 2020, https://soundcloud.com/qanonanonymous/episode-123-international-qanon-the-netherlands-feat-marc-andre-argentino; Mark Scott, 'QAnon Goes European,' *Politico*, October 23, 2020, https://www.politico.eu/article/qanon-europe-coronavirus-protests/.

101. Nationaal Coördinator Terrorismebestrijding en Veiligheid, 'Terrorist Threat Assessment for the Netherlands 53' (Ministerie van Justitie en Veiligheid, The Hague, October 2020), 29, 53.

102. Thomas A. Marks and Paul B. Rich, 'Back to the Future: People's War in the 21st Century,' *Small Wars and Insurgencies* 28, no. 3 (May 4, 2017), 409–10.

103. US Department of the Army, Headquarters, 'Counterinsurgency Operations' (Washington, DC, October 1, 2004), 1–3.

104. George Hawley, *Making Sense of the Alt-Right* (New York: Columbia University Press, 2017), 19.

105. Pete Simi and Robert Futrell, *American Swastika: Inside the White*

Power Movement's Hidden Spaces of Hate (Lanham, MD: Rowman and Littlefield Publishers, 2010), 84–87.

106. A massive leak of material from the site reveals that 'Americans made up most of the new members [and that most] of the activity related to private messages on Iron March was also attributable to American members.' See Jacques Singer-Emery and Rex Bray III, 'The Iron March Data Dump Provides a Window into How White Supremacists Communicate and Recruit,' *Lawfare*, February 27, 2020, https://www.lawfareblog.com/iron-march-data-dump-provides-window-how-white-supremacists-communicate-and-recruit.

107. Belew, 'The White Power Movement at War on Democracy,' 4.

108. The term was coined by American sociologist Diane Vaughan. See Diane Vaughan, *The Challenger Launch Decision: Risky Technology, Culture, and Deviance at NASA* (Chicago: University of Chicago Press, 1996).

109. Simi and Futrell, *American Swastika*, 92–94. These digital counter-states could also be conceived of as illiberal 'counterpublics,' drawing here on the feminist critique of Jürgen Habermas and his work on the public sphere. Fraser defines a counterpublic as 'parallel discursive arenas where members of subordinated social groups invent and circulate counterdiscourses, so as to formulate oppositional interpretations of their identities, interests, and needs.' See Nancy Fraser, 'Rethinking the Public Sphere: A Contribution to the Critique of Actually Existing Democracy,' in *Habermas and the Public Sphere*, ed. Craig J. Calhoun, Studies in Contemporary German Social Thought (Cambridge, MA: MIT Press, 1992), 123.

110. Adolf Hitler, *Mein Kampf* (New York: Reynal and Hitchcock, 1940), 715–16.

111. As cited in Hannah Arendt, *The Origins of Totalitarianism* (New York: Harcourt Publishers, 1973), 357.

112. As cited in Marc Fisher, 'From Memes to Race War: How Extremists Use Popular Culture to Lure Recruits,' *Washington Post*, April 30, 2021, https://www.washingtonpost.com/nation/2021/04/30/extremists-recruiting-culture-community/.

113. Abi Wilkinson, 'We Need to Talk about the Online Radicalisation of Young, White Men,' *The Guardian*, November 15, 2016, sec. Opinion, http://www.theguardian.com/commentisfree/2016/nov/15/alt-right-manosphere-mainstream-politics-breitbart.

114. Nadia M. Brashier and Elizabeth J. Marsh, 'Judging Truth,' *Annual Review of Psychology* 71, no. 1 (January 4, 2020): 503–4, https://doi.org/10.1146/annurev-psych-010419-050807.

115. Farhad Manjoo, 'I Spoke to a Scholar of Conspiracy Theories and I'm Scared for Us,' *New York Times*, October 21, 2020, sec. Opinion, https://www.nytimes.com/2020/10/21/opinion/q-anon-conspiracy.html.

116. Simi and Futrell, *American Swastika*, chap. 4.

117. The Patriot Voice, 'For God and Country Victory Cruise,' Victory Cruise, accessed January 28, 2021, https://www.thepatriotvoice.us. I am grateful to Cracked.com for bringing this event to my attention. See Mark Hill, '4 Reasons We Can't Laugh Away Stupid Conspiracy Theories in 2021,' *Cracked.com*, December 19, 2020, https://www.cracked.com/article_29231_4-reasons-we-cant-laugh-away-stupid-conspiracy-theories-in-2021.html.

118. QAnon Anonymous, 'Undercover at the Save the Children (Again) Rally,' April 28, 2021, https://soundcloud.com/qanonanonymous/episode-140-undercover-at-the-save-the-children-again-rally.

119. Knappenberger, *We Are Legion*.

120. For this history of internet usage by the far right, see Aaron Winter, 'Online Hate: From the Far-Right to the "Alt-Right" and from the Margins to the Mainstream,' in *Online Othering: Exploring Digital Violence and Discrimination on the Web*, ed. Karen Lumsden and Emily Harmer (Cham: Springer International Publishing, 2019), 39–63, https://doi.org/10.1007/978-3-030-12633-9_2.

121. Hawley notes, 'The ability to break out of these isolated Internet ghettos and enter the mainstream discussion is what sets the Alt-Right apart from its predecessors.' Hawley, *Making Sense of the Alt-Right*, 19. See also Marwick and Lewis, 'Media Manipulation and Disinformation Online,' 29. As Stern adds, 'Alt-righters expend a lot of energy reflecting on red-pilling strategies, particularly those that might turn someone.'

122. The dramatic resurgence of this concept during the Trump years reflects the changes that American society was undergoing at this time and the attempt of many to make sense of it all. Derek Robertson, 'How an Obscure Conservative Theory Became the Trump Era's Go-to Nerd Phrase,' *Politico Magazine*, February 25, 2018, http://politi.co/2FunqYx.

123. Joseph G. Lehman, 'An Introduction to the Overton Window of Political Possibility,' Mackinac Center for Public Policy, April 8, 2010, https://www.mackinac.org/12481.

124. Nathan J. Russell, 'An Introduction to the Overton Window of Political Possibilities,' Mackinac Center for Public Policy, January 4, 2006, https://www.mackinac.org/7504.

125. Antonio Gramsci, *Prison Notebooks*, Volume 3. trans. J.A. Buttigieg (New York: Columbia University Press, 2007), 168.

126. Marwick and Lewis, 'Media Manipulation and Disinformation Online,' 36.

127. Alan Rappeport, 'From the Right, a New Slur for G.O.P. Candidates,' *New York Times*, August 13, 2015, sec. U.S., https://www.nytimes.com/2015/08/13/us/from-the-right-a-new-slur-for-gop-candidates.html.

128. Andrew 'weev' Auerheimer, 'Fun with Twitter's Ad Console. (with Images, Tweets),' Storify, June 7, 2015, https://web.archive.org/web/20161114175734/https://storify.com/weev/fun-with-twitter-ads-day-1. 'Weev' is a key figure within the alt-right.

129. J. M. Berger, 'Nazis vs. ISIS on Twitter: A Comparative Study of White Nationalist and ISIS Online Social Media Networks' (George Washington University Program on Extremism, September 2016), 3, https://extremism.gwu.edu/sites/g/files/zaxdzs2191/f/downloads/Nazis%20v.%20ISIS.pdf.

130. Berger, 'The Alt-Right Twitter Census,' 51.

131. Jack Nicas, 'How YouTube Drives People to the Internet's Darkest Corners,' *Wall Street Journal*, February 7, 2018, sec. Tech, https://www.wsj.com/articles/how-youtube-drives-viewers-to-the-internets-darkest-corners-1518020478; Hawley, *Making Sense of the Alt-Right*, 20. See also Marwick and Lewis, 'Media Manipulation and Disinformation Online,' 17, 26.

132. In this instance, a search for 'black on white crime' on Google took Roof to the supremacist website of the Council of Conservative Citizens. As he later commented, 'at this moment I realized that something was very wrong.' See David A. Neiwert, *Alt-America: The Rise of the Radical Right in the Age of Trump* (London: Verso, 2017), 11. See also Jessie Daniels, 'The Algorithmic Rise of the "Alt-Right,"' *Contexts* 17, no. 1 (February 2018): 60–65, https://doi.org/10.1177/1536504218766547.

133. Marwick and Lewis, 'Media Manipulation and Disinformation Online,' 35.

134. As cited in Fisher, 'From Memes to Race War.'

135. 'Want to "redpill" someone? Don't say the edgiest shit you can say. Say the small thing that they're thinking but don't have the courage to say. You'll have a disciple for life.' As cited, alongside other guides, in Alexandra Minna Stern, *Proud Boys and the White Ethnostate: How the Alt-Right Is Warping the American Imagination* (Boston: Beacon Press, 2019), 21.

136. Andrew Anglin, 'A Normie's Guide to the Alt-Right,' *Daily Stormer*

(blog), August 31, 2016, https://dailystormer.su/a-normies-guide-to-the-alt-right/.

137. See S. Peter Davis, 'How Alt-Right Trolls Keep Tricking the Mainstream Media,' Cracked.com, February 28, 2019, https://www.cracked.com/blog/how-alt-right-trolls-keep-tricking-mainstream-media/; 'Okay Hand Gesture,' Anti-Defamation League, accessed February 1, 2021, https://www.adl.org/education/references/hate-symbols/okay-hand-gesture.

138. This is the infamous Pepe the Frog. For full context, see 'Pepe the Frog,' Anti-Defamation League, accessed February 1, 2021, https://www.adl.org/education/references/hate-symbols/pepe-the-frog.

139. As quoted in Hawley, *Making Sense of the Alt-Right*, 99.

140. Eryn J. Newman, Maryanne Garry, Daniel M. Bernstein, Justin Kantner, and D. Stephen Lindsay, 'Nonprobative Photographs (or Words) Inflate Truthiness,' *Psychonomic Bulletin and Review* 19, no. 5 (October 2012): 969–74, https://doi.org/10.3758/s13423-012-0292-0.

141. Both citations are from Friederike Wegener, 'How the Far-Right Uses Memes in Online Warfare,' *Global Network on Extremism and Technology*, May 21, 2020, https://gnet-research.org/2020/05/21/how-the-far-right-uses-memes-in-online-warfare/.

142. Both citations are from ibid.

143. Alice Marwick and Rebecca Lewis, 'The Online Radicalization We're Not Talking About,' *Intelligencer*, May 18, 2017, https://nymag.com/intelligencer/2017/05/the-online-radicalization-were-not-talking-about.html.

144. Hawley, *Making Sense of the Alt-Right*, 86–87.

145. Janet Reitman, 'All-American Nazis: Inside the Rise of Fascist Youth in the U.S.,' *Rolling Stone*, May 2, 2018, https://www.rollingstone.com/politics/politics-news/all-american-nazis-628023/.

146. 8chan poster quoted in Marwick and Lewis, 'Media Manipulation and Disinformation Online,' 34.

147. Wegener, 'How the Far-Right Uses Memes in Online Warfare.' See also Viveca S. Greene, '"Deplorable" Satire: Alt-Right Memes, White Genocide Tweets, and Redpilling Normies,' *Studies in American Humor* 5, no. 1 (2019): 31, https://doi.org/10.5325/studamerhumor.5.1.0031.

148. As cited in Hawley, *Making Sense of the Alt-Right*, 136. In a similar vein, Milo Yiannopoulos and Allum Bokhari, two extreme-right thought leaders, claim in an article that the alt-right is not racist but rather says outrageous things simply 'to fluster their grandparents' (cited in ibid., 145).

149. Ryan Holiday, *Trust Me, I'm Lying: Confessions of a Media Manipulator* (New York: Portfolio/Penguin, 2017).

150. Dafaure, 'The "Great Meme War,"' 14.

151. Davis, 'How Alt-Right Trolls Keep Tricking the Mainstream Media'; *Fox News Tucker Carlson: It's Okay to Be White Goes National*, 2017, https://www.youtube.com/watch?v=aYE_Q9gslVo.

152. Marwick and Lewis, 'Media Manipulation and Disinformation Online,' 36.

153. 'Glenn Beck: Obama Is a Racist,' CBS News, July 29, 2009, https://www.cbsnews.com/news/glenn-beck-obama-is-a-racist/; Hatewatch, 'Ann Coulter: A White Nationalist in the Mainstream?,' Southern Poverty Law Center, May 28, 2015, https://www.splcenter.org/hatewatch/2015/05/27/ann-coulter-%E2%80%93-white-nationalist-mainstream; Simon Clark, 'How White Supremacy Returned to Mainstream Politics,' *Center for American Progress*, July 1, 2020, https://www.americanprogress.org/issues/security/reports/2020/07/01/482414/white-supremacy-returned-mainstream-politics/.

154. 'Fox News Channel Finishes 2018 as Most Watched Cable Network in Total Day and Primetime for Third Consecutive Year and Notches Highest-Rated Primetime Ever,' *Business Wire*, December 12, 2018, https://www.businesswire.com/news/home/20181212005768/en/FOX-News-Channel-Finishes-2018-as-Most-Watched-Cable-Network-in-Total-Day-Primetime-for-Third-Consecutive-Year-and-Notches-Highest-Rated-Primetime-Ever.

155. Christopher Wylie, *Mindf*ck: Cambridge Analytica and the Plot to Break America* (New York: Random House, 2019), 11.

156. Ibid., 118–19.

157. Berger, 'The Alt-Right Twitter Census,' 7.

158. 'Ice-breaker' is the exact term used by several alt-right supporters to describe Trump's effect on the movement. See Hawley, *Making Sense of the Alt-Right*, 119.

159. 'I think if Trump wins … we could really legitimately say that he was associated directly with us, with the 'R'-word [racist], all sorts of things. People will have to recognize us.' Spencer, as cited in Center on Extremism, 'New Hate and Old: The Changing Face of American White Supremacy' (ADL, September 2018), 33.

160. As cited in Hannah Gais, 'The Alt-Right Comes to Washington,' *Washington Spectator*, December 6, 2016, https://washingtonspectator.org/npi-alt-right-dc/; Hawley, *Making Sense of the Alt-Right*, 118–19.

161. *Politico*, 'Transcript: Hillary Clinton's Full Remarks in Reno,

Nevada,' *Politico*, August 25, 2016, https://www.politico.com/story/2016/08/transcript-hillary-clinton-alt-right-reno-227419.

162. Both quoted in Hawley, *Making Sense of the Alt-Right*, 125.

163. Center on Extremism, 'New Hate and Old,' 42.

164. Marwick and Lewis, 'Media Manipulation and Disinformation Online,' 13.

165. Hawley, *Making Sense of the Alt-Right*, 142; Clark, 'How White Supremacy Returned to Mainstream Politics.' See also Nathan J. Robinson, 'Let's Just Stop Writing Long-Form Profiles of Nazis,' *Current Affairs*, November 27, 2017, https://www.currentaffairs.org/2017/11/lets-just-stop-writing-long-form-profiles-of-nazis.

166. Eugen Hadamovsky, *Propaganda und nationale Macht*, 1933, as cited in Arendt, *The Origins of Totalitarianism*, 356.

167. Travis Morris, *Dark Ideas: How Neo-Nazi and Violent Jihadi Ideologues Shaped Modern Terrorism* (Lanham, MD: Lexington Books, 2017). See also Cruickshank and Ali, 'Abu Musab al Suri'; Michael, 'Leaderless Resistance.'

168. Center on Extremism, 'New Hate and Old,' 57.

169. See Karsten Müller and Carlo Schwarz, 'Fanning the Flames of Hate: Social Media and Hate Crime' (Working Paper Series, Centre for Competitive Advantage in the Global Economy, University of Warwick, May 2018), https://www.ssrn.com/abstract=3082972.

170. Andrew Marantz, 'Inside the Daily Stormer's Style Guide,' *New Yorker*, January 8, 2018, https://www.newyorker.com/magazine/2018/01/15/inside-the-daily-stormers-style-guide.

171. Andrew Marantz, 'The Regular Guy Who Almost Challenged Georgia's QAnon Candidate,' *New Yorker*, October 19, 2020, https://www.newyorker.com/magazine/2020/10/26/the-regular-guy-who-almost-challenged-georgias-qanon-candidate. Unsurprisingly, the list of QAnon-related violent incidents has grown as the conspiracy continues to spread. One high-profile example concerns the 'Pizzagate' incident, where a heavily armed man traveled to Comet Pizza in Washington, DC, because he had been led to believe, online, that the pizzeria was the headquarters for a child-trafficking sex ring controlled by Hillary Clinton. Despite his firing three rounds, there were no fatalities in this particular incident. See Amanda Robb, 'Pizzagate: Anatomy of a Fake News Scandal,' *Rolling Stone*, November 16, 2017, https://www.rollingstone.com/politics/news/pizzagate-anatomy-of-a-fake-news-scandal-w511904. For a list of other QAnon violent incidents, see Lois Beckett, 'QAnon: A Timeline of Violence Linked to the Conspiracy Theory,' *The Guardian*, October 16, 2020,

sec. US news, http://www.theguardian.com/us-news/2020/oct/15/qanon-violence-crimes-timeline.

172. As cited in Morris, *Dark Ideas*, xi. Similarly, the man who ran his car into counter-protesters at the Charlottesville rally had previously engaged extensively with the online alt-right community. Alan Blinder, 'Suspect in Charlottesville Attack Had Displayed Troubling Behavior,' *New York Times*, August 13, 2017.

173. See Belew, 'The White Power Movement at War on Democracy,' 7; Seth G. Jones, Catrina Doxsee, and Nicholas Harrington, 'The Escalating Terrorism Problem in the United States' (CSIS Briefs, Center of Strategic and International Studies, June 2020).

174. Mike Levine and Josh Margolin, 'Feds Warn "Violent Opportunists" Infiltrating George Floyd Protests, Could Be "Emboldened" to Attack Police,' ABC News, June 3, 2000, https://abcnews.go.com/Politics/feds-warn-violent-opportunists-infiltrating-protests-emboldened-attack/story?id=71040109.

175. Robert J. Art and Kenneth N. Waltz, *The Use of Force: Military Power and International Politics*, 4th ed. (Lanham, MD: University Press of America, 1993), 8.

176. Ibid., 8.

177. Heather Timmons, 'A Former Skinhead Explains Why It's a Mistake for the US to Stop Targeting Right-Wing Extremists,' *Quartz*, February 2, 2017, https://qz.com/901625/a-former-skinhead-explains-why-its-a-mistake-to-for-the-us-to-stop-targeting-right-wing-terrorists-at-home/.

178. Wesley Lowery and Abigail Hauslohner, '"White Lives Matter" Rally Organizers Adjust Strategy to Avoid Becoming "Another Charlottesville,"' *Washington Post*, October 27, 2017, sec. National, https://www.washingtonpost.com/national/residents-and-organizers-worry-about-violence-at-tennessee-rallies/2017/10/27/554c4e40-bb5d-11e7-a908-a3470754bbb9_story.html. See also Daryl Johnson, *Right Wing Resurgence: How a Domestic Terrorist Threat Is Being Ignored* (Lanham, MD: Rowman and Littlefield Publishers, 2012); Arie Perliger, 'Challengers from the Sidelines: Understanding America's Violent Far-Right' (Combating Terrorism Center, West Point, November 1, 2012), https://doi.org/10.21236/ADA576380.

179. Blout and Burkart show persuasively how 'Unite the Right,' though 'framed by planners and media reporters as a political event,' was in fact 'organized and planned as a simulacrum of a military campaign.' See Emily Blout and Patrick Burkart, 'White Supremacist Terrorism in

Charlottesville: Reconstructing "Unite the Right,"' *Studies in Conflict and Terrorism*, January 4, 2021, 1–22, https://doi.org/10.1080/1057 610X.2020.1862850. See also Sheera Frenkel, 'How the Storming of Capitol Hill Was Organized on Social Media,' *New York Times*, January 6, 2021, sec. U.S., https://www.nytimes.com/2021/01/06/us/politics/protesters-storm-capitol-hill-building.html; Laurel Wamsley, 'On Far-Right Websites, Plans to Storm Capitol Were Made in Plain Sight,' NPR, January 7, 2021, https://www.npr.org/sections/insurrection-at-the-capitol/2021/01/07/954671745/on-far-right-websites-plans-to-storm-capitol-were-made-in-plain-sight.

180. See Nagle, *Kill All Normies*, 119; David French, 'The Price I've Paid for Opposing Donald Trump,' *National Review*, October 21, 2016, https://www.nationalreview.com/2016/10/donald-trump-alt-right-internet-abuse-never-trump-movement/.

181. Arquilla and Ronfeldt, *The Advent of Netwar*, 69.

182. Marwick and Lewis, 'Media Manipulation and Disinformation Online,' 24.

183. Institute for Economics and Peace, 'Global Terrorism Index 2020: Measuring the Impact of Terrorism' (Sydney, November 2020), 3, 40, http://visionofhumanity.org/reports.

184. As commented upon in further detail in chapter 8, the obliqueness with which this discussion has occurred (with references to 'domestic terrorism' rather than anything more politically specific) belies the socio-political can of worms that America will face when dealing with the ideology behind the threat.

185. Marwick and Lewis, 'Media Manipulation and Disinformation Online,' 25.

186. 'Extremist Content Online: ISIS Encouraging Violence with "Available Means,"' Counter Extremism Project, August 4, 2020, https://www.counterextremism.com/press/extremist-content-online-isis-encouraging-violence-%E2%80%98available-means%E2%80%99.

187. The report continues by pointing out that this phenomenon has 'blurred the boundaries of hate groups and far-right ideologies, helping coalesce a broader but more loosely affiliated movement.' See 'The Year in Hate and Extremism: Far-Right Extremists Coalescing in Broad-Based, Loosely Affiliated Movement,' Southern Poverty Law Center, February 5, 2021, https://www.splcenter.org/news/2021/02/05/year-hate-and-extremism-far-right-extremists-coalescing-broad-based-loosely-affiliated. For the aggregate numbers, see 'Hate Map,' Southern Poverty Law Center, accessed February 11, 2021, https://www.splcenter.org/hate-map.

188. Gerlach and Hine, *People, Power, Change Movements of Social Transformation*, 65.

189. Singer and Brooking, *LikeWar*, 22.

190. As cited in Marwick and Lewis, 'Media Manipulation and Disinformation Online,' 2.

191. Clark, 'How White Supremacy Returned to Mainstream Politics.'

192. This is the argument made in Yochai Benkler, Rob Faris, and Hal Roberts, *Network Propaganda: Manipulation, Disinformation, and Radicalization in American Politics* (New York: Oxford University Press, 2018). The main culprit, this study suggests, is the radicalization of right-wing media, stemming from Christian evangelism-turned-political, radio talk shows like Rush Limbaugh, all the way to Fox News and the more radical right-wing outlets that have proliferated more recently.

193. Gary Langer, '1 in 10 Say It's Acceptable to Hold Neo-Nazi Views (Poll),' ABC News, August 21, 2017, https://abcnews.go.com/Politics/28-approve-trumps-response-charlottesville-poll/story?id=49334079.

194. Of those Republicans who had heard of QAnon, 41 percent say it is a somewhat or very good thing for the country (32 percent and 9 percent respectively). One in five self-identified Republicans said they believed in it. See Charles Davis, '30% of Republicans Have "Favorable" View of QAnon Conspiracy Theory, YouGov Poll Finds,' *Business Insider*, January 13, 2021, https://www.businessinsider.com/30-of-republicans-have-favorable-view-of-qanon-conspiracy-theory-poll-2021-1; Pew Research Center, '5 Facts about the QAnon Conspiracy Theories,' *Fact Tank* (blog), November 16, 2020, https://www.pewresearch.org/fact-tank/2020/11/16/5-facts-about-the-qanon-conspiracy-theories/.

195. Tony Romm and Elizabeth Dwoskin, 'Twitter Purged More than 70,000 Accounts Affiliated with QAnon following Capitol Riot,' *Washington Post*, January 11, 2021, https://www.washingtonpost.com/technology/2021/01/11/trump-twitter-ban/.

196. James Oliphant and Chris Kahn, 'Half of Republicans Believe False Accounts of Deadly U.S. Capitol Riot: Reuters/Ipsos Poll,' Reuters, April 6, 2021, https://www.reuters.com/article/us-usa-politics-disinformation-idUSKBN2BS0RZ.

197. David French, 'The Problem Is Bigger than Trump,' *Time Magazine*, August 19, 2019, 33.

198. Philip Bump, 'Biden's Targeting of Racist Extremism Is Being Portrayed as an Attack on the Right Itself,' *Washington Post*, January 21, 2021, sec. Analysis, https://www.washingtonpost.com/

politics/2021/01/21/bidens-targeting-racist-extremism-is-being-portrayed-an-attack-right-itself/.

199. Ibid.

200. Renée DiResta, 'Right-Wing Social Media Finalizes Its Divorce from Reality,' *The Atlantic*, November 23, 2020, https://www.theatlantic.com/ideas/archive/2020/11/right-wing-social-media-finalizes-its-divorce-reality/617177/.

201. William Saletan, 'Americans are Dangerously Divided on the Insurrection,' *Slate*, June 09, 2021, https://slate.com/news-and-politics/2021/06/americans-divided-insurrection-investigation-voter-fraud-polls.html.

202. John Arquilla and David Ronfeldt, 'Cyberwar Is Coming!,' in *In Athena's Camp: Preparing for Conflict in the Information Age*, ed. John Arquilla and David F. Ronfeldt (Santa Monica, CA: RAND Corporation, 1997), 28. Elsewhere, they write: 'a netwar actor may aim to confound people's most fundamental belief about the nature of their society, culture, and government, partly to strike fear but perhaps mainly to disorient people so that they no longer presume to think or act in "normal" terms.' Arquilla and Ronfeldt, *The Advent of Netwar*, 13.

203. Singer and Brooking, *LikeWar*, 22.

204. For a comprehensive analysis, see Dipayan Ghosh and Ben Scott, '#Digitaldeceit: The Technology behind Precision Propaganda on the Internet' (New America and Shorenstein Center on Media, Politics and Public Policy, Harvard Kennedy School, January 2018).

205. Sloan, 'The Challenge of Nonterritorial and Virtual Conflicts: Rethinking Counterinsurgency and Counterterrorism,' 46. The original exploration of this idea appears in Steven Sloan, 'The Changing Face of Insurgency in the Post-Cold War Era: Doctrinal and Operational Implications,' in *Saving Democracies: US Intervention in Threatened Democratic States* ed. Anthony James Joes (Westport, CT: Praeger), 67–80.

206. Alexis de Tocqueville, *The Republic of the United States of America, and Its Political Institutions, Reviewed and Examined*, trans. Henry Reeve (New York: A. S. Barnes and Company, 1863), 122, 199.

207. Walter Lippmann, *Liberty and the News* (Bethlehem, PA: mediastudies. press, 2020), 19–20.

6. MIND THE GAP: COUNTERING LOCALIZED INSURGENCY

1. Zachariah Mampilly, 'A Marriage of Inconvenience: Tsunami Aid and the Unraveling of the LTTE and the GoSL's Complex

Dependency,' *Civil Wars* 11, no. 3 (September 2009): 302, https://doi.org/10.1080/13698240903157545.

2. Zachariah Cherian Mampilly, *Rebel Rulers: Insurgent Governance and Civilian Life during War* (New York: Cornell University Press, 2015), 93–128.
3. Mampilly, 'A Marriage of Inconvenience.'
4. 'Sri Lanka Government Publishes War Death Toll Statistics,' BBC News, February 24, 2012, sec. Asia, https://www.bbc.com/news/world-asia-17156686; 'Sri Lanka Civil War: Rajapaksa Says Thousands Missing Are Dead,' BBC News, January 20, 2020, sec. Asia, https://www.bbc.com/news/world-asia-51184085.
5. Ahmed Hashim, *When Counterinsurgency Wins: Sri Lanka's Defeat of the Tamil Tigers* (Philadelphia: University of Pennsylvania Press, 2013), 188.
6. Ibid., 138–39.
7. Jude Lal Fernando, 'Negotiated Peace versus Victor's Peace: The Geopolitics of Peace and Conflict in Sri Lanka,' *Cambridge Review of International Affairs* 27, no. 2 (June 2014): 206–25.
8. Brian Senewiratne, 'Tamils in the North-East Protest at Last,' *Colombo Telegraph*, October 4, 2016, https://www.colombotelegraph.com/index.php/tamils-in-the-north-east-protest-at-last/; 'Military Occupying over 96% Land Belonging to Tamils: BTF,' *Colombo Telegraph*, April 19, 2016, https://www.colombotelegraph.com/index.php/military-occupying-over-96-land-belonging-to-tamils-btf/. See also '"Why Can't We Go Home?,"' Human Rights Watch, October 9, 2018, https://www.hrw.org/report/2018/10/09/why-cant-we-go-home/military-occupation-land-sri-lanka.
9. International Crisis Group, 'Sri Lanka: Tamil Politics and the Quest for a Political Solution' (Asia Report, Brussels, November 20, 2012), https://www.crisisgroup.org/asia/south-asia/sri-lanka/sri-lanka-tamil-politics-and-quest-political-solution; Nadeeka Arambewela and Rodney Arambewela, 'Post-war Opportunities for Peace in Sri Lanka: An Ongoing Challenge?,' *Global Change, Peace and Security* 22, no. 3 (October 2010): 365–75, https://doi.org/10.1080/14781158.2010.510272.
10. Nirmanusan Balasundaram, 'Sri Lanka: An Ethnocratic State Endangering Positive Peace in the Island,' *Cosmopolitan Civil Societies: An Interdisciplinary Journal* 8, no. 3 (November 30, 2016): 38–58, https://doi.org/10.5130/ccs.v8i3.5194.
11. David Lewis, 'The Failure of a Liberal Peace: Sri Lanka's Counter-insurgency in Global Perspective,' *Conflict, Security and Development*

10, no. 5 (November 2010): 647–71, https://doi.org/10.1080/146
78802.2010.511509.

12. June S. Beittel, 'Peace Talks in Colombia' (Congressional Research Service, Washington, DC, March 31, 2015), 6.

13. Republic of Colombia, 'Democratic Security and Defence Policy' (Presidency of the Republic, Ministry of Defence, Bogotá, 2003), 12.

14. Thomas A. Marks, 'Colombian Military Support for "Democratic Security,"' *Small Wars and Insurgencies* 17, no. 2 (June 2006): 201. See also Thomas A. Marks, 'Colombian Army Adaptation to FARC' (Strategic Studies Institute, Carlisle, PA, 2002), 23.

15. Carlos Ospina and Thomas A. Marks, 'Colombia: Changing Strategy amidst the Struggle,' *Small Wars and Insurgencies* 25, no. 2 (March 4, 2014): 367.

16. Ibid., 367. See also Tom A. Marks, 'At the Front Lines of the GWOT: Colombia Success Builds upon Local Foundation,' *Journal of Counterterrorism and Homeland Security International* 10, no. 2 (2004): 42–50.

17. The 'indiscriminate issue of arms' is a danger raised specifically by classical counterinsurgency theorist and practitioner Robert Thompson: 'When asked towards the end of 1962 what was the total distribution of American weapons to the Vietnamese, an American general informed me that it was equivalent to fifty-one divisions. When I then asked what were the plans for recovering these after victory, he shrewdly replied: "That is a problem which will worry neither you nor me!"' See Robert Thompson, *Defeating Communist Insurgency: The Lessons of Malaya and Vietnam*, Studies in International Security 10 (New York: Frederick A. Praeger, 1966), 56. For other cases, see Austin Long, Stephanie Pezard, Bryce Loidolt, and Todd C. Helmus, *Locals Rule: Historical Lessons for Creating Local Defense Forces for Afghanistan and Beyond* (Santa Monica, CA: RAND and National Defense Research Institute, 2012).

18. Marks, 'Colombian Military Support for "Democratic Security,"' 209–10.

19. Indications of FARC's lack of popularity can be seen in the impressive *No Más* protests, the frustration with FARC's violence and kidnapping, and the high polling for President Álvaro Uribe Vélez, who during his two terms in power successfully decimated the guerrilla organization.

20. Ospina and Marks, 'Colombia.' For the strategy, see Republic of Colombia, 'Democratic Security and Defence Policy.'

21. 'Los consejos comunales, la mejor vitrina que tuvo Uribe,' *El País*, July 4, 2010, https://www.elpais.com.co/colombia/los-consejos-comunales-la-mejor-vitrina-que-tuvo-uribe.html.

22. Carlos Ospina, 'Colombia and the FARC: From Military Victory to Ambivalent Political Reintegration?,' in *Impunity: Countering Illicit Power in War and Transition*, ed. Michelle Hughes and Michael Miklaucic (Washington, DC: Center for Complex Operations (CCO) and the Peacekeeping and Stability Operations Institute (PKSOI), 2016), 163.

23. Angelika Albaladejo, 'Is Colombia Underestimating the Scale of FARC Dissidence?,' *InSight Crime* (blog), October 17, 2017, https://www.insightcrime.org/news/analysis/is-colombia-underestimating-scale-farc-dissidence/; Christopher Woody, 'Colombia Is Trying to Root Out the Cocaine Trade, but Farmers Are Relying on It as an "Insurance Policy,"' *Business Insider*, March 22, 2018, http://www.businessinsider.com/farmers-in-colombia-relying-on-economic-benefits-of-cocaine-production-2018-3; Tracy Wilkinson, 'U.S. Alarmed over Surge in Coca Production in Colombia,' *Los Angeles Times*, February 6, 2018, http://www.latimes.com/nation/la-fg-tillerson-colombia-20180206-story.html.

24. Thomas A. Marks, 'Urban Insurgency,' *Small Wars and Insurgencies* 14, no. 3 (September 2003): 134–35, https://doi.org/10.1080/095923 10410001676925.

25. Republic of Colombia, 'Democratic Security and Defence Policy,' 5–6.

26. Ken Menkhaus, 'Governance without Government in Somalia: Spoilers, State Building, and the Politics of Coping,' *International Security* 31, no. 3 (2006): 78.

27. Volker Boege, Anne Brown, Kevin Clements, and Anna Nolan, 'On Hybrid Political Orders and Emerging States: What Is Failing—States in the Global South or Research and Politics in the West?,' in *Building Peace in the Absence of States: Challenging the Discourse on State Failure*, ed. Martina Fischer and Beatrix Schmelzle, Berghof Handbook Dialogue Series 8 (Berlin: Berghof Forschungszentrum für Konstruktive Konfliktbearbeitung, 2009), 15–36.

28. This perspective builds on the 'political economy of war' lens typical of the literature on conflict, security, and development. See Mats Berdal and Dominik Zaum, 'Power after Peace,' in *Political Economy of Statebuilding: Power after Peace*, ed. Mats R. Berdal and Dominik Zaum, Routledge Studies in Intervention and Statebuilding (New York: Routledge, 2013), 11; Mats Berdal and David Keen, 'The Political Economy of Protectorates and "Post-Conflict" Intervention,' in *The New Protectorates: International Tutelage and the Making of Liberal States*, ed. James Mayall and Ricardo Soares de Oliveira (London: Hurst Publishers, 2011), 221–40.

29. Ken Menkhaus, *Somalia: State Collapse and the Threat of Terrorism*, Adelphi Paper 364 (Oxford: Oxford University Press for the International Institute for Strategic Studies, 2004), 11.

30. Paul Fishstein and Andrew Wilder, 'Winning Hearts and Minds? Examining the Relationship between Aid and Security in Afghanistan' (Feinstein International Center, Tufts University, Medford, MA, January 2012), 30, 37, http://fic.tufts.edu/assets/WinningHearts-Final.pdf. On the aversion to centralized government in Afghanistan, see also Martine van Biljert, 'Between Discipline and Discretion: Policies Surrounding Senior Subnational Appointments' (Briefing Paper Series, Afghanistan Research and Evaluation Unit, May 2009), 5; UK Stabilisation Unit, 'Responding to Stabilisation Challenges in Hostile and Insecure Environments: Lessons Identified by the UK's Stabilisation Unit' (Stabilisation Unit, London, November 2010), 8.

31. David H. Ucko, 'Militias, Tribes and Insurgents: The Challenge of Political Reintegration in Iraq,' *Conflict, Security and Development* 8, no. 3 (October 2008).

32. Dexter Filkins, 'Afghan Offensive Is New War Model,' *New York Times*, February 12, 2010, sec. World, https://www.nytimes.com/2010/02/13/world/asia/13kabul.html.

33. Dion Nissenbaum, 'McChrystal Calls Marjah a "Bleeding Ulcer" in Afghan Campaign,' McClatchy, May 24, 2010, sec. World, https://www.mcclatchydc.com/news/nation-world/world/article24583621.html.

34. Frances Z. Brown, 'The U.S. Surge and Afghan Local Governance' (Special Report, United States Institute of Peace, Washington, DC, September 2012), 6, https://www.usip.org/publications/2012/09/us-surge-and-afghan-local-governance.

35. Michael Shurkin, 'Subnational Government in Afghanistan' (Occasional Paper, RAND Corporation, Santa Monica, CA, 2011), 9–10.

36. Specifically, '82 percent of Malians stated that they have a great deal of trust for traditional authorities, whereas only 50 percent said the same about police and only 43 percent said the same about courts.' See Stéphanie Pézard and Michael Robert Shurkin, *Achieving Peace in Northern Mali: Past Agreements, Local Conflicts, and the Prospects for a Durable Settlement* (Santa Monica, CA: RAND, 2015), 49.

37. Bjoern Hofmann, 'Are Hybrid Political Orders an Appropriate Concept for State Formation? Timor-Leste Revisited,' in *Building Peace in the Absence of States: Challenging the Discourse on State Failure*, ed. Martina Fischer and Beatrix Schmelzle, Berghof Handbook Dialogue

Series 8 (Berlin: Berghof Forschungszentrum für Konstruktive Konfliktbearbeitung, 2009), 82.

38. Ibid., 82.

39. Seymour Martin Lipset, *Political Man: The Social Bases of Politics*, 2nd ed. (London: Heinemann, 1983), 64.

40. Olivier Roy, 'Development and Political Legitimacy: The Cases of Iraq and Afghanistan,' *Conflict, Security & Development* 4, no. 2 (2004), 173.

41. Ibid.

42. As Martine van Biljert explains, 'the provinces were largely seen as ungoverned spaces and few policymakers were aware that there were still functioning, albeit very rudimentary, administrative structures at almost all levels of subnational government.' See van Biljert, 'Between Discipline and Discretion,' 5. See also Shurkin, 'Subnational Government in Afghanistan,' 6.

43. See Ralf Michaels, 'The Mirage of Non-state Governance,' *Utah Law Review* 2010, no. 1 (2010): 42–43; Andreas Mehler, 'Hybrid Regimes and Oligopolies of Violence in Africa: Expectations on Security Provisions "from Below,"' in *Building Peace in the Absence of States: Challenging the Discourse on State Failure*, ed. Martina Fischer and Beatrix Schmelzle, Berghof Handbook Dialogue Series 8 (Berlin: Berghof Forschungszentrum für Konstruktive Konfliktbearbeitung, 2009).

44. Mats Berdal, *Building Peace after War*, Adelphi 407 (London: Routledge, for the International Institute for Strategic Studies, 2009), 27.

45. As Popkin notes, 'Ways of life that may have existed only for lack of alternatives are extolled as virtues. Peasants who have nothing to wear and who go hungry are assumed to have a rich spiritual life. When a son sticks to his father for the sake of survival, this is called filial piety. When people in one village do not talk to their neighbors in another, this is called village solidarity. Somehow what might only have been the necessities and oppressions of one era seem to have become the traditional values of the next.' See Samuel Lewis Popkin, 'The Myth of the Village: Revolution and Reaction in Viet Nam' (Thesis, Massachusetts Institute of Technology, 1969), 61, https://dspace.mit.edu/handle/1721.1/41778.

46. See, respectively, Thomas A. Marks, *Maoist People's War in Post-Vietnam Asia* (Bangkok: White Lotus, 2007), 281–82.

47. In 2017, the International Crisis Group estimated that the country had about 60,000 gang members and a gang social support base of up to 500,000 people—almost 8 percent of the total population. In

2015, its murder rate reached 103 per 100,000 people. International Crisis Group, 'El Salvador's Politics of Perpetual Violence' (Latin America Report, Brussels, December 19, 2017), 8, 11.

48. José Miguel Cruz, 'Government Responses and the Dark Side of Gang Suppression in Central America,' in *Maras: Gang Violence and Security in Central America*, ed. Thomas C. Bruneau, Lucía Dammert, and Elizabeth Skinner (Austin, TX: University of Texas Press, 2011), 137–58.

49. International Crisis Group, 'El Salvador's Politics of Perpetual Violence,' 16.

50. CEJIL, 'Situation of Prison Overcrowding in El Salvador Denounced before the IACHR,' Center for Justice and International Law, March 20, 2015, https://cejil.org/en/situation-prison-overcrowding-salvador-denounced-iachr. On prison-based recruitment, one study notes: 'In 2005, the Salvadoran state imprisoned an estimated 4,000 youths under the age of 18. From this group, 1,630 were pressured into joining MS-13, another 1,000 were recruited by the Barrio 18, and some 400 other youths joined a variety of different street gangs.' See Frank de Waegh, 'Unwilling Participants: The Coercion of Youth into Violent Criminal Groups in Central America's Northern Triangle' (Jesuit Conference of Canada and the United States, 2015), 8.

51. Cruz, 'Government Responses and the Dark Side of Gang Suppression in Central America.'

52. CDDRL, Stanford University, *Mariano Beltrame, Secretary of Security, Rio de Janeiro, Brazil*, 2015, https://www.youtube.com/watch?v=kwMvwiFX47M&feature=youtu.be.

53. Elizabeth Leeds, 'Rio de Janeiro,' in *Fractured Cities: Social Exclusion, Urban Violence and Contested Spaces in Latin America*, ed. Kees Koonings and Dirk Kruijt (London: Zed Books, 2007), 28.

54. Luke Dowdney, *Children of the Drug Trade: A Case Study of Children in Organised Armed Violence in Rio de Janeiro* (Rio de Janeiro: 7Letras, 2003), 82. For more general context on this point, see Stergios Skaperdas, 'The Political Economy of Organized Crime: Providing Protection When the State Does Not,' *Economics of Governance* 2, no. 3 (November 2001): 185.

55. James Cockayne, 'The Futility of Force? Strategic Lessons for Dealing with Unconventional Armed Groups from the UN's War on Haiti's Gangs,' *Journal of Strategic Studies* 37, no. 5 (July 29, 2014): 747.

56. Ibid., 748. Cockayne also cites a classified US cable, made public through a Freedom of Information Act request, that details MINUSTAH's sense of 'paralysis' following the Iron First debacle (p. 748).

57. José Miguel Cruz and Angélica Durán-Martínez, 'Hiding Violence to Deal with the State: Criminal Pacts in El Salvador and Medellin,' *Journal of Peace Research* 53, no. 2 (2016): 206. Emphasis added.

58. International Crisis Group, 'Miracle or Mirage? Gangs and Plunging Violence in El Salvador' (Latin America Report, Brussels, July 8, 2020), 32.

59. Mark Freeman and Vanda Felbab-Brown, 'Negotiating with Violent Criminal Groups: Lessons and Guidelines from Global Practice' (Institute for Integrated Transition, Barcelona, March 2021), 5. Emphasis added.

60. This is one of the main conclusions, and notes of caution, in Vanda Felbab-Brown, 'Bargaining with the Devil to Avoid Hell? A Discussion Paper on Negotiations with Criminal Groups in Latin America and the Caribbean' (Institute for Integrated Transition, Barcelona, July 2020). As she and Freeman put it in a separate report on this topic, 'A militant group can "stay political" at the end of the talks (e.g. by becoming exclusively a political party), but criminal groups cannot "stay criminal."' See Freeman and Felbab-Brown, 'Negotiating with Violent Criminal Groups,' 4.

61. Moritz Schuberth, 'Beyond Gang Truces and Mano Dura Policies: Towards Substitutive Security Governance in Latin America,' *Stability: International Journal of Security and Development* 5, no. 1 (December 28, 2016): 7.

62. José Luis Rocha, 'Street Gangs of Nicaragua,' in *Maras: Gang Violence and Security in Central America*, ed. Thomas C. Bruneau, Lucía Dammert, and Elizabeth Skinner, trans. Michael Solis (Austin, TX: University of Texas Press, 2011), 114.

63. Ibid., 108–9.

64. Ibid., 119.

65. Moritz Schuberth, 'Disarmament, Demobilization and Reintegration in Unconventional Settings: The Case of MINUSTAH's Community Violence Reduction,' *International Peacekeeping* 24, no. 3 (May 27, 2017): 424, https://doi.org/10.1080/13533312.2016.1277145.

66. UN Disarmament, Demobilization and Reintegration (DDR) Section, 'Community Violence Reduction: Creating Space for Peace' (Office of Rule of Law and Security Institutions (OROLSI), Department of Peace Operations (DPO), United Nations, n.d.), 13–15.

67. Moritz Schuberth, 'To Engage or Not to Engage Haiti's Urban Armed Groups? Safe Access in Disaster-Stricken and Conflict-Affected Cities,' *Environment and Urbanization* 29, no. 2 (October 2017): 425–42, https://doi.org/10.1177/0956247817716398.

68. Schuberth, 'Beyond Gang Truces and Mano Dura Policies,' 10.

69. In El Salvador, 'more than 58% of former gang members have received threats against themselves or their families for abandoning the gang.' This number compares with the 19.1 percent who report such experiences while still in the gang. See José Miguel Cruz, Jonathan D. Rosen, Luis Enrique Amaya, and Yulia Vorobyeva, 'The New Face of Street Gangs: The Gang Phenomenon in El Salvador' (Florida International University, 2017), 60–62.

70. International Crisis Group, 'El Salvador's Politics of Perpetual Violence,' 20.

71. Timothy Donais and Geoff Burt, 'Vertically Integrated Peace Building and Community Violence in Haiti' (CIGI Papers, Center for International Governance Innovation, Waterloo, Ontario, February 2014), 12.

72. K. P. S. Gill, 'Endgame in Punjab: 1988–1993,' *Faultlines* 1 (May 1999), https://www.satp.org/satporgtp/publication/faultlines/volume1/Fault1-kpstext.htm.

73. Cockayne, 'The Futility of Force?'

74. Guy Hammond, 'Saving Port-au-Prince: United Nations Efforts to Protect Civilians in Haiti 2006–2007' (Stimson Center, Washington, DC, 2012), 22. As Dorn explains, MINUSTAH used the so-called CARVER methodology of assessing targets based on their Criticality, Accessibility, Return (or Recoverability of adversary), Vulnerability (of UN), Effect (of arrest), and Recognizability.' See A. Walter Dorn, 'Intelligence-Led Peacekeeping: The United Nations Stabilization Mission in Haiti (MINUSTAH), 2006–07,' *Intelligence and National Security* 24, no. 6 (December 2009): 826, https://doi.org/10.1080/02684520903320410.

75. See Dorn, 'Intelligence-Led Peacekeeping,' 805.

76. Michael Dziedzic and Robert M. Perito, 'Haiti: Confronting the Gangs of Port-au-Prince' (Special Report, United States Institute of Peace, Washington, DC, September 2008), 5–6.

77. Cockayne, 'The Futility of Force?,' 766–67.

78. Sarah Oosterbaan and Joris van Wijk, 'Pacifying and Integrating the Favelas of Rio de Janeiro: An Evaluation of the Impact of the UPP Program on Favela Residents,' *International Journal of Comparative and Applied Criminal Justice* 39, no. 3 (July 3, 2015): 182, https://doi.org/10.1080/01924036.2014.973052.

79. CDDRL, Stanford University, *Ignacio Cano, Armed Violence in Rio de Janeiro*, 2011, https://www.youtube.com/watch?v=XBVK1oMafVk.

80. Beatriz Magaloni, Edgar Franco-Vivanco, and Vanessa Melo, 'Killing in the Slums: Social Order, Criminal Governance, and Police Violence in Rio de Janeiro,' *American Political Science Review* 114, no. 2 (May 2020): 571, https://doi.org/10.1017/S0003055419000856.

81. Oosterbaan and van Wijk, 'Pacifying and Integrating the Favelas of Rio de Janeiro.'

82. Antonio Sampaio, 'Out of Control: Criminal Gangs Fight Back in Rio's Favelas,' *Jane's Intelligence Review* 26, no. 12 (December 2014); CDDRL, *Ignacio Cano, Armed Violence in Rio de Janeiro*, 176.

83. Sampaio, 'Out of Control,' 46.

84. CDDRL, Stanford University, *Jailson Silva, Towards a New Paradigm of Public Policy in Rio's Favelas*, 2014, https://www.youtube.com/watch?v=Oyl1nI1TRaA.

85. Ignácio Cano, *Os donos do morro* (Rio de Janeiro: Forum Brasileiro de Segurança Publica, May 2012), 135–38; CDDRL, *Mariano Beltrame, Secretary of Security, Rio de Janeiro, Brazil*; CDDRL, *Jailson Silva, Towards a New Paradigm of Public Policy in Rio's Favelas*.

86. Jefferson Puff, 'Como grupo de jovens virou referência internacional na denúncia de abusos policiais,' BBC Brazil, October 30, 2015, http://www.bbc.com/portuguese/noticias/2015/10/151028_coletivo_papo_reto_alemao_jp; Sampaio, 'Out of Control,' 47; Amnesty International, 'Brazil: Police Killings, Impunity and Attacks on Defenders' (Amnesty International Submission for the UN Universal Periodic Review, 27th Session of the UPR Working Group, May 2017, London, September 2016). See also 'Com Exército no RJ, projeto quer Justiça Militar julgando crimes contra civis,' Poder360, September 14, 2017, https://www.poder360.com.br/congresso/com-exercito-no-rj-projeto-quer-justica-militar-julgando-crimes-contra-civis/; 'Rio's Murder Rate Soared Last Year despite Calm during Olympics,' Reuters, February 1, 2017, https://www.reuters.com/article/us-brazil-violence/rios-murder-rate-soared-last-year-despite-calm-during-olympics-idUSKBN15G5K6.

87. David H. Ucko and Robert Egnell, *Counterinsurgency in Crisis: Britain and the Challenges of Modern Warfare* (New York: Columbia University Press, 2013), 68–72.

88. See, for example, Steven R. Hurst, 'US: Raid of Baghdad's Sadr City Kills 49,' *Washington Post*, October 21, 2007, https://www.washingtonpost.com/wp-dyn/content/article/2007/10/21/AR2007102100159_pf.html.

89. Draws on David E. Johnson, M. Wade Markel, and Brian Shannon, *The 2008 Battle of Sadr City: Reimagining Urban Combat* (Santa Monica, CA: RAND, 2013).

90. Schuberth, 'Beyond Gang Truces and Mano Dura Policies,' 7.

91. Phil Williams and Dan Bisbee, 'Jaish al-Mahdi in Iraq,' in *Impunity: Countering Illicit Power in War and Transition*, ed. Michelle Hughes and Michael Miklaucic (Washington, DC: Center for Complex Operations (CCO) and the Peacekeeping and Stability Operations Institute (PKSOI), 2016), 59.

92. Diaa Jabaili, 'Pollution and Corruption Are Choking the Life out of Basra,' *The Guardian*, September 13, 2018, sec. Opinion, http://www.theguardian.com/commentisfree/2018/sep/13/pollution-corruption-choking-life-out-of-basra. See also Nabih Bulos, 'Basra Was Once a Jewel of a City: Now It's a Symbol of What's Wrong in Iraq,' *Los Angeles Times*, June 17, 2018, sec. World & Nation, https://www.latimes.com/world/la-fg-iraq-basra-20180617-story.html; Arwa Ibrahim and Azhar al-Rubaie, 'Iraqi Journalists Fear for Lives after Basra Reporters Killed,' Al Jazeera, January 12, 2020, https://www.aljazeera.com/news/2020/1/12/iraqi-journalists-fear-for-lives-after-basra-reporters-killed.

93. Isabel Coles and Ghassan Adnan, 'Iraq Kingmaker's Daunting Task: Lift the Poor of Sadr City,' *Wall Street Journal*, June 3, 2018, sec. World, https://www.wsj.com/articles/iraq-kingmakers-daunting-task-lift-the-poor-of-sadr-city-1528023600.

94. The argument here is that counterinsurgency 'restores the sickly body' but 'does not provide it with immunity.' See Thomas A. Marks and Michael S. Bell, 'The U.S. Army in the Iraq War: Volume 1 (Invasion, Insurgency, Civil War 2003–2006),' *Small Wars and Insurgencies* 30, no. 3 (April 16, 2019): 704, https://doi.org/10.1080/09592318.2019.1601873.

7. IN DEFENSE OF DEMOCRACY: COUNTERING INFILTRATIVE INSURGENCY

1.   This section draws on Peter R. Neumann, 'The Bullet and the Ballot Box: The Case of the IRA,' *Journal of Strategic Studies* 28, no. 6 (December 2005): 943–49, https://doi.org/10.1080/01402390500441081.

2.   See for example Christopher Hewitt, 'The Political Context of Terrorism in America: Ignoring Extremists or Pandering to Them?,' *Terrorism and Political Violence* 12, nos. 3–4 (September 2000): 325–44, https://doi.org/10.1080/09546550008427582;   Leonard

Weinberg, Ami Pedahzur, and Arie Perliger, *Political Parties and Terrorist Groups*, 2nd ed., Routledge Studies in Extremism and Democracy. Routledge Research in Extremism and Democracy 10 (London: Routledge, 2009), 17–18.

3.　On the 'political opportunity structure' as concept, see Charles Tilly and Sidney G. Tarrow, *Contentious Politics*, 2nd rev. ed. (New York: Oxford University Press, 2015), 59. As concerns its relationship to violence, see (for example) Ted Robert Gurr, *Why Men Rebel* (Princeton, NJ: Princeton University Press for the Center of International Studies, 1970), chap. 5; Mohammed M. Hafez and Quintan Wiktorowicz, 'Violence as Contention in the Egyptian Islamic Movement,' in *Islamic Activism: A Social Movement Theory Approach*, ed. Quintan Wiktorowicz (Bloomington, IN: Indiana University Press, 2004), 71; Jennifer M. Hazen, 'From Social Movement to Armed Group: A Case Study from Nigeria,' *Contemporary Security Policy* 30, no. 2 (August 2009): 281, https://doi.org/10.1080/13523260903059906.

4.　Samuel Huntington was an early proponent of the thesis that 'democracies have more capacity for absorbing new groups into their political systems.' In later work, he also expounded on the notion of a 'democratic bargain' whereby groups moderate their ways in return for the political openings available through democratic participation. See, respectively, Samuel P. Huntington, *Political Order in Changing Societies* (New Haven, CT: Yale University Press, 1968), 275; Samuel P. Huntington, *The Third Wave: Democratization in the Late Twentieth Century*, Julian J. Rothbaum Distinguished Lecture Series 4 (Norman, OK: University of Oklahoma Press, 1993), 170, 190. Interestingly, Huntington was also an early champion of the 'inclusion-moderation' thesis, though he termed it the 'participation/moderation tradeoff' (see Huntington, *The Third Wave*, 165–70). As Schwedler points out, Huntington treated this hypothesis as a fairly commonsensical proposition, presaging the unquestioned or normative status it has since acquired in some academic circles. See Jillian Schwedler, 'Can Islamists Become Moderates? Rethinking the Inclusion-Moderation Hypothesis,' *World Politics* 63, no. 2 (April 2011): 353, https://doi.org/10.1017/S0043887111000050.

5.　The deduction from this finding is that it is those governments in the middle of true democracy and effective authoritarianism that suffer the greatest risk of rupture. See Demet Yalcin Mousseau, 'Democratizing with Ethnic Divisions: A Source of Conflict?,' *Journal of Peace Research* 38, no. 5 (2001): 547–67; Elena Slinko, Stanislav Bilyuga, Julia Zinkina, and Andrey Korotayev, 'Regime Type and

Political Destabilization in Cross-national Perspective: A Re-analysis,'
Cross-cultural Research 51, no. 1 (February 2017): 26–50, https://doi.
org/10.1177/1069397116676485.

6. See for example, Reto Rufer, 'Disarmament, Demobilisation and
Reintegration (DDR): Conceptual Approaches, Specific Settings,
Practical Experiences' (Working Paper, Geneva Centre for the
Democratic Control of Armed Forces (DCAF), Geneva, 2005), 45.
As Rufer notes, 'The concept of a complete demobilisation therefore
is the precondition for the registration of former parties to the
conflict as political parties, and vice versa, the chance of being able
to "officially" exert political influence is also meant to be an incentive
for the parties involved to turn in their weapons.' See also UN
Disarmament, Demobilization and Reintegration Resource Center,
'The Politics of DDR,' in *Integrated Disarmament, Demobilization and
Reintegration Standards*, 2019, 20, https://www.unddr.org/modules/
IDDRS-2.20-The-Politics-of-DDR.pdf.

7. This moderating effect of inclusion is a major conclusion in Joost van
Spanje and Wouter van der Brug, 'The Party as Pariah: The Exclusion
of Anti-immigration Parties and Its Effect on Their Ideological
Positions,' *West European Politics* 30, no. 5 (November 2007): 1022–
40, https://doi.org/10.1080/01402380701617431.

8. A key exploration of this argument, based on the case studies of
Northern Ireland and Spain's Basque region, is found in Cynthia L.
Irvin, *Militant Nationalism: Between Movement and Party in Ireland and
the Basque Country*, Social Movements, Protest, and Contention 9
(Minneapolis, MN: University of Minnesota Press, 1999).

9. Ibid., 207.

10. Lise Storm, 'Exploring Post-rebel Parties in Power: Political Space and
Implications for Islamist Inclusion and Moderation,' *Open Journal of
Political Science* 10, no. 4 (2020): 638–67, https://doi.org/10.4236/
ojps.2020.104038.

11. Michel Wieviorka, *The Making of Terrorism* (Chicago: University of
Chicago Press, 2004), 63. See also Donatella Della Porta's work on
the organizational and strategic effects of 'clandestinity' (e.g. *Clandestine
Political Violence* (New York: Cambridge University Press, 2013)).

12. Jeremy Weinstein, *Inside Rebellion: The Politics of Insurgent Violence*
(Cambridge: Cambridge University Press, 2006).

13. Using a dataset of 112 cases spread across 12 countries, Heger finds
that 'groups with political wings that participate in elections are less
likely to attack civilians than groups with non-political wings.' The
link, it is proposed, is 'the result of potential losses at the polls [that]

violent groups would suffer if they chose to engage civilian targets.' Lindsay L. Heger, 'Votes and Violence: Pursuing Terrorism While Navigating Politics,' *Journal of Peace Research* 52, no. 1 (January 2015), https://doi.org/10.1177/0022343314552984

14. Sara M.T. Polo, 'The Quality of Terrorist Violence: Explaining the Logic of Terrorist Target Choice,' *Journal of Peace Research* 57, no. 2 (March 2020): 235–50, https://doi.org/10.1177/0022343319829799.

15. Neumann, 'The Bullet and the Ballot Box,' 944.

16. Barbara Geddes, 'Initiation of New Democratic Institutions in Eastern Europe and Latin America,' in *Institutional Design in New Democracies: Eastern Europe and Latin America*, ed. Arend Lijphart and Carlos H. Warisman (Boulder, CO: Westview Press, 1996), 18.

17. Samuel Issacharoff, *Fragile Democracies: Contested Power in the Era of Constitutional Courts* (Cambridge: Cambridge University Press, 2015), 37–38; John Finn, 'Electoral Regimes and the Proscription of Anti-democratic Parties,' *Terrorism and Political Violence* 12, nos. 3–4 (September 2000): 65, https://doi.org/10.1080/09546550008427570.

18. Neumann, 'The Bullet and the Ballot Box,' 967.

19. Ibid., 968.

20. On the intervening variables between democratic inclusion and moderation, see for example Christophe Jaffrelot, 'Refining the Moderation Thesis: Two Religious Parties and Indian Democracy; The Jana Sangh and the BJP between Hindutva Radicalism and Coalition Politics,' *Democratization* 20, no. 5 (August 2013): 876–94, https://doi.org/10.1080/13510347.2013.801256.

21. Finn, 'Electoral Regimes and the Proscription of Anti-democratic Parties,' 53. As but one example, it is worth noting that ETA, the Basque terrorist group, escalated its violence precisely as Spain transitioned from dictatorship to democracy. See Weinberg, Pedahzur, and Perliger, *Political Parties and Terrorist Groups*, 76.

22. As Issacharoff puts it, 'Elections are the shorthand for other factors that we think characterize democratic life, but they are unfortunately not always the pathway to a more tolerant society. Just as likely, elections in a fractured society will serve as the rallying point for intolerance.' See Issacharoff, *Fragile Democracies*, 5. See also discussion in Weinberg, Pedahzur, and Perliger, *Political Parties and Terrorist Groups*, 19–20.

23. As quoted in Gregory H. Fox and Georg Nolte, 'Intolerant Democracies,' *Harvard International Law Journal* 36, no. 1 (Winter 1995): 1.

24. Benedetta Berti, *Armed Political Organizations: From Conflict to Integration* (Baltimore: Johns Hopkins University Press, 2013), 3.

25. Weinberg, Pedahzur, and Perliger, *Political Parties and Terrorist Groups*, 134.
26. Ibid., 133.
27. Mats R. Berdal, *Disarmament and Demobilisation after Civil Wars: Arms, Soldiers and the Termination of Armed Conflicts*, Adelphi Paper 303 (Oxford: Oxford University Press for the International Institute for Strategic Studies, 1996), 24. See also Robert Muggah, 'No Magic Bullet: A Critical Perspective on Disarmament, Demobilization and Reintegration (DDR) and Weapons Reduction in Post-conflict Contexts,' *Round Table* 94, no. 379 (April 2005): 246, https://doi.org/10.1080/00358530500082684.
28. Stina Torjesen and S. Neil MacFarlane, 'Reintegration before Disarmament: The Case of Post-conflict Reintegration in Tajikistan,' in *Reintegrating Armed Groups after Conflict: Politics, Violence and Transition*, ed. Mats Berdal and David H. Ucko (Abingdon: Routledge, 2009), 62.
29. Steve Swerdlow, 'Tajikistan: Why Authoritarian Elections Also Matter,' *The Diplomat*, October 10, 2020, https://thediplomat.com/2020/10/tajikistan-why-authoritarian-elections-also-matter/.
30. Torjesen and MacFarlane, 'Reintegration before Disarmament,' 62. See also Mats Berdal and David H. Ucko, 'Introduction: The Political Reintegration of Armed Groups after War,' in *Reintegrating Armed Groups after Conflict: Politics, Violence and Transition*, ed. Mats Berdal and David H. Ucko (Abingdon: Routledge, 2009), 1–9.
31. Karl Popper, *The Open Society and Its Enemies* (Princeton, NJ: Princeton University Press, 2013), 581.
32. Issacharoff, *Fragile Democracies*, 35.
33. See Karl Dietrich Bracher, *The German Dictatorship: The Origins, Structure and Effects of National Socialism*, trans. Jean Steinberg (New York: Praeger Publishers, 1971), 142.
34. Harvey F. Kline, *Historical Dictionary of Colombia*, Historical Dictionaries of the Americas (Lanham, MD: Scarecrow Press, 2012), 478.
35. Here I draw on Steven S. Dudley, *Walking Ghosts: Murder and Guerrilla Politics in Colombia* (New York: Routledge, 2006).
36. As cited in ibid., 189.
37. Regrets about targeting UP are alluded to in Castaño's memoirs, published in 2001. See Castan Carlos Castaño and Mauricio Aranguren Molina, *Mi confesión: Carlos Castaño revela sus secretos* (Bogotá: Editorial La Oveja Negra, 2001). They are also alluded to, based on direct interviews, in Dudley, *Walking Ghosts*, 140.
38. Neumann, 'The Bullet and the Ballot Box,' 969.

39. PIRA testimony suggests these measures forced activities to a standstill. See Peter Taylor, *Brits: The War against the IRA* (London: Bloomsbury, 2001), 302. For background, see Warren Chin, 'Northern Ireland (1976–1994): Police Primacy,' in *Network Centric Operations (NCO) Case Study: The British Approach to Low-Intensity Operations: Part 2*, 1.0, Transformation Case Study Series (Washington, DC: Department of Defense, 2007), 116–20.

40. Neumann, 'The Bullet and the Ballot Box,' 969.

41. The paragraph draws on Chin, 'Northern Ireland (1976–1994).'

42. Giovanni Capoccia, *Defending Democracy: Reactions to Extremism in Interwar Europe* (Baltimore: Johns Hopkins University Press, 2005), 5.

43. See Francesco Cavatorta and Fabio Merone, 'Moderation through Exclusion? The Journey of the Tunisian *Ennahda* from Fundamentalist to Conservative Party,' *Democratization* 20, no. 5 (August 2013): 857–75, https://doi.org/10.1080/13510347.2013.801255.

44. Jan-Werner Müller, 'Should the EU Protect Democracy and the Rule of Law inside Member States? Protection of Democracy and the Rule of Law,' *European Law Journal* 21, no. 2 (March 2015): 144, https://doi.org/10.1111/eulj.12124.

45. The Avalon Project, 'Thomas Jefferson First Inaugural Address,' Lillian Goldman Law Library, Yale Law School, accessed March 29, 2021, https://avalon.law.yale.edu/19th_century/jefinau1.asp.

46. Capoccia, *Defending Democracy*.

47. Ibid., 216.

48. Daniel Trilling, 'Why Did Golden Dawn's Neo-Nazi Leaders Get Away with It for So Long?,' *The Guardian*, October 8, 2020, sec. Opinion, http://www.theguardian.com/commentisfree/2020/oct/08/golden-dawn-neo-nazi-violence-greece-political-class.

49. Ibid.

50. Cavatorta and Merone, 'Moderation through Exclusion?' In seeking to parse the relative impact of regime repression on the one hand and social isolation on the other, Cavatorta and Merone suggest that 'it is not jail that makes Islamists more moderate, but the realization that, with or without imprisonment, they had to confront a society that was still not at ease with the Manichean views that Islamists had in the 1970s and early 1980s' (p. 869).

51. Take, for example, the mass mobilization of civil-society groupings in support of Stephen Yaxley-Lennon, the founder and former leader of the far-right English Defence League (EDL), also known as Tommy Robinson. See Daniel Trilling, 'Tommy Robinson and the Far Right's New Playbook,' *The Guardian*, October 25, 2018, sec. World news,

http://www.theguardian.com/world/2018/oct/25/tommy-robinson-and-the-far-rights-new-playbook.

52. Capoccia, *Defending Democracy*, 179.

53. Angela K. Bourne and Fernando Casal Bértoa, 'Mapping "Militant Democracy": Variation in Party Ban Practices in European Democracies (1945–2015),' *European Constitutional Law Review* 13, no. 2 (June 2017): fig. 1, https://doi.org/10.1017/S1574019617000098.

54. See, respectively, Karl Loewenstein, 'Militant Democracy and Fundamental Rights, I,' *American Political Science Review* 31, no. 3 (June 1937): 417–32, https://doi.org/10.2307/1948164; Fox and Nolte, 'Intolerant Democracies.' For an abridged compilation of the relevant constitutional clauses from a range of cases, see Finn, 'Electoral Regimes and the Proscription of Anti-democratic Parties,' 70–74.

55. Brad R. Roth, as cited in Issacharoff, *Fragile Democracies*, 77.

56. Popper, *The Open Society and Its Enemies*, 581.

57. Michael Walzer, *On Toleration* (New Haven, CT: Yale University Press, 1997), 8.

58. John Rawls, *A Theory of Justice*, rev. ed. (Cambridge, MA: Belknap Press of Harvard University Press, 1971), 188.

59. Issacharoff, *Fragile Democracies*, 56–57.

60. See ibid., 52.

61. Capoccia, *Defending Democracy*, 3–69.

62. Walzer, *On Toleration*, 81–82.

63. Issacharoff, *Fragile Democracies*, 38.

64. These unaltered laws are called both 'eternity' or 'entrenched' clauses, depending on context.

65. Issacharoff, *Fragile Democracies*, 42.

66. Ibid., 42.

67. As Finn notes, 'proscription is an act of state power: whether informal choices by parties not to interact with anti-democratic parties constitutes state action is at least in part a difficult question about the definition of state power and the relationship of political parties to the constitution and organization of state power.' Finn, 'Electoral Regimes and the Proscription of Anti-democratic Parties,' 59.

68. Fox and Nolte, 'Intolerant Democracies,' 25–26.

69. Valery Gerasimov, 'The Value of Science in Prediction,' *Military-Industrial Kurier*, no. 8 (476) (March 27, 2013), http://vpk-news.ru/sites/default/files/pdf/VPK_08_476.pdf.

70. Carl J. Friedrich, 'Defense of the Constitutional Order,' in *Studies in Federalism*, ed. Robert R. Bowie and Carl J. Friedrich (Boston: Brown and Company, 1954), 683. The comment is made with reference

to the rise of Nazism in Germany. Indeed, it is notable that despite stormtroopers engaging in street brawls, attacks, and intimidation, most observers view Hitler as having navigated a 'legal' path.

71. Stephen Haggard and James Long, 'On Benchmarks: Institutions and Violence in Iraq' (2007). See also David H. Ucko, 'Militias, Tribes and Insurgents: The Challenge of Political Reintegration in Iraq,' *Conflict, Security and Development* 8, no. 3 (October 2008).

72. Friedrich, 'Defense of the Constitutional Order,' 683.

73. Fox and Nolte, 'Intolerant Democracies,' 12.

74. Alexander S. Kirshner, *A Theory of Militant Democracy: The Ethics of Combatting Political Extremism* (New Haven, CT: Yale University Press, 2014), 110.

75. Bourne and Casal Bértoa, 'Mapping "Militant Democracy,"' 239.

76. The German Constitution, as quoted in Issacharoff, *Fragile Democracies*, 47.

77. Bourne and Casal Bértoa, 'Mapping "Militant Democracy,"' 240.

78. Issacharoff, *Fragile Democracies*, 74.

79. Kirshner, *A Theory of Militant Democracy*, 3, 7.

80. Ibid., 112.

81. Fox and Nolte, 'Intolerant Democracies,' 50.

82. Friedrich, 'Defense of the Constitutional Order,' 683.

83. Fox and Nolte, 'Intolerant Democracies,' 66–67.

84. Issacharoff, *Fragile Democracies*, 53.

85. German Federal Constitutional Court, 'Entscheidungen: Kein Verbot der NPD wegen fehlender Anhaltspunkte für eine erfolgreiche Durchsetzung ihrer verfassungsfeindlichen Ziele' (January 17, 2017).

86. Kirshner, *A Theory of Militant Democracy*, 119.

87. Fox and Nolte, 'Intolerant Democracies,' 10.

88. Ibid., 11.

89. Ibid., n. 45.

90. Kirshner, *A Theory of Militant Democracy*, 90. See also Issacharoff, *Fragile Democracies*, 63–64.

91. See a discussion of this case in Kirshner, *A Theory of Militant Democracy*, 107–40.

92. Issacharoff argues, for example, that in asserting Sharia's incompatibility with the fundamental principles of democracy, the ECHR made 'a gratuitous swipe at Islam,' given 'the establishment of Christianity in several of the founding states of the European Union.' See Issacharoff, *Fragile Democracies*, 73.

93. Fox and Nolte, 'Intolerant Democracies,' 53.

94. This was in fact the case in the Weimar Republic, where many 'judges were holdovers from the German monarchy and shared the extreme nationalism and anti-Semitism of the Nazi opposition to Weimar.' See Issacharoff, *Fragile Democracies*, 140.

95. Charles J. Dunlap, Jr, 'Law and Military Interventions: Preserving Humanitarian Values in 21st Century Conflicts' (Humanitarian Challenges in Military Interventions, Carr Center for Human Rights Policy, Harvard Kennedy School, 2001), 5.

96. Issacharoff, *Fragile Democracies*, 68.

97. Capoccia, *Defending Democracy*, 209.

98. Issacharoff, *Fragile Democracies*, 83.

99. Kirshner, *A Theory of Militant Democracy*, 91.

100. Ibid., 91.

101. When Hindenburg issued a presidential decree ordering the immediate dissolution of the SA and the SS, for example, the ban was designed deliberately to avoid a fight with the NSDAP as to its goals and agenda.

102. Ucko, 'Militias, Tribes and Insurgents.'

103. Kirshner, *A Theory of Militant Democracy*, 17.

104. Fox and Nolte, 'Intolerant Democracies,' 13. This is also the conclusion drawn in Matthew J. Goodwin, *Right Response: Understanding and Countering Populist Extremism in Europe* (London: Chatham House, 2012), 95.

105. Donatella Della Porta, *Social Movements, Political Violence, and the State: A Comparative Analysis of Italy and Germany* (Cambridge: Cambridge University Press, 2006).

8. DUELING NARRATIVES: COUNTERING IDEATIONAL INSURGENCY

1. Deborah Orr, 'Anders Behring Breivik's Not a Terrorist, He's a Mass-Murderer,' *The Guardian*, July 27, 2011, sec. World news, http://www.theguardian.com/world/2011/jul/27/breivik-not-terrorist-insane-murderer; Simon Jenkins, 'The Last Thing Norway Needs Is Illiberal Britain's Patronising,' *The Guardian*, July 26, 2011, sec. Opinion, http://www.theguardian.com/commentisfree/2011/jul/26/norway-illiberal-britain-patronising. For contemporaneous discussion, see Robert Lambert, 'Was Anders Breivik a Psychotic Spree Killer or a Calculating Terrorist?,' RUSI, August 18, 2011, https://rusi.org/commentary/was-anders-breivik-psychotic-spree-killer-or-calculating-terrorist.

2. Joseph R. Biden, 'Interim National Security Strategic Guidance' (The White House, Washington, DC, March 2021), 19.

3. Indeed, following both the Charlottesville 'Unite the Right' rally and the Capitol attack of January 6, 2021, filtering through video footage of the event aided law enforcement agencies to apprehend the main culprits and in establishing guilt within a court of law. Even when perpetrators do not themselves film their act, the saturation of smartphones and closed-circuit television in areas where terrorist acts take place means that law enforcement agencies often have abundant evidence with which to pursue those responsible.

4. Jeremy Shapiro and Bénédicte Suzan, 'The French Experience of Counter-terrorism,' *Survival* 45, no. 1 (March 2003): 67–98, https://doi.org/10.1093/survival/45.1.67.

5. 'Switzerland: Draft Anti-terrorism Law Sets "Dangerous Precedent," Rights Experts Warn,' *UN News*, September 11, 2020, https://news.un.org/en/story/2020/09/1072192.

6. European Parliament, Committee on Civil Liberties, Justice and Home Affairs, Directorate General for Internal Policies of the Union, 'EU and Member States' Policies and Laws on Persons Suspected of Terrorism-Related Crimes' (Study, European Parliament, December 2017), 75.

7. 'Macron Anti-terror Law Replaces French State of Emergency,' Deutsche Welle, November 1, 2017, https://www.dw.com/en/macron-anti-terror-law-replaces-french-state-of-emergency/a-41191947.

8. Council of the European Union, 'Consolidated Text: Council Common Position of 27 December 2001 on the Application of Specific Measures to Combat Terrorism' (Pub. L. No. 2001/931/CFSP, 2017), paras. 2–3, http://data.europa.eu/eli/compos/2001/931/2017-11-15.

9. Maxine Bernstein, 'Head of Oregon's FBI: Bureau Doesn't Designate Proud Boys as Extremist Group,' *The Oregonian*, December 4, 2018, sec. Crime, https://www.oregonlive.com/crime/2018/12/head-of-oregons-fbi-bureau-doesnt-designate-proud-boys-as-extremist-group.html.

10. Clint Watts, 'How to Fight the New Domestic Terrorism,' *Wall Street Journal*, August 9, 2019, sec. Life, https://www.wsj.com/articles/how-to-fight-the-new-domestic-terrorism-11565363219; Richard B. Zabel, 'Domestic Terrorism Is a National Problem: It Should Also Be a Federal Crime.,' *Washington Post*, February 2, 2021, sec. Opinion, https://www.washingtonpost.com/opinions/2021/02/02/domestic-terrorism-federal-crime/; Bill Scher, 'It's Time for a

Domestic Terrorism Law,' *Washington Monthly*, January 14, 2021, sec. Politics, https://washingtonmonthly.com/2021/01/14/its-time-for-a-domestic-terrorism-law/.

11. As German argues, 'Definition sections of statutes rarely do [set out penalties]. Section § 2331(1), which defines "international terrorism," likewise does not impose penalties, so this is hardly an argument for a new law … While a handful of federal statutes apply only to foreign terrorist organizations and acts of transnational terrorism, the government needs no new authority to properly respond to domestic terrorism. Congress has already provided powerful tools that give prosecutors multiple options.' See Michael German, 'Why New Laws Aren't Needed to Take Domestic Terrorism More Seriously,' *Just Security*, December 14, 2018, https://www.justsecurity.org/61876/laws-needed-domestic-terrorism/. For a longer and thorough review of domestic counterterrorism laws, see Michael German and Sara Robinson, 'Wrong Priorities on Fighting Terrorism' (Brennan Center for Justice, New York University School of Law), October 2018).

12. Mary McCord, 'It's Time for Congress to Make Domestic Terrorism a Federal Crime,' *Lawfare* (blog), December 5, 2018, https://www.lawfareblog.com/its-time-congress-make-domestic-terrorism-federal-crime.

13. Mary McCord, 'Filling the Gap in Our Terrorism Statutes' (George Washington University Program on Extremism, Washington, DC, August 2019), 2.

14. German, 'Why New Laws Aren't Needed to Take Domestic Terrorism More Seriously'; German and Robinson, 'Wrong Priorities on Fighting Terrorism.' See also Kindy Kimberly, Sari Horwitz, and Devlin Barrett, 'Federal Government Has Long Ignored White Supremacist Threats, Critics Say,' *Washington Post*, September 2, 2017, sec. National, https://www.washingtonpost.com/national/federal-government-has-long-ignored-white-supremacist-threats-critics-say/2017/09/02/bf2ed00c-8698-11e7-961d-2f373b3977ee_story.html?utm_term=.6168f39ad81c.

15. German, 'Why New Laws Aren't Needed to Take Domestic Terrorism More Seriously.'

16. Alice Speri, 'Unredacted FBI Document Sheds New Light on White Supremacist Infiltration of Law Enforcement,' *The Intercept*, September 29, 2020, https://theintercept.com/2020/09/29/police-white-supremacist-infiltration-fbi/; Michael German, 'Hidden in Plain Sight: Racism, White Supremacy, and Far-Right Militancy in Law Enforcement' (Research Report, Brennan Center for Justice,

New York, August 27, 2020), https://www.brennancenter.org/our-work/research-reports/hidden-plain-sight-racism-white-supremacy-and-far-right-militancy-law.

17. Victoria L. Killion, 'Terrorism, Violent Extremism, and the Internet: Free Speech Considerations' (CRS Report for Congress, Congressional Research Service, Washington, DC, May 6, 2019), 14.

18. Maura Conway, 'Routing the Extreme Right: Challenges for Social Media Platforms,' *RUSI Journal* 165, no. 1 (January 2, 2020): 110–11, https://doi.org/10.1080/03071847.2020.1727157.

19. Daniel L. Byman, 'Should We Treat Domestic Terrorists the Way We Treat ISIS?: What Works—and What Doesn't,' Brookings, October 3, 2017, https://www.brookings.edu/articles/should-we-treat-domestic-terrorists-the-way-we-treat-isis-what-works-and-what-doesnt/.

20. See Michael German, 'The Rise of Domestic Terrorism in America' (Committee on the Judiciary, 2021), 4, https://docs.house.gov/meetings/JU/JU08/20210224/111227/HHRG-117-JU08-Wstate-GermanM-20210224.pdf.

21. See Southern Poverty Law Center, 'Klan Leader Jeff Berry Faces Ruin after SPLC Lawsuit,' *Intelligence Report*, 2000, https://www.splcenter.org/fighting-hate/intelligence-report/2000/klan-leader-jeff-berry-faces-ruin-after-splc-lawsuit; 'Klan Group Ordered to Pay $2.5 Million,' NBC News, November 15, 2008, https://www.nbcnews.com/id/wbna27728315.

22. Mike German, 'Behind the Lone Terrorist, a Pack Mentality,' *Washington Post*, June 5, 2005, sec. Opinions, https://www.washingtonpost.com/archive/opinions/2005/06/05/behind-the-lone-terrorist-a-pack-mentality/f9ed5bb8-f18b-429b-b146-1da91a2a37bb/.

23. Merrit Kennedy and Bill Chappell, 'Dominion Voting Systems Files $1.6 Billion Defamation Lawsuit against Fox News,' NPR, March 26, 2021, https://www.npr.org/2021/03/26/981515184/dominion-voting-systems-files-1-6-billion-defamation-lawsuit-against-fox-news.

24. 'Homegrown Threat: FBI Tracks White Supremicists [sic], Domestic Extremists,' NPR, June 28, 2015, Weekend edition Sunday edition, sec. National, https://www.npr.org/2015/06/28/418262038/homegrown-threat-fbi-tracks-white-supremicists-domestic-extremists; Ryan Devereaux, 'How the FBI Increased Its Power after 9/11 and Helped Put Trump in Office,' *The Intercept*, September 14, 2019, https://theintercept.com/2019/09/14/fbi-mike-german-book/.

25. For key known examples of FBI infiltration of the alt-right, see Alan Feuer and Adam Goldman, 'Among Those Who Marched into the Capitol on Jan. 6: An F.B.I. Informant,' *New York Times*, September 25, 2021, https://www.nytimes.com/2021/09/25/us/politics/capitol-riot-fbi-informant.html.

26. Trevor Aaronson, 'The Unlikely Jihadi,' *The Intercept*, September 3, 2017, https://theintercept.com/2017/09/03/the-fbi-pressured-a-lonely-young-man-into-a-bomb-plot-he-tried-to-back-out-now-hes-serving-life-in-prison/.

27. Human Rights Watch, ed., *Illusion of Justice: Human Rights Abuses in US Terrorism Prosecutions* (New York: Human Rights Watch and Columbia Law School Human Rights Institute, 2014), 5. See also Lisa Rose, 'How a Suicidal Pizza Man Found Himself Ensnared in an FBI Terror Sting,' CNN, November 29, 2017, sec. Politics, https://www.cnn.com/2017/11/29/politics/aby-rayyan-fbi-terror-sting-pizza-man; Eric Lichtblau, 'F.B.I. Steps Up Use of Stings in ISIS Cases,' *New York Times*, June 7, 2016, sec. U.S., https://www.nytimes.com/2016/06/08/us/fbi-isis-terrorism-stings.html.

28. Antony Field, 'Ethics and Entrapment: Understanding Counterterrorism Stings,' *Terrorism and Political Violence* 31, no. 2 (March 4, 2019): 260–76, https://doi.org/10.1080/09546553.2016.1213721.

29. Paul Harris, 'Fake Terror Plots, Paid Informants: The Tactics of FBI "Entrapment" Questioned,' *The Guardian*, November 16, 2011, sec. World, http://www.theguardian.com/world/2011/nov/16/fbi-entrapment-fake-terror-plots.

30. For this point and a legal case for review, see Jon Sherman, '"A Person Otherwise Innocent": Policing Entrapment in Preventative, Undercover Counterterrorism Investigations,' *Journal of Constitutional Law* 11, no. 5 (July 2009): 1510, passim. See also Human Rights Watch, *Illusion of Justice*.

31. Parmy Olson, *We Are Anonymous: Inside the Hacker World of LulzSec, Anonymous, and the Global Cyber Insurgency* (New York: Back Bay, 2013), 235.

32. Ibid., 364–65.

33. Ibid., 392.

34. Paul Cooper, 'Lulzsec Leader Turned Informant Helped FBI Foil 300 Cyber Attacks,' ITProPortal, May 27, 2014, https://www.itproportal.com/2014/05/27/lulzsec-leader-turned-informant-helped-fbi-foil-300-cyber-attacks/.

35. Council of Europe, 'Convention on the Prevention of Terrorism – 16.V.2005' (Treaty Series, Council of Europe, 2005), para. 4.

36. As cited and further discussed in Elizabeth M. Renieris, 'Combating Incitement to Terrorism on the Internet: Comparative Approaches in the United States and United Kingdom and the Need for an International Solution,' *Vanderbilt Journal of Entertainment and Technology Law* 11, no. 3 (2009): 687–88.

37. UK Home Office, 'Counter-terrorism and Border Security Act 2019: Terrorism Offences Fact Sheet,' 2019, https://assets.publishing. service.gov.uk/government/uploads/system/uploads/attachment_ data/file/912085/2019-02-11_Terrorist_Offences_Fact_Sheet_ RA.pdf.

38. Michael J Sherman, 'Brandenburg v. Twitter,' *Civil Rights Law Journal* 28, no. 2 (2018): 144–45.

39. Eugene K. B. Tan, 'Singapore,' in *Comparative Counter-terrorism Law*, ed. Kent Roach (Cambridge: Cambridge University Press, 2015), 617–18, https://doi.org/10.1017/CBO9781107298002.022.

40. Martin Redish and Matthew Fisher, 'Terrorizing Advocacy and the First Amendment: Free Expression and the Fallacy of Mutual Exclusivity,' *Fordham Law Review* 86, no. 2 (November 1, 2017): 566.

41. Michal Buchhandler-Raphael, 'Overcriminalizing Speech,' *Cardozo Law Review* 36 (January 1, 2015): 1680–88.

42. As Buchhandler-Raphael explains, 'a publication that praises terrorism would be perceived as one form of support for a terrorist organization … The broadly worded statute provides the government with expansive powers to prosecute individuals for expressing a host of political viewpoints, when it suspects that the expressive messages conveyed by the speech increase the chances that these messages would persuade others to engage in terrorism.' See ibid., 1680.

43. See discussion in Benjamin Wittes and Zoe Bedell, 'Tweeting Terrorists, Part II: Does It Violate the Law for Twitter to Let Terrorist Groups Have Accounts?,' *Lawfare*, February 14, 2016, https://www. lawfareblog.com/tweeting-terrorists-part-ii-does-it-violate-law-twitter-let-terrorist-groups-have-accounts.

44. *Brandenburg v. Ohio* (US Supreme Court, June 9, 1969).

45. Killion, 'Terrorism, Violent Extremism, and the Internet,' 22.

46. Redish and Fisher, 'Terrorizing Advocacy and the First Amendment,' 566, 574.

47. In one key case, far-right radio host Hal Turner was charged for his violent language in an online blog post, as it explicitly threatened three judges and directed violence by revealing their names, photographs, and work addresses. Similarly, in a separate case, the 'doxing' (publication of private information) and violent threats made against

medical personnel performing abortions were found to constitute unprotected speech under the 'true threat' principle. Ibid., 576–82.

48. Anthony Smith and Cooper Fleishman, '(((Echoes))), Exposed: The Secret Symbol Neo-Nazis Use to Target Jews Online,' *Mic*, June 1, 2016, https://www.mic.com/articles/144228/echoes-exposed-the-secret-symbol-neo-nazis-use-to-target-jews-online; Jonathan Weisman, 'The Nazi Tweets of "Trump God Emperor,"' *New York Times*, May 26, 2016, sec. Opinion, https://www.nytimes.com/2016/05/29/opinion/sunday/the-nazi-tweets-of-trump-god-emperor.html.

49. *Sorrell v. IMS Health Inc.* (Syllabus), no. 10-779 (Supreme Court of the United States, June 23, 2011).

50. Buchhandler-Raphael, 'Overcriminalizing Speech,' 1672.

51. Killion, 'Terrorism, Violent Extremism, and the Internet,' 13. For discussion of the relevant conditions, see note 86.

52. Sherman, 'Brandenburg v. Twitter,' 142.

53. Buchhandler-Raphael, 'Overcriminalizing Speech,' 1690, 1704.

54. See, for example, Alan F. Williams, 'Prosecuting Internet Website Development under the Material Support to Terrorism Statutes: Time to Fix What's Broken,' *Journal of Legislation and Public Policy* 11 (2008): 365–403; Redish and Fisher, 'Terrorizing Advocacy and the First Amendment.'

55. Killion, 'Terrorism, Violent Extremism, and the Internet,' 28.

56. 'Armed Toddlers Kill Twice as Many Americans Each Year as Terrorists,' Euronews, January 31, 2017, sec. news_news, https://www.euronews.com/2017/01/31/armed-toddlers-kill-twice-as-many-americans-each-year-than-terrorists.

57. Brian Fishman, 'Crossroads: Counter-terrorism and the Internet,' *Texas National Security Review* 2, no. 2 (February 2019): 83, https://doi.org/10.26153/TSW/1942.

58. Audrey Alexander, 'Digital Decay? Tracing Change over Time among English-Language Islamic State Sympathizers on Twitter' (George Washington University Program on Extremism, Washington, DC, October 2017), 2.

59. Nicholas Confessore and Gabriel J. X. Dance, 'Battling Fake Accounts, Twitter to Slash Millions of Followers,' *New York Times*, July 13, 2018, sec. Technology, https://www.nytimes.com/2018/07/11/technology/twitter-fake-followers.html.

60. Martin Evans, 'Facebook Accused of Introducing Extremists to One Another through "Suggested Friends" Feature,' *The Telegraph*, May 5, 2018, https://www.telegraph.co.uk/news/2018/05/05/facebook-accused-introducing-extremists-one-another-suggested/.

61. 'India Lynchings: WhatsApp Sets New Rules after Mob Killings,' BBC News, July 20, 2018, https://www.bbc.com/news/world-asia-india-44897714.

62. Eshwar Chandrasekharan, Umashanthi Pavalanathan, Anirudh Srinivasan, Adam Glynn, Jacob Eisenstein, and Eric Gilbert, 'You Can't Stay Here: The Efficacy of Reddit's 2015 Ban Examined through Hate Speech,' *Proceedings of the ACM on Human-Computer Interaction* 31, no. 3 (December 6, 2017): 1–22, https://doi.org/10.1145/3134666. As the study concludes, 'By shutting down these echo chambers of hate, Reddit caused the people participating to either leave the site or dramatically change their linguistic behavior' (p. 17).

63. See Ken Schwencke, 'How One Major Internet Company Helps Serve Up Hate on the Web,' *ProPublica*, May 4, 2017, https://www.propublica.org/article/how-cloudflare-helps-serve-up-hate-on-the-web?token=20Tgq0p4nnwC4i13hjc-gV7MRR72yNoe; Matthew Prince, 'Why We Terminated Daily Stormer,' *The Cloudflare Blog* (blog), August 16, 2017, https://blog.cloudflare.com/why-we-terminated-daily-stormer/; Matthew Prince, 'Terminating Service for 8chan,' *The Cloudflare Blog* (blog), August 5, 2019, https://blog.cloudflare.com/terminating-service-for-8chan/.

64. J. M. Berger and Heather Perez, 'The Islamic State's Diminishing Returns on Twitter: How Suspensions Are Limiting the Social Networks of English-Speaking ISIS Supporters' (Occasional Paper, George Washington University Program on Extremism, Washington, DC, February 2016), 4. Because of how Twitter works, the deletion of an account on the basis of a prohibited tweet also removes all other tweets and interactions, thereby producing a far broader sweep of the platform.

65. Maura Conway, Moign Khawaja, Suraj Lakhani, Jeremy Reffin, Andrew Robertson, and David Weir, 'Disrupting Daesh: Measuring Takedown of Online Terrorist Material and Its Impacts,' *Studies in Conflict and Terrorism* 42, nos. 1–2 (February 2019): 151–52, https://doi.org/10.1080/1057610X.2018.1513984.

66. J. M. Berger and Jonathon Morgan, 'The ISIS Twitter Census: Defining and Describing the Population of ISIS Supporters on Twitter' (Analysis Paper, Brookings Project on US Relations with the Islamic World, Center for Middle East Policy, Brookings, March 2015), 55; Conway et al., 'Disrupting Daesh,' 151.

67. Conway et al., 'Disrupting Daesh,' 149–50.

68. Maura Conway, Moign Khawaja, Suraj Lakhani, and Jeremy Reffin, 'A Snapshot of the Syrian Jihadi Online Ecology: Differential Disruption,

Community Strength, and Preferred Other Platforms,' *Studies in Conflict and Terrorism*, January 4, 2021: 13, https://doi.org/10.1080/1057610X.2020.1866736.

69. For comprehensive treatment of the fringe online ecosystem of the far right, see Stephane J. Baele, Lewys Brace, and Travis G. Coan, 'Uncovering the Far-Right Online Ecosystem: An Analytical Framework and Research Agenda,' *Studies in Conflict and Terrorism*, December 30, 2020: 11–15, https://doi.org/10.1080/1057610X.2020.1862895.

70. As Alexander puts it, 'Silencing IS adherents on Twitter may produce unwanted side effects that challenge law enforcement's ability to detect and disrupt threats posed by violent extremists.' Alexander, 'Digital Decay?,' vii, 47–48.

71. Amarnath Amarasingam, Shiraz Maher, and Charlie Winter, 'How Telegram Disruption Impacts Jihadist Platform Migration' (Centre for Research and Evidence on Security Threats, January 2021), 22, https://crestresearch.ac.uk/resources/how-telegram-disruption-impacts-jihadist-platform-migration/.

72. Conway et al., 'A Snapshot of the Syrian Jihadi Online Ecology,' 2.

73. On bugginess, see Kevin Roose, 'The Alt-Right Created a Parallel Internet: It's an Unholy Mess,' *New York Times*, December 11, 2017, sec. Technology, https://www.nytimes.com/2017/12/11/technology/alt-right-internet.html. For a case study of campaign disruption, see Lella Nouri, Nuria Lorenzo-Dus, and Amy-Louise Watkin, 'Following the Whack-a-Mole: Britain First's Visual Strategy from Facebook to Gab' (Global Research Network on Terrorism and Technology, RUSI, London, July 2019).

74. See Amarasingam, Maher, and Winter, 'How Telegram Disruption Impacts Jihadist Platform Migration.' See also Rita Katz, 'ISIS Is Now Harder to Track Online—but That's Good News,' *Wired*, December 16, 2019, https://www.wired.com/story/opinion-isis-is-now-harder-to-track-onlinebut-thats-good-news/. On ways to respond to the encryption challenge, see Bipartisan Policy Center, 'Digital Counterterrorism: Fighting Jihadists Online' (Bipartisan Policy Center, Washington, DC, March 2018), 19–21.

75. Charlie Winter and Jade Parker, 'Virtual Caliphate Rebooted: The Islamic State's Evolving Online Strategy,' *Lawfare*, January 7, 2018, https://www.lawfareblog.com/virtual-caliphate-rebooted-islamic-states-evolving-online-strategy. See also Charlie Winter, 'Inside the Collapse of Islamic State's Propaganda Machine,' *Wired*, December 20, 2017, https://www.wired.co.uk/article/isis-islamic-state-propaganda-content-strategy.

76. Conway et al., 'A Snapshot of the Syrian Jihadi Online Ecology,' 3, passim.

77. Winter and Parker, 'Virtual Caliphate Rebooted.'

78. Audrey Alexander and Helen Christy Powell, 'Gray Media under the Black and White Banner,' *Lawfare*, May 6, 2018, https://www.lawfareblog.com/gray-media-under-black-and-white-banner.

79. Nouri, Lorenzo-Dus, and Watkin, 'Following the Whack-a-Mole,' 3.

80. As Conway puts it, 'the issue is not about the upload and circulation of extreme right-wing *terrorist* content … the issue is more nuanced and contentious, and concerns the appropriateness of removing hostile extreme right-wing content from major platforms prior to attacks due to its potentially radicalising nature.' Conway, 'Routing the Extreme Right,' 113. For the real-world effect of this conundrum, see for example Jessica Guynn, 'Twitter Accused of Political Bias in Right-Wing Crackdown,' *USA Today*, November 18, 2016, https://www.usatoday.com/story/tech/news/2016/11/18/conservatives-accuse-twitter-of-liberal-bias/94037802/.

81. Travis M. Andrews, '"A Great Purge?": Twitter Suspends Richard Spencer, Other Prominent Alt-Right Accounts,' *Washington Post*, November 16, 2016, https://www.washingtonpost.com/news/morning-mix/wp/2016/11/16/a-great-purge-twitter-suspends-richard-spencer-other-prominent-alt-right-accounts/.

82. Twitter Safety, 'An Update Following the Riots in Washington, DC,' Twitter (blog), January 12, 2021, https://blog.twitter.com/en_us/topics/company/2021/protecting--the-conversation-following-the-riots-in-washington--.html. The previous year it had targeted 7,000 QAnon accounts for deletion, then on the grounds of harassment and efforts to evade earlier bans. See Rachel Lerman and Elizabeth Dwoskin, 'Twitter Crackdown on Conspiracy Theories Could Set Agenda for Other Social Media,' *Washington Post*, July 22, 2020, sec. Technology, https://www.washingtonpost.com/technology/2020/07/22/twitter-bans-qanon-accounts/.

83. According to analysis by Zignal Labs, 'online misinformation about election fraud plunged 73 percent after several social media sites suspended President Trump and key allies last week.' See Elizabeth Dwoskin and Craig Timberg, 'Misinformation Dropped Dramatically the Week after Twitter Banned Trump and Some Allies,' *Washington Post*, January 16, 2021, sec. Technology, https://www.washingtonpost.com/technology/2021/01/16/misinformation-trump-twitter/.

84. Sophia Moskalenko and Clark McCauley, 'QAnon: Radical Opinion versus Radical Action,' *Perspectives on Terrorism* 15, no. 2 (April 2021): 142–46.

85. Monika Bickert and Brian Fishman, 'Hard Questions: Are We Winning the War on Terrorism Online?,' Facebook (blog), November 28, 2017, https://about.fb.com/news/2017/11/hard-questions-are-we-winning-the-war-on-terrorism-online/.

86. Brian A. Jackson, Ashley L. Rhoades, Jordan R. Reimer, Natasha Lander, Katherine Costello, and Sina Beaghley, 'Practical Terrorism Prevention: Reexamining U.S. National Approaches to Addressing the Threat of Ideologically Motivated Violence' (Research Reports, RAND Corporation, Santa Monica, CA, February 14, 2019), 81, https://www.rand.org/pubs/research_reports/RR2647.html.

87. Fishman, 'Crossroads,' 89.

88. These questions are discussed in ibid.

89. Conway et al., 'A Snapshot of the Syrian Jihadi Online Ecology,' 2.

90. Fishman, 'Crossroads,' 95.

91. See Moustafa Ayad, 'The Propaganda Pipeline: The ISIS Fuouaris Upload Network on Facebook' (ISD Briefing, London, July 13, 2020).

92. Isabelle van der Vegt, Paul Gill, Stuart Macdonald, and Bennett Kleinberg, 'Shedding Light on Terrorist and Extremist Content Removal' (Global Research Network on Terrorism and Technology, RUSI, London, July 2019), 7–8, https://www.rusi.org/sites/default/files/20190703_grntt_paper_3.pdf.

93. Audrey Alexander and William Braniff, 'Marginalizing Violent Extremism Online,' *Lawfare*, January 21, 2018, https://www.lawfareblog.com/marginalizing-violent-extremism-online.   On redirection, 'Google implemented a pilot effort under the brand "Redirect Method" to describe this, while Facebook calls its initiative "Counter-speech."' For metrics on effectiveness, see Jackson et al., 'Practical Terrorism Prevention,' 82.

94. Fishman, 'Crossroads,' 95–96. See also 'Global Internet Forum to Counter Terrorism,' GIFCT, accessed April 29, 2021, https://gifct.org/about/.

95. Jonathan Greenblatt, 'Examining the Domestic Terrorism Threat in the Wake of the Attack on the U.S. Capitol' (Committee on Homeland Security, 2021), 23, https://homeland.house.gov/imo/media/doc/Testimony-Greenblatt1.pdf.

96. Fishman, 'Crossroads,' 84.

97. Fishman therefore concludes that 'digital counter-terrorism efforts will not and should not be driven primarily by governments.' See ibid., 83, 100.

98. One may, for example, cite the Trump administration's effort to pressure social media companies to boost politically conservative voices and to allow his inflammatory and false tweets. See Jessica Guynn, 'Donald Trump and Joe Biden vs. Facebook and Twitter: Why Section 230 Could Get Repealed in 2021,' *USA Today*, January 4, 2021, https://www.usatoday.com/story/tech/2021/01/04/trump-biden-pelosi-section-230-repeal-facebook-twitter-google/4132529001/.

99. Yochai Benkler as interviewed in Dahlia Scheindlin and Gilad Halpern, 'Who Poisoned My News?,' *Tel Aviv Review*, November 23, 2020, https://tlv1.fm/the-tel-aviv-review/2020/11/23/who-poisoned-my-news/.

100. 'The Call,' Christchurch Call to Eliminate Terrorist and Violent Extremism, accessed April 29, 2021, https://www.christchurchcall.com/call.html.

101. Mathieu Pollet, 'EU Adopts Law Giving Tech Giants One Hour to Remove Terrorist Content,' Euractiv, April 28, 2021, https://www.euractiv.com/section/cybersecurity/news/eu-adopts-law-giving-tech-giants-one-hour-to-remove-terrorist-content/.

102. As Keller puts it with regard to take-down notices more generally (beyond just the issue of terrorism), 'Twenty years of experience with these laws in the United States and elsewhere tells us that when platforms face legal risk for user speech, they routinely err on the side of caution and take it down.' See Daphne Keller, 'Internet Platforms: Observations on Speech, Danger, and Money' (Aegis Series Paper, National Security, Technology, and Law, Hoover Institution, Stanford, CA, June 13, 2018), 2.

103. Pollet, 'EU Adopts Law Giving Tech Giants One Hour to Remove Terrorist Content.' Even then, the resource constraints are daunting. 'The national platform for harmonisation, reports, analysis and checking of digital content, Pharos, has only 28 investigators at its disposal. They monitor various information and communication services in France, and produced more than 228,000 reports in 2019 alone ... Given the scale of Pharos' task, implementing existing rules appears to pose greater challenges than gaps in legislation.' See Boryana Saragerova, 'France: Towards Stronger Counter-terrorism Regulation Online,' *Global Risk Insights*, November 29, 2020, https://globalriskinsights.com/2020/11/france-towards-stronger-counter-terrorism-regulation-online/.

104. 'Bundestag beschließt Gesetz gegen strafbare Inhalte im Internet,' Deutscher Bundestag, 2017, https://www.bundestag.de/dokumente/textarchiv/2017/kw26-de-netzwerkdurchsetzungsgesetz-513398.

105. See, for example, the vitriol within various sections of the British government. Martyn Frampton, 'The New Netwar: Countering Extremism Online' (Policy Exchange, London, 2017), 66–68, https://policyexchange.org.uk/wp-content/uploads/2017/09/The-New-Netwar-1.pdf.

106. This immunity stands so long as the company does not assist in producing this content, nor its platform be used for sex trafficking. As concerns terrorism, Tsesis argues that a social media company could be sued if a user 'can prove [i] that a social media company had received complaints about specific webpages, videos, posts, articles, IP addresses, or accounts of foreign terrorist organizations; [ii] the company's failure to remove the material; [iii] a terrorist's subsequent viewing of or interacting with the material on the website; and [iv] that terrorist's acting upon the propaganda to harm the plaintiff.' As far as barriers go, this one is rather high. See Alexander Tsesis, 'Social Media Accountability for Terrorist Propaganda,' *Fordham Law Review* 86 (2017): 605.

107. Keller, 'Internet Platforms,' 10.

108. Danielle Citron and Benjamin Wittes, 'The Internet Will Not Break: Denying Bad Samaritans § 230 Immunity,' *Fordham Law Review* 86, no. 2 (November 1, 2017): 406.

109. Ibid., 409.

110. Guynn, 'Donald Trump and Joe Biden vs. Facebook and Twitter.' See also Steve Randy Waldman, 'The 1996 Law That Ruined the Internet,' *The Atlantic*, January 3, 2021, https://www.theatlantic.com/ideas/archive/2021/01/trump-fighting-section-230-wrong-reason/617497/.

111. Citron and Wittes, 'The Internet Will Not Break,' 418. Beale proposes a similar amendment, though focused narrowly on the presence and activities of foreign terrorist organizations—a delimitation that would not apply to domestic terrorism. See Steven Beale, 'Online Terrorist Speech, Direct Government Regulation, and the Communications Decency Act,' *Duke Law and Technology Review* 16, no. 1 (2018): 333–50.

112. See, for example, the Eliminating Abusive and Rampant Neglect of Interactive Technologies Act (EARN IT) Act, Platform Accountability and Consumer Transparency (PACT) Act, Raising the Bar Act, and Protecting Americans from Dangerous Algorithms Act.

113. Taylor Owen, 'Sasha Havlicek on Mitigating the Spread of Online Extremism,' *Big Tech*, March 12, 2020, https://www.cigionline.org/big-tech/sasha-havlicek-mitigating-spread-online-extremism. See also Alexander, 'Digital Decay?,' 47.

114. Owen, 'Sasha Havlicek on Mitigating the Spread of Online Extremism.'

115. In one poll, between 66 and 75 percent of respondents said internet companies are not doing enough to tackle online extremism, that it is their responsibility, and that measures should be put in place to compel a more effective response. See Frampton, 'The New Netwar,' 87–110.

116. The phrase is Jack Dorsey's, CEO of Twitter. See Valerie C. Brannon, 'Free Speech and the Regulation of Social Media Content' (Congressional Research Service, March 27, 2019), 2. For a number of recommendations that would meaningfully change social media without destroying it, see Jonathan Haidt and Tobias Rose-Stockwell, 'The Dark Psychology of Social Networks,' *The Atlantic*, December 2019, https://www.theatlantic.com/magazine/archive/2019/12/social-media-democracy/600763/. Specifically, the authors recommend reducing the incentives for moral grandstanding through 'demetrication' ('the process of obscuring like and share counts'), reducing the reach of unverified accounts, and reducing the virality of 'low-quality information' by adding extra steps to its production.

117. See Rachel Briggs and Sebastien Feve, 'Review of Programs to Counter Narratives of Violent Extremism' (Institute for Strategic Dialogue, London, 2013), 6.

118. Kathleen Bouzis, 'Countering the Islamic State: U.S. Counterterrorism Measures,' *Studies in Conflict & Terrorism* 38, no. 10 (2015), 889.

119. See discussion in Greg Miller and Scott Higham, 'In a Propaganda War against ISIS, the U.S. Tried to Play by the Enemy's Rules,' *Washington Post*, May 8, 2015, https://www.washingtonpost.com/world/national-security/in-a-propaganda-war-us-tried-to-play-by-the-enemys-rules/2015/05/08/6eb6b732-e52f-11e4-81ea-0649268f729e_story.html.

120. Bipartisan Policy Center, 'Digital Counterterrorism,' 5. See also Rita Katz, 'The State Department Is Fumbling on Twitter,' *Time*, September 16, 2014, https://time.com/3387065/isis-twitter-war-state-department/.

121. Michael Jones, 'Through the Looking Glass: Assessing the Evidence Base for P/CVE Communications' (Occasional Paper, RUSI, London, July 2020), 22–23.

122. J. McDougall, M. Zezulkova, B. van Driel, and D. Sternadel, 'Teaching Media Literacy in Europe: Evidence of Effective School Pratices in Primary and Secondary Education' (NESET II Report, Publications Office of the European Union, Luxembourg, 2018), 49, https://data.europa.eu/doi/10.2766/613204; Stephan Lewandowsky, Ullrich K.

H. Ecker, and John Cook, 'Beyond Misinformation: Understanding and Coping with the "Post-truth" Era,' *Journal of Applied Research in Memory and Cognition* 6, no. 4 (December 2017): 353–69, https://doi.org/10.1016/j.jarmac.2017.07.008.

123. Hannah Arendt, *The Origins of Totalitarianism* (New York: Harcourt Publishers, 1973), 363.

124. The dilemma is captured in Robert Lambert, 'Empowering Salafis and Islamists against Al-Qaeda: A London Counterterrorism Case Study,' *PS: Political Science and Politics* 41, no. 1 (2008): 31–35; Shiraz Maher and Martyn Frampton, *Choosing Our Friends Wisely: Criteria for Engagement with Muslim Groups* (London: Policy Exchange, 2009).

125. Jones, 'Through the Looking Glass,' 33, 35–36.

126. Matt Freear and Andrew Glazzard, 'Preventive Communication: Emerging Lessons from Participative Approaches to Countering Violent Extremism in Kenya,' *RUSI Journal* 165, no. 1 (2020): 93. The point draws on the treatment of narrative in Steve Lawler, 'Narrative in Social Research,' in *Qualitative Research in Action*, ed. Tim May (London: Sage, 2002), 242–58.

127. Jones, 'Through the Looking Glass,' 24.

128. Ibid., 16. Jones also provides a few key examples of digital engagement that have begun to meet this standard, though, more pessimistically, finds 'a broader lack of socio-psychological considerations in many online interventions' (pp. 16–17, 24).

129. Brendan Nyhan and Jason Reifler, 'The Roles of Information Deficits and Identity Threat in the Prevalence of Misperceptions,' *Journal of Elections, Public Opinion and Parties* 29, no. 2 (April 3, 2019): 222–44, https://doi.org/10.1080/17457289.2018.1465061.

130. See J.-J. van Eerten, B. Doosje, E. Konijn, B. de Graaf, and M. de Goede, 'Developing a Social Media Response to Radicalization: The Role of Counter-narratives in Prevention of Radicalization and de-Radicalization' (Department of Psychology, University of Amsterdam, September 2017), 78, https://dare.uva.nl/search?identifier=4fe0b95f-b5ec-45a1-b50a-2ff8287b4b1c.

131. UK Government, 'Channel Duty Guidance: Protecting People Vulnerable to Being Drawn into Terrorism,' 2020, 6.

132. For full details, see ibid. For commentary, see Ahmed Nazwan, 'The United Kingdom's Effort to Rehabilitate Extremists,' in *Terrorist Deradicalisation in Global Contexts: Success, Failure, and Continuity*, ed. Rohan Gunaratna and Sabariah Hussin, Routledge Studies in the Politics of Disorder and Instability (London: Routledge, 2020), 12–32.

133. For commentary on successful P/CVE practices, see, for example, Sabariah Hussin and Syez Huzaifah bin Othman Alkaff, 'The Los Angeles Model in Deradicalisation,' in *Terrorist Deradicalisation in Global Contexts: Success, Failure, and Continuity*, ed. Rohan Gunaratna and Sabariah Hussin, Routledge Studies in the Politics of Disorder and Instability (London: Routledge, 2020), 197–208; George Selim and Daveed Gartenstein-Ross, 'Save the Terrorism Prevention Toolkit,' *War on the Rocks*, August 28, 2017, https://warontherocks.com/2017/08/save-the-terrorism-prevention-toolkit/.

134. In both contexts, community members attacked the program for its unclear language, its stigmatization of Muslims, its indiscriminate targeting, and its endangerment of civil rights. See Stevan Weine and Ahmed Younis, 'Developing CVE Programs through Building Community Policing Capacities,' in *Countering Violent Extremism: Developing an Evidence-Base for Policy and Practice*, ed. Sara Zeiger and Anne Aly (Perth, Australia: Curtin University, 2015), 147–48, http://apo.org.au/system/files/57458/apo-nid57458-44271.pdf.

135. Beyond issues of integration and marginalization, studies conducted as late as 2018 found that 'about a third of U.S. Muslims still believe that the war on terrorism is a war on Islam.' See Clark R. McCauley, 'Explaining Homegrown Western Jihadists: The Importance of Western Foreign Policy,' *International Journal of Conflict and Violence* 12 (2018): 2, https://doi.org/10.4119/IJCV-3101.

136. As of March 2021, 226 people have been arrested on ISIS-related charges; their religious affiliation was not tracked. Regardless, there are about three million American Muslims. See 'Terrorism in the United States' (GW Extremism Tracker, George Washington University Program on Extremism, Washington, DC, March 2021).

137. Caitlin Ambrozik, 'To Change or Not to Change? The Effect of Terminology on Public Support of Countering Violent Extremism Efforts,' *Democracy and Security* 14, no. 1 (January 2, 2018): 46, https://doi.org/10.1080/17419166.2017.1408010.

138. Trump's Islamophobia can reasonably be derived from his obsession with President Barack Obama's religion and citizenship, his 'Muslim ban,' his amplification of anti-Muslim and white-supremacist content, his theories about Muslims needing tracking or being disloyal, and his association with known bigots. For one summary of this evidence and more, see Brian Klaas, 'A Short History of President Trump's Anti-Muslim Bigotry,' *Washington Post*, March 15, 2019, sec. Opinion, https://www.washingtonpost.com/opinions/2019/03/15/short-history-president-trumps-anti-muslim-bigotry/.

139. Russell Muirhead and Nancy L. Rosenblum, *A Lot of People Are Saying: The New Conspiracism and the Assault on Democracy* (Princeton, NJ: Princeton University Press, 2019), 148.

140. Lisa Hagen, 'Poll: Majority of Republicans Support Trump's Muslim Ban,' *The Hill*, December 9, 2015, https://thehill.com/blogs/ballot-box/presidential-races/262656-poll-majority-of-republicans-support-trumps-muslim-ban; Kristina Wong, 'Poll: Half of American Voters Back Trump's Muslim Ban,' *The Hill*, March 29, 2016, https://thehill.com/policy/defense/274521-poll-half-of-american-voters-back-trumps-muslim-ban.

141. Tom Jensen, 'Trump Still Leads Iowa; Clinton in Good Shape,' Public Policy Polling, September 22, 2015, https://www.publicpolicypolling.com/polls/trump-still-leads-iowa-clinton-in-good-shape/.

142. Of those Republicans who had heard of QAnon, 41 percent say it is a somewhat or very good thing for the country (32 percent and 9 percent respectively). One in five self-identified Republicans said they believed in it. See Davis, '30% of Republicans Have "Favorable" View of QAnon Conspiracy Theory, YouGov Poll Finds'; Pew Research Center, '5 Facts about the QAnon Conspiracy Theories,' *Fact Tank* (blog), November 16, 2020, https://www.pewresearch.org/fact-tank/2020/11/16/5-facts-about-the-qanon-conspiracy-theories/.

143. Kathy Frankovic, 'Belief in Conspiracies Largely Depends on Political Identity,' YouGov, December 27, 2016, https://today.yougov.com/topics/politics/articles-reports/2016/12/27/belief-conspiracies-largely-depends-political-iden.

144. Saletan, 'Americans are Dangerously Divided on the Insurrection.'

145. Eric Rosand, 'Communities First: A Blueprint for Organizing and Sustaining a Global Movement against Violent Extremism' (The Prevention Project: Organizing Against Violent Extremism, Washington, DC, December 2016), 1.

146. Eric Rosand, 'The Global CVE Agenda: Can We Move from Talk to Walk?,' Brookings, *Up Front* (blog), April 20, 2016, https://www.brookings.edu/blog/up-front/2016/04/20/the-global-cve-agenda-can-we-move-from-talk-to-walk/.

147. See, for example, Los Angeles' decision to turn down federal funds for PVE programs following a public outcry. Anadolu Agency, 'Los Angeles Turns Down Funding for Program Targeting Muslims,' *Daily Sabah*, August 17, 2018, sec. Americas, https://www.dailysabah.com/americas/2018/08/17/los-angeles-turns-down-funding-for-program-targeting-muslims.

148. J. M. Berger, 'Making CVE Work: A Focused Approach Based on Process Disruption,' *International Center for Coutner-terrorism, The Hague* 7, no. 5 (May 26, 2016): 7.

149. In this vein, see in particular Yochai Benkler, Rob Faris, and Hal Roberts, *Network Propaganda: Manipulation, Disinformation, and Radicalization in American Politics* (New York: Oxford University Press, 2018).

150. Judit Bayer, Natalija Bitiukova, Petra Bárd, Judit Szakács, Alberto Alemanno, and Erik Uszkiewicz, 'Disinformation and Propaganda: Impact on the Functioning of the Rule of Law in the EU and Its Member States' (Study requested by the LIBE committee, Policy Department for Citizens' Rights and Constitutional Affairs, Directorate General for Internal Policies of the Union, European Union, February 2019), 59.

151. Benkler, Faris, and Roberts, *Network Propaganda*, 6.

152. For a list of the dramatis personae involved in this process, see ibid., 8–20. See also Danah Boyd, 'You Think You Want Media Literacy … Do You?,' *Medium*, March 16, 2018, https://points.datasociety.net/you-think-you-want-media-literacy-do-you-7cad6af18ec2. On the particular virality of outrage, researchers have found that the diffusion of a tweet will increase by a factor of 20 percent for *each* moral-emotional word it includes. See William J. Brady, Julian A. Wills, John T. Jost, Joshua A. Tucker, and Jay J. van Bavel, 'Emotion Shapes the Diffusion of Moralized Content in Social Networks,' *Proceedings of the National Academy of Sciences* 114, no. 28 (July 11, 2017): 7313–18, https://doi.org/10.1073/pnas.1618923114.

153. UN Alliance of Civilizations, 'Report of the High-Level Group' (United Nations, New York, November 13, 2006), 26.

154. Hobbs and McGee note for example the creation of the Institute for Propaganda Analysis (IPA) in 1937 'for the sole purpose of creating teaching methods and curricular material for combatting propaganda.' Much as today, the issue back then was the rise of new forms of mass communication (the spread of newspapers, radio broadcasts) and concern about the effects of these in misleading or manipulating the citizenry. See Renee Hobbs and Sandra McGee, 'Teaching about Propaganda: An Examination of the Historical Roots of Media Literacy,' *Journal of Media Literacy Education* 6, no. 2 (November 9, 2014): 60.

155. Flemming Splidsboel Hansen, 'Russian Hybrid Warfare: A Study of Disinformation' (Danish Institute for International Studies, Copenhagen, 2017), 35.

156. Corneliu Bjola and Krysianna Papadakis, 'Digital Propaganda, Counterpublics and the Disruption of the Public Sphere: The Finnish Approach to Building Digital Resilience,' *Cambridge Review of International Affairs* 33, no. 5 (September 2, 2020): 647, https://doi.org/10.1080/09557571.2019.1704221.

157. As Muirberg and Rosenblum conclude in their study of conspiracy theories, 'the closed conspiracist mind-set is immunized against contradictory evidence and argument, and invulnerable to correction.' See Muirhead and Rosenblum, *A Lot of People Are Saying*, 141.

158. James Pamment, 'The EU Code of Practice on Disinformation: Briefing Note for the New EU Commission' (Policy Perspective Series, Carnegie Endowment for International Peace, Washington, DC, March 2020), 8.

159. OECD, 'Preparing Our Youth for an Inclusive and Sustainable World: The OECD PISA Global Competence Framework' (Directorate for Education and Skills, OECD, Paris, 2018).

160. Alan C. Miller, 'Confronting Confirmation Bias: Giving Truth a Fighting Chance in the Information Age,' *Social Education* 80, no. 5 (October 2016): 276–79.

161. Ibid., 278.

162. W. J. McGuire and D. Papageorgis, 'The Relative Efficacy of Various Types of Prior Belief-Defense in Producing Immunity against Persuasion,' *Journal of Abnormal and Social Psychology* 62, no. 2 (March 1961): 327–37, https://doi.org/10.1037/h0042026. See also Kurt Braddock, 'Vaccinating against Hate: Using Attitudinal Inoculation to Confer Resistance to Persuasion by Extremist Propaganda,' *Terrorism and Political Violence*, November 25, 2019, 1–23, https://doi.org/10.1080/09546553.2019.1693370.

163. Jigsaw, 'Can "Inoculation" Build Broad-Based Resistance to Misinformation?,' *Medium* (blog), March 17, 2021, https://medium.com/jigsaw/can-inoculation-build-broad-based-resistance-to-misinformation-6c67e517e314.

164. Gordon Pennycook, Adam Bear, Evan T. Collins, and David G. Rand, 'The Implied Truth Effect: Attaching Warnings to a Subset of Fake News Headlines Increases Perceived Accuracy of Headlines without Warnings,' *Management Science* 66, no. 11 (November 2020): 4944–57, https://doi.org/10.1287/mnsc.2019.3478.

165. Bjola and Papadakis, 'Digital Propaganda, Counterpublics and the Disruption of the Public Sphere,' 658.

166. Maarit Jaakkola, 'Media Literacy in the Baltics: Different Approaches in Neighbouring Countries,' *Media and Learning* (blog), December 2020,

https://media-and-learning.eu/type/featured-articles/media-literacy-in-the-baltics-similar-backgrounds-but-different-approaches/.

167. Bjola and Papadakis, 'Digital Propaganda, Counterpublics and the Disruption of the Public Sphere,' 658.

168. 'Study: Estonians Have Higher Trust in Government than Latvians, Lithuanians,' ERR News, December 29, 2020, sec. News, https://news.err.ee/1221847/study-estonians-have-higher-trust-in-government-than-latvians-lithuanians; Kalev Stoicescu, 'The Evolution of Russian Hybrid Warfare: Estonia,' *CEPA* (blog), January 29, 2021, https://cepa.org/the-evolution-of-russian-hybrid-warfare-estonia/.

169. W. Lance Bennett and Steven Livingston, 'The Disinformation Order: Disruptive Communication and the Decline of Democratic Institutions,' *European Journal of Communication* 33, no. 2 (April 2018): 127, https://doi.org/10.1177/0267323118760317.

170. Benkler, Faris, and Roberts, *Network Propaganda*, 23.

171. Danah Boyd, 'Did Media Literacy Backfire?,' *Medium* (blog), March 16, 2018, https://points.datasociety.net/did-media-literacy-backfire-7418c084d88d.

172. Cory Doctorow, 'Three Kinds of Propaganda, and What to Do about Them,' *Boing Boing* (blog), February 25, 2017, https://boingboing.net/2017/02/25/counternarratives-not-fact-che.html.

173. Boyd, 'You Think You Want Media Literacy ....'

174. An English-language transcription of the interview is available at 'Hannah Arendt: From an Interview,' *New York Review of Books*, October 26, 1978, http://www.nybooks.com/articles/1978/10/26/hannah-arendt-from-an-interview/.

175. Ibid.

176. Thomas A. Marks, 'Counterinsurgency in the Age of Globalism,' *Journal of Conflict Studies* 27, no. 1 (2007): 26.

CONCLUSION

1.　I am grateful to Christopher Coker for reminding me of this telling script. See also Christopher Coker, 'War and Culture: Cultural Ruthlessness and the War against Terror,' *Australian Army Journal* III, no. 1 (Summer 2005–2006): 160.

2.　Steven Pinker, *The Better Angels of Our Nature: Why Violence Has Declined* (New York: Penguin Books, 2012), 692.

3.　Ibid., 678–79.

4. Bruno Tertrais, 'The Demise of Ares: The End of War as We Know It?,' *Washington Quarterly* 35, no. 3 (August 2012): 7, https://doi.org/10.1080/0163660X.2012.703521.

5. Hedley Bull, *The Anarchical Society: A Study of Order in World Politics* (London: Macmillan, 1977), 25.

6. Elizabeth Cullen Dunn and Michael S. Bobick, 'The Empire Strikes Back: War without War and Occupation without Occupation in the Russian Sphere of Influence,' *American Ethnologist* 41, no. 3 (August 2014): 405–13, https://doi.org/10.1111/amet.12086.

7. Ashley Lane, 'Iran's Islamist Proxies in the Middle East' (The Islamists, Wilson Center, Washington, DC, December 17, 2020), https://www.wilsoncenter.org/article/irans-islamist-proxies.

8. All of this is recognized quite clearly in United States Army Special Operations Command, 'SOF Support to Political Warfare' (White Paper, March 10, 2015), http://www.soc.mil/swcs/ProjectGray/Support%20to%20Political%20Warfare%20White%20Paper%20v2.3-RMT%20(10MAR2015)%20%20%20.pdf. See also Alina Polyakova, 'Strange Bedfellows: Putin and Europe's Far Right,' *World Affairs* 177, no. 3 (2014): 36–40.

9. I am grateful to David Spencer for helping me develop this point.

10. See, for example, Thomas A. Marks, 'Counterinsurgency and Operational Art,' *Low Intensity Conflict and Law Enforcement* 13, no. 3 (2005); Thomas A. Marks, 'Counterinsurgency in the Age of Globalism,' *Journal of Conflict Studies* 27, no. 1 (2007); Thomas A. Marks, *Maoist People's War in Post-Vietnam Asia* (Bangkok: White Lotus, 2007). The approach has been further developed in David H. Ucko and Thomas A. Marks, 'Violence in Context: Mapping the Strategies and Operational Art of Irregular Warfare,' *Contemporary Security Policy* 39, no. 2 (April 3, 2018), https://doi.org/10.1080/13523260.2018.1432922; David H. Ucko and Thomas A. Marks, *Crafting Strategy for Irregular Warfare: A Framework for Analysis and Action* (Washington, DC: National Defense University Press, 2020).

11. For a fuller elaboration on how to use this methodology, see Ucko and Marks, *Crafting Strategy for Irregular Warfare*.

12. For a longer discussion of the center of gravity in irregular warfare, see Ucko and Marks, *Crafting Strategy for Irregular Warfare*, 30–33. Curiously, even in authoritarian counterinsurgency, or where repression is thought to play a more prominent part, legitimacy still plays a surprisingly critical role. See David H. Ucko, '"The People Are Revolting": An Anatomy of Authoritarian Counterinsurgency,' *Journal of Strategic Studies* 39, no. 1 (January 2, 2016): 29–61.

BIBLIOGRAPHY

Aaronson, Trevor. 'The Unlikely Jihadi.' *The Intercept*, September 3, 2017. https://theintercept.com/2017/09/03/the-fbi-pressured-a-lonely-young-man-into-a-bomb-plot-he-tried-to-back-out-now-hes-serving-life-in-prison/.

Abbasi, Waseem. 'Karachi Returning to Peace.' *The News International*, August 2, 2015. https://www.thenews.com.pk/print/54321-karachi-returning-to-peace.

Ackerman, Spencer. 'Badr to Worse.' *New Republic*, July 11, 2005.

Adnani, Abu Muhammad al-. 'Say "Die in Your Rage!"' Al Hayat Media Centre, January 2015.

Agencia de Noticias Fides. 'EEUU confirma presencia de las FARC y ELN de Colombia en Bolivia.' May 8, 2003. https://www.noticiasfides.com/nacional/politica/eeuu-confirma-presencia-de-las-farc-y-eln-de-colombia-en-bolivia-46291.

Agencia de Noticias Fides. 'Las FARC estuvieron en Bolivia y expanden su dominio en la region.' September 25, 2004. https://www.noticiasfides.com/nacional/sociedad/las-farc-estuvieron-en-bolivia-y-expanden-su-dominio-en-la-region-187050.

Agency, Anadolu. 'Los Angeles Turns Down Funding for Program Targeting Muslims.' *Daily Sabah*, August 17, 2018, sec. Americas. https://www.dailysabah.com/americas/2018/08/17/los-angeles-turns-down-funding-for-program-targeting-muslims.

Albaladejo, Angelika. 'Is Colombia Underestimating the Scale of FARC Dissidence?' *InSight Crime* (blog), October 17, 2017. https://www.insightcrime.org/news/analysis/is-colombia-underestimating-scale-farc-dissidence/.

Alexander, Audrey. 'Digital Decay? Tracing Change over Time among English-Language Islamic State Sympathizers on Twitter.' George Washington University Program on Extremism, October 2017.

Alexander, Audrey, and William Braniff. 'Marginalizing Violent Extremism Online.' *Lawfare*, January 21, 2018. https://www.lawfareblog.com/marginalizing-violent-extremism-online.

Alexander, Audrey, and Helen Christy Powell. 'Gray Media under the Black and White Banner.' *Lawfare*, May 6, 2018. https://www.lawfareblog.com/gray-media-under-black-and-white-banner.

Alexander, Robert J. *International Trotskyism, 1929–1985: A Documented Analysis of the Movement.* Durham, NC: Duke University Press, 1991.

Al Jazeera. 'Balochistan: Pakistan's Other War.' January 9, 2012. https://www.aljazeera.com/program/episode/2012/1/9/balochistan-pakistans-other-war/.

Allansson, Marie, Erik Melander, and Lotta Themnér. 'Organized Violence, 1989–2016.' *Journal of Peace Research* 54, no. 4 (July 2017): 574–87. https://doi.org/10.1177/0022343317718773.

Alonso, Rogelio. 'Terrorist Skin, Peace-Party Mask: The Political Communication Strategy of Sinn Féin and the PIRA.' *Terrorism and Political Violence* 28, no. 3 (May 26, 2016): 520–40. https://doi.org/10.1080/09546553.2016.1155934.

Alschuler, Lawrence R. 'The Chiapas Rebellion: An Analysis According to the Structural Theory of Revolution.' *Estudios Interdisciplinarios de América Latina y el Caribe* 10, no. 2 (1999): 131–49.

Alverado, Facundo, Lucas Chancel, Thomas Piketty, Emmanuel Saez, and Gabriel Zucman. 'World Inequality Report 2018.' World Inequality Lab, 2017. http://wir2018.wid.world/files/download/wir2018-full-report-english.pdf.

Amaize, Emma. 'EndSARS: Tension as N'Delta Militants Roll Out 11-Point Demand.' *Vanguard News*, October 25, 2020. https://www.vanguardngr.com/2020/10/endsars-tension-as-ndelta-militants-roll-out-11-point-demand/.

Amarasingam, Amarnath. 'Elton "Ibrahim" Simpson's Path to Jihad in Garland, Texas.' *War on the Rocks*, May 14, 2015. https://warontherocks.com/2015/05/elton-ibrahim-simpsons-path-to-jihad-in-garland-texas/.

Amarasingam, Amarnath. 'What Twitter Really Means for Islamic State Supporters.' *War on the Rocks*, December 30, 2015. https://warontherocks.com/2015/12/what-twitter-really-means-for-islamic-state-supporters/.

Amarasingam, Amarnath, and Marc-André Argentino. 'The QAnon Conspiracy Theory: A Security Threat in the Making?' *CTC Sentinel* 13, no. 7 (July 2020): 37–43.

Amarasingam, Amarnath, Shiraz Maher, and Charlie Winter. 'How Telegram Disruption Impacts Jihadist Platform Migration.' Centre for Research and Evidence on Security Threats, January 2021. https://crestresearch.ac.uk/resources/how-telegram-disruption-impacts-jihadist-platform-migration/.

Ambrozik, Caitlin. 'To Change or Not to Change? The Effect of Terminology on Public Support of Countering Violent Extremism Efforts.' *Democracy and Security* 14, no. 1 (January 2, 2018): 45–67. https://doi.org/10.1080/17419166.2017.1408010.

Amnesty International. 'Bolivia: Crisis and Justice; Days of Violence in February and October 2003.' AMR 18/006/2004, November 2004.

Amnesty International. 'Brazil: Police Killings, Impunity and Attacks on Defenders.' Amnesty International Submission for the UN Universal Periodic Review, 27th Session of the UPR Working Group, May 2017. London, September 2016.

Andrews, Travis M. '"A Great Purge?": Twitter Suspends Richard Spencer, Other Prominent Alt-Right Accounts.' *Washington Post*, November 16, 2016. https://www.washingtonpost.com/news/morning-mix/wp/2016/11/16/a-great-purge-twitter-suspends-richard-spencer-other-prominent-alt-right-accounts/.

Anglin, Andrew. 'A Normie's Guide to the Alt-Right.' *Daily Stormer* (blog), August 31, 2016. https://dailystormer.su/a-normies-guide-to-the-alt-right/.

Anheier, Helmut. 'Movement Development and Organizational Networks: The Role of "Single Members" in the German Nazi Party, 1925–30.' In *Social Movements and Networks*, edited by Mario Diani and Doug McAdam, 49–71. Oxford: Oxford University Press, 2003. https://doi.org/10.1093/0199251789.001.0001.

Anonymous (@YourAnonNews), March 6, 2012. https://twitter.com/YourAnonNews/status/177073022455398400.

Anti-Defamation League. 'The Base.' Accessed February 2, 2021. https://www.adl.org/resources/backgrounders/the-base.

Anti-Defamation League. 'Okay Hand Gesture.' Accessed February 1, 2021. https://www.adl.org/education/references/hate-symbols/okay-hand-gesture.

Anti-Defamation League. 'Pepe the Frog.' Accessed February 1, 2021. https://www.adl.org/education/references/hate-symbols/pepe-the-frog.

Apter, David E. 'Political Violence in Analytical Perspective.' In *The Legitimization of Violence*, edited by David E. Apter. Houndsmills, Basingstoke: Macmillan in association with UNRISD, 1997.

Arambewela, Nadeeka, and Rodney Arambewela. 'Post-War Opportunities for Peace in Sri Lanka: An Ongoing Challenge?' *Global Change, Peace and Security* 22, no. 3 (October 2010): 365–75. https://doi.org/10.1080/14781158.2010.510272.

Arendt, Hannah. *The Origins of Totalitarianism*. New York: Harcourt Publishers, 1973.

Arias, Enrique Desmond. 'How Criminals Govern in Latin America and the Caribbean.' *Current History* 119, no. 814 (February 2020): 43–48.

Arias, Enrique Desmond. 'The Impacts of Differential Armed Dominance of Politics in Rio de Janeiro, Brazil.' *Studies in Comparative International Development* 48, no. 3 (September 2013): 263–84.

Arias, Enrique Desmond, and Corinne Davis Rodrigues. 'The Myth of Personal Security: Criminal Gangs, Dispute Resolution, and Identity in Rio de Janeiro's Favelas.' *Latin American Politics and Society* 48, no. 4 (2006): 53–81.

Arquilla, John, and David F. Ronfeldt. *The Advent of Netwar*. Santa Monica, CA: RAND, 1996.

Arquilla, John, and David Ronfeldt. 'Cyberwar Is Coming!' In *In Athena's Camp: Preparing for Conflict in the Information Age*, edited by John Arquilla and David F. Ronfeldt. Santa Monica, CA: RAND Corporation, 1997.

Arquilla, John, and David F. Ronfeldt. 'Emergence and Influence of the Zapatista Social Netwar.' In *Networks and Netwars: The Future of Terror, Crime, and Militancy*, edited by John Arquilla and David F. Ronfeldt, 171–200. Santa Monica, CA: RAND Corporation, 2001.

Art, Robert J., and Kenneth N. Waltz. *The Use of Force: Military Power and International Politics*. 4th ed. Lanham, MD: University Press of America, 1993.

Asfura-Heim, Patricio, and Julia McQuaid. 'Diagnosing the Boko Haram Conflict: Grievances, Motivations, and Institutional Resilience in Northeast Nigeria.' Occasional Paper, Center for Naval Analysis, January 2015.

Assies, Willem and Ton Salman. *Crisis in Bolivia: The Elections of 2002 and Their Aftermath*. Research Paper 56. London: University of London Institute of Latin American Studies, 2003.

Auerheimer, Andrew 'weev.' 'Fun with Twitter's Ad Console (with Images, Tweets).' Storify, June 7, 2015. https://web.archive.org/web/20161114175734/https://storify.com/weev/fun-with-twitter-ads-day-1.

Avalon Project. 'Thomas Jefferson First Inaugural Address.' Lillian Goldman Law Library, Yale Law School. Accessed March 29, 2021. https://avalon.law.yale.edu/19th_century/jefinau1.asp.

Awan, Akil N. 'The Virtual Jihad: An Increasingly Legitimate Form of Warfare.' *CTC Sentinel* 3, no. 5 (2010): 10–13.

Ayad, Moustafa. 'The Propaganda Pipeline: The ISIS Fuouaris Upload Network on Facebook.' ISD Briefing, ISD, London, July 13, 2020.

Ayoob, Mohammed. 'The Myth of the Islamic State.' *Foreign Affairs*, April 4, 2016. https://www.foreignaffairs.com/articles/2016-04-03/myth-islamic-state.

Aziani, Alberto, Serena Favarin, and Gian Maria Campedelli. 'Security Governance: Mafia Control over Ordinary Crimes.' *Journal of Research in Crime and Delinquency* 57, no. 4 (July 2020): 444–92. https://doi.org/10.1177/0022427819893417.

Baele, Stephane J., Lewys Brace, and Travis G. Coan. 'Uncovering the Far-Right Online Ecosystem: An Analytical Framework and Research Agenda.' *Studies in Conflict and Terrorism*, December 30, 2020, 1–21. https://doi.org/10.1080/1057610X.2020.1862895.

Balasundaram, Nirmanusan. 'Sri Lanka: An Ethnocratic State Endangering Positive Peace in the Island.' *Cosmopolitan Civil Societies: An Interdisciplinary Journal* 8, no. 3 (November 30, 2016): 38–58. https://doi.org/10.5130/ccs.v8i3.5194.

Baldaro, Edoardo. 'A Dangerous Method: How Mali Lost Control of the North, and Learned to Stop Worrying.' *Small Wars and Insurgencies* 29, no. 3 (May 4, 2018): 579–603. https://doi.org/10.1080/09592318.2018.1455323.

Ballentine, Karen, and Heiko Nitzschke. 'Beyond Greed and Grievance: Policy Lessons from Studies in the Political Economy of Armed Conflict.' In *Security and Development: Investing in Peace and Prosperity*, edited by Robert Picciotto and Rachel Weaving, 159–86. Abingdon: Routledge, 2006.

Bansal, Alok. 'Factors Leading to Insurgency in Balochistan.' *Small Wars and Insurgencies* 19, no. 2 (June 2008): 182–200. https://doi.org/10.1080/09592310802061356.

Barbara, Vanessa. 'The Men Who Terrorize Rio.' *New York Times*, May 23, 2018, sec. Opinion. https://www.nytimes.com/2018/05/22/opinion/rio-janeiro-terrorize-militias.html.

Barndt, William T. 'Destroying the Opposition's Livelihood: Pathways to Violence in Bolivia since 2000.' *Journal of Politics in Latin America* 4, no. 3 (December 2012): 3–37. https://doi.org/10.1177/1866802X1200400301.

Bar-On, Tamir. 'The Alt-Right's Continuation of the 'Cultural War' in Euro-American Societies.' *Thesis Eleven* 163, no. 1 (April 2021): 43–70. https://doi.org/10.1177/07255136211005988.

Bauerkämper, Arnd. 'Civil Society History VII: Late 20th and 21st Century.' In *International Encyclopedia of Civil Society*, edited by Helmut K. Anheier, Stefan Toepler, and Regina List, 366–71. Springer Reference. New York: Springer, 2010.

Bayer, Judit, Natalija Bitiukova, Petra Bárd, Judit Szakács, Alberto Alemanno, and Erik Uszkiewicz. 'Disinformation and Propaganda: Impact on the Functioning of the Rule of Law in the EU and Its Member States.' Study requested by the LIBE Committee. Policy Department for Citizens' Rights and Constitutional Affairs, Directorate General for Internal Policies of the Union, European Union, February 2019.

BBC News. 'Boko Haram Crisis: Nigeria Estimates Baga Deaths at 150.' January 12, 2015, sec. Africa. https://www.bbc.com/news/world-africa-30788480.

BBC News. 'Fears over Nepal's Young Maoists.' August 1, 2007. http://news.bbc.co.uk/2/hi/south_asia/6915564.stm.

BBC News. 'India Lynchings: WhatsApp Sets New Rules after Mob Killings.' July 20, 2018. https://www.bbc.com/news/world-asia-india-44897714.

BBC News. 'MQM Denies It Incites Violence.' July 11, 2013. https://www.bbc.com/news/av/uk-23270720.

BBC News. 'Nigeria Arrests "Avengers" Oil Militants.' May 16, 2016, sec. Africa. https://www.bbc.com/news/world-africa-36301835.

BBC News. 'Sri Lanka Civil War: Rajapaksa Says Thousands Missing Are Dead.' January 20, 2020, sec. Asia. https://www.bbc.com/news/world-asia-51184085.

BBC News. 'Sri Lanka Government Publishes War Death Toll Statistics.' February 24, 2012, sec. Asia. https://www.bbc.com/news/world-asia-17156686.

Beale, Steven. 'Online Terrorist Speech, Direct Government Regulation, and the Communications Decency Act.' *Duke Law and Technology Review* 16, no. 1 (2018): 333–50.

Bean, Kevin. 'Endings and Beginnings? Republicanism since 1994.' *Studies in Conflict and Terrorism* 37, no. 9 (September 2, 2014): 720–32. https://doi.org/10.1080/1057610X.2014.931211.

Beckett, Ian. 'The Future of Insurgency.' *Small Wars and Insurgencies* 16, no. 1 (March 2005): 22–36. https://doi.org/10.1080/0959231042000322549.

Beckett, Lois. 'QAnon: A Timeline of Violence Linked to the Conspiracy Theory.' *The Guardian*, October 16, 2020, sec. US news. http://www.theguardian.com/us-news/2020/oct/15/qanon-violence-crimes-timeline.

Beer, D. C. 'Haiti: The Gangs of Cité Soleil.' In *Impunity: Countering Illicit Power in War and Transition*, edited by Michelle Hughes and Michael Miklaucic. Washington, DC: Center for Complex Operations (CCO) & the Peacekeeping and Stability Operations Institute (PKSOI), 2016. http://cco.ndu.edu/News/Article/780129/chapter-3-haiti-the-gangs-of-cit-soleil/.

Beittel, June S. 'Peace Talks in Colombia.' Congressional Research Service, Washington, DC, March 31, 2015.

Belew, Kathleen. 'The White Power Movement at War on Democracy.' Harry Frank Guggenheim Foundation, New York, January 2021.

Benkler, Yochai, Rob Faris, and Hal Roberts. *Network Propaganda: Manipulation, Disinformation, and Radicalization in American Politics*. New York: Oxford University Press, 2018.

Bennett, W. Lance, and Steven Livingston. 'The Disinformation Order: Disruptive Communication and the Decline of Democratic Institutions.' *European Journal of Communication* 33, no. 2 (April 2018). https://doi.org/10.1177/0267323118760317.

Beran, Dale. 'The Return of Anonymous.' *The Atlantic*, August 11, 2020. https://www.theatlantic.com/technology/archive/2020/08/hacker-group-anonymous-returns/615058/.

Berdal, Mats R. *Building Peace after War*. Adelphi 407. London: Routledge, for the International Institute for Strategic Studies, 2009.

Berdal, Mats R. *Disarmament and Demobilisation after Civil Wars: Arms, Soldiers and the Termination of Armed Conflicts*. Adelphi Paper 303. Oxford: Oxford University Press for the International Institute for Strategic Studies, 1996.

Berdal, Mats R. 'How "New" Are "New Wars"? Global Economic Change and the Study of Civil War.' *Global Governance* 9, no. 4 (2003).

Berdal, Mats R. 'The State of UN Peacekeeping: Lessons from Congo.' *Journal of Strategic Studies* 41, no. 5 (July 29, 2018): 721–50. https://doi.org/10.1080/01402390.2016.1215307.

Berdal, Mats R, and David Keen. 'The Political Economy of Protectorates and "Post-Conflict" Intervention.' In *The New Protectorates: International Tutelage and the Making of Liberal States*, edited by James Mayall and Ricardo Soares de Oliveira, 221–40. London: Hurst Publishers, 2011.

Berdal, Mats R, and David H. Ucko. 'Introduction: The Political Reintegration of Armed Groups after War.' In *Reintegrating Armed Groups after Conflict: Politics, Violence and Transition*, edited by Mats R. Berdal and David H. Ucko, 1–9. Abingdon: Routledge, 2009.

Berdal, Mats R, and David H. Ucko. 'The Use of Force in UN Peacekeeping Operations: Problems and Prospects.' *RUSI Journal* 160, no. 1 (March 13, 2015): 6–12.

Berdal, Mats R, and Dominik Zaum. 'Power after Peace.' In *Political Economy of Statebuilding: Power after Peace*, edited by Mats R. Berdal and Dominik Zaum, 1–14. Routledge Studies in Intervention and Statebuilding. New York: Routledge, 2013.

Berger, J. M. 'The Alt-Right Twitter Census: Defining and Describing the Audience for Alt-Right Content on Twitter.' VOX-Pol, 2018.

Berger, J. M. 'Making CVE Work: A Focused Approach Based on Process Disruption.' *International Center for Counter-terrorism, The Hague* 7, no. 5 (May 26, 2016).

Berger, J. M. 'Nazis vs. ISIS on Twitter: A Comparative Study of White Nationalist and ISIS Online Social Media Networks.' George Washington University Program on Extremism, September 2016. https://extremism.gwu.edu/sites/g/files/zaxdzs2191/f/downloads/Nazis%20v.%20ISIS.pdf.

Berger, J. M., and Jonathon Morgan. 'The ISIS Twitter Census: Defining and Describing the Population of ISIS Supporters on Twitter.' Analysis Paper, The Brookings Project on US Relations with the Islamic World, Center for Middle East Policy, Brookings, March 2015.

Berger, J. M., and Heather Perez. 'The Islamic State's Diminishing Returns on Twitter: How Suspensions Are Limiting the Social Networks of English-Speaking ISIS Supporters.' Occasional Paper, George Washington University Program on Extremism, February 2016.

Bernstein, Maxine. 'Head of Oregon's FBI: Bureau Doesn't Designate Proud Boys as Extremist Group.' *The Oregonian*, December 4, 2018, sec. Crime. https://www.oregonlive.com/crime/2018/12/head-of-oregons-fbi-bureau-doesnt-designate-proud-boys-as-extremist-group.html.

Bernstein, Michael S., Andrés Monroy-Hernández, Drew Harry, Paul André, Katrina Panovich, and Greg Vargas. '4chan and /b/: An Analysis of Anonymity and Ephemerality in a Large Online Community.' In *Proceedings of the Fifth International Conference on Weblogs and Social Media*, 8. Barcelona, Spain, 2011.

Berti, Benedetta. *Armed Political Organizations: From Conflict to Integration*. Baltimore: Johns Hopkins University Press, 2013.

Besaw, Clayton. 'Election Violence Spiked Worldwide in 2020: Will This Year Be Better?' *The Conversation*, February 18, 2021. http://

theconversation.com/election-violence-spiked-worldwide-in-2020-will-this-year-be-better-153975.

Bickert, Monika, and Brian Fishman. 'Hard Questions: Are We Winning the War on Terrorism Online?' Facebook (blog), November 28, 2017. https://about.fb.com/news/2017/11/hard-questions-are-we-winning-the-war-on-terrorism-online/.

Biden, Joseph R. 'Interim National Security Strategic Guidance.' The White House, Washington, DC, March 2021.

Biermann, Kai, Luisa Hommerich, Yassin Musharbash, and Karsten Polke-Majewski. 'Anschlag in Halle: Attentäter mordete aus Judenhass.' Die Zeit, October 9, 2019, sec. Gesellschaft. https://www.zeit.de/gesellschaft/zeitgeschehen/2019-10/anschlag-halle-helmkamera-stream-einzeltaeter.

Bipartisan Policy Center. 'Digital Counterterrorism: Fighting Jihadists Online.' Bipartisan Policy Center, Washington, DC, March 2018.

Bjola, Corneliu, and Krysianna Papadakis. 'Digital Propaganda, Counterpublics and the Disruption of the Public Sphere: The Finnish Approach to Building Digital Resilience.' Cambridge Review of International Affairs 33, no. 5 (September 2, 2020): 638–66. https://doi.org/10.1080/09557571.2019.1704221.

Black, Jeremy. Rethinking Military History. London: Routledge, 2004.

Blank, Stephen. 'Imperial Strategies: Russia's Exploitation of Ethnic Issues and Policy in the Middle East.' In Russia in the Middle East, edited by Theodore Karasik and Stephen Blank, 154–82. Washington, DC: Jamestown Foundation, 2018.

Blinder, Alan. 'Suspect in Charlottesville Attack Had Displayed Troubling Behavior.' New York Times, August 13, 2017.

Blout, Emily, and Patrick Burkart. 'White Supremacist Terrorism in Charlottesville: Reconstructing "Unite the Right."' Studies in Conflict and Terrorism, January 4, 2021, 1–22. https://doi.org/10.1080/1057610X.2020.1862850.

Bøås, Morten. 'Crime, Coping, and Resistance in the Mali-Sahel Periphery.' African Security 8, no. 4 (October 2, 2015): 299–319. https://doi.org/10.1080/19392206.2015.1100506.

Bob, Clifford. The Marketing of Rebellion: Insurgents, Media, and International Activism. Cambridge Studies in Contentious Politics. Cambridge: Cambridge University Press, 2005.

Boege, Volker, Anne Brown, Kevin Clements, and Anna Nolan. 'On Hybrid Political Orders and Emerging States: What Is Failing—States in the Global South or Research and Politics in the West?' In Building Peace in the Absence of States: Challenging the Discourse on State Failure, edited by Martina Fischer and Beatrix Schmelzle, 15–36. Berghof Handbook Dialogue Series 8. Berlin: Berghof Forschungszentrum für Konstruktive Konfliktbearbeitung, 2009.

Boeke, Sergei, and Bart Schuurman. 'Operation "Serval": A Strategic Analysis of the French Intervention in Mali, 2013–2014.' *Journal of Strategic Studies* 38, no. 6 (September 19, 2015): 801–25. https://doi.org/10.1080/01402390.2015.1045494.

Bohara, Rameswor. 'An Armless Army.' *Nepali Times*, April 26, 2007.

Bonin, Robson. 'Comando Vermelho vira preocupação do governo Bolsonaro—entenda.' *Veja*, sec. Radar. Accessed September 29, 2020. https://veja.abril.com.br/blog/radar/faccao-criminosa-importa-mercenarios-para-o-rio-de-janeiro/.

Bourne, Angela K., and Fernando Casal Bértoa. 'Mapping "Militant Democracy": Variation in Party Ban Practices in European Democracies (1945–2015).' *European Constitutional Law Review* 13, no. 2 (June 2017): 221–47. https://doi.org/10.1017/S1574019617000098.

Bouzis, Kathleen. 'Countering the Islamic State: U.S. Counterterrorism Measures.' *Studies in Conflict & Terrorism* 38, no. 10 (2015): 885-897. https://www.tandfonline.com/doi/pdf/10.1080/1057610X.2015.1046302.

Bowden, Mark. *Killing Pablo: The Hunt for the World's Greatest Outlaw.* New York: Penguin, 2001.

Bowers, Christopher O. 'Future Megacity Operations: Lessons from Sadr City.' *Military Review*, June 2015, 8–16.

Boyd, Danah. 'Did Media Literacy Backfire?' *Medium* (blog), March 16, 2018. https://points.datasociety.net/did-media-literacy-backfire-7418c084d88d.

Boyd, Danah. 'You Think You Want Media Literacy … Do You?' *Medium*, March 16, 2018. https://points.datasociety.net/you-think-you-want-media-literacy-do-you-7cad6af18ec2.

Bracher, Karl Dietrich. *The German Dictatorship: The Origins, Structure and Effects of National Socialism.* Translated by Jean Steinberg. New York: Praeger Publishers, 1971.

Brachman, Jarret. *Global Jihadism: Theory and Practice.* New York: Routledge, 2009.

Braddock, Kurt. 'Vaccinating against Hate: Using Attitudinal Inoculation to Confer Resistance to Persuasion by Extremist Propaganda.' *Terrorism and Political Violence*, November 25, 2019, 1–23. https://doi.org/10.1080/09546553.2019.1693370.

Brady, William J., Julian A. Wills, John T. Jost, Joshua A. Tucker, and Jay J. van Bavel. 'Emotion Shapes the Diffusion of Moralized Content in Social

Networks.' *Proceedings of the National Academy of Sciences* 114, no. 28 (July 11, 2017): 7313–18. https://doi.org/10.1073/pnas.1618923114.

Brancati, Dawn. 'Democratic Authoritarianism: Origins and Effects.' *Annual Review of Political Science* 17, no. 1 (May 11, 2014): 313–26. https://doi.org/10.1146/annurev-polisci-052013-115248.

Brandenburg v. Ohio (US Supreme Court, June 9, 1969).

Brands, Hal. 'Criminal Fiefdoms in Latin America: Understanding the Problem of Alternatively Governed Spaces.' Western Hemisphere Security Analysis Center, Applied Research Center, Florida International University, Miami, 2010.

Brannon, Valerie C. 'Free Speech and the Regulation of Social Media Content.' Congressional Research Service, March 27, 2019.

Brashier, Nadia M., and Elizabeth J. Marsh. 'Judging Truth.' *Annual Review of Psychology* 71, no. 1 (January 4, 2020): 499–515. https://doi.org/10.1146/annurev-psych-010419-050807.

Brenan, Megan. 'Americans Remain Distrustful of Mass Media.' Gallup, September 30, 2020. https://news.gallup.com/poll/321116/americans-remain-distrustful-mass-media.aspx.

Briggs, Rachel, and Sebastien Feve. 'Review of Programs to Counter Narratives of Violent Extremism.' Institute for Strategic Dialogue, London, 2013.

Brittain, James J. *Revolutionary Social Change in Colombia: The Origin and Direction of the FARC-EP*. London: Pluto Press; New York: Palgrave Macmillan, 2010.

Brown, Alison, and Saeed Ahmed. 'Local Government Dissolution in Karachi: Chasm or Catalyst?' *Third World Thematics: A TWQ Journal* 1, no. 6 (November 2016): 879–97. https://doi.org/10.1080/23802014.2016.1315318.

Brown, Frances Z. 'The U.S. Surge and Afghan Local Governance.' Special Report, United States Institute of Peace, Washington, DC, September 2012. https://www.usip.org/publications/2012/09/us-surge-and-afghan-local-governance.

Buchhandler-Raphael, Michal. 'Overcriminalizing Speech.' *Cardozo Law Review* 36 (January 1, 2015): 1667–737.

Bull, Hedley. *The Anarchical Society: A Study of Order in World Politics*. London: Macmillan, 1977.

Bulos, Nabih. 'Basra Was Once a Jewel of a City. Now It's a Symbol of What's Wrong in Iraq.' *Los Angeles Times*, June 17, 2018, sec. World & Nation. https://www.latimes.com/world/la-fg-iraq-basra-20180617-story.html.

Bump, Philip. 'Biden's Targeting of Racist Extremism Is Being Portrayed as an Attack on the Right Itself.' *Washington Post*, January 21, 2021, sec.

Analysis. https://www.washingtonpost.com/politics/2021/01/21/bidens-targeting-racist-extremism-is-being-portrayed-an-attack-right-itself/.

Bunker, Robert J. *Old and New Insurgency Forms*. Carlisle, PA: Strategic Studies Institute and US Army War College Press, 2016.

Burke, Jason. *The New Threat: The Past, Present, and Future of Islamic Militancy*. New York: New Press, 2015.

Business Wire. 'Fox News Channel Finishes 2018 as Most Watched Cable Network in Total Day and Primetime for Third Consecutive Year and Notches Highest-Rated Primetime Ever.' December 12, 2018. https://www.businesswire.com/news/home/20181212005768/en/FOX-News-Channel-Finishes-2018-as-Most-Watched-Cable-Network-in-Total-Day-Primetime-for-Third-Consecutive-Year-and-Notches-Highest-Rated-Primetime-Ever.

Byman, Daniel L. 'Should We Treat Domestic Terrorists the Way We Treat ISIS? What Works—and What Doesn't.' Brookings, October 3, 2017. https://www.brookings.edu/articles/should-we-treat-domestic-terrorists-the-way-we-treat-isis-what-works-and-what-doesnt/.

Byman, Daniel L., Peter Chalk, Bruce Hoffman, William Rosenau, and David Brannan. *Trends in Outside Support for Insurgent Movements*. Santa Monica, CA: RAND Corporation, 2001.

Cano, Ignácio. *Os donos do morro*. Rio de Janeiro: Forum Brasileiro de Segurança Publica, May 2012.

Capoccia, Giovanni. *Defending Democracy: Reactions to Extremism in Interwar Europe*. Baltimore: Johns Hopkins University Press, 2005.

Carboni, Andrea, and James Moody. 'Between the Cracks: Actor Fragmentation and Local Conflict Systems in the Libyan Civil War.' *Small Wars and Insurgencies* 29, no. 3 (May 4, 2018): 456–90. https://doi.org/10.1080/09592318.2018.1455318.

Castaño, Carlos, and Mauricio Aranguren Molina. *Mi confesión: Carlos Castaño revela sus secretos*. Bogotá: Editorial La Oveja Negra, 2001.

Castells, Manuel. *The Power of Identity*. 2nd ed. The Information Age: Economy, Society, and Culture. Malden, MA: Wiley-Blackwell, 2010.

Cavatorta, Francesco, and Fabio Merone. 'Moderation through Exclusion? The Journey of the Tunisian *Ennahda* from Fundamentalist to Conservative Party.' *Democratization* 20, no. 5 (August 2013): 857–75. https://doi.org/10.1080/13510347.2013.801255.

CBS News. 'Glenn Beck: Obama Is a Racist.' July 29, 2009. https://www.cbsnews.com/news/glenn-beck-obama-is-a-racist/.

CDDRL, Stanford University. *Ignacio Cano, Armed Violence in Rio de Janeiro*. 2011. https://www.youtube.com/watch?v=XBVK1oMafVk.

CDDRL, Stanford University. *Jailson Silva, Towards a New Paradigm of Public Policy in Rio's Favelas*. 2014. https://www.youtube.com/watch?v=Oyl1nI1TRaA.

CDDRL, Stanford University. *Mariano Beltrame, Secretary of Security, Rio de Janeiro, Brazil*. 2015. https://www.youtube.com/watch?v=kwMvwiFX47M&feature=youtu.be.

CEJIL. 'Situation of Prison Overcrowding in El Salvador Denounced before the IACHR.' Center for Justice and International Law, March 20, 2015. https://cejil.org/en/situation-prison-overcrowding-salvador-denounced-iachr.

Cengic, Imelda. 'Brazil Cracks Down on Gangs and Corrupt Government Agents.' OCCRP: Organized Crime and Corruption Reporting Project, August 16, 2019. https://www.occrp.org/en/daily/10493-brazil-cracks-down-on-gangs-and-corrupt-government-agents.

Center for Civilians in Conflict. 'Civilian Perceptions of theYan Gora (CJTF) in Borno State, Nigeria.' July 2018. https://chitrasudhanagarajan.files.wordpress.com/2018/07/civilian-perceptions-of-the-yan-gora.pdf.

Center on Extremism. 'New Hate and Old:The Changing Face ofAmerican White Supremacy.' ADL, September 2018.

Chandrasekharan, Eshwar, Umashanthi Pavalanathan, Anirudh Srinivasan, Adam Glynn, Jacob Eisenstein, and Eric Gilbert. 'You Can't Stay Here: The Efficacy of Reddit's 2015 Ban Examined through Hate Speech.' *Proceedings of the ACM on Human-Computer Interaction* 31, no. 3 (December 6, 2017): 1–22. https://doi.org/10.1145/3134666.

Cheng, Christine. *Extralegal Groups in Post-conflict Liberia: How Trade Makes the State*. NewYork: Oxford University Press, 2018.

Childers, Thomas, and Eugene Weiss. 'Political Violence and the Limits of National Socialist Mass Mobilization.' *German Studies Review* 13, no. 3 (October 1990): 481–98.

Chin, Warren. 'Northern Ireland (1976–1994): Police Primacy.' In *Network Centric Operations (NCO) Case Study: The British Approach to Low-Intensity Operations: Part 2*, 1.0., 101–48. Transformation Case Study Series. Washington, DC: Department of Defense, 2007.

Christchurch Call to Eliminate Terrorist and Violent Extremism. 'The Call.' Accessed April 29, 2021. https://www.christchurchcall.com/call.html.

CIA, Directorate of Intelligence. 'Foreign and Domestic Influences on the Colombian Communist Party, 1957 – August 1966.' Intelligence Report, Central Intelligence Agency, March 1967.

Citron, Danielle, and Benjamin Wittes. 'The Internet Will Not Break: Denying Bad Samaritans § 230 Immunity.' *Fordham Law Review* 86, no. 2 (November 1, 2017).

Clark, Simon. 'How White Supremacy Returned to Mainstream Politics.' Center for American Progress, July 1, 2020. https://www.americanprogress.org/issues/security/reports/2020/07/01/482414/white-supremacy-returned-mainstream-politics/.

Clausen, Maria-Louise. 'Competing for Control over the State: The Case of Yemen.' *Small Wars and Insurgencies* 29, no. 3 (May 4, 2018): 560–78. https://doi.org/10.1080/09592318.2018.1455792.

Clausewitz, Carl von. *On War*. Edited by Michael Eliot Howard and Peter Paret. Princeton, NJ: Princeton University Press, 1989.

CNN. 'Transcript: President Obama's Speech on Combating ISIS.' September 10, 2014. http://www.cnn.com/2014/09/10/politics/transcript-obama-syria-isis-speech/index.html.

Cockayne, James. 'The Futility of Force? Strategic Lessons for Dealing with Unconventional Armed Groups from the UN's War on Haiti's Gangs.' *Journal of Strategic Studies* 37, no. 5 (July 29, 2014): 736–69. https://doi.org/10.1080/01402390.2014.901911.

Cockayne, James. *Hidden Power: The Strategic Logic of Organized Crime*. New York: Oxford University Press, 2016.

Coker, Christopher. *Future War*. Malden, MA: Polity Press, 2015.

Coker, Christopher. 'War and Culture: Cultural Ruthlessness and the War against Terror.' *Australian Army Journal* III, no. 1 (Summer 2005–2006): 145–63.

Colby, Sandra L., and Jennifer M. Ortman. 'Projections of the Size and Composition of the U.S. Population: 2014 to 2060.' Current Population Reports, United States Census Bureau, March 2015.

Coles, Isabel, and Ghassan Adnan. 'Iraq Kingmaker's Daunting Task: Lift the Poor of Sadr City.' *Wall Street Journal*, June 3, 2018, sec. World. https://www.wsj.com/articles/iraq-kingmakers-daunting-task-lift-the-poor-of-sadr-city-1528023600.

Coll, Steve. *Directorate S: The C.I.A. and America's Secret Wars in Afghanistan and Pakistan, 2001–2016*. New York: Penguin Press, 2018.

Collins, Randall. *Violence: A Micro-sociological Theory*. Princeton, NJ: Princeton University Press, 2008.

Colombo Telegraph. 'Military Occupying over 96% Land Belonging to Tamils: BTF.' April 19, 2016. https://www.colombotelegraph.com/index.php/military-occupying-over-96-land-belonging-to-tamils-btf/.

Columbi, Emilia, and Austin C. Doctor. 'Foreign Fighters and the Trajectory of Violence in Northern Mozambique.' *War on the Rocks*, April 13, 2021. https://warontherocks.com/2021/04/foreign-fighters-and-the-trajectory-of-violence-in-northern-mozambique/.

Confessore, Nicholas, and Gabriel J. X. Dance. 'Battling Fake Accounts, Twitter to Slash Millions of Followers.' *New York Times*, July 13, 2018, sec. Technology. https://www.nytimes.com/2018/07/11/technology/twitter-fake-followers.html.

Conway, Maura. 'Routing the Extreme Right: Challenges for Social Media Platforms.' *RUSI Journal* 165, no. 1 (January 2, 2020): 108–13. https://doi.org/10.1080/03071847.2020.1727157.

Conway, Maura, Moign Khawaja, Suraj Lakhani, and Jeremy Reffin. 'A Snapshot of the Syrian Jihadi Online Ecology: Differential Disruption, Community Strength, and Preferred Other Platforms.' *Studies in Conflict and Terrorism*, January 4, 2021: 1–17. https://doi.org/10.1080/1057610X.2020.1866736.

Conway, Maura, Moign Khawaja, Suraj Lakhani, Jeremy Reffin, Andrew Robertson, and David Weir. 'Disrupting Daesh: Measuring Takedown of Online Terrorist Material and Its Impacts.' *Studies in Conflict and Terrorism* 42, no. 1–2 (February 2019): 141–60. https://doi.org/10.1080/1057610X.2018.1513984.

Cooper, Paul. 'Lulzsec Leader Turned Informant Helped FBI Foil 300 Cyber Attacks.' ITProPortal, May 27, 2014. https://www.itproportal.com/2014/05/27/lulzsec-leader-turned-informant-helped-fbi-foil-300-cyber-attacks/.

Corum, James S. 'Development of Modern Counterinsurgency Theory and Doctrine.' In *The Ashgate Research Companion to Modern Warfare*, edited by John Buckley and George Kassimeris. London: Routledge, 2010.

Costello, John, and Peter Mattis. 'Electronic Warfare and the Renaissance of Chinese Informational Operations.' In *China's Evolving Military Strategy*, edited by Joe McReynolds. Washington, DC: Jamestown Foundation, 2017.

Council of Europe. 'Convention on the Prevention of Terrorism – 16.V.2005.' Treaty Series, Council of Europe, 2005.

Council of the European Union. 'Consolidated Text: Council Common Position of 27 December 2001 on the Application of Specific Measures to Combat Terrorism.' Pub. L. no. 2001/931/CFSP, 2017. http://data.europa.eu/eli/compos/2001/931/2017-11-15.

Council on Foreign Relations. 'The Eastern Congo.' CFR InfoGuide Presentation, n.d. https://on.cfr.org/21SfJBh.

Council on Hemispheric Affairs (blog). 'Gangs Are the New Law in Urban Trinidad & Tobago.' October 11, 2013. https://www.coha.org/gangs-are-the-new-law-in-urban-trinidad-and-tobago/.

Counter Extremism Project. 'Extremist Content Online: ISIS Encouraging Violence with "Available Means."' August 4, 2020. https://www.

counterextremism.com/press/extremist-content-online-isis-encouraging-violence-%E2%80%98available-means%E2%80%99.

Cruickshank, Paul, and Mohannad Hage Ali. 'Abu Musab Al Suri: Architect of the New Al Qaeda.' *Studies in Conflict and Terrorism* 30, no. 1 (January 2007): 1–14. https://doi.org/10.1080/10576100601049928.

Cruz, José Miguel. 'Government Responses and the Dark Side of Gang Suppression in Central America.' In *Maras: Gang Violence and Security in Central America*, edited by Thomas C. Bruneau, Lucía Dammert, and Elizabeth Skinner, 137–58. Austin, TX: University of Texas Press, 2011.

Cruz, José Miguel, and Angélica Durán-Martínez. 'Hiding Violence to Deal with the State: Criminal Pacts in El Salvador and Medellin.' *Journal of Peace Research* 53, no. 2 (2016): 197–210.

Cruz, José Miguel, Jonathan D. Rosen, Luis Enrique Amaya, and Yulia Vorobyeva. 'The New Face of Street Gangs: The Gang Phenomenon in El Salvador.' Florida International University, 2017.

Dafaure, Maxime. 'The "Great Meme War": The Alt-Right and Its Multifarious Enemies.' *Angles*, no. 10 (April 1, 2020). https://doi.org/10.4000/angles.369.

Daily Star. 'Riot Police Called In to Halt Nepali Student Violence.' August 16, 2007. https://www.thedailystar.net/news-detail-194.

Daisley, Stephen. 'Why Putin Wants Scottish Independence.' *The Spectator*, July 22, 2020. https://www.spectator.co.uk/article/why-putin-wants-scottish-independence.

Daniels, Jessie. 'The Algorithmic Rise of the "Alt-Right."' *Contexts* 17, no. 1 (February 2018): 60–65. https://doi.org/10.1177/1536504218766547.

Darling, Juanita. *Latin America, Media, and Revolution: Communication in Modern Mesoamerica.* Palgrave Macmillan Series in International Political Communication. New York: Palgrave Macmillan, 2008.

Davies, James C. 'Toward a Theory of Revolution.' *American Sociological Review* 27, no. 1 (February 1962): 5–19.

Davies, Thomas. 'Civil Society History VI: Early and Mid 20th Century.' In *International Encyclopedia of Civil Society*, edited by Helmut K. Anheier, Stefan Toepler, and Regina List. Springer Reference. New York: Springer, 2010.

Davis, Charles. '30% of Republicans Have "Favorable" View of QAnon Conspiracy Theory, YouGov Poll Finds.' *Business Insider.* January 13, 2021. https://www.businessinsider.com/30-of-republicans-have-favorable-view-of-qanon-conspiracy-theory-poll-2021-1.

Davis, S. Peter. 'How Alt-Right Trolls Keep Tricking the Mainstream Media.' Cracked.com, February 28, 2019. https://www.cracked.com/blog/how-alt-right-trolls-keep-tricking-mainstream-media/.

de Zeeuw, Jeroen and Georg Frerks, Proceedings, Seminar on the Political Economy of Internal Conflict, 22 November 2000, Netherlands Institute of International Relations (Clingendael), December 2000.

Della Porta, Donatella. *Clandestine Political Violence*. New York: Cambridge University Press, 2013. https://doi.org/10.1017/CBO9781139043144.

Della Porta, Donatella. *Social Movements, Political Violence, and the State: A Comparative Analysis of Italy and Germany*. Cambridge: Cambridge University Press, 2006.

Demirjian, Karoun. 'Putin Denies Russian Troops Are in Ukraine, Decrees Certain Deaths Secret.' *Washington Post*, May 28, 2015, sec. World. https://www.washingtonpost.com/world/putin-denies-russian-troops-are-in-ukraine-decrees-certain-deaths-secret/2015/05/28/9bb15092-0543-11e5-93f4-f24d4af7f97d_story.html.

Desilver, Drew. 'Coups Have Become Less Common Worldwide.' *Pew Research Center* (blog), November 17, 2017. https://www.pewresearch.org/fact-tank/2017/11/17/egypts-coup-is-first-in-2013-as-takeovers-become-less-common-worldwide/.

Desilver, Drew. 'Despite Global Concerns about Democracy, More than Half of Countries Are Democratic.' FactTank, Pew Research Center, May 14, 2019. https://www.pewresearch.org/fact-tank/2019/05/14/more-than-half-of-countries-are-democratic/.

Deutsche Welle. 'Macron Anti-terror Law Replaces French State of Emergency.' November 1, 2017. https://www.dw.com/en/macron-anti-terror-law-replaces-french-state-of-emergency/a-41191947.

Devereaux, Ryan. 'How the FBI Increased Its Power after 9/11 and Helped Put Trump in Office.' *The Intercept*, September 14, 2019. https://theintercept.com/2019/09/14/fbi-mike-german-book/.

Devermont, Judd. 'Politics at the Heart of the Crisis in the Sahel.' CSIS Briefs, Center for Strategic and International Studies, December 2019. https://csis-website-prod.s3.amazonaws.com/s3fs-public/publication/191206_Devermont_SahelCrisis_layout_v5.pdf.

Diamond, Larry. *Squandered Victory: The American Occupation and the Bungled Effort to Bring Democracy to Iraq*. New York: Henry Holt and Company, 2013. http://rbdigital.oneclickdigital.com.

Dickson, Peter. 'One Million Passports: Putin has Weaponized Citizenship in Occupied Eastern Ukraine.' *UkraineAlert*, Atlantic Council, June 17, 2020. https://www.atlanticcouncil.org/blogs/ukrainealert/

one-million-passports-putin-has-weaponized-citizenship-in-occupied-eastern-ukraine/.

DiResta, Renée. 'Right-Wing Social Media Finalizes Its Divorce from Reality.' *The Atlantic*, November 23, 2020. https://www.theatlantic.com/ideas/archive/2020/11/right-wing-social-media-finalizes-its-divorce-reality/617177/.

Doctor, Austin C. 'The Looming Influx of Foreign Fighters in Sub-Saharan Africa.' *War on the Rocks*, August 18, 2020. https://warontherocks.com/2020/08/the-looming-influx-of-foreign-fighters-in-sub-saharan-africa/.

Doctorow, Cory. 'Three Kinds of Propaganda, and What to Do about Them.' *Boing Boing* (blog), February 25, 2017. https://boingboing.net/2017/02/25/counternarratives-not-fact-che.html.

Dodge, Toby. 'Securing America's Interest in Iraq: The Remaining Options.' Pub. L. no. S. HRG 110–153, Committee on Foreign Relations, United States Senate, 2007.

Dodge, Toby. 'The Iraq Transition: Civil War or Civil Society?' Testimony before the Committee on Foreign Relations, Washington, DC, April 20, 2004.

Donais, Timothy, and Geoff Burt. 'Vertically Integrated Peace Building and Community Violence in Haiti.' CIGI Papers, Center for International Governance Innovation, Waterloo, Ontario, February 2014.

Dorn, A. Walter. 'Intelligence-Led Peacekeeping: The United Nations Stabilization Mission in Haiti (MINUSTAH), 2006–07.' *Intelligence and National Security* 24, no. 6 (December 2009): 805–35. https://doi.org/10.1080/02684520903320410.

Dowdney, Luke. *Children of the Drug Trade: A Case Study of Children in Organised Armed Violence in Rio de Janeiro*. Rio de Janeiro: 7Letras, 2003.

Doyle, Damian, and Tristan Dunning. 'Recognizing Fragmented Authority: Towards a Post-Westphalian Security Order in Iraq.' *Small Wars and Insurgencies* 29, no. 3 (May 4, 2018): 537–59. https://doi.org/10.1080/09592318.2018.1455324.

Droogan, Julian, and Shane Peattie. 'Reading Jihad: Mapping the Shifting Themes of *Inspire* Magazine.' *Terrorism and Political Violence* 30, no. 4 (July 4, 2018): 684–717. https://doi.org/10.1080/09546553.2016.1211527.

Droz-Vincent, Philippe. 'Competitive Statehood in Libya: Governing Differently a Specific Setting or Deconstructing Its Weak Sovereign State with a Fateful Drift toward Chaos?' *Small Wars and Insurgencies* 29, no. 3 (May 4, 2018): 434–55. https://doi.org/10.1080/09592318.2018.1455322.

Dudley, Steven S. *Walking Ghosts: Murder and Guerrilla Politics in Colombia.* New York: Routledge, 2006.

Dunlap, Charles J., Jr. 'Law and Military Interventions: Preserving Humanitarian Values in 21st Century Conflicts.' Carr Center for Human Rights Policy, Harvard Kennedy School, 2001.

Dunn, Elizabeth Cullen, and Michael S. Bobick. 'The Empire Strikes Back: War without War and Occupation without Occupation in the Russian Sphere of Influence.' *American Ethnologist* 41, no. 3 (August 2014): 405–13. https://doi.org/10.1111/amet.12086.

Dunning, Thad. 'Fighting and Voting: Violent Conflict and Electoral Politics.' *Journal of Conflict Resolution* 55, no. 3 (June 2011): 327–39. https://doi.org/10.1177/0022002711400861.

Durkheim, Emile. *The Division of Labor in Society.* New York: Free Press, 2014.

Durkheim, Emile. *Suicide; A Study in Sociology.* New York: Free Press, 1951.

Dwoskin, Elizabeth, and Craig Timberg. 'Misinformation Dropped Dramatically the Week after Twitter Banned Trump and Some Allies.' *Washington Post*, January 16, 2021, sec. Technology. https://www.washingtonpost.com/technology/2021/01/16/misinformation-trump-twitter/.

Dziedzic, Michael, and Robert M. Perito. 'Haiti: Confronting the Gangs of Port-au-Prince.' Special Report, United States Institute of Peace, Washington, DC, September 2008.

Eaton, Kent. 'The Downside of Decentralization: Armed Clientelism in Colombia.' *Security Studies* 15, no. 4 (October 2006): 533–62. https://doi.org/10.1080/09636410601188463.

Economist, The. 'The Bottom Line.' October 22, 2009. http://www.economist.com/the-americas/2009/10/22/the-bottom-line.

Economist, The. 'The Gulf of Guinea Is Now the World's Worst Piracy Hotspot.' June 29, 2019. http://www.economist.com/international/2019/06/29/the-gulf-of-guinea-is-now-the-worlds-worst-piracy-hotspot.

Economist, The. 'Mafias Run by Rogue Police Officers Are Terrorising Rio.' May 30, 2019.http://www.economist.com/the-americas/2019/05/30/mafias-run-by-rogue-police-officers-are-terrorising-rio.

Economist, The. 'Mixing the Modern and the Traditional.' July 26, 2014. https://www.economist.com/middle-east-and-africa/2014/07/26/mixing-the-modern-and-the-traditional.

Economist, The. 'The Peace Prize.' November 23, 2006. https://www.economist.com/asia/2006/11/23/the-peace-prize.

Economist, The. 'Shining Light on Latin America's Homicide Epidemic.' April 5, 2018. https://www.economist.com/news/briefing/21739954-latin-americas-violent-crime-and-ways-dealing-it-have-lessons-rest.

Edsall, Thomas B. 'White Riot.' *New York Times,* January 13, 2021, sec. Opinion. https://www.nytimes.com/2021/01/13/opinion/capitol-riot-white-grievance.html.

Egnell, Robert. 'A Western Insurgency in Afghanistan.' *Joint Force Quarterly* 70, no. 3 (2013): 8–14.

Eju! 'Un abogado dice que las FARC actuaron el 2003.' October 17, 2018, sec. Política. http://eju.tv/2008/10/un-abogado-dice-que-las-farc-actuaron-el-2003/.

Elgar, Frank J., and Nicole Aitken. 'Income Inequality, Trust and Homicide in 33 Countries.' *European Journal of Public Health* 21, no. 2 (April 2011): 241–46. https://doi.org/10.1093/eurpub/ckq068.

Elizondo, Gabriel. 'Bolivians Vote to "Decolonise Courts."' Al Jazeera, October 16, 2011, sec. Opinion. https://www.aljazeera.com/indepth/opinion/2011/10/201110169924243497.html.

Ellinas, Antonis A. 'The Rise of Golden Dawn: The New Face of the Far Right in Greece.' *South European Society and Politics* 18, no. 4 (December 2013): 543–65. https://doi.org/10.1080/13608746.2013.782838.

El País. 'Los consejos comunales, la mejor vitrina que tuvo Uribe.' July 4, 2010. https://www.elpais.com.co/colombia/los-consejos-comunales-la-mejor-vitrina-que-tuvo-uribe.html.

English, Richard. *Armed Struggle: The History of the IRA.* London: Pan Macmillan, 2008.

ERR News. 'Study: Estonians Have Higher Trust in Government than Latvians, Lithuanians.' December 29, 2020, sec. News. https://news.err.ee/1221847/study-estonians-have-higher-trust-in-government-than-latvians-lithuanians.

Estes, Adam Clark. 'How Neo-Nazis Used the Internet to Instigate a Right-Wing Extremist Crisis.' *Vox,* February 2, 2021. https://www.vox.com/recode/22256387/facebook-telegram-qanon-proud-boys-alt-right-hate-groups.

Euronews. 'Armed Toddlers Kill Twice as Many Americans Each Year as Terrorists.' January 31, 2017, sec. news_news. https://www.euronews.com/2017/01/31/armed-toddlers-kill-twice-as-many-americans-each-year-than-terrorists.

European Parliament, Committee on Civil Liberties, Justice and Home Affairs, Directorate General for Internal Policies of the Union. 'EU and Member States' Policies and Laws on Persons Suspected of Terrorism-Related Crimes.' Study, European Parliament, December 2017.

Evans, Martin. 'Facebook Accused of Introducing Extremists to One Another through "Suggested Friends" Feature.' *The Telegraph*, May 5, 2018. https://www.telegraph.co.uk/news/2018/05/05/facebook-accused-introducing-extremists-one-another-suggested/.

Evans, Robert, and Jason Wilson. 'The Boogaloo Movement Is Not What You Think.' *Bellingcat*, May 27, 2020. https://www.bellingcat.com/news/2020/05/27/the-boogaloo-movement-is-not-what-you-think/.

Fairfield, Tasha. *Private Wealth and Public Revenue in Latin America: Business Power and Tax Politics.* New York: Cambridge University Press, 2015.

Farah, Douglas. 'Into the Abyss: Bolivia under Evo Morales and the MAS.' International Assessment and Strategy Center, Alexandria, VA, June 18, 2009. http://www.offnews.info/downloads/20090618_IASCIntoTheAbyss061709.pdf.

Farah, Douglas, and Kathryn Babineau. 'The Evolution of MS 13 in El Salvador and Honduras.' *PRISM* 7, no. 2 (September 14, 2017): 59–73.

Farrell, Michael. 'We Have Now Established a Sort of Republican Veto.' *Magill*, June 30, 1983. https://magill.ie/archive/we-have-now-established-sort-republican-veto.

Farrell, Theo. 'Unbeatable: Social Resources, Military Adaptation, and the Afghan Taliban.' *Texas National Security Review* 1, no. 3 (May 2018): 58–75.

Farwell, James P. 'The Media Strategy of ISIS.' *Survival* 56, no. 6 (November 2, 2014): 49–55. https://doi.org/10.1080/00396338.2014.985436.

Fearon, James D., and David D. Laitin. 'Ethnicity, Insurgency, and Civil War.' *American Political Science Review* 97, no. 1 (February 2003): 75–90. https://doi.org/10.1017/S0003055403000534.

Feinberg, Andrew. 'Intelligence Officials Warn of What Comes Next after Pro-Trump Capitol Riots.' *The Independent*, January 7, 2021, sec. Voices. https://www.independent.co.uk/voices/capitol-riots-trump-dc-shooting-cia-b1783607.html.

Felbab-Brown, Vanda. 'Bargaining with the Devil to Avoid Hell? A Discussion Paper on Negotiations with Criminal Groups in Latin America and the Caribbean.' Institute for Integrated Transition, Barcelona, July 2020.

Felbab-Brown, Vanda. 'Conceptualizing Crime as Competition in State-Making and Designing an Effective Response.' *Security and Defense Studies Review* 10 (Spring–Summer 2010): 155–58.

Feldman, Brian. 'Inside /Pol/, the 4chan Politics Board Shouted Out in Minneapolis Gun Video.' *Intelligencer*, November 25, 2015. https://nymag.com/intelligencer/2015/11/inside-pol-4chans-racist-heart.html.

397

Fernando, Jude Lal. 'Negotiated Peace versus Victor's Peace: The Geopolitics of Peace and Conflict in Sri Lanka.' *Cambridge Review of International Affairs* 27, no. 2 (June 2014): 206–25. https://www. tandfonline.com/doi/abs/10.1080/09557571.2014.888540.

Feuer, Alan and Adam Goldman. 'Among Those Who Marched into the Capitol on Jan. 6: An F.B.I. Informant.' *New York Times*, September 25, 2021. https://www.nytimes.com/2021/09/25/us/politics/capitol-riot-fbi-informant.html.

Field, Antony. 'Ethics and Entrapment: Understanding Counterterrorism Stings.' *Terrorism and Political Violence* 31, no. 2 (March 4, 2019): 260–76. https://doi.org/10.1080/09546553.2016.1213721.

Filkins, Dexter. 'Afghan Offensive Is New War Model.' *New York Times*, February 12, 2010, sec. World. https://www.nytimes. com/2010/02/13/world/asia/13kabul.html.

Finn, John E. *Constitutions in Crisis: Political Violence and the Rule of Law*. New York: Oxford University Press, 1991.

Finn, John E. 'Electoral Regimes and the Proscription of Anti-democratic Parties.' *Terrorism and Political Violence* 12, nos. 3–4 (September 2000): 51–77. https://doi.org/10.1080/09546550008427570.

Fischer, Martina, and Beatrix Schmelzle, eds. *Building Peace in the Absence of States: Challenging the Discourse on State Failure*. Berghof Handbook Dialogue Series 8. Berlin: Berghof Forschungszentrum für Konstruktive Konfliktbearbeitung, 2009.

Fisher, Marc. 'From Memes to Race War: How Extremists Use Popular Culture to Lure Recruits.' *Washington Post*, April 30, 2021. https:// www.washingtonpost.com/nation/2021/04/30/extremists-recruiting-culture-community/.

Fishman, Brian. 'Crossroads: Counter-terrorism and the Internet.' *Texas National Security Review* 2, no. 2 (February 2019): 82–101. https://doi. org/10.26153/TSW/1942.

Fishstein, Paul, and Andrew Wilder. 'Winning Hearts and Minds? Examining the Relationship between Aid and Security in Afghanistan.' Feinstein International Center, Tufts University, Medford, MA, January 2012. http://fic.tufts.edu/assets/WinningHearts-Final.pdf.

Foundation for Partnership Initiatives in the Niger Delta. 'Niger Delta Annual Conflict Report: January to December 2020.' PIND, February 9, 2021.

Fox, Gregory H., and Georg Nolte. 'Intolerant Democracies.' *Harvard International Law Journal* 36, no. 1 (Winter 1995): 1–70.

Fox News. *Fox News Tucker Carlson: It's Okay to Be White Goes National*, 2017. https://www.youtube.com/watch?v=aYE_Q9gslVo.

Frampton, Martyn. 'The New Netwar: Countering Extremism Online.' Policy Exchange, London, 2017. https://policyexchange.org.uk/wp-content/uploads/2017/09/The-New-Netwar-1.pdf.

Frankovic, Kathy. 'Belief in Conspiracies Largely Depends on Political Identity.' YouGov, December 27, 2016. https://today.yougov.com/topics/politics/articles-reports/2016/12/27/belief-conspiracies-largely-depends-political-iden.

Fraser, Nancy. 'Rethinking the Public Sphere: A Contribution to the Critique of Actually Existing Democracy.' In *Habermas and the Public Sphere*, edited by Craig J. Calhoun, 109–42. Studies in Contemporary German Social Thought. Cambridge, MA: MIT Press, 1992.

Freear, Matt, and Andrew Glazzard. 'Preventive Communication: Emerging Lessons from Participative Approaches to Countering Violent Extremism in Kenya.' *RUSI Journal* 165, no. 1 (2020): 90–106.

Freeman, Mark, and Vanda Felbab-Brown. 'Negotiating with Violent Criminal Groups: Lessons and Guidelines from Global Practice.' Institute for Integrated Transition, Barcelona, March 2021.

French, David. 'The Price I've Paid for Opposing Donald Trump.' *National Review*, October 21, 2016. https://www.nationalreview.com/2016/10/donald-trump-alt-right-internet-abuse-never-trump-movement/.

French, David. 'The Problem Is Bigger than Trump.' *Time Magazine*, August 19, 2019.

Frenkel, Sheera. 'How the Storming of Capitol Hill Was Organized on Social Media.' *New York Times*, January 6, 2021, sec. U.S. https://www.nytimes.com/2021/01/06/us/politics/protesters-storm-capitol-hill-building.html.

Friedrich, Carl J. 'Defense of the Constitutional Order.' In *Studies in Federalism*, edited by Robert R. Bowie and Carl J. Friedrich, 676–711. Boston: Brown and Company, 1954.

Friesen, John, Lea Rausch, Peter F. Pelz, and Johannes Fürnkranz. 'Determining Factors for Slum Growth with Predictive Data Mining Methods.' *Urban Science* 2, no. 3 (September 2018). https://doi.org/10.3390/urbansci2030081.

Fürstenau, Marcel. 'Walter Lübcke: ein politischer Mord erschüttert Deutschland.' Deutsche Welle, June 2, 2020. https://www.dw.com/de/walter-l%C3%BCbcke-ein-politischer-mord-ersch%C3%BCttert-deutschland/a-53604759.

Gais, Hannah. 'The Alt-Right Comes to Washington.' *Washington Spectator*, December 6, 2016. https://washingtonspectator.org/npi-alt-right-dc/.

Galeotti, Mark. *Hybrid War or Gibridnaya Voina? Getting Russia's Non-linear Military Challenge Right*. Mayak Intelligence, Prague, 2016.

Galeotti, Mark. 'I'm Sorry for Creating the "Gerasimov Doctrine."' *Foreign Policy*, March 5, 2018. https://foreignpolicy.com/2018/03/05/im-sorry-for-creating-the-gerasimov-doctrine/.

Gall, Carlotta. *The Wrong Enemy: America in Afghanistan, 2001–2014*. Boston: Houghton Mifflin Harcourt, 2014.

Galliéni, Général. *Neuf ans à Madagascar*. Paris: Librairie Hachette, 1908.

Gamson, William A. *The Strategy of Social Protest*. Homewood, IL: Dorsey Press, 1990.

Gardell, Mattias. 'Crusader Dreams: Oslo 22/7, Islamophobia, and the Quest for a Monocultural Europe.' *Terrorism and Political Violence* 26 (2014): 129–55.

Gayer, Laurent. *Karachi: Ordered Disorder and the Struggle for the City*. New York: Oxford University Press, 2014.

Geddes, Barbara. 'Initiation of New Democratic Institutions in Eastern Europe and Latin America.' In *Institutional Design in New Democracies: Eastern Europe and Latin America*, edited by Arend Lijphart and Carlos H. Warisman. Boulder, CO: Westview Press, 1996.

Gerasimov, Valery. 'The Value of Science in Prediction.' *Military-Industrial Kurier*, no. 8 (476) (March 27, 2013). http://vpk-news.ru/sites/default/files/pdf/VPK_08_476.pdf.

Gerlach, Luther P. 'Protest Movements and the Construction of Risk.' In *The Social and Cultural Construction of Risk*, edited by B. B. Johnson and V. T. Covello, 103–45. Boston: D. Reidel, 1987.

Gerlach, Luther P, and Virginia H. Hine. *People, Power, Change: Movements of Social Transformation*. Indianapolis, IN: Bobbs-Merrill, 1970.

German, Michael. 'Behind the Lone Terrorist, a Pack Mentality.' *Washington Post*, June 5, 2005, sec. Opinions. https://www.washingtonpost.com/archive/opinions/2005/06/05/behind-the-lone-terrorist-a-pack-mentality/f9ed5bb8-f18b-429b-b146-1da91a2a37bb/.

German, Michael. 'Hidden in Plain Sight: Racism, White Supremacy, and Far-Right Militancy in Law Enforcement.' Research Report, Brennan Center for Justice, New York, August 27, 2020. https://www.brennancenter.org/our-work/research-reports/hidden-plain-sight-racism-white-supremacy-and-far-right-militancy-law.

German, Michael. 'The Rise of Domestic Terrorism in America.' US House of Representatives Committee on the Judiciary, 2021. https://docs.house.gov/meetings/JU/JU08/20210224/111227/HHRG-117-JU08-Wstate-GermanM-20210224.pdf.

German, Michael. 'Why New Laws Aren't Needed to Take Domestic Terrorism More Seriously.' *Just Security*, December 14, 2018. https://www.justsecurity.org/61876/laws-needed-domestic-terrorism/.

German, Michael, and Sara Robinson. 'Wrong Priorities on Fighting Terrorism.' Brennan Center for Justice, New York University School of Law, October 2018.

German Federal Constitutional Court. 'Entscheidungen: Kein Verbot der NPD wegen fehlender Anhaltspunkte für eine erfolgreiche Durchsetzung ihrer verfassungsfeindlichen Ziele.' January 17, 2017.

German Parliament. 'Bundestag beschließt Gesetz gegen strafbare Inhalte im Internet.' 2017. https://www.bundestag.de/dokumente/textarchiv/2017/kw26-de-netzwerkdurchsetzungsgesetz-513398.

Gestión. 'Los Ponchos Rojos, la milicia aymara que se planta como la 'retaguardi' de Bolivia.' December 16, 2019, sec. Internacional. https://gestion.pe/mundo/internacional/los-ponchos-rojos-la-milicia-aymara-que-se-planta-como-la-retaguardia-de-bolivia-noticia/.

Getmansky, Anna. 'You Can't Win If You Don't Fight: The Role of Regime Type in Counterinsurgency Outbreaks and Outcomes.' *Journal of Conflict Resolution* 57, no. 4 (August 2013): 709–34. https://doi.org/10.1177/0022002712449326.

Ghosh, Dipayan, and Ben Scott. '#Digitaldeceit: The Technology behind Precision Propaganda on the Internet.' New America and Shorenstein Center on Media, Politics and Public Policy, Harvard Kennedy School, January 2018.

Gilbert, David. 'Anonymous Declared War on Trump, and Then Disappeared.' *Vice*, November 28, 2016. https://www.vice.com/en/article/ywna4w/anonymous-declared-war-on-trump-and-then-disappeared.

Gill, K. P. S. 'Endgame in Punjab: 1988–1993.' *Faultlines* 1 (May 1999). https://www.satp.org/satporgtp/publication/faultlines/volume1/Fault1-kpstext.htm.

Gilman, Nils. 'The Collapse of Racial Liberalism.' *American Interest* 13, no. 5 (March 2, 2018). https://www.the-american-interest.com/2018/03/02/collapse-racial-liberalism/.

Gilman, Nils. 'The Twin Insurgency.' *American Interest* 9, no. 6 (2014): 3–11.

GIFCT. 'Global Internet Forum to Counter Terrorism.' Global Internet Forum to Counter Terrorism. Accessed April 29, 2021. https://gifct.org/about/.

Gobyn, Winne. 'From War to Peace: The Nepalese Maoists' Strategic and Ideological Thinking.' *Studies in Conflict and Terrorism* 32, no. 5 (May 2009): 420–38. https://doi.org/10.1080/10576100902831578.

Godwin, Ameh Comrade. 'Asari-Dokubo Establishes University in Benin Republic.' *Daily Post Nigeria*, October 11, 2013. https://dailypost. ng/2013/10/11/asari-dokubo-establishes-university-in-benin-republic/.

Golden-Timsar, Rebecca. 'Amnesty and New Violence in the Niger Delta.' *Forbes*, March 20, 2018. https://www.forbes.com/sites/ uhenergy/2018/03/20/amnesty-and-new-violence-in-the-niger-delta/.

Gollo, Luiz Augusto. 'Vigilante Groups in Brazil Trump Drug Gangs and Become Rio's New Authority.' *Brazzil*, November 11, 2009. https:// www.brazzil.com/23490-vigilante-groups-in-brazil-trump-drug-gangs-and-become-rio-s-new-authority/.

Goodwin, Matthew J. *Right Response: Understanding and Countering Populist Extremism in Europe*. London: Chatham House, 2012.

Gramsci, Antonio. *Prison Notebooks*. Volume 3. trans. J. A. Buttigieg. New York: Columbia University Press, 2007.

Grare, Frederic. 'Balochistan: The State versus the Nation.' Carnegie Papers: South Asia, Carnegie Endowment for International Peace, Washington, DC, April 2013. https://carnegieendowment.org/2013/04/11/ balochistan-state-versus-nation-pub-51488.

Greenblatt, Jonathan. 'Examining the Domestic Terrorism Threat in the Wake of the Attack on the U.S. Capitol.' US House of Representatives Committee on Homeland Security, 2021. https://homeland.house. gov/imo/media/doc/Testimony-Greenblatt1.pdf.

Greene, Viveca S. '"Deplorable" Satire: Alt-Right Memes, White Genocide Tweets, and Redpilling Normies.' *Studies in American Humor* 5, no. 1 (2019). https://doi.org/10.5325/studamerhumor.5.1.0031.

Grey, Stephen. *Operation Snakebite: The Explosive True Story of an Afghan Desert Siege*. London: Viking, 2009.

Grier, Kevin B., and Robin M. Grier. 'The Washington Consensus Works: Causal Effects of Reform, 1970–2015.' *Journal of Comparative Economics*, September 2020, S0147596720300639. https://doi.org/10.1016/j. jce.2020.09.001.

Guáqueta, Alexandra. 'The Way Back In: Reintegrating Illegal Armed Groups in Colombia Then and Now.' In *Reintegrating Armed Groups after Conflict: Politics, Violence and Transition*, edited by Mats Berdal and David H. Ucko. Abingdon: Routledge, 2009.

Guardian, The. 'Commander Says Nigerian Army Completely Defeated Boko Haram.' February 4, 2018. https://guardian.ng/news/commander-says-nigerian-army-completely-defeated-boko-haram/.

Gurr, Ted Robert. *Why Men Rebel*. Princeton, NJ: Princeton University Press for the Center of International Studies, 1970.

Gutierrez, Eric Dante. 'The Paradox of Illicit Economies: Survival, Resilience, and the Limits of Development and Drug Policy Orthodoxy.' *Globalizations* 17, no. 6 (August 17, 2020): 1008–26. https://doi.org/10.1080/14747731.2020.1718825.

Guynn, Jessica. 'Donald Trump and Joe Biden vs. Facebook and Twitter: Why Section 230 Could Get Repealed in 2021.' *USA Today*, January 4, 2021. https://www.usatoday.com/story/tech/2021/01/04/trump-biden-pelosi-section-230-repeal-facebook-twitter-google/4132529001/.

Guynn, Jessica. 'Twitter Accused of Political Bias in Right-Wing Crackdown.' *USA Today*, November 18, 2016. https://www.usatoday.com/story/tech/news/2016/11/18/conservatives-accuse-twitter-of-liberal-bias/94037802/.

Gventer, Celeste Ward, David Martin Jones, and M.L.R. Smith, eds. *The New Counter-Insurgency Era in Critical Perspective*. New York: Palgrave Macmillan, 2014.

GW Extremism Tracker. 'Terrorism in the United States.' George Washington University Program on Extremism, March 2021.

Hafez, Mohammed M, and Quintan Wiktorowicz. 'Violence as Contention in the Egyptian Islamic Movement.' In *Islamic Activism: A Social Movement Theory Approach*, edited by Quintan Wiktorowicz, 61–88. Bloomington, IN: Indiana University Press, 2004.

Hagen, Lisa. 'Poll: Majority of Republicans Support Trump's Muslim Ban.' *The Hill*, December 9, 2015. https://thehill.com/blogs/ballot-box/presidential-races/262656-poll-majority-of-republicans-support-trumps-muslim-ban.

Haggard, Stephen, and James Long. 'On Benchmarks: Institutions and Violence in Iraq.' 2007.

Haidt, Jonathan, and Tobias Rose-Stockwell. 'The Dark Psychology of Social Networks.' *The Atlantic*, December 2019. https://www.theatlantic.com/magazine/archive/2019/12/social-media-democracy/600763/.

Halliday, Fred. 'Terrorism in Historical Perspective.' *Arab Studies Quarterly* 9, no. 2 (1987): 139–48.

Hammes, Thomas X. *The Sling and the Stone: On War in the 21st Century*. St. Paul, MN: Zenith Press, 2006.

Hammond, Guy. 'Saving Port-au-Prince: United Nations Efforts to Protect Civilians in Haiti 2006–2007.' Stimson Center, Washington, DC, 2012.

Hankes, Keegan, and Alex Amend. 'The Alt-Right Is Killing People.' Southern Poverty Law Center, February 5, 2018. https://www.splcenter.org/20180205/alt-right-killing-people.

Hansen, Flemming Splidsboel. 'Russian Hybrid Warfare: A Study of Disinformation.' Danish Institute for International Studies, Copenhagen, 2017.

Hansen, William. 'Boko Haram: Religious Radicalism and Insurrection in Northern Nigeria.' *Journal of Asian and African Studies* 52, no. 4 (June 2017): 551–69. https://doi.org/10.1177/0021909615615594.

Harris, Paul. 'Fake Terror Plots, Paid Informants: The Tactics of FBI "Entrapment" Questioned.' *The Guardian*, November 16, 2011, sec. World. http://www.theguardian.com/world/2011/nov/16/fbi-entrapment-fake-terror-plots.

Hashim, Ahmed. *When Counterinsurgency Wins: Sri Lanka's Defeat of the Tamil Tigers*. Philadelphia: University of Pennsylvania Press, 2013.

Hassan, Idayat. 'The Danger of a Better-Behaved Boko Haram.' *New Humanitarian*, August 21, 2018, sec. Opinion. http://www.thenewhumanitarian.org/opinion/2018/08/21/opinion-nigeria-militancy-peace-boko-haram.

Hassan, Syed Raza. 'Fearful for Decades, Pakistan's Main Parties Now Openly Campaign in Karachi.' Reuters, July 19, 2018. https://www.reuters.com/article/us-pakistan-election-karachi-idUSKBN1K9162.

Hatewatch Staff. 'Ann Coulter: A White Nationalist in the Mainstream?' Southern Poverty Law Center, May 28, 2015. https://www.splcenter.org/hatewatch/2015/05/27/ann-coulter-%E2%80%93-white-nationalist-mainstream.

Hawley, George. *Making Sense of the Alt-Right*. New York: Columbia University Press, 2017.

Haysom, Simone. 'Where Crime Compounds Conflict: Understanding Northern Mozambique's Vulnerabilities.' Global Institution Against Transnational Organized Crime, Geneva, October 2018.

Hazen, Jennifer M. 'From Social Movement to Armed Group: A Case Study from Nigeria.' *Contemporary Security Policy* 30, no. 2 (August 2009): 281–300. https://doi.org/10.1080/13523260903059906.

Heger, Lindsay L. 'Votes and Violence: Pursuing Terrorism While Navigating Politics.' *Journal of Peace Research* 52, no. 1 (January 2015): 32–45. https://doi.org/10.1177/0022343314552984.

Heller, Sam. 'When Measuring ISIS's "Resurgence", Use the Right Standard.' Commentary, International Crisis Group, May 13, 2020. https://www.crisisgroup.org/middle-east-north-africa/gulf-and-arabian-peninsula/iraq/when-measuring-isiss-resurgence-use-right-standard.

Herbst, Jeffrey. *States and Power in Africa: Comparative Lessons in Authority and Control*. 2nd ed. Princeton, NJ: Princeton University Press, 2014. http://hdl.handle.net/2027/heb.34113.

Hewitt, Christopher. 'The Political Context of Terrorism in America: Ignoring Extremists or Pandering to Them?' *Terrorism and Political Violence* 12, no. 3–4 (September 2000): 325–44. https://doi.org/10.1080/09546550008427582.s

Hill, Mark. '4 Reasons We Can't Laugh Away Stupid Conspiracy Theories in 2021.' Cracked.com, December 19, 2020. https://www.cracked.com/article_29231_4-reasons-we-cant-laugh-away-stupid-conspiracy-theories-in-2021.html.

Himalayan Times. 'YCL Cadres Injure Nepali Congress Leader in Rukum.' April 14, 2016. https://thehimalayantimes.com/nepal/ycl-cadres-injure-nepali-congress-leader-rukum/.

Hinnebusch, Raymond. 'From Westphalian Failure to Heterarchic Governance in MENA: The Case of Syria.' *Small Wars and Insurgencies* 29, no. 3 (May 4, 2018): 391–413. https://doi.org/10.1080/09592318.2018.1455330.

Hitchens, Christopher. 'The Old Man.' *The Atlantic*, July 1, 2004. https://www.theatlantic.com/magazine/archive/2004/07/the-old-man/302984/.

Hitler, Adolf. *Mein Kampf*. New York: Reynal and Hitchcock, 1940.

Hobbs, Renee, and Sandra McGee. 'Teaching about Propaganda: An Examination of the Historical Roots of Media Literacy.' *Journal of Media Literacy Education* 6, no. 2 (November 9, 2014): 56–67.

Hoffman, Frank G. 'Hybrid vs. Compound War.' *Armed Forces Journal*, October 1, 2009. http://armedforcesjournal.com/hybrid-vs-compound-war/.

Hoffmann, Leena Koni. 'Who Speaks for the North? Politics and Influence in Northern Nigeria.' Research Paper, Royal Institute of International Affairs, Chatham House, July 2014.

Hofmann, Bjoern. 'Are Hybrid Political Orders an Appropriate Concept for State Formation? Timor-Leste Revisited.' In *Building Peace in the Absence of States: Challenging the Discourse on State Failure*, edited by Martina Fischer and Beatrix Schmelzle, 79–86. Berghof Handbook Dialogue Series 8. Berlin: Berghof Forschungszentrum für Konstruktive Konfliktbearbeitung, 2009.

Holiday, Ryan. *Trust Me, I'm Lying: Confessions of a Media Manipulator*. New York: Portfolio/Penguin, 2017.

Horwitz, Jeff. 'Facebook Knew Calls for Violence Plagued "Groups," Now Plans Overhaul.' *Wall Street Journal*, January 31, 2021, sec. Tech. https://www.wsj.com/articles/facebook-knew-calls-for-violence-plagued-groups-now-plans-overhaul-11612131374.

Howard, Philip N., Bharath Ganesh, and Dimitra Liotsiou. 'The IRA, Social Media and Political Polarization in the United States, 2012-2018.'

University of Oxford: Computational Propaganda Research Project, December 2018.

Huey, Laura. 'This Is Not Your Mother's Terrorism: Social Media, Online Radicalization and the Practice of Political Jamming.' *Journal of Terrorism Research* 6, no. 2 (May 25, 2015). https://doi.org/10.15664/jtr.1159.

Human Rights Watch, ed. *Illusion of Justice: Human Rights Abuses in US Terrorism Prosecutions.* New York: Human Rights Watch and Columbia Law School Human Rights Institute, 2014.

Human Rights Watch. '"Why Can't We Go Home?"' October 9, 2018. https://www.hrw.org/report/2018/10/09/why-cant-we-go-home/military-occupation-land-sri-lanka.

Huntington, Samuel P. *Political Order in Changing Societies.* New Haven, CT: Yale University Press, 1968.

Huntington, Samuel P. *The Third Wave: Democratization in the Late Twentieth Century.* The Julian J. Rothbaum Distinguished Lecture Series 4. Norman, OK: University of Oklahoma Press, 1993.

Hurst, Steven R. 'US: Raid of Baghdad's Sadr City Kills 49.' *Washington Post*, October 21, 2007. https://www.washingtonpost.com/wp-dyn/content/article/2007/10/21/AR2007102100159_pf.html.

.Hussain, Abid. 'Dialogue: Laurent Gayer and Omar Shahid Hamid on Karachi.' *Herald Magazine*, October 26, 2016. http://herald.dawn.com/news/1153570.

Hussain, Naveed. 'Fiddling While Balochistan Burns.' *Express Tribune*, August 15, 2012.

Hussin, Sabariah, and Syez Huzaifah bin Othman Alkaff. 'The Los Angeles Model in Deradicalisation.' In *Terrorist Deradicalisation in Global Contexts: Success, Failure, and Continuity*, edited by Rohan Gunaratna and Sabariah Hussin, 197–208. Routledge Studies in the Politics of Disorder and Instability. London: Routledge, 2020.

Ibrahim, Arwa, and Azhar al-Rubaie. 'Iraqi Journalists Fear for Lives after Basra Reporters Killed.' *Al Jazeera*, January 12, 2020. https://www.aljazeera.com/news/2020/1/12/iraqi-journalists-fear-for-lives-after-basra-reporters-killed.

Ingram, Haroro J. 'The Strategic Logic of Islamic State Information Operations.' *Australian Journal of International Affairs* 69, no. 6 (November 2, 2015): 729–52. https://doi.org/10.1080/10357718.2015.1059799.

Ingram, Haroro J., Craig Whiteside, and Charlie Winter. *The ISIS Reader: Milestone Texts of the Islamic State Movement.* New York: Oxford University Press, 2020.

Institute for Economics and Peace. 'Global Terrorism Index 2020: Measuring the Impact of Terrorism.' Sydney, November 2020. http://visionofhumanity.org/reports.

International Campaign to Ban Landmines and Human Rights Watch. *Landmine Monitor Report 2004: Toward a Mine-Free World*. Washington: Human Rights Watch, 2004.

International Crisis Group. 'Electoral Violence and Illicit Influence in Mexico's Hot Land.' Latin America Report, Brussels, June 2, 2021.

International Crisis Group. 'El Salvador's Politics of Perpetual Violence.' Latin America Report, Brussels, December 19, 2017.

International Crisis Group. 'Facing the Challenge of the Islamic State in West Africa Province.' Africa Report, Brussels, May 16, 2019.

International Crisis Group. 'Iraq's Civil War, the Sadrists and the Surge.' Middle East Report, Brussels, February 7, 2008.

International Crisis Group. 'Iraq's Muqtada al-Sadr: Spoiler or Stabiliser?' Middle East Report, Brussels, July 11, 2006.

International Crisis Group. 'Iraq's Paramilitary Groups: The Challenge of Rebuilding a Functioning State.' Middle East Report, Brussels, July 30, 2018.

International Crisis Group. 'Miracle or Mirage? Gangs and Plunging Violence in El Salvador.' Latin America Report, Brussels, July 8, 2020.

International Crisis Group. 'Nepal's Maoists: Purists or Pragmatists?' Asia Report, Brussels, May 18, 2007.

International Crisis Group. 'The Next Iraqi War? Sectarianism and Civil Conflict.' Middle East Report, Brussels, February 27, 2006.

International Crisis Group. 'Pakistan: Stoking the Fire in Karachi.' Asia Report, Brussels, February 15, 2017.

International Crisis Group. 'Sri Lanka: Tamil Politics and the Quest for a Political Solution.' Asia Report, Brussels, November 20, 2012. https://www.crisisgroup.org/asia/south-asia/sri-lanka/sri-lanka-tamil-politics-and-quest-political-solution.

Irvin, Cynthia L. *Militant Nationalism: Between Movement and Party in Ireland and the Basque Country*. Social Movements, Protest, and Contention 9. Minneapolis, MN: University of Minnesota Press, 1999.

Isacson, Adam. 'Why Colombia's Historic Peace Breakthrough Was the "Easy Part."' *World Politics Review*, September 6, 2016. https://www.worldpoliticsreview.com/articles/19826/why-colombia-s-historic-peace-breakthrough-was-the-easy-part.

Issacharoff, Samuel. *Fragile Democracies: Contested Power in the Era of Constitutional Courts*. Cambridge: Cambridge University Press, 2015.

Jaakkola, Maarit. 'Media Literacy in the Baltics: Different Approaches in Neighbouring Countries.' *Media and Learning* (blog), December 2020. https://media-and-learning.eu/type/featured-articles/media-literacy-in-the-baltics-similar-backgrounds-but-different-approaches/.

Jabaili, Diaa. 'Pollution and Corruption Are Choking the Life out of Basra.' *The Guardian*, September 13, 2018, sec. Opinion. http://www.theguardian.com/commentisfree/2018/sep/13/pollution-corruption-choking-life-out-of-basra.

Jackson, Brian A., Ashley L. Rhoades, Jordan R. Reimer, Natasha Lander, Katherine Costello, and Sina Beaghley. 'Practical Terrorism Prevention: Reexamining U.S. National Approaches to Addressing the Threat of Ideologically Motivated Violence.' Research Reports, RAND Corporation, Santa Monica, CA, February 14, 2019. https://www.rand.org/pubs/research_reports/RR2647.html.

Jaffrelot, Christophe. 'Refining the Moderation Thesis: Two Religious Parties and Indian Democracy; The Jana Sangh and the BJP between Hindutva Radicalism and Coalition Politics.' *Democratization* 20, no. 5 (August 2013): 876–94. https://doi.org/10.1080/13510347.2013.801256.

Jamal, Umair. 'Amid a Pandemic, Pakistan Focuses on a Baloch Insurgency.' *The Diplomat*, June 16, 2020. https://thediplomat.com/2020/06/amid-a-pandemic-pakistan-focuses-on-a-baloch-insurgency/.

Jardina, Ashley. *White Identity Politics*. Cambridge: Cambridge University Press, 2019.

Jardine, Eric. 'The Insurgent's Dilemma: A Theory of Mobilization and Conflict Outcome.' Doctoral thesis, Carleton University, 2014. https://curve.carleton.ca/4043e1a5-90ab-4835-bafe-96274c75ce2a.

Jenkins, Simon. 'The Last Thing Norway Needs Is Illiberal Britain's Patronising.' *The Guardian*, July 26, 2011, sec. Opinion. http://www.theguardian.com/commentisfree/2011/jul/26/norway-illiberal-britain-patronising.

Jensen, Tom. 'Trump Still Leads Iowa; Clinton in Good Shape.' Public Policy Polling, September 22, 2015. https://www.publicpolicypolling.com/polls/trump-still-leads-iowa-clinton-in-good-shape/.

Jigsaw. 'Can "Inoculation" Build Broad-Based Resistance to Misinformation?' *Medium* (blog), March 17, 2021. https://medium.com/jigsaw/can-inoculation-build-broad-based-resistance-to-misinformation-6c67e517e314.

Joes, Anthony James. *Urban Guerrilla Warfare*. Lexington: University Press of Kentucky, 2007.

Johnson, Daryl. *Right Wing Resurgence: How a Domestic Terrorist Threat Is Being Ignored*. Lanham, MD: Rowman and Littlefield Publishers, 2012.

Johnson, David E., M. Wade Markel, and Brian Shannon. *The 2008 Battle of Sadr City: Reimagining Urban Combat*. Santa Monica, CA: RAND, 2013.

Jones, Michael. 'Through the Looking Glass: Assessing the Evidence Base for P/CVE Communications.' Occasional Paper, RUSI, London, July 2020.

Jones, Seth G. *Waging Insurgent Warfare: Lessons from the Vietcong to the Islamic State*. New York: Oxford University Press, 2017.

Jones, Seth G., Catrina Doxsee, and Nicholas Harrington. 'The Escalating Terrorism Problem in the United States.' CSIS Briefs, Center of Strategic and International Studies, June 2020.

Kalyvas, Stathis N., and Laia Balcells. 'International System and Technologies of Rebellion: How the End of the Cold War Shaped Internal Conflict.' *American Political Science Review* 104, no. 3 (August 2010): 415–29. https://doi.org/10.1017/S0003055410000286.

Karlsen, Geir Hågen. 'Divide and Rule: Ten Lessons about Russian Political Influence Activities in Europe.' *Palgrave Communications* 5, no. 1 (February 8, 2019): 1–14. https://doi.org/10.1057/s41599-019-0227-8.

Katz, Rita. 'ISIS Is Now Harder to Track Online—but That's Good News.' *Wired*, December 16, 2019. https://www.wired.com/story/opinion-isis-is-now-harder-to-track-onlinebut-thats-good-news/.

Katz, Rita. 'The State Department Is Fumbling on Twitter.' *Time*, September 16, 2014. https://time.com/3387065/isis-twitter-war-state-department/.

Kaválek, Tomáš. 'From al-Qaeda in Iraq to Islamic State: The Story of Insurgency in Iraq and Syria in 2003–2015.' *Alternatives : Turkish Journal of International Relations* 14, no. 1 (December 26, 2015): 1–32.

Keller, Daphne. 'Internet Platforms: Observations on Speech, Danger, and Money.' Aegis Series Paper: National Security, Technology, and Law, Hoover Institution, Stanford, CA, June 13, 2018.

Kennan, George F. 'The Inauguration of Organized Political Warfare [redacted version].' April 30, 1948. Wilson Center Digital Archive. https://digitalarchive.wilsoncenter.org/document/114320.

Kennedy, Merrit, and Bill Chappell. 'Dominion Voting Systems Files $1.6 Billion Defamation Lawsuit against Fox News.' NPR, March 26, 2021. https://www.npr.org/2021/03/26/981515184/dominion-voting-systems-files-1-6-billion-defamation-lawsuit-against-fox-news.

Khosrokhavar, Farhad. *Quand Al-Qaïda parle: Témoignages derrière les barreaux*. Paris: Seuil, 2007.

Kilcullen, David J. 'Countering Global Insurgency.' *Journal of Strategic Studies* 28, no. 4 (August 2005): 597–617.

Kilcullen, David J. *The Dragons and the Snakes: How the Rest Learned to Fight the West*. London: Hurst Publishers, 2020.

Kilcullen, David J. *Out of the Mountains:The Coming Age of the Urban Guerrilla*. London: Hurst Publishers, 2013.

Killion, Victoria L. 'Terrorism, Violent Extremism, and the Internet: Free Speech Considerations.' CRS Report for Congress, Congressional Research Service, Washington, DC, May 6, 2019.

Kimberly, Kindy, Sari Horwitz, and Devlin Barrett. 'Federal Government Has Long Ignored White Supremacist Threats, Critics Say.' *Washington Post*, September 2, 2017, sec. National. https://www.washingtonpost. com/national/federal-government-has-long-ignored-white-supremacist-threats-critics-say/2017/09/02/bf2ed00c-8698-11e7-961d-2f373b3977ee_story.html?utm_term=.6168f39ad81c.

Kirshner, Alexander S. *A Theory of Militant Democracy:The Ethics of Combatting Political Extremism*. New Haven, CT:Yale University Press, 2014.

Kissinger, Henry A. 'The Viet Nam Negotiations.' *Foreign Affairs* 11, no. 2 (1969): 38–50.

Kiszely, John. 'Post-Modern Challenges for Modern Warriors.' Shrivenham Paper, Defence Academy of the United Kingdom, December 2007.

Klaas, Brian. 'A Short History of President Trump's Anti-Muslim Bigotry.' *Washington Post*, March 15, 2019, sec. Opinion. https://www.washingtonpost.com/opinions/2019/03/15/short-history-president-trumps-anti-muslim-bigotry/.

Kline, Harvey F. *Historical Dictionary of Colombia*. Historical Dictionaries of the Americas. Lanham, MD: Scarecrow Press, 2012.

Knappenberger, Brian. *We Are Legion: The Story of Hacktivists*. FilmBuff, 2012.

Knights, Michael. 'Soleimani Is Dead: The Road Ahead for Iranian-Backed Militias in Iraq.' *CTC Sentinel*, January 2020.

Koch, H. W. '1933: The Legality of Hitler's Assumption of Power.' In *Aspects of the Third Reich*, edited by H. W. Koch, 39–61. London: Macmillan, 1985.

Kohut, Andrew, and James Bell. 'Muslim Publics Share Concerns about Extremist Groups.' Pew Research Center, Washington, DC, September 10, 2013. https://www.pewresearch.org/global/2013/09/10/muslim-publics-share-concerns-about-extremist-groups/.

Kreutz, Joakim. 'How and When Armed Conflicts End: Introducing the UCDP Conflict Termination Dataset.' *Journal of Peace Research* 47, no. 2 (March 2010): 243–50. https://doi.org/10.1177/0022343309353108.

LADB. 'Bolivia Expels Cocaleros Leader.' Latin America Database, February 1, 2002. https://digitalrepository.unm.edu/cgi/viewcontent.cgi?article=13988&context=notisur.

Lambert, Robert. 'Empowering Salafis and Islamists against al-Qaeda: A London Counterterrorism Case Study.' PS: Political Science and Politics 41, no. 1 (2008): 31–35.

Lambert, Robert. 'Was Anders Breivik a Psychotic Spree Killer or a Calculating Terrorist?' RUSI, August 18, 2011. https://rusi.org/commentary/was-anders-breivik-psychotic-spree-killer-or-calculating-terrorist.

Lane, Ashley. 'Iran's Islamist Proxies in the Middle East.' The Islamists, Wilson Center, Washington, DC, December 17, 2020. https://www.wilsoncenter.org/article/irans-islamist-proxies.

Langer, Gary. '1 in 10 Say It's Acceptable to Hold Neo-Nazi Views (Poll).' ABC News, August 21, 2017. https://abcnews.go.com/Politics/28-approve-trumps-response-charlottesville-poll/story?id=49334079.

Laqueur, Walter. Guerrilla Warfare: A Historical and Critical Study. London: Transaction Publishers, 1998.

Lartéguy, Jean. The Centurions. Translated by Alexander Wallace Fielding. New York: Penguin, 2015.

Lasswell, Harold D. Politics: Who Gets What, When, How. New York: Meridian Books, 1958.

Law, Vincent. 'What Exactly Does Modern Society Offer Young White Men Anymore?' AltRight.com (blog), December 28, 2017. https://altright.com/2017/12/28/what-exactly-does-modern-society-offer-young-white-men-anymore/.

Lawler, Steve. 'Narrative in Social Research.' In Qualitative Research in Action, edited by Tim May, 242–58. London: Sage, 2002.

Lawrence, T. E. Seven Pillars of Wisdom. Ware: Wordsworth, 1977.

Leeds, Elizabeth. 'Rio de Janeiro.' In Fractured Cities: Social Exclusion, Urban Violence and Contested Spaces in Latin America, edited by Kees Koonings and Dirk Kruijt, 23–35. London: Zed Books, 2007.

Lehman, Joseph G. 'An Introduction to the Overton Window of Political Possibility.' Mackinac Center for Public Policy, April 8, 2010. https://www.mackinac.org/12481.

Lenin, V. I. 'Against Boycott: Notes from a Social-Democratic Publicist.' 1907. Marxist Internet Archive. https://www.marxists.org/archive/lenin/works/1907/boycott/i.htm#fwV13E005.

Lenin, V. I. '"Left-Wing" Communism: An Infantile Disorder.' June 1920. Marxist Internet Archive. https://www.marxists.org/archive/lenin/works/1920/lwc/index.htm.

Lenin, V. I. *V. I. Lenin: Selected Works*. New York: International Publishers, 1968.

LeRiche, Matthew, and Matthew Arnold. *South Sudan: From Revolution to Independence*. Oxford: Oxford University Press, 2013.

Lerman, Rachel, and Elizabeth Dwoskin. 'Twitter Crackdown on Conspiracy Theories Could Set Agenda for Other Social Media.' *Washington Post*, July 22, 2020, sec. Technology. https://www.washingtonpost.com/technology/2020/07/22/twitter-bans-qanon-accounts/.

Levine, Mike, and Josh Margolin. 'Feds Warn "Violent Opportunists" Infiltrating George Floyd Protests, Could Be "Emboldened" to Attack Police.' ABC News, June 3, 2000. https://abcnews.go.com/Politics/feds-warn-violent-opportunists-infiltrating-protests-emboldened-attack/story?id=71040109.

Levite, Ariel E., and Jonathan (Yoni) Shimshoni. 'The Strategic Challenge of Society-Centric Warfare.' *Survival* 60, no. 6 (November 2, 2018): 91–118. https://doi.org/10.1080/00396338.2018.1542806.

Levitsky, Steven, and Lucan Way. 'The Rise of Competitive Authoritarianism.' *Journal of Democracy* 13, no. 2 (2002): 51–65. https://doi.org/10.1353/jod.2002.0026.

Lewandowsky, Stephan, Ullrich K. H. Ecker, and John Cook. 'Beyond Misinformation: Understanding and Coping with the "Post-truth" Era.' *Journal of Applied Research in Memory and Cognition* 6, no. 4 (December 2017): 353–69. https://doi.org/10.1016/j.jarmac.2017.07.008.

Lewis, David. 'The Failure of a Liberal Peace: Sri Lanka's Counter-insurgency in Global Perspective.' *Conflict, Security and Development* 10, no. 5 (November 2010): 647–71. https://doi.org/10.1080/14678802.2010.511509.

Lichtblau, Eric. 'F.B.I. Steps Up Use of Stings in ISIS Cases.' *New York Times*, June 7, 2016, sec. U.S. https://www.nytimes.com/2016/06/08/us/fbi-isis-terrorism-stings.html.

Linden, Sander, Costas Panagopoulos, Flávio Azevedo, and John T. Jost. 'The Paranoid Style in American Politics Revisited: An Ideological Asymmetry in Conspiratorial Thinking.' *Political Psychology* 42, no. 1 (June 24, 2020): 23–51. https://doi.org/10.1111/pops.12681.

Lindholm, Charles, and José Pedro Zúquete. *The Struggle for the World: Liberation Movements for the 21st Century*. Stanford, CA: Stanford University Press, 2010.

Lippmann, Walter. *Liberty and the News*. Bethlehem, PA: Mediastudies. press, 2020.

Lipset, Seymour Martin. *Political Man: The Social Bases of Politics*. 2nd ed. London: Heinemann, 1983.

Lister, Tim, and Clare Sebastian. 'Stoking Islamophobia and Secession in Texas—from an Office in Russia.' CNN. October 5, 2017. https://www.cnn.com/2017/10/05/politics/heart-of-texas-russia-event/index.html.

Littlejohn, David. *The SA 1921–45: Hitler's Stormtroopers.* Men-at-Arms 220. Oxford: Osprey, 2001.

Loewenstein, Karl. 'Militant Democracy and Fundamental Rights, I.' *American Political Science Review* 31, no. 3 (June 1937): 417–32. https://doi.org/10.2307/1948164.

Long, Austin, Stephanie Pezard, Bryce Loidolt, and Todd C. Helmus. *Locals Rule: Historical Lessons for Creating Local Defense Forces for Afghanistan and Beyond.* Santa Monica, CA: RAND and National Defense Research Institute, 2012.

López-Fonseca, Óscar, and Fernando J. Pérez. 'Spain's High Court Opens Investigation into Russian Spying Unit in Catalonia.' *El País*, November 21, 2019. https://english.elpais.com/elpais/2019/11/21/inenglish/1574324886_989244.html.

Lowery, Wesley, and Abigail Hauslohner. '"White Lives Matter" Rally Organizers Adjust Strategy to Avoid Becoming "Another Charlottesville."' *Washington Post*, October 27, 2017, sec. National. https://www.washingtonpost.com/national/residents-and-organizers-worry-about-violence-at-tennessee-rallies/2017/10/27/554c4e40-bb5d-11e7-a908-a3470754bbb9_story.html.

Luhn, Alec. 'Russia Funds Moscow Conference for US, EU and Ukraine Separatists.' *The Guardian*, September 20, 2015. https://www.theguardian.com/world/2015/sep/20/russia-funds-moscow-conference-us-eu-ukraine-separatists.

Luitel, Guna Raj. 'Nepalese Journalist Defiant after Razor Slashing.' CPJ, January 12, 2010. https://cpj.org/blog/2010/01/tika-bista-heard-the-word.php.

Mackinlay, John. *The Insurgent Archipelago: From Mao to Bin Laden.* London: Hurst Publishers, 2009.

Maclean, Ruth, and Finbarr O'Reilly. 'Crisis in the Sahel Becoming France's Forever War.' *New York Times*, March 29, 2020, sec. World. https://www.nytimes.com/2020/03/29/world/africa/france-sahel-west-africa-.html.

Magaloni, Beatriz, Edgar Franco-Vivanco, and Vanessa Melo. 'Killing in the Slums: Social Order, Criminal Governance, and Police Violence in Rio de Janeiro.' *American Political Science Review* 114, no. 2 (May 2020): 552–72. https://doi.org/10.1017/S0003055419000856.

Maher, Shiraz, and Martyn Frampton. *Choosing Our Friends Wisely: Criteria for Engagement with Muslim Groups*. London: Policy Exchange, 2009.

Mahmood, Amna. 'Regional Political Parties: Challenge to Political Stability of Pakistan.' *Pakistan Vision* 15, no. 2 (2014).

Mampilly, Zachariah Cherian. 'A Marriage of Inconvenience: Tsunami Aid and the Unraveling of the LTTE and the GoSL's Complex Dependency.' *Civil Wars* 11, no. 3 (September 2009): 302–20. https://doi.org/10.1080/13698240903157545.

Mampilly, Zachariah Cherian. *Rebel Rulers: Insurgent Governance and Civilian Life during War*. New York: Cornell University Press, 2015.

Manjoo, Farhad. 'I Spoke to a Scholar of Conspiracy Theories and I'm Scared for Us.' *New York Times*, October 21, 2020, sec. Opinion. https://www.nytimes.com/2020/10/21/opinion/q-anon-conspiracy.html.

Manwaring, Max G. *A Contemporary Challenge to State Sovereignty: Gangs and Other Illicit Transnational Criminal Organizations in Central America, El Salvador, Mexico, Jamaica, and Brazil*. Security Issues in the Western Hemisphere. Carlisle Barracks, PA: Strategic Studies Institute, US Army War College, 2007.

Manwaring, Max G. *Street Gangs: The New Urban Insurgency*. Carlisle, PA: Strategic Studies Institute, US Army War College, 2005.

Mao Tse-tung. 'Problems of Strategy in China's Civil War.' In *Strategic Studies: A Reader*, 2nd ed., 274–308. Abingdon: Routledge, 2014.

Mao Tse-tung. 'Unite All Anti-Japanese Forces and Combat the Anti-Communist Die-Hards.' In *Selected Works of Mao Tse-Tung*, vol. 2, 389–94. Peking: Foreign Languages Press, 1967. http://marxism.halkcephesi.net/Mao/CACD40.html.

Marantz, Andrew. 'Inside the Daily Stormer's Style Guide.' *New Yorker*, January 8, 2018. https://www.newyorker.com/magazine/2018/01/15/inside-the-daily-stormers-style-guide.

Marantz, Andrew. 'The Regular Guy Who Almost Challenged Georgia's QAnon Candidate.' *New Yorker*, October 19, 2020. https://www.newyorker.com/magazine/2020/10/26/the-regular-guy-who-almost-challenged-georgias-qanon-candidate.

Marashi, Ibrahim al-. 'The Future of Militias in Post-ISIL Iraq.' Al Jazeera, March 27, 2017, sec. Opinion. https://www.aljazeera.com/opinions/2017/3/27/the-future-of-militias-in-post-isil-iraq.

Marcuse, Herbert. *Counterrevolution and Revolt*. Boston: Beacon Press, 1972.

Marks, Thomas A. 'At the Front Lines of the GWOT: Colombia Success Builds upon Local Foundation.' *Journal of Counterterrorism and Homeland Security International* 10, no. 2 (2004): 42–50.

Marks, Thomas A. 'Back to the Future: Nepali People's War as "New War."' In *Countering Insurgencies and Violent Extremism in South and South East Asia*, edited by Shanthie D'Souza. London: Routledge, 2019.

Marks, Thomas A. 'Colombian Army Adaptation to FARC.' Carlisle, PA: Strategic Studies Institute, 2002.

Marks, Thomas A. 'Colombian Military Support for "Democratic Security."' *Small Wars and Insurgencies* 17, no. 2 (June 2006): 197–220.

Marks, Thomas A. 'Counterinsurgency and Operational Art.' *Low Intensity Conflict and Law Enforcement* 13, no. 3 (2005).

Marks, Thomas A. 'Counterinsurgency in the Age of Globalism.' *Journal of Conflict Studies* 27, no. 1 (2007).

Marks, Thomas A. 'FARC, 1982–2002: Criminal Foundation for Insurgent Defeat.' *Small Wars and Insurgencies* 28, no. 3 (May 4, 2017): 488–523.

Marks, Thomas A. 'For Nepal's Maoists, the Cold War Continues.' *World Politics Review*, February 22, 2011. https://www.worldpoliticsreview.com/articles/7943/for-nepals-maoists-the-cold-war-continues.

Marks, Thomas A. 'Mao Tse-tung and the Search for 21st Century Counterinsurgency.' *CTC Sentinel* 2, no. 10 (October 2009): 17–20.

Marks, Thomas A. 'Maoist Conception of the United Front with Particular Application to the United Front in Thailand since October 1976.' *Issue and Studies* 16, no. 3 (March 1980): 46–69.

Marks, Thomas A. *Maoist People's War in Post-Vietnam Asia*. Bangkok: White Lotus, 2007.

Marks, Thomas A. '"Post-Conflict" Terrorism in Nepal.' *Journal of Counter Terrorism* 21, no. 1 (2015): 24–31.

Marks, Thomas A. 'Tenuous Security in the Himalayas: A Focus on Nepal.' In *Terrorism, Security and Development in South Asia: National, Regional and Global Implications*, edited by M. Raymond Izarali and Dalbir Ahlawat. New Regionalisms. Abingdon: Routledge, 2021.

Marks, Thomas A. 'Terrorism as Method in Nepali Maoist Insurgency, 1996–2016.' *Small Wars and Insurgencies* 28, no. 1 (January 2, 2017): 81–118.

Marks, Thomas A. 'Urban Insurgency.' *Small Wars and Insurgencies* 14, no. 3 (September 2003): 100–157. https://doi.org/10.1080/0959231041 0001676925.

Marks, Thomas A., and Rodney S. Azama. 'Cyberterrorism.' In *The Fundamentals of Counterterrorism Law*, edited by Lynne K. Zusman, 253–66. Chicago: American Bar Association, 2014.

Marks, Thomas A., and Michael S. Bell. 'The U.S. Army in the Iraq War: Volume 1 (Invasion, Insurgency, Civil War 2003–2006).' *Small Wars and Insurgencies* 30, no. 3 (April 16, 2019): 703–18. https://doi.org/10.1 080/09592318.2019.1601873.

Marks, Thomas A., and Paul B. Rich. 'Back to the Future: People's War in the 21st Century.' *Small Wars and Insurgencies* 28, no. 3 (May 4, 2017): 409–25. https://doi.org/10.1080/09592318.2017.1307620.

Marwick, Alice, and Rebecca Lewis. 'Media Manipulation and Disinformation Online.' Data and Society Research Institute, May 15, 2017.

Marwick, Alice, and Rebecca Lewis. 'The Online Radicalization We're Not Talking About.' *Intelligencer*, May 18, 2017. https://nymag.com/intelligencer/2017/05/the-online-radicalization-were-not-talking-about.html.

Mason, Paul. 'Golden Dawn Verdict: No Sunset for the Far Right.' *International Politics and Society*, October 14, 2020. https://www.ips-journal.eu/topics/human-rights/golden-dawn-verdict-no-sunset-for-the-far-right-4718/.

Matanock, Aila M., and Paul Staniland. 'How and Why Armed Groups Participate in Elections.' *Perspectives on Politics* 16, no. 3 (September 2018): 710–27. https://doi.org/10.1017/S1537592718001019.

Matsinhe, David. 'Mozambique: The Forgotten People of Cabo Delgado.' *Daily Maverick*, May 28, 2020, sec. Opinion. https://www.dailymaverick.co.za/article/2020-05-29-mozambique-the-forgotten-people-of-cabo-delgado/.

Matsinhe, David, and Estacio Valoi. 'The Genesis of Insurgency in Northern Mozambique.' Southern Africa Report, Institute for Security Studies, October 2019.

Mazarr, Michael J. *Mastering the Gray Zone: Understanding a Changing Era of Conflict*. Carlisle Barracks, PA: Strategic Studies Institute and US Army War College Press, 2015. http://www.strategicstudiesinstitute.army.mil/pubs/display.cfm?pubID=1303.

Mazzetti, Mark, Jane Perlez, Eric Schmitt and Andrew W. Lehren. 'Pakistan Aids Insurgency in Afghanistan, Reports Assert.' *New York Times*, July 25, 2010.

McAllister, Ian. '"The Armalite and the Ballot Box": Sinn Fein's Electoral Strategy in Northern Ireland.' *Electoral Studies* 23, no. 1 (March 2004): 123–42. https://doi.org/10.1016/j.electstud.2003.10.002.

McCauley, Clark R. 'Explaining Homegrown Western Jihadists: The Importance of Western Foreign Policy.' *International Journal of Conflict and Violence* 12 (2018): 1–10. https://doi.org/10.4119/IJCV-3101.

McCord, Mary. 'Filling the Gap in Our Terrorism Statutes.' George Washington University Program on Extremism, Washington, DC, August 2019.

McCord, Mary. 'It's Time for Congress to Make Domestic Terrorism a Federal Crime.' *Lawfare* (blog), December 5, 2018. https://www.

lawfareblog.com/its-time-congress-make-domestic-terrorism-federal-crime.

McDougall, J., M. Zezulkova, B. van Driel, and D. Sternadel. 'Teaching Media Literacy in Europe: Evidence of Effective School Practices in Primary and Secondary Education.' NESET II Report, Publications Office of the European Union, Luxembourg, 2018. https://data. europa.eu/doi/10.2766/613204.

McGuire, W. J., and D. Papageorgis. 'The Relative Efficacy of Various Types of Prior Belief-Defense in Producing Immunity against Persuasion.' *Journal of Abnormal and Social Psychology* 62, no. 2 (March 1961): 327–37. https://doi.org/10.1037/h0042026.

Mehler, Andreas. 'Hybrid Regimes and Oligopolies of Violence in Africa: Expectations on Security Provisions "from Below."' In *Building Peace in the Absence of States: Challenging the Discourse on State Failure*, edited by Martina Fischer and Beatrix Schmelzle, 57–66. Berghof Handbook Dialogue Series 8. Berlin: Berghof Forschungszentrum für Konstruktive Konfliktbearbeitung, 2009.

Mendez, Zeus Hans. 'Repression and Revolt in Balochistan: The Uncertainty and Survival of a People's National Aspirations.' *Journal of Indo-Pacific Affairs* 3, no. 3 (Fall 2020): 43–61.

Menkhaus, Ken. 'Governance without Government in Somalia: Spoilers, State Building, and the Politics of Coping.' *International Security* 31, no. 3 (2006): 74–106.

Menkhaus, Ken. *Somalia: State Collapse and the Threat of Terrorism*. Adelphi Paper 364. Oxford: Oxford University Press for the International Institute for Strategic Studies, 2004.

Merkl, Peter H. 'Approaches to Political Violence: The Stormtroopers, 1925–33.' In *Social Protest, Violence, and Terror in Nineteenth- and Twentieth-Century Europe*, edited by Wolfgang J. Mommsen and Gerhard Hirschfeld, 367–83. London: Macmillan Press, 1982.

Merom, Gil. *How Democracies Lose Small Wars: State, Society, and the Failures of France in Algeria, Israel in Lebanon, and the United States in Vietnam*. Cambridge: Cambridge University Press, 2003.

Merton, Robert K. 'Social Structure and Anomie.' *American Sociological Review* 3, no. 5 (October 1938): 672–82. https://doi.org/10.2307/2084686.

Metz, Steven. 'The Future of Insurgency.' Carlisle Barracks, PA: Strategic Studies Institute, US Army War College, 1993.

Metz, Steven, and Raymond Millen. 'Insurgency and Counterinsurgency in the 21st Century: Reconceptualizing Threat and Response.' Carlisle, PA: Strategic Studies Institute, US Army War College, November 2004.

Michael, George. 'Leaderless Resistance: The New Face of Terrorism.' *Defence Studies* 12, no. 2 (June 2012): 257–82. https://doi.org/10.10 80/14702436.2012.699724.

Michaels, Ralf. 'The Mirage of Non-state Governance.' *Utah Law Review* 2010, no. 1 (2010): 31–46.

Middle East Eye. 'Iran Denies Providing Missiles to Yemen's Houthi Rebels.' Accessed May 13, 2020. http://www.middleeasteye.net/news/iran-denies-providing-missiles-yemens-houthi-rebels.

Milbank, Dana. 'Rumsfeld's War on "Insurgents."' *Washington Post*, November 30, 2005, sec. Opinions. http://www.washingtonpost.com/wp-dyn/content/article/2005/11/29/AR2005112901405.html.

Miller, Alan C. 'Confronting Confirmation Bias: Giving Truth a Fighting Chance in the Information Age.' *Social Education* 80, no. 5 (October 2016): 276–79.

Miller, Greg and Scott Higham. 'In a Propaganda War against ISIS, the U.S. Tried to Play by the Enemy's Rules.' *Washington Post*, May 8, 2015. https://www.washingtonpost.com/world/national-security/in-a-propaganda-war-us-tried-to-play-by-the-enemys-rules/2015/05/08/6eb6b732-e52f-11e4-81ea-0649268f729e_story.html.

Miller, Joanne M., Kyle L. Saunders, and Christina E. Farhart. 'Conspiracy Endorsement as Motivated Reasoning: The Moderating Roles of Political Knowledge and Trust.' *American Journal of Political Science* 60, no. 4 (October 2016): 824–44. https://doi.org/10.1111/ajps.12234.

Mirovalev, Mansur. 'Moscow Welcomes the (Would-Be) Sovereign Nations of California and Texas.' *Los Angeles Times*. September 27, 2016. https://www.latimes.com/world/europe/la-fg-russia-separatists-snap-story.html.

Molnar, Andrew R., William A. Lybrand, Lorna Hahn, James L. Kirkman, and Peter B. Riddleberger. *Undergrounds in Insurgent, Revolutionary, and Resistance Wars*. Washington, DC: Special Operations Research Office, 1963.

Monthly Review. 'Interview with Baburam Bhattarai: Transition to New Democratic Republic in Nepal.' November 21, 2009. https://monthlyreview.org/commentary/interview-with-baburam-bhattarai/.

Morris, Travis. *Dark Ideas: How Neo-Nazi and Violent Jihadi Ideologues Shaped Modern Terrorism*. Lanham, MD: Lexington Books, 2017.

Moskalenko, Sophia, and Clark McCauley. 'QAnon: Radical Opinion versus Radical Action.' *Perspectives on Terrorism* 15, no. 2 (April 2021): 142–46.

Mousseau, Demet Yalcin. 'Democratizing with Ethnic Divisions: A Source of Conflict?' *Journal of Peace Research* 38, no. 5 (2001): 547–67.

Mowle, Thomas S. 'Iraq's Militia Problem.' *Survival* 48, no. 3 (October 2006): 41–58. https://doi.org/10.1080/00396330600905528.

MQM. 'Empowering People: MQM Manifesto 2013.' January 4, 2013. http://www.mqm.org/Manifesto2013.

MQM. 'Life and Death of Mohajirs Is Associated with Sindh Province.' January 6, 2006. http://www.mqm.org/English-News/Jan-2006/news060107.htm.

Muggah, Robert. 'Fragile Cities Rising.' *IPI Global Observatory* (blog), July 10, 2013. https://theglobalobservatory.org/2013/07/fragile-cities-rising/.

Muggah, Robert. 'No Magic Bullet: A Critical Perspective on Disarmament, Demobilization and Reintegration (DDR) and Weapons Reduction in Post-conflict Contexts.' *Round Table* 94, no. 379 (April 2005): 239–52. https://doi.org/10.1080/00358530500082684.

Muirhead, Russell, and Nancy L. Rosenblum. *A Lot of People Are Saying: The New Conspiracism and the Assault on Democracy*. Princeton, NJ: Princeton University Press, 2019.

Muller, Edward N., and Mitchell A. Seligson. 'Inequality and Insurgency.' *American Political Science Review* 81, no. 2 (June 1987). https://doi.org/10.2307/1961960.

Müller, Jan-Werner. 'Should the EU Protect Democracy and the Rule of Law inside Member States? Protection of Democracy and the Rule of Law.' *European Law Journal* 21, no. 2 (March 2015): 141–60. https://doi.org/10.1111/eulj.12124.

Müller, Karsten, and Carlo Schwarz. 'Fanning the Flames of Hate: Social Media and Hate Crime.' Working Paper Series, Centre for Competitive Advantage in the Global Economy, University of Warwick, May 2018. https://www.ssrn.com/abstract=3082972.

Nagle, Angela. *Kill All Normies: The Online Culture Wars from Tumblr and 4chan to the Alt-Right and Trump*. Winchester, UK: Zero Books, 2017.

Nasution, Abdul Haris. *Fundamentals of Guerrilla Warfare*. New York: Praeger, 1965.

Nationaal Coördinator Terrorismebestrijding en Veiligheid. 'Terrorist Threat Assessment for the Netherlands 53.' Ministerie van Justitie en Veiligheid, The Hague, October 2020.

NATO. 'Allied Joint Doctrine for Counterinsurgency (COIN).' Brussels, 2009.

Nazwan, Ahmed. 'The United Kingdom's Effort to Rehabilitate Extremists.' In *Terrorist Deradicalisation in Global Contexts: Success, Failure, and Continuity*, edited by Rohan Gunaratna and Sabariah Hussin, 12–32. Routledge Studies in the Politics of Disorder and Instability. London: Routledge, 2020.

NBC News. 'Klan Group Ordered to Pay $2.5 Million.' November 15, 2008. https://www.nbcnews.com/id/wbna27728315.

Neiwert, David A. *Alt-America: The Rise of the Radical Right in the Age of Trump*. London: Verso, 2017.

Nepali Times. 'Maoists Tricked UNMIN.' May 8, 2009. https://archive. nepalitimes.com/news.php?id=15924.

Neumann, Peter R. 'The Bullet and the Ballot Box: The Case of the IRA.' *Journal of Strategic Studies* 28, no. 6 (December 2005): 941–75. https:// doi.org/10.1080/01402390500441081.

Newman, Eryn J., Maryanne Garry, Daniel M. Bernstein, Justin Kantner, and D. Stephen Lindsay. 'Nonprobative Photographs (or Words) Inflate Truthiness.' *Psychonomic Bulletin and Review* 19, no. 5 (October 2012): 969–74. https://doi.org/10.3758/s13423-012-0292-0.

New York Review of Books. 'Hannah Arendt: From an Interview.' October 26, 1978. http://www.nybooks.com/articles/1978/10/26/hannah-arendt-from-an-interview/.

Nguyên Giáp Võ. *People's War, People's Army: The Viet Công Insurrection Manual for Underdeveloped Countries*. Praeger Publications in Russian History and World Communism 119. New York: Praeger, 1962.

Nicas, Jack. 'How YouTube Drives People to the Internet's Darkest Corners.' *Wall Street Journal*, February 7, 2018, sec. Tech. https://www. wsj.com/articles/how-youtube-drives-viewers-to-the-internets-darkest-corners-1518020478.

Nickerson, Raymond S. 'Confirmation Bias: A Ubiquitous Phenomenon in Many Guises.' *Review of General Psychology* 2, no. 2 (June 1998): 175–220. https://doi.org/10.1037/1089-2680.2.2.175.

Nissenbaum, Dion. 'McChrystal Calls Marjah a "Bleeding Ulcer" in Afghan Campaign.' McClatchy. May 24, 2010, sec. World. https://www. mcclatchydc.com/news/nation-world/world/article24583621.html.

Noriega, Roger F. 'Evo Morales's Reelection: Last Stand for Democracy?' Latin American Outlook, American Enterprise Institute, Washington, DC, December 2009. http://www.aei.org/wp-content/uploads/2011/10/No-%204-LAOg.pdf.

Notezai, Muhammad Akbar. 'The Rise of Religious Extremism in Balochistan.' *The Diplomat*, January 9, 2017. https://thediplomat. com/2017/01/the-rise-of-religious-extremism-in-balochistan/.

Nouri, Lella, Nuria Lorenzo-Dus, and Amy-Louise Watkin. 'Following the Whack-a-Mole: Britain First's Visual Strategy from Facebook to Gab.' Global Research Network on Terrorism and Technology, RUSI, London, July 2019.

Novosseloff, Alexandra. 'The Many Lives of a Peacekeeping Mission: The

UN Operation in Côte D'Ivoire.' International Peace Institute, June 2018. https://doi.org/10.2139/ssrn.3261285.

NPR. 'Homegrown Threat: FBI Tracks White Supremicists [sic], Domestic Extremists.' June 28, 2015, Sunday edition, sec. National. https://www.npr.org/2015/06/28/418262038/homegrown-threat-fbi-tracks-white-supremicists-domestic-extremists.

Nyhan, Brendan, and Jason Reifler. 'The Roles of Information Deficits and Identity Threat in the Prevalence of Misperceptions.' *Journal of Elections, Public Opinion and Parties* 29, no. 2 (April 3, 2019): 222–44. https://doi.org/10.1080/17457289.2018.1465061.

O'Doherty, Malachi. *The Trouble With Guns: Republican Strategy and the Provisional IRA*. Belfast: Blackstaff Press, 1998.

OECD. 'Preparing Our Youth for an Inclusive and Sustainable World: The OECD PISA Global Competence Framework.' Directorate for Education and Skills, OECD, Paris, 2018.

Oliphant, James, and Chris Kahn. 'Half of Republicans Believe False Accounts of Deadly U.S. Capitol Riot—Reuters/Ipsos Poll.' Reuters, April 6, 2021. https://www.reuters.com/article/us-usa-politics-disinformation-idUSKBN2BS0RZ.

Ollivant, Douglas A. 'Why Washington Should Side with the Protesters in Iraq.' *Washington Post*, November 5, 2019, sec. Opinion. https://www.washingtonpost.com/opinions/2019/11/05/why-washington-should-side-with-protesters-iraq/.

Olson, Mançur. *Power and Prosperity: Outgrowing Communist and Capitalist Dictatorships*. New York: Basic Books, 2000.

Olson, Parmy. *We Are Anonymous: Inside the Hacker World of LulzSec, Anonymous, and the Global Cyber Insurgency*. New York: Back Bay, 2013.

Ooi, Giok Ling, and Kai Hong Phua. 'Urbanization and Slum Formation.' *Journal of Urban Health* 84, no. S1 (May 2007): 27–34. https://doi.org/10.1007/s11524-007-9167-5.

Oosterbaan, Sarah, and Joris van Wijk. 'Pacifying and Integrating the Favelas of Rio de Janeiro: An Evaluation of the Impact of the UPP Program on Favela Residents.' *International Journal of Comparative and Applied Criminal Justice* 39, no. 3 (July 3, 2015): 179–98. https://doi.org/10.1080/01924036.2014.973052.

Orr, Deborah. 'Anders Behring Breivik's Not a Terrorist, He's a Mass-Murderer.' *The Guardian*, July 27, 2011, sec. World news. http://www.theguardian.com/world/2011/jul/27/breivik-not-terrorist-insane-murderer.

Ospina, Carlos. 'Colombia and the FARC: From Military Victory to Ambivalent Political Reintegration?' In *Impunity: Countering Illicit Power in War and Transition*, edited by Michelle Hughes and

Michael Miklaucic, 150–69. Washington, DC: Center for Complex Operations (CCO) and the Peacekeeping and Stability Operations Institute (PKSOI), 2016.

Ospina, Carlos A., Thomas A. Marks, and David H. Ucko. 'Colombia and the War-to-Peace Transition: Cautionary Lessons from Other Cases.' *Military Review* 96, no. 4 (2016). http://usacac.army.mil/CAC2/MilitaryReview/Archives/English/MilitaryReview_20160831_art010.pdf.

Ospina, Carlos, and Thomas A. Marks. 'Colombia: Changing Strategy amidst the Struggle.' *Small Wars and Insurgencies* 25, no. 2 (March 4, 2014): 354–71.

Owen, Taylor. 'Sasha Havlicek on Mitigating the Spread of Online Extremism.' *Big Tech* (podcast), March 12, 2020. https://www.cigionline.org/big-tech/sasha-havlicek-mitigating-spread-online-extremism.

Paley, Amit R., and Zaid Sabah. 'Case Is Dropped against Shiites in Sunni Deaths.' *Washington Post*, March 4, 2008. http://www.washingtonpost.com/wp-dyn/content/article/2008/03/03/AR2008030300311.html.

Palmer, Bryan D. 'The French Turn in the United States: James P. Cannon and the Trotskyist Entry into the Socialist Party, 1934–1937.' *Labor History* 59, no. 5 (September 3, 2018): 610–38. https://doi.org/10.1080/0023656X.2018.1436946.

Pamment, James. 'The EU Code of Practice on Disinformation: Briefing Note for the New EU Commission.' Policy Perspective Series, Carnegie Endowment for International Peace, Washington, DC, March 2020.

Parker, Ned. 'The Iraq We Left Behind: Welcome to the World's Next Failed State.' *Foreign Affairs* 91, no. 2 (2012): 94–110.

Patel, Ronak B., and David P. Palotty. 'Climate Change and Urbanization: Challenges to Global Security and Stability.' *Joint Force Quarterly* 89, no. 2 (2018): 93–98.

Patriot Voice. 'For God and Country Victory Cruise.' Accessed January 28, 2021. https://www.thepatriotvoice.us.

Payne, Kenneth. 'Building the Base: Al Qaeda's Focoist Strategy.' *Studies in Conflict and Terrorism* 34, no. 2 (January 24, 2011): 124–43.

Pennycook, Gordon, Adam Bear, Evan T. Collins, and David G. Rand. 'The Implied Truth Effect: Attaching Warnings to a Subset of Fake News Headlines Increases Perceived Accuracy of Headlines without Warnings.' *Management Science* 66, no. 11 (November 2020): 4944–57. https://doi.org/10.1287/mnsc.2019.3478.

Perliger, Arie. 'Challengers from the Sidelines: Understanding America's

Violent Far-Right,' Combating Terrorism Center, West Point, November 1, 2012. https://doi.org/10.21236/ADA576380.

Pew Research Center. '5 Facts about the QAnon Conspiracy Theories.' *Fact Tank* (blog), November 16, 2020. https://www.pewresearch.org/fact-tank/2020/11/16/5-facts-about-the-qanon-conspiracy-theories/.

Pézard, Stéphanie, and Michael Robert Shurkin. *Achieving Peace in Northern Mali: Past Agreements, Local Conflicts, and the Prospects for a Durable Settlement.* Santa Monica, CA: RAND, 2015.

Phillips, P. Michael. 'Deconstructing Our Dark Age Future.' *Parameters* 39, no. 2 (Summer 2009): 94–110. https://doi.org/10.21236/ADA501234.

Pinker, Steven. *The Better Angels of Our Nature: Why Violence Has Declined.* New York: Penguin Books, 2012.

Poder360. 'Com Exército no RJ, projeto quer Justiça Militar julgando crimes contra civis.' September 14, 2017. https://www.poder360.com.br/congresso/com-exercito-no-rj-projeto-quer-justica-militar-julgando-crimes-contra-civis/.

Pokalova, Elena. 'Framing Separatism as Terrorism: Lessons from Kosovo.' *Studies in Conflict and Terrorism* 33, no. 5 (April 9, 2010): 429–47. https://doi.org/10.1080/10576101003691564.

Polese, Abel, and Ruth Hanau Santini. 'Limited Statehood and Its Security Implications on the Fragmentation Political Order in the Middle East and North Africa.' *Small Wars and Insurgencies* 29, no. 3 (May 4, 2018): 379–90. https://doi.org/10.1080/09592318.2018.1456815.

Politico. 'Transcript: Hillary Clinton's Full Remarks in Reno, Nevada.' August 25, 2016. https://www.politico.com/story/2016/08/transcript-hillary-clinton-alt-right-reno-227419.

Pollack, Kenneth M. 'The Seven Deadly Sins of Failure in Iraq: A Retrospective Analysis of the Reconstruction.' *Middle East Review of International Affairs* 10, no. 4 (December 2006): 1–20.

Pollet, Mathieu. 'EU Adopts Law Giving Tech Giants One Hour to Remove Terrorist Content.' Euractiv, April 28, 2021. https://www.euractiv.com/section/cybersecurity/news/eu-adopts-law-giving-tech-giants-one-hour-to-remove-terrorist-content/.

Polo, Sara MT. 'The Quality of Terrorist Violence: Explaining the Logic of Terrorist Target Choice.' *Journal of Peace Research* 57, no. 2 (March 2020): 235–50. https://doi.org/10.1177/0022343319829799.

Polyakova, Alina. 'Strange Bedfellows: Putin and Europe's Far Right.' *World Affairs* 177, no. 3 (2014): 36–40.

Popkin, Samuel Lewis. 'The Myth of the Village: Revolution and Reaction in Viet Nam.' Thesis, Massachusetts Institute of Technology, 1969. https://dspace.mit.edu/handle/1721.1/41778.

Popper, Karl. *The Open Society and Its Enemies*. Princeton, NJ: Princeton University Press, 2013.

Prince, Matthew. 'Terminating Service for 8chan.' *The Cloudflare Blog* (blog), August 5, 2019. https://blog.cloudflare.com/terminating-service-for-8chan/.

Prince, Matthew. 'Why We Terminated Daily Stormer.' *The Cloudflare Blog* (blog), August 16, 2017. https://blog.cloudflare.com/why-we-terminated-daily-stormer/.

Puff, Jefferson. 'Como grupo de jovens virou referência internacional na denúncia de abusos policiais.' BBC Brazil, October 30, 2015. http://www.bbc.com/portuguese/noticias/2015/10/151028_coletivo_papo_reto_alemao_jp.

QAnon Anonymous. 'International QAnon (The Netherlands) Feat. Marc-André Argentino.' December 30, 2020. https://soundcloud.com/qanonanonymous/episode-123-international-qanon-the-netherlands-feat-marc-andre-argentino.

QAnon Anonymous. 'Undercover at the Save the Children (Again) Rally.' April 28, 2021. https://soundcloud.com/qanonanonymous/episode-140-undercover-at-the-save-the-children-again-rally.

Quenallata, René. 'El Mallku revela que falló una emboscada para matar a Sánchez Berzaín.' Eju!, August 4, 2013, Opinion edition. https://eju.tv/2013/08/el-mallku-revela-que-fall-una-emboscada-para-matar-a-snchez-berzan/.

Rafiq, Arif. 'Operation Karachi: Pakistan's Military Retakes the City.' *National Interest*, August 24, 2015. https://nationalinterest.org/feature/operation-karachi-pakistans-military-retakes-the-city-13660.

Raleigh, Clionadh. 'Political Hierarchies and Landscapes of Conflict across Africa.' *Political Geography* 42 (2014): 92–103.

Ramos da Cruz, Claudio, and David H. Ucko. 'Beyond the Unidades de Polícia Pacificadora: Countering Comando Vermelho's Criminal Insurgency.' *Small Wars and Insurgencies* 29, no. 1 (January 2, 2018): 38–67.

Rappeport, Alan. 'From the Right, a New Slur for G.O.P. Candidates.' *New York Times*, August 13, 2015, sec. U.S. https://www.nytimes.com/2015/08/13/us/from-the-right-a-new-slur-for-gop-candidates.html.

Radio Free Europe. 'Leaked NATO Report Shows Pakistan Support For Taliban,' February 01 2012. https://www.rferl.org/a/leaked_nato_report_shows_pakistan_support_for_taliban_awire/24469649.html.

Rathmell, Andrew, Olga Oliker, Terrence K. Kelly, David Brannan, and Keith Crane. *Developing Iraq's Security Sector: The Coalition Provisional Authority's Experience*. Santa Monica, CA: RAND Corporation, 2005.

Rawls, John. *A Theory of Justice*. Rev. ed. Cambridge, MA: Belknap Press of Harvard University Press, 1971.

Rayburn, Joel, and Frank K. Sobchak, eds. *The U.S. Army in the Iraq War*. Carlisle, PA: Strategic Studies Institute, US Army War College Press, 2019.

Redish, Martin, and Matthew Fisher. 'Terrorizing Advocacy and the First Amendment: Free Expression and the Fallacy of Mutual Exclusivity.' *Fordham Law Review* 86, no. 2 (November 1, 2017).

Refugee Review Tribunal, Australia. 'RRT Research Response: Nepal.' March 4, 2008. https://www.justice.gov/sites/default/files/eoir/legacy/2013/06/11/npl32984.pdf.

Reichardt, Sven. 'Violence and Community: A Micro-study on Nazi Storm Troopers.' *Central European History* 46, no. 2 (June 2013): 275–97. https://doi.org/10.1017/S0008938913000617.

Reitman, Janet. 'All-American Nazis: Inside the Rise of Fascist Youth in the U.S.' *Rolling Stone*, May 2, 2018. https://www.rollingstone.com/politics/politics-news/all-american-nazis-628023/.

Renieris, Elizabeth M. 'Combating Incitement to Terrorism on the Internet: Comparative Approaches in the United States and United Kingdom and the Need for an International Solution.' *Vanderbilt Journal of Entertainment and Technology Law* 11, no. 3 (2009): 673–709.

Reno, William. 'Clandestine Economies, Violence and States in Africa.' *Journal of International Affairs* 53, no. 2 (Spring 2000): 433–59.

Reno, William. *Warfare in Independent Africa*. Cambridge: Cambridge University Press, 2011.

Republic of Colombia. 'Democratic Security and Defence Policy.' Presidency of the Republic: Ministry of Defence, Bogotá, 2003.

Reuters. 'Rio's Murder Rate Soared Last Year despite Calm during Olympics.' February 1, 2017. https://www.reuters.com/article/us-brazil-violence/rios-murder-rate-soared-last-year-despite-calm-during-olympics-idUSKBN15G5K6.

Rich, Paul B. 'People's War Antithesis: Che Guevara and the Mythology of Focismo.' *Small Wars and Insurgencies* 28, no. 3 (May 4, 2017): 451–87. https://doi.org/10.1080/09592318.2017.1307616.

Richards, Anthony. 'Terrorist Groups and Political Fronts: The IRA, Sinn Fein, the Peace Process and Democracy.' *Terrorism and Political Violence* 13, no. 4 (December 2001): 72–89. https://doi.org/10.1080/09546550109609700.

Ricks, Thomas E. *Fiasco: The American Military Adventure in Iraq*. New York: Penguin Books, 2007.

Ricks, Thomas E. *The Gamble: General Petraeus and the American Military Adventure in Iraq*. New York: Penguin Books, 2010.

Risse, Thomas, ed. *Governance without a State? Policies and Politics in Areas of Limited Statehood*. New York: Columbia University Press, 2011.

Roach, Kent. *The 9/11 Effect: Comparative Counter-terrorism*. Cambridge: Cambridge University Press, 2011.

Robb, Amanda. 'Pizzagate: Anatomy of a Fake News Scandal.' *Rolling Stone*, November 16, 2017. https://www.rollingstone.com/politics/news/pizzagate-anatomy-of-a-fake-news-scandal-w511904.

Roberts, James Q. 'Need Authorities for the Gray Zone?' *PRISM* 6, no. 3 (December 2016): 21–32.

Roberts, Paul. 'Chats, Car Crushes and Cut 'N Paste Sowed Seeds of LulzSec's Demise.' *Threatpost*, March 7, 2012. https://threatpost.com/chats-car-crushes-and-cut-n-paste-sowed-seeds-lulzsecs-demise-030712/76298/.

Robertson, Derek. 'How an Obscure Conservative Theory Became the Trump Era's Go-to Nerd Phrase.' *Politico Magazine*, February 25, 2018. http://politi.co/2FunqYx.

Robinson, Nathan J. 'Let's Just Stop Writing Long-Form Profiles of Nazis.' *Current Affairs*, November 27, 2017. https://www.currentaffairs.org/2017/11/lets-just-stop-writing-long-form-profiles-of-nazis.

Rocha, José Luis. 'Street Gangs of Nicaragua.' In *Maras: Gang Violence and Security in Central America*, edited by Thomas C. Bruneau, Lucía Dammert, and Elizabeth Skinner, translated by Michael Solis, 105–21. Austin, TX: University of Texas Press, 2011.

Rodriguez, Alberto K. 'Evitar la confrontación: Entrevista con Filemón Escobar.' *Encuentro* 44 (July 20, 2007): 99–104.

Romm, Tony, and Elizabeth Dwoskin. 'Twitter Purged More than 70,000 Accounts Affiliated with QAnon Following Capitol Riot.' *Washington Post*, January 11, 2021. https://www.washingtonpost.com/technology/2021/01/11/trump-twitter-ban/.

Ronfeldt, David F., John Arquilla, Graham E. Fuller, and Melissa Fuller. *The Zapatista 'Social Netwar' in Mexico*. Santa Monica, CA: RAND, 1998.

Roose, Kevin. 'The Alt-Right Created a Parallel Internet: It's an Unholy Mess.' *New York Times*, December 11, 2017, sec. Technology. https://www.nytimes.com/2017/12/11/technology/alt-right-internet.html.

Rosand, Eric. 'Communities First: A Blueprint for Organizing and Sustaining a Global Movement against Violent Extremism.' Prevention

Project: Organizing Against Violent Extremism, Washington, DC, December 2016.

Rosand, Eric. 'The Global CVE Agenda: Can We Move from Talk to Walk?' *Up Front* (blog), April 20, 2016. https://www.brookings.edu/blog/up-front/2016/04/20/the-global-cve-agenda-can-we-move-from-talk-to-walk/.

Rose, Lisa. 'How a Suicidal Pizza Man Found Himself Ensnared in an FBI Terror Sting.' CNN, November 29, 2017, sec. Politics. https://www.cnn.com/2017/11/29/politics/aby-rayyan-fbi-terror-sting-pizza-man.

Roy, Olivier. 'Development and Political Legitimacy: The Cases of Iraq and Afghanistan.' *Conflict, Security & Development* 4, no. 2 (2004): 167-179. https://www.tandfonline.com/doi/abs/10.1080/14678800420002 59095

Rufer, Reto. 'Disarmament, Demobilisation and Reintegration (DDR): Conceptual Approaches, Specific Settings, Practical Experiences.' Working Paper, Geneva Centre for the Democratic Control of Armed Forces (DCAF), Geneva, 2005.

Russell, Nathan J. 'An Introduction to the Overton Window of Political Possibilities.' Mackinac Center for Public Policy, January 4, 2006. https://www.mackinac.org/7504.

Sabat, Ahmad, Muhammad Shoaib, and Abdul Qadar. 'Religious Populism in Pakistani Punjab: How Khadim Rizvi's Tehreek-e-Labbaik Pakistan Emerged.' *International Area Studies Review* 23, no. 4 (December 2020): 365–81. https://doi.org/10.1177/2233865920968657.

Saletan, William. 'Americans are Dangerously Divided on the Insurrection.' *Slate*, June 09, 2021. https://slate.com/news-and-politics/2021/06/americans-divided-insurrection-investigation-voter-fraud-polls.html.

Salhy, Suadad al-. 'Iraq Shi'ite Militia Splinters into Hit Squads, Gangs.' Reuters, July 21, 2011. https://www.reuters.com/article/us-iraq-violence-mehdi-idUSTRE76K22E20110721.

Sampaio, Antonio. 'Out of Control: Criminal Gangs Fight Back in Rio's Favelas.' *Jane's Intelligence Review* 26, no. 12 (December 2014): 44–48.

Sánchez, W. Alejandro. 'Sangre Joven? Understanding the New Wave of Armed Groups in Latin America.' *Security and Defense Studies Review* 12 (Fall–Winter 2011): 135–53.

Sapolsky, Robert M. *Behave: The Biology of Humans at Our Best and Worst.* New York: Penguin Press, 2017.

Saragerova, Boryana. 'France: Towards Stronger Counter-terrorism Regulation Online.' *Global Risk Insights*, November 29, 2020. https://globalriskinsights.com/2020/11/france-towards-stronger-counter-terrorism-regulation-online/.

Sayari, Sabri, and Bruce Hoffman. *Urbanization and Insurgency: The Turkish Case, 1975–1980*. Santa Monica, CA: RAND Corporation, 1991.

Scheindlin, Dahlia, and Gilad Halpern. 'Who Poisoned My News?' *Tel Aviv Review*. November 23, 2020. https://tlv1.fm/the-tel-aviv-review/2020/11/23/who-poisoned-my-news/.

Scher, Bill. 'It's Time for a Domestic Terrorism Law.' *Washington Monthly*, January 14, 2021, sec. Politics. https://washingtonmonthly.com/2021/01/14/its-time-for-a-domestic-terrorism-law/.

Schuberth, Moritz. 'Beyond Gang Truces and Mano Dura Policies: Towards Substitutive Security Governance in Latin America.' *Stability: International Journal of Security and Development* 5, no. 1 (December 28, 2016): 1–20.

Schuberth, Moritz. 'Disarmament, Demobilization and Reintegration in Unconventional Settings: The Case of MINUSTAH's Community Violence Reduction.' *International Peacekeeping* 24, no. 3 (May 27, 2017): 410–33. https://doi.org/10.1080/13533312.2016.1277145.

Schuberth, Moritz. 'To Engage or Not to Engage Haiti's Urban Armed Groups? Safe Access in Disaster-Stricken and Conflict-Affected Cities.' *Environment and Urbanization* 29, no. 2 (October 2017): 425–42. https://doi.org/10.1177/0956247817716398.

Schuurman, Bart, Edwin Bakker, Paul Gill, and Noémie Bouhana. 'Lone Actor Terrorist Attack Planning and Preparation: A Data-Driven Analysis.' *Journal of Forensic Sciences* 63, no. 4 (July 2018): 1191–200. https://doi.org/10.1111/1556-4029.13676.

Schwedler, Jillian. 'Can Islamists Become Moderates? Rethinking the Inclusion-Moderation Hypothesis.' *World Politics* 63, no. 2 (April 2011): 347–76. https://doi.org/10.1017/S0043887111000050.

Schwencke, Ken. 'How One Major Internet Company Helps Serve Up Hate on the Web.' *ProPublica*, May 4, 2017. https://www.propublica.org/article/how-cloudflare-helps-serve-up-hate-on-the-web?token=20Tgq0p4nnwC4i13hjc-gV7MRR72yNoe.

Scott, Mark. 'QAnon Goes European.' *Politico*, October 23, 2020. https://www.politico.eu/article/qanon-europe-coronavirus-protests/.

Selim, George, and Daveed Gartenstein-Ross. 'Save the Terrorism Prevention Toolkit.' *War on the Rocks*, August 28, 2017. https://warontherocks.com/2017/08/save-the-terrorism-prevention-toolkit/.

Selznick, Philip. *The Organizational Weapon: A Study of Bolshevik Strategy and Tactics*. Santa Monica, CA: RAND Corporation, 1952. https://www.rand.org/pubs/reports/R201.html.

Senewiratne, Brian. 'Tamils in the North-East Protest at Last.' *Colombo*

Telegraph, October 4, 2016. https://www.colombotelegraph.com/index.php/tamils-in-the-north-east-protest-at-last/.

Shapiro, Jacob N. *The Terrorist's Dilemma: Managing Violent Covert Organizations*. Princeton, NJ: Princeton University Press, 2017. https://doi.org/10.23943/princeton/9780691157214.001.0001.

Shapiro, Jeremy, and Bénédicte Suzan. 'The French Experience of Counter-terrorism.' *Survival* 45, no. 1 (March 2003): 67–98. https://doi.org/10.1093/survival/45.1.67.

Shearer, Elisa, and Amy Mitchell. 'News Use across Social Media Platforms in 2020.' *Pew Research Center's Journalism Project* (blog), January 12, 2021. https://www.journalism.org/2021/01/12/news-use-across-social-media-platforms-in-2020/.

Sherman, Jon. '"A Person Otherwise Innocent": Policing Entrapment in Preventative, Undercover Counterterrorism Investigations.' *Journal of Constitutional Law* 11, no. 5 (July 2009): 1475–510.

Sherman, Michael J. 'Brandenburg v. Twitter.' *Civil Rights Law Journal* 28, no. 2 (2018): 127–72.

Shipley, Thomas. 'Mali: Overview of Corruption and Anti-Corruption.' U4 Helpdesk Answers. Chr. Michelsen Institute, 2017. https://www.u4.no/publications/mali-overview-of-corruption-and-anti-corruption.

Shiraef, Mary. 'From Fighting Nazis to Electing Nazis: The Rise of Golden Dawn in Greece.' *Cornell International Affairs Review* 7, no. 1 (2013). http://www.inquiriesjournal.com/articles/1486/from-fighting-nazis-to-electing-nazis-the-rise-of-golden-dawn-in-greece.

Shurkin, Michael. 'Subnational Government in Afghanistan.' Occasional Paper, RAND Corporation, Santa Monica, CA, 2011.

Shy, John W. *A People Numerous and Armed: Reflections on the Military Struggle for American Independence*. Rev. ed. Ann Arbor: University of Michigan Press, 1990.

Siddiqui, Niloufer. 'The MQM and Identity Politics in Pakistan.' *Criterion Quarterly* 3, no. 3 (November 20, 2020). https://criterion-quarterly.com/the-mqm-and-identity-politics-in-pakistan/.

Siddiqui, Niloufer. 'Strategic Violence among Religious Parties in Pakistan.' In *Oxford Research Encyclopedia of Politics*. Oxford: Oxford University Press, 2019. https://doi.org/10.1093/acrefore/9780190228637.013.842.

Siemens, Daniel. *Stormtroopers: A New History of Hitler's Brownshirts*. New Haven, CT: Yale University Press, 2017.

Silke, Andrew. 'Rebel's Dilemma: The Changing Relationship between the IRA, Sinn Féin and Paramilitary Vigilantism in Northern Ireland.' *Terrorism and Political Violence* 11, no. 1 (March 1999): 55–93. https://doi.org/10.1080/09546559908427495.

Silverman, Craig. 'This Analysis Shows How Viral Fake Election News Stories Outperformed Real News on Facebook.' *BuzzFeed News*, November 16, 2016. https://www.buzzfeednews.com/article/craigsilverman/viral-fake-election-news-outperformed-real-news-on-facebook.

Simi, Pete, and Robert Futrell. *American Swastika: Inside the White Power Movement's Hidden Spaces of Hate*. Lanham, MD: Rowman and Littlefield Publishers, 2010.

Simon, Steven. 'The Price of the Surge.' *Foreign Affairs* 87, no. 3 (May 3, 2008). https://www.foreignaffairs.com/articles/iraq/2008-05-03/price-surge.

Singer, P. W., and Emerson T. Brooking. *LikeWar: The Weaponization of Social Media*. Boston: Eamon Dolan/Houghton Mifflin Harcourt, 2018.

Singer-Emery, Jacques, and Rex Bray III. 'The Iron March Data Dump Provides a Window into How White Supremacists Communicate and Recruit.' *Lawfare* (blog), February 27, 2020. https://www.lawfareblog.com/iron-march-data-dump-provides-window-how-white-supremacists-communicate-and-recruit.

Skaperdas, Stergios. 'The Political Economy of Organized Crime: Providing Protection When the State Does Not.' *Economics of Governance* 2, no. 3 (November 2001).

Slinko, Elena, Stanislav Bilyuga, Julia Zinkina, and Andrey Korotayev. 'Regime Type and Political Destabilization in Cross-national Perspective: A Re-analysis.' *Cross-cultural Research* 51, no. 1 (February 2017): 26–50. https://doi.org/10.1177/1069397116676485.

Sloan, Stephen. 'The Challenge of Nonterritorial and Virtual Conflicts: Rethinking Counterinsurgency and Counterterrorism.' JSOU Report, Joint Special Operations University, MacDill AFB, Florida, March 2011.

Sloan, Steven. 'The Changing Face of Insurgency in the Post-Cold War Era: Doctrinal and Operational Implications.' In *Saving Democracies: US Intervention in Threatened Democratic States*, edited by Anthony James Joes, 67–80. Westport, CT: Praeger.

Smith, Anthony, and Cooper Fleishman. '(((Echoes))), Exposed: The Secret Symbol Neo-Nazis Use to Target Jews Online.' *Mic*, June 1, 2016. https://www.mic.com/articles/144228/echoes-exposed-the-secret-symbol-neo-nazis-use-to-target-jews-online.

Smith, M. L. R. *Fighting for Ireland?: The Military Strategy of the Irish Republican Movement*. Abingdon: Routledge, 2003.

Smith, M. L. R. and David Martin Jones. *The Political Impossibility of Modern Counterinsurgency: Strategic Problems, Puzzles, and Paradoxes*. New York: Columbia University Press, 2015.

Smith, Paul Hubert. *Loyalists and Redcoats: A Study in British Revolutionary Policy*. Durham: University of North Carolina Press, 1964.

Smyth, Philip. 'Beware of Muqtada al-Sadr.' Policy Analysis, Washington Institute, October 19, 2016. https://www.washingtoninstitute.org/policy-analysis/view/beware-of-muqtada-al-sadr.

Solomon, Evan. 'Fighting in Afghanistan: "You Have the Watches. We Have the Time."' *Maclean's*, September 2, 2017. https://www.macleans.ca/news/fighting-in-afghanistan-you-have-the-watches-we-have-the-time/.

Sorrell v. IMS Health Inc. (Syllabus), no. 10-779, Supreme Court of the United States June 23, 2011.

South Asia Terrorism Portal. 'Nepal Terrorist Groups: Young Communist League (YCL).' Accessed August 6, 2018. http://www.satp.org/satporgtp/countries/nepal/terroristoutfits/YCL.html.

Southern Poverty Law Center. 'Hate Map.' Accessed February 11, 2021. https://www.splcenter.org/hate-map.

Southern Poverty Law Center. 'Klan Leader Jeff Berry Faces Ruin after SPLC Lawsuit.' *Intelligence Report*, 2000. https://www.splcenter.org/fighting-hate/intelligence-report/2000/klan-leader-jeff-berry-faces-ruin-after-splc-lawsuit.

Southern Poverty Law Center. 'The Year in Hate and Extremism: Far-Right Extremists Coalescing in Broad-Based, Loosely Affiliated Movement.' February 5, 2021. https://www.splcenter.org/news/2021/02/05/year-hate-and-extremism-far-right-extremists-coalescing-broad-based-loosely-affiliated.

Spencer, David E., and Hugo Acha Melgar. 'Bolivia, a New Model Insurgency for the 21st Century: From Mao Back to Lenin.' *Small Wars and Insurgencies* 28, no. 3 (May 4, 2017): 629–60.

Spencer, David J. *Colombia's Paramilitaries: Criminal or Political Force?* Carlisle, PA: Strategic Studies Institute, US Army War College, 2001.

Spencer, David J. 'The Evolution and Implementation of FARC Strategy: Insights from Its Internal Documents.' *Security and Defense Studies Review* 12, nos. 1–2 (Fall–Winter 2011): 73–98.

Speri, Alice. 'Unredacted FBI Document Sheds New Light on White Supremacist Infiltration of Law Enforcement.' *The Intercept*, September 29, 2020. https://theintercept.com/2020/09/29/police-white-supremacist-infiltration-fbi/.

Spyridon, Tsoutsoumpis. 'The Far Right in Greece. Paramilitarism, Organized Crime and the Rise of "Golden Dawn."' *Südosteuropa: Journal of Politics and Society* 66, no. 4 (2018): 503–31.

Staniland, Paul. 'Cities on Fire: Social Mobilization, State Policy, and Urban Insurgency.' *Comparative Political Studies* 43, no. 12 (December 2010): 1623–49. https://doi.org/10.1177/0010414010374022.

Staniland, Paul. 'Political Violence in South Asia: The Triumph of the State?' Carnegie Endowment for International Peace, September 3, 2020. https://carnegieendowment.org/2020/09/03/political-violence-in-south-asia-triumph-of-state-pub-82641.

Staniland, Paul. 'States, Insurgents, and Wartime Political Orders.' *Perspectives on Politics* 10, no. 2 (June 2012): 243–64. https://doi.org/10.1017/S1537592712000655.

Steele, Abbey. *Democracy and Displacement in Colombia's Civil War*. Ithaca, NY: Cornell University Press, 2017.

Stern, Alexandra Minna. *Proud Boys and the White Ethnostate: How the Alt-Right Is Warping the American Imagination*. Boston: Beacon Press, 2019.

Stern, Jessica, and J. M. Berger. *ISIS: The State of Terror*. New York: Ecco Press/HarperCollins, 2016.

Stewart, Frances, and E. V. K. Fitzgerald, eds. *War and Underdevelopment*. 2 vols. Oxford: Oxford University Press, 2001.

Stochastic Terrorism (blog). 'Stochastic Terrorism: Part 1, Triggering the Shooters.' January 26, 2011. http://stochasticterrorism.blogspot.com/2011/01/stochastic-terrorism-part-1-triggering.html.

Stoicescu, Kalev. 'The Evolution of Russian Hybrid Warfare: Estonia.' *CEPA* (blog), January 29, 2021. https://cepa.org/the-evolution-of-russian-hybrid-warfare-estonia/.

Storm, Lise. 'Exploring Post-rebel Parties in Power: Political Space and Implications for Islamist Inclusion and Moderation.' *Open Journal of Political Science* 10, no. 4 (2020): 638–67. https://doi.org/10.4236/ojps.2020.104038.

Straubhaar, Rolf. 'A Broader Definition of Fragile States: The Communities and Schools of Brazil's Favelas.' *Current Issues in Comparative Education* 15, no. 1 (2012): 41–51.

Straziuso, Jason. 'US Team Using Twitter, Facebook to Fight Militants.' *Taiwan News*, April 13, 2012. https://www.taiwannews.com.tw/en/news/2195115.

Subramanian, Nirupama. 'Explained: How Radical Outfit Forced Pakistan Hand in Move to Expel French Envoy.' *Indian Express*, April 27, 2021. https://indianexpress.com/article/explained/tehreek-e-labbaik-pakistan-saad-hussain-rizvi-protests-imran-khan-7281260/.

Sullivan, John P. 'How Illicit Networks Impact Sovereignty.' In *Convergence: Illicit Networks and National Security in the Age of Globalization*, edited by

Michael Miklaucic and Jacqueline Brewer, 171–88. Washington, DC: NDU Press, 2013.

Sullivan, John P. 'Narco-Cities: Mexico and Beyond.' *Small Wars Journal*, March 3, 2014. https://smallwarsjournal.com/jrnl/art/narco-cities-mexico-and-beyond#_edn17.

Sullivan, John P., and Robert J. Bunker. 'Drug Cartels, Street Gangs, and Warlords.' *Small Wars and Insurgencies* 13, no. 2 (August 2002): 40–53. https://doi.org/10.1080/09592310208559180.

Sullivan, John P., and Robert J. Bunker 'Rethinking Insurgency: Criminality, Spirituality, and Societal Warfare in the Americas.' *Small Wars and Insurgencies* 22, no. 5 (December 2011): 742–63. https://doi.org/10.1080/09592318.2011.625720.

Sullivan, John P, and Adam Elkus. 'State of Siege: Mexico's Criminal Insurgency.' *Small Wars Journal*, 2008, 12.

Summers, Harry G. *American Strategy in Vietnam: A Critical Analysis*. Mineola, NY: Dover Publications, 2012. http://public.eblib.com/choice/publicfullrecord.aspx?p=1890088.

Suri, Abu Musab al-. 'Lessons Learned from the Armed Jihad in Syria.' Harmony Program, West Point Combating Terrorism Center, n.d. https://ctc.usma.edu/wp-content/uploads/2013/10/AFGP-2002-600080-Translation.pdf.

Swerdlow, Steve. 'Tajikistan: Why Authoritarian Elections Also Matter.' *The Diplomat*, October 10, 2020. https://thediplomat.com/2020/10/tajikistan-why-authoritarian-elections-also-matter/.

Tamini, Aymenn Jawad al-. 'Islamic State Insurgent Tactics: Translation and Analysis.' *Aymenn Jawad al-Tamini's Blog*, April 26, 2019. http://www.aymennjawad.org/2019/04/islamic-state-insurgent-tactics-translation.

Tamini, Aymenn Jawad al-. 'Review of "ISIS: The State of Terror."' *Syria Comment* (blog), March 27, 2015. https://www.joshualandis.com/blog/review-of-isis-the-state-of-terror/.

Tan, Eugene K. B. 'Singapore.' In *Comparative Counter-terrorism Law*, edited by Kent Roach, 610–49. Cambridge: Cambridge University Press, 2015. https://doi.org/10.1017/CBO9781107298002.022.

Tavernise, Sabrina. 'Why the Announcement of a Looming White Minority Makes Demographers Nervous.' *New York Times*, November 22, 2018, sec. U.S. https://www.nytimes.com/2018/11/22/us/white-americans-minority-population.html.

Taw, Jennifer M., and Bruce Hoffman. *The Urbanization of Insurgency: The Potential Challenge to U.S. Army Operations*. Santa Monica, CA: RAND Corporation, 1994.

Taylor, Adam. 'New Zealand Suspect Allegedly Claimed "Brief Contact" with Norwegian Mass Murderer Anders Breivik.' *Washington Post*, March 15, 2019. https://www.washingtonpost.com/world/2019/03/15/new-zealand-suspect-allegedly-claimed-brief-contact-with-norwegian-mass-murderer-anders-breivik/.

Taylor, Peter. *Brits: The War against the IRA*. London: Bloomsbury, 2001.

Taylor, Peter. *Provos: The IRA and Sinn Fein*. Rev. and Updated. London: Bloomsbury, 1998.

Terrill, Andrew W. *The United States and Iraq's Shi'ite Clergy: Partners or Adversaries?* Carlisle, PA: US Strategic Studies Institute, 2004.

Tertrais, Bruno. 'The Demise of Ares: The End of War as We Know It?' *Washington Quarterly* 35, no. 3 (August 2012): 7–22. https://doi.org/10.1080/0163660X.2012.703521.

Thapa, Manish. 'Nepal's Maoists: From Violent Revolution to Nonviolent Political Activism.' In *Civil Resistance and Conflict Transformation: Transitions from Armed to Nonviolent Struggle*, edited by Véronique Dudouet, 190–201. London: Routledge, 2015.

Thomas, Charles G, and Toyin Falola. *Secession and Separatist Conflicts in Postcolonial Africa*. Calgary, Alberta: University of Calgary Press, 2020. http://www.deslibris.ca/ID/459176.

Thompson, Robert. *Defeating Communist Insurgency: The Lessons of Malaya and Vietnam*. Studies in International Security 10. New York: Frederick A. Praeger, 1966.

Tilly, Charles. 'War Making and State Making as Organized Crime.' In *Bringing the State Back In*, edited by Peter B. Evans, Dietrich Rueschemeyer, and Theda Skocpol, 169–91. Cambridge: Cambridge University Press, 1985. https://doi.org/10.1017/CBO9780511628283.008.

Tilly, Charles, and Sidney G. Tarrow. *Contentious Politics*. 2nd rev. ed. New York: Oxford University Press, 2015.

Tilly, Charles, Louise Tilly, and Richard H. Tilly. *The Rebellious Century, 1830–1930*. Cambridge, MA: Harvard University Press, 1975.

Timmons, Heather. 'A Former Skinhead Explains Why It's a Mistake for the US to Stop Targeting Right-Wing Extremists.' *Quartz*, February 2, 2017. https://qz.com/901625/a-former-skinhead-explains-why-its-a-mistake-to-for-the-us-to-stop-targeting-right-wing-terrorists-at-home/.

Tocqueville, Alexis de. *The Republic of the United States of America, and Its Political Institutions, Reviewed and Examined*. Translated by Henry Reeve. New York: A. S. Barnes and Company, 1863.

Torjesen, Stina, and S. Neil MacFarlane. 'Reintegration before Disarmament: The Case of Post-conflict Reintegration in Tajikistan.' In *Reintegrating*

Armed Groups after Conflict: Politics, Violence and Transition, edited by Mats Berdal and David H. Ucko, 47–66. Abingdon: Routledge, 2009.

Trilling, Daniel. 'Golden Dawn: The Rise and Fall of Greece's Neo-Nazis.' *The Guardian*, March 3, 2020, sec. News. https://www.theguardian.com/news/2020/mar/03/golden-dawn-the-rise-and-fall-of-greece-neo-nazi-trial.

Trilling, Daniel. 'Tommy Robinson and the Far Right's New Playbook.' *The Guardian*, October 25, 2018, sec. World news. http://www.theguardian.com/world/2018/oct/25/tommy-robinson-and-the-far-rights-new-playbook.

Trilling, Daniel. 'Why Did Golden Dawn's Neo-Nazi Leaders Get Away with It for So Long?' *The Guardian*, October 8, 2020, sec. Opinion. http://www.theguardian.com/commentisfree/2020/oct/08/golden-dawn-neo-nazi-violence-greece-political-class.

Trotsky, Leon. *What Next? Vital Questions for the German Proletariat*. 1932. Marxist Internet Archive. https://www.marxists.org/archive/trotsky/germany/1932-ger/index.htm.

Tsesis, Alexander. 'Social Media Accountability for Terrorist Propaganda.' *Fordham Law Review* 86 (2017): 605–31.

Tucker, David. *Revolution and Resistance: Moral Revolution, Military Might, and the End of Empire*. Baltimore: Johns Hopkins University Press, 2016.

Twitter Safety. 'An Update Following the Riots in Washington, DC.' Twitter (blog), January 12, 2021. https://blog.twitter.com/en_us/topics/company/2021/protecting--the-conversation-following-the-riots-in-washington--.html.

Ucko, David H. 'Beyond Clear-Hold-Build: Rethinking Local-Level Counterinsurgency after Afghanistan.' *Contemporary Security Policy* 34, no. 3 (December 2013): 526–51.

Ucko, David H. 'Militias, Tribes and Insurgents: The Challenge of Political Reintegration in Iraq.' *Conflict, Security and Development* 8, no. 3 (October 2008): 341–73.

Ucko, David H. '"The People Are Revolting": An Anatomy of Authoritarian Counterinsurgency.' *Journal of Strategic Studies* 39, no. 1 (January 2, 2016): 29–61.

Ucko, David H. 'The Role of Economic Instruments in Ending Conflict: Priorities and Constraints.' International Institute for Strategic Studies roundtable, National Press Club, Washington, DC, 2009.

Ucko, David H., and Robert Egnell. *Counterinsurgency in Crisis: Britain and the Challenges of Modern Warfare*. New York: Columbia University Press, 2013.

Ucko, David H., and Thomas A. Marks. *Crafting Strategy for Irregular Warfare: A Framework for Analysis and Action*. Washington, DC: National Defense University Press, 2020.

Ucko, David H., and Thomas A. Marks. 'Violence in Context: Mapping the Strategies and Operational Art of Irregular Warfare.' *Contemporary Security Policy* 39, no. 2 (April 3, 2018): 206–33. https://doi.org/10.1080/13523260.2018.1432922.

UK Government. 'Channel Duty Guidance: Protecting People Vulnerable to Being Drawn into Terrorism.' 2020.

UK Government, Home Office. 'Counter-terrorism and Border Security Act 2019: Terrorism Offences Fact Sheet.' 2019. https://assets.publishing.service.gov.uk/government/uploads/system/uploads/attachment_data/file/912085/2019-02-11_Terrorist_Offences_Fact_Sheet_RA.pdf.

UK Stabilisation Unit. 'Responding to Stabilisation Challenges in Hostile and Insecure Environments: Lessons Identified by the UK's Stabilisation Unit.' London, November 2010.

UN Alliances of Civilizations. 'Report of the High-Level Group.' New York: United Nations, November 13, 2006.

UN Department of Economic and Social Affairs. *World Social Report: Inequality in a Rapidly Changing World*. New York: United Nations, 2020.

UN Department of Economic and Social Affairs. *World Urbanization Prospects: The 2018 Revision*. New York: United Nations, 2019. https://population.un.org/wup/Publications/Files/WUP2018-Report.pdf.

UN Disarmament, Demobilization and Reintegration Resource Center. 'The Politics of DDR.' In *Integrated Disarmament, Demobilization and Reintegration Standards*. 2019. https://www.unddr.org/modules/IDDRS-2.20-The-Politics-of-DDR.pdf.

UN Disarmament, Demobilization and Reintegration (DDR) Section. 'Community Violence Reduction: Creating Space for Peace.' Office of Rule of Law and Security Institutions (OROLSI), Department of Peace Operations (DPO), United Nations, n.d.

UN Habitat. *Urbanization and Development: Emerging Futures; World Cities Report 2016*. Nairobi: UN Habitat, 2016.

UN High-Level Panel on Threats, Challenges, and Change. *A More Secure World: Our Shared Responsibility*. New York: United Nations Publications, 2004.

UN Human Settlements Programme, ed. *The Challenge of Slums: Global Report on Human Settlements, 2003*. London: Earthscan Publications, 2003.

UN News. 'Switzerland: Draft Anti-terrorism Law Sets "Dangerous Precedent," Rights Experts Warn.' September 11, 2020. https://news.un.org/en/story/2020/09/1072192.

US Army Special Operations Command. 'SOF Support to Political Warfare.' White Paper, March 10, 2015. http://www.soc.mil/swcs/ProjectGray/Support%20to%20Political%20Warfare%20White%20Paper%20v2.3-RMT%20(10MAR2015)%20%20%20.pdf.

US Bureau of Citizenship and Immigration Services. 'Pakistan: Information on Mohajir/Muttahida Qaumi Movement-Altaf (MQM-A).' February 9, 2004. https://www.refworld.org/docid/414fe5aa4.html.

US Department of the Army, Headquarters. 'Counterinsurgency Operations.' Washington, DC, October 1, 2004.

US Department of the Army and United States Marine Corps. *FM 3-24/MCWP 3- 33.5. Counterinsurgency*. Washington, DC, 2006.

US Department of State. 'Foreign Terrorist Organizations.' Accessed June 14, 2017. http://www.state.gov/j/ct/rls/other/des/123085.htm.

US Embassy, La Paz. 'Bolivia: Morales Manipulates Media Owners.' La Paz, December 22, 2008. Wikileaks Public Library of US Diplomacy. https://wikileaks.org/plusd/cables/08LAPAZ2623_a.html.

US General Accounting Office. 'Efforts to Develop Alternatives to Cultivating Illicit Crops in Colombia Have Made Little Progress and Face Serious Obstacles.' Report to Congressional Requesters, Washington, DC, February 2002.

US Joint Chiefs of Staff. 'Counterinsurgency.' Department of Defense, Washington, DC, April 25, 2018.

Uscinski, Joseph E., and Joseph M. Parent. *American Conspiracy Theories*. Oxford: Oxford University Press, 2014.

Van Biljert, Martine. 'Between Discipline and Discretion: Policies Surrounding Senior Subnational Appointments.' Briefing Paper Series, Afghanistan Research and Evaluation Unit, May 2009.

Van Cott, Donna Lee. 'From Exclusion to Inclusion: Bolivia's 2002 Elections.' *Journal of Latin American Studies* 35, no. 4 (2003): 751–75.

Van der Veen, Jacco. 'A Very Private War: The Failure of Mozambique's Approach to Defeating an Islamist Insurgency.' *JASON Institute for Peace and Security Studies* (blog), July 19, 2020. https://jasoninstitute.com/2020/07/19/a-very-private-war-the-failure-of-mozambiques-approach-to-defeating-an-islamist-insurgency/.

Van der Vegt, Isabelle, Paul Gill, Stuart Macdonald, and Bennett Kleinberg. 'Shedding Light on Terrorist and Extremist Content Removal.' Global Research Network on Terrorism and Technology, RUSI, London, July 2019.

Van Eerten, J.-J., B. Doosje, E. Konijn, B. de Graaf, and M. de Goede. 'Developing a Social Media Response to Radicalization: The Role of Counter-narratives in Prevention of Radicalization and De-radicalization.' Department of Psychology, University of Amsterdam, September 2017. https://dare.uva.nl/search?identifier=4fe0b95f-b5ec-45a1-b50a-2ff8287b4b1c.

Vanguard News. 'Ateke Tom Receives Winners of 2018 MBMN, Gets National Merit Impact Award.' January 4, 2019. https://www.vanguardngr.com/2019/01/ateke-tom-receives-winners-of-2018-mbmn-gets-national-merit-impact-award/.

Van Spanje, Joost, and Wouter van der Brug. 'The Party as Pariah: The Exclusion of Anti-immigration Parties and Its Effect on Their Ideological Positions.' *West European Politics* 30, no. 5 (November 2007): 1022–40. https://doi.org/10.1080/01402380701617431.

Vaughan, Diane. *The Challenger Launch Decision: Risky Technology, Culture, and Deviance at NASA*. Chicago: University of Chicago Press, 1996. https://www.rusi.org/sites/default/files/20190703_grntt_paper_3.pdf.

Veilleux-Lepage, Yannick. 'Paradigmatic Shifts in Jihadism in Cyberspace: The Emerging Role of Unaffiliated Sympathizers in Islamic State's Social Media Strategy.' *Journal of Terrorism Research* 7, no. 1 (February 5, 2016). https://doi.org/10.15664/jtr.1183.

Venhaus, John M. 'Why Youth Join al-Qaeda.' Special Report, United States Institute of Peace, Washington, DC, May 2010. https://www.usip.org/sites/default/files/SR236Venhaus.pdf.

Vieira, Gilberto, and Marta Harnecker. *Combinación de todas las formas de lucha*. Bogotá: Ediciones Suramérica, 1988.

Waegh, Frank de. 'Unwilling Participants: The Coercion of Youth into Violent Criminal Groups in Central America's Northern Triangle.' Jesuit Conference of Canada and the United States, 2015.

Waldman, Matt. 'The Sun in The Sky: The Relationship Between Pakistan's ISI And Afghan Insurgents.' Discussion Paper 18. Crisis States Research Centre, London School of Economics (June 2010).

Waldman, Steve Randy. 'The 1996 Law That Ruined the Internet.' *The Atlantic*, January 3, 2021. https://www.theatlantic.com/ideas/archive/2021/01/trump-fighting-section-230-wrong-reason/617497/.

Walzer, Michael. *On Toleration*. New Haven, CT: Yale University Press, 1997.

Wamsley, Laurel. 'On Far-Right Websites, Plans to Storm Capitol Were Made in Plain Sight.' NPR, January 7, 2021. https://www.npr.org/sections/insurrection-at-the-capitol/2021/01/07/954671745/on-far-right-websites-plans-to-storm-capitol-were-made-in-plain-sight.

Watts, Clint. 'How to Fight the New Domestic Terrorism.' *Wall Street Journal*, August 9, 2019, sec. Life. https://www.wsj.com/articles/how-to-fight-the-new-domestic-terrorism-11565363219.

Wegener, Friederike. 'How the Far-Right Uses Memes in Online Warfare.' *Global Network on Extremism and Technology*, May 21, 2020. https://gnet-research.org/2020/05/21/how-the-far-right-uses-memes-in-online-warfare/.

Weinberg, Leonard, Ami Pedahzur, and Arie Perliger. *Political Parties and Terrorist Groups*. 2nd ed. Routledge Studies in Extremism and Democracy. London: Routledge, 2009.

Weine, Stevan, and Ahmed Younis. 'Developing CVE Programs through Building Community Policing Capacities.' In *Countering Violent Extremism: Developing an Evidence-Base for Policy and Practice*, edited by Sara Zeiger and Anne Aly. Perth, Australia: Curtin University, 2015. http://apo.org.au/system/files/57458/apo-nid57458-44271.pdf.

Weinstein, Jeremy. *Inside Rebellion: The Politics of Insurgent Violence*. Cambridge: Cambridge University Press, 2006.

Weisman, Jonathan. 'The Nazi Tweets of "Trump God Emperor."' *New York Times*, May 26, 2016, sec. Opinion. https://www.nytimes.com/2016/05/29/opinion/sunday/the-nazi-tweets-of-trump-god-emperor.html.

White, Joshua T. 'Vigilante Islamism in Pakistan: Religious Party Responses to the Lal Masjid Crisis.' *Current Trends in Islamist Ideology* 7 (2008): 50–65.

Whiteside, Craig. 'The Islamic State and the Return of Revolutionary Warfare.' *Small Wars and Insurgencies* 27, no. 5 (September 2, 2016): 743–76. https://doi.org/10.1080/09592318.2016.1208287.

Whiteside, Craig. 'Nine Bullets for the Traitors, One for the Enemy: The Slogans and Strategy behind the Islamic State's Campaign to Defeat the Sunni Awakening (2016–2017).' *Terrorism and Counter-terrorism Studies*, 2018: 1–36. https://doi.org/10.19165/2018.1.07.

Wieviorka, Michel. 'Terrorism in the Context of Academic Research.' In *Terrorism in Context*, edited by Martha Crenshaw. University Park, PA: Pennsylvania State University Press, 1995.

Wieviorka, Michel. *The Making of Terrorism*. Chicago: University of Chicago Press, 2004.

Wilkinson, Abi. 'We Need to Talk about the Online Radicalisation of Young, White Men.' *The Guardian*, November 15, 2016, sec. Opinion. http://www.theguardian.com/commentisfree/2016/nov/15/alt-right-manosphere-mainstream-politics-breitbart.

Wilkinson, Tracy. 'U.S. Alarmed over Surge in Coca Production in Colombia.' *Los Angeles Times*, February 6, 2018. http://www.latimes.com/nation/la-fg-tillerson-colombia-20180206-story.html.

Williams, Alan F. 'Prosecuting Internet Website Development under the Material Support to Terrorism Statutes: Time to Fix What's Broken.' *Journal of Legislation and Public Policy* 11 (2008): 365–403.

Williams, Phil, and Dan Bisbee. 'Jaish al-Mahdi in Iraq.' In *Impunity: Countering Illicit Power in War and Transition*, edited by Michelle Hughes and Michael Miklaucic, 40–66. Washington, DC: Center for Complex Operations (CCO) and the Peacekeeping and Stability Operations Institute (PKSOI), 2016.

Wilson, Andrew J. 'The Conflict between Noraid and the Friends of Irish Freedom.' *Irish Review*, no. 15 (1994). https://doi.org/10.2307/29735731.

Winter, Aaron. 'Online Hate: From the Far-Right to the "Alt-Right" and from the Margins to the Mainstream.' In *Online Othering: Exploring Digital Violence and Discrimination on the Web*, edited by Karen Lumsden and Emily Harmer, 39–63. Cham: Springer International Publishing, 2019. https://doi.org/10.1007/978-3-030-12633-9_2.

Winter, Charlie. 'Inside the Collapse of Islamic State's Propaganda Machine.' *Wired*, December 20, 2017. https://www.wired.co.uk/article/isis-islamic-state-propaganda-content-strategy.

Winter, Charlie. 'Media Jihad: The Islamic State's Doctrine for Information Warfare.' London: The International Centre for the Study of Radicalisation and Political Violence, 2017.

Winter, Charlie, and Jade Parker. 'Virtual Caliphate Rebooted: The Islamic State's Evolving Online Strategy.' *Lawfare*, January 7, 2018. https://www.lawfareblog.com/virtual-caliphate-rebooted-islamic-states-evolving-online-strategy.

Wittes, Benjamin, and Zoe Bedell. 'Tweeting Terrorists, Part II: Does It Violate the Law for Twitter to Let Terrorist Groups Have Accounts?' *Lawfare*, February 14, 2016. https://www.lawfareblog.com/tweeting-terrorists-part-ii-does-it-violate-law-twitter-let-terrorist-groups-have-accounts.

Wolff, Michael Jerome. 'Building Criminal Authority: A Comparative Analysis of Drug Gangs in Rio de Janeiro and Recife.' *Latin American Politics and Society* 57, no. 2 (2015): 21–40. https://doi.org/10.1111/j.1548-2456.2015.00266.x.

Wong, Kristina. 'Poll: Half of American Voters Back Trump's Muslim Ban.' *The Hill*, March 29, 2016. https://thehill.com/policy/defense/274521-poll-half-of-american-voters-back-trumps-muslim-ban.

Woody, Christopher. 'Colombia Is Trying to Root Out the Cocaine Trade, but Farmers Are Relying on It as an "Insurance Policy."' *Business Insider*, March 22, 2018. http://www.businessinsider.com/farmers-in-colombia-relying-on-economic-benefits-of-cocaine-production-2018-3.

Wyke, Thomas. '"Sharpen Your Knives. Prepare Your Explosive Devices" Urges Canadian ISIS Fighter.' *International Business Times UK*, December 7, 2014, sec. Society. https://www.ibtimes.co.uk/sharpen-your-knives-prepare-your-explosive-devices-urges-canadian-isis-fighter-1478447.

Wylie, Christopher. *Mindf*ck: Cambridge Analytica and the Plot to Break America*. New York: Random House, 2019.

Zabel, Richard B. 'Domestic Terrorism Is a National Problem: It Should Also Be a Federal Crime.' *Washington Post*, February 2, 2021, sec. Opinion. https://www.washingtonpost.com/opinions/2021/02/02/domestic-terrorism-federal-crime/.

Zee News. 'Maoist Chief Prachanda to Get Nepal's Top Peace Award.' June 16, 2008. https://zeenews.india.com/news/south-asia/maoist-chief-prachanda-to-get-nepals-top-peace-award_449170.html.

Zogg, Benno. 'Organized Crime: Fueling Corruption and Mali's Desert War.' *IPI Global Observatory* (blog), February 27, 2018. https://theglobalobservatory.org/2018/02/organized-crime-corruption-mali/.

INDEX

Note: Page numbers followed by "*n*" refer to notes.

meaning, 15
militarized, 17–23
narratives, role of, 57, 115–16
as necessary, 17
political nature of, 17–23
as a politico-military campaign, 5
root causes of, 29–33
shifting context, 33–9
sponsorship, 35–6, 37, 272
terrorism vs. insurgency, 19–22
See also individual insurgencies by their name
insurgents
adaptation, 6, 10, 13
counter-states usage to inculcate propaganda, 140
dilemma after 9/11 attacks, 40–1
'dilemma of conflicting goals', 36–7
emerging trends, 1–4
military strength, difficulties in achieving, 40–1
and social movements, 17–18
strategic contradictions, 8
terrorists vs. insurgents, 19–22
theories of victory, 6, 10, 15–16, 130, 270
use of violence, 17–23, 30–1, 35, 270
victories and regime changes, 25–8
International Crisis Group, 108, 176, 343–4n47
internationalization, 66–7, 69
internet, 113
birth of, 114–15
-enabled insurgency, 116–19
evolution of, 116
power of, 133

and value of ideas in insurgency, 115–19
See also ideational insurgency
intra-state conflicts, 28
Iran, 36, 103, 106, 272
Iraq, 5, 28, 130, 194, 272
armed political competition in post-Saddam Iraq, 103–6
counterinsurgency in, 23, 24
Operation Charge of the Knights (2008), 183–4
post-war Iraq, 169
pre- and post-Islamic State governance, 58
al-Sadr's Sadr City control, 48–9, 65, 271
sectarian conflict in, 105–6, 169
Shia against the Sunnis, 104, 105
Sunnis views on constitution, 105
unemployment problem, 182, 183
Iraqi Army, 48, 182, 183
Iraqi Governing Council, 104
Iraqi Police Service, 182
Iron March, 139
irredentism, 60
irregular warfare, 273
Irvin, Cynthia, 88
ISIS/Islamic State, 4, 5, 16, 39, 106, 116, 140, 184, 225, 231, 267–8
communications strategy, commentary on, 125
counter-state, military dismantling of, 24
defeat of, 16, 28
de-platforming online contents of, 235, 239, 241
digital counter-state, operating through, 127–8

INDEX

Roof, Dylann, 143, 151, 261
Rosand, Eric, 256
Roy, Olivier, 171–2
Royal Nepalese Army, 80
Rumsfeld, Donald, 20–1
rural insurgency, 31, 54–62, 267–8
Russia, 10, 269
  in eastern Ukraine, 36, 68
  Finland and Estonia defense against, 261–2
  Gerasimov Doctrine, 10–11, 85–8
  global power re-establishment efforts, 67–8
  information operations (US, 2016), 68, 126, 272
  insurgency sponsorship, 272
  Kurdish 'cultural autonomy', calling for, 68
  'passportification', 68
  separatist-irredentist groupings, supporting, 68
Russian Revolution (1917), 74
Rwanda, 58

SA. See *Sturmabteilung* (SA)
Sadr City (Baghdad)
  joint Iraqi–US operation (Mar 2008), 49
  Operation Charge of the Knights (2008), 183–4
  al-Sadr's control over, 48–9, 65, 271
al-Sadr, Mohammad Mohammad-Sadeq, 48
al-Sadr, Moqtada, 48–9, 51, 65, 104, 271
  loyalists gained control of the ministries, 105
  Operation Charge of the Knights (2008), 182–3

Sadr City control, 48–9, 65, 271
  See also Jaish al-Mahdi (JAM)
Salo Forum, 139
Sampaio, Antonio, 65
Sayari, Sabri, 49
schism, 141
Schuberth, Moritz, 177, 178
SCIRI. *See* Supreme Council for the Islamic Revolution in Iraq (SCIRI, later ISCI)
Scotland, 68
secessionism, 59–60
Shapiro, Jacob, 5
Sherman, Jon, 233–4
Shia communities (Iraq), 48–9, 104, 105
Siddiqui, Niloufer, 107, 109
Siemens, Daniel, 92
Sierra Leone, 189
Silke, Andrew, 100
Simi, Pete, 141
Sindh Province, 107
Singapore: "Sedition Act 28", 231
Singer, P. W., 155
Sinhala Buddhist chauvinism, 164
Sinn Féin (political party), 99–102, 190, 193, 194, 195–6, 202
Sloan, Stephen, 158
slum dwellers, 52–3
slums
  Baghdad, 183
  and insurgency nexus, 45–7, 49–50
  rise of, 52–3
  See also favelas of Rio de Janeiro (Brazil)
Social Democrats, 91
social media
  companies de-platforming initiatives, 243–7